Manchester Medieval Sources Series

series advisers Rosemary Horrox and Simon MacLean

This series aims to meet a growing need amongst students and teachers of medieval history for translations of key sources that are directly usable in students' own work. It provides texts central to medieval studies courses and focuses upon the diverse cultural and social as well as political conditions that affected the functioning of all levels of medieval society. The basic premise of the new series is that translations must be accompanied by sufficient introductory and explanatory material and each volume therefore includes a comprehensive guide to the sources' interpretation, including discussion of critical linguistic problems and an assessment of the most recent research on the topics being covered.

THE ANNALS OF LAMPERT OF HERSFELD

MANCHESTER
1824

Manchester University Press

MedievalSources*online*

Complementing the printed editions of the Medieval Sources series, Manchester University Press has developed a web-based learning resource which is now available on a yearly subscription basis.

Medieval Sources*online* brings quality history source material to the desktops of students and teachers and allows them open and unrestricted access throughout the entire college or university campus. Designed to be fully integrated with academic courses, this is a one-stop answer for many medieval history students, academics and researchers keeping thousands of pages of source material 'in print' over the Internet for research and teaching.

titles available now at MedievalSources*online include*

Trevor Dean *The towns of Italy in the later Middle Ages*

John Edwards *The Jews in Western Europe, 1400–1600*

Paul Fouracre and Richard A. Gerberding *Late Merovingian France: History and hagiography 640–720*

Chris Given-Wilson *Chronicles of the Revolution 1397–1400: The reign of Richard II*

P. J. P. Goldberg *Women in England, c. 1275–1525*

Janet Hamilton and Bernard Hamilton *Christian dualist heresies in the Byzantine world, c. 650–c. 1450*

Rosemary Horrox *The Black Death*

David Jones *Friars' Tales: Thirteenth-century exempla from the British Isles*

Graham A. Loud and Thomas Wiedemann *The history of the tyrants of Sicily by 'Hugo Falcandus', 1153–69*

A. K. McHardy *The reign of Richard II: From minority to tyranny 1377–97*

Simon MacLean *History and politics in late Carolingian and Ottonian Europe: The Chronicle of Regino of Prüm and Adalbert of Magdeburg*

Anthony Musson with Edward Powell *Crime, law and society in the later Middle Ages*

Janet L. Nelson *The Annals of St-Bertin: Ninth-century histories, volume I*

Timothy Reuter *The Annals of Fulda: Ninth-century histories, volume II*

R. N. Swanson *Catholic England: Faith, religion and observance before the Reformation*

Elisabeth van Houts *The Normans in Europe*

Jennifer Ward *Women of the English nobility and gentry 1066–1500*

Visit the site at *www.medievalsources.co.uk* for further information and subscription prices.

THE ANNALS OF
LAMPERT OF HERSFELD

translated and annotated with an introduction

by I. S. Robinson

Manchester University Press

Published by Manchester University Press
Altrincham Street, Manchester M1 7JA, UK
www.manchesteruniversitypress.co.uk

British Library Cataloguing-in-Publication Data
A catalogue record for this book is available from the British Library

Library of Congress Cataloging-in-Publication Data applied for

ISBN   978 0 7190 8437 9 *hardback*
       978 0 7190 8438 6 *paperback*

First published 2015

The publisher has no responsibility for the persistence or accuracy of URLs for any external or third-party internet websites referred to in this book, and does not guarantee that any content on such websites is, or will remain, accurate or appropriate.

Typeset in Monotype Bell
by Koinonia, Manchester
Printed in Great Britain
by Bell & Bain Ltd, Glasgow

CONTENTS

ACKNOWLEDGEMENTS

This translation of the *Annals* of Lampert of Hersfeld and the accompanying commentary is the culmination of half a century of reading the *Annals*. I first studied Lampert's work in a special subject on Pope Gregory VII, taught by Eric John, a very astute critic of the text. Subsequently I had the great good fortune of studying the *Annals* under the guidance of Dr Beryl Smalley, the most erudite doctoral supervisor that could ever be imagined. I also enjoyed the privilege of discussing Lampert's work with those most distinguished ecclesiastical historians, the Reverend Dr H. E. J. Cowdrey, Professor Christopher Brooke and Professor Horst Fuhrmann, the President of the Monumenta Germaniae Historica. More recently I have benefited from reading the translated passages from the *Annals* that Professor G. A. Loud has generously made available in electronic form to students of eleventh-century history.

I have received much encouragement and learned much from fellow students of narrative sources of the Central Middle Ages: Dr Detlev Jasper (Munich), Dr Patrick Healy (Toronto), Dr Conor Kostick (Nottingham), Dr Thomas McCarthy (Sarasota) and my friends and colleagues in Dublin, Dr Léan Ní Chléirigh, Dr Stephen Hanaphy, Dr Conor McCann, Dr Felim McGrath, Michael Burke, Steffen Magister, Axel Kelly, Brian McNamee, Yan Bourke and Dr Eimhín Walsh (who also very kindly helped me with the technicalities of preparing this manuscript). I am most grateful for the help of my friends from the Library of Trinity College, Dublin, Mary Higgins and Séan Hughes. I also owe a great debt of gratitude to their predecessor, the late Anne Walsh, to whom so many researchers in the History collection are deeply indebted.

Above all, I record my thanks to my wife, Dr Helga Robinson-Hammerstein, for the wise advice and tireless help that she has given me for most of the half-century in which I have been reading and re-reading Lampert's *Annals*.

ABBREVIATIONS

D H III	*Diploma Heinrici III*
D H IV	*Diploma Heinrici IV*
Die Salier und das Reich	*Die Salier und das Reich* ed. S. Weinfurter, 3 volumes (Sigmaringen, 1991)
Investiturstreit und Reichsverfassung	*Investiturstreit und Reichsverfassung* ed. J. Fleckenstein (Vorträge und Forschungen 17: Sigmaringen, 1973)
JE, JK, JL	P. Jaffé, *Regesta pontificum Romanorum* ed. W. Wattenbach, S. Loewenfeld, F. Kaltenbrunner, P. Ewald (second edition, Leipzig, 1885)
Lamperti Opera	*Lamperti monachi Hersfeldensis Opera, MGH SS rer. Germ.* [38] (1894)
Livy	Titus Livius Patavinus, *Ab urbe condita libelli*
MGH	*Monumenta Germaniae Historica*
Briefe	*Briefe der deutschen Kaiserzeit*
Briefsammlungen	*Briefsammlungen der Zeit Heinrichs IV., MGH Briefe* 5 (1950)
Constitutiones	*Constitutiones et acta publica imperatorum et regum*
DD	*Diplomata*
Libelli	*Libelli de lite imperatorum et pontificum*
SS	*Scriptores* (in Folio)
SS rer. Germ.	*Scriptores rerum Germanicarum in usum scholarum separatim editi*
MPL	J. P. Migne (ed.), *Patrologiae cursus completus. Series Latina*

1 The kingdom of Germany in the lifetime of Lampert of Hersfeld

2 Places mentioned in Lampert of Hersfeld's *Annals*

INTRODUCTION

Lampert of Hersfeld, according to the standard work on the German narrative sources of the Middle Ages, 'was one of the best stylists and the most erudite authors whom the Middle Ages produced: indeed among the medieval historians of Germany none could come near his linguistic artistry, his great literary elegance. Moreover in terms of content Lampert captivated by his pleasing way of narrating, the charming stories that he knew so well how to tell, the great importance of the events, of which he seemed to have a remarkably accurate, often almost intimate knowledge.' He was 'a superb story-teller, who wished to fascinate and to entertain'.[1] Lampert's principal work, the *Annals*, contains the most detailed account of the minority of King Henry IV of Germany and of the first decade of his personal rule (October 1056 – January 1077), which is indeed the most detailed narrative source of the Central Middle Ages. During the five centuries since the appearance of the first printed edition of the *Annals* Lampert's work has been more studied and has also been more controversial than any other medieval chronicle.

Biographical information about the author, almost all deriving from his own narrative, is very limited; so limited indeed that there is uncertainty even about his name. The author included autobiographical material in his narrative, as when, in the annal for 1058, he recorded his entry into the monastery of Hersfeld and his subsequent ordination as a priest. The principal textual tradition here reads: 'I, N., ... abandoned domestic concerns ... and received the sacred garment ...' and 'I, N., was ordained priest by Archbishop Liutpold [of Mainz]'. Here the letter N (for *nomen*, 'name') appears either through the author's deliberate reticence or more probably through the intervention at some stage in the transmission of the text of a scribe who either could not decipher the name or considered anonymity more decorous and appropriate to monastic authorship. In the exemplars of the *Annals* in the manuscripts of Würzburg and Göttingen, copied *circa* 1500, however, a name is supplied in the first of these autobiographical references: *Lampertus*.[2]

1 Wattenbach-Holtzmann-Schmale (1967) pp. 463–4, 469.

2 Lampert, *Annals* 1058, below, pp. 72, 73. See Holder-Egger in *Lamperti Opera* p. 73 variant *; Holder-Egger (1894) pp. 152–4, 170.

The Würzburg manuscript also provides a title for the work: 'The chronicle of Lampert, monk of Hersfeld of the order of St Benedict in the diocese of Mainz'. Furthermore a twelfth-century manuscript of Gotha containing numerous extracts from the *Annals* refers to 'the chronicle of brother Lampert, monk of Hersfeld'. All these manuscripts were linked with the monastery of St Peter in Erfurt, from which the whole of the extant manuscript tradition derives.[3]

In Erfurt at least the identification of Lampert with the author of the *Annals* survived throughout the Middle Ages, so that *circa* 1490 an Erfurt monk and historian, borrowing from the *Annals*, could cite his source: 'as Lampert, monk of Hersfeld, stated clearly and lucidly in his chronicle'.[4] Others who owed their knowledge of the *Annals* to St Peter's, Erfurt, however – the fourteenth-century Dominican historian, Henry of Herford, who identified the author as *Egkardus*, the scribes who copied the Dresden manuscript of the *Annals circa* 1500, the distinguished physician and humanist scholar Hartman Schedel, who made lengthy extracts from the *Annals* in 1507 – either did not know or did not trust the attribution.[5] No contemporary record confirms the existence of a monk named Lampert in the monastery of Hersfeld during the years 1058–77. Indeed since there is no complete necrology and since charters from the abbey survive only in small numbers, the names of very few eleventh-century monks of Hersfeld are known. How reliable, therefore, was the Erfurt tradition that ascribed the *Annals* to Lampert?

In fact the author of the *Annals* himself left a clue to his identity in the autobiographical passages in the annals for 1058 and 1059. In 1059 he recorded that after his pilgrimage to Jerusalem, 'I returned to the monastery on 17 September'. In the previous annal he reported his ordination to the priesthood 'during the Ember Days of autumn'.[6] In 1058 these Ember Days fell on 16, 18 and 19 September. It was surely not a coincidence that in these two autobiographical passages the author sought to fix the reader's attention on the date 17 September and the days immediately surrounding that date – which is the Feast of St Lambert, bishop and martyr. This was perhaps the clue that led

3 Holder-Egger (1894) pp. 169–70.

4 Nicolaus of Siegen, *Chronicon ecclesiasticum* p. 231, cited by Holder-Egger (1894) p. 171.

5 Holder-Egger (1894) pp. 154–7, 162–3, 169–71.

6 Lampert, *Annals* 1059, below, p. 75; 1058, below p. 73. A. Schmidt in *Lamperti Annales* p. 66 and Struve (1969) p. 12 wrongly translated the date as '17 October'.

the more alert readers of the *Annals* in St Peter's, Erfurt, to the secret of Lampert's authorship.[7] It should be noted that all the references to the author deriving from the Erfurt tradition render his name in the form *Lampertus* rather than *Lambertus*.[8] Similarly, in the single instance in which the name occurs in the text of the *Annals* (referring to the church of St Lambert in Liège), it appears in all the manuscripts as *sancto Lamperto*.[9] It is appropriate, therefore, to call our author *Lampert* of Hersfeld.

The *Annals* offer no clue to the author's birthplace. Historians' favourite conjectures have been Thuringia, Hesse or Franconia.[10] Lampert's explanation of his entry into the monastic life – 'I ... abandoned domestic concerns so as not to be weighed down by them on the road to God' – has been interpreted as evidence that he came from a wealthy and noble family.[11] Readers of the *Annals* have found confirmation of this interpretation in the stridently aristocratic viewpoint expressed in Lampert's pronouncements on political and social developments in Germany. This is especially apparent in his denunciation of the advisers of King Henry IV. The king 'raised very many of [the Swabians] – who were descended from low-born ancestors and had virtually no ancestors at all – to the highest offices and made them into men of the first importance in the palace'. He had 'excluded the princes from his friendship and had raised men of the lowest rank and of no ancestry to the highest honours'.[12] These and many similar statements have prompted the judgement that Lampert was a 'reactionary aristocrat'.[13] For Lampert's birth date we are dependent on the report of his ordination to the priesthood in the annal for 1058. If he had reached the age prescribed by canon law for ordination and was at least thirty years old, he must have been born no later than 1028.[14]

---

7 This was the solution suggested by Ernst Dümmler to Lampert's editor, Oswald Holder-Egger: see Holder-Egger (1894) p. 179.

8 Holder-Egger (1894) pp. 170–3.

9 Lampert, *Annals* 1071, below, p. 142 and n. 684. See Holder-Egger (1894) p. 180.

10 Holder-Egger in *Lamperti Opera* pp. IX–X; Wattenbach-Holtzmann-Schmale (1967) p. 457; Struve (1969) p. 12.

11 Lampert, *Annals* 1058, below, p. 72. See Holder-Egger in *Lamperti Opera* p. IX; Struve (1969) p. 12.

12 Lampert, *Annals* 1073, below, p. 173; 1076, below pp. 335–6.

13 Bosl (1950) p. 70. See also the much more nuanced assessment of Struve (1970a) pp. 39–47.

14 Lampert, *Annals* 1058, below, p. 73. See Holder-Egger in *Lamperti Opera* p. IX and n. 2; Wattenbach-Holtzmann-Schmale (1967) p. 457; Struve (1969) p. 12.

Lampert reported nothing about his career before his admission to Hersfeld on 15 March 1058. His failure directly to identify his school or his schoolmasters has inevitably led scholars to speculate where he could have acquired the education that made him 'one of the best stylists and the most erudite authors whom the Middle Ages produced'.[15] The most convincing arguments point to the outstanding cathedral school of Bamberg and its remarkable library. That school, richly endowed by Bamberg's founder, Emperor Henry II, and by his Salian successors, educated some of Lampert's most distinguished contemporaries. Among the Bamberg alumni scholars have identified the historian Adam of Bremen, the canonist and pro-papal polemicist Bernard (master of the cathedral school of Constance and subsequently of Hildesheim), Williram of Ebersberg (author of a celebrated metrical paraphrase of the Song of Solomon in Latin and Middle High German) and, in particular, Meinhard of Bamberg, theologian, letter-writer, master of the Bamberg school and a key figure in the history of eleventh-century scholarship.[16] It has indeed been suggested that 'entry into the cathedral school of Bamberg, membership of the Bamberg clergy signified ... in this period the prospect of a great career'.[17] The prosopographical evidence for the eleventh century reveals at least the regularity with which clerks from Bamberg were recruited to the imperial chapel and the imperial episcopate.[18]

The evidence for Lampert's education in Bamberg has been found both in the content and in the literary style of the *Annals*. The keen interest shown by the author in events in Bamberg is characterised by detailed local knowledge. For example, writing of Bishop Herman's foundation, the religious house of St James, Lampert noted that it 'was situated in a much frequented place in the midst of streams of people ... and separated from the cathedral church of Bamberg by thirty paces at most and therefore much more suitable for clerks than for monks'. Lampert's estimate, equivalent to about 45 metres, is accurate and suggests a personal knowledge of the topography of the city.[19] Lampert's detailed

---

15 Wattenbach-Holtzmann-Schmale (1967) pp. 463–4.

16 Erdmann (1938) pp. 16–24; Märtl (1991) pp. 327–32.

17 Meyer (1973) p. 35.

18 Zielinski (1984) pp. 84–6, 145–7, 151, 158, 164, 268–9; Märtl (1991) p. 329; Wende-horst (1991) p. 237.

19 Lampert, *Annals* 1075, below, p. 244 and n. 1292. See Struve (1969) pp. 29–31, con-cluding: 'Only someone personally acquainted with the locality could give these precise specifications.'

account of the experiences of Bishop Gunther of Bamberg on 'the great German pilgrimage' to Jerusalem of 1064–5 seems to depend on the testimony of eyewitnesses from the bishop's entourage. The author's admiration for Gunther prompted him to compose one of the very few physical descriptions found in the *Annals*. 'Both in his stature and in the beauty, elegance and health of his whole body he was so superior to other mortals that during that journey to Jerusalem people came running from the cities and from the fields in their eagerness to gaze at him.'[20] Equally significant is the central role in the *Annals* of Archbishop Anno of Cologne, to whom Lampert devoted more space than to any other churchman. For, until he was appointed provost of SS Simon and Jude in Goslar in 1054, Anno served as master (*magister scholarum*) 'in the school of Bamberg, which at that time surpassed all the others in Germany in the fervour of its discipline, piety and zeal'.[21] It is likely that, when Lampert composed the very lengthy eulogy of the archbishop that closes his annal for 1075 (in which he noted that Anno 'was educated both in divine and in secular literature in the school of the church of Bamberg'), it was of his former schoolmaster that he was writing.[22]

If Lampert was educated in Bamberg while Anno was master, he is likely to have been the school fellow of Meinhard, whom a younger Bamberg contemporary described as 'virtually second to none in erudition, genius and eloquence'.[23] From a comparison of the style of the *Annals* and that of the letters composed by Meinhard as master of the Bamberg school Carl Erdmann (1938) drew the 'obvious conclusion' that Lampert had received his education in the cathedral school in which Meinhard had also studied. He noted, for example, that both authors used the 'historic infinitive' (the present infinitive used instead of the imperfect indicative in order to convey sudden and rapid action), which is extremely rare in medieval Latin. Both Meinhard and Lampert avoided the rhyming prose fashionable among contemporary writers.[24] The detailed comparison by Tilman Struve (1969) of the use of classical quotations by Meinhard and Lampert and of their characteristic idioms

20 Lampert, *Annals* 1065, below, p. 107. See Holder-Egger in *Lamperti Opera* p. X; Struve (1969) pp. 28–9.

21 *Vita Annonis archiepiscopi Coloniensis* I.1, pp. 467–8. See Holder-Egger in *Lamperti Opera* pp. X–XII; Wattenbach-Holtzmann-Schmale (1967) p. 457; Struve (1969) pp. 25–6; Märtl (1991) p. 331.

22 Lampert, *Annals* 1075, below, p. 291.

23 Frutolf of Michelsberg, *Chronica* 1085, p. 98.

24 Erdmann (1938) pp. 113–14 and n. 4, noting that the 'historic infinitive' is 'totally un-medieval'.

and word associations strongly supports Erdmann's conclusion. Most convincingly, Meinhard and Lampert used the same *mis*-quotations of classical authors and the same 'mixed quotations', combining two distinct passages on similar topics.[25] This cannot have been a coincidence: the two authors had learned the art of composition in the same school. Perhaps there was a further parallel in the careers of the two authors. No record has survived of the name of the master of the Bamberg school in the years between the departure of Anno in 1054 and 1058, the earliest date at which Meinhard is known to have held the office. It is possible that Lampert served as *magister scholarum* in these years and that Meinhard succeeded him when Lampert entered the monastery of Hersfeld.[26]

The instruction in the art of Latin composition in the school of Bamberg made Lampert 'the unrivalled master among medieval historians: even his critics admit that'.[27] Only a library as rich in manuscripts of the Latin classics as that of Bamberg could have introduced him to the poets Horace, Ovid, Vergil and Lucan, to the comedies of Terence and above all to the historians Livy, Sallust, Ammianus Marcellinus, Justinus and Suetonius.[28] It was the Latin historians who most strongly influenced Lampert's style (while that of his schoolfellow Meinhard was influenced by the poets).[29] How Lampert valued these ancient historians is apparent in an observation about Charlemagne in his biography of St Lul (bishop of Mainz and founder of Hersfeld). 'In fact if [Charlemagne] had acquired either Titus Livy or Crispus Sallust as the writer of his deeds, I should say without violating my faith that he would have equalled the glory of Julius or Augustus Caesar or any of the most illustrious Roman emperors both in war and in the arts of peace.'[30] Lampert's editor, Oswald Holder-Egger, identified as the principal influences on Lampert's style Sallust and his imitator, Sulpicius Severus (the author of the *Life of St Martin of Tours*, the pre-eminent model for

---

25 Struve (1969) pp. 22–5. The most obvious example is the deliberate inversion, *o mores, o tempora* (cf. Cicero, *Orationes in Catilinam* I.1.2) in Meinhard of Bamberg, *Letters* 9, 24, 28, pp. 202, 221, 226; Lampert, *Annals* 1075, below p. 289 and n. 1531.

26 Holder-Egger in *Lamperti Opera* pp. XI–XII; Struve (1969) p. 26; Märtl (1991) p. 331.

27 Struve (1969) p. 12.

28 Holder-Egger in *Lamperti Opera* p. XLV; Holder-Egger (1894) pp. 415–16; Struve (1969) pp. 25–8. Some of these manuscripts of the classics have survived to the present day: see the exhibition catalogue edited by Fauser and Gerstner (1953).

29 Struve (1969) p. 22.

30 Lampert, *Vita Lulli* c. 14 in *Lamperti Opera* p. 327 ('both in war and in the arts of peace' is a quotation from Livy I.21.6).

medieval hagiography).[31] It was from Sallust that Lampert imitated the method of composing an apparently objective presentation of events in which opposing figures are each given the opportunity to argue their cases. (This was the method of presentation that would earn Lampert the reputation of a non-partisan historian in the historiography of the early nineteenth century.)[32]

The study of Guido Billanovich (1945), however, demonstrated in the most precise detail that Livy's *History* exercised the most important stylistic influence on Lampert's works and especially on the *Annals*. Lampert never quoted extensive passages from Livy (or from any other of his classical models) but instead produced sentences composed of many partial quotations. These were drawn especially from the first decade of Livy – the first books of which Lampert seems to have known by heart – and to a lesser extent from the third and fourth decades. Lampert was also 'the first and perhaps the only' medieval author to show knowledge of the fifth decade. Billanovich suggested that for every situation in the history of his own times Lampert found in his memory an analogous passage in Livy's *History* and in this way he made the language of Livy his own.[33]

Livy and his other classical models provided Lampert with his most dramatic effects in the *Annals*. In particular, a scene of political crisis or armed conflict is always narrated with a cluster of quotations from Livy. The most striking examples are the dissensions involving the abbey of Fulda in 1063; the Arab attack on the 'great German pilgrimage' to Jerusalem in 1065; the rebellion of Margrave Dedi I of Lower Lusatia in 1069; the rebellion of Otto of Northeim, duke of Bavaria in 1070–1; the adventurous early career attributed to Count Robert I of Flanders in the annal for 1071; the conspiracy of the Saxons and the march on the Harzburg in 1073; the capture of royal castles by the Saxon rebels in 1073–4; the rebellion of the citizens of Cologne against Archbishop Anno in 1074; the battle of Homburg in 1075; the conflict within the Saxon rebel army, when 'the common people' opposed the princes in 1075; the Saxon and Thuringian debate about continued resistance and their surrender to the king in 1075 and the renewed outbreak of

---

31 Holder-Egger (1884) pp. 296–7; Holder-Egger in *Lamperti Opera* p. XLV; Holder-Egger (1894) pp. 415–16.

32 See below p. 36.

33 Billanovich (1945) pp. 6–9, 15–16, 39–43, 46, 51. The parallels between Lampert's *Annals* and Livy's *History* are given in full in Billanovich (1945) pp. 55–195.

the Saxon rebellion in 1076.[34] The best-known passage in Lampert's *Annals* is also that in which the influence of Livy is most obvious. The account of Henry IV crossing the Alps, intending to intercept the pope in January 1077, borrows frequently from Livy's account of Hannibal crossing the Alps in the *History* XXI.32–8. Many of the 'realistic' details that have convinced historians of Lampert's reliability as a narrator – the hiring of local guides, the treacherous weather conditions and the perils of the journey, the measures taken to transport the horses – were actually taken from Livy.[35]

Lampert's editor, Holder-Egger, noting the borrowings from Livy in the account of Henry IV's victory over the Saxon rebels at Homburg (9 June 1075), criticised Lampert's narrative severely for its dependence on 'memorised passages' from his classical model.[36] In fact Lampert's account of Homburg does not differ in essentials from the parallel sources for the battle, in particular that of *The Saxon War* of Bruno of Merseburg.[37] The authentic information about the battle that had reached Lampert was, however, one-sided: it referred only to the conduct of the royal army. Perhaps it came to him in the form of the eyewitness accounts of the knights of the contingent sent by the abbey of Hersfeld or of the contingent of the neighbouring abbey of Fulda.[38] Desiring to report also the actions of the Saxon and Thuringian rebel army, with whose cause he strongly sympathised, Lampert gathered his material from the battle scenes of Livy's *History*. Hence at the beginning of the battle Lampert placed the rebel army in a fortified Roman

---

34 Lampert, *Annals* 1063, below pp. 85–91 (Fulda); 1065, below pp. 99–107 (pilgrimage); 1069, below pp. 118–21 (Dedi); 1070–1, below pp. 131–3 (Otto); 1071, below pp. 138–42 (Robert I); 1073, below pp. 177–84 (Harzburg); 1073–4, below pp. 202–6 (royal castles); 1074, below pp. 222–31 (Cologne); 1075, below pp. 260–6 (Homburg); 1075, below pp. 273–4 (Saxon conflict); 1075, below pp. 279–87 (surrender); 1076, below pp. 319, 328 (renewed rebellion).

35 Lampert, *Annals* 1077, below pp. 346–7. See Billanovich (1945) pp. 5, 189–93.

36 Lampert, *Annals* 1075, below pp. 260–6. See Holder-Egger (1894) pp. 533–4; Billanovich (1945) pp. 154–62.

37 Bruno of Merseburg, *Saxon War* c. 46, pp. 44–5. Cf. Lampert, *Annals* 1075, below pp. 261–6 nn. 1369, 1388, 1400, 1401, 1408, 1410. See Holder-Egger (1894) p. 534; Meyer von Knonau (1894) pp. 874–7, 878–9; Struve (1970a) p. 87.

38 Although Lampert did not report this, it seems certain that Abbot Hartwig of Hersfeld participated in person in the Homburg expedition, since Abbot Widerad of Fulda was not exempted from participation despite his extremely poor health. Lampert reported Widerad's presence in the army, adding that 'the king was concerned above all to make this the most impressive of expeditions by including the banners and insignia of all his princes' (*Annals* 1075, below p. 258). See Holder-Egger (1894) p. 194; Struve (1970a) p. 87.

camp; he caused the Saxons to 'burst out of the gates' at the approach of the royal army and arranged for them to attack the enemy 'without waiting for the signal, as is the custom with those about to engage in battle' – the custom, that is, in Livy's Roman armies.[39] It was in the interests of narrative completeness that Lampert borrowed details from Livy to fill in the gaps in his knowledge of Homburg and Henry IV's crossing of the Alps.

Lampert's works seem all to have been written in the abbey of Hersfeld but the classical erudition that characterises them must have owed much to his studies and perhaps also his teaching in the school of Bamberg. Hersfeld indeed possessed a richly endowed library in the eleventh century: Lampert himself reported 'the great abundance of books' furnished by Abbot Gozbert (970–84).[40] Very little of the library survived the fifteenth century, however, and today only fragments of Tacitus, Suetonius and Ammianus Marcellinus remain of the classical holdings of Hersfeld in Lampert's lifetime.[41] Much more survives of the classical collection of the renowned library of the Bamberg cathedral school, probably the richest in the German kingdom and including manuscripts of Livy's *History*, a great rarity in eleventh-century Europe. Among the survivals are fragments of a fifth-century codex of Livy's fourth decade in an uncial script. Bamberg, Staatsbibliothek, Codex Class. 35 also contains Livy's fourth decade, this time written in several hands of the eleventh century. This manuscript is evidently a copy of the fifth-century codex prepared in the Bamberg scriptorium, presumably because the latter had faded so much that it was difficult to read (not least because of the unfamiliar uncial script). The more competent pupils of the cathedral school could well have been co-opted into the labour of copying and – the conjecture is irresistible – Lampert and Meinhard may have been among their number. Perhaps Bamberg Codex Class. 35 reveals something of the process by which Lampert and his putative schoolfellow so successfully internalised the language of Livy.[42]

These two distinguished intellectuals, probably the products of the same educational system and so alike in their erudition and their fascination with the classics, would follow markedly different careers. Meinhard of Bamberg, after serving as *magister* of the Bamberg cathedral school

39 Lampert, *Annals* 1075, below p. 262 and nn. 1375, 1377. See Struve (1970a) p. 86.

40 Lampert, *Libelli de institutione Herveldensis ecclesiae* I, p. 348.

41 Struve (1969) pp. 31–2.

42 *Ibid.*, pp. 26–7. See also Munk Olsen (1985) pp. 13–14. I owe this reference to Dr Stephen Hanaphy.

(1058–71), seems to have achieved a higher rank in the cathedral chapter, perhaps that of provost, and ended his life as a bishop – to be precise, imperial anti-bishop of Würzburg (1085–8), appointed by Henry IV to oust the pro-papal incumbent, Adalbero. His contemporaries, both pro-imperial and pro-papal, connected Meinhard's elevation with his outstanding erudition.[43] As we have seen, Lampert – perhaps after serving as master of the Bamberg cathedral school (1054–8) – did not pursue a career in the secular clergy but entered the abbey of Hersfeld in 1058.

This departure from secular life clearly did not involve Lampert's abandonment of secular literature. His near contemporary, the Bamberg-educated Bernard, schoolmaster in Constance and Hildesheim, who ultimately became a monk of Corvey, ceased 'to cherish the frivolous lyre of Horace' and turned instead to 'the mystical cithern of David, to the greater advantage of himself and his pupils'. Bernard, that is to say, renounced the pagan literature that he had studied in the school of Bamberg in favour of Scripture and canon law.[44] His fellow pro-papal polemicist Manegold of Lautenbach, dean of the house of regular canons in Rottenbuch, denounced the adherents of pagan learning with the same acerbity that he directed against the supporters of King Henry IV, regarding the two sets of opponents as equally heretical.[45] For Lampert of Hersfeld, however, the highest commendation that he could confer on a distinguished prelate was that he was learned in secular as well as divine literature. Thus Lampert recorded of Anno of Cologne, evidently his own schoolmaster, that 'he was educated both in divine and in secular literature'. Of Abbot Meginher, whose 'renown' had drawn Lampert himself to Hersfeld in 1058, the author wrote that 'he was skilled in all the arts'.[46]

Having 'converted to religion' (to use the medieval expression for entering the monastic life), Lampert would henceforward, according to his own words, live 'enclosed, as it were, in the prison of the monastery'.[47]

43 Frutolf of Michelsberg, *Chronica* 1085, p. 98; Continuation of Frutolf's *Chronica* 1105, *ibid.*, p. 230. Hostile references to Meinhard: Bonizo of Sutri, *To a Friend* IX, p. 254; Bernold of St Blasien, *Chronicle* 1088, p. 293. See Erdmann (1938) pp. 16–24; Märtl (1991) pp. 331–40.

44 Bernold of St Blasien, *De damnatione scismaticorum* III, p. 47. For Bernard as the pupil of Meinhard of Bamberg see Erdmann (1938) pp. 218–21, 308–11.

45 Manegold of Lautenbach, *Liber contra Wolfelmum* c. 2 (concerning Macrobius, Cicero and Vergil), c. 3 (Pythagoras, Plato, Aristotle, Boethius and fourteen other ancient philosophers), pp. 47–51. See also the summary by W. Hartmann, *ibid.*, pp. 12–32.

46 Lampert, *Annals* 1075, below p. 291; 1058, below p. 72; Lampert, *Libelli de institutione Herveldensis ecclesiae* I, p. 350.

47 Lampert, *Libelli de institutione Herveldensis ecclesiae* I, p. 348.

The renunciation of the world for 'the purity of the monastic way of life' is a recurrent theme of Lampert's *Annals*, which consistently celebrates the desire to live 'as a simple monk and to seek rest forever from all the noise of worldly affairs in the name of voluntary poverty'.[48] The monk followed 'the holy and apostolic way of life', superior to any other. 'Monks indeed are set apart from the multitude'; 'as the more honourable and the more exalted part of the body of Christ, they cling more closely to God'. Monks abandon the world 'so that, if they sacrifice what laymen revere and regard as of the utmost importance, they do not do so before the eyes of laymen, who would be tempted to evil and would pelt them with the stones of their derision and defame the holy and apostolic life'.[49] The *Annals* contain a record of the incompatibility of monastic values and those of the world and of 'the hatred directed against monasticism, which secular men always try with deep-seated malice to degrade and crush'.[50]

When he renounced the world in 1058, however, Lampert entered an illustrious institution that had long enjoyed great prosperity and influence. Hersfeld had long been one of the foremost Benedictine abbeys in the German kingdom. Like its neighbour and great rival, Fulda, Hersfeld was an eighth-century foundation, enriched by the Carolingians and Ottonians. An imperial abbey, it enjoyed the protection and patronage of the emperors, received its abbots from their hands and was reformed by them. It was the intervention of the eleventh-century German kings and emperors that introduced to the imperial abbeys the reformed monasticism particularly associated with the Lotharingian monastery of Gorze. Hersfeld experienced monastic reform when Emperor Henry II imposed reforming abbots on the monastery in 1005 (Godehard of Niederaltaich) and in 1012 (Arnold of Tegernsee), just as he imposed reformers on the imperial abbeys of Fulda, Corvey, Reichenau and Prüm. Lampert recorded that Abbot Godehard 'began to reform [the monastery] for the better' and that his pupil and successor, Arnold, was 'a man of the strictest severity'.[51] A far more congenial reformer was Abbot Meginher of Hersfeld, who had received Lampert into the monastery on 15 March 1058. Lampert had come to

---

48 Lampert, *Annals* 1075, below p. 243; 1072, below p. 162.

49 *Ibid.*, 1063, below p. 90; 1075, below p. 244. Cf. 1071, below p. 146: 'the holy and angelic profession of the monks'.

50 *Ibid.*, 1063, below p. 86. Cf., for example, the persecution of Hersfeld by King Henry IV's favourite, Count Werner: *ibid.*, 1064, below p. 97.

51 Lampert, *Libelli de institutione Herveldensis ecclesiae* I, pp. 349, 350. See Hallinger (1950) p. 169; Vogtherr (1991) p. 430.

Hersfeld expressly 'to follow the way of life of Abbot Meginher, which was pleasing to God and renowned throughout the whole world'. 'He was a man of great virtues in Christ and truly – and I say this without offence to all the abbots of modern times – the unique model of correct monastic living in the German territories in his generation.'[52]

One of the four autobiographical passages in Lampert's *Annals* deals with the author's relations with Meginher. Lampert recorded that after his ordination to the priesthood by Archbishop Liutpold of Mainz in September 1058 he 'immediately set out on a pilgrimage to Jerusalem' without the permission of his abbot. This 'great crime', as the author called it, an act of disobedience in breach of the *Rule* of Benedict, Lampert explained by reference to the scriptural text Romans 10:2: he had acted 'with *zeal for God*, but would that it was *according to knowledge!*'[53] Lampert's motives were perhaps those of two contemporary monastic pilgrims, Werner and Liuthar of Reichenau, who set out for Jerusalem in 1053: 'burning with zeal for a life of greater perfection, [they] secretly undertook a pilgrimage for Christ's sake'.[54] Like the 'extremely learned' Werner of Reichenau, Lampert seems immediately after the experience of his ordination to the priesthood to have concluded that the pilgrimage to Jerusalem represented 'a life of greater perfection' than the monastic routine of Hersfeld. Nevertheless he began to fear that he would be 'found guilty before God of a great crime, if [Meginher] at his death had been displeased and unreconciled'. To his relief, on his return to Hersfeld on 17 September 1059 the abbot 'joyfully received' him and 'pardoned [his] sin'.[55]

During the abbatiate of Meginher of Hersfeld (1035–59) the wealth and influence of the abbey greatly increased. This was evidently the consequence of the personal friendship of Meginher with Emperor Henry III. According to Lampert, 'Henry revered [Meginher] as a holy man and made him his intimate associate'.[56] It is known that Henry III visited Hersfeld in 1040 (for the consecration of the new buildings undertaken by Meginher) and in 1051 and that Meginher

---

52 Lampert, *Annals* 1058, below p. 72; 1059, below p. 75.

53 *Ibid.*, 1058, below p. 73; 1059, below p. 75.

54 Herman of Reichenau, *Chronicle* 1053, p. 96 and n. 322. Unlike Lampert, they obtained the abbot's permission, 'which was granted in a letter'. Werner was the younger brother of the chronicler Herman.

55 Lampert, *Annals* 1059, below p. 75.

56 Lampert, *Libelli de institutione Herveldensis ecclesiae* I, p. 352.

was present in the imperial entourage in Mainz in 1047 and 1049.[57] The evidence of Henry III's diplomas reveals that Hersfeld received more imperial privileges than any other imperial abbey during the reign.[58] Of particular importance are the two diplomas of 1043 and 1044 that link substantial donations of property to Hersfeld with the obligation to institute prayers in perpetuity for the memory of Henry's parents, Emperor Conrad II and Empress Gisela. These Hersfeld diplomas bear witness to the well attested preoccupation of the Salian emperors with the perpetuation of the *memoria* of their dynasty. It was a process in which the clergy of the imperial churches and the monks of the imperial abbeys played an indispensable role and may indeed have been intended to strengthen the ties between the dynasty and the churches.[59] Certainly the abbots of Hersfeld (as we shall see) remained steadfastly loyal to the dynasty for the rest of the century. In the case of Lampert, however, his writings reveal an individual whose loyalty was given not to the Salian dynasty but to the *memoria* of Henry III.

In Lampert's account of the history of Hersfeld Henry III appears as the generous benefactor who granted the abbey 'the tithes of the lands of the royal fisc as long as he lived'.[60] Lampert represented Henry as 'like another Charles, virtuous and pious', the equal, that is to say, of Charlemagne, the protector and benefactor of Hersfeld, whose virtues Lampert celebrated in his biography of Lul, the founder of Hersfeld.[61] 'Very many men likened [Henry] to Charles the Great himself: since indeed he possessed that excellent character, that magnificence in his actions, that humility, piety, clemency, affability and generosity in giving alms.'[62] Lampert, born no later than 1028, grew to maturity in the reign of Henry III and seems ever afterwards to have conceived of that reign as a golden age of harmony in Church and kingdom.

---

57 Vogtherr (1991) pp. 440–1.

58 *MGH DD.H.III* 63, 100, 127, 274. On the significance of the transaction recorded in *D.H.III* 302 (by restoring in 1053 property in eastern Saxony that had been alienated by Margrave Ekkehard of Meissen, Henry III was able to redeem a crown that he had previously left in pawn to the abbey of Hersfeld) see Vogtherr (1991) pp. 441–2. See also Kehr (1930) p. 25.

59 *DD.H.III* 100, 127. See Schmid (1984b) pp. 666–726.

60 Lampert, *Libelli de institutione Herveldensis ecclesiae* I, p. 352. No record survives of this grant among the diplomas of Henry III.

61 Lampert, *Libelli de institutione Herveldensis ecclesiae* I, p. 351. Cf. Lampert, *Vita Lulli archiepiscopi Mogontiacensis* c. 14, 19, pp. 326–8, 332–3.

62 Lampert, *Libelli de institutione Herveldensis ecclesiae* I, pp. 351–2 (a fragment surviving only in Paul Lang's *Chronicon Citizense*).

What Lampert believed himself to be recording in the *Annals* was the disastrous decline in standards in public life that followed the death of Henry III. Lampert's consistently hostile portrayal of Henry IV was prompted by his idealised memory of the king's father.[63] A similar idealisation of Henry III is visible in the revised version of the chronicle of Lampert's contemporary, Berthold, monk of the imperial abbey of Reichenau in Swabia.[64] Most importantly, this was also the view of 'Emperor Henry of pious memory' held by the papal reform party in Rome. The reformers honoured him as a sincere opponent of the practice of simony in ecclesiastical appointments: Henry III 'had cut off all the heads of the many-headed hydra, simoniacal heresy, with the sword of heavenly virtue'.[65]

The rumours and later the open accusations of simony levelled against the regime of Henry IV in the 1060s and 1070s heightened the contrast between the young king and his reform-minded father. Lampert was keen to emphasise the evil reputation of Henry IV at the papal court: the king 'had been denounced to the apostolic see as guilty of the heresy of simony for having sold ecclesiastical offices'.[66] It is to Lampert's *Annals* that we owe much of our information about the accusations of simony in the German Church. The annal for 1063 already reports that 'bishoprics and abbacies and all manner of ecclesiastical and secular offices were sold' by the young king's advisers, Archbishop Adalbert of Hamburg-Bremen and his ally, Count Werner.[67] In 1071 the king's confidant Bishop Charles of Constance was proved by his clergy to have obtained his office by means of 'simoniacal heresy' and lost his office despite the efforts of Henry IV to protect him 'with the majesty of his royal authority'.[68] The *cause célèbre* in the *Annals* is that of Bishop Herman of Bamberg. Lampert's detailed account of the allegations that Herman became bishop 'by means of simoniacal heresy and the squandering of huge sums of money' and of the protracted proceedings that ended in his deposition by the pope (1075) reveals his keen interest in the affairs of Bamberg.[69]

---

63 See Struve (1970a) p. 34: 'The reign of Henry III set the standard according to which Lampert henceforward judged the kingdom and the empire.'

64 Berthold of Reichenau, *Chronicle* 1056, pp. 113–14. See Robinson (2008) pp. 25–7.

65 Peter Damian, *Letter* 40, p. 501.

66 Lampert, *Annals* 1074, below p. 232.

67 *Ibid.*, 1063, below p. 92.

68 *Ibid.*, 1069, 1071, below pp. 124, 150.

69 *Ibid.*, 1065, 1070, 1075, below pp. 108, 125–6, 245–51.

Lampert's severest denunciations of simony relate to the appointments of abbots of imperial abbeys. He reported the abbatial election of 1075 in Fulda with the *Schadenfreude* characteristic of his accounts of the troubles of Hersfeld's illustrious neighbour and rival. 'As if in a contest in officially convened public games, each man ran the race to the utmost of his ability. One man promised mountains of gold, another promised vast benefices from the lands of Fulda, a third promised more than the customary services to the State.... What morals, what times!'[70] Even more polemical is Lampert's account of the two successive abbatial appointments in Reichenau that were tainted by simony. After the resignation of the simoniac Abbot Meginward, 'Abbot Rupert of Bamberg, nicknamed "the money-changer", intruded into his place ... through the underground passage of simoniacal heresy, after paying out 1,000 pounds of the purest silver into the king's treasury'.

Lampert's portrait of Rupert, abbot of St Michael's in Bamberg and subsequently abbot of Reichenau, must owe much to Bamberg gossip, to which the author evidently still had access. 'This man had amassed for himself an enormous sum of money by means of the most squalid methods of profiteering and usury, which he had practised even when he was still an ordinary monk in the monastery.' In 'his unbridled ambition' for high office he longed for the deaths of bishops and abbots and, when they disappointed him by their obstinate longevity, he produced 'the secret gifts by means of which the favour of the confidential advisers of the king must be purchased' and 'promised the king himself 100 pounds of gold' if he would remove the abbot of Fulda and give his abbey to Rupert himself. Henry IV was prevented from agreeing to this proposal by 'a few men who valued the laws of the Church more than money'. The example of Abbot Rupert proved to be contagious. 'This false monk ... so dishonoured, corrupted and injured the holy and angelic profession of the monks that in our times and in these lands ... in the election of abbots the question is not who is the most worthy to hold office but who can purchase the abbacy at the higher price. Thus through the device invented by this man ... this custom has been introduced into the Church, according to which abbeys are prostituted by being offered for sale publicly in the palace.' The hostile portrait of Rupert has broadened into a violent polemic against the prevalence of monastic simony in the reign of Henry IV. 'To lament over these matters as they deserve would,' Lampert concluded, 'in view of their

---

70 *Ibid.*, 1075, below, p. 289. On the Ciceronian quotation see above p. 6 n. 25.

great importance, necessitate a book devoted to them alone and a tragic work of greater length.'[71]

Just as Henry III, the generous benefactor of Hersfeld and the active opponent of simony, represented for Lampert the ideal of kingship, so his friend Abbot Meginher of Hersfeld was 'the unique model of correct monastic living in the German territories in his generation', a model from whom the subsequent generation of abbots had sadly deviated. This was certainly true, in Lampert's opinion, of Meginher's immediate successors in Hersfeld, Abbot Ruthard (1059–72) and Hartwig (1072–90).[72] In his history of his monastery Lampert introduced Meginher as 'a monk [of Hersfeld who] succeeded as abbot, a serious and good man, whose teaching harmonised with his life'. Lampert emphasised that Meginher 'was skilled in all the arts' and 'established a school'. One of the most eloquent passages in Lampert's works is devoted to this school. 'What shall I say of the scholarly exercises? At that time studies were pursued with such passion that other monasteries sent their most promising pupils there to be taught. Everywhere mother Hersfeld diffused the perfume of her fame through the respect shown for the sons brought up in that dwelling-place of philosophy *from*, as they say, *earliest childhood.*'[73] Other authors testified to the flourishing condition of the school in the later eleventh century. Hersfeld was 'the fortunate sanctuary of philosophy', 'a royal place, outstandingly excellent in the studies of the liberal arts and of secular knowledge'.[74]

It has been suggested that at some point during the third quarter of the eleventh century Lampert himself was the master of this school.[75] Lampert's encomium on 'mother Hersfeld' as the 'dwelling-place of philosophy' certainly encourages this conjecture. Its rhetorical exuberance is a pointed reminder of that mastery of the *artes* that seems previously to have qualified him to be *magister scholarum* in Bamberg. Support for this conjecture is found in the writings of the only other known Hersfeld authors of the later eleventh century. Both Ekkebert, monk of

---

71 Lampert, *Annals* 1069, below p. 124; 1071, below pp. 145–6.

72 See below pp. 21–4.

73 Lampert, *Libelli de institutione Herveldensis ecclesiae* I, p. 350 (the encomium on the school is a fragment surviving in Paul Lang's *Chronicon Citizense.* The quotation is from Horace, *Carmina* III.6.24). Cf. Lampert, *Annals* 1059, below p. 75.

74 The descriptions respectively of Ekkebert of Hersfeld, *Vita sancti Haimeradi*, prologue, p. 598; Rudolf of St Trond, *Gesta abbatum Trudonensium* c. 5, p. 232.

75 See Holder-Egger in *Lamperti Opera* p. XIV; Wattenbach-Holtzmann-Schmale (1967) p. 458; Struve (1969) p. 56.

Hersfeld, in his *Life* of the hermit Haimerad of Hasungen (composed between 1085 and 1090), and the anonymous monk of Hersfeld who composed the anti-papal polemic *The preservation of the unity of the Church* (composed in 1092–3), were careful imitators of Lampert's style, as well as borrowers from his works.[76] That such imitation was associated with the relationship of pupil and master has been observed in the case of some of these authors' contemporaries: for example, the chronicler Berthold, pupil of Herman 'the Lame' of Reichenau, and the chronicler Bernold of St Blasien, pupil of Bernard of Hildesheim.[77] It is possible, therefore, that both Ekkebert of Hersfeld and the Hersfeld anonymous were among the younger pupils taught by Lampert as *magister scholarum* in the abbey.

The respect for Lampert's erudition and his influence in Hersfeld are evident in the last of the autobiographical passages included in his *Annals*. In the annal for 1071 (the penultimate year of the abbatiate of Ruthard of Hersfeld) Lampert described his visit to the abbeys of Siegburg and Saalfeld, products of the reforming initiatives of Archbishop Anno of Cologne. Lampert 'came there to consult [the monks] about the order and discipline of the monastic life, since popular report ascribed great and distinguished qualities to them'. 'I ... came to them and stayed with them for fourteen weeks, partly in Saalfeld and partly in Siegburg. I observed that our customs corresponded better than theirs to the *Rule* of St Benedict, if we were willing to hold as firmly to our principles and follow as rigorously and zealously the traditions of our predecessors.'[78] The context of Lampert's visit was a new movement of monastic reform in Germany, originating not in the imperial abbeys like Hersfeld but in the monastic foundations of princes who, like Anno of Cologne, were sympathetic to reform. They were sympathisers like Archbishop Siegfried of Mainz, Dukes Rudolf of Swabia and Berthold I of Carinthia

---

76 On Lampert's stylistic influence in Ekkebert, *Vita sancti Haimeradi* pp. 595–607 see Holder-Egger in *Lamperti Opera* p. VIII n. 1; Holder-Egger (1894) pp. 181, 206, 567–9; Struve (1969) p. 62 n. 14. On Lampert's stylistic influence in the Hersfeld anonymous, *Liber de unitate ecclesiae conservanda* pp. 173–284, see Struve (1969) pp. 65–71; Robinson (1978b) pp. 545–6.

77 Berthold identified himself as the pupil of Herman in his biography of his master: Berthold, *Chronicle* 1054, p. 111. On Berthold's imitation of his master's style see I. S. Robinson, introduction, *Die Chroniken Bertholds von Reichenau und Bernolds von Konstanz* pp. 44–9. On Bernold as the pupil of Bernard see Robinson (1989) pp. 169–70, 177–8; on Bernold's style, *ibid.*, pp. 166–8.

78 Lampert, *Annals* 1071, below pp. 152, 154. Semmler (1959) pp. 217–23 wished to date Lampert's visit to 1077, by which year he believed that the author had moved to the abbey of Hasungen. See the counter arguments of Struve (1969) pp. 86–7.

and Count Adalbert of Calw, who were soon to become the political opponents of King Henry IV.[79]

In his analysis of this monastic reform movement Lampert identified its origins in a reaction against the recent cases of simony in the imperial abbeys that he associated in particular with Abbot Rupert of Bamberg and Reichenau. 'The shameful personal conduct of certain false monks had branded the name of monk with extreme infamy, since they abandoned the study of godliness and devoted all their efforts to money and profit.'[80] 'For this reason the princes of the kingdom summoned monks from beyond the Alps to establish a school of divine service in Gaul,' who imposed 'a stricter way of life' in their monasteries. Consequently 'the ordinary people' and to an even greater extent the princes 'regarded us' – that is, the monks of the imperial abbeys – 'with whom they had long been familiar, as worthless and thought that these monks – because they seemed to offer something new and unusual – were not men but angels, not flesh but spirit'.[81]

These 'monks from beyond the Alps' came from the north Italian abbey of Fruttuaria, the foundation of the distinguished reformer William 'of Volpiano', abbot of St-Bénigne, Dijon, notable for his extreme austerity. The abbey enjoyed royal protection but was not an imperial abbey, owing the services characteristic of the 'imperial Church system'. Lampert recorded that Archbishop Anno of Cologne, while travelling in Italy 'on the business of the State', visited Fruttuaria, where 'he admired the way of life of the monks, which was very strict and accorded with the traditions of the *Rule*, and on his return he brought away with him some of those who were most practised in the service of God'. Anno entrusted the reform of his foundation of Siegburg to twelve monks of Fruttuaria (perhaps in 1068) 'in order', wrote Lampert, 'to transmit the model of that same discipline to Gaul'.[82] It was the monastic 'customs' (*consuetudines*) of Fruttuaria that also provided the model for the reform of the monastery of St Blasien, which commemorated Duke Rudolf of Swabia as its founder.[83] Lampert reported that Anno's innovation was widely

79 See Jakobs (1968) pp. 239–90; Jakobs (1973) pp. 87–115; Schmid (1973) pp. 295–319; Vogel (1984) pp. 1–30; Robinson (1999) pp. 126–7.

80 Lampert, *Annals* 1071, below p. 153. See above pp. 15–16 and n. 71.

81 Lampert, *Annals* 1071, below pp. 154, 152. On 'Gaul' (*Gallia*) as a designation for Germany see Lugge (1960) pp. 132–40 and n. 238.

82 Lampert, *Annals* 1075, below p. 294. See Semmler (1959) pp. 35–50, 60–3, 118–20; Schieffer (1971) pp. 154–6.

83 See Jakobs (1968) pp. 39–42, 160, 266–90; Jakobs (1973) pp. 106–12; Vogel (1984) pp. 1–5, 24–30.

imitated. 'The rest of the bishops of Gaul' recruited monks, 'some from Gorze, some from Cluny, some from Siegburg', 'and each bishop established a new school of divine service in his monasteries'.[84]

The importation into Germany of the monastic 'customs' of Fruttuaria – that is, the precise way in which the *Rule* of Benedict was interpreted in the daily life of the monastery – seemed to offer a challenge to the validity of the 'customs' of the imperial abbeys. Hence Lampert was sent by his abbey to Saalfeld and Siegburg to investigate whether the 'customs' so much admired by Anno of Cologne truly 'accorded with the traditions of the *Rule*'. Lampert's judgement was, as we have seen, unequivocal. 'I observed that our customs corresponded better than theirs to the *Rule* of St Benedict.'[85] Despite his sincere veneration for the memory of Anno of Cologne, Lampert could not approve of the 'life of the strictest discipline' that he had imposed on his monastic foundations. Lampert's account of the rapid dissemination of the monastic reform, although included in his lengthy eulogy of the archbishop in the annal for 1075, is ironical in tone. 'The desire to imitate this fortunate development so grew in strength that we now see few monasteries in Gaul that have not already submitted to the yoke of this new institution.'[86] It is not so much the image of submission to the yoke but the adjective 'new' that is damning. In Lampert's vocabulary the terms 'new' and 'modern' always have a pejorative meaning. For example, according to Lampert, King Henry IV was condemned by the pope for his 'new and extraordinary rebellion against the apostolic see' in 1076; while the Saxon rebels in 1073 accused him of having 'defiled our land with unheard-of inventions'.[87] Lampert characterised 'the common people' (whom he regarded with hostility and contempt) as 'eager for novelties' and noted their enthusiasm for the reformed monks, who 'seemed to offer something new and unusual'.[88]

In the years following Lampert's visit to Saalfeld and Siegburg and his confident rejection of their 'customs' Hersfeld continued to investigate 'this new institution' of monastic reform. The evidence is a letter from the monks of Monte Cassino addressed to Hartwig of Hersfeld, from which it appears that the abbot had written to this most prestigious

---

84 Lampert, *Annals* 1075, below p. 294.

85 *Ibid.*, 1071, below p. 154.

86 *Ibid.*, 1075, below p. 294.

87 *Ibid.*, 1076, below p. 307; 1073, below p. 182.

88 *Ibid.*, 1071, below p. 152 and n. 751. Cf. *ibid.*, 1074, below p. 224 and n. 1178; 1075, below p. 252 and n. 1329. See Struve (1970a) pp. 51–5, 41–2 and nn. 21–2.

of Benedictine monasteries, regarded as the foundation of St Benedict himself, about the 'customs' of reformed monasteries. Hartwig must have referred specifically to the 'customs' of Cluny, the best known of the reformed abbeys of the eleventh century, since the Cassinese monks replied: 'regarding what you say in particular about the tonsure and habit of the Cluniacs, we can briefly reply that they do not please us nor ought they to please anyone who wishes to live a regular life, for they seem entirely contrary to the *Rule*.'[89] 'We are amazed in no small degree,' wrote the Cassinese monks, 'that some men, puffed up by immoderate pride and contempt, rashly dare, by means of one [custom], albeit good, to destroy another that is no less good and is perhaps better.' Since it would be difficult to set down all the Cassinese 'customs' and send them to Hersfeld, as Hartwig had requested, one of the Hersfeld monks should be sent to Monte Cassino to spend a year or more, studying the life of the abbey. (It is not known whether such a visit – along the lines of Lampert's visit to Saalfeld and Siegburg – was ever undertaken.)

Meanwhile the attitude of Monte Cassino was: 'we observe the commands of our father, blessed Benedict, and we do not wish to deviate from the path of so great a truth for the sake of any alien and new custom'. The advice to Hersfeld was: 'do not be eager to change your customs and ordinances for any others, unless they differ from the *Rule*.'[90] This was, of course, the same conclusion that Lampert reached in his annal for 1071. Perhaps he was consciously echoing the letter from Monte Cassino in this annal, which, like the rest of his *Annals*, was written (as we shall see) in the later 1070s.[91] This letter has generally been dated in 1072 or 1073, at the beginning of the abbatiate of Hartwig[92] but its precise reference to Cluny might well suggest that the correspondence was prompted by the gradual adoption of the 'customs' of Cluny by the reformed monastery of Hirsau during the later 1070s. This was

89 *Die ältere Wormser Briefsammlung* p. 15. The editor, W. Bulst, rejected the argument of Hallinger (1950) pp. 175, 450–1, that this was a 'circular letter' from Monte Cassino to the German imperial abbeys, since copies from the abbeys of Fulda and Lorsch also survive. Bulst p. 14 emphasised that the letter was a response to particular questions from Abbot Hartwig and that its further dissemination was the work of Hersfeld. See also Feierabend (1913) pp. 20–1; Semmler (1959) pp. 217–19; Struve (1970a) pp. 68–9.

90 *Die ältere Wormser Briefsammlung* p. 15.

91 See below pp. 31–4.

92 See Feierabend (1913) p. 20; Bulst (as n. 89) p. 13; Hallinger (1950) pp. 175, 450; Struve (1970a) p. 68 n. 57.

the process that transformed Hirsau into the most important centre of monastic reform in southern Germany during the Investiture Contest.[93]

The 'customs' of Hirsau are the target of a polemic that reveals the continuation of Hersfeld's preoccupation with monastic reform into the early 1090s. This was *The preservation of the unity of the Church*, the work of the anonymous monk of Hersfeld who (as we have seen) was a careful imitator of Lampert's style and perhaps his pupil in the Hersfeld school.[94] He defended the traditions of the imperial abbeys against the monastic reformers, whose 'customs, which are the commands of men, carry more weight in their monasteries than the Gospel of Christ and the commandment of God'.[95] At their head were 'the monks of Hirsau, from whose school came ... that civil war by which that single order of monks has long been split into very many sects'. In an extraordinary escalation of Lampert's criticisms of the 'new' monasticism, the polemic of the anonymous monk of Hersfeld ascribes to the proponents of monastic reform responsibility not only for the disputes about 'customs' in the German monasteries but also for the divisions of the Investiture Contest itself. The reformers were 'the promoters or authors of the schisms that were caused a while ago both in the Church and in the State'.[96]

After the annal of 1071 containing Lampert's defence of the monastic traditions of Hersfeld, the work contains no further autobiographical information. The conjectures of Lampert's editor, Oswald Holder-Egger (1894), about the author's later career focused on the likelihood of his growing estrangement from his abbot and brethren in Hersfeld. Throughout the abbatiate of Hartwig (1072–90) Hersfeld remained consistently loyal to the king and indeed the abbey became one of Henry IV's most reliable supporters during the Saxon wars. (Hence the historian Abbot Rudolf of St Trond would subsequently describe Hersfeld as 'the royal place'.)[97] On the basis of Lampert's narrative of events in Saxony and Thuringia in the *Annals* Holder-Egger suggested that already in 1074 Lampert 'was suspected in the circle of his royalist

---

93 See Hallinger (1950) pp. 428–42; Büttner (1966) pp. 321–38; Cowdrey (1970) pp. 196–209.

94 See above p. 17.

95 *Liber de unitate ecclesiae conservanda* II.41, p. 271.

96 *Ibid.*, II.38, p. 266. See Hallinger (1950) pp. 454–6; Semmler (1959) p. 218.

97 Rudolf of St Trond, *Gesta abbatum Trudonensium* I.5, p. 232. See Feierabend (1913) pp. 109–20; Vogtherr (1991) pp. 451–3.

brethren of leanings towards the rebellious Saxons and Thuringians'.[98]
That Lampert encountered criticism in the abbey around this time is
clear from his preface to his history of Hersfeld, which survives only in
fragmentary form. Here he referred to another of his works – no longer
extant – 'in heroic metre' (that is, hexameters) concerning the recent
history of Hersfeld. For reasons that are not specified the work was
not well received: 'I am accused of having written in the verses very
many falsehoods instead of truths.' He consequently judged himself to
be 'unsuitable' to record 'the deeds enacted in modern times' despite
his keen interest in them. (Here Lampert blended his reference to the
criticism of his earlier readers with the 'humility *topos*' conventional in
the writing of eleventh-century prefaces.)[99] The divergence in opinion
between Lampert and his royalist brethren can only have been intensified by the conflicts between the king and the pope and the king and
the princes in 1076, which Lampert attributed in his *Annals* entirely to
the malice of Henry IV. It is significant, as Holder-Egger (1894) noted,
that 'in the entire long narrative of the events of the year 1076 and the
first months of 1077 [Lampert] makes no mention at all of his abbot
and his monastery'.[100]

Lampert's attitude towards Abbot Hartwig of Hersfeld is indeed mainly
to be inferred from the silence of the *Annals*. Reporting the resignation of the ailing Abbot Ruthard (December 1072), Lampert added
the briefest of statements about his successor: 'according to his wish,
H., a monk of the same monastery, immediately succeeded him'. In all
the manuscripts of the *Annals* the abbot's name is represented only by
the initial letter, which suggests that Lampert wrote only 'H.' in his
autograph.[101] In the other four references to Hartwig he appears simply
as 'the abbot of Hersfeld' without his name.[102] Three of these references
are neutral in tone but the first reference is critical of Hartwig's failure
to defend the interests of Hersfeld in the Thuringian tithes dispute.
In the synod of Erfurt (March 1073) Hartwig was frightened by the

98 See Holder-Egger (1894) p. 209.

99 Lampert, *Libelli de institutione Herveldensis ecclesiae* I, prologue, p. 345. Holder-Egger
    (1894) pp. 210–11 suggested that the controversial subject was the Thuringian
    tithes dispute. On the date of this work see Struve (1969) pp. 38–9. On the 'humility
    topos' see Arbusow (1963) pp. 98, 104–6; Simon (1958) pp. 108–19. I am grateful to
    Dr Conor McCann for drawing my attention to the latter work.

100 See Holder-Egger (1894) pp. 195–6.

101 Lampert, *Annals* 1072, below p. 162. On the manuscripts see Holder-Egger (1894)
    p. 205 n. 2.

102 Lampert, *Annals* 1073, below pp. 165–8, 188; 1074, below pp. 207, 211.

king's threats and was 'compelled to pass under the yoke'. His conduct is juxtaposed to that of his neighbour, Abbot Widerad of Fulda, who 'remained steadfast and firm in his purpose for some days' after Hartwig had deserted their common cause.[103]

There is an obvious contrast with the admiring portrait of Hartwig in *The preservation of the unity of the Church*, the work of the anonymous monk of Hersfeld, the imitator of Lampert and possibly his pupil. In this portrait of 1092–3 Hartwig appears as 'extremely educated and learned both in moral disciplines and in the holy Scriptures': 'through the application of his wisdom and ingenuity the unity of the evil men [who opposed Henry IV] was destroyed'.[104] There is a similar contrast between Lampert's view of Hartwig and that of Ekkebert, monk of Hersfeld, another imitator and perhaps also a pupil of Lampert. Ekkebert dedicated his *Life* of Haimerad of Hasungen 'to the unique model of true virtue, his lord and father, Hartwig', in a passage adapted from Lampert's description of Abbot Meginher of Hersfeld in the *Annals*.[105]

Meginher, as we have seen, constituted Lampert's ideal of monastic virtue: 'renowned throughout the whole world', he was 'the unique model of correct monastic living in the German territories in his generation'.[106] By comparison, Meginher's successor, Ruthard, 'was rather more negligent in his observance of the holy *Rule* than morals and the times required'. Nevertheless Lampert declared that 'he was extremely learned in the holy Scriptures and so skilful in speaking that no man of that time discoursed of the word of God with more eloquence or with more penetration or with more refinement'.[107] To Hartwig Lampert attributed no qualities whatsoever and he seems to have concealed his full name. It is significant that he included the information that on his deathbed Abbot Ruthard 'repented and deplored' his decision to resign his office. Whether this means that he regretted the succession, 'according to his wish', of Hartwig is not clear.[108]

Holder-Egger (1894) conjectured that Lampert himself hoped to become Ruthard's successor.[109] His conjecture was partly inspired by

103 *Ibid.*, 1073, pp. 167–8.
104 *Liber de unitate ecclesiae conservanda* II.28, p. 249.
105 Ekkebert, *Vita sancti Haimeradi* p. 598.
106 Lampert, *Annals* 1058, below p. 72; 1059, below p. 75.
107 *Ibid.*, 1074, below p. 236.
108 *Ibid.*, 1074, below p. 236; 1072, below p. 162.
109 Holder-Egger in *Lamperti Opera* p. XVI.

the discrepancy between the two versions of the succession composed by Lampert, that in the history of Hersfeld being written before the account in the *Annals*. The fragmentary earlier version, composed at the request of Abbot Hartwig himself, reads: 'Abbot Ruthard was enfeebled by old age and resigned Hersfeld to Henry [IV] on his arrival. The monk Hartwig was put in his place by the same Henry. This pleased [Archbishop] Anno [of Cologne].' The version in the *Annals* says nothing either of the presence of the king on the occasion of Ruthard's resignation or of Archbishop Anno's approval of Hartwig's succession.[110] Holder-Egger suggested that 'Anno had formerly been on friendly terms with Lampert' – that is, as his teacher in the cathedral school of Bamberg – and 'strove then to appoint Lampert abbot'. The king opposed the appointment and Anno was forced to accept the election of Hartwig. Such an event would explain Lampert's intense hostility towards Henry IV and his strained relations with Abbot Hartwig.[111] The most striking piece of evidence used by Holder-Egger to support his conjecture derives from Lampert's account of the Christmas festivities in Bamberg in 1072, just a fortnight after Ruthard's resignation and Hartwig's succession. 'There also the archbishop of Cologne, who was displeased by much that happened in the palace that was contrary to justice and fairness, requested from the king that he should thereafter be given an exemption from participating in the government of the State.'[112] Perhaps Lampert believed that Anno's failure to influence the election in Hersfeld was the factor that prompted his sudden withdrawal from the royal court.

There is considerable agreement with the suggestion of Holder-Egger that the author of the violently anti-Henrician *Annals* could not have remained in the royalist abbey of Hersfeld for the rest of his life. Having failed to persuade his brethren by means of the *Annals* to abandon Henry IV, he departed or was expelled from the congregation.[113] In the opinion of Haller (1938), 'Lampert left Hersfeld voluntarily or under compulsion at the latest in 1077.'[114] Apart from these conjectures, in attempting to reconstruct the later career of Lampert we are dependent on a few scraps of evidence from outside the text of the *Annals* that are difficult to

---

110 Lampert, *Libelli de institutione Herveldensis ecclesiae* II, p. 354; Lampert, *Annals* 1072, below p. 162.

111 Holder-Egger in *Lamperti Opera* pp. XVI–XVII.

112 Lampert, *Annals* 1073, below p. 163.

113 Holder-Egger in *Lamperti Opera* p. XIX and n. 1; Holder-Egger (1894) pp. 169 and n. 1, 202–4.

114 Haller (1938) p. 422. See also Stengel (1955) p. 251; Struve (1969) pp. 59, 86.

interpret. Firstly, the early sixteenth-century Göttingen manuscript of the *Annals* originally bore the title, 'The chronicle of Lampert, formerly abbot of Hasungen'.[115] Secondly, two early sixteenth-century humanist historians referred to Lampert by the same title. Hartman Schedel entitled his extracts from the *Annals*, 'From the chronicle of Lampert, formerly abbot of Hasungen, which is held in the monastery of St Peter in Erfurt in an ancient script'. Schedel seems to be referring here to the lost Erfurt manuscript from which the extant Göttingen manuscript was copied.[116] Schedel's contemporary, Andreas of Michelsberg, noted that 'Lampert, monk of Hersfeld and abbot of Hasungen, wrote a very famous chronicle'.[117] Finally, there is the problematical evidence of the forged foundation charter of the abbey of Hasungen, claiming to have been granted by Archbishop Siegfried of Mainz in 1082. Although a forgery of *circa* 1100, the charter undoubtedly refers to an actual event, briefly recorded in narrative sources. Archbishop Siegfried is said to have transformed into a Benedictine abbey in 1081 the house of canons that he had founded seven years before in Hasungen (west of Kassel).[118] The forged charter represents Siegfried as saying that 'we have chosen the order of most holy religion of Cluny' and 'we have followed this order with Abbot Lampert as the guide'.[119]

From these unpromising materials Stengel (1955) reconstructed his narrative of the last years of the career of Lampert as abbot of Hasungen. That Lampert, monk of Hersfeld, did indeed become an abbot was confirmed for Stengel by the fragment of the necrology of Hersfeld that commemorated the death of an Abbot *Lambhertus* on 2 October. Since there was no one of this name in the sequence of the abbots of Hersfeld, this must refer to a monk of Hersfeld who exercised the office elsewhere and the 'Abbot Lampert of Hasungen' remembered in Erfurt and identified in the forged foundation charter of Hasungen is the only available candidate.[120] Stengel deduced that, when Lampert left

---

115 The place-name was altered by a later hand to 'Hirsau'. See Stengel (1955) p. 248 and n. 30; Struve (1969) p. 85.

116 See Stengel (1955) p. 247 n. 26; Struve (1969) p. 85. On the lost Erfurt codex see Holder-Egger in *Lamperti Opera* p. L; Holder-Egger (1894) pp. 150–1.

117 See Holder-Egger in *Lamperti Opera* pp. LVII–LVIII; Holder-Egger (1894) p. 249; Stengel (1955) p. 247 n. 27; Struve (1969) p. 85.

118 Cf. *Annals of Iburg* 1074, p. 436; *Annals of Ottobeuren* 1081, p. 7. See Büttner (1949) p. 46; Hallinger (1950) pp. 260, 267–8; Stengel (1955) p. 249; Struve (1969) p. 85.

119 *Mainzer Urkundenbuch* no. 358, pp. 253–8. See Hallinger (1950) pp. 542–3; Stengel (1955) pp. 250–4; Semmler (1959) pp. 219–20.

120 See Stengel (1955) p. 247 and n. 25; Semmler (1959) pp. 220–1; Struve (1969) pp. 91–4.

Hersfeld, he 'found refuge' in Hasungen, the proprietary monastery of Archbishop Siegfried of Mainz. As abbot of Hasungen, Lampert played the leading role in converting the congregation of canons that Siegfried had founded in Hasungen in 1074 into a community following the *Rule* of Benedict.[121]

In the pages of Lampert's *Annals* Siegfried of Mainz is seen to act against the interests of Hersfeld in the Thuringian tithes dispute and he is castigated for 'his private hatred of the Thuringians'. The archbishop's demand for the payment of tithes 'was the source and starting-point of all the disasters by which the State had now been very unhappily tormented for very many years'.[122] Stengel argued that Lampert was reconciled to Siegfried when the latter changed his political allegiance. In 1076 'the archbishop of Mainz and very many others who had hitherto vigorously supported the party of the king, abandoned him and joined the princes' who were conspiring to depose Henry IV.[123] In Stengel's opinion, Lampert underwent 'a change of mind, which is very probably to be attributed to a man like him, who ... never had any mental reservations about sacrificing truth to his own inclination'.[124] Stengel also ascribed to Lampert a more extreme 'change of mind': the acceptance of what the forged foundation charter of 1082 calls 'the order of most holy religion of Cluny' when he became abbot of Hasungen.[125]

There is independent evidence of the presence in Hasungen in the 1080s of monks of Hirsau, whose abbot, the distinguished reformer William of Hirsau, had adopted the 'customs' of Cluny in 1079.[126] A Hirsau tradition records that 'Abbot Giselbert was sent to Hasungen.' This undated report refers to the distinguished monastic reformer who, before becoming abbot of St Peter's in Erfurt and simultaneously abbot of Reinhardsbrunn (✝1101), had been abbot of Hasungen. It is also recorded that he was compelled to leave Hasungen with about fifty monks at some point during the archiepiscopate of the pro-Henrician Wezilo of Mainz (1084–8).[127] That the Hirsau–Cluniac reform could

121 Stengel (1955) p. 252.

122 Lampert, *Annals* 1073, below pp. 165–8; 1069, below p. 119; 1074, below p. 240.

123 *Ibid.*, 1076, below p. 331.

124 Stengel (1955) p. 252.

125 *Ibid.*, p. 253.

126 See Hallinger (1950) pp. 309, 840; Semmler (1956) pp. 261–76; Jakobs (1961) p. 40.

127 *Codex Hirsaugiensis* p. 263; Haimo, *Vita Willihelmi abbatis Hirsaugiensis* c. 16, p. 217. See Hallinger (1950) pp. 260, 384–7; Semmler (1956) pp. 261–76; Semmler (1959) pp. 129, 220, 350–1; Struve (1969) pp. 87–9.

also have been promoted by Lampert has, however, been strongly doubted by scholars.[128] As we have seen, his analysis in the *Annals* of 'this new institution' of monastic reform patronised by 'the bishops of Gaul' concluded that the traditions of the imperial abbeys were superior to the practice of the reformers. Lampert agreed with the monks of Monte Cassino, who considered that some of the 'customs' of Cluny 'seem entirely contrary to the *Rule*'.[129]

The likely explanation of this discrepancy is that the forged foundation charter of Hasungen – which refers to the introduction to Hasungen of 'the order of most holy religion of Cluny', 'with Abbot Lampert as the guide' – conflated two distinct stages of the history of Hasungen as a Benedictine monastery. The first stage was the introduction of the Benedictine *Rule* into the congregation of canons founded by Siegfried of Mainz in 1074. The second stage was the adoption of the 'customs' of Cluny with the help of monks of Hirsau. As we have seen, Hirsau tradition associates this second stage with the reformer Giselbert. It was probably to this later development that the annalist of Ottobeuren referred in his annal for 1081: 'There began to be monks on the mountain of Hasungen.' For the Ottobeuren annalist, compiling his work in the early twelfth century, principally from the *Annals of Hasungen*, now lost, the arrival of Abbot Giselbert marked the true beginning of the Benedictine observance in Hasungen. The annalist would have known that, although they had been excluded from Hasungen in the mid-1080s, Hirsau monks and Cluniac 'customs' had been reintroduced in the time of Archbishop Ruthard of Mainz (1089–1109).[130]

Before the arrival of Abbot Giselbert and the Cluniac 'customs' in 1081, however, it is likely that there had been an earlier stage of Benedictine observance in Hasungen 'with Abbot Lampert as the guide'. The suggestion is that at a date between 1074 and 1081 Lampert brought to Hasungen from Hersfeld the 'customs' of the imperial abbeys that he defended in the *Annals* as superior to those of the reforming monasteries. There is certainly some evidence of links between Hersfeld and Hasungen both before and after Lampert's abbatiate: notably

---

128 See Semmler (1956) p. 263; Semmler (1959) p. 220; Hallinger (1958–60) p. 225; Struve (1969) pp. 86–9.

129 See above pp. 17–20 and nn. 77, 80, 88.

130 *Annals of Ottobeuren* 1081, p. 7. See Hallinger (1950) p. 260; Jakobs (1961) p. 41. For the view that the lost *Annals of Hasungen* were a continuation of Lampert's *Annals*, perhaps preceded by an abridged version of Lampert's work, see Robinson (1978b) pp. 538–50.

the concern in Hersfeld with the cult of Haimerad of Hasungen. In his annal for 1072 Lampert reported that the tomb of Haimerad in Hasungen was 'renowned and held in the highest honour throughout Gaul and ... visited every day by great crowds of people because of the divine healing that was granted there again and again to the sick'.[131] Continued interest in the cult is evident in the *Life of St Haimerad* composed between 1085 and 1090 by the monk Ekkebert of Hersfeld at the request of Abbot Hartwig.[132] It is tempting to connect the commissioning of this *Life* with the suggestion of Holder-Egger (1894) that Hartwig sent Hersfeld monks to Hasungen at the request of Archbishop Wezilo of Mainz after the departure of Abbot Giselbert and his fifty supporters.[133] Hersfeld may well have provided Hasungen with a *Life* of its saint on the occasion in the mid-1080s when Hersfeld monks assisted the pro-Henrician Abbot Wigbert in ensuring the continuity of monastic life in Hasungen.[134] Given the imperialist allegiance of Abbot Wigbert and his patron, Archbishop Wezilo, it seems likely that the 'customs' of the imperial abbeys were followed in Hasungen during the interlude between two periods of Cluniac–Hirsau 'customs'.

Perhaps this was a restoration of the 'customs' of imperial monasticism after the first introduction of the Cluniac–Hirsau 'customs' in 1081. Perhaps indeed this Hersfeld mission of the mid-1080s was Abbot Hartwig's *second* intervention in the history of Hasungen as a Benedictine abbey, the first being the sending of Hersfeld monks with Lampert as their abbot at a date between 1074 and 1081, presumably at the request of Archbishop Siegfried of Mainz. Tilman Struve, in his convincing reassessment of the evidence for Lampert's abbatiate in Hasungen (1969), argued that, despite the anti-Henrician opinions in the *Annals* and the author's coolness in his allusions to his abbot, there was no overt hostility between Hartwig and Lampert. For it was Hartwig who commissioned Lampert's first work, *The Life of Lul, archbishop of Mainz*, and his subsequent history of the abbey (which survives only as fragments), both works devoted to the defence of the rights of Hersfeld. 'Hartwig would never have entrusted Lampert with

---

131 Lampert, *Annals* 1072, below p. 161.

132 Ekkebert, *Vita sancti Haimeradi* pp. 595–607. See above pp. 17 and n. 76, 23 and n. 105.

133 Holder-Egger (1894) p. 573. See also Semmler (1956) p. 275; Struve (1969) p. 90.

134 Abbot Wigbert of Hasungen (?1085–?1088) is identified in *Mainzer Urkundenbuch* no. 371, p. 270 (praising 'the constancy of Abbot Wigbert of that place, together with his tiny flock'). See Hallinger (1950) p. 260; Struve (1969) pp. 89–90.

the composition of the *Vita Lulli* and the history of the monastery if he had not regarded him as reliable.'[135] According to this interpretation of the evidence, Lampert neither fled nor was expelled from Hersfeld for his political opinions but was entrusted by Abbot Hartwig with the task of introducing the Benedictine *Rule* to Hasungen. Perhaps it was here that he died in 1081 and was succeeded by Abbot Giselbert.[136]

While much of the monastic career of Lampert remains conjectural, his literary career is well known to us. As we have seen, his first three works were concerned exclusively with the history of his own abbey. The earliest was a hagiographical work, *The Life of Lul, archbishop of Mainz*, the Anglo-Saxon pupil of St Boniface, whom he succeeded as archbishop, and the founder of Hersfeld (†786). Holder-Egger, who was the first to identify the *Life* as the work of Lampert, drew attention to its polemical character, noting the biographer's emphasis on Hersfeld's independence and his attack on the pretensions of the abbey of Fulda, the old rival of his own abbey.[137] Even more evident is the political purpose of the *Life*. The portrayal of Lul of Mainz and Charlemagne as the most active of benefactors and defenders of Hersfeld was clearly intended to serve as a model of correct conduct for contemporaries and doubtless also to provide a contrast with the failure of Archbishop Siegfried of Mainz and King Henry IV to imitate the example of their renowned predecessors. Hence Tilman Struve (1969), in dating the *Life*, placed it in the context of the Thuringian tithes dispute, which culminated in 1073.[138]

The tithes dispute was perhaps also the subject of Lampert's second work, no longer extant: a metrical work dealing with the recent history of Hersfeld. Of this poem we know only that it aroused such sharp criticism from its readers – presumably the brethren of Hersfeld – that Lampert declared that he doubted his ability to report 'the deeds of modern times'. This declaration appears in the preface of his third

---

135 Struve (1969) p. 90; see also pp. 48–51.

136 Unless the appearance of the name Lampert in the necrology of the monastery of Helmarshausen (in the diocese of Paderborn) indicates that Lampert of Hersfeld ended his life as a monk of Helmarshausen: see Freise (1981) p. 247. For the date of Lampert's death in the Hersfeld necrology as 2 October see above p. 25 and n. 120. The same date is given in the necrology of the monastery of Abdinghof (Paderborn): see Semmler (1959) pp. 220–1; Struve (1969) p. 93.

137 Holder-Egger (1884) pp. 283–320; Holder-Egger in *Lamperti Opera* pp. XXV–XXVI.

138 Lampert, *Vita Lulli* c. 19, pp. 332–3. See Struve (1969) p. 37. On the Thuringian tithes dispute see Lampert, *Annals* 1073, below pp. 164–8.

work, the history of Hersfeld commissioned by Abbot Hartwig.[139] How Lampert treated 'the deeds of modern times' in this work is not known since the history survives only in excerpts made in the early sixteenth century. The prologue and the greater part of book I were excerpted by a monk of Hamersleben in 1513, who called the work *Libellus de institutione Herveldensis ecclesiae*, a title that draws attention to the foundation of the abbey, recorded in the opening pages of book I.[140] Book II, which begins in 1056, survives only in fragments in the chronicles of the humanist historians Paul Lang and Wigand Gerstenberg, of which the latest refers to the year 1076.[141]

The *Annals* was Lampert's final work. Like his three previous works, it seems to have been undertaken to meet the needs of Hersfeld: in this instance, as a continuation of the old Hersfeld Annals (no longer extant).[142] Hence Tilman Struve (1969) suggested that, like the *Life of Lul* and the history of the abbey, the *Annals* was commissioned by Abbot Hartwig.[143] Since, unlike the two previous works, the *Annals* contains no prologue explaining the circumstances of its composition, it must remain a matter of speculation whether Hartwig actually prompted the composition of a work, the opinions of which were to prove so much at odds with his own views. It is clear from the resultant work that Lampert saw himself as a *contemporary* historian, concerned above all with 'the study of deeds enacted in modern times'.[144] Although he retained from the old Hersfeld Annals the traditional format of the 'world chronicle', a historical narrative beginning with the Creation, he did not share the interest in antiquity of, for example, his older contemporary, Herman of Reichenau, or his younger contemporary, Bernold of St Blasien.[145]

The centuries preceding Lampert's own lifetime receive the most perfunctory treatment in the *Annals*. Lampert added very little to the

---

139 Lampert, *Libelli de institutione Herveldensis ecclesiae* I, prologue, p. 345. See above p. 22 and n. 99.

140 Lampert, *Libelli de institutione Herveldensis ecclesiae* I, pp. 345–7.

141 *Ibid.*, pp. 353–4. See Holder-Egger in *Lamperti Opera* pp. XXIX–XXXIV. Additional fragments were identified by Struve (1969) pp. 40–2.

142 The old Hersfeld Annals have been reconstructed from their numerous derivatives: see the edition of G. H. Pertz under the title *Annales Hildesheimenses, Quedlinburgenses, Weissenburgenses et Lamberti pars prior*, MGH SS 3, 18–102. See also Wattenbach-Holtzmann-Schmale (1967) p. 463; Struve (1969) pp. 51–4.

143 Struve (1969) p. 51.

144 Lampert, *Libelli de institutione Herveldensis ecclesiae* I, prologue, p. 345.

145 Robinson (2008) pp. 9, 11, 50.

single annalistic source that he found in the library of Hersfeld and there is no evidence of historical research. The events from the Creation to 702 (a synopsis derived from Isidore of Seville and Bede, which preceded the old Hersfeld Annals) occupy only six pages of Holder-Egger's edition. The events of 708–984 (derived from the original Hersfeld Annals) fill twenty-four pages. The events of 984–1040 (derived from a continuation of the Hersfeld Annals composed in Hildesheim) fill eleven pages. The first two decades of Lampert's independent composition, from the accession of Henry III to 1063, occupy twenty-four pages. Thereafter the individual annals swell in size, the decade 1063–73 filling sixty pages and the last four-and-a-half years of the *Annals* (from 1073 to the beginning of 1077) being nearly three times as long, with 162 pages. Lampert began his task of continuator following the traditional annalistic form. From his annal for 1063 onwards, however, his enthusiasm for narrating the events of his own times burst through the restraints of the format. Nevertheless Lampert always adhered to a strict chronological narrative. Thus he noted in his obituary of Archbishop Anno of Cologne at the end of his annal for 1075: 'If the reader wishes to know more about what he achieved or what he suffered in the course of administering the State, he should return to the earlier pages of this little book and he will find the individual events set out in detail in the order and according to the time at which they happened.'[146]

Lampert's work ends with the decision of the 'deposition faction' of German princes to summon an assembly to meet in Forchheim on 13 March 1077. The concluding sentence invites a future continuator of the *Annals* to resume the work with an account of this assembly. 'If ... it happens that some one who comes after us should choose to put his hand to writing the remaining part of this narrative, he will find a suitable beginning for his work in the election of King Rudolf.' It is evident that Lampert was aware of the outcome of the assembly of Forchheim but he declared that he could write no more because he was 'now faint with exhaustion' and – a *topos* borrowed from Sulpicius Severus – 'overwhelmed by the sheer quantity of the subject-matter'.[147] The abruptness of the ending of the *Annals* has prompted the suggestion that it was his new duties as abbot of Hasungen that prevented his continuing the work.[148] There is general agreement among scholars that the work was completed in a single burst of composition in the

146 Lampert, *Annals* 1075, below p. 296.
147 *Ibid.*, 1077, below p. 367. Cf. Sulpicius Severus, *Vita Martini episcopi Turonensis* c. 26.
148 See Schieffer (1985) col. 519.

years 1077–8.[149] Lampert was clearly aware of the events of 1073–6, the Saxon rebellion and the deposition of the king, when he composed his account of the earlier years of Henry IV's reign.

This hindsight is apparent, for example, in the report of Count Otto of Weimar-Orlamünde's succession to his brother's office of margrave of Meissen in 1062. Otto 'could obtain the benefices of the archbishopric of Mainz only if he promised that he would give tithes from his possessions in Thuringia and would compel the rest of the Thuringians to do the same. This fact was the source of many evils; since all the Thuringians denounced his action and declared that they would rather die than lose the rights of their forefathers.'[150] The annal for 1067 notes that 'all the Thuringians rejoiced exceedingly at [Otto's] death because he was the first of the Thuringian princes (as was mentioned above) to agree to pay tithes from his possessions in Thuringia and he was seen thereby to have brought the greatest misfortune on his people'.[151] Lampert composed these reports with full knowledge of the Thuringian tithes dispute between Hersfeld and the archbishop of Mainz that was to culminate in the synod of Erfurt (March 1073). When describing Margrave Otto's concessions to Mainz as 'the source of many evils', Lampert had already formulated his view that the Thuringian tithes dispute was the principal cause of the Saxon rebellion of 1073–5. 'This issue was the source and starting-point of all the disasters by which the State had now been very unhappily tormented for very many years,' he wrote in the annal for 1074.[152] It was because Henry IV had attempted to force the Thuringians to pay tithes 'by means of the power of royal majesty' that 'he had almost lost both his kingdom and his life' in the Saxon wars.[153]

Henry IV's deposition in 1076 is foreshadowed in the *Annals* by a series of incidents in which the king is represented as being in imminent danger of losing his throne. As early as the first year of the reign the Saxons had 'decided to kill the king, whenever fortune gave them the opportunity' and seize the kingship from the seven-year-old boy 'while his age still provided an opportunity to inflict that injury'.[154] In his account

---

149 See Holder-Egger in *Lamperti Opera* pp. XXXIV–XXXV; Wattenbach-Holtzmann-Schmale (1967) pp. 462–3; Struve (1969) pp. 55–6.

150 Lampert, *Annals* 1062, below p. 80.

151 *Ibid.*, 1067, below pp. 114–15.

152 *Ibid.*, 1074, below p. 240.

153 *Ibid.*, 1073, below pp. 165, 205.

154 *Ibid.*, 1057, below pp. 69–70. The last clause was imitated from Livy II.13.10.

of the conspiracy of princes that succeeded in expelling Archbishop Adalbert of Bremen from the imperial court in January 1066, Lampert claimed that the young king was presented with an ultimatum, 'that either he should abdicate from the kingship or he should banish the archbishop of Bremen from his counsels'.[155] The annal for 1073 presents a (similarly uncorroborated) account of negotiations in Gerstungen on 20 October between the rebel Saxon princes and envoys from Henry IV, who 'finally all agreed on this decision: that they should reject the king and elect another, who was suitable to govern the kingdom'.[156] In the annal for 1074 the Saxon rebels are represented as 'unanimously' deciding to meet in Fritzlar in February 'to take counsel with the rest of the princes of the kingdom and set up a ruler for the endangered State who would be acceptable to all men'. The following month the Saxon army was reported to be marching on the palace of Goslar, wishing 'to bid [Henry IV] farewell and set up a king whom they would thereafter have as their leader in war'.[157]

The election of Rudolf of Swabia as anti-king in the assembly of Forch-heim in March 1077 is similarly presaged in the *Annals* by accounts (uncorroborated by any other source) of earlier attempts by the princes to elect him king. On the occasion of the negotiations between the Saxon rebels and the envoys of Henry IV in Gerstungen in October 1073 'they would certainly have appointed Duke Rudolf as king without any delay in that very place, had the latter not stubbornly resisted and sworn that he would never consent to this, unless an assembly was held, in which it was decided by all the princes that this could be done without incurring the disgrace of perjury and with his good name unimpaired'. Here Rudolf is portrayed as the archetypal reluctant candidate, such reluctance being regarded in the eleventh century as proof of the candidate's suitability for office.[158] The duke is also represented as insisting

---

155 Lampert, *Annals* 1066, below p. 111 and n. 469.

156 *Ibid.*, below p. 196. The king's envoys are identified as the archbishops of Mainz and Cologne, the bishops of Metz and Bamberg and the dukes of Swabia, Carinthia and Lower Lotharingia, including therefore Henry's most loyal adherents, Duke Godfrey IV of Lotharingia and Bishop Herman of Bamberg. Lampert added that the princes did not make their decision public.

157 Lampert, *Annals* 1074, below pp. 206–7, 217.

158 *Ibid.*, 1073, below p. 197 and n. 1026, for the *topos* of the reluctant candidate for high office. For Lampert's commendation of reluctance to assume office cf. also *Annals* 1073, below p. 170 (Pope Gregory VII); 1075, p. 290 (Abbot Ruozelin of Fulda). For Lampert's condemnation of ambition for office cf. 1064, p. 96 (Cadalus of Parma and Pope Alexander II); 1071, p. 145 (Abbot Rupert of Reichenau); 1071, p. 153 ('infamous' monks); 1075, pp. 289–90 (competitors for the abbacy of Fulda).

on the holding of an assembly of princes like that which was to meet in Forchheim in 1077. Later in the annal for 1073 Lampert claimed that Archbishop Siegfried of Mainz 'summoned the princes from the whole kingdom to Mainz, so that according to their common counsel he might set up Duke Rudolf as king'. The proximity of Henry IV's army, however, deterred the princes from assembling in Mainz, so that Archbishop Siegfried was unable to play the role that he would play four years later in Forchheim.[159] While the narrative of the years 1057–74 contains these allusions to the events of the crisis years 1076–7, however, there is no allusion to any event later than the election in Forchheim, no sign that the author knew of the second excommunication of Henry IV (7 March 1080) and of the death of the anti-king Rudolf (15 October 1080). As his editor Holder-Egger concluded, it could only have been in Rudolf's lifetime that Lampert would 'have written and hoped that his reign would be happy and prosperous'.[160]

'Lampert's *Annals* appeared, to use a modern expression, at an unfavourable moment,' wrote Johannes Haller (1938). For not long after the completion of 'a historical work, the narrative of which culminated in the elevation of the anti-king', Rudolf died after failing to impose his authority beyond the frontiers of Saxony. Lampert's work 'was written from the viewpoint of a particular party and this party was defeated'. His partisan account was unacceptable not only to supporters of Henry IV but also to the king's pro-papal enemies, since 'Lampert was not a true Gregorian and he had expressly rejected [in the *Annals*] the new direction in monasticism' patronised by the opposition princes. 'He was a man of a former age and the new age saw everything differently.'[161] This was presumably the reason for the surprisingly sparse manuscript tradition of the *Annals*.

Of central importance in the transmission of the text of the *Annals* was the lost manuscript on which the *editio princeps* of 1525 was based. This first edition, under the title *History of the Germans* and without the author's name, was the work of Caspar Churrer, professor in the university of Tübingen. His edition was prompted by a letter of 30 May 1525 from his friend, the great reformer Philip Melanchthon in Wittenberg, advising him of the existence of the '*historia*, of which there is a copy in the library of the Augustinian monks'. It is gener-

---

159 Lampert, *Annals* 1073, below pp. 197, 200.

160 Holder-Egger in *Lamperti Opera* p. XXXV.

161 Haller (1938) pp. 420–1. For Lampert's attitude towards the 'modern' monastic reform movements see above pp. 17–19.

ally assumed that this was a Wittenberg manuscript (perhaps drawn to Melanchthon's attention by Martin Luther, a former Augustinian friar). An Erfurt connection has also been suggested, given the close links between the Wittenberg Augustinians and Erfurt in the early sixteenth century.[162] As we have already seen, it was only in the monastery of St Peter in Erfurt that the name of the author of the *Annals* was preserved and it is with this monastery that all the existing manuscripts of the work are linked. At the beginning of the sixteenth century St Peter's, Erfurt, possessed a complete exemplar of the *Annals*, written 'in an ancient script' and attributing the work to *Lampertus*.[163] It was from this manuscript, no longer extant, that the three fullest surviving codices were copied at the beginning of the sixteenth century that are now found in Würzburg, Göttingen and Dresden. There survive also some excerpts from the *Annals* copied in the later twelfth century in a manuscript of Gotha (containing material from the years 705–1056) and a manuscript of Pommersfelden (material from the years 1039–75), both derived from the lost manuscript of St Peter's, Erfurt. The oldest surviving witness to the text of the *Annals* is an early twelfth-century fragment of the annal for 1076, now in Worms, likewise deriving from the Erfurt textual tradition.[164]

The earliest modern assessment of the value of Lampert's *Annals* as a historical source is found in Philip Melanchthon's letter of 30 May 1525 to Caspar Churrer. The distinguished humanist scholar wrote that he had never before seen a work by a German author 'more carefully composed, although [Lampert] introduced certain material concerning private affairs that is unworthy of being remembered by posterity'. The dedication of Churrer's edition praises the *Annals* as 'most felicitous both in the value of the material and the elegance of the language'.[165] The keen interest that Lampert's work inspired among German scholars is evident from the numerous editions published in the following three

---

162 *Historiae Germanorum* ed. Caspar Churrer (Tübingen: Ulrich Morhart, 1525). The letter of Philip Melanchthon was printed by Holder-Egger in *Lamperti Opera* p. XLVIII n. 2. The lost codex is designated 'A' in Holder-Egger's edition, pp. XLVII–L. Haller (1938) pp. 417–20 argued that this manuscript was found in the library of the Augustinians in Tübingen.

163 Thus Hartman Schedel, excerpting the *Annals* in his manuscript Munich, Staatsbibliothek Clm 901, fol. 134, compiled in 1507. See Holder-Egger (1894) pp. 156–7; Haller (1938) p. 415. See also above p. 2.

164 Holder-Egger in *Lamperti Opera* pp. L–LIX; Holder-Egger (1894) pp. 150–4; Haller (1938) pp. 411–16; Stengel (1955) pp. 245–6 and n. 16. The Dresden codex suffered severe water damage in the Second World War and is now barely legible.

165 Holder-Egger in *Lamperti Opera* p. XLVIII nn. 2, 3.

centuries. Already in 1533 a second edition appeared, again in Tübingen. The work of the notary Ludwig Schradin, it was the first to give a name to the author of the *Annals*: 'Lambert of Aschaffenburg'.[166] Four more editions followed in 1566 (Frankfurt), 1569 (Basel), 1574 (Basel) and 1583 (Frankfurt, reprinted in 1613). Reprints of earlier editions appeared in 1609 (Strasbourg), 1673 (Giessen) and 1726 (Regensburg) and a new edition in 1797 (Halle and Leipzig).[167] The first critical edition of Lampert's *Annals* was that of the Monumenta Germaniae Historica: the annals from the Creation to 1039 edited by G. H. Pertz in volume 3 of the *Scriptores* (Hanover, 1839) and the annals for 1040–77 prepared by L. F. Hesse and printed with additions by Georg Waitz in volume 5 of the *Scriptores* (Hanover, 1844).[168]

After the publication of the *editio princeps* in 1525, wrote Georg Waitz, Lampert's *Annals* 'seemed to learned men a very precious treasure so that thereafter all authors recounted the history of these years with Lampert as their principal authority. Would that they had also imitated and endeavoured to equal his good judgement!'[169] Early nineteenth-century German historians had indeed no reservations about the value of the *Annals*. In his account of the Salian emperors (1828) G. A. H. Stenzel praised Lampert's 'impartiality and honesty'.[170] For A. F. Gfrörer, who used the *Annals* extensively in his voluminous biography of Pope Gregory VII (1861), Lampert was 'the truthful and honour-able historian of the first rank'.[171] In his widely read *History* Wilhelm von Giesebrecht explained: 'From the year 1069 onwards I have adhered pre-eminently to Lampert's account, unless serious doubts were definitely discovered.' He added in a footnote: 'It seems to me the only means of protecting the delineation of the history of the years 1069–1076 from arbitrariness.'[172] Most famously, Giesebrecht followed Lampert closely in his description of the submission of King Henry

---

166 *Res gestae Germanorum* ed. Ludwig Schradin (Tübingen: Ulrich Morhart, 1533). The identification *Lambertus Schafnaburgensis* was suggested to the editor by Lampert, *Annals* 1058, below p. 73.

167 Holder-Egger in *Lamperti Opera* pp. LXIV–LXV.

168 *Lamberti Hersfeldensis Annales, MGH SS* 3, 18–102 (edited together with other annals using the old Hersfeld Annals: see above p. 30 and n. 142); *MGH SS* 5, 134–263; reprinted in *MGH Scriptores rerum Germanicarum* (Hanover, 1843; corrected version: Hanover, 1874).

169 G. Waitz, introduction, *Lamberti Hersfeldensis Annales, MGH SS* 5, 148–9.

170 Stenzel (1828) p. 101.

171 Gfrörer (1861) p. 602.

172 Giesebrecht (1890) p. 1036 and n. 1.

IV to Pope Gregory VII in Canossa (January 1077). When Otto von Bismarck announced to the German Reichstag on 14 May 1872, 'Do not be afraid: we are not going to Canossa – neither physically nor spiritually', his image of the events at Canossa was drawn from Giesebrecht – that is, from Lampert of Hersfeld.[173]

In his confident dependence on Lampert's *Annals*, however, Giesebrecht was not taking full account of the reservations expressed by his great contemporary Leopold von Ranke in his famous paper of 1854 to the Prussian Academy on the criticism of Frankish and German annalistic works. This ground-breaking work of source criticism included a study of Lampert's *Annals*, concluding that despite 'all the admiration inspired by his gifts as an author', Lampert's work was vitiated by his fierce partisanship. Ranke's analysis of eight important passages in the latter pages of the *Annals* demonstrated the unreliability of the annalist's judgements and the inaccuracy of his information. Lampert's bias sprang from his loyalty to the traditions of the imperial monasteries and above all of his own monastery of Hersfeld and from his hatred of King Henry IV. Ranke suggested indeed that one of Lampert's concerns in his *Annals* was to justify the election of Duke Rudolf of Swabia as anti-king by the anti-Henrician faction of German princes in March 1077.[174] Ranke would subsequently write in more positive terms of Lampert's *Annals*: 'In respect of the form of his account Lampert is highly esteemed: as far as the industry involved in its preparation is concerned, Lampert's work is the best achievement of the annalistic historiography of the Middle Ages. It is, however, thoroughly biased against Henry [IV].'[175] Ranke's paper of 1854 inspired a stream of articles and dissertations that accumulated further evidence of the unreliability of Lampert's narrative. The judgement of Harry Bresslau, for example, was that in many instances Lampert could have possessed no accurate information about the events that he recorded. 'His reports could only have originated from rumours..., from that monastic gossip (*Klosterklatsch*) that played as great a role in the writing of annals in the eleventh century as ... the gossip of newspapers in our own days.'[176]

---

173 Bismarck drew his information from his correspondent Baroness von Spitzemberg, an avid reader of Giesebrecht's *Kaiserzeit*. See Schneider (1972) p. 202 n. 655.

174 L. von Ranke, 'Zur Kritik fränkisch-deutscher Reichsannalisten. 2: Über die Annalen des Lambertus von Hersfeld', *Abhandlungen der Preußischen Akademie, phil.-hist. Klasse* (1854) pp. 436–58; expanded in Ranke (1888) pp. 125–49.

175 Ranke (1886) p. 266 n. 1.

176 Bresslau (1878) p. 145.

These studies culminated in the magisterial contribution of Oswald Holder-Egger. In 1894 he published his magnificent edition of the works of Lampert – the *Life* of Archbishop Lul of Mainz, Hersfeld's founder, and the surviving fragments of the history of Hersfeld (*Libellus de institutione Herveldensis ecclesiae*) as well as the *Annales* – with a 61-page introduction. This edition with its detailed commentary provided the soundest possible basis for subsequent Lampert studies.[177]

Simultaneously Holder-Egger published a two-hundred-page article on the life and works of Lampert.[178] He concluded that Lampert was a deliberate liar who had systematically falsified his account of events in the reign of Henry IV. 'This man had no historical conscience; he had not the slightest inkling of fidelity to historical truth.'[179] Holder-Egger adopted the suggestion of Ranke, that Lampert wished to justify the election of Rudolf of Swabia as anti-king, and transformed it into the *raison d'être* of the *Annals*. It was a polemic against Henry IV, intended to persuade the abbot and monks of Hersfeld, an imperial abbey with Henrician sympathies, that Henry was a tyrant who must be deposed and that Rudolf was his lawfully elected replacement. Lampert 'endeavoured, in drawing the character of King Henry, to apply blacker and blacker colouring, not so much through judgements pronounced on him and his doings as through the seemingly objective presentation of his actions until the negative picture is so complete that the unfortunate situation in which the king found himself at the end of 1076 seemed to be the natural consequence and just punishment of his vindictiveness, his breach of faith, his cruelty and all his other misdeeds'.[180] Nevertheless in the introduction to his edition Holder-Egger concluded that amidst all the falsehood 'there remains much that he had on good authority, which he recorded truthfully and which must be believed.... This book will, therefore, always be regarded as of great worth.'[181]

It was, however, the negative aspects of Holder-Egger's judgement that most influenced subsequent Lampert studies. During the half-century following his publications only Gerold Meyer von Knonau, in an immediate response published in 1894, rejected Holder-Egger's version of Lampert's intentions and polemical methods. From his

---

177 *Lamperti Opera, MGH Scriptores rerum Germanicarum in usum scholarum separatim editi* 38 (Hanover–Leipzig, 1894; reprinted 1956).

178 Holder-Egger (1894) pp. 141–213, 369–430, 507–74.

179 *Ibid.*, p. 517.

180 *Ibid.*, pp. 681–2.

181 Holder-Egger in *Lamperti Opera* p. XLVII.

detailed analysis of Lampert's account of Henry IV's relations with the
archbishops Adalbert of Bremen and Anno of Cologne, with the Saxon
rebels, with Pope Gregory VII and with the opposition princes in 1076
Meyer von Knonau concluded that there was no evidence of the single-
minded partisan work that Holder-Egger imagined. Instead the work
was full of the kind of internal contradictions 'that a deliberate liar
would certainly have avoided'.[182] Holder-Egger's view of the *Annals* as
a partisan work seemed, however, to be confirmed by the findings of
Edmund Stengel (1955), who, as we have seen, established that Lampert
became the first abbot of the monastery of Hasungen in Hesse. Stengel
argued from Holder-Egger's view of the *Annals* that its publication must
have brought Lampert into open conflict with Abbot Hartwig and his
brethren, so that he was forced to flee from Hersfeld: Hasungen was his
'refuge'.[183] This speculation was based entirely on the interpretation of
the *Annals* as a venomous anti-Henrician polemic.

The publication of Tilman Struve's monograph in 1969/70 brought a
very detailed reappraisal of the career and writings of Lampert, which
offered a convincing explanation of the paradox noted by Ranke and
Holder-Egger, of the author apparently without 'the slightest inkling
of fidelity to historical truth', who produced a 'book [that] will always
be regarded as of great worth'.[184] Struve's study was not concerned
primarily with the question of 'reliability', of the literal exactness of
Lampert's narrative, which dominated the later nineteenth-century
historiography, but concentrated instead on the 'literary personality'
and the 'world-picture' of the author. His starting-point was the observation of Helmut Beumann, that the medieval historian consciously or
unconsciously followed a particular bias, a 'perspective informed by
his personality and by the awareness of the time in which he wrote'
(*Zeitbewußtsein*).[185] Struve also paid close attention to the judgement of
Martin Lintzel, that medieval historians produced a 'well-upholstered
literary narrative' rather than an objective historical account, not
because of their intellectual limitations or their dishonesty but because
'they actually had no desire to know any better or to be able to do
otherwise'. For the authors of the Central Middle Ages the boundary

182 Meyer von Knonau (1894) p. 851.

183 Stengel (1955) pp. 251–2. Haller (1938) p. 422 had already assumed that Lampert
   must have left Hersfeld 'voluntarily or under compulsion' by 1077 at the latest. See
   above p. 24.

184 Struve (1969) pp. 1–123; Struve (1970a) pp. 32–142.

185 Beumann (1965) pp. 136–7. Cf. Beumann (1950) pp. VIII–IX, 205–65. I owe this
   reference to Mr Steffen Magister. See also Struve (1969) p. 10.

between 'history' and 'imaginative literature' (*Dichtung*) was still remarkably fluid.[186]

Hence Struve could conclude that, despite all the evidence quoted
by Holder-Egger, Lampert 'did not manipulate historical truth, for
whatever he presented was for him reality'.[187] Above all, as Ranke had
been the first to point out, Lampert's point of view was that of a monk,
loyal to the interests of his monastery of Hersfeld and devoted to the
monastic 'customs' (*consuetudines*) of the imperial monastic reform of
early eleventh-century Germany.[188] Lampert was also of noble birth
and his ideas and attitudes were those of the aristocracy, whose status
and rights were, in his view, coming under threat in the reign of Henry
IV.[189] Struve's summary of the standpoint from which Lampert viewed
contemporary history is entirely convincing. 'As a representative of the
nobility and as a representative of the imperial monasticism, Lampert
showed himself to be an anti-reformist traditionalist.... His general
outlook is probably to be characterised most effectively with the label
"conservative idealist".'[190]

It was especially the tribulations of Lampert's monastic *patria* of
Hersfeld that influenced his treatment of the history of his own times. In
the *Annals* Henry IV is portrayed as the persecutor of Hersfeld. Thus in
the annal for 1064 the king is blamed for the grant to the royal adviser
Count Werner of the abbey's estate of Kirchberg 'without consulting
the abbot'.[191] Lampert must, however, have been aware that this grant
must have been initiated not by the fourteen-year-old king but by his
principal adviser, Archbishop Adalbert of Bremen, on whom (according
to the annal for 1063) 'the king depended exclusively' and who 'seemed to
usurp almost sole power'. Lampert must have been equally aware of the
royal diploma of 5 April 1065 in which the king conferred on Hersfeld
an estate in the village of Hohenburg, presumably as compensation for
the loss of Kirchberg.[192] Lampert deliberately omitted information that
would have palliated the king's offence against the abbey.

186 Lintzel (1956) p. 166. See also Struve (1970a) p. 134.

187 Struve (1970a) p. 82.

188 Ranke (1888) p. 149. See also Struve (1970a) pp. 66–9.

189 See above p. 3 and n. 13.

190 Struve (1970a) p. 139.

191 Lampert, *Annals* 1064, below p. 97.

192 *Ibid.*, 1063, below p. 92; *D.H.IV* 146. Lampert, *Annals* 1066, below p. 110, reported
that after Werner was mortally wounded in an affray – having 'been destroyed by
the prayers of the monks of Hersfeld' – he restored Kirchberg to the abbey on his
deathbed. See Holder-Egger (1894) pp. 183–4.

Similarly, the misfortunes of Hersfeld in the Thuringian tithes dispute are attributed in the *Annals* primarily to the malice of the king. When after two centuries of quiescence Archbishop Liutpold of Mainz and his successor Siegfried laid claim to tithes throughout Thuringia, their intervention seriously threatened the material interests of Hersfeld. For the abbeys of Hersfeld and Fulda possessed extensive estates in Thuringia from which they had drawn the tithes now claimed by Mainz.[193] The tithes dispute, as we have seen, prompted the composition of Lampert's *Life of Lul*, commissioned by Abbot Hartwig and intended to prove the legality of his abbey's claims by describing the origins of the Thuringian tithes in the time of Lul, abbot of Hersfeld and archbishop of Mainz.[194] In the version of the tithes dispute given in the *Annals* the threat to Hersfeld is represented as coming not from the archbishop but from Henry IV. The annal for 1069 reports the 'secret talks' in which the king requested Archbishop Siegfried's 'help in achieving the scheme that he had in mind', the divorce of his queen, Bertha of Turin. In return Henry 'would obey [Siegfried's] every word; in addition, he would compel the Thuringians by armed force, if there was no other possibility, to pay tithes without any opposition in perpetuity'.[195]

After the royal divorce was forbidden by the pope, according to Lampert, Henry returned to the issue of the Thuringian tithes in 1073, in the context of his 'great stratagem ... to reduce all the Saxons and Thuringians to slavery'.[196] To this end he built 'strongly fortified castles on all the mountains and on the little hills of Saxony and Thuringia' and permitted their garrisons to plunder the neighbouring villages. 'Lest he be branded with open tyranny ..., in order to cloak his ungodliness with some appearance of religion, he urged the archbishop of Mainz by all the means at his disposal to demand the tithes of Thuringia, as he had determined to do many years before.' Henry promised Siegfried 'that he would compel the unwilling to obey the command by means of the power of royal majesty, on condition, however, that the archbishop granted him a portion of those tithes appropriate to royal magnificence'.

193 See Meyer von Knonau (1890) pp. 661–3; Meyer von Knonau (1894) p. 795; Holder-Egger (1894) pp. 185–90; Struve (1969) pp. 46–9; Struve (1970a) pp. 76–8; Staab (1991) pp. 52–3; Robinson (1999) pp. 76–7.

194 See above p. 29.

195 Lampert, *Annals* 1069, below p. 116. See Struve (1970a) p. 76: Lampert 'linked [the dispute] with areas that had nothing whatever to do with the Mainz demand for tithes, such as Henry IV's plan for a divorce'.

196 Lampert, *Annals* 1073, below p. 171.

It was for this reason that Archbishop Siegfried summoned the synod of Erfurt (10 March 1073), in which the king's wishes prevailed. The consequence was the outbreak of the great rebellion of the Saxons and Thuringians. By the end of 1073 'the king lamented that through his unbridled eagerness to obtain the tithes, he had almost lost both his kingdom and his life'.[197] Lampert's partisan monastic viewpoint thus inflated Hersfeld's dispute with the church of Mainz into the principal cause of the Saxon rebellion of 1073. In the opinion of Holder-Egger (1894), 'Lampert's entire narrative [of the tithes dispute] ... is a poisonously malicious representation of the proceedings and motives of the persons concerned.... It was only a fantasy on Lampert's part to bring the Thuringian tithes controversy into a close causal connection with the Saxon rebellion.'[198]

Lampert's implacable hostility towards the king seems to have been prompted by the distress inflicted on Hersfeld by the rebellion of the Saxons and Thuringians, in response to the 'tyranny' of Henry IV. In the summer of 1073 the Thuringian rebels 'gave notice to the abbot of Fulda and the abbot of Hersfeld and to the other princes who possessed any property in Thuringia that they should come on the appointed day to swear an oath with them to bring help to their people. If they did not do so, the rebels would immediately seize all their possessions.'[199] Nevertheless Hersfeld remained loyal to the king throughout the Saxon wars. It was to Hersfeld that Henry IV came after he was compelled by the rebels to flee from his castle of the Harzburg (13 August 1073).[200] It was Abbot Hartwig of Hersfeld who was commissioned by the king in January 1074 to negotiate the removal of Queen Bertha from the royal castle of *Vokenroht* when it was besieged by the Thuringian rebels. He brought her to Hersfeld – 'for because of the disorder in the State the king did not know where he could send her to be kept in safety' – and it was here that she gave birth to the future King Conrad (✝1101). On 26 January Hartwig was sent by the king to the camp of the Saxon rebels to settle the preliminaries of peace negotiations. He was able to report success to the king, who had now returned to Hersfeld.[201] Hartwig of Hersfeld was thus already launched on the career of royal service that would culminate in his appointment as the Henrician archbishop of

197 *Ibid.*, 1073, below pp. 164–5, 205. See also above p. 32 and nn. 152–3.
198 Holder-Egger (1894) p. 186.
199 Lampert, *Annals* 1073, below p. 188.
200 *Ibid.*, 1073, below p. 184.
201 *Ibid.*, 1074, below pp. 207, 209–11.

Magdeburg (1085), while his abbey had proved itself 'one of the most durable pillars of the power of King Henry'.[202]

Nevertheless when the king's army assembled in the vicinity of the abbey (27 January – 2 February 1074) royalist Hersfeld suffered severe losses. The troops 'scoured the villages in the neighbourhood of Hersfeld far and wide and plundered them as if they were in enemy territory.... The king did not prevent this injustice since this was the price that he paid to make the troops more loyal to him.' Both Hersfeld and neighbouring Fulda 'were so weakened and exhausted by this devastation that it was with great difficulty that the brethren were restrained from leaving the monasteries as the food shortage grew worse'.[203] Lampert had already referred to this grievance in the prologue of his history of Hersfeld. Among 'the many miseries and calamities' that the abbey had recently suffered he emphasised 'the violence of the plunderers, who had left [the abbey] nothing except the walls and the stones'. These 'plunderers' remained unidentified since the prologue was addressed to Abbot Hartwig.[204] The animosity of Lampert towards Henry IV is attributable in particular to this misfortune and the grievance of the Thuringian tithes, for which the historian held the king responsible. It was the king's duty to protect the imperial abbey of Hersfeld but Henry IV had allowed the monastery to be victimised by his own troops, just as he had conspired with the archbishop of Mainz to defraud the monastery in the Thuringian tithes dispute.

Lampert's fullest discussion of the failings of Henry IV appears in his account of the developing crisis of summer 1076. It is part character sketch, part exposition of Lampert's political ideas and it is presented as the thoughts that passed through the mind of the leader of the Saxon rebels, Otto of Northeim, as he tried to negotiate with Henry IV. 'This was the difference between a king and a tyrant: the latter extorted obedience from unwilling subjects by means of force and cruelty, while the former governed his subjects and issued his commands according to the laws and customs of his forefathers. But that king had been born and brought up to exercise power and, as befitted such high birth and the high offices and titles of his lineage, he always showed a royal spirit in all

---

202 Holder-Egger (1894) p. 201. Hartwig was invested as imperial anti-archbishop of Magdeburg, in opposition to the pro-papal candidate, also named Hartwig. See Feierabend (1913) pp. 111–12; Vogtherr (1991) pp. 447, 452–4; Robinson (1999) pp. 95, 247.

203 Lampert, *Annals* 1074, below p. 210.

204 Lampert, *Libelli de institutione Herveldensis ecclesiae* I, prologue, pp. 343, 344.

his troubles and he would rather die than suffer defeat. He thought it a blot of irremediable disgrace if he received an injury and did not avenge it.... For this purpose he had drawn to himself men who were skilled in such endeavours, born indeed of middling rank but very ready to give advice and to act.... Through their flatteries they inflamed his diseased mind, which was in any case inclined to wrath and rashness.... The king used these most wicked men as his advisers; he strongly resisted the princes of the kingdom when they urged him to do what was right.... On the contrary, he desired, if the opportunity arose, to suppress their authority and to obliterate it entirely, so that no one would oppose and no one would condemn him when he threw himself with unbridled freedom into every activity that suggested itself to him.'[205]

Lampert's portrait of the imperious, vengeful, wrathful, violent Henry IV is the product of his training in the art of rhetoric. He used the rhetorical devices of *vituperatio* and *damnatio* perfected by 'the rhetoricians of the schools who' – in the words of a contemporary critic of rhetoric – 'when they have taken up a theme, pay no attention to what actually happened or did not happen but sharpen up their tongues on fictitious cases and keep up their flow of speech only as long as one or other of them inflicts or sustains an insult'.[206] 'Rhetorical skill presents not so much the truth as verisimilitude,' wrote an early eleventh-century teacher of rhetoric.[207] This is the technique visible, for example, in Lampert's version of the king's intentions towards Saxony. On the eve of the Saxon rebellion of 1073 'he began to plan a great stratagem that had not been attempted by any of his ancestors in former times: namely, to reduce all the Saxons and Thuringians to slavery and to add their estates to the public fisc'. After his victory over the rebels at the battle of Homburg (9 June 1075) 'the king had set his mind inexorably on the extermination of the whole Saxon people'. By 1076, 'as the king had always intended, the whole Saxon people had been driven under the yoke of servitude'.[208]

Lampert intensified his negative portrayal of Henry IV by means of the Sallustian device of dramatic confrontations between the king and prominent subjects. The device is already apparent in the annal for 1065, reporting the ceremony of the king's coming of age (29 March 1065)

---

205 *Ibid.*, 1076, below pp. 326–7.

206 Manegold of Lautenbach, *Liber contra Wolfelmum* c. 24, p. 107.

207 Anselm of Besate, *Rhetorimachia* p. 103

208 Lampert, *Annals* 1073, below p. 171; 1075, below p. 279; 1076, below p. 313.

in Worms. 'It was there by the permission of [Archbishop Adalbert of Bremen] that the king first girded himself with the weapons of war. He would immediately have made a trial of the arms that he had received upon the archbishop of Cologne and would have thrown himself on him head foremost to avenge himself on him with sword and fire, had not the empress [Agnes] calmed the disturbance with exceedingly timely advice.' Here the fifteen-year-old Henry is already represented as the violent, vengeful king of the later annals. This anecdote is not found in any other source and the scene is likely to have been invented by Lampert. He wished to dramatise the young king's hostility towards Anno of Cologne, which he believed (no doubt correctly) stemmed from the archbishop's seizure of power at the imperial court in spring 1062, when 'he had almost flung the king himself into the utmost danger' by abducting him from the palace of Kaiserswerth.[209]

Lampert expressed the deepest reverence for Anno of Cologne, who, as we have seen, had probably been his schoolmaster in Bamberg. When the archbishop once more became the king's principal adviser in 1072, 'it was then that the State first began to be restored to its former condition and dignity'. Anno behaved towards the king as 'a father and the guardian of his welfare' and 'conducted affairs with such mastery, such diligence and authority that you would certainly find it difficult to decide whether he was more suited to the title of bishop or that of king'.[210] When, however, old age compelled Anno's retirement from secular affairs, 'the king, like someone who had been set free from a very strict schoolmaster, immediately threw himself headlong into every kind of shameful act, breaking down all the restraints of moderation and discretion'.[211] In Lampert's opinion, it was characteristic of Henry IV that he should hate the saintly archbishop of Cologne and adhere to Anno's great political rival, Archbishop Adalbert of Bremen.

Lampert described the latter as 'a man of such very evil reputation among the people, who did not lead a virtuous life' and 'whom everyone accused of having, under the pretence of close friendship with the king, usurped the royal power in an act of manifest tyranny'.[212] The conspiracy of princes at the assembly of Tribur in January 1066 that

209 *Ibid.*, 1065, below p. 98. For the dramatic scene of the abduction cf. *ibid.*, 1062, below pp. 81–2. See Meyer von Knonau (1890) pp. 400–2, 404–6; Jenal (1974) p. 275; Robinson (1999) p. 52.

210 Lampert, *Annals* 1072, below pp. 156–7.

211 *Ibid.*, 1073, below p. 164.

212 *Ibid.*, 1065, below p. 98; 1066, below p. 109.

drove Adalbert of Bremen from the imperial court inspired another of Lampert's dramatic 'scenes'. The princes demanded that Henry IV 'should abdicate from the kingship or he should banish the archbishop of Bremen from his counsels'. 'While [the king] twisted and turned and while he hesitated about what course of action to choose, the archbishop advised that on the following night he should flee in secret, taking with him the insignia of the kingship.' The king's attempt to follow this advice was thwarted and 'amidst reproaches and invective the archbishop was driven out of the royal court'. Once again Lampert's version of events finds no corroboration in the other sources. The princes' ultimatum – abdication or the dismissal of the favourite – is surely a polemical invention, intended to anticipate and justify the actions of the 'deposition faction' of princes at Forchheim in March 1077.[213]

The best-known and most widely criticised of all the 'scenes' in the *Annals* is Lampert's account of Pope Gregory VII's absolution of Henry IV at Canossa in January 1077. It was one of the passages singled out in Ranke's analysis of 1854, which first demonstrated how Lampert's polemical distortions are exposed by the immediately contemporary testimony of Gregory VII's letter of 28 January 1077, reporting the absolution to the German princes.[214] Lampert's dramatisation of the events at Canossa was intended to emphasise, firstly, that Henry IV had been utterly defeated and humiliated (if he regained the kingship, it would only be on condition that 'he should always be subject to the Roman pontiff and obedient to his orders') and, secondly, that the king's negotiations with the pope were conducted in bad faith ('there was no strong inclination to trust the man who made the promise'). The most controversial aspect of Lampert's version of events is his claim that immediately after the absolution of the king, Gregory VII, in celebrating mass, chose to ascribe to the receiving of communion the character of a trial by ordeal. Lampert interpolated the customary formula for the ordeal into the pope's invitation to the king to receive the sacrament: '*If you know that you are innocent* ... eat this remaining part of the Lord's body so that you may prove your innocence with God as your witness.' The king feared to undertake the ordeal and declined the sacrament.[215]

213 *Ibid.*, 1066, below p. 111. See Meyer von Knonau (1894) pp. 810–11; Robinson (1999) pp. 59–60. See also above p. 33.

214 Lampert, *Annals* 1077, below pp. 355–60. See Ranke (1888) p. 147; Holder-Egger (1894) pp. 557–9; Meyer von Knonau (1894) pp. 900–1; Struve (1970a) pp. 118–21; Robinson (1999) pp. 161–4.

215 Lampert, *Annals* 1077, below p. 358 and n. 1882, for the formula of the ordeal (italicised).

No other source corroborates Lampert's version of events and the letter of Gregory VII clearly states that the pope 'received [Henry] into the grace of communion'.[216] The scene of the trial by ordeal was in fact borrowed from a literary model: the description of the encounter of King Lothar II and Pope Hadrian II in 869 in the chronicle of Regino of Prüm.[217] The theatricality of the event reported by Regino clearly appealed to Lampert and seemed exactly to correspond to his conception of the momentous confrontation of king and pope that concluded his *Annals*. Above all it gave him the opportunity to dramatise the exposure of Henry IV's guilt in his shocked reaction to the pope's offer of the sacrament. 'The king was thunderstruck by this unexpected development. His response was to become violently agitated, to be evasive, to take counsel with his intimate friends apart from the rest of the company and in his agitation to consider ... how he might escape the need to undergo so fearful a trial.'[218]

Theatricality is the hallmark of Lampert's narrative and theatrical imagery came easily to his pen. He reported, for example, Henry IV's accusation against Anno of Cologne in 1074, that he had incited King William I of England to invade Germany, which the historian denounced as 'a false tale, like the fictions of the theatre'.[219] Similarly, the charges brought against Gregory VII in the synod of Worms (24 January 1076) were 'something like a tragedy ... with theatrical inventions'.[220] The clergy of Bamberg urged the deposition of their bishop, Herman I, 'about whose way of life and whose appointment they had published a mournful tragedy, to be recited in a theatre whose audience was this whole world'.[221] Lampert used Sallust's expression 'the drama of human affairs' in reporting the rebellion of the citizens of Cologne against Archbishop Anno in 1074 and in commenting on the decision of Henry IV to cross the Alps in the winter of 1076–7 in order to intercept

216 Gregory VII, *Register* IV.12, p. 313. The pro-papal chronicler, Berthold of Reichenau, *Chronicle* 1077, p. 162, claimed that 'the king declared that he was unworthy to share [the eucharist] and he went away without receiving communion' but there is no reference here to a trial by ordeal.

217 Regino of Prüm, *Chronicon* 869, p. 97. Cf. Lampert, *Annals* 1077, below p. 357 and n. 1880. See Holder-Egger (1894) pp. 561–2.

218 Lampert, *Annals* 1077, below p. 359.

219 *Ibid.*, 1074, below p. 234.

220 *Ibid.*, 1076, below p. 305.

221 *Ibid.*, 1075, below p. 289.

Gregory VII on his journey to Germany.[222] Lampert's imitation of Sallust has already been noted.[223] His predilection for interpolated speeches in the manner of Sallust is a further aspect of Lampert's dramatisation of the events in his narrative. He used this device to explain motivation or to present the accusations and the defence presented by rival parties: as when the Saxons defended their rebellion to the royal envoys in August 1073 and again in October 1075; when the king's opponents described his misdeeds to the assembly of Tribur in October 1076 or when at Canossa Gregory VII urged the king to demonstrate his innocence in a trial by ordeal.[224]

Lampert's dramatic 'scenes' explain his reputation as a spinner of tales and that delight in *Fabulieren* deplored by those critics who forgot that, for its author, a medieval chronicle was first and foremost a work of literature.[225] It is the sheer exuberance of Lampert's story-telling that holds the attention of the general reader: the kidnapping of the twelve-year-old Henry IV at Kaiserswerth in 1062; the rebellion of the monks of Fulda against Abbot Widerad in 1063; the narrow escape of the bishops on the 'great German pilgrimage' to Jerusalem in 1065; the adventure story of the resourceful and fortunate young nobleman that Lampert grafted on to the early career of Count Robert I of Flanders; the epic history of the sword of Attila, which the queen of Hungary gave to Count Otto of Northeim in 1063; the rebellion of the citizens of Cologne against Archbishop Anno in 1074; the imprisonment of Bishop Bucco (Burchard II) of Halberstadt, a leader of the Saxon rebellion, and his daring escape in 1076; the equally adventurous escape of the two little Saxon hostages, sons of Margrave Udo II of the Saxon Nordmark and Margrave Dedi I of Lower Lusatia.[226] Lampert of Hersfeld is the most eminently readable of all medieval historians.

222 *Ibid.*, 1074, below p. 228; 1076, below p. 344, citing Sallust, *Jugurtha* 14. See Struve (1970a) pp. 122–3 and n. 49.

223 See above p. 7.

224 Lampert, *Annals* 1073, below pp. 182–3; 1075, below pp. 283–5; 1076, below pp. 337–9; 1077, below pp. 357–9.

225 Hainer (1914) p. 85.

226 Lampert, *Annals* 1062, below p. 81; 1063, below pp. 88–91; 1065, below pp. 100–6; 1071, below pp. 138–41, 150; 1074, below pp. 222–8; 1076, below pp. 320–3, 331–4.

THE ANNALS OF
LAMPERT OF HERSFELD

1039

Emperor Conrad died in Utrecht on the second day of Whitsuntide[1] and his son Henry succeeded him.[2] Abbot Richard of Fulda died[3] and Sigeward succeeded him.[4] Bishop Reginbold of Speyer died[5] and Sibicho succeeded him.[6]

1040

King Henry led an army into Bohemia and there Count Werner[7] and Reginhard, the standard-bearer of Fulda,[8] together with many others, were slain. Peter, king of the Hungarians[9] was driven out by his subjects and took refuge with King Henry, seeking his help. Bishop Eberhard of Bamberg died[10] and Suidger succeeded him.[11] In Hersfeld the crypt was dedicated and the relics of the holy confessors Wigbert and Lul were translated to it.[12]

1 Conrad II, king (1024–39), emperor (1027), +4 June.

2 Henry III, king (1039–56), emperor (1046).

3 Richard, abbot of Fulda (1018–39), +20 July.

4 Sigeward, abbot of Fulda (1039–43).

5 Reginbold II, abbot of Ebersberg, bishop of Speyer (?1032–1039), +13 October.

6 Sibicho (Sigibodo), bishop of Speyer (1039–54).

7 Werner, count in Hesse, '*maior domus* of the church of Fulda' (*Annalista Saxo* p. 684), 'the instigator of this act of daring' (*Annales Sangallenses maiores* 1040, p. 84). See Metz (1991) pp. 344, 360, 362 ('Werner I.').

8 Reginhard, count in Hesse, steward of the household of the abbey of Fulda. On this battle (22 August 1040): Herman of Reichenau, *Chronicle* 1040, p. 72. See Steindorff (1874) pp. 94–5.

9 Peter, king of Hungary (1038–41, 1044–6, +1059). On his expulsion in 1041: Herman, *Chronicle* 1041, p. 73. See Steindorff (1874) pp. 114–18.

10 Eberhard, bishop of Bamberg (1007–40), +13 August.

11 Suidger, bishop of Bamberg (1040–7); Pope Clement II (1046–7).

12 Wigbert, abbot of Fritzlar (+746) and Lul, archbishop of Mainz, founder of Hersfeld (+786). Cf. Lampert, *Libellus de institutione Herveldensis ecclesiae* I, pp. 351–2: 'The tender and as yet unconsecrated king [Henry III] was present at the dedication of the repaired church of Hersfeld, which the bishops Hunfrid of Magdeburg, Khazo [Kadeloh] of Naumburg and Hunold of Merseburg dedicated with the consent of Bardo, archbishop of the see of Mainz, under Abbot Meginher, whom the same

1041

King Henry entered Bohemia for the second time. He received the surrender of its duke, whose name was Bretislav,[13] and caused the country to pay tribute to him. He returned from there through Bavaria and celebrated the feast of St Michael[14] in Regensburg. Aba,[15] who had usurped the kingdom of the Hungarians, attacked the frontiers of Bavaria and Carinthia and made off with much plunder. The Bavarians, however, gathered their forces together, pursued them, seized back the plunder and, after killing many of them, forced the rest to flee.

1042

The king undertook his first expedition into Hungary and put to flight the aforementioned Aba. He proceeded as far as the River Raab, captured three very great fortresses[16] and, after taking an oath from the people of that province, he returned home in peace. Bishop Herman of Münster died[17] and Rupert succeeded him.[18] Bishop Heribert of Eichstätt died[19] and his brother Gezman succeeded him.[20] When the latter died after a few weeks, Gebhard succeeded him.[21]

Henry revered as a holy man and placed at his side.' See Steindorff (1874) pp. 92–3; Vogtherr (1991) pp. 440–1.

13 Bretislav I, duke of Bohemia (1034–55). Cf. Herman, *Chronicle* 1041, p. 73. See Steindorff (1874) pp. 111–13.

14 29 September. Steindorff (1874) p. 109 n. 4 argued, on the evidence of the *Annals of Niederaltaich* 1041, p. 27, and *Annalista Saxo* 1042 [=1041], p. 685, that on this day Henry III was in Prague. The king was in Regensburg on 22 October: *D.H.III* 86.

15 Aba-Samuel, king of Hungary (1041–4). This is a reference to the Hungarian expedition of February 1042 and the victory of Margrave Adalbert of Austria described by Herman, *Chronicle* 1042, p. 73, and *Annals of Niederaltaich* 1042, p. 30. See Steindorff (1874) pp. 148–52.

16 Hainburg and Pressburg were destroyed 'in the autumn': Herman, *Chronicle* 1042, pp. 73–4. Steindorff (1874) p. 160 n. 3 noted that Lampert's claim that Henry III 'proceeded as far as the River Raab', uncorroborated by the parallel sources, suggests a confusion with the expedition of 1044.

17 Herman I, bishop of Münster (1032–42), †22 July.

18 Rupert, bishop of Münster (1042–63).

19 Heribert, bishop of Eichstätt (1021/2–42), †24 July.

20 Gezman, bishop of Eichstätt (1042), †17 October.

21 Gebhard I, bishop of Eichstätt (1042–57); Pope Victor II (1054–7).

1043

The king celebrated Christmas in Goslar. When the duke of Bohemia arrived there, he was courteously received by the king and honourably entertained for some time and at last dismissed in peace.[22] There among the envoys of various provinces the envoys of the Russians returned home sorrowfully because they brought back a definite rejection of their king's daughter, whom they had hoped to marry to King Henry.[23] There also the envoys of the king of the Hungarians humbly begged for peace but did not obtain it since King Peter – whom Aba had driven from the kingdom by force – was present and humbly implored King Henry's help against Aba's violence.[24]

Abbot Sigeward of Fulda died[25] and Rohing succeeded him.[26] Empress Gisela died and was buried in Speyer.[27] Undertaking his second expedition against the Hungarians, the king forced the aforementioned Aba to accept the settlement that he desired and received from him oaths confirming the peace and hostages.[28] On his return he celebrated in Ingelheim his *union and wedding*[29] with Agnes, daughter of Count William of Poitou.[30]

22 25 December 1042. Cf. *Annals of Niederaltaich* 1043, p. 32: 'Among other princes Duke Bretislav of Bohemia was present; he brought the king appropriate gifts; he was treated in a magnificent manner and departed after a few days, honoured with royal gifts.'

23 The envoys of Jaroslav I, grand prince of Kiev (1019–54). (The second of his three daughters, Anna, would in 1049 marry King Henry I of France.) Lampert was alone in linking this Russian embassy with marriage negotiations: see Steindorff (1874) pp. 98, 164.

24 Since the usually well informed *Annals of Niederaltaich* 1043, pp. 32–3, placed these events in Paderborn at Whitsun (22 May 1043), Steindorff (1874) pp. 163 n. 2, 177, concluded that Lampert confused these two occasions.

25 Sigeward (see above n. 4) died on 28 March 1043.

26 Rohing, abbot of Fulda (1043–7).

27 Gisela, queen (1024), empress (1027), widow of Conrad II, +15 February 1043.

28 August–September 1043. Cf. *Annals of Niederaltaich* 1043, p. 33. See Steindorff (1874) pp. 176–80.

29 Esther 2:18.

30 Agnes of Poitou (?1025–1077), queen (1043), empress (1046), daughter of William V, duke of Aquitaine-Poitou (995–1029). The wedding in Ingelheim was probably in late November 1043: Steindorff (1874) pp. 192–3.

1044

The king celebrated Christmas in Trier and there he pardoned the offences of all those who had transgressed against the royal majesty and promulgated throughout the whole kingdom the same law, that all should pardon each other's offences.[31]

Gozelo, duke of the Lotharingians, died.[32] His son Godfrey, a youth of most noble character and extremely experienced in military affairs, took up arms against the State because he could not obtain his father's duchy.[33] He defeated in battle and killed Duke Adalbert, whom the king had appointed in his father's place.[34] He caused the slaughter of men and the devastation of fields on an enormous scale and reduced to ashes the whole region as far as the Rhine, except for those places that escaped hostile attack with the help of their walls or that ransomed themselves with money.

On his third expedition into Hungary the king defeated and expelled the aforementioned Aba and restored the kingdom to Peter.[35] Bishop Azecho of Worms died[36] and Adelger succeeded him.[37] When shortly afterwards he was likewise released from human existence, Arnold succeeded him.[38] Bishop Thietmar of Hildesheim died[39] and Azelin was his successor.[40]

---

31 25 December 1043. *Annals of Niederaltaich* 1044, p. 34 confirms that 'the king celebrated Christmas in Trier with his new bride' but Lampert was alone in recording a 'peace council' on this occasion. Lampert's terminology resembles that of Herman's account of Henry III's measures in Constance: *Chronicle* 1043, p. 74. See Steindorff (1874) pp. 195–6; Wadle (1973) pp. 159–62.

32 Gozelo I, duke of Lower Lotharingia (1023–44), duke of Upper Lotharingia (1033–44) †(?)19 April 1044.

33 Godfrey III ('the Bearded'), duke of Upper Lotharingia (1044–7), duke of Lower Lotharingia (1065–9), margrave of Tuscany (1054–69). On the Lotharingian succession and Godfrey's claims: *Annals of Niederaltaich* 1044, p. 34; Herman, *Chronicle* 1044, p. 75 and nn. 167–8. See Steindorff (1874) pp. 201, 215–16; Boshof (1978a) pp. 65–70.

34 Adalbert (of Châtenois), duke of Upper Lotharingia (1047–8), was killed at Thuin on the Sambre in 1048: see Steindorff (1881) pp. 24, 46; Boshof (1978a) p. 96. Lampert conflated the events of 1044 and 1047–8.

35 Henry III's victory was at Menfö on 5 July 1044. Cf. Herman, *Chronicle* 1044, pp. 75–6. See Steindorff (1874) pp. 205–9.

36 Azecho, bishop of Worms (1025–44) †17 January.

37 Adelger, bishop of Worms (1044) †20 July (?).

38 Arnold (Arnulf) I, bishop of Worms (1044–65).

39 Thietmar, bishop of Hildesheim (1038–44) †14 November.

40 Azelin, bishop of Hildesheim (1044–54).

1045

Duke Godfrey surrendered to the king and was sent to Giebichenstein to be imprisoned there and thus for a short time the kingdom remained calm and peaceful.[41] King Peter of the Hungarians captured Aba, his rival and the usurper of his kingdom, and beheaded him.[42] Bishop Bruno of Würzburg died[43] and Adalbero succeeded him.[44] Bishop Kathelo of Zeitz died[45] and Eppo was his successor.[46] Archbishop Alebrand died[47] and Adalbert succeeded him.[48]

1046

The king celebrated Christmas in Goslar[49] and his mother-in-law from Poitou[50] was present there with the nobility of her nation. King Peter of the Hungarians was seized by the cunning of his kinsman Andreas[51] and blinded. Margrave Ekkehard died a sudden death by suffocation.[52] Abbot Druthmar of Corvey died[53] and Ruthard was his successor.[54]

Duke Godfrey was released from imprisonment. When he saw, however, that neither the intercession of the princes nor the act of surrender that he had willingly performed had been of any benefit to him, he was incited by his indignation on this account and by disgust at his own poverty to begin the war afresh.[55] Among the other disasters that he

41 July 1045. Cf. Herman, *Chronicle* 1045, p. 78. Giebichenstein near Halle was 'the usual prison for princely offenders against the State': Steindorff (1874) p. 237.

42 In 1044, according to Herman, *Chronicle* 1044, p. 76. See Steindorff (1874) p. 212.

43 Bruno, bishop of Würzburg (1034–45) †27 May.

44 Adalbero, bishop of Würzburg (1045–90).

45 Kathelo (Cadalus), bishop of Zeitz (Naumburg) (1030–44).

46 Eppo (Eberhard), bishop of Zeitz (Naumburg) (1045–79).

47 Alebrand-Becelin, archbishop of Hamburg-Bremen (1035–43) †15 April 1043.

48 Adalbert, archbishop of Hamburg-Bremen (1043–72).

49 25 December 1045. Cf. Herman, *Chronicle* 1046, p. 78.

50 Agnes, widow of William V, duke of Aquitaine-Poitou, wife of Count Geoffrey II of Anjou.

51 Andreas I (son of Vaszoly, nephew of King Stephen I), king of Hungary (1046–60). Cf. Herman, *Chronicle* 1046, p. 79; *Annals of Niederaltaich* 1046, pp. 42–3. See Steindorff (1874) pp. 305–6.

52 Ekkehard II, margrave of Meissen (1032–46), last of the Ekkehardiner dynasty, †24 January.

53 Druthmar, abbot of Corvey (1014–46), †15 February.

54 Ruthard, abbot of Corvey (1046–50), abbot of Hersfeld (1059–72) †1074.

55 Godfrey III was released in May and the king restored to him the duchy of Upper Lotharingia: Herman, *Chronicle* 1046, p. 79; *Annals of Niederaltaich* 1046, p. 41. See

inflicted on the State, he burned down the royal palace in Nymwegen,
a building of marvellous and incomparable beauty; he captured the city
of Verdun and burned the cathedral church there. Shortly afterwards,
however, he so greatly repented of his action that he caused himself to
be scourged in public and paid a large sum of money so that his hair
should not be cut off; he paid the cost of rebuilding the church and very
frequently participated personally in the building work, performing the
duties of a poor serf.[56]

1047

The king celebrated Christmas in Rome.[57] There he deposed three
men who had usurped the apostolic see, contrary to the regulations of
the Church, and appointed Bishop Suidger of Bamberg as the vicar of
the apostles.[58] The king himself in his turn was endowed by the pope
with the imperial title and office on that holy day, together with Queen
Agnes. Travelling from there through Benevento and the neighbouring
regions,[59] on his return journey he celebrated the holy festival of Easter
in Mantua[60] and the Ascension in Augsburg.[61] There, since Bishop Eppo
had died,[62] he put Henry in his place.[63] Then he led a naval expedition on
the Rhine to Frisia against Godfrey and his abettor Theoderic[64] and there
he captured two very well fortified castles, Rijnsburg and Vlaardingen.

Steindorff (1874) p. 295; Boshof (1978a) pp. 85–6. Godfrey renewed his rebellion in
    1047: see Steindorff (1881) p. 19; Boshof (1978a) p. 94.

56 Cf. Herman, *Chronicle* 1047, p. 83; *Annals of Niederaltaich* 1047, p. 44; Hugh of
    Flavigny, *Chronicon* II, p. 406 . See Steindorff (1881) pp. 19–21; Boshof (1978a) p. 95.
    Lampert alone gave the details of Godfrey's penance. On the date of his reconciliation
    see Steindorff (1881) p. 21.

57 25 December 1046. On Lampert's version of the events of the synods of Sutri and
    Rome see Schmale (1979) p. 68. See also Steindorff (1874) pp. 313–14, 456–510;
    Poole (1934) pp. 185–222; Zimmermann (1968) pp. 119–39.

58 The three popes Benedict IX (1032–46), Silvester III (1045), Gregory VI (1045–6).
    For Suidger–Clement II see above n. 11.

59 Cf. *Annals of Benevento* 1047 (codex 3), p. 179; *Chronicle of Monte Cassino* II.78, p. 323.
    See Steindorff (1874) pp. 328–9.

60 19 April. Cf. Herman, *Chronicle* 1047, p. 81. See Steindorff (1874) pp. 332–4.

61 28 May. Cf. Herman, *Chronicle* 1047, p. 81; *Annals of Niederaltaich* 1047, pp. 43–4;
    Annals of Augsburg 1047, p. 126. See Steindorff (1881) p. 7.

62 Eppo (Eberhard), bishop of Augsburg (1029–47) †26 May.

63 Henry II, bishop of Augsburg (1047–63).

64 Theoderic IV, count of Holland (1039–49). On this expedition 'in the autumn':
    Herman, *Chronicle* 1047, p. 83; *Annals of Niederaltaich* 1047, p. 47. See Steindorff
    (1881) p. 18.

Pope Suidger, who was also called Clement, died and was buried in Bamberg.[65] Abbot Rohing of Fulda died.[66] He had been consecrated by Pope Suidger in Rome that same year on Christmas day. The hermit Gunther died.[67]

1048

The emperor celebrated Christmas in Pöhlde.[68] Envoys of the Romans appeared there, announcing the death of Pope Suidger and requesting a successor to him. The emperor gave them Bishop Poppo of Brixen[69] but conferred the bishopric of Bamberg on the chancellor Hezekin.[70] The emperor celebrated the feast of St Michael again in Pöhlde.[71] Here on the following day Count Thietmar, the brother of Duke Bernard,[72] was accused by his vassal Arnold[73] of planning a conspiracy against the emperor. Thietmar fought with him in order to clear himself of the alleged crime with his own hands but he was defeated and killed. Ekbert became abbot of Fulda immediately after Christmas.[74]

65 9 October. See Hauck (1959) pp. 265–74.

66 Rohing (above n. 26) died 29 November. Cf. the papal privileges for Fulda: Clement II, *JL* 4133, 4134, *MPL* 142, col. 577B–581B (29, 31 December 1046).

67 Gunther, from the Thuringian comital family of Schwarzburg and Käfernburg, monk, founder of a settlement of hermits at Rinchnach, +9 October 1045. Cf. Lampert, *Annales* 1006: 'Gunther, a nobleman from Thuringia, became a monk in Hersfeld but subsequently he went to Niederaltaich on the advice of Abbot Godehard [of Niederaltaich and Hersfeld]'; 1008: 'The monk Gunther sought out a hermitage' (ed. Holder-Egger p. 50). See Steindorff (1874) p. 289.

68 25 December 1047. Cf. *Annals of Niederaltaich* 1048, p. 44.

69 Poppo, bishop of Brixen (?1039–1048), Pope Damasus II (1047–8). For the accounts of his election see Steindorff (1881) p. 29.

70 Hezekin (Hartwig), bishop of Bamberg (1047–53).

71 29 September 1048.

72 Thietmar Billung, count, brother of Duke Bernard II of Saxony.

73 'Arnold, formerly his vassal (*miles*)': *Annals of Niederaltaich* 1048, p. 45; 'his armed retainer (*satelles*) named Arnold': Adam of Bremen, *Gesta* III.8, p. 149. See Steindorff (1881) pp. 16, 40–1; Fenske (1977) pp. 19–20; Althoff (1991) p. 320; Althoff (1997) p. 44.

74 Ekbert (Eppo), monk of Hersfeld, abbot of Tegernsee (1046–7), abbot of Fulda (1047–58).

1049

The emperor celebrated Christmas in Freising.[75] There envoys of the Romans appeared again, announcing the death of Pope Poppo[76] and requesting a ruler of the Roman church. The emperor gave them Bishop Bruno of Toul.[77]

1050

Pope Leo left Rome so as to set the state of the churches in order and to restore peace to Gaul. He celebrated a synod in Mainz under the presidency of the emperor, together with forty-two bishops.[78] There Bishop Sibicho of Speyer cleared himself by means of holy communion of the offences of which he was accused.[79] Duke Godfrey obtained the emperor's pardon through the intervention of the pope and the princes.[80] When the synod was over, the emperor undertook an expedition against Baldwin.[81] The pope, however, awaited his return in Aachen.[82]

1051

The emperor celebrated Christmas in Worms.[83] There Pope Leo bade him farewell and, when they had with moderation put the affairs of

---

75 25 December 1048. Cf. Herman, *Chronicle* 1049, p. 85; *Annals of Niederaltaich* 1049, p. 45.

76 9 August 1048.

77 Bruno, bishop of Toul (1026–51); Pope Leo IX (1048–54). He was elected at an imperial assembly in Worms in December 1048: see Steindorff (1881) pp. 54–5. On the different versions of his papal election see Robinson (2004a) pp. 33–5, 57.

78 Council of Mainz, 19–26 October 1049. See *MGH Constitutiones* 1, 97 (no. 51); Steindorff (1881) pp. 93–9; Munier (2002) pp. 130–1.

79 Sibicho (see above n. 6), 'accused of the offence of adultery, was purged by the ordeal of the holy wafer': Adam of Bremen, *Gesta* III.30, p. 172. Cf. the anonymous *Life of Leo IX* II.12, p. 139: Sibicho 'was accused of a crime and wished to exculpate himself with a fearful oath on the body of the Lord. It is said, however, that his jaw was seized by paralysis and so it remained as long as he lived.' On Sibicho's evil reputation: Herman, *Chronicle* 1039, 1052, pp. 72, 92.

80 In July 1049 in Aachen: see Steindorff (1881) p. 83.

81 Baldwin V, count of Flanders (1035–67), who had become the ally of Godfrey III in 1047. Henry III invaded Flanders in April/May 1050: see Steindorff (1881) pp. 106–7.

82 Lampert confused the sequence of events. After the council of Mainz Leo IX travelled to Alsace, probably escorted by Henry III, and then to Swabia and Bavaria, reaching Verona by 25 December 1049: Herman, *Chronicle* 1049, p. 86. See Steindorff (1881) p. 103.

83 25 December 1050. In Pöhlde, according to *Annals of Niederaltaich* 1051, p. 47; in Goslar, according to Herman, *Chronicle* 1051, p. 88. See Steindorff (1881) p. 118.

the Church and the business of the empire in order, he returned to Rome.[84] He took with him Duke Godfrey[85] and his brother Frederick,[86] who afterwards succeeded Gebhard[87] in the apostolic see, and also very many others, both clergy and laymen very experienced in military matters, with whose strength he planned to attack the Normans, who had seized Apulia.[88]

The church in Goslar was consecrated by Archbishop Herman of Cologne.[89] The emperor celebrated Whitsun in Paderborn.[90] There Archbishop Bardo[91] preached a sermon during the mass, in which he predicted that his death was at hand and commended himself to the prayers of the faithful. He died that same month and Liutpold succeeded him.[92] Bishop Dietrich of Constance died[93] and Rumold succeeded him.[94] Bishop Hunfrid of Magdeburg died[95] and Engelhard succeeded him.[96]

A son, King Henry IV,[97] was born to the emperor on 11 November.

---

84 Lampert here conflated Leo IX's first and second visits to Germany (June–December 1049 and September 1050 – February 1051). See Steindorff (1881) pp. 134–9; Munier (2002) pp. 135–6.

85 There is no evidence that Godfrey III entered Italy before his expedition to marry Margravine Beatrice of Tuscany (1054): see below p. 61. Lampert seems to have confused this occasion with the return of Pope Victor II to Italy, perhaps escorted by Godfrey III, in 1057: see Meyer von Knonau (1890) p. 25.

86 Frederick of Lotharingia (brother of Godfrey III), chancellor of the Roman church (1051), abbot of Monte Cassino (1057), cardinal priest of S. Grisogono (1057), Pope Stephen IX (1057–8). He is first identified as chancellor of Leo IX in a papal diploma of 9 March 1051: Hüls (1977) p. 248.

87 Gebhard–Victor II (see above n. 21).

88 This seems to be a confused reminiscence of the 'very many Germans' who followed Leo IX to Italy after his third visit to Germany (August 1052 – February 1053), when he sought military aid from Henry III against the Normans: Herman, *Chronicle* 1053, pp. 93–4. See Steindorff (1881) pp. 214–16; Munier (2002) pp. 138–9.

89 Herman II, archbishop of Cologne (1036–56). He consecrated the church of SS Simon and Jude in Goslar on 2 July 1050: see Steindorff (1881) p. 116.

90 19 May 1051.

91 Bardo, abbot of Hersfeld (1031), archbishop of Mainz (1031–51) †10/11 June. This anecdote also appears in the *Vita maior Bardonis* c. 24, p. 339, which Holder-Egger, *Lamperti Annales* p. 63 n. 2 suggested as Lampert's possible source.

92 Liutpold, archbishop of Mainz (1051–9).

93 Dietrich, bishop of Constance (1047–51) †22 June.

94 Rumold, bishop of Constance (1051–69).

95 Hunfrid, archbishop of Magdeburg (1023–51), †28 February.

96 Engelhard, archbishop of Magdeburg (1051–63).

97 Henry IV, king (1056–1106), emperor (1084), born 11 November 1050.

1052

The emperor celebrated Christmas in Pöhlde.[98] There he caused the princes of the kingdom to promise their fealty on oath to his son Henry, who was still unbaptised.[99] He celebrated Easter in Cologne and there the aforementioned boy was baptised by Herman, the archbishop of that city.[100] Bishop Rudolf of Paderborn died[101] and Imad was his successor.[102]

1053

The emperor celebrated Christmas in Goslar and there Imad was consecrated by Archbishop Liutpold. There also heretics were discovered and hanged by Duke Godfrey.[103]

Pope Leo marched against the Normans and joined battle with them near Benevento. The Lombards fled immediately at the first attack and the Germans were almost all killed to the last man. The pope himself was besieged in Benevento and he was at last and with difficulty freed from the siege after many troubles.[104] After surviving this disaster he spent all his days in affliction and mourning.

---

98 25 December 1051, in Goslar: Herman, *Chronicle* 1052, p. 90; *Annals of Niederaltaich* 1052, p. 48. See Steindorff (1881) p. 165.

99 Fealty was sworn to the still unbaptised Henry IV on 25 December 1050: Herman, *Chronicle* 1051, p. 88 (Goslar); *Annals of Niederaltaich* 1052, p. 47 (Pöhlde). See Steindorff (1881) p. 118; Meyer von Knonau (1890) p. 4. On the significance of the oath-taking see Robinson (1999) pp. 20–1.

100 The baptism took place on Easter day (31 March) 1051: see Steindorff (1881) pp. 139–40; Meyer von Knonau (1890) p. 5. Henry III celebrated Easter in 1052 (19 April) in Speyer: see Steindorff (1881) p. 168.

101 Rudolf, abbot of Hersfeld (1031–6), bishop of Paderborn (1036–51) †6 November. Cf. Lampert, *Libellus de institutione Herveldensis ecclesiae* I, p. 350: 'Rudolf from the monastery of Stablo was appointed abbot here, an Italian by birth, a mild and kindly father, most careful and provident in the service of God.'

102 Imad, bishop of Paderborn (1051–76).

103 The Christmas in question in this report was that of 1051: see Steindorff (1881) p. 165. On the 'heretics' see Herman, *Chronicle* 1052, p. 90: 'certain heretics ... who among other wicked and erroneous doctrines detested the eating of all animal flesh, like the Manichean sect'. Lampert was alone in recording the role of Godfrey III of Lotharingia. The contemporary preoccupation of Bishop Wazo of Liège with Lotharingian heretics was emphasised by Anselm of Liège, *Gesta episcoporum Leodiensium* c. 64, p. 228. See Steindorff (1881) pp. 165–6; Moore (1977) pp. 39, 244, 252.

104 The papal expedition culminated in the battle of Civitate (18 June 1053), in which the German forces and those of the Italian princes (the duke of Gaeta and the counts of Aquino, Teano and Teate) were defeated by the Norman troops of Count Humphrey of Apulia, Robert Guiscard and Richard of Aversa. See Steindorff (1881) pp. 245–50; Taviani-Carozzi (1996) pp. 181–211; Munier (2002) pp. 212–15.

At that time the brother of Godfrey, Frederick, archdeacon of the Roman church,[105] set out for Constantinople on a legation of the apostolic see. There he announced a synod, to which he summoned the emperor of Constantinople[106] and the patriarch.[107] When they claimed that their primacy was supreme and scorned to obey his summons, he left the city and publicly *shook the dust from* his *sandals against them*[108] in the manner of the apostles. This action struck all the inhabitants of Constantinople with such great terror that on the following day the emperor and the patriarch, together with the clergy and people, clad in sackcloth and ashes, went in procession to him and, sinking to the ground, showed their reverence for the apostolic authority in him.[109]

Boniface, margrave of the Italians died.[110] Duke Godfrey married his widow, Beatrice,[111] and claimed for himself his march and his other possessions on the pretext of this marriage. When Emperor Henry learned of this, he began to be oppressed by painful anxiety, since he thought that the Italians, whose minds were always *eager for novelties*,[112] might be incited by Godfrey to break away from the kingdom of the Germans.[113]

---

105 Frederick (above n. 86) had previously been archdeacon of Liège; in 1053 his office in the Roman Church was that of cardinal deacon and chancellor. His colleagues on this legation (24 June – 18 July 1054) were Cardinal bishop Humbert of Silva Candida and Archbishop Peter of Amalfi. See Petrucci (1977) pp. 90–6; Munier (2002) pp. 217–46.

106 Emperor Constantine IX Monomachus (1042–55).

107 Michael Cerullarius, patriarch of Constantinople (1043–58).

108 Acts 13:51

109 On the fictitious character of Lampert's account see Steindorff (1881) p. 270 n. 3.

110 Boniface II (of Canossa), margrave of Tuscany (1030–52) †6 May. See Steindorff (1881) pp. 172–3; Goez (1995) pp. 20, 201.

111 Beatrice of Lotharingia, margravine of Tuscany (†1076), daughter of Duke Frederick II of Upper Lotharingia, married (1) Boniface of Tuscany (n. 110); (2) Godfrey III of Lotharingia (n. 33). The marriage was contracted in summer or autumn 1054: see Steindorff (1881) pp. 272–3; Goez (1995) pp. 22–3, 202.

112 Sallust, *Jugurtha* 19.46. Cf. Livy I.8.6.

113 Lampert alone reported such a development: see Goez (1995) p. 23. Cf. Herman, *Chronicle* 1054, p. 98: 'Duke Godfrey once more raised up a tyrannical power against the emperor.' Another version of Godfrey's plans is found in the claim of the *Chronicle of Monte Cassino* II.97, p. 355, that Pope Stephen IX planned to confer on [Godfrey] the imperial crown'.

1054

Pope Leo IX died a blessed death in the Lord on 19 April and was buried in Rome.[114] The emperor was petitioned by the Romans to provide a bishop for the apostolic see and sent Bishop Gebhard of Eichstätt.[115] The emperor secretly sent letters to all the men in Italy who could claim preeminence by virtue of their wealth or their military ability and entreated them to keep a close watch on Duke Godfrey, lest he chanced to have any evil designs against the State[116] and he promised that, if he was still alive, he himself would be there the next year and see what it was necessary to do.

[A subdeacon gave him[117] poison in the chalice. When after the consecration he wished to lift it and could not do so, he threw himself on the ground to pray, together with the people, in order to ask the Lord the reason for this circumstance and immediately his poisoner was seized by a demon. The reason was thus made clear and the lord pope commanded that the chalice, together with the Lord's blood, should be enclosed in a certain altar and should be preserved forever as a relic. Then, together with the people, he threw himself on the ground again to pray until the subdeacon was liberated from the demon.]

When Archdeacon Frederick returned from Constantinople and learned that Pope Leo had departed this human life and that another man had already assumed the rights of the government of the Church, he delivered to the Roman church the very splendid gifts that he brought from the emperor of Constantinople[118] and, immediately leaving the city, he entered the monastery of Monte Cassino in order thenceforward

---

114 See Steindorff (1881) p. 267.

115 On the election of Gebhard – Victor II (above n. 21) see Steindorff (1881) pp. 285, 292–4.

116 Steindorff (1881) p. 297 preferred the version of events given by Sigebert of Gembloux, *Chronica* 1053, p. 359: 'Godfrey ... was driven out of Lombardy by the command of the emperor.' Cf. *Annals of Niederaltaich* 1054, p. 50. See Goez (1995) p. 141.

117 This passage, referring to Victor II, is also found verbatim in Bernold of St Blasien, *Chronicle* 1054, p. 245. Holder-Egger, *Lamperti Annales* p. 65 n. 1, concluded that the passage was not the work of Lampert himself but a later interpolation in the chronicle, originally in the form of a marginal gloss. On the poisoning of popes in the mid-eleventh century see Hauck (1959) pp. 265–74.

118 'Frederick ... had brought back a huge sum of money from Constantinople': *Chronicle of Monte Cassino* II.86, p. 336. Cf. *Annales Romani* p. 470: he 'returned with a great treasure from Constantinople, where he had been a legate'.

to serve there as a warrior of Christ under a holy vow.[119] Very many people put an evil interpretation on this action. No one of sound understanding, however, believed anything other than that he had done this because of his ardent love of the faith and his weariness of worldly affairs, especially since at that time he was both fatigued by the exertion of a long journey and struck down by a serious physical disorder and he had given up hope of being able to live any longer.

Bishop Azelin of Hildesheim died[120] and Hezelo succeeded him.[121] Bishop Sibicho of Speyer died[122] and Arnold was his successor.[123] Bishop Hezekin of Bamberg died[124] and Adalbero succeeded him.[125]

Henry, the emperor's son, was anointed king in Aachen by Archbishop Herman of Cologne.[126] The latter with difficulty obtained a reluctant consent for this from Archbishop Liutpold, to whom, because of the primacy of the see of Mainz, the consecration of the king and the direction of the other affairs of the kingdom principally belonged.[127] The emperor, however, preferred to claim this privilege for Archbishop Herman because of his distinguished birth[128] and because the consecration had happened to be performed in his diocese.

---

119 *Ca.* June 1055, according to *Chronicle of Monte Cassino* II.86, p. 336. On the subject of Frederick's motives the *Chronicle* claimed that 'the emperor began to regard him with great suspicion' because he was Godfrey III's brother and ordered Victor II to take him prisoner. Frederick therefore sought refuge in Monte Cassino. See Steindorff (1881) p. 312.

120 Azelin (above n. 40) †8 March.

121 Hezelo, bishop of Hildesheim (1054–79).

122 Sibicho (above n. 6) †11/12 April.

123 Arnold I, bishop of Speyer (1054–5).

124 Hezekin (Hartwig) (above n. 70) †6 November 1053.

125 Adalbero, bishop of Bamberg (1053–7).

126 17 July 1054 (on the evidence of *D.H.IV* 471 of 1101). See Steindorff (1881) p. 279; Meyer von Knonau (1890) p. 9; Reinhardt (1975) pp. 235–8.

127 Lampert returned to this theme in his annal for 1073, below p. 200 and n. 1038: 'the archbishop of Mainz – to whom, before all others, by virtue of the primacy of the see of Mainz, the authority to elect and to consecrate a king was granted'. From the early tenth century the archbishops of Mainz claimed precedence in the German Church and usually played a leading role in coronations until 1028, when Mainz lost the right of crowning the king to Cologne: see Thomas (1970) pp. 371–2, 384; Boshof (1978b) pp. 36–43.

128 Herman II (above n. 89) was a member of the family of the *Ezzones*: he was the son of Emperor Otto II's daughter Matilda and the Lotharingian count palatine Ezzo.

1055

Emperor Henry celebrated Christmas in Goslar and, as soon as the feast days were over, he set out for Italy.[129] He was summoned there by an embassy of the Romans who had reported that the power and influence of Duke Godfrey in Italy was growing enormously at the expense of the State and unless he quickly took steps to deal with the disturbances, Godfrey would very soon lose all his shame and seize the kingdom from him. When the emperor entered Italy, however, Duke Godfrey sent envoys to meet him, informing him that nothing was further from his mind than rebellion: he was on the contrary prepared to undergo every kind of misfortune for the good of the State and the wellbeing of the emperor. He was grateful that, as an exile from his fatherland, who had been dispossessed of his ancestral property, he might at least be supported in a foreign land by the resources of his wife, whom he had joined to himself in matrimony not by deceit or by force but according to her wishes and in a formal wedding ceremony.[130]

Beatrice also, hiding her fear, went to meet the emperor and, obtaining with difficulty the opportunity to speak to him, said that she had done nothing except what was permitted to her by the law of nations. Deprived of her first husband, she had provided her desolate house with a protector; as a free-born woman, she had married a free-born man without deceit or criminal conspiracy. The emperor was forgetting justice and goodness if he would not grant her peace and permit her what had always been permitted to noblewomen in the Roman empire. The emperor, therefore, took the advice of the princes and declared Godfrey innocent of the accusation, not so much because he was satisfied with his explanation as because he was afraid that he might be provoked by his recent misfortunes to offer himself as a military commander to the Normans, who were destroying Italy, and the evils *that were to come* would *be worse than the earlier ones.*[131] Nevertheless the emperor took Beatrice away with him, as if he had received her surrender, since he blamed her for contracting a marriage without consulting him and for

---

129 25 December 1054: cf. *Annals of Niederaltaich* 1055, p. 50; Berthold of Reichenau, *Chronicle* 1055, pp. 99, 112. Henry III was in Brixen by 22 March and in Trient by 27 March: *D.H.III 335–6.*

130 'The fullest account of the conflict ... is found in Lampert of Hersfeld but ... what appear to be the most important details are nothing but tendentious tales, for which a partisan Lotharingian source used by Lampert must be responsible', according to Steindorff (1881) p. 303, preferring the version of events in Berthold, *Chronicle* 1055, p. 100; *Annals of Niederaltaich* 1055, p. 51; Sigebert, *Chronica* 1054, p. 360.

131 Matthew 12:45; Luke 11:26.

betraying Italy to an enemy of the State.[132] He then remained in Italy for a whole year and magnificently imposed order in all matters as seemed useful and necessary, according to the needs of the time and the place.[133]

1056

Gunther, the chancellor at that time,[134] saw a vision worth remembering. God sat on the throne of His majesty and, raising His arm on high, He brandished His drawn sword with a great effort and said to those who stood around: *I will render vengeance to mine enemies and will reward them that hate me.*[135] This vision was immediately followed by many deaths among the princes of the kingdom.[136] And after the vision had been fulfilled, he again saw the Lord in the same posture but He had now put the sword back into its sheath and laid it on His knees and He said to those who stood around: *A fire is kindled in mine anger and shall burn unto the lowest hell.*[137]

Archbishop Herman of Cologne died[138] and Anno, the provost of Goslar, succeeded him.[139]

After he had returned from Italy, the emperor celebrated the holy festival of Easter in Paderborn[140] and after a short stay in Goslar he proceeded to the village of Ivois, situated on the frontier of the kingdom of the

132 The earliest account, *Annals of Niederaltaich* 1055, p. 51, indicates that it was in Florence, where Henry III held a synod on Whit Sunday (4 June), that 'he commanded that Beatrice should be held prisoner'. Cf. Berthold, *Chronicle* 1055, p. 100: 'Beatrice came to surrender to the emperor and, although she had sworn fidelity, she was held prisoner because of her husband.' On Lampert's version see Goez (1995) pp. 141, 203.

133 Having arrived in Italy at the end of March 1055, Henry III remained in the kingdom until November 1055. By 20 November he was in Brixen: see Müller (1901) pp. 107–10. Henry III's judicial proceedings in these months: *D.H.III* 339, 348. See Steindorff (1881) pp. 300–2; Goez (1995) pp. 141–2 ('The bustling judicial activity documents the intention of Henry III to demonstrate the significance of the crown as the authoritative source of order in northern Italy').

134 Gunther, chancellor of the Italian kingdom (1054–7), bishop of Bamberg (1057–65). On his vision see Struve (1970a) pp. 37, 58. On Lampert and Bamberg see above p. 5.

135 Deuteronomy 32:41.

136 Struve (1970a) p. 37 n. 26 found here an allusion to the murder of the Saxon count palatine Dedi of Goseck in 1056 (below p. 68). A number of German princes had died in 1055: Duke Conrad II of Bavaria, the emperor's infant second son (10 April), Margrave Adalbert of Austria (26 May), Duke Welf III of Carinthia (13 November), the deposed Duke Conrad I of Bavaria (?15 December).

137 Deuteronomy 32:22.

138 Herman II (above n. 89) †11 February.

139 Anno II, archbishop of Cologne (1056–75).

140 7 April. Cf. *Annals of Niederaltaich* 1056, p. 52.

French and that of the Germans, in order to hold a conference there with the king of the French.[141] The latter rebuked him in an insolent and hostile manner, saying that he had very often deceived him and had long delayed the restoration of the extensive part of the kingdom of the French that had been seized from his ancestors by cunning. When the emperor said that he was ready to refute these accusations by engaging in single combat with him, the king fled in haste the following night and returned to his own territory.[142]

The emperor celebrated the nativity of St Mary in Goslar and there he prepared a magnificent welcome for Pope Victor (who was also called Gebhard). He assembled indeed almost all the treasures and the princes of the kingdom to add to the splendours of the festive day.[143] From there he set out for Bodfeld and, while he was spending some time there engaged in hunting,[144] he learned that Margrave William[145] and Count Theoderic,[146] together with an infinite number of the Saxon army, whom he had dispatched against the Liutizi,[147] had been defeated and killed.[148]

141 Henry I, king of France (1031–60). The conference, soon after Whitsun (26 May), was at Ivois on the River Chiers, where the two rulers had made a treaty of friendship in 1048: see Steindorff (1881) p. 43.

142 Lampert thus represented this as a dispute over the revival of the French claim to Lotharingia. The *Annals of Niederaltaich* 1056, p. 52 attributed the dispute to Henry I's repudiation of the treaty of 1048: 'he soon met the king of the *Charalingi* to hold a conference on the frontiers of the two kingdoms. There the king began to reject a certain agreement that had previously been made between himself and the emperor. But since the emperor was prepared to fight with an army rather than give up the truth, once he had acknowledged it, he finally proposed a trial by single combat to be fought by himself and [the king]. When the king realised that he was now vanquished by this means, he secretly fled by night with all his followers.' See Steindorff (1881) pp. 340–1. This incident echoes the similar challenge to single combat made by the west Frankish king Lothar to Emperor Otto II in the war of 978 (*Deeds of the bishops of Cambrai* I.98, p. 441).

143 8 September. Cf. Anonymous of Hasenried, *On the bishops of Eichstätt* c. 39, p. 265. Victor II 'was honoured by a reception of unheard-of glory'; 'the royal magnificence advanced to meet him with the most exquisite accoutrements'. See Steindorff (1881) p. 351.

144 *D.H.III* 378–81: Bodfeld, 15–28 September. Cf. Anonymous of Hasenried, *On the bishops of Eichstätt* c. 40, p. 265: the emperor was 'preoccupied with autumn hunting, an exertion most pleasing to him, in the forest called the Harz'. See Steindorff (1881) p. 351; Müller (1901) p. 117.

145 William ('of Haldensleben'), margrave of the Saxon Nordmark (✝1056).

146 Theoderic I, count of Katlenburg (✝1056).

147 The Liutizi were a confederation of the Slav tribes of the Zirzipani, Tollensi, Kessini and Redarii, living between the Rivers Elbe and Oder. See Reuter (1991a) pp. 178–9, 213, 256–7, 260, 262.

148 10 September: battle at the confluence of the Rivers Havel and Elbe. See Steindorff

Not long afterwards the emperor himself was afflicted by illness and, after he had been confined to his bed for seven days or more, he breathed his last.[149] Those who were present, as though summoned expressly to attend the deathbed of so great a man, were the Roman pontiff,[150] the patriarch of Aquileia,[151] the bishop of Regensburg, the emperor's uncle,[152] and innumerable other persons holding high office, both of the secular and of the ecclesiastical order. It was observed that never before in the memory of man had so many illustrious persons assembled together in one place without an official summons. His body was brought to Speyer and, after the funeral service had been performed in the royal manner, he was given burial on the day of the nativity of the apostles Simon and Jude, which was in fact the day on which he was born.[153] His son Henry, a little child, five years old,[154] obtained the kingship in place of his father, in the third year after he had been anointed king. Nevertheless the supreme power and the administration of all necessary business remained in the hands of the empress. Although the State was in danger, she protected it with such skill that the great novelty of the situation produced no disturbance and no animosity in the State.[155]

(1881) pp. 352–3.

149 5 October. See Steindorff (1881) pp. 355–6; Struve (1984a) pp. 21–3 (no. 72).

150 Cf. *Annals of Niederaltaich* 1056, p. 53; Anonymous of Hasenried, *On the bishops of Eichstätt* c. 40, p. 265.

151 Gotebald, patriarch of Aquileia (1048–63).

152 Gebhard III, bishop of Regensburg (1036–60) was the stepbrother of Emperor Conrad II, son of Adelaide of Metz by her second husband (unknown). In July 1056 Henry III had pardoned his uncle for his participation in the rebellion of 1055: see Steindorff (1881) pp. 318–19, 323, 345–6, 354.

153 28 October. Cf. Berthold, *Chronicle* 1056, p. 101: Henry III was 'buried next to his father and mother in the [cathedral] church of St Mary [in Speyer], which he himself had built'. See Steindorff (1881) p. 357; Struve (1984a) p. 28 (no. 81).

154 Lampert's calculation was based on his misdating the birth of Henry IV in 1051 (see above p. 59).

155 Cf. Lampert, *Libellus de institutione Herveldensis ecclesiae* II, p. 353: 'On his death Emperor Henry left his little son Henry as his heir under the guidance of his mother Agnes, the most prudent queen.' On Agnes's role of regent see Meyer von Knonau (1890) pp. 13–15; Bulst-Thiele (1933) pp. 33–4; Robinson (1999) pp. 27–8. Meyer von Knonau (1890) pp. 647–51 noted that Lampert was alone in presenting a positive view of the situation in 1056. Cf. Otloh of St Emmeram, *Liber Visionum* 15, p. 384: 'For in this little king of ours we can, alas, the sorrow of it! have no government for a long time to come'; Adam of Bremen, *Gesta* III.33, p. 176: 'On [Henry III's] death not only was the Church thrown into disorder but also the State seemed to be coming to an end … A woman with a boy succeeded to the government of the kingdom, to the great detriment of the empire'; *Annals of Niederaltaich* 1060, p. 56: 'These were the beginnings of our griefs'.

Bishop Arnold of Speyer died[156] and Conrad succeeded him.[157] The emperor's son Conrad, the duke of Bavaria, died.[158] The emperor conferred his duchy on the empress as a private possession for as long as she wished.[159] The count palatine Dedi was killed by a certain clerk of Bremen, whom he had received from his brother, the archbishop, to be banished into exile because of the offences of which he was accused.[160] He was buried in Goslar at the emperor's command. Margrave William was succeeded by Count Udo, an extremely active man and a very close kinsman of the king.[161]

1057

The king celebrated Christmas in Regensburg, still in the presence of Pope Victor.[162] The latter returned from there to Italy, since the affairs of the kingdom had in some degree been set in order, as far as was possible at that time. He departed to the Lord on 28 July.[163] The bishopric of Eichstätt, which he had not relinquished on becoming pope, was received by Gunzo.[164] Then indeed all men, whether princes or the Roman people, with one mind and one will agreed on the election of Frederick, the brother of Duke Godfrey.[165] They dragged him from the monastery

---

156 Arnold I (above n. 123) †2 October 1055.

157 Conrad, bishop of Speyer (1056–60).

158 Conrad II, duke of Bavaria (1054–5), born 1052; †10 April 1055.

159 I.e. this grant, made before the death of Henry III, allowed Agnes to enjoy the ducal revenues of Bavaria. See Meyer von Knonau (1890) p. 14; Bulṣt-Thiele (1933) pp. 27–8; Robinson (1999) p. 28. The evidence of Agnes's itinerary suggests that she did not play an active role in the administration of the duchy: Black-Veldtrup (1995) pp. 84–90.

160 Dedi (of Goseck), Saxon count palatine (†5 May 1056), brother of Archbishop Adalbert of Bremen (above n. 48). Cf. Adam of Bremen, *Gesta* III.56, p. 200: 'The archbishop's full brother, the count palatine named Dedo, was killed by a certain priest of his diocese.' See Steindorff (1881) pp. 338–9.

161 Liuder-Udo I, count of Stade, margrave of the Saxon Nordmark (†1057). His wife Adelaide was the niece of Henry III's paternal grandmother, Adelaide of Metz: see Jakobs (1968) genealogical table A.

162 25 December 1056. Cf. *Annals of Niederaltaich* 1057, p. 53; Berthold, *Chronicle* 1057, p. 102. On the presence of Victor II: Otloh of St Emmeram, *Liber Visionum* 15, p. 86. See Meyer von Knonau (1890) pp. 19–20.

163 In Arezzo: see Meyer von Knonau (1890) pp. 28–9.

164 Gunzo (Gundechar II), bishop of Eichstätt (1057–75). On the significance of the retention of their German dioceses by the popes of 1046–57 see Frech (1991) pp. 303–32.

165 Frederick – Stephen IX (above n. 86) was elected on 2 August (the feast day of Pope Stephen I) and consecrated on 3 August. Cf. *Annals of Niederaltaich* 1057, p. 54:

of Monte Cassino, where, as *a light* of God, *burning* and giving light, he was hidden *under a bed* of monastic tranquillity, and raised him *on* the *candlestick*[166] of the apostolic see. No man had for many years past advanced to the government of the Roman Church with more joyful approval and with greater expectations on the part of all men. But alas! a premature death disappointed such high hopes.

Margrave Udo died[167] and his son, the younger Udo, succeeded him.[168] The princes of Saxony engaged in frequent meetings concerning the injuries that had been inflicted on them under the emperor and they considered that they would be admirably compensated for these injuries if they seized the kingship from his son, while his *age* still *provided an opportunity to inflict* that *injury*;[169] and they were not far from believing that the son *in his character and way of life would tread,* as they say, in his father's *footsteps.*[170] A great source of help in creating a disturbance came unexpectedly to hand in the person of Otto, the brother of Margrave William[171] but born of an unequal marriage (that is to say, his mother was a Slav), a man of keen understanding and *quick to resort to arms.*[172] He had since his boyhood lived in exile among the Bohemian people. When he heard of his brother's death, however, he returned to Saxony with high hopes of obtaining his inheritance and was received in a kindly manner by all the princes there. They all gave him great encouragement and incited him not only to strive for the march, which belonged to him

---

'Frederick, named Stephen, was substituted by the Romans, without the knowledge of the king, who nevertheless afterwards approved his election.' See Meyer von Knonau (1890) pp. 30–1.

166 Luke 8:16. Cf. *Chronicle of Monte Cassino* II.94, p. 353: the Romans 'violently dragged Frederick from the Pallaria [S. Maria in Pallaria, where he was staying during his visit to Rome] and led him to the basilica of blessed Peter called *ad Vincula*'.

167 Liuder-Udo I (above n. 161) ✝7 November.

168 Udo II, count of Stade, count of Dithmarschen, margrave of the Saxon Nordmark (✝1082).

169 Livy II.13.10.

170 *Ibid.,* V.9.2; IX.8.13.

171 Otto, half-brother of Margrave William of the Saxon Nordmark (above n. 145). On the Saxon conspiracy see Meyer von Knonau (1890) pp. 39–41; Fenske (1977) pp. 23–4; Giese (1991) pp. 284–5; Robinson (1999) pp. 63–4. Struve (1984a) p. 42 (no. 109) noted that this account was composed 'unmistakably under the impression made by later events, the Saxon war and the discussion of the deposition of Henry IV'. Struve (1970a) pp. 36–7, 56, noted that this was the only passage in Lampert's writings admitting criticism of Henry III's regime.

172 Livy XXIX.32.1.

by hereditary right, but also *to aspire to the kingdom*[173] itself. When they observed that he was eager and ready for the enterprise, they all swore fidelity to him, each promising homage and support, and they decided to kill the king, whenever fortune gave them the opportunity.

All who had any *responsibility for affairs of State*[174] were struck by fear and were above all eager to calm the disturbance that was just beginning. It was their opinion that the king should come to Saxony as soon as possible and take whatever measures he could against the danger that threatened the State. He therefore formed the intention of celebrating the feast of the holy apostles Peter and Paul[175] in Merseburg and *he commanded* that those *princes* who were in Saxony should be *summoned to a conference.*[176] While they were travelling there, each individual being accompanied, according to his means, by a large force of knights, it happened that Bruno and Ekbert, the king's cousins,[177] chanced to encounter the army of the aforementioned Otto, which was moving with serried ranks towards the royal court.[178] They felt extremely hostile towards him, not only on political grounds but also for personal reasons of enmity. Without delay they gave the knights the signal to fight, they *spurred on their horses*[179] and each side rushed with equal daring and equal hatred to inflict wounds on each other. There in the forefront Bruno and Otto – both *full of wrath*,[180] both *neglecting to defend themselves while* they rained blows on their *enemy*[181] – made such a violent attack on each other that *at the first onset*[182] each *ran the other through, inflicting a* mortal *wound*[183] and *throwing* him *off*

---

173 *Ibid.,* II.7.6; XXIV.25.4.

174 *Ibid.,* II.41.2; II.49.5.

175 29 June.

176 Livy XXIV.1.5; XXX.12.8; XXXI.27.3.

177 Bruno, count of Brunswick (✝1057), and Ekbert I, count of Brunswick, margrave of Meissen (✝1068), were the sons of Count Liudolf of Brunswick (✝1038), the half-brother of Emperor Henry III. They were *Brunones,* the descendants of Empress Gisela by her first marriage to Count Bruno of Brunswick (✝1010/12).

178 26 June, 'near the village called Neindorf [Haus-Neindorf] beside the River Selke', north-east of Quedlinburg: *Annalista Saxo* p. 692. See Meyer von Knonau (1890) pp. 40–2 and n. 33; Struve (1984a) p. 43 (no. 113): 'Otto presumably aimed to overtake the young king on the way to Merseburg.'

179 Livy II.20.2.

180 *Ibid.,* II.38.6.

181 *Ibid.,* II.6.5.

182 *Ibid.,* II.25.4; XXV.19.5.

183 *Ibid.,* II.6.9.

his horse.[184] *After the leaders were lost,*[185] for some considerable time *an indecisive battle*[186] held the two armies in its grip. But Ekbert, although he was seriously wounded, nevertheless threw himself headlong with reckless haste into the crowded ranks of the enemy, driven wild by grief at the death of his brother, and he killed the son of Count Bernard,[187] an excellent youth but scarcely old enough for military service. The others were fighting more faintheartedly since they had lost their leader and he put them to flight. Thus the State *was freed from* very *great anxiety*[188] and, now that the standard-bearer of rebellion had been eliminated, the Saxons undertook no further hostile enterprise against the king.

Cuno, a kinsman of the king, was made duke of the Carinthians.[189] His brother, Henry, count palatine of the Lotharingians,[190] at the instigation of a demon, took the monastic vows in Gorze. After a few days, however, when the demon that had deluded him had made its identity known, he abandoned the habit of the religious life, in which the angel of *Satan had transformed* himself *into an angel of light,*[191] and, like a deserter of God and a renegade, took back his wife[192] and his possessions.

184 Vergil, *Aeneid* XI.640.

185 Livy XXX.30.7.

186 *Ibid.,* XXVII.14.6; XXVIII.14.12; XXXIII.18.16.

187 This Saxon count may be the Count Bernard mentioned in the imperial diploma of 1052, *D.H.III* 281. See also Fenske (1977) p. 88 n. 344. His son may be the *Liudierus* recorded in the necrology of the monastery of St Michael, Lüneburg, together with Count Bruno, Otto 'and the others killed with them': Meyer von Knonau (1890) p. 41 n. 33.

188 Livy XXXIII.15.16.

189 Cuno (Conrad III), duke of Carinthia (1056–61). The appointment was made in December 1056: Meyer von Knonau (1890) p. 19; Struve (1984a) pp. 30–1 (no. 86). A member of the family of the *Hezelini,* a branch of the *Ezzones,* Cuno was the son of Hezel, count in Zülpichgau, brother of the Lotharingian count palatine Ezzo (see above n. 128).

190 Henry I, Lotharingian count palatine (1045–61) entered Gorze in 1059: see Meyer von Knonau (1890) pp. 163–4.

191 II Corinthians 11:14.

192 Matilda (✝1060), daughter of Duke Gozelo II of Lower Lotharingia, niece of Godfrey III ('the Bearded') of Lotharingia.

1058

The king celebrated Christmas in Merseburg.[193] Present there among the other princes of the kingdom was Hildebrand, abbot of St Paul, bearing instructions from the apostolic see, a man who was truly admirable for his eloquence and his knowledge of sacred literature.[194]

I, [Lampert], striving to follow the way of life of Abbot Meginher,[195] which was pleasing to God and renowned throughout the whole world, abandoned domestic concerns so as not to be weighed down by them on the road to God and received the sacred garment from his most holy hands on 15 March, being alas! utterly unworthy to *put on* such *armour*.[196]

While Pope Stephen of pious memory (who was also called Frederick) was staying in the city of Florence, on 29 March he paid his debt to mortal nature and truly, as we hope, passed from this *vale of tears*[197] to the joy of the angels.[198] Evidence of this are *the tokens and wonders*[199] for which his tomb in the same city is famous up to this very day. Immediately, without consulting the king and the princes, a certain Benedict[200] of the Lateran church usurped the apostolic see, aided by *a faction* of the people, whom *he had corrupted*[201] with money.

193 25 December 1057 in Goslar, according to the evidence of the *Annals of Niederaltaich* 1058, p. 54, which is followed by Meyer von Knonau (1890) p. 52 and nn. 53–4; Struve (1984a) p. 50 (no. 129), since Henry IV was reported in Pöhlde on 27 December.

194 Hildebrand, archdeacon of the Roman Church (1059–73), Pope Gregory VII (1073–85). From 1050 until at least the mid–1060s he was administrator (with the title of *rector* or *economus*) of the monastery of S. Paolo fuori le Mura but 'he was never called *abbas*': Cowdrey (1998) pp. 31, 38, 58. His presence in Pöhlde on 27 December was recorded by Gundechar, *Liber pontificalis Eichstetensis* p. 246. This papal legation, in which Hildebrand accompanied Bishop Anselm I of Lucca, was intended to secure royal recognition of the election of Stephen IX: see Meyer von Knonau (1890) p. 52; Struve (1984a) pp. 50–1 (no. 130); Cowdrey (1998) p. 35.

195 Meginher, abbot of Hersfeld (1035–69). See Vogtherr (1991) pp. 440–1. On Lampert's entry into Hersfeld: Holder-Egger, *Lamperti Annales* p. IX; Struve (1969) p. 12. Lampert's name is supplied here only by the Würzburg and Göttingen manuscripts: see above p. 1.

196 Cf. Ephesians 6:11, 13.

197 Psalm 83:7.

198 See Meyer von Knonau (1890) pp. 81–2.

199 Psalm 134:9.

200 John II Mincius, cardinal bishop of Velletri (✝ *ca.* 1073), Pope Benedict X (1058–9), a member or adherent of the Tusculan family, which dominated the papacy 1012–46. See Meyer von Knonau (1890) pp. 85–6; Hüls (1977) p. 144; Schmidt (1977) pp. 78–80. On Lampert's version of the papal election see Struve (1970a) pp. 80, 100.

201 Livy I.51.2.

Otto of Schweinfurt, the duke of the Swabians, died.[202] Rudolf obtained his duchy[203] and, in order in those uncertain times to make him more devoted to the king and more loyal to the State by means of a marriage alliance, he was also betrothed to the king's sister, who was still of tender age.[204] She was entrusted to the bishop of Constance[205] to be brought up until she was of marriageable age.

Duke Cuno of the Carinthians assembled a huge force in order to take possession of his duchy, which he had not visited for so long for fear of a rebellion, and he prepared a first expedition. But he was overtaken by death and did not complete the campaign that he had undertaken.[206]

I, [Lampert] was ordained priest by Archbishop Liutpold in Aschaffenburg during the Ember Days of autumn[207] and immediately set out on a pilgrimage to Jerusalem with *zeal for God*, but would that it was *according to knowledge!*[208]

Ekbert, who was also called Eppo, the abbot of Fulda, died on 17 November[209] and Siegfried, a monk of that same monastery, was his successor.[210]

---

202 Otto III (of Schweinfurt), duke of Swabia (1048–57) †28 September 1057.

203 Rudolf of Rheinfelden, duke of Swabia (1057–79), anti-king (1077–80). On the hostile version of Rudolf's appointment and marriage by Frutolf of Michelsberg, *Chronica* 1057, p. 74 (composed 1098/9) see Meyer von Knonau (1890) pp. 48–50; Struve (1984a) pp. 48–9 (no. 126); Robinson (1999) pp. 33–4 and n. 48. On Rudolf's kinship with the Salian dynasty see Hlawitschka (1991) p. 209.

204 Matilda (1048–60), daughter of Henry III and Agnes. The wedding was probably in April/May 1059: see Black-Veldtrup (1995) pp. 108–9.

205 Rumold (above n. 94).

206 Cuno (above n. 189) †1061. On his defeat in 1058 see *Annals of Niederaltaich* 1058, p. 55: 'In the autumn Duke Cuno of the Carinthians entered Lombardy with a strong force but, when the inhabitants of the province resisted him, he retreated in a shameful manner.' Cf. Berthold, *Chronicle* 1061, p. 104: 'Conrad ... was duke of the Carinthians in name only'. See Meyer von Knonau (1890) pp. 98–9.

207 16 or 18 or 19 September. Lampert's name is supplied here only by the Würzburg and Göttingen manuscripts: see above p. 1. Holder-Egger, *Lamperti Annales* p. IX noted that, if Lampert was now at the canonical age of at least thirty, he must have been born before 1028. See also Struve (1969) p. 12. For Archbishop Liutpold of Mainz see above n. 92.

208 Romans 10:2. Holder-Egger, *Lamperti Annales* p. IX, noted the report by Ekkebert of Hersfeld, *Vita sancti Haimeradi* c. 32, p. 606, that Meginfrid, burgrave of Magdeburg, with many others had made a pilgrimage to Jerusalem and conjectured that Lampert had joined this expedition. See Struve (1970a) p. 58.

209 Ekbert (above n. 74).

210 Siegfried of Eppenstein, abbot of Fulda (1058–60); Archbishop Siegfried I of Mainz (1060–84).

1059

I celebrated Christmas in the city of *Marouwa*, situated on the frontier of the Hungarians and the Bulgarians.[211]

The Roman princes sent an explanation to the king: namely, that the fidelity that they had sworn to the father would be kept to the son, as far as they could, and with this intention they had not up to the present time appointed a pontiff in the vacant Roman church. Instead they awaited his decision in this matter and they begged him earnestly to send whom he wished.[212] There was nothing to hinder his installation, unless *he had not entered by the door* of lawful election *into the sheepfold but climbed up some other way.*[213] The king held a consultation with the princes and designated as pope Bishop Gerard of Florence,[214] on whom the Romans and the Germans had concurred in their choice, and sent him to Rome by the agency of Margrave Godfrey.[215] Thus Benedict, who, unbidden by the king and the princes, had usurped the priesthood, was rejected and Gerard, who was also called Nicholas, obtained the papacy.[216] In the same year he received a petition from Abbot Meginher on the subject of the tithes of Saxony and sent a letter commanding Bishop Burchard of Halberstadt[217] not to *go beyond the boundaries* established by *his fathers*[218] and not to disturb the monastery of Hersfeld with unnecessary disputes. If he continued to be troublesome, the pope would be compelled to use the rod of apostolic authority against his disobedience, especially since the privileges of so many of his predecessors bore witness that that monastery lay under the jurisdiction of the

---

211 25 December 1058. The place name cannot be identified. See Struve (1969) p. 12; Struve (1970a) p. 91.

212 Whitsun (7 June) 1058 in Augsburg: *Annals of Niederaltaich* 1058, p. 54. See Meyer von Knonau (1890) pp. 92, 674–7; Krause (1960) pp. 63–9; Schmidt (1977) pp. 72–80; Struve (1984a) pp. 52–3 (no. 136). On Lampert's version of the papal election see Meyer von Knonau (1894) p. 842; Struve (1970a) pp. 80, 100.

213 John 10:1.

214 Gerard, bishop of Florence (1045–61), Pope Nicholas II (1058–61).

215 Margrave Godfrey ('the Bearded') of Tuscany (above n. 33).

216 Nicholas II was elected 6(?) December 1058 in Siena and consecrated 24 January 1059 in Rome. Benedict X was deprived of the papal, episcopal and priestly offices in March/April 1060. See Meyer von Knonau (1890) pp. 100–2, 119–22; Krause (1960) pp. 65–9; Hüls (1977) p. 144; Robinson (1999) pp. 37–8.

217 Burchard I, bishop of Halberstadt (1036–58). The papal letter (Nicholas II, *JL* 4409) is not extant. On the Saxon tithes dispute see Meyer von Knonau (1890) pp. 656–7; Lübeck (1947) p. 312; Struve (1970a) pp. 73–4.

218 Proverbs 22:28.

Roman pontiff.[219] The pope also sent the abbot a letter with words of consolation, which is preserved at the present time in the archive of the monastery of Hersfeld.[220]

After completing the pilgrimage to Jerusalem, I returned to the monastery on 17 September[221] and found – what I had especially prayed to God to find throughout my whole journey – that Abbot Meginher was still alive. For I feared that, since I had set out without his blessing, I should have been found guilty before God of a great crime, if at his death he had been displeased and unreconciled. But the divine power graciously accompanied the returning traveller, just as it had often most mercifully protected him even when threatened by the greatest danger. I found him alive; he pardoned my sin and I arose, as it were, from the dead, alive again and thus he joyfully received me (as they say) *with open hands.*[222] *In a wonderful manner,*[223] however, you might say that his life had been preserved expressly for the sake of my absolution. On the same day on which he absolved me from my sins, he was seized by a fever and thus for eight days he was consumed by a grave illness and on 26 September he joyfully *finished his course*[224] and rested in the Lord. He was a man of great virtues in Christ and truly – and I say this without offence to all the abbots of modern times – the unique model of correct monastic living in the German territories in his generation.[225]

He (as was mentioned before) had been involved in a long drawn out dispute with Bishop Burchard of Halberstadt concerning the tithes of Saxony, which the latter snatched away from the monastery of Hersfeld and claimed for himself on the pretext of his episcopal authority. Since neither secular nor ecclesiastical laws could achieve anything in the face

---

219 This claim is made in the spurious papal privileges for Hersfeld, Stephen III, *JE* 2384, John XIII, *JL* 3723.

220 The papal letter (Nicholas II, *JL* 4410) is not extant.

221 The feast of St Lambert, bishop and martyr: see Holder-Egger, *Lamperti Annales* p. XIV. The date '17 October' in the German translation of A. Schmidt and W. D. Fritz, *Lamperti Annales* p. 67, and in Struve (1969) p. 12 is a misreading.

222 Jerome, *Letter 53* (to Paulinus) c. 10, *MPL* 22, col. 549. Lampert's offence was to have departed on pilgrimage immediately after his ordination in Aschaffenburg without first seeking his abbot's permission: see Holder-Egger, *Lamperti Annales* p. XIV.

223 Caesar, *Bellum Gallicum* I.41.

224 II Timothy 4:7.

225 Cf. Lampert, *Libellus de institutione Herveldensis ecclesiae* I, p. 350: 'Meginher, a monk of [Hersfeld], succeeded as abbot, a man venerable and good, whose teaching agreed with his life. He established a school and was skilled in all the arts.'

of his dishonesty and, often going to law with his complaint, he had *told his tale to deaf*[226] law courts, at last, shortly before the end of his life, he had sent word to the bishop by Frederick, the count palatine,[227] that as he was certainly *the inferior in strength,*[228] his case would fail but nevertheless God would not lack the strength to defend justice. They should both, therefore, be prepared within a few days to defend their cause before the judgement seat of God, the most righteous judge: there the victor would be not he who was more powerful but he whose cause was the more just. And the outcome proved this to be true. For only a few days had passed after the abbot's death and the bishop had summoned a synod to deal with the aforementioned case; his horse was brought to him and he wished to hasten there, when, lo and behold! struck down by divine punishment, he fell to the ground. He was carried back to his bedchamber and, quickly assembling his priests, he implored them by God to restore his tithes to the monastery of Hersfeld and to end the whole dispute about this matter forever. They should know that all those who attempted to behave in the same way would share the unhappy fate that had befallen him, who learned that God Himself was so harsh an avenger of his unjust demand. And when the bishops of Magdeburg[229] and Hildesheim[230] had arrived to visit him, he confessed with loud lamentation that, according to the prediction of the excellent abbot, he was already dragged before the judgement seat of God and called to account for seizing the possessions of others and he asked with all his might that envoys should be sent to Hersfeld and humbly beg pardon for what he had done. Not long afterwards his internal organs were torn asunder by a pitiable disease and he breathed his last.[231] Similarly his archpriest Uto, whose encouragement in particular had kindled this harsh conduct and who had been the most eager enforcer and superintendent of this chicanery, in the same year succumbed to a sudden death without confession, without holy communion, strangled (as *was widely rumoured*)[232] by the devil.[233]

226 Terence, *Heautontimorumenos* II.1.10.

227 Frederick II (of Goseck), Saxon count palatine (brother of Archbishop Adalbert of Bremen) +1088.

228 Livy XXV.27.8; XXVI.25.10; XLII.65.6.

229 Engelhard (above n. 96).

230 Hezelo (above n. 121).

231 18 October. See Meyer von Knonau (1890) pp. 164–5.

232 Livy I.7.2; XXV.17.4.

233 The archpriest Uto is otherwise unknown. This version of Burchard I's death is

In place of Abbot Meginher, Ruthard was installed on 8 November. He was a monk of the Corvey observance, who had formerly been appointed abbot in the monastery of Corvey but had subsequently been accused of certain offences – falsely, it is believed – and had lost the abbacy and had now spent some years in various monasteries without an office.[234] Bucco, provost of Goslar, succeeded Bishop Burchard.[235] Struck with horror by the recent disastrous end of his predecessor, he refrained from troubling the monastery of Hersfeld. Nevertheless he frequently threatened that he would do great things but he went no further than words.

Archbishop Liutpold of Mainz died on 7 December.[236] He left behind him as his memorial the monastery of St James, which he had built at his own expense in Mainz, outside the walls on the mountain that is called 'Beautiful'.[237] Abbot Siegfried of Fulda succeeded him.[238] Widerad, a monk of that same monastery and also originating from the same family, obtained the office of abbot.[239]

---

found only in Lampert's *Annals*. On the partisan character of the account see Meyer von Knonau (1890) pp. 165 n.85, 656–7; Struve (1970a) pp. 73–4.

234 Ruthard (above n. 54). Cf. Lampert, *Libellus de institutione Herveldensis ecclesiae* II, p. 353: 'Ruthard, the former abbot of Corvey, succeeded Meginher as abbot of Hersfeld, a clever and highspirited man; he knew how to command, not how to be commanded. He acted shrewdly in secular affairs, unremarkably in spiritual affairs. Meginher had proceeded by the opposite route.' See Holder-Egger, *Lamperti Annales* p. XV; Struve (1970a) p. 103 n. 13; Vogtherr (1991) p. 437 and nn. 50, 52, 447. Cf. *Annals of Corvey* p. 6: 'Our deposed abbot Ruthard was appointed in Hersfeld.'

235 Bucco (Burchard II), provost of Henry III's foundation of SS Simon and Jude, Goslar; bishop of Halberstadt (1059–88). Lampert noted, below 1075, p. 257, that Burchard II was the nephew (son of the sister) of Archbishop Anno II of Cologne (cf. Adam of Bremen, *Gesta* III.35, p. 177; *Gesta archiepiscoporum Magdeburgensium* c. 21, p. 400).

236 Liutpold (above n. 92).

237 Monastery of St James (St Jakobskloster), Mainz: see Meyer von Knonau (1890) p. 167; Hauck (1954) p. 1013. Abbot Ruthard of Hersfeld was identified in a charter of 1070 as the 'ruler' (*rector*) of St James, Mainz: see Vogtherr (1991) p. 447 n. 113.

238 Siegfried I (above n. 210) was invested on 7 January 1060: Meyer von Knonau (1890) p. 175; Struve (1984a) p. 75 (no. 184).

239 Widerad, abbot of Fulda (1060–75). His kinship with Siegfried: Meyer von Knonau (1890) p. 175; Vogtherr (1991) p. 445.

1060

The king celebrated Christmas in Worms.[240] Here a synod was announced but it did not take place, the bishops pleading as an excuse both sickness and the plague that was then fiercely raging in Gaul.[241]

Bishop Sizzo of Verden died[242] and Richbert succeeded him.[243] Bishop Gebhard of Regensburg died[244] and Otto was his successor.[245] Bishop Conrad of Speyer died[246] and Einhard was promoted to his office.[247]

1061

Andreas, king of the Hungarians, seeing that one of his kinsmen, Bela,[248] sought to obtain the kingship and that the Hungarians were gradually abandoning him, sent his wife[249] and his son Salomon[250] – to whom the emperor had betrothed his daughter[251] while they were both children – together with much treasure, to King Henry, entreating him to send an army to help him and to keep his loved ones safe until peace was restored to the land. The king sent there William, margrave of the Thuringians[252] and Bishop Eppo of Zeitz,[253] together with the duke

---

240 25 December 1059 in Freising, according to *Annals of Niederaltaich* 1060, p. 55. See Meyer von Knonau (1890) p. 157 and n. 75; Struve (1984a) p. 74 (no. 182).

241 Cf. *Annals of Niederaltaich* 1059, p. 55: 'a severe plague of men and animals raged throughout the whole province [of Bavaria]'; Berthold, *Chronicle* 1059, p. 102: 'there were many deaths among men and a sickness among cattle'; 1060, p. 103: 'in this year, as in the previous one, many perished from disease'. On Gaul (*Gallia*) as a designation for Germany see Lugge (1960) pp. 132–40, especially p. 132 n. 238.

242 Sizzo (Sigebert), bishop of Verden (1049–60) †9 October.

243 Richbert, bishop of Verden (1060–76[?]).

244 Gebhard III (above n. 152) †2 December.

245 Otto, bishop of Regensburg (1060/1–89).

246 Conrad (above n. 157) †12 December.

247 Einhard II, bishop of Speyer (1060–7).

248 Bela I, king of Hungary (1061–3), brother of Andreas I (above n. 51). See Meyer von Knonau (1890) pp. 192–8; Boshof (1986) p. 185.

249 Anastasia, daughter of Jaroslav, grand prince of Kiev (above n. 23), queen of Hungary.

250 Salomon, king of Hungary (1063–74, †1087).

251 Judith (?1054–92/6), known in Hungary as Sophia, married (1) Salomon, (2) Duke Vladislav-Herman of Poland. The treaty had been concluded in September 1058 (not, as Lampert claimed, in the reign of Henry III): Meyer von Knonau (1890) pp. 95–6; Boshof (1986) p. 185; Robinson (1999) p. 35.

252 William IV, count of Weimar-Orlamünde, margrave of Meissen (†1062).

253 Eppo (Eberhard) of Zeitz (Naumburg): see above n. 46.

of the Bohemians[254] and the Bavarian army. But the margrave and the bishop were the first to enter Hungary and, without waiting for the duke of the Bohemians, they engaged in battle with Bela and destroyed an infinite number of Hungarians. Then when the Hungarians arrived in great numbers, crowding together on all sides to bring help to their compatriots, the king's envoys saw that they were *inferior in numbers and strength*[255] to so great a host and they wished to withdraw from the land of their enemies. But the Hungarians had closed to them all the places through which they could escape and they had seen to it that neither food nor drink was to be found on their route. As they retreated, moreover, the Hungarians harassed them with frequent attacks and they always repelled danger courageously, inflicting great slaughter on the enemy. Finally, however, their strength was exhausted by constant killing; Andreas was accidentally thrown from his horse and trampled by the feet of the fighting men;[256] the bishop was captured;[257] the margrave surrendered, overcome by hunger rather than by the sword. His courage was so greatly admired by the barbarians that Geisa, the son of Bela[258] – a young man whose abilities inspired high hopes, considering the state of civilisation of his nation at that time – spontaneously entreated his father not only to leave him *unharmed, according to the law of war,*[259] but also to connect himself with him by marriage, betrothing him to his daughter, Geisa's sister.[260]

The empress gave the duchy of Bavaria (which up to that time she herself had administered after the death of her son Conrad) to Otto,[261]

---

254 Spitignev II, duke of Bohemia (1055–61).

255 Livy XXV.27.3; XXXI.33.9; XLII.65.6.

256 In 1060 at Moson. Cf. *Annals of Niederaltaich* 1060, p. 57: 'the king was captured alive there but at the same moment he was trampled on by horses and chariots and died'. But see Berthold, *Chronicle* 1060, p. 103: 'Andreas … was at last struck down by fever.' See Meyer von Knonau (1890) pp. 193–8; Struve (1984a) p. 82 (no. 202).

257 Eppo (Eberhard) of Zeitz (Naumburg). Cf. *Annals of Niederaltaich* 1060, p. 57: 'Of our men, Bishop Eppo, the Saxon margrave William, [the Bavarian] count Boto and very many others were captured.'

258 Geisa (Magnus), king of Hungary (1074–7), son of Bela I (above n. 248).

259 Livy II.12.14.

260 Sophia (†1095), daughter of King Bela I, married (1) Margrave Udalric of Carniola and Istria; (2) Magnus Billung, duke of Saxony.

261 Otto, count of Northeim, [II] duke of Bavaria (1061–70; †1083). Cf. *Annals of Niederaltaich* 1060, p. 57: Agnes 'voluntarily gave up the duchy of Bavaria, which she had long held, and took care that it should be conferred on the prudent man Otto'. See Meyer von Knonau (1890) pp. 210–11; Lange (1961) pp. 10–14; Struve (1984a) p. 86 (no. 214). On Empress Agnes and Duke Conrad II of Bavaria see above p. 68 and nn. 158, 159.

seeing in him an active man, well qualified to assist in the affairs of the kingdom.

Henry, count palatine of the Lotharingians, murdered his wife with his own hands and thus at last made it entirely clear that he was in the power of a demon, which he had long concealed. He was sent to the monastery of Echternach and there he perished, consumed by long torments.[262]

1062

Margrave William returned to Thuringia and, while he was preparing to return to Hungary and to bring back his bride with the great pomp of her riches, he was struck down by disease on the second stage of his journey and died.[263] His kinsman Udalric, margrave of the Carinthians, received his bride;[264] his brother Otto obtained the march.[265] The latter, however, could obtain the benefices of the archbishopric of Mainz only if he promised that he would give tithes from his possessions in Thuringia and would compel the rest of the Thuringians to do the same. This fact was the source of many evils, since all the Thuringians denounced his action and declared that they would rather die than lose the rights of their forefathers.[266]

While the empress was still bringing up her son, she herself administered the government of the kingdom and she made excessive use of the advice of Bishop Henry of Augsburg.[267] She could not, therefore, escape the suspicion of incestuous love and the rumour publicly circulated everywhere that they could not be involved in so close an

262 The Lotharingian count palatine Henry I (above n. 190) murdered his wife Matilda (above n. 192) in 1060: see Meyer von Knonau (1890) pp. 199–200.

263 Margrave William of Meissen (above n. 252) had been released from captivity by King Bela I of Hungary after agreeing to marry the latter's daughter, Sophia (above n. 260): *Annals of Niederaltaich* 1061, p. 58. See Meyer von Knonau (1890) pp. 206, 294; Struve (1984a) p. 86 (no. 212).

264 Udalric I of Weimar-Orlamünde, margrave of Carniola and Istria (✝1070), son of Count Poppo of Weimar-Orlamünde, the brother of Margrave Otto (below n. 265).

265 Otto, count of Weimar-Orlamünde, margrave of Meissen (✝1067).

266 See Meyer von Knonau (1890) pp. 295–6, 659; Struve (1969) p. 47 n. 74.

267 Henry II (above n. 63). Cf. Berthold, *Chronicle* 1058, p. 102: 'Bishop Henry of Augsburg had the role of chief adviser of the empress, which greatly displeased some of the princes of the kingdom, who would not tolerate his arrogance.' Criticism of the avarice of Henry II ('who hitherto was in command in the palace') and of his dealings with Bishop Cadalus of Parma: *Annals of Niederaltaich* 1060, p. 56. See Meyer von Knonau (1890) pp. 85, 168–9, 270–1, 354–5; Bulst-Thiele (1933) pp. 36–7, 46, 48; Black-Veldtrup (1995) pp. 356–60.

intimacy without indulging in a scandalous liaison.[268] This circumstance seriously offended the princes, for they saw that, because of private affection for a single individual, their own authority – which should have been the most powerful in the State – had been almost obliterated. They therefore did not tolerate the indignity; they held frequent meetings;[269] they performed their public duties rather negligently; they *stirred up the minds of the people*[270] against the empress and finally they endeavoured by all means to separate the boy from his mother and to transfer the administration of the kingdom into their own hands. At last, after consulting Count Ekbert[271] and Otto, duke of the Bavarians,[272] the archbishop of Cologne[273] came by ship on the Rhine to the place that is called the island of St Suitbert.[274] The king was then there. When one day after a festive banquet he was particularly cheerful, the archbishop began to urge him to go to look at a certain ship, which he had caused to be built with remarkable workmanship for this very purpose.

He easily persuaded the artless boy, who did not at all suspect a trap. As soon as he had set foot on the ship, he was surrounded by those whom the archbishop had recruited from among the associates of his faction and his servants; suddenly the oarsmen sprang up and applied themselves to their oars and, *more quickly than can be told,*[275] impelled the ship into the middle of the river. The king *was thrown into confusion* by the unexpected turn of events and his *mind was full of doubt;*[276] he believed that nothing less than violence and murder was planned for him and he threw himself headlong into the river. The turbulent water would very

---

268 Lampert was alone in making this allegation. Cf. his positive assessment of Agnes's administration above p. 67 and *Libellus de institutione Herveldensis ecclesiae* II, p. 353 ('Agnes, the most prudent queen'). Critics of Agnes disapproving of female government: Sigebert of Gembloux, *Chronica* 1062, p. 360 ('the kingdom was not governed with manly vigour by Agnes'); Bonizo of Sutri, *To a Friend* VI, p. 209 ('They judged it unfitting that the kingdom should be subject to a female ruler'). See Struve (1984a) p. 97 (no. 238); Black-Veldtrup (1995) p. 356.

269 Cf. *Annals of Niederaltaich* 1062, p. 59: 'they held frequent meetings'.

270 Livy XXI.48.2.

271 Count Ekbert I of Brunswick, the cousin of Henry IV (above n. 177). His involvement in the conspiracy is also mentioned in *Annalista Saxo* p. 693.

272 Otto of Northeim (above n. 261). His involvement in the conspiracy is also mentioned in the *Annals of Augsburg* 1062, p. 127, and *Annalista Saxo* p. 693.

273 On the central role of Archbishop Anno II (above n. 139) in this conspiracy see Jenal (1974) pp. 177–81; Struve (1984a) p. 98 (no. 239).

274 The site of the royal palace of Kaiserswerth.

275 Vergil, *Aeneid* I.142; Horace, *Satirae* II.2.80.

276 Livy I.7.6. Cf. Tacitus, *Annales* 6.46.

rapidly have drowned him, had not Count Ekbert jumped in after the endangered boy, placing himself also in the greatest danger, and with extreme difficulty snatched him from death and brought him back to the ship.[277] Afterwards they soothed him with what blandishments they could and brought him to Cologne.[278] The rest of the company followed by land and very many of them complained that the royal majesty had been dishonoured and was no longer master of itself.[279] In order to soften the ill will caused by his action – so that it should not seem that he had done this because of personal ambition rather than for the sake of the common good – the archbishop decreed that any bishop in whose diocese the king was residing at that particular time should take care that *the State* suffered *no harm*[280] and should have a special responsibility for the cases that were referred to the king.

The empress wished neither to follow her son nor to complain of the injuries inflicted on her with an appeal to the law of nations. Instead she withdrew to her own estates and resolved henceforward to live a life removed from State affairs. Not long afterwards, having suffered the hardships of the world and having also learned from her personal misfortunes how soon and how swiftly *the grass* of temporal glory *withers because the spirit of the Lord blows on it,*[281] she planned to renounce the world and she would immediately have rushed headlong to perform what she had planned, had not her friends restrained the impulse of her spirit with their more appropriate advice.[282]

---

277 For most of the details of Lampert's account there is no corroboration from the parallel sources. It is, however, known 'that three months after the king's abduction Lampert himself encountered Henry IV and Anno and presumably on that occasion learned of the events at first hand': Jenal (1974) p. 183, referring to *D.H.IV* 88 (diploma of 13 July 1062). Cf. Lampert, *Libellus de institutione Herveldensis ecclesiae* II, p. 353: 'Archbishop Anno of Cologne took away her son Henry from his mother, to the distress of both of them. The archbishop, together with the king, transferred the government to himself.' Berthold of Reichenau alone, by connecting these events with Easter (31 March), gave an approximate date for the abduction of Henry IV: *Chronicle* 1062, p. 104. See Meyer von Knonau (1890) pp. 274–9; Jenal (1974) pp. 175–6, 183–5; Struve (1984a) p. 98 (no. 239); Robinson (1999) pp. 43–4.

278 Cf. *D.H.IV* 87, diploma of 1062, issued in Cologne (precise date missing); *Annals of Niederaltaich* 1062, p. 59: 'they brought him as far as Cologne without meeting any resistance'; Berthold, *Chronicle* 1062, p. 104.

279 Cf. *Triumphus sancti Remacli Stabulensis* I.2, p. 438: Anno 'did not hesitate to transfer to himself with rash daring the right to govern, not without injury to the royal dignity'.

280 Livy III.4.10; VI.19.3.

281 Isaiah 40:7.

282 Empress Agnes in a letter to Abbot Albert and the monks of Fruttuaria inter-

1063

The king celebrated Christmas in Goslar.[283] There on that day, while the seats of the bishops were being set in place for vespers, a serious dispute arose between the chamberlains of Bishop Hezelo of Hildesheim and the chamberlains of Abbot Widerad of Fulda,[284] which was conducted at first with abusive language, then with blows and they would quickly have resorted to swords, had it not been for the intervention of the authority of Otto, duke of the Bavarians, who upheld the cause of the abbot. The reason was as follows. There was a custom in the kingdom observed by many of our ancestors in times past that in an assembly of bishops the abbot of Fulda should sit next to the archbishop of Mainz. But the bishop claimed that nobody in his diocese ought to take precedence of him after the archbishop.[285] He was incited to act both by pride in his wealth, in which he far surpassed his predecessors,[286] and by the opportunity presented by the times: because the king was still in his minority, individuals could do with impunity whatever their inclination prompted.

preted the abduction of Henry IV as a punishment for her sins: Struve (1984b) p. 424. Meyer von Knonau (1890) pp. 280–4, 320–1, and Bulst-Thiele (1933) pp. 81–2, 84–6, suggested that in winter 1062–3 she travelled to Italy, first to Fruttuaria, then to Rome. Struve (1985) pp. 1–29 argued that Agnes did not leave Germany until summer/autumn 1065. See also the itinerary in Black-Veldtrup (1995) pp. 27–36, 92–4.

283 25 December 1062 in Freising, according to *Annals of Niederaltaich* 1063, p. 61. See Meyer von Knonau (1890) p. 305 n. 135; Struve (1984a) p. 119 (no. 276). Meyer von Knonau (1890) p. 328 suggested that the incident recorded by Lampert occurred in a provincial synod in Mainz in late December 1062: see also Struve (1984a) p. 119 (no. 277).

284 Hezelo (above n. 121) and Widerad (above n. 239). On the precedence dispute between Fulda and Hildesheim see Meyer von Knonau (1890) pp. 328–9, 664–8 (excursus 4); Struve (1970a) pp. 75–6; Vogtherr (1991) pp. 445–6.

285 Cf. the polemic of the anonymous monk of Hersfeld, composed in the early 1090s, *Liber de unitate ecclesiae conservanda* II.33, p. 259: the bishop's chamberlains claimed precedence for their lord 'on account of the privilege of his diocese', the abbot's chamberlains made their claim 'on account of the primacy of the abbey of Fulda'. On the primacy claimed by Fulda, based on the privilege of Pope John XIII of 968, see Lübeck (1942) pp. 96–133; Franke (1987) pp. 162–4.

286 Hezilo was of a noble Franconian family, the kinsman of Bishop Cuno of Brescia: see Schwartz (1913) p. 108; Zielinski (1984) p. 63. Another kinsman was Abbot Meginward of Reichenau. Cf. *Annals of Niederaltaich* 1071, p. 83: 'when the abbot of Reichenau [Udalric] died, the bishop of Hildesheim gave a large quantity of money to the king and obtained the same abbey for his kinsman'.

Pope Gerard, who was also called Nicholas, died.[287] The bishop of
Parma[288] was put in his place through the election of the king and of
certain princes and was sent to Rome, escorted by Bishop Bucco of
Halberstadt.[289] On his return the latter received from him, as a reward
for a well conducted embassy, the pallium and certain other archiepiscopal insignia.[290] The archbishop of Mainz reacted to this with the
greatest indignation, interpreting it as an attempt to eclipse his exalted
rank of primate.[291] But amends was made to him through the intervention of the archbishop of Cologne[292] and his *wrath was pacified.*[293]

The king celebrated Whitsun in Goslar.[294] There, when the king and
the bishops had assembled for the vesper service, an uproar broke out
again about the placing of the episcopal seats not, as on the previous
occasion, through a chance encounter but through a long premeditated
plot.[295] For the bishop of Hildesheim, mindful of the affront that he had
suffered previously, had concealed behind the altar Count Ekbert,[296]
together with knights ready for a fight. When the latter heard the noise

---

287 Nicholas II (above n. 214) †20 July (?) 1061 in Florence.

288 Cadalus, bishop of Parma (?1046–?1071), anti-pope Honorius II, elected in Basel, 28
    October 1061. See Meyer von Knonau (1890) pp. 224–7; Schmidt (1977) pp. 108–10,
    126–7; Struve (1984a) pp. 92–3 (no. 227). Lampert does not mention the election
    of Pope Alexander II (by the cardinals on 1 October 1061) until his annal for 1064:
    below p. 96.

289 Burchard II of Halberstadt (above n. 235) did not escort Cadalus to Rome but was
    sent by the council of Augsburg (October 1062) to Rome to investigate the papal
    schism and eventually recognised the claims of Cadalus's rival, Pope Alexander II.
    See Meyer von Knonau (1890) pp. 300–1; Jenal (1974) pp. 231–40; Schmidt (1977)
    pp. 119–21; Struve (1984a) p. 116 (no. 269).

290 This grant was made by Alexander II, *JL* 4498: *Gesta episcoporum Halberstadensium* p.
    97 (13 January 1063). See Meyer von Knonau (1890) pp. 306–7; Jenal (1974) p. 238;
    Schmidt (1977) pp. 120–1; Zotz (1982) pp. 155–6; Struve (1984a) p. 120 (no. 279).

291 Siegfried of Mainz (above n. 210), letter to Alexander II: *Codex Udalrici* 28, p. 55.
    See Meyer von Knonau (1890) pp. 327–8; Thomas (1970) pp. 384–5 and n. 72.

292 Jenal (1974) pp. 238–40 suggested that Siegfried's grievance was that he himself had
    not yet received the pallium and that Anno (above n. 139) intervened with the pope,
    by virtue of his honorific post of archchancellor of the Roman church, to obtain the
    pallium for Siegfried.

293 Esther 7:10; Ezekiel 24:13.

294 8 June. See Meyer von Knonau (1890) p. 328; Struve (1984a) p. 123 (no. 285).

295 In the church of SS Simon and Jude, Goslar. Cf. the brief reports in *Annals of Nieder-
    altaich* 1063, p. 61; Berthold, *Chronicle* 1063, p. 118. On Lampert's account of the
    violence see Meyer von Knonau (1890) pp. 328–31, 664–8 (excursus 4); Lübeck
    (1942) pp. 123–4; Struve (1970a) pp. 75–6; Leyser (1979) p. 97; Franke (1987) pp.
    162–4; Vogtherr (1991) pp. 445–6.

296 Count Ekbert I of Brunswick (above n. 177).

of the chamberlains contending against each other, they quickly sprang out, striking some of the men of Fulda with their fists, others with their cudgels; they threw them to the ground and easily drove them out of the sanctuary of the church, stupefied as they were by the unexpected danger. Immediately *giving the call to arms*,[297] the men of Fulda, whose weapons were near at hand, formed a band and burst into the church. In the midst of the choir and the brethren chanting psalms they engaged in close combat, wielding now not cudgels but swords. *A savage fight*[298] began and instead of hymns and spiritual songs the shouts of those urging on the fight and the moans of the dying were heard throughout the church. Dismal sacrifices were perpetrated on the altars of God and everywhere rivers of blood ran through the church, shed not as in former times in lawful rituals but by the cruelty of enemies.

The bishop of Hildesheim took possession of a more elevated place and urged his men as if with a war-trumpet to fight bravely and, lest they should be frightened to use their weapons because of the holiness of the place, he provided them with the pretext of his authority and permission. Many were wounded on both sides and many were killed, the most eminent among them being Reginbodo, the standard bearer of Fulda,[299] and Bero, a knight most dear to Count Ekbert. Meanwhile the king, shouting and entreating the people in the name of the royal majesty, seemed to be *telling a tale to deaf ears*.[300] At last he was warned by his followers to protect his own life and withdraw from the fight; with difficulty he forced his way through the closely packed crowd and reached the palace. The men of Hildesheim, who had come prepared and equipped for a fight, were victorious. The men of Fulda, who had been caught unawares and defenceless by *the storm of sedition*[301] when it suddenly arose, were thrown to the ground, put to flight and driven out of the church. The doors were immediately barred. The men of Fulda, who at the outbreak of the disturbance had drawn back some little distance to fetch their weapons, now appeared *armed and in great numbers*.[302] They occupied the churchyard and drew up their battle line so as to attack them at once as

---

297 Livy III.50.11. See Billanovich (1945) p. 67.

298 Livy I.30.9; VII.26.6. See Billanovich (1945) p. 67.

299 The Fulda necrology records for 1063: 'Counts Reginbodo and Wignand' (*Annales necrologici Fuldenses* p. 215).

300 Terence, *Heautontimorumenos* II.1.10.

301 Livy XXVIII.25.8.

302 *Ibid.*, I.52.5.

they left the church. But *night interrupted*[303] the strife.

The next day a very rigorous investigation was held and Count Ekbert easily cleared himself of any charge not so much with the support of justice and the laws as through the favour and indulgent fondness of the king, whose cousin he was.[304] The whole weight of the accusation fell upon the abbot.[305] They said that he was the head and the instigator of everything that had happened; that he had come with premeditated rage to disturb the peace of the royal court. The evidence for this assertion was that he had come there provided with so large a force of his followers and so great a display of military preparation when there was no need for him to fear any danger. Then of course he was hard pressed by that bishop of apostolic sanctity and Mosaic gentleness, who had consecrated his hands to God with so much bloodshed and avenged the injuries of the profaned church more savagely and more inexorably than the king avenged his own injuries.[306] After he had visited his rage on their bodies with the sword, he now hurled his thunderbolts to destroy their souls with the sword of the spirit, cutting off from the body of the Church both the dead and those who had survived the slaughter.

The abbot was oppressed not only by the anguish caused by this event but also by the hatred directed against monasticism, which secular men always try with deep seated malice to degrade and crush.[307] He was thus assailed on all sides, attacked, oppressed and after so many and such great hardships he would have been deprived of his office and would have departed, had not money protected one whom neither law nor a blameless life could protect. For he sold and squandered the property of the monastery of Fulda and ransomed himself and his followers at a very high price. How much was given to the king, how much to his advisers, how much to the bishop we have not learned for certain.[308] For care was taken lest it became known far and wide. This, however, is established beyond doubt: the property of that monastery, which until

303 *Ibid.*, IX.23.4. See Billanovich (1945) p. 68.

304 See above n. 177. Meyer von Knonau (1890) p. 666 argued that Ekbert, as a conspirator in the abduction at Kaiserswerth, owed his pardon to Anno of Cologne.

305 Widerad of Fulda (above n. 239).

306 Lampert 'lashed the conduct of the bishop of Hildesheim with bitter irony': Struve (1970a) p. 75.

307 On the defence of monastic values in Lampert's work see Struve (1970a) pp. 72–82.

308 Holder-Egger, *Lamperti Annales* p. 84 n. 1; Meyer von Knonau (1890) p. 666 argued that this payment was lawful compensation for the damage wrought in Goslar, not a series of bribes to the king, the courtiers and the bishop of Hildesheim.

that period was in a most prosperous condition and towered over all the churches of Gaul, was at that time impoverished and weakened so that at this moment you will find scarcely any traces of its previous wealth.

Afterwards the abbot received permission to return to Fulda, his mind embittered and utterly ground down by such great disasters. And lo! he was received there almost with more roughness and asperity and according to the saying of the prophet, *fleeing from the iron weapons, he* ran *into the bow of steel.*[309] His austere nature, less congenial than was appropriate, had from the outset offended the brethren of Fulda. He *increased their ill will*[310] and added much fuel to their animosity by impiously granting the estates of the church to knights and by reducing the amount of the provisions established by the liberality of the previous abbots. Day after day they murmured[311] about these matters and the monastery was agitated by internal dissensions. Nevertheless they put up with their misfortunes out of fear rather than love, lest their grievances should become known to the world prematurely and the favour of the king and the princes should protect the abbot.

When, however, the news came to Fulda of the disaster that he had suffered in Goslar, they were all moved to voice their complaints aloud, incited both by the pain of this new wound and by the memory of past grievances and they urged each other not to lose such a favourable opportunity offered to them by heaven.[312] Nothing was lacking to accomplish their business except some exertion and diligence on their part: the man would be driven to destruction by his own misdeeds. Let each of them participate now to the utmost of his ability and free their monastery from one who was not their father but their fiercest enemy, who had exposed the name of Fulda, which had previously been the equal of heaven, to the ridicule of all men. While discord was being kindled in this way, a fresh injury added (as it were) oil to the flames. Reginbodo, who had died in that affray in Goslar, had given a horse of great value to the brethren of Fulda for the remembrance of his soul but the abbot immediately gave it to a certain layman without consulting them. The brethren demanded it back *with minds full of violence*[313] and

309 Job 20:24.

310 Livy III.59.4.

311 Cf. *Rule of Benedict* c. 5: 'Above all there is to be no murmuring for any cause whatsoever, by any word whatsoever or any gesture.' Cf. c. 34.

312 On Lampert's account of the tensions in Fulda see Meyer von Knonau (1890) p. 331; Struve (1970a) pp. 75–6; Oexle (1978) p. 173; Vogtherr (1991) p. 446.

313 II Maccabees 5:11.

intemperate cries, declaring that they had endured his authority – or rather his tyranny – for a long time with servile patience but they would bear it no longer. He should quickly return the pious donation, the result of another's generosity, which had been snatched away from them by force. If he hesitated, they would no longer content themselves with secret mutterings but would openly go to the courts of law and beg for divine and human help against his violence.

At first the weight of these misfortunes robbed the abbot of the power to reply. Then he *gave himself up entirely to prayers* and tears *and begged*[314] and implored them by God not, in the words of the old proverb, to *poke about in the fire with a sword*[315] and not to aggravate the wound of the assault in Goslar, which was still fresh and had not yet healed into a scar, with new sources of grief. They should remember that *a bruised reed* is *not* to be *broken and the smoking flax*[316] is not to be reduced to cinders and ashes; they should show mercy if not for the sake of their own reputation, then at least for the sake of his misfortune and his wretchedness, which was so great that it could force tears even from his enemies. If *the angel of the Lord that pursued*[317] him would release him for a while, if he survived such great evils and could ever recover his breath, not only would he restore what had been taken from them but he would increase their property by doubling his gifts to them.

These words quickly satisfied those who were more mature in age and understanding. But the young, according to their custom, admitted of *no forgiveness*, no *mitigation*.[318] He had long practised on their ingenuous natures with his gentle words but he could no longer betray their fidelity, which had been tried and tested for so long a time and on so many occasions. The character, the depravity of the man was such that whatever he had not done under the pressure of present evils, would never be done unless force was again applied. They would, therefore, not give up their right until they had tried all the resources of divine and human aid to overcome his hardness of heart. The abbot hesitated for a long time when he saw that he was achieving nothing by begging and that he did not possess the resources to pay back what was demanded, especially since almost all the wealth of the monastery was used up and

314 Livy VI.24.8.
315 Horace, *Satirae* II.3.275.
316 Isaiah 42:3.
317 Psalm 34:6.
318 Livy II.3.4.

was not even sufficient to satisfy the voracious greed of those who had been injured in the disturbance in Goslar. At last, summoned by the king's command, he set out for the royal court *after giving his* friends *the task*[319] of calming the minds of the enraged young men by means of threats and flattery, in whatever way they could.

Finally after his departure *the leaders of the young men*,[320] at whose insti-gation above all that great evil had broken out, addressed the whole congregation. They declared that they had made up their minds, *when they had broken out*[321] of the monastery, to seek out the king, *wherever in the world*[322] he was to be found, and beg for the protection of his power against the abbot's cruelty and they requested that those whose state of health did not prevent it, should set out with them, while those who could not do so because they were burdened by age or sickness should support their action by means of their written agreement. To the older brethren this declaration seemed shameful and horrible even to speak of. They flung themselves on the ground and beseeched them in God's name not to *let* both themselves and what little hope remained for Fulda *go to ruin*.[323] If they departed from the confines of the monastery with that purpose, the condition of Fulda, which was thrown into serious disorder by the calamity in Goslar, would not only be troubled once more but would fall into total destruction. The young men were not at all affected by these words, for their obstinacy had already *turned* into folly and *into madness*.[324] They rapidly ran to and fro through the monas-tery, urging each other to dare to perpetrate the outrage and so at length their conspiracy reached maturity and, sixteen in number, having the cross carried before them and while the antiphon was being intoned, they burst out of the monastic buildings. The older brethren, who were of sounder mind, followed them at a distance with such great lamenta-tion and wailing that it was as if a funeral procession was bearing them away to a burial to hear *the last farewell*.[325] In order that the king should not be struck with *astonishment* by the sudden news of *this* strange and *dreadful affair*,[326] they sent one of their number in advance on horseback,

319 *Ibid.*, III.18.9. See Billanovich (1945) p. 74.

320 Livy II.12.15. See Billanovich (1945) p. 74.

321 Livy XXII.6.8. See Billanovich (1945) p. 74.

322 Cicero, *De deorum natura* I.44.121.

323 Livy XXVI.27.10; XXXII.22.6.

324 *Ibid.*, VIII.30.1. See Billanovich (1945) p. 75.

325 Cf. Ovid, *Metamorphoses* 10.62.

326 Livy III.47.6.

as fast as he could, who carried to the king a letter describing this great misfortune and instructing him under what compulsion and in what necessity they were forced to resort to these extreme measures. They themselves followed on foot in a regular line.

After the messenger had arrived there and the letter had been read, all those who were in the palace were horrorstruck at such a shameless deed and they were astonished that such disgraceful conduct could be found among those excellent men following the apostolic way of life, that they would avenge the wrongs inflicted on them personally *by injuring the State*[327] and that the sons felt no pity for their father, especially in that calamitous situation that could move even his enemies to compassion and to tears. Everyone decided, therefore, that this extraordinary crime should be avenged by an extraordinary punishment. The king then sought the advice of the archbishop of Cologne and Duke Otto of Bavaria (for at that time the State was governed according to their judgement)[328] and commanded that the bearer of the letter, together with three others, who were *the leaders of the uprising*,[329] should be sent to various monasteries to be kept in custody. The abbot was to use military power to restrain the rest of the crowd, since they could be corrected neither by the spirit of gentleness nor by the rod of monastic discipline. The abbot then sent knights to meet them and ordered them to be brought back to Fulda without any violent disturbances; they were to be placed under guard and were to await his return outside the monastery. He himself bade farewell to the king and immediately followed them. The brethren and the foremost knights of Fulda assembled and discussed at length whether they ought to be subject to the judgement of laymen or of monks. *The dominant opinion was that of those who believed*[330] that, since they had shaken off the yoke of the *Rule* and, in

---

327 *Ibid.*, II.1.3; IV.4.5..

328 The dominant position at court of Archbishop Anno (above n. 139) from the abduction at Kaiserswerth until July 1064 is evident in the 'intervention clauses' of the royal diplomas. In eight of these diplomas he is given the honorific title 'master' (*magister*). Cf. *D.H.IV* 104 (14 July 1063) granted to the church of Cologne 'especially on account of the indefatigable merit and faithful service' of Anno. See Gawlik (1970) pp. 24–32; Jenal (1974) pp. 218–24; Robinson (1999) pp. 45–51. Otto of Northeim (above n. 261) appears sporadically in the 'intervention clauses' of diplomas of this period: *DD.H.IV* 89, 97, 112–13: see Gawlik (1970) pp. 25, 27, 29–30, 150. Otto's intervention in the affairs of Fulda prompted the suggestion of Lange (1961) p. 20 n. 54 that he may have had the office of advocate there but Lange could find no evidence that the counts of Northeim exercised such an office in Fulda.

329 Livy VII.39.4. See Billanovich (1945) p. 77.

330 Livy II.4.3. See Billanovich (1945) p. 77.

defiance of their abbot, had departed through their own arrogance and had not yet been received back into the monastery, they ought rather to be judged according to the law of the laity.[331] Thus the abbot, following the judicial practice of laymen, ordered two of them – one of them distinguished by the office of the priesthood, the other by the office of deacon – to be publicly beaten with rods, to be tonsured and expelled. The rest he sent, after a severe flogging, to neighbouring monasteries, each man to a different place. Nevertheless *the punishment was chosen* in individual cases not according to the degree of guilt but was milder or severer according to *the distinction* or obscurity of their *birth.*[332] Perhaps the abbot saw that, moved by the strength of his grievance, he had *overstepped the bounds of moderation*[333] by avenging his own injuries more harshly than was fitting. It is certain that at that time the monastery of Fulda was *branded with disgrace*[334] that perhaps cannot be cleansed and purified in the long series of years to come.

Bela, who had usurped the kingdom of the Hungarians, died. His son Geisa considered it better to enjoy moderate power in peace than to bring calamity and ruin on his nation by striving for boundless power. He therefore sent word to King Henry that, if Salomon, the son of King Andreas, showed him the honour due to his birth and his merits, he would be a faithful subject to him, preferring to strive with good deeds rather than with weapons, with fidelity rather than with warfare. All the Hungarians in frequent embassies made the same promise. King Henry, therefore, entered Hungary with an army and restored Salomon to the throne of his father, after Henry's sister had been joined to him in marriage. After sweeping away all the problems that could cause the king uneasiness or damage the state of the kingdom, he returned in peace to Gaul.[335]

331 Cf. Burchard of Worms, *Decretum* VIII.6, 26, 57.

332 Livy III.18.10; XXXIII.28.15: see Billanovich (1945) p. 78. Cf. Tacitus, *Historia* 1.49.

333 Livy II.2.2; XXVIII.25.8. See Billanovich (1945) p. 78.

334 Livy III.58.2.

335 Cf. Lampert, *Libellus de institutione Herveldensis ecclesiae* II, p. 353: 'Meanwhile King Salomon of the Hungarians, who was himself a boy, was expelled from the kingdom by his uncle and took refuge with Henry. Each of them was betrothed to the sister of the other. [Henry] restored [Salomon] to his kingdom with the help of Anno.' The correct sequence of events can be reconstructed from the *Annals of Niederaltaich* 1063, pp. 62–3. King Bela I (above n. 248) sent peace envoys to the German court, offering the restoration of Salomon (above n. 250) to the Hungarian throne, but the offer was rejected and Henry IV's army invaded Hungary (September). At this juncture Bela died and his son Geisa (above n. 258) fled 'and thus by God's providence the people and the whole of that land were restored by King Henry to

The education of the king and the administration of all State affairs was in the hands of the bishops, among whom the authority of the archbishops of Mainz and Cologne was paramount.[336] After they had received Archbishop Adalbert of Bremen into their counsels, both because of the distinction of his family and because of the prerogative belonging to his age and his archbishopric,[337] he had soon so completely won over the king to his side by frequent conversations and also by honouring and flattering him that the king depended on him exclusively,[338] pushing the other bishops aside, and in the general administration he seemed to usurp almost sole power. A role second to his was played by Count Werner,[339] a young man with *the wild disposition* characteristic *of his age.*[340] These two men ruled in the place of the king: bishoprics and abbacies and all manner of ecclesiastical and secular offices were sold by them. There was no *hope of obtaining preferment*, even *for a* diligent and excellent *man*,[341] unless he first paid these men with a large-scale

---

Salomon without bloodshed'. Thereupon Salomon was married to Henry IV's sister, Judith (above n. 251). See Meyer von Knonau (1890) pp. 342–8; Struve (1984a) pp. 132–3 (no. 304); Boshof (1986) pp. 185–6; Robinson (1999) p. 53. On 'Gaul' as a term for Germany see above n. 241.

336 For Anno of Cologne see above n. 328. Archbishop Siegfried of Mainz (above n. 210) is described in a letter of Meinhard of Bamberg (*Briefsammlungen der Zeit Heinrichs IV.* p. 202) as 'the head of a conspiracy' to remove Anno from power, possibly in December 1062: see Struve (1984a) p. 119 (no. 277). Siegfried appears in the 'intervention clauses' of the following diplomas of the period of Anno's ascendancy at court: *DD.H.IV* 88–9, 94, 103, 112–13, 120, 121. See Gawlik (1970) pp. 24–7, 29–31, 130.

337 Adalbert (above n. 48) belonged to the Thuringian family of the counts of Goseck, counts palatine of Saxony (see above n. 227). Cf. Adam of Bremen, *Gesta* III.34, p. 176: 'Archbishops Adalbert and Anno were proclaimed consuls and henceforward the whole government depended on their counsel'; III.43, p. 186: at the time of the Hungarian expedition of 1063 Adalbert was 'the teacher (*magister*) of the king and the chief adviser'; III.45, p. 187: 'At that time the archbishop [of Bremen] held the primary position in the court'. Cf. *Triumphus sancti Remacli Stabulensis* I.3, p. 439. The evidence of the royal diplomas suggests that in 1063 Adalbert's influence had increased (three diplomas give him the honorific title *patronus*, 'protector') but had not yet eclipsed that of Anno. Cf. *DD.H.IV* 104–5, 107–10: Gawlik (1970) pp. 28–9, 142. See Meyer von Knonau (1890) p. 333; Glaeske (1962) pp. 65–6; Jenal (1974) pp. 278–9; Struve (1984a) p. 124 (no. 287); Robinson (1999) pp. 45–6.

338 Bruno of Merseburg, *Saxon War* c. 5, p. 16: as the king's confidant, Adalbert 'nourished the seeds of the vices [in Henry IV] with the water of flattery'. See Meyer von Knonau (1890) pp. 387–8 and n. 42; Glaeske (1962) pp. 93–4; Struve (1984a) p. 149 (no. 336).

339 Werner, count in Hesse (†1066). Lampert subsequently recorded (1065, below p. 99) that he was 'the kinsman' of Bishop Werner II of Strasbourg. See Meyer von Knonau (1890) pp. 466, 484–6; Zielinski (1984) p. 58; Metz (1991) pp. 337, 342–3, 347, 355, 360, 362 ('Werner III., Graf im Hessengau').

340 Livy VI.23.3.

341 *Ibid.*, I.34.1.

expenditure of his own money. These men indeed spared the bishops and dukes, although they did so out of fear rather than piety. In the case of the abbots, however – because they could not *resist the injustice*[342] – they proceeded entirely without restraint, declaring that the king possessed no less authority and power over abbots than over his stewards or over any other administrators of the crown lands.

At first indeed they distributed the estates of the monasteries to their supporters just as they pleased and they drained to the final dregs whatever remained by means of the frequent exaction of royal services. Then as their insolence increased, they made an attack on the monasteries themselves and shared them out among themselves like provinces, while the king showed a childlike readiness to agree to whatever had been ordered.[343] The archbishop of Bremen, therefore, took possession of two abbeys, Lorsch and Corvey, declaring that this was a reward for his fidelity and devotion towards the king.[344] Lest this should excite envy among the other princes of the kingdom, after persuading the king he gave two abbeys to the archbishop of Cologne, Malmédy and Kornelimünster,[345] one in Seligenstadt to the archbishop of Mainz,[346] one to Otto, duke of the Bavarians in Altaich,[347] one to Rudolf, duke

---

342 Sallust, *Jugurtha* 14.25.

343 The consequence of these transactions of 1063 and 1065 was that these 'royal abbeys' lost their characteristic *libertas*: i.e. royal protection and the associated rights (immunity from intervention by secular officials, freedom to elect the abbot etc.). Lampert's account is incomplete: similar grants are recorded in six royal diplomas of 1065 (*DD.H.IV* 101, 155, 164–6, 192) and the grant of Vilich to Anno of Cologne in *Codex Laureshamensis* c. 123C, p. 392. See Meyer von Knonau (1890) pp. 443–4, 462–3, 466–9; Seibert (1991) pp. 537–50; Robinson (1999) pp. 56–7, 254.

344 *DD.H.IV* 168 (6 September 1065), 169 (8 September). Cf. *Annals of Weissenburg* 1066, p. 53: 'Bishop Adalbert of Bremen, a worthless man, an adviser of King Henry, among the very many evil deeds that he perpetrated, caused provostships and everything that he could extort from the houses of the saints to be surrendered to the supporters of his wickedness by the hand of the king and in addition he claimed for himself the two abbeys of Corvey and Lorsch'; Adam of Bremen, *Gesta* III.28, 45, 61, pp. 171, 188, 206–7. See Meyer von Knonau (1890) pp. 474–7; Lange (1961) pp. 22–4.

345 July/August 1065. Cf. *Triumphus sancti Remacli Stabulensis* I.4, p. 440. See Meyer von Knonau (1890) pp. 462–6; Jenal (1974) pp. 56–109; Seibert (1991) pp. 541–3.

346 Cf. *DD.H.IV* 101 (14 June 1063). See Meyer von Knonau (1890) pp. 332–3: 'it cannot be doubted that Henry IV's favour towards Siegfried ... was instigated by Anno', who in 1063 was the dominant influence at court; similarly Seibert (1991) pp. 536–7.

347 Cf. *Annals of Niederaltaich* 1065, p. 71: 'In this year the abbey of Niederaltaich was given as a benefice to the Bavarian duke Otto, which many soon began to think and say would not turn out prosperously.' See Meyer von Knonau (1890) pp. 468–9; Feierabend (1913) p. 131; Lange (1961) pp. 22–3; Seibert (1991) p. 548.

of the Swabians in Kempten.[348] In order, therefore, to make the abbey
of Corvey entirely subject to his tyranny, the archbishop of Bremen
made up a ridiculous story. He spread rumours through the royal court,
announcing that the bishop of a certain city beyond the Alps named
Pola had departed from this world.[349] After persuading the king, he
appointed the abbot of Corvey[350] as his successor and ordered him as
soon as possible to go and look after the church that had been deprived
of its ruler. During the delay in which he made the necessary preparations for the journey, however, men arrived from Italy and announced
that the bishop who had been reported dead was alive and well and
everyone began both to mock and to curse the archbishop's deception.
Then Duke Otto of the Bavarians was moved by the spirit of God to
prevent such a wicked deed and, after making every kind of endeavour,
he brought it about, but with the greatest difficulty, that the honour
and the dignity both of the abbot and of the monastery of Corvey were
preserved unharmed.[351]

When moreover the archbishop's accomplices had come to the monastery of Lorsch, announcing that the monastery had been consigned
by royal gift to the jurisdiction and power of the archbishop, and
commanded that the abbot[352] should not delay in meeting him at the
appointed place, such great *distress and indignation*[353] seized them all
that they would not have *refrained from laying hands* on the envoys, had
not *the law of nations weighed*[354] more with them than their anger. They
were heard with contempt and they were dismissed with even greater
contempt. This was subsequently reported to the king and he sent other
envoys and ordered the abbot – uttering threats against his life – to

348 On Rudolf (above n. 203) see Meyer von Knonau (1890) pp. 468–9; Feierabend
    (1913) p. 75; Seibert (1991) p. 549, dating the grant in 1065.

349 Megingaud (Megingoz), bishop of Pola (diocese in Istria belonging to the province
    of Aquileia) ✝ after 17 August 1061 and before 2 August 1075, probably no later
    than 1067: see Schwartz (1913) pp. 40–1. Meyer von Knonau (1894) p. 810 n. 70
    noted that Wolfram, the new bishop of Treviso (a diocese also in the province of
    Aquileia) was in Corvey on 19 November 1065 and may have brought the news that
    inspired Lampert's anecdote.

350 Saracho, abbot of Corvey (1056–71).

351 Meyer von Knonau (1890) p. 479 and n. 166; Meyer von Knonau (1894) pp. 809–10,
    813; Lange (1961) pp. 23–4; Vogtherr (1991) p. 443 argued that Otto of Northeim
    was motivated by the fact that his rights as advocate of Corvey were threatened by
    Adalbert of Bremen's acquisition of the abbey.

352 Udalric, abbot of Lorsch (1056–75).

353 Livy XXXIV.7.5; XLI.10.2.

354 *Ibid.*, II.23.10; II.4.7.

resign his office and to leave the monastery with all haste. Learning of the king's decision before the envoys arrived, the abbot gave orders that they were to be received in a friendly manner and he deferred until the next day his hearing of what they were commissioned to say. During the night he left there with only a few companions and, unnoticed by all except for a very small number, went to a very safe place, after first secretly carrying away all the treasures of the church and placing them in safety. On the next day, therefore, the envoys found no one to whom they might convey the king's commands and, full of admiration at the sagacity of the man, they returned without achieving the purpose of their mission.[355] Then the abbot's knights, who at that time were very famous, both for their wealth and for their military abilities, gathered their forces and took possession of a mountain situated close to the monastery, built a castle, placed a garrison there and were prepared to prevent the archbishop from troubling the monastery even at the risk of their own lives.[356]

1064

The Roman princes were complaining that the king had appointed a pontiff of the Roman Church without consulting them and they seemed to be planning a rebellion because of this affront. For this reason he decided that the archbishop of Cologne should be sent to Rome. On his arrival, since he could find no other remedy for the disorders, he declared that the appointment that had been made without the knowledge of the Roman senate was invalid and, setting aside the bishop of Parma,[357]

355 The twelfth-century history of Lorsch, *Codex Laureshamensis*, used Lampert's account and supplemented it with additional materials, including three purported letters of Henry IV of 1065: *Letters* 2, 3, pp. 7–8, to Abbot Udalric, demanding obedience to the king and his 'protector' (*patronus*) Adalbert of Bremen, and *Letter* 4, pp. 7–8, to the monks of Lorsch, forbidding them to obey Udalric as their abbot. *Codex Laureshamensis* c. 123C, p. 392, records the presence of Henry IV and Adalbert in Lorsch on 20 March 1065, when the archbishop secured Udalric's acceptance of his acquisition of Lorsch. See Meyer von Knonau (1890) pp. 400, 475–6; Struve (1984a) p. 159 (no. 358).

356 Cf. *Annals of Weissenburg* 1066, p. 53: 'The knights of the abbot of Lorsch, taking this ill [above n. 344], built fortresses to resist him and placed garrisons in them.' *Codex Laureshamensis* c. 123C, p. 392, identified a castle on 'the mountain called *Burcheldon*, not far from the monastery'. On the wealth and military resources of Lorsch see Feierabend (1913) p. 100 and n. 2.

357 For Cadalus of Parma (anti-pope Honorius II) and the circumstances of the papal schism of 1061–4 see above p. 84 and n. 288. Anno of Cologne's mission was not to Rome (as Bonizo of Sutri, *To a Friend* VI, p. 209, likewise claimed). He participated in the synod of Mantua (31 May 1064), which recognised the papal title of Alexander II and condemned Cadalus in his absence. See Meyer von Knonau (1890)

he resolved that Bishop Anselm of Lucca[358] should be put in his place
by means of their election. Hardly had he completed his mission and
returned to Gaul, however, than the bishop of Parma, together with a
considerable host of armed men, attempted to drive the bishop of Lucca
from the apostolic see by force.[359] For their part, the latter's supporters
quickly had recourse to their weapons, a battle took place and *many men
on both sides received wounds*[360] and fell to the ground. Thus was the rigour
of ecclesiastical conduct corrupted: unlike former times, when men had
to be seized on and compelled to rule over the Church of God,[361] they
now fought with weapons in their hands for fear that they would not
rule over the Church and they shed each other's blood not for the sake
of Christ's sheep but for fear that they would not have dominion over
Christ's sheep.[362] Nevertheless Anselm, who was also called Alexander,
obtained the see through the courage of his knights and the favour of
the princes. As for the other man: although he had been driven out with
contempt, he never, as long as he lived,[363] gave up his claim and he always
disparaged Alexander, calling him an adulterer of the Church of God
and a false apostle. He also celebrated masses outside the Church and
did not cease to perform ordinations and to issue his decrees and letters
throughout the churches in the manner of the apostolic see.[364] But no
one paid any heed to them since everyone accused him of having stained

pp. 375–8; Schmidt (1977) p. 120; Struve (1984a) p. 148 (nos 334–5); Robinson (1999) pp. 49–51.

358 Anselm I, bishop of Lucca (1057–72); Pope Alexander II (1061–73).

359 An allusion either to the battle on the field of Nero (14 April 1062) during Cadalus's first expedition to Rome or to the seizure of the Leonine city in May/June 1063 during his second expedition. See Meyer von Knonau (1890) pp. 254–6, 312–17; Schmidt (1977) pp. 117–18, 121–2. On 'Gaul' (Germany) see above n. 241.

360 Livy XXXII.10.12.

361 For the principle that the candidate must be reluctant to assume ecclesiastical office see Schmid (1926) pp. 44–6. Eleventh-century reformers remembered above all the election of Pope Gregory I (590), as described in John the Deacon, *Vita Gregorii Magni* I.44, *MPL* 75, col. 81B: he was 'seized, dragged away and consecrated supreme pontiff'. See Robinson (1978a) pp. 31–9.

362 Cf. *Annals of Niederaltaich* 1065, p. 71: Cadalus 'inflicted war and armed force on Rome, the mother of churches, and thus under his leadership and by his advice murder and the hewing of many limbs was perpetrated there'. While the adherents of Alexander II brought this charge against Cadalus (e.g. Peter Damian, *Letter* 89, p. 533), Cadalus's supporter, Bishop Benzo of Alba, made the same accusation against Alexander (*Ad Heinricum IV* II.2, p. 198). Lampert alone made the same charge against both parties: see Erdmann (1935) pp. 118–19.

363 Cadalus †(?)1071: see Schwartz (1913) pp. 186–7.

364 See Meyer von Knonau (1890) pp. 436 n. 80 (Bardi, 1065), 603 n. 52 (Parma, 20 April 1069: a charter describing him as 'pope elect').

the apostolic see with murder to avenge a personal insult.

Bishop Henry of Augsburg died,[365] detested by the king, detested by all the bishops because of the arrogance with which he governed the kingdom in the time of the empress. His successor was Embriko, provost of Mainz, a man of the discretion and dignity befitting a bishop.[366]

Count Werner[367] sought and obtained from the king the village belonging to our monastery which is called Kirchberg, without consulting the abbot.[368] We exerted ourselves in a long-lasting struggle to recover it, fighting against the cruelty of so great an enemy not with carnal weapons but with fasting and frequent prayers. For this reason he was accustomed to jest with more acerbity than wit that he deserved a great reward from the king because he had applied a new stimulus to stir up his monks – who had previously been feeble and lukewarm in God's work – and had forced them against their will to fast and to go barefoot.

During the autumn Archbishop Siegfried of Mainz and the bishops Gunther of Bamberg and Otto of Regensburg and William of Utrecht[369] and very many others, the pillars and the heads of Gaul, set out for Jersualem.[370]

365 Henry II (above n. 63) +3 September 1063. Cf. *Annals of Augsburg* 1063, p. 129: 'afflicted with many injuries by the confidants of the king'. For criticism of his regime: see above p. 80 and n. 267.

366 Embriko, bishop of Augsburg (1063–77). Cf. *Annals of Augsburg* 1063, p. 129: 'exceedingly pious and praiseworthy'.

367 Werner: see above n. 339. Lampert omitted to mention that Hersfeld received in compensation an estate in Homberg on the Ohm (in Werner's county in Hesse): *D.H.IV* 146 (5 April 1065). See Meyer von Knonau (1890) p. 403 and n. 18; Holder-Egger (1894) pp. 183–4; Struve (1970a) p. 174.

368 Ruthard (above n. 54).

369 William, bishop of Utrecht (1054–76).

370 This pilgrimage, including 'a multitude of counts and princes, rich and poor' (*Annals of Niederaltaich* 1065, p. 66), 'many rich and poor ... more than seven thousand' (Marianus Scottus, *Chronicon* 1086 [=1064], pp. 558–9), began in November 1064. Cf. Marianus Scottus p. 558: 'after the passing of St Martin' (11 November). On 'the great German pilgrimage' of 1064–5 see Meyer von Knonau (1890) pp. 390–4, 445–50; Joranson (1928) pp. 3–43.

1065

The king celebrated Christmas in Goslar[371] and Easter in Worms.[372] It was there during the holy ceremony of the mass that the archbishop of Bremen,[373] while he was delivering a sermon appropriate to so great a festival, cleansed a man from possession by a demon, after both he and all the people present had poured out their prayers on his behalf. That event appeared to them all a great miracle, for they were astonished that a man of such very evil reputation among the people, who did not lead a virtuous life, should perform miraculous works. But his enemies interpreted it in an envious manner, ascribing so remarkable an occurrence not to his deserts but to the prayers of the people who were present.

It was there by the permission of that same archbishop that the king first girded himself with the weapons of war.[374] He would immediately have made a trial of the arms that he had received upon the archbishop of Cologne and would have thrown himself on him head foremost to avenge himself on him with sword and fire, *had* not the empress *calmed the disturbance*[375] with exceedingly timely advice. Among other grievances against the archbishop, the most important was that some years before, when the archbishop wished to seize power over the kingdom and rights of government from the empress,[376] he had almost flung the king

371 25 December 1064 in Goslar, according to Berthold, *Chronicle* 1065, p. 105; 'in Cologne', according to *Annals of Niederaltaich* 1065, p. 66. See Meyer von Knonau (1890) p. 395 and n. 57.

372 27 March. Cf. Berthold, *Chronicle* 1065, p. 105.

373 Adalbert (see above n. 48). See Meyer von Knonau (1890) p. 400; Glaeske (1962) p. 69: Struve (1984a) p. 159 (no. 359). For Lampert's criticisms of Adalbert see Struve (1970a) pp. 106–7.

374 Easter Tuesday, 29 March. Cf. *Annals of Weissenburg* 1065, p. 53: 'On the third day of Easter Henry IV girded on the sword in Worms with the blessing of Archbishop Eberhard of Trier'; Berthold, *Chronicle* 1065, p. 105; 'in the same place [Worms] he was girded with the sword in the ninth year of his reign but in the fourteenth year of his life and Duke Godfrey was chosen as his shieldbearer'; Bernold of St Blasien, *Chronicle* 1065, pp. 248–9. According to the ancient law of the Ripuarian Franks the fifteenth year marked the end of a minority. See Meyer von Knonau (1890) pp. 400–2; Bulst-Thiele (1933) p. 91; Struve (1984a) pp. 159–60 (no. 360); Robinson (1999) pp. 51–2.

375 Livy IV.10.6.

376 I.e. the abduction at Kaiserswerth: see above p. 81. This anecdote, recorded only by Lampert, should be seen in the context of the polemical representation of Henry IV in the *Annals*: see Meyer von Knonau (1890) pp. 404–5 and n. 20; Holder-Egger, *Lamperti Annales* p. 93 n. 2. Cf. Lampert, *Libellus de institutione Herveldensis ecclesiae* II, p. 353: 'When Henry had reached the age of maturity, he abandoned the bishop [Anno of Cologne] and lived according to his own will and, while promising

himself *into the utmost danger.*[377]

Werner,[378] the kinsman of Count Werner, was appointed the successor of Bishop Hezelo of Strasbourg, who had died a little before.[379]

Meanwhile the aforementioned bishops continued their expedition to Jerusalem. When they very unwisely displayed the extent of their wealth to the people among whom they were travelling, they would have brought the utmost danger upon themselves, had not divine mercy *rescued a situation* that human *rashness had threatened with ruin.*[380] For the barbarians came flocking *from the cities and the fields*[381] to gaze at such illustrious men and they were attracted at first by the great marvel of foreign apparel and splendid equipment and then, as tends to happen, by a strong hope and desire for plunder.[382] When they had passed through Cilicia, therefore, and entered the territory of the Saracens[383] and when they were already one day's march or a little more from the city named Ramleh on the Good Friday next following, around the third hour of the day[384] they suffered an attack from the Arabs, who had learned of the arrival of such eminent men and flocked together from all sides *in great numbers and in arms,*[385] seeking plunder.[386] Very many of the Christians

---

that he would play the role of Charlemagne in his own age, he played the role of Rehoboam (II Chronicles 12:1). Anno renounced the court and went into retirement. Archbishop Adalbert of Bremen succeeded to his place but not to his diligence.'

377 Livy XLV.8.1; XXVIII.32.9.

378 Werner II, bishop of Strasbourg (1065–77). His kinsman, Count Werner: above n. 339. Meyer von Knonau (1890) p. 486 suggested that Bishop Werner II was the younger brother of Count Werner's wife, Willibirg (of the family of the counts of Achalm).

379 Hezelo (Herrand), bishop of Strasbourg (1046–65) †12/13 January.

380 Livy VI.22.6.

381 *Ibid.*, I.1.5.

382 Cf. *Annals of Niederaltaich* 1065, pp. 66–7: 'as soon as they crossed the river called Morava, the dangers of thieves and brigands immediately became frequent' – i.e. in Bulgaria. The 'barbarians' were Bulgarians or invading Ogúz. See Joranson (1928) pp. 16–17.

383 The more detailed account of the *Annals of Niederaltaich* 1065, pp. 67–8, traces the pilgrims' route from Constantinople through Asia Minor to Laodicea, Tripoli, Caesarea and Ramleh, north-west of Jerusalem. See Meyer von Knonau (1890) p. 445; Joranson (1928) pp. 17–20.

384 25 March. Cf. *Annals of Niederaltaich* 1065, p. 68: 'almost at the second hour of the day'. At this date, a few days after the vernal equinox, the second hour would begin at 7 a.m., the third at 8 a.m. by modern reckoning: see Joranson (1928) p. 20 n. 58.

385 Livy I.52.5.

386 Cf. Marianus Scottus, *Chronicon* 1086 [=1064], p. 559: 'the Arabs were brought together by the rumour of money'.

– thinking it impious to help themselves with their own hands and to defend with material weapons their safety, which they had devoted to God when they set out on pilgrimage[387] – were *immediately* overthrown *at the first attack*,[388] exhausted by many wounds and plundered of everything that they had *from a thread even to a shoe latchet*.[389] One of them was Bishop William of Utrecht, whose arm was almost crippled by blows and who was left naked and half-dead.[390] The other Christians, by throwing stones (a kind of missile that the place happened to supply in abundance), did not so much ward off danger as attempt to delay the death that immediately threatened them. They gradually withdrew and turned aside to a village, which was a moderate distance from their route. From the similarity of the name they conjectured that this was Capernaum.[391]

As soon as they entered the village, all the bishops took possession of a certain courtyard, surrounded by a low wall, which was so unstable that it might easily fall down, even if no force was applied. In the middle of the courtyard was a house, having an upper storey sufficiently elevated and *prepared as if expressly*[392] for the purposes of defence.[393] The bishops of Mainz and Bamberg took possession of the upper part, together with their clergy, while the other bishops[394] took the lower. All the laymen ran quickly to and fro *to ward off the enemy's attack*[395] and to defend the

---

387 Cf. *Annals of Niederaltaich* 1065, p. 68: 'Our men at first attempted to resist but, as they were unarmed, they were very quickly forced to flee back into the village [of Kafar Sallâm].' The 'evidence, direct as well as indirect, ... conclusively proves that our pilgrims were unarmed': Joranson (1928) pp. 14–15, also pp. 22, 40. On the requirement that pilgrims should not bear arms see Erdmann (1935) p. 281.

388 Livy IV.33.1.

389 Genesis 14:23.

390 The author of the *Annals of Niederaltaich*, who did not make Lampert's distinction between non-resisting and resisting groups of pilgrims, represented William (above n. 369) as being 'seriously wounded' during the retreat to Kafar Sallâm (1065, p. 68).

391 *Capharsala* (*Annals of Niederaltaich* 1065, p. 68), *Carvasalim* (Marianus Scottus, *Chronicon* 1086 [=1064], p. 559), identified by Meyer von Knonau (1890) p. 446 and Holder-Egger, *Lamperti Annales* p. 94 n.2 as Kafar Sâba and by Joranson (1928) p. 23 n. 74 as Kafar Sallâm, which was not the Capernaum of Matthew 4:13 etc.

392 Livy I.9.6.

393 *Annals of Niederaltaich* 1065, p. 68 describes 'a walled courtyard and two stone towers'. See Joranson (1928) pp. 23–4.

394 Otto of Regensburg (above n. 245) was presumably the only bishop in the lower storey since both Lampert and the *Annals of Niederaltaich* recorded that William of Utrecht did not return to Kafar Sallâm.

395 Livy II.53.1; cf. I.1.5; III.8.7; XXV.30.9.

wall and indeed they *withstood the violence of the first*[396] engagement, as previously stated, by throwing stones. Then, when the barbarians had *hurled a* dense *cloud of missiles*[397] into the camp and the defenders had made very many incursions against them and had forcibly wrested the shields and swords from their hands, they were now not only strong enough to defend the wall but they even dared meanwhile to burst out of the gates and to fight them hand to hand. When the Arabs were *unable to withstand their attack anywhere*[398] with any of their forces, they at last *altered their strategy from* one of disorganised attack *to one of siege*[399] and they prepared to destroy by hunger and fatigue those whom they could not overcome by the sword.

They therefore divided their superabundant forces – they had in fact gathered together about twelve thousand men – so that they might take turns in the labours of the siege and allow the defenders no opportunity to recover their breath even for a moment, suspecting that they would not long endure the hardship of fighting because they *lacked all the resources*[400] by which human life is usually sustained. Thus the Christians were attacked without a pause during the whole of Good Friday, during the whole of Holy Saturday almost until the third hour of Easter Day[401] and the audacious enemy did not allow them even a little time in which to recover their strength by sleeping. For, having *death before their eyes*,[402] they desired neither food nor drink and even if they had greatly longed for them, they were *totally lacking in anything to eat or drink.*[403]

When on the third day[404] they were worn out by hunger and exertion and had come to the extreme limit of their endurance and when their strength was so broken down by fasting that deeds of bravery and further efforts were rendered more or less useless, one of the priests in their company cried out that they were not acting rightly in *placing their*

396 *Ibid.,* II.10.7; XLIII.10.6.

397 *Ibid.,* XXXVIII.26.7.

398 *Ibid.,* II.50.5; IV.18.8; V.28.12. See Billanovich (1945) pp. 86–7.

399 Livy II.11.10.

400 *Ibid.,* IX.4.1.

401 Cf. *Annals of Niederaltaich* 1065, p. 69: 'For three days in succession the battle was fought with the greatest violence on both sides'. See Meyer von Knonau (1890) p. 446; Joranson (1928) pp. 28–9.

402 Livy II.53.6. See Billanovich (1945) p. 89.

403 Livy XXXVII.15.3.

404 27 March. Cf. *Annals of Niederaltaich* 1065, p. 69: 'on the very Sunday of holy Eastertide'.

hope and strength *in their weapons* rather *than in God*[405] and in attempting to ward off with their own forces the calamity that had befallen them by God's permission. For this reason it seemed to him appropriate that they should surrender, especially since three days of fasting had already made them utterly unfit for military service. God – who had so often miraculously freed His own when they were in the greatest need – would have no difficulty in showing mercy to them, once they had surrendered and *had been forced under the yoke of slavery*[406] by the enemy. This might also be inferred: that the barbarians were exerting themselves with such fury not to kill them but to rob them of their money and, if they could gain possession of it, they would then allow them to depart free and unharmed, without any violence or annoyance. They all welcomed this advice and, *turning* immediately *from* weapons *to entreaties, they begged*[407] the enemy through an interpreter to accept their surrender.

When he learned of this, the leader of the Arabs, *setting his horse in motion, flew*[408] to the front ranks of his men and caused the rest to withdraw farther off, fearing that if he was rash enough to give the crowd access to it, the plunder would be distributed in a disorderly manner. Taking with him seventeen of the most distinguished of his people, he entered the camp,[409] which now stood open, but *left* his son *at the gates to stand guard*,[410] lest someone *in his greed for plunder*[411] should rush in, unbidden, after him. After a ladder had been brought, he went up with a few followers into the upper room where the bishops of Mainz and Bamberg were hiding. The bishop of Bamberg (to whom, although he was the younger in years, special honour was nevertheless shown by everyone, because of the pre-eminence of his virtues and because of the admirable dignity of his whole person)[412] began to beg him that,

405 Livy II.39.8; III.53.3.

406 Cicero, *De officiis* III.30.109. Cf. Livy I.26.13; II.34.9.

407 Livy III.28.9; IV.10.4. See Billanovich (1945) p. 90.

408 Livy I.57.8.

409 Cf. *Annals of Niederaltaich* 1065, p. 69: on Easter Sunday 'at around the ninth hour of the day, when peace had been declared among them, eight chiefs of the pagans were permitted to go up into the tower where the bishops were'; Marianus Scottus, *Chronicon* 1086 [=1064], p. 559: 'they admitted the leader of the Arabs with sixteen men and as many swords'. See Meyer von Knonau (1890) p. 448 n. 102; Holder-Egger, *Lamperti Annales* p. 96 n.2; Joranson (1928) pp. 30–1.

410 Livy I.59.5; III.18.5.

411 *Ibid.*, XXV.25.5.

412 Cf. *Annals of Niederaltaich* 1065, p. 69: the chieftain of 'the pagans' 'thought that [Gunther] was the chief of them all' (cf. p. 67: the inhabitants of Constantinople

when he had taken away everything that they had, even to *the uttermost farthing*,[413] he might give them leave to depart without any of their possessions. The Arab, however, was *rendered haughty by victory*[414] and rendered extremely fierce, even beyond the inborn savagery of his nature, by the injuries suffered in so many attacks. He said that he had waged war against them now for three days with great losses to his army and his purpose was to impose his own conditions on the vanquished rather than those that they had stipulated. They should, therefore, not be deluded by any false hopes, for, when he had taken everything that they had, he would eat their flesh and drink their blood.[415]

Without delay he unwound the linen cloth that he had wrapped round his head according to the custom of his people, made it into a noose and put it around the bishop's neck.[416] The bishop was, however, a man of noble feelings and of fitting gravity of demeanour and he would not suffer any dishonour. He punched the enemy in the face with such force that *with one blow* he dashed the astonished man *headlong*[417] to the floor,[418] at the same time loudly exclaiming that he must first be punished for his impiety in daring, as a profane idolater, to lay his filthy hands on a priest of Christ. Immediately the other clergy and the laymen rushed forward and tied both him and the others who had climbed up into the upper room with their hands behind their backs, so tightly that in most cases their skin was torn and blood flowed from their fingernails. As soon as news of this bold deed reached those who were standing in the lower part of the house, they also did the same to those Arab princes who

---

'gazed at Bishop Gunther as a great wonder and believed that he was not a bishop but the king of the Romans'); Marianus Scottus, *Chronicon* 1086 [=1064], p. 559: he treated Gunther 'as the lord of our men because of the size and beauty of his person'. Cf. Lampert's eulogy of Gunther below p. 106. On Lampert's view of Gunther see Struve (1969) pp. 28–9 and above p. 5.

413 Matthew 5:26.

414 Livy II.51.5; III.62.6.

415 Cf. Marianus Scottus, *Chronicon* 1086 [=1064], p. 559: the Arab chieftain 'said, "I shall suck this beautiful blood from your throat".'

416 I.e. his turban. Cf. *Annals of Niederaltaich* 1065, p. 69: the chieftain 'unloosed the linen cloth with which his head was wrapped and placed it around the neck of the seated bishop'; Marianus Scottus, *Chronicon* 1086 [=1064], p. 559: 'he stretched his belt around the neck of the bishop of Bamberg'.

417 Livy IX.22.7.

418 Cf. *Annals of Niederaltaich* 1065, p. 69: Gunther 'suddenly sprang up and with one blow he threw him to the floor and set his foot on the man's neck'; Marianus Scottus, *Chronicon* 1086 [=1064], p. 559: 'the bishop, seizing the head of the chieftain, knocked him to the ground with a blow of his fist'. See Meyer von Knonau (1890) pp. 446–7; Joranson (1928) pp. 32–3.

were with them. Then all the laymen raised a cry to heaven and called upon the Creator of all things for His aid. Once more they snatched up their weapons, took possession of the wall, engaged in combat *with those who had been set to guard the gates*,[419] vanquished and put them to flight and everywhere carried out their duties with such eagerness and with their strength so renewed by their unexpected success that you would think that they had experienced no fatigue and no inconvenience from the three days of fasting and toil.

The Arabs were utterly amazed by such eager activity, which suddenly sprang out of a situation of peril and complete despair, and they conjectured that the cause of this strange turn of events could only be that their princes had been killed. *With the most savage ferocity* they hurled themselves *into battle*[420] and, *forming themselves into a body*, fully armed, they prepared to *force their way*[421] through the defenders into the camp. And it would have been all over, had not the idea occurred to the Christians in the nick of time to place the princes, restrained by their bonds, in that place where the enemy's most savage attack and their heaviest *shower of missiles*[422] would make themselves felt. They stationed over the heads of the princes an executioner, who held a drawn sword in his hands and who cried out through the interpreter that, unless they ceased their attack, they would be resisted not with weapons but with the heads of the princes. Then the princes themselves, who were suffering not only from the pain of their bonds but also from the sword that hovered over their necks, implored their men with loud lamentations to behave with more restraint, lest by stubbornly continuing to attack their enemies, they might provoke them to torture and kill their prisoners *when hope of pardon had gone*.[423] The son of the Arab leader (who, as I mentioned above, *had been left* by his father *to guard the gate*[424] of the courtyard) was aghast at his father's danger and flung himself *at full speed*[425] into the most densely packed troops of his countrymen. He held back the forward movement of the enraged army, checking them with voice and hand, and forbade them to throw missiles at the enemy, for these would strike not the enemy themselves, as they supposed, but the breasts of their princes.

419 Livy XXX.12.10.
420 *Ibid.*, X.31.5.
421 Sallust, *Catilina* 50.2; cf. Sallust, *Jugurtha* 58.3; Livy VIII.24.13.
422 Vergil, *Aeneid* XII.284.
423 Livy III.58.6; XXXV.31.7.
424 *Ibid.*, I.59.5; III.18.5; VII.37.13.
425 *Ibid.*, XXVIII.14.17.

As a result of this intervention there was a brief period of freedom from weapons and conflict. There then came to the Christians in their camp a messenger, who had been sent by those of their number who had lost all their possessions and on Good Friday had pushed on, naked and wounded, all the way to Ramleh.[426] This messenger brought great consolation for minds consumed by sorrow and fear. He informed them that the ruler of the aforementioned city[427] – who, although a pagan, was nevertheless (so they believed) moved by divine inspiration[428] – was coming with a huge army to free them. *The rumour of the approach of their enemies*[429] could not be concealed from the Arabs. They immediately all melted away, their thoughts diverted from attacking others by the need to save themselves, in headlong flight wherever there was a hope of escape. In this state of confusion, while some ran this way, others that way, each pursuing different concerns, one of the bound prisoners escaped with the help of a certain Saracen, whom the Christians used as a guide on their journey. This caused such vexation and sorrow to them all that it was with difficulty that they restrained themselves from violence against the man who had mercifully released the prisoner.

Not long afterwards[430] the ruler himself arrived with his army, just as it had been announced, and he was received in peace by the Christians in the courtyard. Nevertheless they were all *held in suspense between hope and fear*[431] lest perhaps their misfortunes were not over and they had *only exchanged* one enemy *for another.*[432] Given the strangeness of the situation, they found it difficult to believe that *Satan* would *cast out Satan,*[433] that is, that one pagan would restrain another from troubling Christians. First of all, the ruler commanded that the bound prisoners should be shown to him. When he had inspected them and had listened

---

426 See above p. 100. See also Meyer von Knonau (1890) p. 447; Joranson (1928) p. 35.

427 Cf. *Annals of Niederaltaich* 1065, p. 69: 'the general of the king of the Babylonians, who ruled in the city of Ramleh'. See Joranson (1928) p. 35 and below n. 435.

428 The motive ascribed by the *Annals of Niederaltaich* 1065, p. 69, is that the general in Ramleh 'thought that if these men perished in so wretched a massacre, no one would henceforward come through that land for the sake of prayer [i.e. on pilgrimage] and he and his followers would in consequence incur serious losses'.

429 Livy V.17.10.

430 'On the following day [Monday, 28 March] around the ninth hour [2 p.m.]' (*Annals of Niederaltaich* 1065, p. 69); 'on the second feast day of Easter' (Marianus Scottus, *Chronicon* 1086 [=1064], p. 559).

431 Livy VIII.13.7.

432 *Ibid.*, XXVIII.46.12.

433 Matthew 12: 26.

to an account of the correct sequence of events, he expressed his most grateful thanks to the Christians for their magnificent military feats and for defeating the most ferocious enemies of the State, who had disturbed the kingdom of the Babylonians[434] now for many years with their constant plundering and who had very often crushed great armies drawn up in battle array against them when they engaged in combat. Consigning them to guards, he ordered them to be kept alive for the king of the Babylonians.[435] When he had received from the Christians the sum of money on which they had agreed,[436] he brought them with him to Ramleh. From there he commanded them to be conducted all the way to Jerusalem, after arranging for them a guard of *lightly armed young men*[437] so that they would in no way be endangered a second time by an attack by brigands. Thereafter they experienced no difficulty on their outward journey and none on their return journey.[438] They arrived in Cilicia, giving thanks to God for having restored them to safety after they had passed through so many adversities alive and unharmed. They returned from here through Christian lands and everything happened according to their wishes.

When they afterwards came to Hungary, however, Bishop Gunther of Bamberg was, alas! overtaken by an untimely death and thus the conclusion of the fortunate and joyful homecoming was an occasion of sorrow for everyone. He died on 23 July in the flower of his age,[439] when he was still able to enjoy this world to the full. He was a man who was notable for the renown of his personal conduct and the riches of his soul but who was also adorned with great physical advantages. He had been born of the most eminent personages of the royal palace[440] and

---

434 The Fatimid caliphate of Egypt: see below n. 435. Cf. Marianus Scottus, *Chronicon* 1086 [=1064], p. 559: 'the captive leader of the Arabs, for a long time the enemy of the king of the Saracens'.

435 According to Holder-Egger, *Lamperti Annales* p. 98 n. 3, the Seldjuk sultan, Alp-Arslan (1063–73). According to Joranson (1928) p. 36 and n. 122, the Fatimid caliph in Cairo, Mustansir (1036–94). In 1065 (and until 1071) Ramleh and the rest of southern Palestine were under Fatimid jurisdiction.

436 Cf. Marianus Scottus, *Chronicon* 1086 [=1064], p. 559: 'the general of Ramleh ... received 500 golden bezants' (Byzantine gold coins).

437 Livy XXXVII.16.8.

438 The pilgrims entered Jerusalem on 12 April and remained there for thirteen days before returning to Ramleh: *Annals of Niederaltaich* 1065, p. 70.

439 Cf. *Annals of Niederaltaich* 1065, p. 70: 'he arrived at the city that is called Oedenburg ... and died on 23 July'.

440 Cf. the epitaph of Gunther of Bamberg in *Codex Udalrici* 30, p. 57: 'He was renowned for his distinguished appearance, stature, pedigree, pattern of life.' He was perhaps

in addition to his bishopric he was immensely rich in private properties.[441] He was *adroit in speech*[442] and counsel and learned in both divine
and secular literature.[443] Both in his stature and in the beauty, elegance
and health of his whole body he was so superior to other mortals that
during that journey to Jerusalem people came running *from the cities
and from the fields*[444] in their eagerness to gaze at him and everyone
who had happened to see him, believed himself to be fortunate. For this
reason, whenever they were staying in an inn and too large a crowd
gathered on his account (as was very often the case) and became too
troublesome, he was at various times forced by the other bishops to
appear in public so that the sight of him would distract the crowd
laying siege outside from inconveniencing the others.[445] The innocence
of his way of life and the sobriety of his character caused the splendour
of this transitory happiness *only to complete and perfect* his *renown*.[446]
While everyone was filled with wonder at the great glory of these two
aspects of his character, he alone regarded it with contempt for God's
sake, so that he behaved in a courteous and affable manner even to men
of the lowest rank and very often endured the most abusive language
from his servants and did not punish them.[447] He was brought back to
the fatherland, therefore, in a solemn funeral procession and received
with great lamentations on the part of all who had known him. He
was buried in the church of Bamberg, where he had grown up from his
boyhood.[448] He was succeeded in the bishopric by Herman, the admin-

---

a member of the Saxon family of the Ekkehardiner: see Zielinski (1984) p. 39.

441 Cf. the charter in *Codex Udalrici* 25, pp. 50–2, referring to Gunther's estates between
the rivers Enns and Ips and between the Enns and the Traun. On Gunther's foundation of the church of St Mary and St Gangolf in Bamberg see Meyer von Knonau
(1890) p. 452.

442 Livy II.45.15.

443 On the importance of Gunther's role in the Bamberg cathedral school see Märtl
(1991) pp. 339–40. On Lampert's emphasis on erudition see Struve (1970a) p. 102.

444 Livy I.1.5.

445 See above p. 102 and n. 412.

446 Livy II.47.11.

447 A similar forbearance was attributed to Bishop Bruno of Toul (Pope Leo IX): *Life
of Pope Leo IX* I.15, p. 122 ('Bruno repaid the insulting words [of subjects] not
with blows but with tears of condolence'); Anonymous of Hasenried, *On the bishops
of Eichstätt* c. 37, pp. 264–5. For instances of bishops personally inflicting corporal
punishment see Ralph Glaber, *Vita domni Willelmi abbatis* c. 11, p. 284 (Bishop
Herman of Toul); Adam of Bremen, *Gesta* III.38, p. 180 (Archbishop Adalbert of
Bremen). See Weinfurter (1992) p. 65.

448 Cf. *Annals of Niederaltaich* 1065, p. 71: he was buried 'before the altar of St Gertrude,
as he had arranged during his lifetime'.

istrator of the church of Mainz.[449] The latter had taken part in the same pilgrimage to Jerusalem and, when he saw that the bishop's illness was growing worse and that he was hastening to his death, he sent envoys to his kinsmen, to whom, on leaving the fatherland, he had assigned the management of his household affairs. He begged them to open up a way for him to the bishopric by whatever means they could. This they performed sedulously and squandered an incalculable amount of silver and gold in purchasing it.[450]

Bishop Eilbert of Passau died[451] and Altman, the chaplain of the empress, succeeded him. He had travelled to Jerusalem at the same time as the other princes and was designated bishop by the empress in his absence.[452]

Bishop Arnold of Worms, a man whose propriety of conduct and sanctity was fitting for a bishop, departed to the Lord.[453] He was succeeded by Adalbero, a monk of the monastery of St Gallen, the brother of Duke Rudolf,[454] completely lame in one foot and a man who was in all respects a sight to behold. For he was a man of great strength, of extreme gluttony and of such obesity that he struck beholders with horror rather than admiration. *No hundred-handed giant* or any other monster of antiquity, if *it rose up from the underworld*,[455] would *turn the eyes* and *gaze* of the astonished populace *upon himself to this degree.*[456]

---

449 Herman I, bishop of Bamberg (1065–75). As *vicedominus* of Mainz, he was the administrator of the possessions of the church: see Niermeyer – van de Kieft (2002) p. 1425.

450 Cf. Berthold of Reichenau, *Chronicle* 1065, p. 106: 'Ricimann [Herman] succeeded [Gunther] by means of simony'; Bruno of Merseburg, *Saxon War* c. 15, p. 22: '[Henry IV] gave, or rather sold for an enormous sum of money, the bishopric of Bamberg ... to a certain swindler, who knew better how to count the various sorts of money than to read the text of any book correctly, let alone understand or expound it'. For the allegations of simony against Herman see Schieffer (1972) pp. 22–46; Schieffer (1975) pp. 55–76; Cowdrey (1998) pp. 110–14, 124–7.

451 Egilbert, bishop of Passau (1045–65) †17 May.

452 Altman, bishop of Passau (1065–91). Cf. *Vita Altmanni episcopi Pataviensis* c. 5, p. 230: Empress Agnes (above n. 30) 'and the most noble men of the kingdom took counsel and all chose Altman in place of the deceased bishop'. See Meyer von Knonau (1890) pp. 457–8; Boshof (1991) p. 130. (Bishop Egilbert had also been the chaplain of Agnes before his accession.)

453 Arnold (Arnulf) I (above n. 38) †30 April.

454 Adalbero (1065–70), brother of Duke Rudolf of Swabia (above n. 203). See Zielinski (1984) p. 43.

455 Horace, *Carmina* II.17.14 ('no hundred-handed giant'), combined with Sulpicius Severus, *Vita Martini Turonensis* c. 26 ('rose up from the underworld').

456 Livy XXXIII.23.6; XLV.19.1. See Billanovich (1945) p. 98.

1066

The king celebrated Christmas in Goslar.[457] He had remained there already from the very beginning of the autumn until that period of the winter, as if in a stationary camp,[458] although his expenditure did not correspond at all to the splendour of a king. For apart from the small sums that came from the revenues of the royal fisc and that the abbots supplied through their enforced service, everything else that was purchased for the needs of the day came from the income of that day. This happened because of the hatred felt for the archbishop of Bremen, whom everyone accused of having, under the pretence of close friendship with the king, usurped the royal power in an act of manifest tyranny.[459] For this reason the customary services to the king were withheld and the archbishop refused to take the king into the other regions of the kingdom lest by being obliged to share with the other princes his dominant role of adviser and friend of the king, he should somewhat diminish the supreme and unique power that he had usurped. But the princes of the kingdom *seemed unwilling to endure* this injury *any longer*.[460] The archbishops of Mainz and Cologne, together with others who were concerned for the welfare of the State, held frequent meetings and asked them all to deliberate together about what needed to be done.[461] Then,

---

457 25 December 1065, 'in Mainz', according to the *Annals of Niederaltaich* 1066, p. 71, which Kilian (1886) p. 35 and Meyer von Knonau (1890) p. 483 considered more likely.

458 For Henry IV's movements in autumn–winter 1065 see Kilian (1886) pp. 34–5. Cf. the evidence of the diplomas: *DD.H.IV* 164 (Gerstungen, 18 August), 165–7 (Goslar, 30 August), 168–9 (Oschersleben, 6 September), 170 (Magdeburg, no date), 171 (Bossleben, 27 September), 172–3 (Goslar, 16 and 19 October), 174–5 (Corvey, 19 November, 8 December). For Lampert on Goslar see also below 1070, 1071, 1075, pp. 133, 135, 270. See Rothe (1940) pp. 21–31; Wilke (1970) pp. 18–24, 30–3; Robinson (1999) p. 80.

459 Cf. Adam of Bremen, *Gesta* III.47, p. 190: Adalbert (above n. 48) 'had now obtained the office of consul; having pushed his rivals aside, he alone now possessed the citadel of the Capitol, but not without the envy that always follows glory'. The evidence of the 'intervention clauses' in the royal diplomas suggests that in 1065 Adalbert dominated the court: see Gawlik (1970) pp. 32–8, 142. See also Meyer von Knonau (1890) pp. 479–80; Glaeske (1962) pp. 89–90; Jenal (1974) pp. 294–5, 297–8. On the claim that the crown's income was depleted: Meyer von Knonau (1890) pp. 695–9; Hauck (1954) pp. 728–9; Seibert (1991) p. 540.

460 Livy II.63.2.

461 On the role of Anno of Cologne (above n. 139) and Siegfried of Mainz (above n. 210) see Meyer von Knonau (1890) p. 488; Jenal (1974) pp. 305–6. Cf. Adam of Bremen, *Gesta* III.47, p. 190: 'nearly all the bishops and princes of the kingdom ... were unanimous in their hatred and conspired that he should perish'. The fellow conspirators are identified in the letter of Anno to Pope Alexander II in Giesebrecht (1890) pp. 1258–9 (document 5): see below n. 471.

when the conspiracy was fully matured, they announced the meeting of
a general assembly to all the princes of the kingdom.[462] They would thus
meet in Tribur and through their combined efforts they would all attack
the archbishop of Bremen, the common enemy of every one of them,
and would declare to the king that either he must give up the kingship
or he must put an end to his close association and his friendship with
the archbishop of Bremen.

When news of this dreadful development reached Goslar,[463] the king
hastened with all speed to the meeting that had been decreed. With
him was Count Werner,[464] who came to the village of Ingelheim, part
of which belongs to our monastery, and claimed the right of lodging
there. When his knights began to rob the villagers there and they in
turn gave the call to arms and strove to defend themselves, *a violent
fight*[465] broke out. Count Werner *quickly intervened in* the fight *to help his
men;*[466] he was struck on the head with a cudgel by a serf of our monastery, a man of very low station, or, as some say, by a female dancer. He
fell to the ground and was brought back to the king only half-alive.
He was exhorted by the bishops who were present that, now that he
was breathing his last, he should make amends to God for his sins.
He should recognise that he had been destroyed by the prayers of the
monks of Hersfeld and he should return to them the village of Kirchberg, of which he had taken possession unjustly.[467] He would in no way
agree to this until the bishops united in threatening that they would
not give him holy communion when he was dying unless he had first
unburdened himself of so great a weight of sin. Thus it was because he
was overcome by shame rather than piety that he finally relinquished
the property and he immediately departed this life.

---

462 The assembly of Tribur was summoned by the king. See the letter of Anno to
   Alexander II (above n. 461) p. 1258: 'after the octave of Epiphany [13 January
   1066] our lord king held a conference with certain princes'.

463 For Henry IV's itinerary in late 1065 see above n. 458. Kilian (1886) pp. 35–6 and
   Meyer von Knonau (1890) p. 484 and n. 176 placed these events before Christmas
   1065, when the royal entourage was en route from Corvey to Mainz.

464 The fate of Werner (above n. 339) was recorded only by Lampert, who represented
   it as a divine judgement on an enemy of the abbey of Hersfeld: see Struve (1970a)
   p. 74.

465 Livy I.30.9; VII.26.6. See Billanovich (1945) p. 67.

466 Livy XXXV.11.5; XXII.6.2. See Billanovich (1945) p. 100.

467 See above n. 367 for Lampert's failure to mention the compensation received by
   Hersfeld for the loss of Kirchberg.

On the appointed day[468] the faces of all men looked sternly on the king
and stern was their decision that either he should abdicate from the
kingship[469] or he should banish the archbishop of Bremen from his
counsels and from participation in the government of the kingdom.
While he twisted and turned and while he hesitated about what course
of action to choose, the archbishop advised that on the following night
he should flee in secret, taking with him the insignia of the kingship, and
go to Goslar or to some other place where he would be safe from injury,
until this disturbance died down. As evening came, he had already begun
to carry away the royal treasure by means of the aiders and abettors
of his deceit, when suddenly this plan became known (I do not know
who disclosed it) to the royal officials. They immediately seized their
weapons, surrounded the royal residence and afterwards, remaining
watchful all night, they kept guard, lest anything unusual happened.
When morning came, everyone rounded upon the archbishop with
such hostility that they *would not have restrained themselves from striking
him*,[470] had not the royal majesty with the greatest difficulty checked
their anger. Amidst reproaches and invective the archbishop was, therefore, driven out of the royal court, together with all the supporters of
his tyranny, and the king sent a large company of his friends with him
so that he would not fall victim to an ambush by his enemies during
his journey.[471] Thus the management of public affairs returned once

---

468 'After the octave of Epiphany [13 January 1066]': see above n. 462. On the fall of
    Adalbert of Bremen at Tribur see Meyer von Knonau (1890) pp. 487–9; Glaeske
    (1962) p. 73; Jenal (1974) pp. 303–6: Robinson (1999) pp. 59–60.

469 This claim was made only by Lampert. Influenced by the events of the assembly
    of princes at Tribur in October 1076 (below pp. 334–42), the account is charac-
    teristic of his polemical presentation of Henry IV. Cf. Lampert's version of the
    Saxon conspiracy of 1057: above p. 69 and n. 171. See Meyer von Knonau (1894) pp.
    810–11; Robinson (1999) p. 60 and above p. 33.

470 Livy II.23.10.

471 Cf. *Annals of Weissenburg* 1065, p. 53: 'Archbishop Siegfried of Mainz and the other
    bishops, dukes and princes and all the adherents of justice, conspiring together,
    exhorted the king in Tribur to cancel whatever had been enacted on the advice of the
    archbishop [Adalbert] and to have done with him, which was not concealed from
    the archbishop; for he fled at night, no one pursuing him'; Adam of Bremen, *Gesta*
    III.47, p. 191: 'nearly all the bishops and princes of the kingdom ... were unanimous
    in their hatred and conspired that he should perish ... They all assembled together,
    therefore, in Tribur, when the king was present, and expelled our archbishop from
    the court as if he was a magician and seducer'; *ibid.*, III.55, p. 199: 'our archbishop
    was expelled from the court, so they say, through the jealousy of the archbishop of
    Cologne'. The conspirators are identified in the letter of Anno to Pope Alexander II
    in Giesebrecht (1890) pp. 1258–9 (document 5) as the archbishops of Cologne and
    Mainz, Archbishop Gebhard of Salzburg and the dukes Otto of Bavaria, Rudolf of
    Swabia, Berthold of Carinthia and Godfrey III of Lotharingia.

again to the bishops so that each of them in his turn made provision for whatever was necessary for the king and the State.[472]

The king celebrated Easter in Utrecht.[473] On Holy Saturday after Archbishop Eberhard of Trier had solemnly presented to the people the eucharist of so important a day, he retired to the sacristy and, resting his head on the bosom of the archdeacon, he breathed his last, surrounded by the brethren.[474] Cuno, the provost of Cologne obtained his archbishopric through the intervention of the archbishop of Cologne.[475] Both the clergy and the people of Trier responded with the most violent indignation to the fact that they had not been involved and consulted in his election and they strongly urged each other to wash out the stain of this extraordinary insult in a manner that was equally extraordinary.[476] The advocate of the church of Trier at that time was Count Theoderic,[477] a young man who was *savage* both in his natural disposition and *because of his time of life*.[478] On the day on which

---

472 Cf. above, 1062, p. 82, where Lampert attributed such a scheme of government to the intervention of Anno of Cologne. For Lampert's view of Anno as the proponent of the highest ideals of government see Struve (1970a) pp. 107–8 and n. 47. Holder-Egger, *Lamperti Annales* p. 102 n. 2, claimed that 'supreme power' returned to Anno himself in 1066. According to Jenal (1974) p. 351: 'certainly after Adalbert's fall Anno was one of the most influential figures ... but there were opposing forces, which now impeded such powerful individual politicians as were possible before [Henry IV's coming of age].' Particularly noteworthy is the prominence of Siegfried of Mainz in the 'intervention clauses' of the royal diplomas of 1066: see Gawlik (1970) pp. 38–40, 130.

473 16 April. Cf. Berthold of Reichenau, *Chronicle* 1066, p. 106; but *Annals of Niederaltaich* 1066, p. 71: 'in Speyer'. Kilian (1886) p. 37 and Meyer von Knonau (1890) p. 498 and n. 15 concluded that the evidence of the itinerary made Utrecht more likely.

474 Eberhard, archbishop of Trier (1047–66) +15 April.

475 Cuno (Conrad) of Pfullingen, provost of Cologne, archbishop elect of Trier (1066). Lampert omitted to mention that he was the nephew of Archbishop Anno. The central role of Anno in his appointment was emphasised by the hostile *Triumphus sancti Remacli Stabulensis* I.17, p. 446 (Anno 'put his own provost in [Eberhard's] place and on this account just cause of hatred against [Anno] arose among the men of Trier, because he had shown contempt for their choice and imposed his own choice on them'), by Adam of Bremen, *Gesta* III.35, p. 178 ('by the exertions and through the favour of Anno') and by the hagiographer Theoderic of Tholey, *Vita et passio Conradi* c. 2, p. 214. See Meyer von Knonau (1890) p. 499; Zielinski (1984) pp. 24 and n. 33, 178–9.

476 Cf. *Annals of Weissenburg* 1066, p. 53: 'the people of Trier in their anger refused to receive him'; *Annals of Niederaltaich* 1067, p. 73: 'both the clergy and people took [his election] ill'; Berthold of Reichenau, *Chronicle* 1066, p. 106: Conrad 'was opposed by the clergy and citizens of Trier'; Adam of Bremen, *Gesta* III.35, p. 177: Cuno was 'crowned with martyrdom by the envy of the clergy before he was enthroned'.

477 Theoderic, burgrave of Trier, advocate of the church of Trier (+1073). On Lampert's term for him (*maior domus*) see Niermeyer–van de Kieft (2002) p. 821.

478 Livy VI.23.3.

the archbishop was expected to enter the city this Theoderic set out to meet him with a very large force of men. In the darkness before dawn he forced his way into the archbishop's presence before he had left his lodgings;[479] he killed the few men who tried to resist and he scattered the rest, who were *thrown into confusion by this* unexpected *terror*,[480] and easily put them to flight and he plundered the splendid treasures that the archbishop had brought with him. He captured the archbishop himself and delivered him into the hands of executioners and commanded that he should be thrown headfirst from a very high rock and thus killed.[481] His body was retrieved by pious men and buried in the monastery of Tholey. There (it is said) he is often honoured by heaven with great miracles even to the present time.[482] He was succeeded in the archbishopric by Udo, on whose election both clergy and people agreed.[483]

During the Easter festival a comet appeared for almost fourteen consecutive nights.[484] At that time *an extremely savage* and lamentable *battle took place*[485] in the lands of the north, in which the king of the Anglo-Saxons utterly destroyed three kings, together with their innumerable army.[486]

After arriving in Fritzlar, the king fell victim to an illness of such great severity that the physicians despaired of his life and the princes had begun to consult together about the succession to the kingship.[487]

479 18 May in Bitburg (north of Trier): see Meyer von Knonau (1890) pp. 503–4.

480 Livy I.14.9.

481 After imprisonment in the castle of Uerzig, he was killed on 1 June. For the different accounts of the manner of his death see Meyer von Knonau (1890) pp. 504–5 and n. 25.

482 Cuno was buried in the village of Losenich before being brought by Bishop Theoderic of Verdun to the abbey of Tholey: see Meyer von Knonau (1890) p. 505 and n. 25. Miracles were recorded by *Annals of Weissenburg* 1067, p. 53; *Annals of Niederaltaich* 1067, p. 73; Berthold of Reichenau, *Chronicle* II, 1066, p. 119.

483 Udo of Nellenburg, archbishop of Trier (1066–78).

484 Cf. Berthold of Reichenau, *Chronicle* 1066, p. 119: 'Comets were seen … on 23 April and they remained for thirty days'. This was Halley's Comet. On the various sightings in German and Italian narrative sources: Meyer von Knonau (1890) p. 523 n. 55.

485 Livy II.40.13. See Billanovich (1945) p. 67.

486 Lampert perhaps conflated the battles of Stamford Bridge (25 September) and Hastings (14 October) and the deaths of the kings Harald Hardrada of Norway (1047–66) and Harold II of England (1066). An indication of the identity of Lampert's third king is given in the version of Stamford Bridge in Adam of Bremen, *Gesta* III.52, p. 196: 'Tostig [earl of Northumbria] was killed and also the king of Ireland and Harald [Hardrada]'.

487 In mid-May, according to Kilian (1886) p. 38 and Meyer von Knonau (1890) p. 524. Cf. *Triumphus sancti Remacli Stabulensis* I.16, p. 445: 'the king was staying in the town

He had hardly made a full recovery from this indisposition when he celebrated Whitsun in Hersfeld.[488] Not long afterwards he celebrated his wedding with royal magnificence in Tribur[489] *on the occasion of his marriage*[490] with Queen Bertha, the daughter of Margrave Otto of the Italians.[491]

Bishop Reginher of Meissen died[492] and Craft, the provost of Goslar succeeded him.[493] When he had received the bishopric, the latter had come to Goslar and after a meal, as though wishing to rest a little, he shut himself in his bedchamber, where, unknown to anyone, he had buried his treasure, which he loved far too much. As the day was already declining towards evening and he seemed to have yielded to sleep to an immoderate degree and contrary to his custom, the chamberlains, wondering at this unusual circumstance, began to knock at the door. But there was no reply to their knocking or their shouts. When at last they broke down the doors and burst in, they found him lifeless, with a broken neck and an unwholesome colour, lying in a pitiable manner on his treasure. Benno, canon of the aforementioned church of Goslar, received the bishopric in his place.[494]

1067

Margrave Otto of the Thuringians died.[495] All the Thuringians rejoiced exceedingly at his death because he was the first of the Thuringian princes (as was mentioned above) to agree to pay tithes from his possessions in Thuringia and he was seen thereby to have brought the

---

of Fritzlar, where he was seized and tortured by a serious and troublesome illness'; *Annals of Niederaltaich* 1066, p. 71: 'the king began to be so ill that the doctors entirely despaired of him and certain of the princes had already taken possession of the throne of the kingdom in their hopes and desires'.

488 4 June. Cf. *D.H.IV* 179 (issued on 5 June in Hersfeld).

489 Before the issue of *D.H.IV* 181, dated 13 July in Tribur (in which Bertha appeared in an 'intervention clause' for the first time). Cf. Berthold of Reichenau, *Chronicle* 1066, p. 120: 'in Tribur'; but *Annals of Niederaltaich* 1066, p. 72: 'in Ingelheim'. See Kilian (1886) p. 38; Meyer von Knonau (1890) p. 526 ('probably in Tribur').

490 Esther 2:18.

491 Bertha of Turin (1051–87), queen (1066), empress (1084), daughter of Odo, count of Savoy (†1057/1060) and Margravine Adelaide of Turin.

492 Reginher, bishop of Meissen (?1063–1066).

493 Craft, bishop of Meissen (1066). This anecdote was recorded only by Lampert: see Meyer von Knonau (1890) p. 532.

494 Benno, bishop of Meissen (1066–1105/7).

495 Margrave Otto of Meissen (above n. 265). On the issue of tithes see above p. 80 and n. 266.

greatest misfortune on his people. His march was received by Ekbert, the kinsman of the king.[496]

Bishop Einhard of Speyer died[497] and was succeeded by Henry, a canon of the church of Goslar.[498] The latter was hardly old enough for so important an office and he was promoted to it not so much by the choice of the princes as by the fondness of the king, who in his boyhood had been on the closest terms of friendship with him.

Bishop Benno of Osnabrück died[499] and a second Benno succeeded him.[500]

The king came to Goslar on the feast of the nativity of St Martin[501] and succumbed to a serious illness. He lay in bed for many days, suffering from that same infirmity.

1068

The king celebrated Christmas in Goslar, although he had not yet fully recovered his health.[502] After the feast days were over, Margrave Ekbert took leave of him and, when he had returned to his own land, he contracted a slight fever and this caused his death.[503] But while he was still alive, he had secured his march for his son, a little child of very tender age,[504] born to him by the widow of Duke Otto of Schweinfurt.[505] A few days before he departed this life, however, he had considered obtaining a divorce from her and, contrary to the laws and the

---

496 Count Ekbert I of Brunswick, margrave of Meissen (above n. 177), first cousin of Henry IV.

497 Einhard II (above n. 247) +23 March.

498 Henry I, bishop of Speyer (1067–75). See Fleckenstein (1973) p. 125 n. 40, 126 n. 45; Zielinski (1984) p. 141 and n. 414.

499 Benno I, bishop of Osnabrück (?1052–1068) +19/20 September 1068.

500 Benno II, bishop of Osnabrück (1068–88).

501 11 November. Lampert alone recorded this illness: see Kilian (1886) p. 41; Meyer von Knonau (1890) p. 573.

502 25 December 1067. Cf. *Annals of Niederaltaich* 1067, p. 74: 'in Goslar'; but Berthold of Reichenau, *Chronicle* 1067, p. 122: 'in Cologne'. Kilian (1886) p. 41 and Meyer von Knonau (1890) p. 573 and n. 47 accepted Lampert's report.

503 Margrave Ekbert I of Meissen (above n. 177) +11 January 1068. See Meyer von Knonau (1890) p. 583.

504 Ekbert II, count of Brunswick, margrave of Meissen (+1090). Lampert described him in the annal for 1073 as 'a boy still under the age of knighthood' (below p. 176; cf. 1076, p. 330 and n. 1740), i.e. still under fifteen.

505 Immula (Irmgard) of Susa (+1077/8), daughter of Margrave Olderich Manfred II of Turin, widow of Duke Otto III of Swabia (above n. 202).

canons, joining himself in matrimony to the widow of Margrave Otto[506] because that woman seemed to be of greater elegance and beauty and more suited to his own *ferocious disposition*.[507] But death opportunely intervened to prevent his impious efforts.

Patriarch Ravenger of Aquileia died[508] and the chancellor Sigehard succeeded him,[509] while Pibo was appointed as chancellor in the latter's place.[510]

1069

The king celebrated Christmas in Goslar,[511] Easter in Quedlinburg[512] and Whitsun in Cologne.[513] After Whitsun he held an assembly with the princes of the kingdom in Worms.[514] There he first held secret talks with the archbishop of Mainz and begged most earnestly for his help in achieving the scheme that he had in mind. If this request was granted, the king would thereafter be subject to him and would obey his every word. In addition he would compel the Thuringians by armed force, if there was no other possibility, to pay tithes without any opposition in perpetuity.[515] When the archbishop had given his promise and an agree-

---

506 Adela of Louvain (✝1083), daughter of Count Lambert of Louvain, widow of Margrave Otto of Meissen (above n. 265). Lampert alone recorded these matrimonial plans: see Meyer von Knonau (1890) pp. 583–4.

507 Livy XXXIV.24.4.

508 Ravenger, patriarch of Aquileia (1063–8).

509 Sigehard, chancellor of the German kingdom (1064–8), patriarch of Aquileia (1068–77).

510 Pibo, chancellor of the German kingdom (1068–9), bishop of Toul (1069–1107).

511 25 December 1068. Cf. Berthold of Reichenau, *Chronicle* 1069, p. 122: 'in Goslar'; but *Annals of Niederaltaich* 1069, p. 76: 'in Mainz'. Kilian (1886) p. 42 and Meyer von Knonau (1890) p. 599 and n. 42 decided on Goslar, on the basis of *D.H.IV* 214, issued in Goslar on 3 January 1069.

512 12 April. Henry IV's elder sister was Abbess Adelaide II of Quedlinburg and Gandersheim.

513 31 May. In Mainz, according to Kilian (1886) pp. 43–4 and Meyer von Knonau (1890) p. 612 and n. 11, on the basis of *D.H.IV* 217 (for Hersfeld), issued in Mainz on 1 June.

514 Cf. Siegfried of Mainz, letter to Pope Alexander II in *Codex Udalrici* 34, p. 65: an assembly 'of as many magnates as were then in the palace'. See Kilian (1886) p. 44 and Meyer von Knonau (1890) p. 612.

515 On Siegfried of Mainz (above n. 210) and the demand for Thuringian tithes see above p. 80 and n. 266. See also Meyer von Knonau (1890) pp. 661–3; Meyer von Knonau (1894) p. 795; Struve (1969) p. 47 n. 74; Struve (1970a) p. 76 (Lampert 'linked the [tithes dispute] with areas that had nothing whatever to do with the Mainz demand for tithes, such as Henry IV's plan for a divorce').

ment was confirmed between them, the king announced in public that he did not live in harmony with his wife. He had long concealed this from the eyes of men but he was unwilling to conceal it any longer. He could not allege any offence on her part that justly merited a divorce but – he was uncertain through what misfortune or what divine judgement – he was unable to have marital relations with her.[516] For that reason he begged them in God's name to free him from the chains of this ill-omened marriage and patiently to allow a separation to take place so that she might open the way for him, and he for her, to a happier marriage, if God so willed it. And lest anyone should object that once her chastity had been violated, there was an obstacle to her marrying again, he confirmed on oath that he had kept her as he received her, undefiled and in a state of unimpaired virginity. This subject seemed to all who were present to be unseemly and utterly inconsistent with royal authority. Nevertheless they all felt that it was a serious matter to reject a plan to which the king had devoted himself with such fervour. The archbishop, whose agreement had been purchased by so precious a promise, also willingly gave his support to the king's cause, as far as was compatible with his honour.[517] Since they all decided that this should be

516 Queen Bertha (above n. 491). Cf. Siegfried of Mainz, letter to Pope Alexander II (above n. 514): 'Your son Henry, our king, a few days ago wished to renounce his wife ... putting forward no fault or cause of division ... because he could associate with her in neither a natural nor a marital compact of intercourse.' See Schmeidler (1920) pp. 141–9: 'This is a compelling argument, the only irrefutable grounds that the Catholic Church recognises for a divorce.' Cf. *Annals of Niederaltaich* 1069, p. 78: the king 'was accustomed to resort to the unlawful embraces of concubines and he therefore planned to renounce the queen, whom he had lawfully married as the consort of the kingdom'; Berthold of Reichenau, *Chronicle* 1068, p. 122: Henry was 'forgetful of his lawful wife'; Bruno of Merseburg, *Saxon War* c. 6, pp. 16–17: 'His wife, the noble and beautiful woman whom he had married unwillingly at the recommendation of the princes, was so hated by him that after the wedding he never saw her of his own free will'. For two years after the wedding in 1066 Bertha appeared in the 'intervention clauses' of diplomas but after 5 August 1068 her name disappeared for more than a year: see Gawlik (1970) pp. 39–43, 128. See also Meyer von Knonau (1890) pp. 612–17; Robinson (1999) pp. 109–13; Bühler (2001) pp. 43–6.

517 Cf. *Annals of Niederaltaich* 1069, p. 78: 'His wicked purpose was strengthened by the encouragement of the bishop of Mainz, who had promised that he would permit him to do this by means of a synodal judgement.' But see Siegfried of Mainz, letter to Pope Alexander II (above n. 514): 'astonished and deeply moved ..., on the advice of as many magnates as were then in the palace we resisted him face to face and declared that, unless he put forward a valid case for a divorce, we – if [papal] authority was forthcoming – would separate him from the bosom and communion of the Church, without respect for the royal power, without fear of the threat of the sword'. This contradiction provided Ranke (1888) pp. 133–4 with one of his principal arguments against Lampert's veracity. See also Meyer von Knonau (1890) pp. 615–17; Schmeidler (1920) pp. 144–8.

done, therefore, he announced that a synod would be held to complete this business in Mainz in the week after the feast of St Michael.[518] While affairs remained in suspense in anticipation of this synod, the queen was sent to Lorsch, to wait there until the appointed time.[519] The king went somewhere else,[520] where the business of the kingdom summoned him.

Meanwhile, after he had married the widow of Margrave Otto[521] in the third year after the latter's death, the Saxon Margrave Dedi[522] strove with all his might to gain possession also of the estates that Margrave Otto had held as benefices from various lords.[523] Since none of them gave him what he demanded, he would not endure this insulting treatment and made preparations for war against the king, whom he regarded as principally responsible for their not giving him the land, and he held frequent conferences with the Thuringians, urging them *to make a military alliance*[524] with him. He hoped that this would be easy to achieve because the king, in assisting the archbishop in his demand for tithes, had done much to alienate their sympathies from him.[525] Dedi's rage, however, was above all encouraged by his wife, a woman of the utmost cruelty. This woman instilled youthful passions into her husband, whose disposition was peaceful and tamed by age, and she very often deafened him with her taunts that, *if he was a true man,*[526]

518 I.e. the week after 29 September.

519 Cf. *Annals of Niederaltaich* 1069, p. 78: 'While this synod was awaited, the queen was ordered to stay in Lorsch.' On Henry IV's relations with Lorsch in 1069 see Meyer von Knonau (1890) p. 616 n. 19; Feierabend (1913) p. 100.

520 To Regensburg, according to the *Annals of Niederaltaich* 1069, p. 77. See Kilian (1886) p. 44; Meyer von Knonau (1890) p. 617.

521 Adela of Louvain (above n. 506), widow of Margrave Otto of Meissen (above n. 265).

522 Dedi, margrave of Lower Lusatia (1046–75).

523 On the estates of Otto of Meissen see above 1062, p. 80 ('benefices of the archbish-opric of Mainz'). Meyer von Knonau (1890) p. 620 n. 29 identified these as Thuringian possessions of the house of Weimar-Orlamünde, which Adela brought to her marriage with Dedi, including the castle of Beichlingen, mentioned by Lampert below p. 120. Fenske (1977) p. 35 suggested that these were 'imperial benefices of Margrave Otto, denied [Dedi] by Henry IV but to which the Wettin [Dedi] believed that he had a right through his marriage to [Otto's] widow'. On Dedi's rebellion see Meyer von Knonau (1890) pp. 617–23; Fenske (1977) pp. 34–6; Giese (1991) pp. 288–9; Robinson (1999) pp. 64–5.

524 Livy X.11.11.

525 Holder-Egger, *Lamperti Annales* pp. 106 n. 1 and 107 n. 2 noted that if the agreement between king and archbishop was secret, as Lampert claimed, the Thuringians (and Lampert himself) could know nothing of it. See also Struve (1970a) pp. 76–7.

526 Livy XXV.18.11. For Lampert's portrayal of Adela of Louvain see also above p. 116 and below pp. 176, 279.

he would not let injuries go unavenged and that he should not behave less courageously than her first husband, to whom he was superior in strength and riches.

When the king received this news,[527] he was deeply troubled and he very quickly assembled large numbers of troops that would even have been sufficient for very many wars. It was in these circumstances that the archbishop of Mainz calculated that the time had come to indulge his private hatred for the Thuringians, using the opportunity of this public war. He appeared before the king in the most aggressive frame of mind and urged him to proceed with the greatest severity. He also devoted his own energies to the undertaking, drawing on all the resources of his friends and of the archbishopric of Mainz.[528] The Thuringians were well aware of the archbishop's savage attitude towards them and their own feelings towards him were no milder. They sent envoys to the king to inform him that they had no hostile plans and no evil designs against him and that they had given neither their advice nor their approval to anyone's taking up arms against the State. On the contrary, they were prepared to confront the enemy of the State even at the risk of their own lives. They would, however, do so more readily and more easily if he were to confirm that the laws concerning tithes that had been established for them as a concession by kings and bishops in earlier times would remain fixed and inviolable. If the archbishop came to them to accomplish a divine purpose not with divine but with human weapons and wished to extort from them by right of war the tithes that he could not have obtained by ecclesiastical law or by secular law, they were bound by an oath[529] and under an obligation now, just as they were long ago, *not to let* robbers and plunderers *go unpunished.*[530] It was

---

527 'In the summer', according to the *Annals of Niederaltaich* 1069, p. 77: 'When the king, who was stationed in Regensburg, heard this news, he assembled a host and hastened to hinder the endeavours' of Dedi and 'Count Adalbert' of Ballenstedt, his son-in-law.

528 Meyer von Knonau (1890) p. 620 n. 30 used this reference to Archbishop Siegfried's participation as a means of dating the expedition. Siegfried was still in Mainz on 10 July; Henry IV had left Thuringia and was in Tribur on 15 August (*D.H.IV* 218–19).

529 Cf. below 1070, p. 132: 'the Thuringians (who some years before had bound themselves by an oath not to allow robbers and plunderers to go unpunished)'. Meyer von Knonau (1890) pp. 599 n. 43, 662 n. 23, linked the Thuringians' 'oath' with the report in Berthold of Reichenau, *Chronicle* 1069, p. 122: 'Peace and reconciliation were confirmed among the people on oath by royal edict at Christmas [25 December 1068] in Goslar.' I.e. it was a local manifestation of the royal 'peace movement', inspired by the measures of Henry III, 1043–7: see Holder-Egger, *Lamperti Annales* p. 108 n. 1; Wadle (1973) p. 159.

530 Livy II.9.2.

preferable for them to die in battle than to lose the rights of their ancestors and live as oath-breakers.

To this the king gave a favourable answer and told them to rely with the utmost certainty upon his help, if they remained faithful to him. Then, when *the time seemed ripe*,[531] he marched into Thuringia with a hostile force. There he took possession of two castles in which the margrave had placed garrisons, Beichlingen and Burgscheidungen, the former surrendering, the latter being taken by assault.[532] The army was immediately ordered to advance on the other castles. The margrave, however, realised that there was *no locality* and no fortress *where he could withstand an attack*[533] by the king and, since *all hope* of resistance *was taken from him*,[534] he surrendered himself and all his possessions.[535] Although the Thuringians, as they had promised, were obedient and faithful to the king and the cause of the State, they nevertheless indulged in every kind of hostile behaviour towards the archbishop of Mainz. They challenged him to his face with insults and loud reproaches; they very often formed bands to attack his knights when the latter were engaged in plundering, wrested the booty from their hands, routed and put them to flight; finally they apprehended some of his officials, when they had turned aside for plunder at some distance from the king's army – and these were men of considerable property and not of low birth – and they hanged them.[536] Nevertheless the king commanded them *without hesitation* and *in a contemptuous manner*[537] to pay the tithes, not because he was planning to use force against those who refused to pay but in order not to offend the archbishop by failing to keep his promise.

---

531 *Ibid.*, II.45.11.

532 Cf. *Annals of Niederaltaich* 1069, p. 77: 'In Thuringia the king besieged a castle of the margrave named Beichlingen, captured it in the first attack and ordered it to be burned. Moving from there, he reached Burgscheidungen and, although it also was stormed, nevertheless during the first attack many men on the king's side were wounded and lost their lives.' See Meyer von Knonau (1890) p. 622.

533 Livy II.50.5; IV.18.8; V.28.12. See Billanovich (1945) pp. 86–7.

534 Livy III.58.6; XXXV.31.7.

535 Cf. *Annals of Niederaltaich* 1069, p. 77: 'the margrave and Adalbert [of Ballenstedt] … gave a great part of their estates to the king and gained his favour'. *D.H.IV* 224 (for the church of SS Simon and Jude, 26 October 1069) records that after 'Margrave Dedi had been at odds with us in recent tumults and in rash warfare, regaining time and peace for himself', he restored the estate of Sollnitz to the king. See Meyer von Knonau (1890) p. 623.

536 Meyer von Knonau (1890) p. 623 n. 38: 'because of his aversion towards Siegfried', Lampert's account contains 'obvious exaggerations'.

537 Livy II.56.12.

Margrave Dedi was held for some time in prison but he was finally released after he had been deprived of a considerable part of his possessions and revenues. His son, the younger Dedi, at that time pursued his father with greater hostility and bitterness than anyone else[538] and for this reason, when the war was over, he began to be held *in the highest honour*[539] by the king. He was a young man of outstanding abilities if only he had not been driven headlong by the spirit of ambition and by a precocious desire for dominance. Not long afterwards, one night when he had withdrawn to answer a call of nature, a man who was lying in wait for him outside stabbed him in the abdomen and killed him. It is not known for certain who was the instigator of his murder, although *it was rumoured far and wide*[540] among the common people that he had been killed through the guile of his stepmother.[541] One fact, however, is beyond doubt. When he died, the monasteries and churches were freed from a great burden of fear, since the belief had very firmly taken possession of everyone's mind that, in his efforts to increase his power, he would spare neither God nor man, since he had not spared his own father.

As the day drew near that had been appointed for ending the king's marriage, the king travelled with great haste to Mainz. And lo and behold! in the course of the journey he learned that a legate of the apostolic see was awaiting his arrival in Mainz.[542] The legate was to forbid the divorce and to threaten the archbishop of Mainz with the sentence of papal censure because he promised to perform such an unlawful separation. The king was dismayed that the plan that he had cherished for so long had slipped through his hands and he

---

538 Dedi (+1069), son of Margrave Dedi of Lower Lusatia and Oda, his former wife. (Cf. the contrasting version of the *Annals of Ottobeuren* 1068, p. 7: 'Dedi, the son of Dedi, reconciled his father to the king.' See Meyer von Knonau (1890) pp. 622–3 and n. 40.

539 Livy II.16.7; II.22.6.

540 *Ibid.*, VIII.29.2.

541 Adela of Louvain: see above nn. 506, 526. See Fenske (1977) p. 74 ('she was accused of instigating the murder of her stepson ... to secure the succession in the margraviate to her own progeny'). Cf. *Annals of Ottobeuren* 1068, p. 7: 'Dedi the younger was secretly killed'; *Genealogia Wettinensis* p. 227: 'Dedi the younger ... was killed in his boyhood, being stabbed through the buttocks'. See Meyer von Knonau (1890) p. 623; Reuter (1991b) pp. 305–6.

542 On 15 August he was not far from Mainz, in Tribur (*D.H.IV* 219). See Kilian (1886) p. 44 and Meyer von Knonau (1890) p. 624. Cf. the different version of the *Annals of Niederaltaich* 1069, p. 78: 'When the day of the synod had come and the archbishop had already taken his seat and had begun the proceedings, lo and behold! an envoy of the lord pope appeared.'

immediately wished to return to Saxony by the same route by which he
had come. Nevertheless with the greatest difficulty he was overruled
by the advice of his friends and, so as not to disappoint the princes of
the kingdom, whom he had commanded to meet him in Mainz in very
great numbers, he went to Frankfurt[543] and ordered those who had
assembled in Mainz to appear in Frankfurt on a specific day. When
they had arrived there in a large crowd, Peter Damian[544] – for he was
the legate of the apostolic see, a man most venerable in his age and
in the blamelessness of his life – informed them of the commands of
the Roman pontiff. What the king was endeavouring to do was most
injurious and entirely inconsistent with the conduct of a Christian,
to say nothing of a king. If he was not afraid of human laws and the
decrees of the canons, he should at least refrain from injuring his own
reputation and honour, lest the poison *of such a disgraceful example,*[545]
originating with the king, should contaminate the whole Christian
people and he who ought to be the punisher of wrongdoing would
himself become the instigator and standard bearer of shameful deeds.[546]
Finally, if *he was not prevailed upon* by this advice, the pope would be
compelled *to resort to the power*[547] of the Church and to prevent wickedness by means of canon law. For his hands would never consecrate as

---

543 The evidence of the royal diplomas shows him in Frankfurt on 23 September
(*D.H.IV* 220) and on 6–8 October (*D.H.IV* 221–2). See Kilian (1886) p. 45 and Meyer
von Knonau (1890) pp. 625–7. The 'intervention clause' of *D.H.IV* 221 indicates the
presence of the archbishops Siegfried of Mainz and Anno of Cologne and Bishop
Herman of Bamberg in Frankfurt on 6 October.

544 Peter Damian, cardinal bishop of Ostia (1057–72). Lampert alone identified Peter
Damian as the legate of Pope Alexander II. The *Annals of Niederaltaich* 1069, p. 78
mentions only 'an envoy of the lord pope'. Cf. Siegfried of Mainz, letter to Pope
Alexander II (above n. 514): 'may you deign to send from your side persons with
your written authority to investigate and judge so great a case'. See Schumann
(1912) pp. 12–13; Gresser (2006) pp. 94–6. Dr Eimhín Walsh (who is preparing a
study of the writings of Peter Damian) has pointed out to me that there is no reference to this legation in any extant papal document or in any letter of Peter Damian
or in his biography by John of Lodi.

545 Livy XXVIII.26.2.

546 On Lampert's thought process here see Keller (1986) p. 171: 'It was a consequence
of the Ottonian-Salian royal theology that the strictest standards must be imposed
on him who, as king, was elevated far above all men. The king must not through his
conduct give a bad example to those who were subject to his lordship and endanger
the welfare of all by bringing down God's anger on himself.' Cf. Bishop Wido of
Ferrara, *On the schism of Hildebrand* I.3, p. 536 (written in 1086): 'How is [the king]
to be a punisher of crime, an avenger of sin, when he himself is in the toils of the
same errors? Under what covenant will he preserve the law for others, when he has
destroyed the rule of justice in himself?' See Robinson (1999) p. 112.

547 Livy V.43.1.

emperor a man who had done his utmost to betray the Christian faith by setting so pernicious an example.

Then indeed all the princes who were present rounded upon the king and said that the decision of the Roman pontiff was just.[548] They begged him in God's name *not* to *leave any reproach on* his *honour*[549] and not to stain the majesty of the title of king with the impurity of such a shameful deed. Moreover he should not give the queen's kinsmen a reason for rebellion and a just motive for throwing the State into disorder. For *if they were true men*,[550] they would undoubtedly – since they disposed of very many weapons and extensive property – cause so great an insult to their daughter to be expiated by some extraordinary outrage.[551] The king was ground down rather than converted by this speech. He replied: 'If you are immovably and stubbornly resolved upon this, I for my part shall bear, as best I can, the burden of which I cannot rid myself.' Thus his hatred was intensified as a result of the effort of reconciliation. To be sure, he agreed that the queen should be recalled to partnership in the kingship but he himself rapidly returned to Saxony, taking barely forty knights with him, so as to avoid meeting and seeing her. The queen followed at a slow pace with the rest of the forces and with the royal insignia. When she came to him in Goslar,[552] it was with difficulty that

548 Cf. *Annals of Niederaltaich* 1069, p. 77: 'an envoy of the lord pope appeared, who with dreadful threats declared to [the achbishop] that if he himself became the author of this unjust separation, as long as the pope lived, he would never participate in the priestly ministry. Hearing this, the synod was dissolved and the queen was once more restored to the royal marriage-bed.' See Meyer von Knonau (1890) pp. 626–7; Robinson (1999) pp. 111–12; Gresser (2006) pp. 95–6.

549 I Maccabees 9:10.

550 Livy I.58.7; II.38.5.

551 Bertha's father, Count Odo of Savoy (above n. 491) was dead (†1057/1060). On her brothers, Count Peter of Savoy, margrave of Turin and Count Amadeus of Savoy, see Meyer von Knonau (1890) p. 626 n. 44. On the situation of Bertha's mother, Margravine Adelaide of Turin (above n. 491), in 1069 see the uncorroborated report of *Annals of Niederaltaich* 1069, p. 78: 'Adelaide, the king's mother-in-law, was enraged with the men of Lodi and she therefore laid waste to the province and besieged the city of Lodi itself with a great host and, after capturing it, caused it to be burned.' See Meyer von Knonau (1890) pp. 632–3; Robinson (1999) p. 111.

552 Lampert's account is contradicted by the evidence of the 'intervention clauses' of the royal diplomas: *D.H.IV* 224, issued in Merseburg on 26 October 1069 through the intervention of 'Bertha, consort of our marriage-bed and kingdom'; *D.H.IV* 227, issued in Allstedt on 4 December 1069 through the intervention of 'our beloved Queen Bertha, consort of our kingdom and our marriage-bed'; *D.H.IV* 228, issued in Haina (east of Eisenach) on 14 December 1069 through the intervention of Queen Bertha. See Gawlik (1970) p. 190. Lampert alone placed the king and queen in Goslar at the end of the year.

his close associates forced him to go to meet her, whereupon he received her far more kindly than was his custom. But his love immediately grew cold again and he *returned to his old courses*[553] and to his former hardheartedness. Because the plan of ending his marriage, which he had now often attempted, had proved ineffectual, he decided that henceforward he would share with her only the royal title and thus behave as though she was not his wife.[554]

In that year the vines and all the woodland trees were to a very large extent unfruitful.[555]

Abbot Meginward of Hildesheim received the abbey of Reichenau, after gaining access to it by lavishing large sums of money.[556]

Bishop Rumold of Constance, a man of great dignity befitting his years, died[557] and was succeeded by Charles, a canon of Magdeburg.[558] He was at first received in a friendly manner by the clergy of Constance but with the passing of time, since he carried out his duties entirely as he pleased rather than in a reasonable manner, the clergy became angry and began to abstain from communion with him because of the simoniacal heresy by means of which he was said to have gained possession of the bishopric. They also charged him with having secretly carried off

---

553 Terence, *Adelphi* I.1.46.

554 As well as the evidence of the royal diplomas (above n. 552 and subsequently *DD.H.IV* 229, 230–1, issued 29 December 1069 and 11 April 1070 through the intervention of Bertha), there is the fact, noted by Ranke (1888) p. 135, that Lampert himself recorded the birth of a son, below 1071, p. 151. Even more striking is the evidence of *D.H.IV* 426 (21 September 1091), which, in commemorating the members of the imperial family buried in the cathedral of Speyer, mentions 'our daughter Adelaide and our son Henry'. Meyer von Knonau (1894) p. 85 n. 82 identified the latter as the son born in 1071 and the former as a daughter born earlier and therefore already in 1070.

555 Cf. *Annals of Weissenburg* 1068, p. 53; *Annals of Augsburg* 1069, p. 128 ('A grave famine').

556 Meginward, prior of the abbey of St Michael, Hildesheim; abbot of Reichenau (1070), abbot of St Michael, Hildesheim (1079). Cf. Berthold of Reichenau, *Chronicle* 1069, p. 123: 'In [Udalric's] place a certain Meginward of Hildesheim was with difficulty appointed abbot by the king, for the appointment was simoniacal and the brethren rebelled against him.' *Annals of Niederaltaich* 1071, p. 83, identified 'the abbot of Hildesheim, named Siegfried' as the simoniacal successor, confusing abbot and prior: see Giesebrecht in *Annales Altahenses maiores* p. 83 n. 4. See also above n. 286. On his simony see Meyer von Knonau (1894) pp. 2–3; Feierabend (1913) p. 37.

557 Rumold (above n. 94) +4 November. Cf. Berthold of Reichenau, *Chronicle* 1069, p. 123: 'an extremely pious and humane man ... and the most careful enlarger and steward of the church's treasure'.

558 Charles (Carloman), bishop of Constance (1070–1).

most of the treasures of the church.[559] When this accusation reached Rome, the Roman pontiff commanded the archbishop of Mainz that he was by no means to consecrate Charles until the case had been very carefully investigated in his presence.[560]

The bishop of Toul died[561] and the chancellor Pibo succeeded him.[562] Adalbero, canon of Metz, was appointed as chancellor in his place.[563]

1070

The king celebrated Christmas in Freising.[564]

The bishops of Mainz, Cologne and Bamberg came to Rome, summoned by the lord pope.[565] There the bishop of Bamberg was accused of having

559 Cf. *Acta* of the Synod of Mainz (1071) in *Codex Udalrici* 37, p. 72: the canons of the cathedral of Constance 'unanimously' opposed Charles's consecration 'because ... he had bestowed on them none of the care of the pastoral office, ... he had been unsparing in his plundering of the treasures of the church'; Berthold of Reichenau, *Chronicle* 1070, p. 124: 'that simoniac ... usurped the cathedral church.... he secretly divided up the sacred vessels, the ceremonial vestments and the altar-fronts ...; he scattered gold, jewels and all the treasure of the church among his followers'; *Annals of Niederaltaich* 1071, p. 82: 'as soon as he came to Constance, he began to take their benefices from the clergy and the laity and to confiscate their possessions, wishing to recover from their property the money that he seemed previously to have spent in acquiring the bishopric'. See Meyer von Knonau (1894) pp. 1–3, 5; Schieffer (1972) pp. 46–50; Robinson (1999) p. 118.

560 Cf. Berthold of Reichenau, *Chronicle* 1070, p. 124: 'When Pope Alexander [II] was fully informed of this by the brethren in a letter of complaint, ... he sent a letter to the archbishop of Mainz, with the command that he should by no means consecrate him as bishop unless he cleared himself of the aforesaid heresy according to canon law.' *Annals of Niederaltaich* 1071, p. 82: the pope 'ordered the archbishop of Mainz, whose suffragan [Carloman] was, that he should by no means receive episcopal consecration from him unless he had first investigated his case with a synodal judgement'. The papal letter to Siegfried of Mainz is not extant.

561 Udo, bishop of Toul (1051–69) +14 July.

562 Pibo (above n. 510).

563 Adalbero, chancellor of the German kingdom (1069–76). See Gawlik (1978) pp. XXXVI–XXXVIII.

564 25 December 1069. Cf. Berthold of Reichenau, *Chronicle* 1070, p. 124; *D.H.IV* 229 (29 December 1069). See Meyer von Knonau (1890) p. 631.

565 Siegfried of Mainz (above n. 210), Anno of Cologne (above n. 139) and Herman I of Bamberg (above n. 449). No other source refers to a summons by Alexander II. Corroboration of Siegfried of Mainz's presence in Rome is found in his letter to Alexander II (of winter 1070–1) in *Codex Udalrici* 36, p. 68: 'For when I was in Rome ... you forbade me to consecrate him who was designated bishop of Constance.' The report in Frutolf of Michelsberg, *Chronica* 1073, p. 82, seems to refer to the same occasion: 'Bishop Anno of Cologne and Herman of Bamberg were sent to Rome to collect the money that was owed to the king.' See the analysis of Lampert's account in Schieffer (1971) pp. 152–74, who argued that the three prelates happened to be in Rome at the same time.

paid money and seized the bishopric by means of simoniacal heresy. He gave many precious gifts to the pope and thereby transformed his hostility towards himself to such great kindness that this man, who was thought to be unlikely to escape without the loss of his office and the priesthood, not only went unpunished for the offence with which he had been charged but also received as a gift from the apostolic see the pallium and certain other archiepiscopal insignia.[566] For his part, the archbishop of Mainz greatly desired to resign from his archbishopric and to retire to the freedom of private life but with the greatest difficulty he was dissuaded from his purpose both by the authority of the Roman pontiff and by the more considered advice of those who were present.[567] They were all in general sharply reprimanded for selling holy orders in an act of simoniacal heresy and for indiscriminately sharing communion with those who bought them and laying their hands on them in consecration. Finally the pope received an oath from them that they would no longer do such things[568] and they were allowed to depart in peace to their own land.

Duke Godfrey of the Lotharingians, who was well known and admired in almost all the lands for the greatness of his deeds, died and was buried in Verdun.[569] He was succeeded by his son Gozelo, who was indeed a young man of outstanding abilities but a hunchback.[570]

Margrave Udalric of the Carinthians died.[571]

566 Cf. Bonizo of Sutri, *To a Friend* VII, p. 223: 'a certain Herman, bishop of Bamberg, came to Rome for the purpose of receiving the pallium' (here dated *ca.* 1074). Schieffer (1971) pp. 158–60 argued that this was the purpose of Herman's journey in 1070. The pallium had been conferred on the previous bishops of Bamberg, Hartwig (1053) and Gunther (early 1060s): Zotz (1982) pp. 156–7. Schieffer (1971) pp. 158–9 considered that there was no question in 1070 of the accusations of simony for which Herman was condemned in 1075 (see below pp. 243–51).

567 'It is precisely in [Siegfried's] aim of resignation ... that the reason for his journey to Rome is most likely to be found': Schieffer (1971) p. 164. Cf. below 1072, p. 161.

568 This seems to be an exaggerated account of the oath administered on the reception of the pallium. Cf. the oath of Archbishop Ralph of Tours to Alexander II: 'I ... received the election and the investiture of the bishopric of Tours neither by making a gift nor any other bargain contrary to the holy canons, to the best of my knowledge', cited Schieffer (1971) p. 168 n. 88.

569 Godfrey III, 'the Bearded' (above n. 33) †24 December 1069. Cf. Berthold of Reichenau, *Chronicle* 1069, p. 123: 'Duke Godfrey, who was entirely outstanding among secular men' See Meyer von Knonau (1890) p. 637; Goez (1995) p. 213.

570 Godfrey IV ('the Hunchback'), duke of Lower Lotharingia (1069–76). Cf. Sigebert of Gembloux, *Chronica* 1070, p. 362: 'although small in his body, nevertheless excellent in his intellect'; *Song of the Saxon War* III.80, p. 17: 'bearing the heart of his father, although unequal in his body'.

571 Margrave Udalric I of Carniola and Istria (above n. 264) †6 March. See Meyer von Knonau (1894) p. 34.

The king celebrated Easter in Hildesheim.[572] There a fight broke out between the king's knights and the knights of the bishop.[573] But the king's knights gained the upper hand in the encounter; they killed very many of the bishop's knights, captured *the instigators of the conflict*[574] and, on the king's orders, put them in chains. The king celebrated the Lord's Ascension in Quedlinburg[575] and Whitsun in Merseburg.[576] *The most venerable temple*[577] in Quedlinburg, together with all its neighbouring buildings, caught fire and was reduced to ashes. It is uncertain whether this occurred through divine punishment or through an unfortunate accident.[578]

At that time Duke Otto of the Bavarians *was* of high renown in the palace and *of great authority*[579] in the State.[580] But, as *envy* is always accustomed *to follow glory*,[581] he was envied by very many worthless men, who lamented that his power and his boundless fame should stand in the way of their wickedness. They were anxiously on the watch for an opportunity to crush him. They therefore secretly incited an individual named Egino,[582] who was a noble man but branded with

---

572 4 April. *Annals of Niederaltaich* 1070, p. 79 place the celebrations 'in Speyer' but *DD.H.IV* 230–1, dated 11 April, was issued in Goslar. Hence Kilian (1886) p. 46 and Meyer von Knonau (1894) pp. 7–8 preferred Lampert's version.

573 Hezelo (above n. 121). See Meyer von Knonau (1894) p. 7.

574 Livy XXVIII.26.10. See Billanovich (1945) p. 77.

575 13 May. See Kilian (1886) p. 46; Meyer von Knonau (1894) p. 8.

576 23 May. But cf. *Annals of Niederaltaich* 1070, p. 79: 'at Whitsun he held an assembly of princes in Meissen'. Kilian (1886) p. 46 and Meyer von Knonau (1894) p. 8 n. 19 preferred Lampert's version.

577 Livy XLII.3.6; XLII.12.6. See Billanovich (1945) p. 109.

578 Cf. *Annals of Corvey* 1070, p. 6: 'Quedlinburg was burned down.'

579 Livy XXIX.29.9; XXXVIII.32.9.

580 Otto of Northeim, [II] duke of Bavaria (above n. 261). Cf. Frutolf of Michelsberg, *Chronica* 1071, p. 80: 'He was of Saxon birth, a man of the most renowned nobility, with whom very few could compare in wisdom and military ability and who was held in … high regard by all the princes.' On the extent of Otto's influence (cf. *DD.H.IV* 209–10, 215) see Meyer von Knonau (1894) pp. 9–11 and n. 23; Lange (1961) p. 33; Robinson (1999) p. 65.

581 Sallust, *Jugurtha* 55.

582 Cf. *Annals of Niederaltaich* 1069, p. 77: 'a certain man named Egino'; Bruno of Merseburg, *Saxon War* c. 19, p. 25: 'a certain man named Egino, who possessed no virtue except boldness'; Frutolf of Michelsberg, *Chronica* 1071, p. 80: 'a certain Egino, born in the middling rank, lacking in property, well known only for his boldness and wickedness, crept into the court under the protection of certain of the king's faithful followers'. Lampert subsequently identified 'Count Giso [of Gudensberg?] and Adalbert [of Schaumburg?]' as having 'incited that same reprobate [Egino] to fabricate this tragic story' (below, 1073, p. 205 and nn. 1073–4). See Meyer von Knonau (1894) pp. 9–13; Lange (1961) pp. 31–3; Fenske (1977) pp. 92–4; Robinson (1999) pp. 65–8.

every kind of wrongdoing, to bring about his ruin and murder. He brought against Otto the accusation that he had repeatedly urged Egino with many pleas and promises to kill the king and as evidence of his credibility he produced the sword that he claimed to have been given by Otto for such a wicked and impious purpose.[583] If Otto denied the charge, he was prepared to support his statement by volunteering any proof that was required. When this accusation became common knowledge, all those whom Otto had offended in his pursuit of the general good came forward, enraged and combative, and tried with all their might and using all their influence to inflame the king's anger against him. The king, therefore, summoned Otto to Mainz, together with the rest of the princes, to an assembly.[584] He there made public this allegation and, when Otto denied it, allowed him a delay in proceedings of six weeks, so that he was to come to Goslar on 1 August to disprove the charge brought against him by personal combat with his accuser.[585]

Departing after this pronouncement, the princes began to debate the injustice of this stipulation, saying that it was neither good nor just that a man of the highest nobility, of the most blameless reputation in the eyes of all men and never touched by the stain of an adverse rumour, should be ordered to fight with a most infamous villain who had long ago obliterated whatever nobility he had inherited from his ancestors by theft, highway robbery, in short by every kind of shameful and vicious act.[586] Otto himself was exasperated by this insulting treatment. Nevertheless he trusted to God as a witness fully aware of his innocence and preferred to fight with anyone, even an unworthy opponent, regardless of his own lineage, rather than remain under the suspicion of so evil a deed. He therefore came on the appointed day *with a troop of*

---

583 Lampert, *Libellus de institutione Herveldensis ecclesiae* II, p. 354: 'Duke Otto of the Bavarians was accused of a crime against the king.' Cf. *Annals of Niederaltaich* 1069, p. 77: Egino 'declared that he had received from the duke's hand a sword with which he had promised that he would be the killer of the king'; Bruno of Merseburg, *Saxon War* c. 19, p. 25: Egino would 'say that the duke had negotiated with him the death of the king'.

584 On 19 June, according to Kilian (1886) p. 46; 'approximately three weeks after Whitsun', according to Meyer von Knonau (1894) p. 14.

585 Cf. *Annals of Niederaltaich* 1070, p. 79: Otto 'was commanded to go home in order to appear in Goslar on a certain day and to clear himself of that same charge before the king and the princes by single combat'. See Meyer von Knonau (1894) p. 15; Lange (1961) p. 34; Robinson (1999) p. 68. Kilian (1886) pp. 46–50 argued that the journey would require more than seven weeks. Cf. *D.H.IV* 236 (6 August, Goslar).

586 Cf. Frutolf of Michelsberg, *Chronica* 1071, p. 80: 'Otto scorned to fight with Egino, as a duke with a brigand, a man of the highest nobility with one of none'.

armed men[587] to the neighbourhood of Goslar. He sent envoys to the king, declaring that, if he was granted a safe conduct to come there and to defend his cause, he was prepared to appear immediately, subject to the conditions that the princes of the kingdom had judged to be fair, and to disprove the charge that had been brought against him. To this the king replied violently and harshly that he promised him peace or safety neither in coming there nor in defending his cause. He expected only this: that Otto was to come to Goslar at once, according to the agreement, and, if he supposed himself to be innocent, he should engage in combat with his opponent and commit his cause to God, the most just of judges. If Otto did not do this, the king would have no regard for the contradictory state of the laws and pay no heed to the clash of opinions, but would consider him as having been convicted and as having acknowledged that he was guilty of the enormity of so great a crime.[588] When this reply was brought to the duke, it seemed to those who wished to give him appropriate advice that it was neither safe nor honourable for him to expose himself to be abused and harassed by the anger of the king that was thus inflamed against him. For in a situation in which no decision had yet been made and no charge had yet been proved, the king had not granted him safe conduct to come there, although according both to divine law and to human law[589] this had always been granted to all defendants in all cases. *His hope* of pardon thus *came to nothing*[590] and he returned home with nothing accomplished, thinking it better to preserve his life by means of weapons, as long as he could, than to be shamefully killed, just as cattle are slaughtered, to satisfy the hatred of his enemies.

587 Livy I.52.5.

588 Cf. *Annals of Niederaltaich* 1070, p. 79: Otto 'was indeed present on the appointed day but nevertheless declined to come into the king's presence, sending word to the king that he could not come to the court unless the king granted him sureties of an assured peace in coming and departing. The king said to him, "Peace will be guaranteed to him when he comes to me and afterwards, provided that the accused appears to be innocent." Reflecting on this answer very deeply, he again sent to ask for a further delay and he immediately mounted his horse and departed in haste'; Berthold of Reichenau, *Chronicle* 1070, p. 125: 'an opportunity was given to [Otto] to clear himself in a judicial duel. Since he did not wish to do so, he seized on this as a pretext for rebellion'; Bruno of Merseburg, *Saxon War* c. 19, p. 25: 'When a day had been appointed for that fight, Otto was warned by his friends, bishops and other princes, that if he came to Goslar, where the duel was to be fought, he would not escape from there with his life even if he defeated his adversary. He therefore chose to lose his office through injustice, rather than to undergo a trial in which he would encounter violence rather than justice.'

589 On Lampert's term *ius fori*, meaning secular law, as opposed to ecclesiastical law, see Niermeyer – van de Kieft (2002) p. 587.

590 Livy III.58.6; XXXV.31.7.

The next day the king asked the princes of Saxony to pronounce sentence on Otto, because he was of Saxon birth and because they were particularly hostile towards him on account of their private feuds.[591] They judged that he was guilty of the offence of treason and they decreed that, if he was taken prisoner, he was to be punished by the imposition of a capital sentence.[592] The king's friends instantly undertook, each to the utmost of his ability, to hunt him down with fire and sword. Very many men also took up arms against him, not out of loyalty towards the king nor out of devotion to the State nor in revenge for any private injury but solely out of greed for booty.[593] Thus on all sides the *reins of wrath*[594] were loosened, or rather torn asunder. All men rushed to attack him, *plundered* his estates and other possessions, laid them waste and burned them; they *cut down*, mutilated and murdered his servants and the labourers in the fields, *if they chanced to meet with*[595] them. Thus, finally, unbridled anger raved beyond all bounds and all shame so that the violence of their savage hostility did not spare even the churches and places of worship that Otto had built for God at his own expense.

Then the king assembled an army[596] and set out so that he himself should put *the finishing touches to the work.*[597] Either by taking hostages or by imposing an oath, he bound the princes whom he knew to be under an obligation to Otto through kinship or some other connection, so that they would not go over to him. He ordered the total destruction

591 2 August. He was judged according to Saxon law: Meyer von Knonau (1894) p. 18; Mitteis (1927) pp. 34–5; Höss (1945) p. 19; Lange (1961) p. 36.

592 Cf. *Annals of Niederaltaich* 1070, p. 79: 'According to the judgement of [the princes] it was decided that he was guilty of treason and, his duchy returning to the king's control, it was ordered that he should be pursued by all men'; Frutolf of Michelsberg, *Chronica* 1071, p. 80: 'Thus Otto lost the duchy of Bavaria, like one guilty of treason'; 1072, p. 80: the king 'strove to destroy him utterly, as one who was truly an enemy of the State'.

593 Cf. *Annals of Niederaltaich* 1070, pp. 79–80: 'Certain of the king's close friends fell upon his estates and, when they had laid waste to them all, they burned his buildings and villages.'

594 Vergil, *Aeneid* XII.499.

595 Livy XXV.29.9.

596 Cf. Siegfried of Mainz, letter to Pope Alexander II in *Codex Udalrici* 36, p. 69: 'the command of the royal power prevented the holding of a council, compelling me and the other princes of the kingdom to participate in his military expedition'. See Kilian (1886) p. 50; Meyer von Knonau (1894) p. 19.

597 Cicero, *Brutus sive de claris oratoribus* 33.126.

of Otto's castle of Hanstein,[598] from which the garrison had been withdrawn *immediately at the first shock of war.*[599] He had already moved the army to another castle, which is called Desenberg.[600] Although they were *unassailable because of their location*[601] and they were abundantly supplied with all the resources that were necessary for the conduct of the war, they thought it better to surrender of their own accord rather than try *the doubtful fortunes of war.*[602] Leaving a garrison there, the king led his army into more remote areas to destroy also the possessions of Otto's wife;[603] he burned many estates splendidly furnished with buildings and all the signs of wealth; he plundered property; he perpetrated many cruel and hostile acts against women and children, for the men had hidden themselves in the mountains and unfrequented woodlands. Innocent men over whom there was not the slightest suspicion of any offence suffered such great violence and cruelty during that expedition at the hands of their own king that they could not have suffered worse violence or worse cruelty from barbarians.

At last Duke Otto was grief-stricken and his patience and perseverance were overcome by the weight of his misfortunes. Taking with him three thousand picked men, trained in every branch of military discipline, he therefore made an attack on Thuringia.[604] He burned the estates of the royal fisc, which abounded in all kinds of riches; he brought away much booty and in the first place he used this reward to satisfy his knights – the majority of whom only *the hope of plunder had enticed* to be his comrades

598 Hanstein, east of Witzenhausen. 'Through [the castle's] dominant position on the right bank of the Werra ... Otto had control of the lower course of this river': Meyer von Knonau (1894) p. 20.

599 Livy XXVII.32.7; cf. I.2.4.

600 Desenberg, near Warburg, north of the River Diemel.

601 Livy V.6.9; XXIV.37.2; XLII.67.7.

602 Cicero, *Oratio pro Marcello* 5; Sallust, *Catilina* 57; Lucan III.51, IV.390. See Struve (1970a) p. 115 n. 6.

603 Richenza, daughter of Duke Otto II of Swabia (of the family of the Ezzones), married (1) Count Herman of Werl; (2) Otto of Northeim (*ca.* 1050). These possessions were probably the Westphalian estates inherited from her father in 1047: see Lange (1961) p. 10.

604 Cf. *Annals of Niederaltaich* 1070, p. 80: Otto 'fled to the mountainous regions of the forest called *Chetil,* gathered together such associates as he could and from there made sallies now here, now there and laid waste episcopal lands and royal villages with fire and plunder'. Otto 'regarded the proceedings against him and his condemnation as unlawful and, because he evidently felt himself to be guiltless, he resorted to self-help, according to the Germanic right of resistance': Lange (1961) p. 40. See also Höss (1945) p. 25; Robinson (1999) p. 69.

in *war*[605] – and made them faithful and true to him. Thus laying waste the countryside, he advanced beyond Eschwege. There he *was joined by crowds* of peasants *from his estates,*[606] whom the king's knights had left with nothing except a wretched existence. Otto distributed part of his booty among them, admonished them to endure the blows of heaven's chastisement with a courageous spirit and entreated them, since they could not bear arms, to address prayers to God on his behalf.

Meanwhile the Thuringians (who some years before had bound themselves by an oath not to *allow* robbers and plunderers *to go unpunished*)[607] were exasperated by the pillaging of their property and *issued a call to arms.*[608] Huge crowds of troops rapidly assembled and immediately followed the enemy. They found them not far from Eschwege and joined battle with them on 2 September.[609] *The outcome of the battle* was not *long in doubt.*[610] For when those who were with Duke Otto eagerly attacked them, they were barely able *to withstand the first violent onset*[611] of the battle and were put to flight. Some tried *to escape into the nearby mountains and forests;*[612] others made a very great effort to return *at full gallop*[613] along the road by which they had come, cursing this most inauspicious throw of the dice of fortune. Finally, the man who had at first been the most active originator and instigator of the decision to join battle, that is, Count Ruotger,[614] now took on the role of *the first originator* and standard bearer *of flight*[615] and crossed over the mountains and hills (to use the common expression) *faster than any wind,*[616] like a modern-day

---

605 Sallust, *Catalina* 57.1

606 Livy V.46.4.

607 *Ibid.,* II.9.2. See above 1069, p. 119.

608 Livy III.50.11; VII.12.3; X.32.9; XLI.26.2. See Billanovich (1945) p. 67.

609 Cf. *Annals of Corvey* 1070, p. 6: Otto 'caused a great slaughter of men at Eschwege'; *Annals of Ottobeuren* 1070, p. 7: 'Duke Otto caused great slaughter against the king at Eschwege'. See Meyer von Knonau (1894) pp. 21–2; Lange (1961) pp. 40–1; Fenske (1977) p. 81. On the partisanship revealed in this account and Lampert's ironic presentation of Ruotger see Meyer von Knonau (1894) p. 22 n. 35; Eckhardt (1964) p. 67.

610 Livy XXVII.14.6; XXVIII.14.12; XXXIII.18.16.

611 *Ibid.,* II.10.7; XLIII.10.6.

612 *Ibid.,* XXVIII.16.6; cf. XXVIII.8.9.

613 *Ibid.,* I.5.8.

614 Ruotger (Rucker/Rugger), count in the Werratal in western Thuringia (*fl.* 1070–5), whose family figured in the twelfth century as counts of Bilstein.

615 Livy XXVIII.16.6.

616 C. Silius Italicus, *Punica* IV.6.

Jeduthun.[617] Three hundred of the Thuringians, more or less, fell in that encounter. On the other side one man was killed and two were wounded.

After Duke Otto had *given the signal for retreat*[618] and after he had with the greatest difficulty called off his troops from the work of slaughtering the enemy, he remained for some time in that same camp. *As the day was already declining into evening*,[619] he discharged the majority of the princes in his army in peace, each to his own home. He himself, taking with him as many troops as the situation seemed to demand, rapidly made for the more distant parts of Saxony and there he spent the whole winter until Christmas.[620] He lived partly on plundering and pillaging and partly on the property of Count Magnus,[621] in whom he found a comrade in war and in all perils and a most faithful defender of his innocence. Magnus was the son of Duke Otto of Saxony, an excellent young man, who in peacetime was *most attentive to what was* good and *just*[622] beyond his years and in wartime was second to none in boldness and martial courage. When news of the defeat inflicted in Eschwege reached the king, he paid no further attention to other business but returned in great haste to Goslar and never left that place until Christmas.[623] He was evidently afraid that in his absence the enemy might reduce to glowing embers and ashes that estate which was so dear and so agreeable to him and in which the German kings were accustomed to reside as their home and domestic hearth;[624] for his enemies were said to have threatened this and to have insisted on it in their frequent discussions.

Bishop Adalbero of Worms died, suffocated (so it is said) by his own

617 I Chronicles 16:41; 25:3, 6. Cf. the explanation of the name in Isidore of Seville, *Etymologiae* VII.8.28: '*Jeduthun*: "leaping over them" or "jumping over them".'

618 Livy II.62.2. See Billanovich (1945) p. 112.

619 Suetonius, *De vita Caesarum: Otho* 7.

620 Cf. *Annals of Augsburg* 1071, p. 128: 'Duke Otto of the Bavarians withdrew to the Liutizi'. See Meyer von Knonau (1894) pp. 22–3; Lange (1961) p. 41.

621 Magnus Billung, duke of Saxony (1073/4–1106), son of Ordulf (Otto) Billung, duke of Saxony (1059–72). Cf. Berthold of Reichenau, *Chronicle* 1070, p. 125: 'Magnus, son of Duke Otto of northern Saxony, joined with [Otto]'; Bruno of Merseburg, *Saxon War* c. 19, p. 25: Otto 'made an alliance with Magnus, duke of Saxony, together with whom he waged a cruel war against the king for almost two years'; Adam of Bremen, *Gesta* III.60, p. 206. See Meyer von Knonau (1894) p. 23; Lange (1961) p. 41; Fenske (1977) p. 64; Robinson (1999) p. 69.

622 Vergil, *Aeneid* II.427.

623 See Kilian (1886) p. 51; Meyer von Knonau (1894) pp. 23–4. See also below n. 629.

624 For Lampert on Goslar see also above, 1066 and below, 1071, 1075, pp. 109, 135, 270. See Rothe (1940) pp. 21–31; Wilke (1970) pp. 18–24, 30–3; Robinson (1999) p. 80.

obesity.[625] Adalbert was his successor.[626]

The deacon Aribo, brother of the margraves William and Otto,[627] was killed by his own serfs. This was a man who was exceedingly learned both in divine and in secular literature but because of his wantonness and the lack of moderation in his character, he was deservedly regarded by all good men as burdensome and detestable.

The woodland trees were as unfruitful as in the previous year.[628] But the fertility of the vines was so great that in very many places the grapes could scarcely be harvested because of their sheer numbers.

1071

The king celebrated Christmas in Goslar.[629] There, through the inter-cession of Duke Rudolf of the Swabians, Welf, the son of Margrave Azzo of Italy,[630] received the duchy of Bavaria. He had married the daughter of Duke Otto of the Bavarians and on another occasion he had again sworn an oath of marital fidelity.[631] As long as the situation was calm, therefore, and also as long as he hoped that the war, which had been begun so rashly, could be brought to an end without a great alteration in public affairs, he bestowed conjugal love and honour on his wife and

---

625 Adalbero (see above n. 454) ✝6 August. Hartman Schedel's collection of extracts from the *Annals* (see above pp. 2 and n. 5, 35 and n. 163) reads: 'Bishop Adalbero of Worms, a monk of St Gallen and brother of the duke of the Swabians'.

626 Adalbert, bishop of Worms (1070–1107).

627 Aribo, of the family of the counts of Weimar-Orlamünde, brother of the Margraves William (above n. 252) and Otto (above n. 265) of Meissen.

628 See above, 1069, p. 124.

629 25 December 1070. Cf. *Annals of Niederaltaich* 1071, p. 80: 'The king celebrated Christmas in Bamberg.' Kilian (1886) p. 51 and Meyer von Knonau (1894) pp. 24 n. 38, 41, accepted Lampert's version, on the basis of *D.H.IV* 238, issued on 6 January 1071 in Goslar.

630 Welf IV, count in Swabia = Welf I, duke of Bavaria (1070–7, 1096–1101), son of Albert Azzo II, margrave of Este (✝1097), and Cuniza, daughter of Count Welf II. See Meyer von Knonau (1894) pp. 24–6; Störmer (1991) pp. 516–17; Robinson (1999) pp. 70–1. On the role of Duke Rudolf of Swabia (above n. 203) see Meyer von Knonau (1894) pp. 27–8; Lange (1961) p. 41 (evidence of 'the ever clearer antago-nism of the Rheinfeldener towards Otto of Northeim'); Jakobs (1968) pp. 183, 193 (evidence of the kinship of Rudolf and Welf).

631 Ethelinde, married (1) Welf IV; (2) Count Herman I of Kalvelage (Westphalia). Cf. *Annals of Niederaltaich* 1071, p. 80: 'This Welf had married the daughter of that same Otto ... and had confirmed on oath that he would keep her according to the laws. When, therefore, he was already striving for his father-in-law's duchy and this did not seem to the royal advisers to be safe, he sent that wife back to her father and afterwards swore that he would never go near her again.' See Meyer von Knonau (1894) p. 25; Lange (1961) pp. 41–2.

upheld the cause of his father-in-law with his weapons and his advice, as far as he was able. But when he learned of the sentence that was passed on Otto and saw that from day to day war intensified and the king's anger against Otto became more violent, he broke all the agreements that they had made and all the bonds by which they had in turn strengthened their friendship, believing it to be better to endure the reproach of oath-breaking and the shame of a breach of faith than to involve his own most prosperous fortunes with Otto's hopelessly lost cause. And firstly, when Otto asked for help *in such a critical situation,*[632] he refused it; then he separated Otto's daughter from his embraces and from the companionship of the marriage bed and sent her back to her father. Finally he devoted all his efforts to taking possession of Otto's duchy, caring nothing about how much gold, how much silver, how much of his income and possessions he squandered, as long as he obtained what he desired.[633] It was, *therefore, sent into his hand* and he had power *and he prevailed*[634] but all men hated him because he had defiled the most glorious and most renowned office in the State by such dishonourable ambition. The king knew that this would not greatly please the princes of Bavaria both because it was contrary to their custom and their rights and because it had been done without consulting them.[635] For that reason he was disposed to go to Bavaria as quickly as possible, so that, if there chanced to be an uprising, he might suppress it in person. But on the other hand, he was not unaware that, if he went so far away, the enemy would immediately attack Goslar and reduce that residence, the most renowned in the kingdom, to ashes. After taking the advice of his close friends, *he left* certain princes of Saxony *there as a garrison,*[636] while he himself made preparations, as he had decided, to set out for Bavaria. Meanwhile Duke Otto saw that he had no hope left, since the fires of his enemies had consumed all his possessions and another man had taken possession of his duchy, primarily as a way of insulting him. He decided to *bring his affairs to a final crisis*[637] and, when the first oppor-

---

632 Livy IV.13.4.

633 Cf. *Annals of Niederaltaich* 1071, p. 80: after repudiating Ethelinde, Welf 'gave a quantity of his estates and his money to the king'.

634 A conflation of Daniel 8:25 and Hosea 12:3–4.

635 On the idea of the Bavarians' right of electing their duke cf. Thietmar of Merseburg, *Chronicon* V.14, p. 236: 'the Bavarians from the beginning possessed the power freely to elect their duke' (speech attributed to King Henry II). See Meyer von Knonau (1894) p. 40 n. 2; Störmer (1991) pp. 512–17.

636 Livy VII.37.13.

637 Cicero, *Orationes Philippicae in Marcum Antonium* VII.1. Cf. Livy III.17.10; XXII.9.6.

tunity occurred, to *engage in close fight*[638] with the king. He therefore
occupied the mountain called Hasungen,[639] so that it would be a place
of refuge for his knights, whatever might be the event of the battle.
Although it was very *secure by virtue of the natural conditions* and *the site*,[640]
he nevertheless made it even more secure by constructing fortifications.
He caused booty from the surrounding fields to be carried there and
then waited for the king.

When the king received the news, he did not delay but very rapidly assembled as many troops as he could in that situation of haste and confusion,
from Saxony, from Thuringia and from Hesse. He commanded the other
princes who lived further away to hasten to meet him fully armed, as fast
as they could, if it happened that the conflict could not be brought to an
end without a considerable delay. At that time the king made extensive
use of the advice of Count Eberhard, an exceedingly wise man.[641] The
latter saw that the enemy were so well trained in war and had already
been rendered so ferocious through sheer desperation (which very often
tends to *give courage even to the faint-hearted*)[642] that they neither could
be conquered nor could conquer without great damage to the State. He
therefore went to Duke Otto and began to implore him not to throw
himself and his followers into so great a danger: all hope of pardon, all
power of recovery had not yet been taken away from him. If he removed
his army from the mountain which he had seized and if he surrendered
to the king on reasonable conditions, Eberhard would promise him on
his oath that he would obtain from the king both pardon for the offence
of which he had been accused and the restoration of everything that he
had lost according to the law of war. As Otto agreed to this, Eberhard
brought the matter to the king and had no difficulty in persuading him,
since he had indeed already begun to be weary of the war, because he
saw that the princes were using their ingenuity to prolong the war and
to wage it in a dilatory fashion, on account of their personal sympathy

638 Livy I.33; II.50.

639 West of Kassel in northern Hesse. See Meyer von Knonau (1894) p. 42 and n. 4;
    Lange (1961) p. 42.

640 Livy XXIV.3.8; XLIV.31.6.

641 Probably Count Eberhard 'the Bearded' (+1078), who figures in royal diplomas
    of 1068–77. Cf. his intervention in *D.H.IV* 245 of 28 November 1071. See Gawlik
    (1970) pp. 43, 48, 159; Robinson (1999) p. 361. Holder-Egger, *Lamperti Annales* p.
    119 n. 3 and Lange (1961) p. 42 identified this 'Count Eberhard' as Count Eberhard
    III of Nellenburg (see below pp. 190 and n. 994, 263). Gawlik (1970) p. 48 and
    Tellenbach (1988) p. 359 identified him as Eberhard 'the Bearded'.

642 Statius, *Thebais* IV.12.

for that man. Peace was declared by both sides on oath and a truce was granted to Duke Otto until Easter,[643] when he would come to Cologne and perform the act of surrender according to the conditions that the princes had judged to be just. During this truce, after Duke Otto had dismissed his army and sent each man to his own home, Count Retheri,[644] who was a figure of no small importance in his party, was killed by his enemies as the result of a private feud.

Abbot Saracho of Corvey died[645] and he was succeeded by Werner, a monk of the same monastery.[646]

The king went to Bavaria,[647] as he had intended, and after he had to a limited extent settled the affairs of the kingdom there, as far as he was able, he returned to the Rhine.[648] He made a supreme effort to repair the castle of Hammerstein, which had long ago been demolished by previous kings.[649] He celebrated Easter in Cologne[650] and there he again granted Duke Otto a truce until Whitsun.[651] When the Easter festivities were over, he went to Liège.[652] There the widow of Count Baldwin[653] came to him, requesting the protection of the royal majesty against the ferocity and wickedness of Robert, the brother of Baldwin,[654] who had defeated

---

643 24 April. See Meyer von Knonau (1894) p. 43; Lange (1961) p. 43.

644 A Saxon count, otherwise unknown: see Meyer von Knonau (1894) p. 44 n.7.

645 Saracho, abbot of Corvey (1056–71) †9 January 1071.

646 Werner, abbot of Corvey (1071–9).

647 Cf. *Annals of Augsburg* 1071, p. 128: 'The king stayed in Augsburg on Quinquagesima Sunday', i.e. 6 March. See Kilian (1886) p. 51; Meyer von Knonau (1894) p. 44.

648 Cf. *DD.H.IV* 239–40, issued in Basel on 26 March and Strasbourg on 3 April. See Kilian (1886) p. 51; Meyer von Knonau (1894) p. 44.

649 The castle of Hammerstein (on the Rhine near Neuwied) had been partially dismantled by Henry II after a siege in December 1020: see Holtzmann (1941) p. 471. On the death of Count Otto of Hammerstein in 1036, the castle had come into the possession of the crown: see Bresslau (1884) pp. 360–1.

650 24 April. Cf. *Annals of Niederaltaich* 1071, p. 80: 'the king celebrated Easter Sunday in Liège'; likewise *Triumphus sancti Remacli Stabulensis* II.1, p. 450 and *D.H.IV* 408 of 22 November 1089 ('at our court assembled in Liège in Eastertide of the year 1071'). But see Kilian (1886) pp. 51–2 and Meyer von Knonau (1894) p. 46 n. 14. See also below n. 652.

651 I.e. 12 June. See Meyer von Knonau (1894) p. 46 and n. 15.

652 He was in Liège from 7 to 11 May, according to *Triumphus sancti Remacli Stabulensis* II.1–38, pp. 449–61; cf. *D.H.IV* 242, issued in Liège on 11 May. See Kilian (1886) p. 52 and Meyer von Knonau (1894) p. 47.

653 Richilde (†1086) married (1) Count Herman of Hainault and (2) Count Baldwin VI of Flanders (1067–71).

654 Robert I (Friso), count of Flanders (1071–93).

his brother in battle, robbed him of his life[655] and seized his county with tyrannical cruelty, expelling his wife and children.[656]

Perhaps it will not be disagreeable to the reader if *I complete* the history of these events *as briefly*[657] as I can. In the county and in the family of Baldwin there was a custom, preserved for many centuries, as though it had been sanctioned by a permanent law, that whichever of the sons found most favour with the father was to take the father's name and was to be the sole recipient of the office of prince in the whole of Flanders by hereditary succession.[658] The other brothers, however, were to lead a life without any distinction, subject to this brother and obeying his commands or were to travel to foreign parts and attempt to achieve eminence through their own deeds rather than abandon themselves to *idleness and folly*,[659] consoling themselves for their extreme poverty with empty fancies about their ancestry. This was done, of course, so that the province would not be divided into many parts and the splendour of that family decay through the dwindling of the family property.

When the elder Baldwin[660] had fathered two sons, Baldwin and Robert, therefore, he appointed Baldwin as the heir of all that he possessed. As soon as Robert seemed to be of an age fit for performing military service, the elder Baldwin prepared ships, supplied gold and other means sufficient for the expenses of a long journey and ordered him to go to the foreign peoples and, *if he was a true man*,[661] to acquire for himself a kingdom and riches by means of his own military talents. Acquiescing in his father's wish, Robert brought with him a crowd of men, by whom the region seemed to be oppressed, took ship and planned to go to Galicia and, if God responded favourably to his prayers, to conquer

---

655 It was not Count Baldwin VI but his son, Count Arnulf III of Flanders and Hainault, who died in the battle of Cassel on 22 February 1071. See Meyer von Knonau (1894) pp. 61–2.

656 Baldwin II, count of Hainault (1071–98), was the only surviving child of Baldwin VI and Richilde.

657 Sallust, *Jugurtha* 17.2 (a formulation frequently used by Sallust).

658 See Struve (1970a) pp. 91–2: 'Lampert's story about Robert Friso ... is an early example of the fixing in literary form of a tale of adventure with "jongleuresque" characteristics in the Latin language. The sources on which he drew are not known to us but it is quite conceivable that a vernacular version was available to him.' Cf. Meyer von Knonau (1890) pp. 374 n. 17; 573 n. 46; (1894) p. 37 n. 60. See also Struve (1970b) pp. 395–404.

659 Sallust, *Catilina* 4.1; *Auctor ad Herennium* 2.23.35.

660 Baldwin V ('the Islander'), count of Flanders (1035–67).

661 Livy XXV.18.11.

it. After a few days he reached an unknown coast, he went ashore and began to carry off plunder from the inhabitants of the place. The latter immediately gathered together from all directions, *fully armed, to ward off the attack*;[662] there was a fight and, although he valiantly withstood the assault for some time, they forced him to flee, pursued him as he fled back to the ships and slaughtered almost all of his companions. He himself barely escaped with a few men and returned to his father as the bearer of the news of so great a disaster. He was driven away by his father, who was full of reproaches for the ill success of his venture and, since he had not prospered by that route, he set off again to *try his fortune*[663] by another route, ready to brave every circumstance, even the very worst, in order to wash away the old stain by means of fresh deeds.

After he had repaired the ships and restored his troops to their former numbers, he entrusted himself once more to the waves of the sea to journey to a remote land where God would show the wanderer a dwelling place. And lo and behold! after a few days he was overtaken by a most violent storm and lost many of his men in a shipwreck, while he himself, naked and destitute of all possessions, escaped with great difficulty to the shore. He then put on the clothing of a common man and planned to go to Constantinople in the company of those who made the journey to Jerusalem for the sake of prayer. He had been invited there by frequent embassies from the Normans who served as the soldiers of the emperor of Constantinople and who promised him dominion over the whole of Greece if he came there.[664] But the emperor of Constantinople learned of this plan and placed guards on all the rivers by means of which a traveller can gain access to Greece, to keep watch so that he might be intercepted and killed on the spot. His efforts and endeavours were thus in vain.

Finally he perceived that whatever way he attempted to increase his renown turned out unhappily for him. He then turned his attention once and for all away from making war on foreign peoples and carried out an invasion of Frisia, which borders on Flanders and which had been ruled by the former Count Theoderic[665] and, after him, by

662 *Ibid.*, I.1.5.

663 *Ibid.*, XL.27 (Cf. Caesar, *Bellum Gallicum* III.6; 7.4; Sallust, *Jugurtha* 7.1). On the motif of *fortuna* in Lampert's work see Struve (1970a) pp. 91 n. 28; 114–17; on Robert I p. 115 n. 6.

664 Holder-Egger, *Lamperti Annales* p. 122 n. 1, suggested that Lampert erroneously ascribed to Robert I the journeys of Harald Hardrada of Norway to Constantinople and Jerusalem *ca.* 1045.

665 Count Theoderic IV of Holland (above n. 64).

Florentius, his brother.[666] He fought two battles there, in which he was defeated and put to flight. When at last the inhabitants of the place, exhausted by many battles, realised that his mind was inflexibly set either on death or on victory, they voluntarily surrendered to him.[667] As soon as his brother Baldwin learned of this – for his father, *weakened by disease and old age*, had already *yielded up his spirit to nature*[668] – he made preparations with great vigour and huge exertions to drive Robert from that land with a large force of armed men.[669] As he advanced with his army, Robert sent envoys to meet him, beseeching him to remember that he was Robert's brother and not to violate the laws of brotherhood, which are always sacred and inviolable even among barbarians. He should instead feel pity for the wanderings in foreign lands, the sufferings and the misfortunes in which he had worn out his whole life; he should rejoice that he himself was fortunate in his destiny, since he alone obtained the inheritance of their father without sharing it with his brother, although according to the law of nations he ought to have divided it with him. Robert, however, had been exiled from his fatherland, robbed of his father's inheritance and driven from the summit of renown enjoyed by his ancestors *down to the uttermost poverty*.[670] He had made war on foreign peoples; he had thrown land and sea into an uproar; he had, in short, left nothing undone in his efforts to avoid troubling his brother with respect to the share of their father's property that belonged to him. Now, worn out by his exertions, exhausted by his hardships, he had with great difficulty settled down in a very small corner of the world, no part of which – as was very well known – was under Baldwin's authority. Finally, he was firmly resolved and could not be diverted by any force or compulsion from his decision, that here he was to find either repose for his approaching old age or at least a burial place after an honourable death. Baldwin was not at all affected by these words and moved his army at a rapid pace towards Frisia.

---

666 Florentius I, count of Holland (1049–61).

667 Robert I did not acquire the territory by conquest. Cf. *Annales Egmundani* 1063, p. 447: 'Robert ... joined to himself in marriage Countess Gertrude, the widow of Count Florentius, and thus acquired the county of Holland and Frisia'. See Meyer von Knonau (1890) pp. 373–4.

668 Sallust, *Jugurtha* 14.15. Baldwin V †1 September 1067.

669 Baldwin VI never waged war on Robert I. In 1070 Baldwin obtained an oath from his brother in an assembly in Bruges to protect the rights of his heir, Arnulf: Meyer von Knonau (1894) p. 36.

670 Livy IX.22.8; XXVII.9.5.

Then Robert was compelled by circumstances to arm the most promising of the young men whom he had with him and to advance to meet him. When they joined battle, many were killed and very many wounded on Baldwin's side and all were put to flight. Baldwin himself made a supreme effort to arrest the flight of these fugitives and to renew the battle but, as he *rashly forced his way*[671] into the closely packed ranks of the enemy, he was killed.[672] When he learned of his death, Robert immediately invaded Flanders and made the whole country subject to himself, as if by right of due succession. Baldwin had a son,[673] who was still a beardless youth, not yet of the age to bear arms. Stunned by the dreadful news of his father's death and the hostile invasion, he at once sought refuge with the king of the French, whose name was Philip,[674] seeking help and revenge for the killing of his father. For his father had often given both the king and his forefathers the most valuable support in hard times[675] and he had received from him as a gift some of those cities that Robert had seized. The king, utterly outraged by this shameful conduct, immediately and *rashly* led into Flanders *an army* that had been gathered together only *in a very hurried manner*,[676] presuming too much on the great numbers of his own forces and on the weakness of the enemy. When Robert was *inferior in strength*,[677] however, he was all the more eager *to use cunning*.[678] He *pretended* for some time *to be afraid* and eager *to flee*,[679] then unexpectedly and by means of an ambush he released his troops against the king's army and filled them with so great a terror that they threw away their weapons and strove with all their might to secure their safety by running away.[680]

671 *Ibid.*, II.20.1.

672 Baldwin VI died in his residence in Bruges on 17 July 1070: see Meyer von Knonau (1894) pp. 36–7 and n. 60.

673 Baldwin VI left two sons, Arnulf III, count of Flanders and Hainault (1070–1), and Count Baldwin II of Hainault (above n. 656).

674 Philip I, king of France (1060–1108), the feudal lord of the western provinces of the county of Flanders ('royal Flanders'), received a request for help from Arnulf III. See Meyer von Knonau (1894) p. 59.

675 Baldwin V, who was married to Adela, sister of the Capetian King Henry I, had been the guardian of his nephew, Philip I, during his minority. See Meyer von Knonau (1890) pp. 235–6; (1894) p. 59.

676 Livy VII.11.10.

677 *Ibid.*, XXV.27.8; XXVI.25.10; XLII.65.6.

678 Terence, *Eunuchus* V.4.2.

679 Livy VI.24.11.

680 This was the battle of Cassel, 22 February 1071, in which Philip I's army was defeated and Count Arnulf III died. See Meyer von Knonau (1894) pp. 61–2.

The son of Baldwin[681] subsequently *placed* little *hope in the weapons*[682] of the French and, taking his mother with him, he came to Henry, king of the Germans, who was at that time (as was mentioned before)[683] stationed in Liège, and humbly begged for his help against the violent conduct of his uncle. In order to place the king under a greater obligation to him, he gave up to St Lambert[684] the county of the former Count Reginher[685] together with the strongly fortified castle named Mons, which were the properties that his mother had received from her previous husband[686] as a marriage portion. The bishop of Liège[687] in his turn gave it to Duke Godfrey[688] and the latter in a similar fashion gave it as a benefice to the son of Baldwin himself. This was the price at which the king's support was, so to speak, purchased and he commanded the bishop of Liège and Duke Godfrey and also other princes of Lotharingia to provide help for Baldwin's son in adversity and to drive Robert out by force of arms if he would not voluntarily withdraw from the lands that he had unjustly seized. They immediately gathered an army and set out for Flanders.[689] When, however, they heard the news that Robert had already been restored to the favour of the king of the French, had made amends for his old offences and had committed himself to be steadfast and faithful to him,[690] they returned to their own land without accomplishing

681 The ten-year-old Count Baldwin II of Hainault (above n. 656).

682 Livy II.39.8; III.53.3.

683 7 –11 May 1071: see above p. 137 and n. 652.

684 I.e. to the bishopric of Liège.

685 Reginher V, count of Hainault (1013–39), father of Richilde.

686 Herman, count of Hainault (1039–50/1).

687 Dietwin, bishop of Liège (1048–75).

688 Duke Godfrey IV ('the Hunchback') of Lower Lotharingia (above n. 570). The trans-action is recorded in *D.H.IV* 242 (11 May 1071) and in a probably contemporary report: 'King Henry, coming to Liège, ... gave to St Mary and St Lambert the county of Hainault and the march of Valenciennes ... in the presence and with the agreement of Countess Richilde, together with her son Baldwin. And in the same place in the presence of the king and of all the princes Duke Godfrey became the vassal of the lord Bishop Dietwin, after receiving this benefice from him. The countess herself, however, ... received this same benefice from the duke' (*MGH Constitutiones* 1, 650). See Meyer von Knonau (1894) pp. 65–6.

689 Cf. *Annales Egmundani* 1071, p. 447: 'Duke Godfrey the Hunchback, together with Bishop William [of Utrecht] and a royal army, expelled Robert from Holland and powerfully subdued it to himself'; similarly Sigebert of Gembloux, *Chronica* 1071, p. 362; *Annales Patherbrunnenses* 1071, p. 95. See Meyer von Knonau (1894) pp. 68–9 and n. 53 ('Lampert exaggerates' in this account); Werner (1991) pp. 382–3.

690 Robert I was reconciled to Philip I and received investiture with the county of Flanders in March/April 1071: see Verlinden (1935) pp. 70–2.

anything. For they considered it foolhardy *to enter into combat*[691] against a most powerful king with only a private army. Thus Robert continued thereafter in undisturbed possession of the principality of Flanders.

The brethren of the monastery of Stablo dinned into the king's ears every day their demand for the return of the monastery of Malmédy, which the king had taken away from the abbot and, on the advice of the archbishop of Bremen (as mentioned above), had conferred on the archbishop of Cologne as a gift.[692] When the king remained unmoved by prayers, by tears and even by their importunate urging, they took counsel together and were inspired by a divine revelation (so it is said)[693] to put into effect this plan. They took out the bones of the blessed Remaclus, brought them to Liège and, while the king was holding a banquet in a certain famous place, they set the bones before him on the very table.[694] They implored him in God's name to show compassion, if not for the sons, then at least for so great a father,[695] who now reigned with Christ and every day proclaimed the wrongs that had been inflicted on him before the judgement-seat of the eternal Judge. If the king did not restore the saint's possessions, they would no longer be able to serve him simply because they lacked the necessities of life. This form of supplication, which had been devised to *obtain his good will*,[696] on the contrary greatly exasperated the king.[697] Enraged, he abandoned

691 Livy XXX.19.11.

692 Archbishops Adalbert of Bremen (above n. 48) and Anno of Cologne (above n. 139): see above p. 93 and n. 345. The sister-monasteries of Stablo (in the diocese of Liège) and Malmédy (in that of Cologne) had been intended by their founder to be under the rule of the same abbot. This principle was violated by the granting of Malmédy to Anno in 1065. In 1068 in Rome Abbot Theoderic of Stablo, in Anno's presence, had petitioned Pope Alexander II in vain for the return of Malmédy. See Meyer von Knonau (1890) pp. 587–9; (1894) pp. 48–54; Feierabend (1913) pp. 161–2; Semmler (1959) pp. 43–4, 180; Seibert (1991) pp. 541–3.

693 Cf. *Triumphus sancti Remacli Stabulensis* II.2, pp. 450–1: a miraculous occurrence experienced by the monks on the night of 6–7 May in Louvegnée, while en route for Liège.

694 8 May. The banquet was held in an orchard neighbouring the palace in Liège: *Triumphus sancti Remacli Stabulensis* II.8, p. 452. Cf. Bishop Dietwin of Liège, letter to Bishop Imad of Paderborn p. 434; *Annals of Niederaltaich* 1071, p. 81. See Meyer von Knonau (1894) pp. 49–50.

695 Remaclus (✝673/9), abbot of Solignac, founder and abbot of Stablo and Malmédy, bishop of Maastricht.

696 On the significance of Lampert's phrase *ad captandam benivolentiam* see Arbusow (1963) p. 98, on the rhetorical figure of *captatio benevolentiae*.

697 Holder-Egger, *Lamperti Annales* p. 126 n. 3, noted that Lampert – unlike the *Triumphus sancti Remacli Stabulensis* II.10, p. 453, and the *Annals of Niederaltaich* 1071, p. 81, which criticised Anno of Cologne – 'in transferring all the odium of the affair to

the banquet, rushed into the palace and pondered, full of wrath, what exemplary punishment he ought to inflict on the abbot,[698] the instigator of such a presumptuous act. But lo and behold! the table on which the holy relics had been placed was smashed in pieces by divine power, fell on the ground and crushed the legs and feet of a royal dignitary (a man whose reputation was far from obscure).[699] God's mercy was, however, obtained through the intercession of the blessed Remaclus and he was so fully restored to his former good health that not even a scar was left as evidence of the wound that had disappeared. And during the whole of the following night and the next day so great a host of miracles shone round about the holy body[700] that the blessed Remaclus seemed to be demanding his rights by making, as it were, a personal appeal. Everyone was *thunderstruck by* this great and *unprecedented event*[701] and the king was seized by the very strong fear that, if he should chance to hesitate, the punishment of heaven would instantly fall upon him. He not only restored what had been taken away but also generously overwhelmed the abbey with new gifts in keeping with royal munificence.[702]

Departing from here, he celebrated Whitsun in Halberstadt.[703] There he received the surrender of Duke Otto and the other noblemen who were accused together with him of having taken up arms against the State and he entrusted them to the princes of the kingdom to be kept in custody and to be delivered up to him on the appointed day.[704]

the king, took care not to mention Anno's role in this shameful business'. Cf. Feiera-bend (1913) p. 162: 'In Stablo itself there was a feeling that the abbey had Henry IV's good will in this affair and therefore never reproached him.' In 1065 Henry IV had issued *D.H.IV* 160, confirming the privilege of Henry III (*D.H.IV* 51), which assumed the continuing union of Stablo and Malmédy: see Seibert (1991) p. 543.

698 Theoderic, abbot of Stablo-Malmédy and of St Maximin in Trier (1048–80).

699 According to *Triumphus sancti Remacli Stabulensis* II.11, p. 454: 'a servant lad' (*servulus*) Gonterulus, 'one of our servants of [Remaclus's] own household', who was miracu-lously healed immediately afterwards. Cf. *Annals of Niederaltaich* 1071, p. 81: 'one of the bystanders , who had ranted against the saint of God' and who was not healed.

700 Cf. *Triumphus sancti Remacli Stabulensis* II.24–7, pp. 457–8; Bishop Dietwin of Liège, letter to Bishop Imad of Paderborn p. 434; *Annals of Niederaltaich* 1071, p. 81.

701 Livy I.479.

702 Cf. *Annals of Niederaltaich* 1071, p. 81: 'the king immediately restored the monastery that he had taken away and added as much again in estates from his own possessions'.

703 12 June. So also *Annals of Niederaltaich* 1071, p. 81. See Kilian (1886) pp. 52–3 and Meyer von Knonau (1894) p. 69.

704 See above p. 137 and n. 643. Cf. Berthold of Reichenau, *Chronicle* 1071, p. 125; *Annals of Niederaltaich* 1071, p. 81; Bernold of St Blasien, *Chronicle* 1071, p. 251, gave the date 14 June, on which see Meyer von Knonau (1894) p. 70 n. 60. According to Adam of Bremen, *Gesta* III.60, p. 206, and Bruno of Merseburg, *Saxon War* c. 19, p. 25,

Abbot Meginward of Reichenau voluntarily resigned his office. He was displeased both by the troublesome conduct of certain of his knights, who had inflicted serious injuries on him, and by the insistence of the king, who in his frequent communications urged him to confer the estates of the monastery on his knights as benefices, even though these estates had been squandered through Meginward's prodigality and that of the previous abbots so that they were now barely sufficient for the needs of the brethren.[705] Abbot Rupert of Bamberg, nicknamed 'the money-changer',[706] immediately intruded into his place, not *through the door*[707] of election but through the underground passage of simoniacal heresy, after paying out 1,000 pounds of the purest silver into the king's treasury.[708] This man had amassed for himself an enormous sum of money by means of the most squalid methods of profiteering and usury, which he had practised even when he was an ordinary monk in the monastery, and moreover he had for a long time yearned with anxious longing for the deaths of bishops and abbots. He felt vexation and the utmost impatience because by living too long they were delaying the fulfilment of his wishes and hindering the advance of his unbridled ambition, which dragged him headlong in full career.[709] He ventured

---

Magnus Billung also surrendered on this occasion. Magnus was imprisoned in the Harzburg: see Lampert, *Annals* 1073, below p. 177. The place of Otto of Northeim's imprisonment is unknown. See Meyer von Knonau (1894) p. 70; Lange (1961) p. 43; Althoff (1991) p. 323; Robinson (1999) p. 71.

705 On Meginward see above p. 124 and n. 556. Cf. Berthold of Reichenau, *Chronicle* 1070, p. 125: 'Meginward, who was unwilling to tolerate the exactions and commands and services imposed on him by the king, voluntarily gave up the office of abbot of Reichenau.' *Annals of Niederaltaich* 1071, p. 83 ascribed his resignation to the fact that Liupold of Meersburg, a knight of the king's household, had demanded, in the king's name, to be given one of the abbey's estates as a benefice. See Meyer von Knonau (1894) p. 33; Robinson (1999) pp. 121, 355.

706 Rupert, abbot of Michelsberg in Bamberg (1066–71), abbot of Reichenau (1071–2), abbot of Gengenbach (1074–5). See Meyer von Knonau (1894) pp. 45, 165–6; Feierabend (1913) pp. 38–40; Schieffer (1972) p. 47.

707 Cf. John 10:9.

708 Cf. Berthold of Reichenau, *Chronicle* 1071, p. 126: 'having given the king much gold'; *Annals of Niederaltaich* 1071, pp. 83–4: 'offered the king 30 pounds of gold, so they say, and bought that same abbey of Reichenau'; Gregory VII, *Register* I.82, p. 117: 'Rupert, the simoniac and the invader of this monastery', who had 'left another abbey and striven after this one for a price'.

709 Lampert seems here to be repeating Bamberg gossip about Rupert. For Lampert's studies in the cathedral school of Bamberg see Holder-Egger, *Lamperti Annales* pp. X–XII; Wattenbach and Holtzmann (1967–71) p. 457 n. 54; Struve (1969) pp. 22–31 and above p. 4. On Lampert's polemic against Rupert see Meyer von Knonau (1894) pp. 816–17: 'The picture of this monk whom Lampert personally hated is distorted into pure caricature ... This Reichenau issue clearly has for Lampert a

so far into madness that, above and beyond the secret gifts by means
of which the favour of the confidential advisers of the king must be
purchased, he promised the king himself 100 pounds of gold if he would
expel Abbot Widerad,[710] a man of extraordinary sanctity, and hand over
the abbey of Fulda to Rupert himself. And assuredly he would most
infamously have obtained what he had impiously striven for, had not a
few men who valued the laws of the Church more than money *opposed*
the king *to his face*,[711] saying that he should not do it.

This false monk – moved by the intensity of my distress I shall say
more plainly: this angel of *Satan disguised as an angel of light*[712] – so
dishonoured, corrupted and injured the holy and angelic profession of
the monks that in our times and in these lands monks are measured
not according to their innocence and the purity of their way of life
but according to the amount of their money and in the election of
abbots the question is not who is most worthy to hold office but who
can purchase the abbey at the higher price. Thus through the device
invented by this man and his *new* and inauspicious *method of hunting*[713]
for office this custom has been introduced into the Church, according
to which abbeys are prostituted by being offered for sale publicly in the
palace and no one can set so high a price that he does not immediately
find a buyer. Meanwhile the monks do not strive among themselves
with a worthy zeal for the observance of the *Rule* but *contend with bitter
jealousy*[714] in profiteering and usury. But to lament over these matters
as they deserve would, in view of their great importance, necessitate a
book devoted to them alone and a tragic work of greater length. Let us
return instead to the account that we have begun.

After he learned that this money-loving abbot was approaching and
heard of the scale of the expenditure by means of which *the ravening
wolf* had opened up for himself a way *into the sheepfold*[715] of Christ, the
advocate of the monastery of Reichenau sent messengers to meet him,
threatening his safety if he presumed to approach the possessions of

---

wider significance, extending far beyond Rupert's personality. For in his opinion
"the holy and angelic profession of the monks" is entirely dishonoured by Rupert.'

710 For Widerad of Fulda see above n. 239.

711 Galatians 2:11.

712 II Corinthians 11:14.

713 Terence, *Eunuchus* II.2.16.

714 James 3:14.

715 John 10:12 and 1.

the monastery of Reichenau:[716] if he did so, the advocate would oppose him and with an armed band obtain liberty for those whom Rupert had bought as slaves at so dear a price. When he heard this, Rupert was struck with the deepest dismay, both because of his serious loss of money and because the office was, so to speak, snatched away from his jaws, which had for so long anxiously gaped for it. At first indeed he had made up his mind to allow the matter to be settled by weapons and (as men are accustomed to say) *to poke about in the fire with a sword*,[717] that is, to outdo simoniacal heresy by committing murders. But when those who were with him declared that the enterprise was beyond his strength, he went away with a perplexed (as he deserved) and weakened spirit, to his brother's estates, there to await what outcome fate would bring from such melancholy beginnings. For in the meantime Ekbert, a monk of the Gorze discipline, had received the abbey of Bamberg.[718] The brethren had been trained by the previous abbot in his own discipline, that is, in the arts of commerce and usury, and he had taught them as a father teaches his sons (as they say) with regard to their *character and way of life* to *tread in his footsteps*.[719] On Ekbert's accession they all scattered like *leaves that are seized by the wind*.[720]

Charles, to whom the king had given the bishopric of Constance,[721] continually addressed appeals to the apostolic see on the subject of his ordination.[722] For their part, however, the brethren of Constance fought with inflexible hostility to prevent a man who was charged not only with simoniacal heresy but also with theft from being appointed as their bishop. Since they were troublesome to him, the pope referred the

716 Perhaps 'the advocate Hezelo' first identified in a charter of Abbot Ekkehard II of Reichenau of 2 May 1075: see Meyer von Knonau (1894) pp. 407 n. 144, 816 n. 84. This Hezelo (+1088) was the founder of the abbey of St Georgen in the Black Forest, where he became a monk: Bernold of St Blasien, *Chronicle* 1088, p. 292. See Jakobs (1968) pp. 228–30.

717 Horace, *Satirae* II.3.275.

718 Ekbert, abbot of Münsterschwarzach (1046–75), abbot of Michelsberg (1071–5), abbot of St James, Bamberg (1074–5), introduced the stricter 'new Gorze reform', to the discomfiture of the congregation, accustomed to the 'old Gorze' customs: see Hallinger (1950–1) pp. 348–50.

719 Livy V.9.2; IX.8.13.

720 Job 13:25.

721 Bishop Charles of Constance: see above pp. 124–5 and nn. 558–60.

722 Cf. Archbishop Siegfried of Mainz, letter to Pope Alexander II in *Codex Udalrici* 36, p. 69: 'it was reported to us that a royal embassy is bringing that same designated bishop to you to be investigated and consecrated'.

examination of the case to the archbishop of Mainz.[723] He commanded
that both parties should be summoned to a synod, that he was to investigate the case with the utmost care and that, if Charles was unable to rebut
the charges that were brought against him, he should on no account
consecrate him. For this reason the archbishop of Mainz announced a
synod to take place in the month of August. The king viewed this dispute
with hostility because of his friendship with Charles and also because of
the very many services that he had very frequently and most opportunely
performed for him in his personal affairs and he therefore wished most
eagerly that the office would be confirmed and remain his. He was therefore extremely angry with the archbishop of Mainz for not having consecrated him immediately[724] and shown his contempt for the arguments of
the obstreperous brethren. But the archbishop remained immovable and
steadfast in his purpose,[725] bearing in mind how dreadfully he had been
rebuked by the pope in a similar case the previous year and with what
great difficulty he had escaped without the loss of his office[726] and how
he had been admonished in a recent letter from the apostolic see not to
perform his consecration without a most careful investigation.

As 1 August now drew near, the king hastened to Mainz since he
himself desired to sit side by side with the archbishop as a judge in the
examination of such an important case. In the course of the journey he
came to Hersfeld. Departing from here on the following day, he halted
in the village called Udenhausen[727] to break his fast. After they had eaten,
they were all most impetuous in their eagerness to hasten the journey
and returned to their horses as if competing in a race. It now happened
that a certain Liupold of Meersburg,[728] who was very dear to the king

---

723 The letter of Alexander II to Siegfried of Mainz is not extant but is acknowledged
      in Siegfried of Mainz, letter to Alexander II in *Codex Udalrici* 36, p. 69. Cf. Berthold
      of Reichenau, *Chronicle* 1071, p. 125; *Annals of Niederaltaich* 1071, p. 82. See Meyer
      von Knonau (1894) pp. 78–9; Schieffer (1972) pp. 46–50; Robinson (1999) p. 118.

724 Cf. Siegfried of Mainz, letter to Alexander II in *Codex Udalrici* 36, p. 69: 'I shall
      appear to have sinned against my prince, in that I refused to consecrate him out of
      hatred rather than a just cause and your command.'

725 Cf. *Acta* of the Synod of Mainz (1071) in *Codex Udalrici* 37, p. 72: 'the metropolitan
      ... was firmly immovable in his praiseworthy constancy'.

726 This is a polemical version of the events reported above p. 126 and nn. 565–8.

727 A village three miles southwest of Hersfeld: see Kilian (1886) pp. 53–4 and Meyer
      von Knonau (1894) p. 76.

728 Liupold of Meersburg, Swabian nobleman: 'our most faithful and most dear knight
      (*miles*)' (*D.H.IV* 243), 'a familiar of the king' (*Annals of Niederaltaich* 1071, p. 83),
      'brother of Berthold, the king's adviser, and himself an adviser' (Bruno of Merse-
      burg, *Saxon War* c. 81, p. 78). See Schmid (1984a) pp. 247–9; Tellenbach (1988) pp.

and on whose aid and advice he was accustomed to rely in the most confidential affairs, chanced to fall from his horse; he was pierced by his own sword and immediately died.[729] This accident overwhelmed the king with unbearable grief and sorrow. He brought him back at once to Hersfeld and caused him to be buried with a magnificent and solemn funeral service in the middle of the church. He also conferred on the monastery thirty manses in the place called Martinfeld for the repose of his soul.[730]

It should be noted that this was the very sword with which that most famous Attila, the king of the Huns in olden times,[731] had raged with wild fury, slaughtering Christians and bringing ruin to Gaul. This sword had in fact been given by the queen of the Hungarians,[732] the mother of King Salomon, to Duke Otto of the Bavarians as a gift when, on Otto's advice and with his support, King Henry had restored her son to the throne of his father.[733] Duke Otto had entrusted it for a while to the younger Dedi, the son of Margrave Dedi, as a proof and a pledge of his unalterable affection. After the younger Dedi was killed (as was mentioned above),[734] the sword had come into the hands of the king and through the king it had come by chance to this Liupold. Hence the majority of the supporters of Duke Otto drew the conclusion that it was through a divine judgement that this man was killed by that sword that belonged to Duke Otto. For it was said that it was he above all who had incited the king to initiate proceedings against Otto and to drive him out of the palace.[735] Concerning this sword, however, we read in the

---

357–8; Robinson (1999) pp. 67, 359. A kinsman of Liupold of the same name in the early twelfth century was identified as a vassal of the bishop of Constance: see Maurer (1991) p. 175.

729 Cf. *Annals of Niederaltaich* 1071, p. 83; Bruno of Merseburg, *Saxon War* c. 81, p. 78 (reporting this as an accident while hawking and apparently dating it in 1076). See Meyer von Knonau (1894) pp. 76–7.

730 *D.H.IV* 243 (30 July 1071). See Meyer von Knonau (1894) p. 77; Schmid (1984a) pp. 247–9; Vogtherr (1991) p. 447.

731 Attila, khan of the Huns (✝453).

732 Anastasia, daughter of Jaroslav, grand prince of Kiev, wife of King Andreas I of Hungary (above n. 51), mother of King Salomon of Hungary (above n. 250).

733 A reference to Otto of Northeim's role in the expedition of September 1063: see above p. 91 and n. 335. The sword was one of the most precious objects in the Hungarian treasury: see Schramm (1955) pp. 485–91.

734 The death of Dedi, son of Margrave Dedi of Lower Lusatia, in 1069: see above p. 121 and n. 538.

735 Cf. above p. 127: Otto 'was envied by very many worthless men', who incited Egino to accuse Otto of plotting the king's assassination. Cf. Lampert's judgement on

Deeds of the Getae,[736] who are also called the Goths, that it once belonged to Mars, who, according to the false tales told by the pagans, was the patron of warfare and the original inventor of weapons of war. After a long lapse of time a certain herdsman discovered the sword, partially hidden in the earth after seeing the blood of an ox, whose foot had been injured by it, while grazing in the pasture. The herdsman brought the sword to King Attila, to whom the oracles of all the soothsayers of that time prophesied that this same sword was destined to bring about the destruction of the whole world and the overthrow of many peoples. The truth of this prophecy is evident to this day from the ruins of many most noble cities in Gaul, to such an extent that this sword was also called by the barbarians 'the avenger of God's wrath' or 'the scourge of God'. Thus much may be said by way of a digression since I happened to mention this sword.

After the funeral was held with royal magnificence, the king hastened to Mainz, as he had intended. On the appointed day, when he had taken his seat with the bishops in the synod,[737] Charles appeared and there also appeared the brethren of Constance, bringing a huge number of accusations against him. The king deliberately opposed them, as far as he could do so without dishonour. Sometimes he tried to clear Charles of particular charges; sometimes he tried by means of cunning arguments to lessen the importance of charges of which he could not clear him. He also very often reproved with harsh words the insolence of those men who pursued their case so persistently and attempted to check their impudent boldness by countering it with the majesty of his royal authority. He used up a first and a second day in this undertaking.[738] When he proved unable *to undermine* the stead-

---

'Count Giso and Adalbert' in 1073: below p. 205. See Robinson (1999) p. 67. On the motif of divine judgement on evildoers in Lampert's work see Struve (1970a) pp. 117–118 and n. 18.

736 Cf. Jordanes, *Getica* c. 35, 183, pp. 104–5. For the exemplar of the *Getica* in the cathedral library of Bamberg see Struve (1969) p. 27.

737 Synod of Mainz, 15–18 August. Lampert's account refers only to three days of proceedings. (See Holder-Egger, *Lamperti Annales* p. 131 n. 2, on Lampert's preference for councils and conferences to last three days.) Cf. *Acta* of the synod (1071) in *Codex Udalrici* 37, pp. 70–7; Siegfried of Mainz, letter to Alexander II in *Codex Udalrici* 38, pp. 77–81; Berthold of Reichenau, *Chronicle* 1071, pp. 125–6; *Annals of Niederaltaich* 1071, pp. 82–3; Marianus Scottus, *Chronicon* 1093 [=1071], p. 560. See Meyer von Knonau (1894) pp. 79–84; Gresser (2006) pp. 99–103.

738 Cf. *Acta* of the Synod of Mainz (1071) p. 75: God 'so restrained the mind of the prince, so attuned him to the words of holy exhortation, that he was not moved to youthful harshness and, which is difficult for powerful men, he did not wound the priests with an insolent reply.' The discrepancy between Lampert's account and the

fast demeanour of the accusers either by a truthful refutation or by *skilful oratory*[739] and when the charges brought against Charles were proved, he finally took back the bishop's staff from him.[740] He nevertheless comforted his sadness with the most carefully chosen words and promised that, as soon as it became convenient for him, he would compensate him for this disaster with a generous recompense.

During these days the queen, who was in Mainz with the king, gave birth to a son.[741] But he died immediately after being baptised and was brought to the Harzburg and buried there.[742]

The king gave the bishopric of Constance to Otto, a canon of Goslar,[743] and, being *frightened by the case of the recent*[744] scandal, he caused him to be consecrated without delay, lest once again some doubt should arise against him as a result of a delay in his consecration.

There was a most violent dispute between the duke of the Poles[745] and the duke of the Bohemians.[746] For this reason the king summoned them during the autumn to the city of Meissen.[747] He rebuked them very sternly and commanded them, invoking the royal majesty, each henceforward to be content with his own frontiers and not to provoke each

---

Acta prompted Ranke (1888) p. 136 to conclude that Lampert had no exact information about the events of the synod. See also Meyer von Knonau (1894) pp. 814–15.

739 Livy III.10.10; XLIV.36.3.

740 On 18 August Charles voluntarily resigned his office: *Acta* p. 76. Cf. Berthold of Reichenau, *Chronicle* 1071, p. 126: Charles 'was cast out … not … by an act of public deposition' but 'resigned the episcopal staff'. See Meyer von Knonau (1894) p. 83; Gresser (2006) p. 102.

741 This was presumably the son commemorated in *D.H.IV* 426 of 21 September 1091: 'our son Henry'. Cf. *Annals of Niederaltaich* 1071, p. 84: 'This autumn … the queen gave birth to a son, who departed this life in his christening robe.' See Meyer von Knonau (1894) p. 85. This report contradicts Lampert's statement about Queen Bertha above, 1069, p. 124 and n. 554.

742 The Harzburg was a royal fortress on the northern border of the Harz mountains: see Fenske (1977) pp. 29, 31–2; Schneider (1991) p. 122; Weinfurter (1991) p. 86. On the grave in the Harzburg see below 1074, p. 220.

743 Otto I, bishop of Constance (1071–86). See Meyer von Knonau (1894) p. 84; Gresser (2006) p. 103.

744 Livy XXXI.12.2.

745 Boleslav II, duke of Poland (1058–76), king (1076–83).

746 Vratislav II, duke of Bohemia (1061–85), king (1085–92).

747 Cf. *D.H.IV* 244, dated 4 October in Merseburg; *Chronicae Polonorum* I.24, p. 439: 'the deception of the Bohemians against Boleslav'. See Kilian (1886) p. 55 and Meyer von Knonau (1894) pp. 85–6.

other with rash attacks: otherwise he *who was the first to take up arms*[748] against the other would learn from experience that the king was an enemy and avenger.

Archbishop Anno of Cologne expelled the canons from Saalfeld and introduced the monastic life there, sending there monks from Siegburg and St Pantaleon.[749] At that time I also came there to consult them about the order and discipline of the monastic life,[750] since popular report ascribed great and distinguished qualities to them. Consequently, as in the world's opinion everything loses its value through over-familiarity and as the minds of the people, *eager for novelties*,[751] are always more struck by what is unknown, they regarded us,[752] with whom they had long been familiar, as worthless and thought that these monks – because they seemed to offer something new and unusual – were not men but angels, not flesh but spirit.[753] And this belief had taken possession of the minds of the princes more deeply and more strongly than those of the ordinary people.[754] A report spreading from the princes to the people

---

748 Livy XXXII.10.6.

749 Anno had established the canonical foundation in Saalfeld in 1063–4: see Semmler (1959) pp. 61–2 and n. 5. According to a charter of Anno of 1072(?), the archbishop did not 'expel' the canons but summoned them to Cologne and a tradition of the canons of the foundation of St George in Cologne records that the Saalfeld canons settled there: *ibid.*, pp. 61 n. 8, 178. The earliest extant charter of Saalfeld, dated 1071, states that the monks had settled there and an abbot had already been established there by 1071: Semmler (1959) p. 61. On Anno's reform of Siegburg (1068?) and St Pantaleon (1068/70) see Hallinger (1950–1) pp. 127, 449–50; Semmler (1959) pp. 36–8, 118–19.

750 On Lampert's visit to Saalfeld and Siegburg see Holder-Egger, *Lamperti Annales* p. XV; Semmler (1959) pp. 219–23; Struve (1969) p. 12; Struve (1970a) pp. 67–8; Vogtherr (1991) p. 453.

751 Sallust, *Jugurtha* 19.46. Cf. Livy I.8.6.

752 I.e. monks of the early eleventh-century Gorze reform tradition, like those of Hersfeld. See Hallinger (1950–1) pp. 169–70; Struve (1970a) pp. 67–8; Vogtherr (1991) pp. 430–2, 453–4.

753 Cf. anonymous monk of Hersfeld, *Liber de unitate ecclesiae conservanda* II.41, p. 271, attacking, *ca.* 1090, the monks of the Hirsau reform, who 'have greatly degenerated from the paternal practice of the blessed Benedict, which they professed ... and who also declare that they are righteous monks, following the *Rule*, and boast that they are heavenly and spiritual'. On this anonymous polemicist's use of Lampert's *Annals* see Robinson (1978b) pp. 538–50.

754 See Struve (1970a) p. 66 and below n. 765. Cf. Bernold of St Blasien's account of the role of the nobility in the monastic reform movement in southwest Germany a decade later, *Chronicle* 1083, p. 272: 'a wonderful host of noble and prudent men fled for refuge to these monasteries.... Those who were formerly counts or margraves in the world now considered it the greatest delight to serve the brethren.'

caused such great alarm[755] in most of the monasteries in this region that at their approach numerous monks – in one place thirty, in another forty, elsewhere fifty – were led astray by their fear of the imposition of a stricter way of life and withdrew from their monasteries. They thought it better to risk the salvation of their souls in the world than to *enter the kingdom of heaven by violence*[756] beyond the limits of their strength.

And indeed the Lord seemed not undeservedly to *pour contempt*[757] on the monks of our land. For the shameful personal conduct of certain false monks had branded the name of monk with extreme infamy, since they abandoned the study of godliness and devoted all their efforts to money and profit.[758] They churlishly dinned the ears of the princes with talk of abbacies and bishoprics and aimed at ecclesiastical offices not by means of virtuous conduct, as was the custom of our ancestors, but by the dangerous path of flattery and the lavish expenditure of ill-gotten sums of money. In short, every day they *promised mountains of gold*[759] in purchasing even a minor office and excluded secular purchasers by the prodigality of their expenditure: a seller did not dare to demand as much as the buyer was prepared to pay. The world asked in amazement what might be the source of so great a river of money and how the wealth of Croesus and Tantalus[760] had accumulated in the possession of ordinary men and in particular of those men who chose *the stumbling-block of the cross*[761] and embraced poverty as a sign of honour and who falsely claimed that they had no personal possessions except plain food and clothing. Those *weeds in the field*[762] of the Lord, these withered twigs and stalks of the vine of God, prepared for the eternal fires, had infected the whole body of the holy flock like a plague and, according to the Apostle, *a little leaven* had *leavened the whole lump,*[763] so that we were all considered to be like them and it was believed that there was among us *none that did good, no, not one.*[764]

---

755 Livy XXXVIII.16.10.

756 Luke 16:16.

757 Job 12:21.

758 See the case of Abbot Rupert of Reichenau, above pp. 145–7.

759 Terence, *Phormio* I.2.18.

760 Croesus, king of Lydia, was renowned for his riches. Tantalus, king of Phrygia, was the son of Jupiter, entertained by his father at the feasts of the gods.

761 Galatians 5:11.

762 Matthew 13:25.

763 Galatians 5:9; I Corinthians 5:6.

764 Psalm 14:1.

For this reason the princes of the kingdom summoned monks from beyond the Alps to establish a school of divine service in Gaul[765] but, if any of our compatriots would not voluntarily submit to their ordinances, the princes drove them ignominiously out of the monasteries. I, however (as I mentioned before), came to them and stayed with them for fourteen weeks, partly in Saalfeld and partly in Siegburg.[766] I observed that our customs corresponded better than theirs to the *Rule* of St Benedict, if we were willing to hold as firmly to our principles and follow as rigorously and zealously the traditions of our predecessors.[767]

The archbishop of Mainz was afflicted by a severe illness from the feast of St Michael until Whitsun[768] so that the doctors even despaired of his life and very many men most eagerly applied themselves to the matter of the succession.

Charles, whose expulsion from the bishopric of Constance we mentioned above, returned to the diocese of Magdeburg and died on 27 December.[769]

---

765 The late eleventh-century monastic reform movement in southwest Germany, which established a monasticism independent of the early eleventh-century Gorze tradition, was supported by secular princes (including later opponents of Henry IV). Notable was Duke Rudolf of Swabia, who in 1072 introduced monks of Fruttuaria into his 'ducal monastery' of St Blasien. See Jakobs (1961) pp. 152–89; Jakobs (1968) pp. 1, 258 and n. 21, 271–90 ; Jakobs (1973) pp. 102–8; Schmid (1973) pp. 295–319. On 'Gaul' (Germany) see above n. 241.

766 Meyer von Knonau (1894) p. 173 n. 106 noted that Lampert could 'not have been absent for fourteen weeks without the knowledge and wish of the abbot'. Feierabend (1913) pp. 19, 110, wrote that this visit was 'most probably commissioned by Abbot Ruthard' (above n. 54). Struve (1970a) p. 68 n. 57 linked the visit with the correspondence of Ruthard's successor, Hartwig, with the abbey of Monte Cassino (below n. 767). Semmler (1959) pp. 219–23 wished to date Lampert's visit in 1077.

767 Cf. the letter of the monks of Monte Cassino to the abbeys of Hersfeld, Fulda and Lorsch, dated in 1072 by the editor, W. Bulst, *Die ältere Wormser Briefsammlung* no. 1, pp. 13–16: 'do not be eager to change your customs and ordinances for any others, unless they differ from the *Rule*'. The new monastic reforms 'do not please us nor ought they to please anyone who wishes to live a regular life, for they seem entirely contrary to the *Rule*.' Bulst, like Feierabend (1913) p. 20 and Struve (1970a) p. 68 n. 57, interpreted this letter as a reply to a question addressed to Monte Cassino by Abbot Hartwig of Hersfeld on the validity of the new monastic reforms. Hallinger (1950–1) pp. 450–1 interpreted it as a circular letter offering instruction to several German monasteries. See above p. 20 and n. 89.

768 29 September 1071 – 27 May 1072. On Archbishop Siegfried (above n. 210) see Meyer von Knonau (1894) p. 95.

769 See above p. 151 and Meyer von Knonau (1894) pp. 84–5.

1072

The king celebrated Christmas in Worms.[770] From there he travelled through a considerable part of the kingdom[771] before returning to Goslar, where he spent the whole of Lent.[772]

Burchard, the chamberlain of the archbishop of Mainz, was consecrated bishop in Basel.[773]

The first man in the palace was then Archbishop Adalbert of Bremen, who had triumphed over the rivals who had driven him out of the palace some years before.[774] He alone now had access to the king and he had been received not only into his favour and friendship but virtually into participation in the royal power and involvement in all affairs both public and private.[775] He had thus by his crafty deceptions made the king subject to his will. But he was worn out by sickness and age. After he had for a long time struggled against death through the most extraordinary efforts on the part of the doctors,[776] as if he could *cheat* nature *by means of art*,[777] in the middle of Lent, on 17 March, he paid his debt to the human condition[778] and at long last by dying gave satisfaction

---

770 25 December 1071. *Annals of Niederaltaich* 1072, p. 84: 'in Regensburg'. But Kilian (1886) p. 55 and Meyer von Knonau (1894) p. 88 and n. 88 accept Lampert's version, in the light of *D.H.IV* 247, issued in Worms on 29 December 1071.

771 Henry IV was in Lorsch on 1 January 1072 (*D.H.IV* 249) and in Regensburg on 9 January (*DD.H.IV* 251–2) and 4 February (*D.H.IV* 253). See Kilian (1886) p. 56 and Meyer von Knonau (1894) pp. 117–18.

772 I.e. 21 February – 7 April. But Lampert also states, below p. 156 and n. 782, that Henry IV was in Cologne on 1 April.

773 Burchard, bishop of Basel (1072–1107).

774 See above 1066, p. 111.

775 Cf. Adam of Bremen, *Gesta* III.59, p. 205: 'three years after his expulsion he fulfilled his wishes and was restored to his former rank at the court', i.e.1069. *Ibid.*, III.60, p. 206: 'it redounded to the prelate's glory that … that famous conference of the emperor with the king of the Danes … was held in Lüneburg', i.e. July (?) 1071 (see below 1073, p. 172). *Ibid.*, III.61, p. 206: 'thus placed in a position of supreme glory, although he was troubled by frequent bodily ailments, he nevertheless refused to neglect public affairs and he was carried in a litter in the king's entourage from the Rhine to the Danube and from there into Saxony', i.e. January–February 1072. For evidence of Adalbert in the 'intervention clauses' of royal diplomas in 1071 see Gawlik (1970) p. 142. See also Meyer von Knonau (1894) pp. 89–92, 123; P. Johanek (1991) p. 102; Robinson (1999) pp. 85–6.

776 Cf. Adam of Bremen, *Gesta* III.63, p. 209: 'while he strove to recover his health with the help of doctors, he soon fell into a more serious illness because of frequent experiments with medication'.

777 Livy III.10.10; XLIV.36.3.

778 16 March, according to Adam of Bremen, *Gesta* III.67, p. 214. See Meyer von Knonau (1894) p. 122.

to the men who had perseveringly hated him, which he could never
have done while he was alive. He was clearly a man admirable for his
expressions of remorse: in particular, when he offered to God the life-
giving host, he completely dissolved in tears. It was also said that from
his mother's womb he remained a virgin.[779] But the arrogance of his
manners and his capricious boasting greatly obscured these virtues of
his in men's eyes.[780] His body was brought from Goslar to his episcopal
see and buried there.[781]

The king celebrated Palm Sunday in Cologne and Easter in Utrecht.[782]
There the people furiously cried out against him because of the injuries
and hardships that overwhelmed the innocent everywhere throughout
the whole kingdom, the orphans and widows who were plundered, the
monasteries and churches that were laid waste and the unbridled injustice
that raged with impunity, committing every crime that it wished. At last
the king was moved to act either by the painful nature of these events or
by the savage demeanour of those making the complaints, supported as
they were in this matter by all the princes of the kingdom. He prevailed
on the archbishop of Cologne to undertake the administration of the
State, second only to himself.[783] The archbishop long resisted his request,
partly because of the memory of his old injuries, partly because, as a
man totally devoted to God, he would have preferred to be involved in
divine rather than worldly affairs. Nevertheless he was overcome by
the unanimous wish of those who petitioned him and made his personal
convenience secondary to public service.[784] It was then that the State
first began to be restored *to its former condition and dignity*[785] and *bridle*

---

779 Cf. Adam of Bremen, *Gesta* III.2, p. 144: 'he was a lover of chastity'.

780 Cf. Adam of Bremen, *Gesta* III.2, p. 144: 'such a man could be and be called blessed,
   had not one vice prevented it, the ugliness of which clouded all the prelate's comeli-
   ness. That was vainglory, the common fault of the rich.'

781 In the cathedral of Bremen: Adam of Bremen, *Gesta* III.68, pp. 214–15.

782 Respectively 1 and 8 April. See Kilian (1886) p. 56 and Meyer von Knonau (1894) p.
   151.

783 Lampert alone reported this incident and the subsequent restoration of Archbishop
   Anno to the government. For evidence of Anno in the 'intervention clauses' of royal
   diplomas in 1072 see Gawlik (1970) p. 136. See also Meyer von Knonau (1894) pp.
   151 and 803–4 (an analysis of Lampert's bias in the presentation of Anno); Schieffer
   (1991) p. 13.

784 See Struve (1970a) p. 108: 'Lampert thus consciously represented [Anno] as the
   ideal model of the bishop and saint, who did not thrust himself into ecclesiastical
   or secular offices – in order to remind contemporaries accustomed to simony of the
   primitive condition of the Church.'

785 Livy III.37.1; XXXV.32.10.

and bit were placed on licentious conduct that hitherto had *wandered freely.*[786] For when the king adopted the custom of referring the judgement of all cases from himself to the archbishop, as though to a father and the guardian of his welfare, the latter could never be led away by friendship or hatred for any individual from right to wrong but *judged* all cases, as it is written, *without respect of persons,*[787] *not respecting the person of the poor* in his judgement, *nor honouring the person of the mighty.*[788] He inflicted a very severe punishment on any rich men who had been accused of using their power to oppress the poor; he ordered their castles, which were places of refuge for evildoers, to be destroyed from the very foundations and very many of them, who were most distinguished both for their noble birth and for their wealth, he threw into prison. Among the latter was that Egino, very well known in our times, who had been the cause of that great disaster that befell Duke Otto of the Bavarians.[789] After many men had come into the king's presence to accuse Egino of personal injuries and robberies, the archbishop caused him to be taken prisoner and commanded him to be led about, laden with chains, as a public show – in order, in fact to gain approval in the people's minds for the stern application of royal power. In short, he conducted affairs with such mastery, such diligence and authority that you would certainly find it difficult to decide whether he was more suited to the title of bishop or that of king[790] and, in brief, he revived the strength of character and the morals of his ancestors in the king himself, who through negligence and indolence had virtually fallen into a decline.

The king set out for Aachen[791] and there took possession of the holy confessor Speus[792] and an arm of the righteous man Simeon, who is mentioned in the Gospel,[793] and the head of Anastasius, monk and

786 Horace, *Carmina* IV.15.10.

787 I Peter 1:17.

788 Leviticus 19:15.

789 On the accusation of Egino against Otto of Northeim see above 1070, p. 128. See Meyer von Knonau (1894) p. 152 and n. 74: Lampert 'perhaps saw with his own eyes' the fate of Egino, on which he based his generalisations on 'the strict preservation of the law by Anno'.

790 Meyer von Knonau (1894) p. 804 noted that in his obituary of Anno Lampert stated that Anno secured his release from secular affairs in July 1072 – see below 1075, p. 296 – so that this period of administration lasted for only a quarter of the year.

791 Cf. *D.H.IV* 254, issued on 27 April in Aachen. See Kilian (1886) p. 56 and Meyer von Knonau (1894) p. 152.

792 Otherwise unknown: see *Acta Sanctorum Ianuarii* 2, 891.

793 Luke 2: 25–32.

martyr,[794] and relics of other saints and brought them to the Harzburg.

Also in Trier at St Paulinus thirteen bodies were found – so it is believed – of the saints of the Theban legion[795] *and their names, inscribed on lead tablets, were found in the same place: Palmatius, Thyrsus, Maxentius, Constantius, Crescentius, Justinus, Leander, Alexander, Soter, Hormista, Papirius, Constans, Jovianus. And while earth was being carried out of the crypt where the saints were resting, one of the bones was carelessly dropped on the ground and it shed a considerable quantity of blood and it continues to be full of blood up to the present day.* This written account of their passion has reached us from the men of Trier themselves. '*Rictiovarus, the prefect of Emperor Maximian, persecuted the Theban legion everywhere on the emperor's orders. It was on their account that he entered Trier on 4 October and on the same day he killed there Thyrsus, the leader of that same legion, with all his retinue. On the following day he slew Palmatius, consul of the city of Trier and patrician, together with all the princes of that same city. On the third day he carried out a slaughter of the people, both men and women. The countless bodies of these martyrs, however, are lying in the church of the holy Archbishop Paulinus.*'[795]

The king celebrated the Lord's Ascension in Goslar and Whitsun in Magdeburg.[796] There he appointed a successor to Archbishop Adalbert of Bremen, who (as was mentioned above)[797] had died during Lent. This was Liemar, a young man on whom the greatest hopes were placed and who was above all distinguished by his learning in all the liberal arts.[798] There also Duke Otto of the Bavarians a full year after his surrender

---

794 Anastasius (✝628) Persian martyr. On the foundation in the Harzburg see Spier (1962) pp. 31–7; Weinfurter (1991) pp. 86–7. On the relic collection see also below, 1074, p. 220.

795 These two passages are also found as an interpolation in some of the codices of the *Gesta Treverorum* p. 166 n. * and in the Vatican codex Palatinus latinus 482, fol. 63v. The text perhaps originated as a letter of Archbishop Udo of Trier, describing the *inventio* of the martyrs in February 1072 in the church of St Paulinus, Trier: see Holder-Egger (1892) pp. 487–8. On the *inventio* see *Historia martyrum Trevirensium* c. 3, pp. 220–3; Sigebert of Gembloux, *Chronica* 1071, p. 362. On the massacre of the Theban legion (in 291), the legendary persecutor Rictiovarus and Bishop Paulinus of Trier (*ca.* 350) see Thomas (1968) pp. 28–33. See also Meyer von Knonau (1894) p. 168 and n. 101; Heyen (1964) pp. 23–66.

796 17 May; 27 May. See Kilian (1886) p. 56 and Meyer von Knonau (1894) p. 156.

797 See above p. 155 and n. 778.

798 Liemar, archbishop of Hamburg-Bremen (1072–1101). On his learning: Adam of Bremen, *Gesta*, preface, p. 2: Liemar's 'worldly wisdom' and 'study of divine philosophy'; epilogue, p. 281: 'you adorn your speech with rhetoric, ... your tongue is the key to holy Scripture'; Bonizo of Sutri, *To a Friend* VII, p. 222: 'a most eloquent man, exceptionally learned in liberal studies'; IX, p. 254: 'the wisest of men, most skilled in all the arts'.

recovered the favour of the king, after giving a considerable part of his estates either to the king or to those persons who had interceded with the king on his behalf.[799]

On the feast of the Nativity of St James in Worms the king met his mother, Empress Agnes, who had returned from the lands beyond the Alps.[800] She had remained there now for six years or more[801] and had established a way of life of such extreme rigour that her endurance in fasting and nightly vigils exceeded the usual capacity of human strength.[802] This, however, was the reason for her return to Gaul. Duke Rudolf of Swabia had been denounced to the king by those who wished to harm him, alleging that he had hostile designs against the king and against the State. He therefore received frequent messages summoning him to the royal court to state his defence.[803] But although he knew that he was very far from being guilty, he was nevertheless *very frightened by the recent case*[804] of Duke Otto of Bavaria and of certain other men on whom the king had given an over-hasty judgement and had condemned

---

799 See above p. 144 and n. 704. Cf. *Annals of Niederaltaich* 1071, p. 81: 'He lost the greatest part of the benefices, of which he possessed an immense number, and the abbey of Niederaltaich was also restored to its former liberty'; *Annals of Ottobeuren* 1072, p. 7. See Meyer von Knonau (1894) p. 159 and n. 86 (on the reliability of Lampert's account); Lange (1961) pp. 43–4.

800 25 July. Cf. *D.H.IV* 255 (Worms, 27 July). See Kilian (1886) p. 57 and Meyer von Knonau (1894) pp. 159–60. On the role of Empress Agnes see also Bulst-Thiele (1933) pp. 92–3; Jakobs (1968) pp. 40, 269–71; Jakobs (1973) pp. 110–11; Vogel (1984) pp. 1–30; Black-Veldtrup (1995) pp. 96, 303–7; Robinson (1999) pp. 125–6.

801 Agnes had perhaps left Germany for Italy in summer/autumn 1065, according to Struve (1985) pp. 1–29, countering the arguments for 1063 in Meyer von Knonau (1890) pp. 280–4, 320–1 and Bulst-Thiele (1933) pp. 81–2, 84–6. See above p. 82 and n. 282. There is evidence that the empress was in Rome, Farfa, Fruttuaria and Monte Cassino during the years 1065–72 but it is possible that she was also intermittently in Germany (in Regensburg and Speyer in 1067): see Black-Veldtrup (1995) pp. 27–36, 92–4.

802 Cf. Berthold of Reichenau, *Chronicle* 1077, pp. 191–4; *Annals of Niederaltaich* 1062, p. 59. See Meyer von Knonau (1900) p. 93; Bulst-Thiele (1933) pp. 104–10; Black-Veldtrup (1995) pp. 330, 377–8.

803 Rudolf (above n. 203). Cf. *Annals of Niederaltaich* 1072, p. 84: the king 'rarely admitted any of the nobility into his secrets and, because many things were done in an irregular manner, the bishops, dukes and other princes of the kingdom withdrew from royal affairs. Among them, Dukes Rudolf and Berthold were often summoned to the king but nevertheless refused to come until the king began to suspect that they were preparing to rebel against him. When the rumour also spread that an expedition was in preparation against them, they regularly sent messengers seeking a delay and thus put off an attack by the king.' See Meyer von Knonau (1894) pp. 153–6.

804 Livy XXX.12.2.

without the investigation prescribed by law[805] and he was therefore unwilling to throw himself heedlessly into danger. And since he was very dear to the empress because of his former meritorious service and since he was also connected through kinship on account of her daughter (who, as was mentioned above, had married him but who had died within a few days of the celebration of the marriage),[806] he sent a message to her, most urgently requesting her to come to Gaul to calm the brewing *storm of civil war*.[807] For he had taken the irrevocable decision that, unless peace was agreed, he would take up arms to defend his safety, as long as he could, rather than surrender himself to the royal power and allow himself to be dishonoured by insults and reproaches. Although the empress had forsworn all secular affairs forever on religious grounds, she nevertheless judged that it would not be too inconsistent with her resolution nor at odds with her duties to the Church if she gave her support in a difficult situation to a man who had deserved very well of her and if she imposed restrictions on the youthful disorders of her son.

She therefore came to Worms, attended by a most impressive number of abbots and monks[808] and when the aforementioned duke had appeared in person, the archbishops of Cologne and Mainz pledging their words for him,[809] she freed him from all suspicion of a crime. And immediately after the settlement of the matter about which she had come, she took leave of her son in order to make quite clear to everyone that she had been drawn to undertake this secular business not so much by an inclination towards worldly affairs as by the motive of the common good. The duke was also bidden by the king to depart in peace and he returned immediately to his own estates. He was convinced that the king had not banished his enmity entirely from his mind but that he had for a while been deprived of the power of doing harm.

805 On this polemical version of the proceedings against Otto of Northeim see above p. 130 and nn. 591–2.

806 Matilda (✝1060): see above p. 73 and n. 204.

807 Livy III.7.3.

808 In their reconstruction of the events of 1072, Jakobs (1968) pp. 39–42, 160, 266–90; Jakobs (1973) pp. 106–12; Vogel (1984) pp. 1–5, 24–30; Hlawitschka (1991) pp. 219–20; Black-Veldtrup (1995) p. 311; Robinson (1999) pp. 125–6 noted that during the empress's visit she and Rudolf co-operated in the reform of his 'ducal monastery' of St Blasien: Agnes assisted in introducing the monastic customs of Fruttuaria, perhaps at Rudolf's request.

809 Anno of Cologne (above n. 139) and Siegfried of Mainz (above n. 210). On the friendship of Rudolf with Anno see Meyer von Knonau (1890) pp. 490–1; Jakobs (1968) pp. 265–6. On Rudolf's relations with Siegfried see below, 1073, pp. 195, 200. See also Jakobs (1968) p. 270; Jakobs (1973) p. 110; Black-Veldtrup (1995) pp. 303–4.

There also Abbot Hugh of Cluny,[810] who had arrived there with the empress, delivered to Abbot Rupert of Reichenau the written commands of the Roman pontiff:[811] namely, that he was separated from the body of the Church by the anathema of the apostolic see; that the performance of every divine office was forbidden to him, except the singing of psalms; that all access to the abbacy of Reichenau or to any ecclesiastical office was closed to him forever,[812] because he had been charged with simoniacal heresy and, having been summoned to a synod twice and three times to clear himself of the charge against him, he had declined to come. He was thus compelled by the king to give up the pastoral staff, which he had seized *not as a shepherd but as a hireling*,[813] which he did with the greatest acrimony.

At this time the tombs of St Sebald in Nuremberg[814] and St Haimerad in Hasungen[815] were renowned and held in the highest honour throughout Gaul and they were visited every day by great crowds of people because of the divine healing that was granted there again and again to the sick.

The archbishop of Mainz set out from Mainz on the feast of the Nativity of St Mary. After pretending to set out for Galicia to pray there, he withdrew to the monastery of Cluny.[816] He sent away all those who had accompanied him and also renounced all that he possessed

---

810 Hugh I ('the Great'), abbot of Cluny (1049–1109), godfather of King Henry IV. Cf. *D.H.IV* 255 (Worms, 27 July), confirming the donation of the monastery of Rüeggisberg to Cluny. See Diener (1959) p. 363; Kohnle (1993) pp. 91, 304. On Agnes's close personal relationship with Cluny see Black-Veldtrup (1995) pp. 310–12.

811 On the case of Abbot Rupert of Reichenau see above p. 145 and n. 706. This letter of Alexander II is not extant: see *JL* 4703*, 4704*. Cf. Gregory VII, *Register* I.82, p. 117.

812 But see below, 1076, p. 312 and n. 1666: Rupert subsequently became abbot of Gengenbach.

813 John 10:12.

814 Cf. *Annals of Weissenburg* 1070, p. 55; *Annals of Augsburg* 1070, p. 128. See Meyer von Knonau (1894) p. 167.

815 Cf. Ekkebert of Hersfeld, *Vita sancti Haimeradi* c. 27–39, pp. 606–7. See Meyer von Knonau (1894) p. 168. On Lampert's connection with Hasungen see Stengel (1955) pp. 245–58; Struve (1969) pp. 84–96 and above pp. 25–9.

816 8 September. Cf. Marianus Scottus, *Chronicon* 1094 [=1072], p. 560: 'On Sunday, 6 September Bishop Siegfried of Mainz set off for Galicia to St James [Santiago di Compostella], as though for the sake of prayer. When, however, he was in the monastery of Cluny, on the Sunday before Michaelmas [23 September], he entered the cloister and renounced the world.' Gregory VII, *Register* II.29, p. 162 ('you wished to spend the rest of your life in the monastery of Cluny'). See Meyer von Knonau (1894) pp. 168–70.

and decided to spend the rest of his life there as a simple monk and to seek rest forever from all the noise of worldly affairs in the name of voluntary poverty. But he did not persevere for very long in this resolution. Both the clergy and the people of Mainz called him back and he was extracted from the monastery with the greatest difficulty.[817] He returned to Mainz on the feast of the Nativity of St Andrew the apostle[818] and hastily resumed the burdensome task that he had equally hastily abandoned, since he could not resist the general will of all the men of Mainz.

Abbot Ruthard of Hersfeld began to be ill in the month of January and throughout the year he was weakened by unremitting sickness. After he had given up hope of recovery, on 11 December he voluntarily resigned the abbacy and the pastoral office, which he could not perform because of his infirmity, precisely in the thirteenth year after he had succeeded Abbot Meginher.[819] And according to his wish, H[artwig], a monk of the same monastery, immediately succeeded him.[820]

Bishop Adalbero of Metz died[821] and Herman, the provost of Liège, succeeded him.[822]

---

817 Cf. the letter of 'the whole clergy and people of the see of Mainz' to Archbishop Siegfried: *Codex Udalrici* 39, pp. 81–4.

818 30 November. Cf. Marianus Scottus, *Chronicon* 1094 [=1072], p. 560: 'he returned to Mainz on 6 December'.

819 See above p. 55 and n. 54, p. 77 and n. 234. He died on 9 June 1074: see below p. 236 and n. 1246. Cf. Lampert, *Libellus de institutione Herveldensis ecclesiae* II, p. 354: 'Abbot Ruthard, worn out by old age, gave up Hersfeld on the arrival of Henry [IV].' See Meyer von Knonau (1894) p. 173 and n. 107. See also above p. 24.

820 Hartwig, abbot of Hersfeld (1072–90), anti-archbishop of Magdeburg (1085). The name appears as 'H' in all the manuscripts, including that on which the *editio princeps* was based. Cf. Lampert, *Libellus de institutione Herveldensis ecclesiae* II, p. 354: 'The monk Hartwig was put in his place by Henry [IV]. This was pleasing to Anno [of Cologne].' See Feierabend (1913) pp. 109–10. On Lampert's attitude to Hartwig's succession see Holder-Egger (1894) pp. 205–7 and above pp. 22–4.

821 Adalbero III, bishop of Metz (1047–72).

822 Herman, bishop of Metz (1072–90).

1073

The king celebrated Christmas in Bamberg.[823] There he took away the duchy of Berthold, duke of the Carinthians,[824] in the latter's absence and without the proceedings required by law, and entrusted it to a certain Markward, who was his kinsman.[825] It was also feared that Duke Rudolf of the Swabians was plotting a rebellion against the State. But frequent envoys ran to and fro between the two sides and *through their salutary management*[826] they restrained both Rudolf from rushing headlong into war and the king from the stubborn and insolent conduct that would provoke the hesitant duke into action.[827] There also the archbishop of Cologne, who was displeased by much that happened in the palace that was contrary to justice and fairness, requested from the king that he should thereafter be given an exemption from participating in the government of the State, pleading his time of life, which was now declining into old age and every day was becoming less and less equal to the wearisome business of the kingdom.[828] The king had no difficulty

823 25 December 1072. Cf. *Annals of Niederaltaich* 1073, p. 84. See Kilian (1886) p. 57; Meyer von Knonau (1894) p. 174.

824 Berthold I (of Zähringen), duke of Carinthia (1061–77, ✝1078). Cf. Berthold of Reichenau, *Chronicle* 1073, p. 127 (see below n. 827); *Annals of Niederaltaich* 1072, p. 84 (above, n. 803); 1073, p. 85: on 24 March the king 'restored his favour to the dukes Rudolf and Berthold'. Lampert alone reported this deposition, which is evidently a polemical exaggeration: see Meyer von Knonau (1894) pp. 174 n. 108, 818. According to Heyck (1891) p. 80, Berthold never effectively established himself as duke in Carinthia.

825 Markward IV, count of Eppenstein (✝1076). He and the king had a common ancestor in Duke Herman II of Swabia, Markward's grandfather and Henry IV's great-grandfather. Lampert subsequently offered an alternative version of this event (below p. 181: 'it was on his own initiative that Markward had seized the territory of another man'). Meyer von Knonau (1894) pp. 34–5, 195 suggested that on the death of Margrave Udalric I in 1070 (above p. 126) the marches of Carniola and Istria were placed under the administration of Markward without the title of margrave.

826 Livy XLV.18.6.

827 Cf. Berthold of Reichenau, *Chronicle* 1073, p. 127: 'Duke Rudolf of Swabia, Duke Berthold of Carinthia and Duke Welf of Bavaria dissociated themselves from the king because they perceived that their advice carried no weight with him'; *Annals of Niederaltaich* 1072, p. 84 (above, n. 803); 1073, p. 85 and also above p. 159. See Meyer von Knonau (1894) p. 174.

828 Anno's presence in Bamberg on 25 December is corroborated by the *Vita Annonis archiepiscopi Coloniensis* I.38, p. 483, which reported that Anno came to Bamberg to receive from Abbot Reginger of Elwangen relics for his new foundation of Siegburg. Lampert's polemical purpose in this passage was to distance his hero Anno from the measures taken by the king in Saxony, which must, however, have already been in operation while the archbishop was the principal royal adviser. See Meyer von Knonau (1894) p. 174 n. 110, 804; Struve (1970a) pp. 107–9.

in agreeing to this, because he had noticed a long while ago that the archbishop was seriously offended by his vicious inclinations and his youthful follies and very often opposed them as far as he could without injuring the royal dignity. When the archbishop had returned to his own estates, therefore, the king, like someone who had been set free from a very strict schoolmaster, immediately threw himself headlong into every kind of shameful act, breaking down all the restraints of moderation and discretion.

On all the mountains and on the little hills of Saxony and Thuringia he constructed strongly fortified castles and placed a garrison in each.[829] Since the necessary provisions were insufficient, he permitted them *to take plunder* from the nearby villages and fields, *like enemy raiders,*[830] and to compel those who were settled in the area round about to build the fortifications of those castles and to gather together building materials in sufficient quantities and even to sweat and labour like slaves themselves.[831] But lest he be branded with open tyranny if he raged against the innocent and against his own kingdom with such savage cruelty, in order to cloak his ungodliness with some appearance of religion, he urged the archbishop of Mainz by all the means at his disposal to demand the tithes of Thuringia, as he had determined to do very many years before.[832] He promised that he would give him

829 Cf. *Annals of Niederaltaich* 1072, p. 85: the king 'had already begun to build many castles in the forest called the Harz'; Berthold of Reichenau, *Chronicle* 1072, p. 127: 'The king built for himself many very strongly fortified castles in the regions of Saxony and Thuringia'; Bruno of Merseburg, *The Saxon War* c. 16, p. 22: Henry IV 'began to seek out high mountains with natural defences in deserted localities and began to build on them castles which, had they only stood in suitable places, would have been a great defence and ornament to the kingdom'. On Henry IV's castles see Baaken (1961) pp. 81–4; Fenske (1977) pp. 28–32; Robinson (1999) pp. 82–4.

830 Livy I.5.4.

831 Cf. Archbishop Werner of Magdeburg, letter to Archbishop Siegfried of Mainz of 1074/5 (cited in Bruno of Merseburg, *The Saxon War* c. 42, p. 41): the king 'fortified the more inaccessible places in our region with very strong castles, in which he placed considerable numbers of armed men who compelled us to serve them like slaves'; *Annals of Niederaltaich* 1072, p. 85: 'because [the king] had few estates or none at all in the neighbourhood of those fortresses, the men who guarded the castles, because of the scarcity of provisions, always plundered the possessions of the inhabitants of the province'; Bruno of Merseburg, *The Saxon War* c. 16, p. 23: 'garrisons were placed in the castles and began to plunder the country roundabout, so as to harvest where they had not sown, to force free men to do the work of serfs'.

832 On Siegfried of Mainz and the demand for Thuringian tithes see above pp. 80 and n. 266, 116 and n. 515. See Holder-Egger (1894) pp. 185–90 (especially p. 186: 'Lampert's entire narrative ... is a poisonously malicious misrepresentation of the proceedings and motives of the persons concerned.... It was only a fantasy on Lampert's part to bring the Thuringian tithes controversy into a close causal connection with the

the utmost assistance in his demands and that he would compel the unwilling to obey the command by means of the power of royal majesty, on condition, however, that the archbishop granted him a portion of those tithes appropriate to royal magnificence and to the great efforts made by the king. Thus encouraged by the vainest of hopes, the archbishop summoned a synod to meet in Erfurt on 10 March.[833]

On the appointed day the king was present, the archbishop was present and each was surrounded by a large swarm of philosophers, or rather of sophists, whom they had taken the greatest pains to gather around them from various places. Their purpose was to interpret the canons for them, not according to the truth of the texts but according to the will of the archbishop, and to strengthen his case by sophistries and polemic since they could not do so by means of truthful statements.[834] Together with the king and the archbishop of Mainz, Bishop Herman of Bamberg,[835] Bishop Hezelo of Hildesheim,[836] Bishop Eppo of Zeitz[837] and Bishop Benno of Osnabrück[838] were in attendance. They had been summoned not to debate the case according to ecclesiastical law but by means of their rhetorical skill and the weight of their arguments, ultimately by whatever reasoning and stratagem they could, to achieve what the king wished, although most of them very strongly disapproved of the king's undertaking. But they were restrained from expressing their opinions freely both by their great fear of the king and by their personal friendship with the archbishop. Moreover the king had a considerable force of armed men around him, so that he might use their military strength to coerce any who might perhaps attempt to disrupt business.

The hope and reliance of the Thuringians depended especially on the

Saxon rebellion'); Meyer von Knonau (1894) p. 795; Struve (1969) pp. 46–9; Struve (1970a) pp. 76–8; Staab (1991) pp. 52–3; Robinson (1999) pp. 76–7.

833 Cf. *Annalista Saxo* p. 699 and *Annals of Iburg* 1073, p. 436: 'In the middle of Lent a synod was held in Erfurt in order to demand tithes from the Thuringians.' Lampert alone gave a detailed account of the synod. On his version of events see Meyer von Knonau (1894) pp. 186–90, 795–6, 811; Struve (1969) pp. 47–8; Staab (1991) p. 53; Robinson (1999) p. 76. Gresser (2006) pp. 107–10 referred to the synod of Erfurt as 'the Mainz synod of 1073'.

834 On the polemical character of Lampert's account see Holder-Egger (1894) p. 186. Lampert's *Life* of St Lul, the founder of Hersfeld, composed in the decade 1063–73, was intended to strengthen the legal position of the abbey in the tithes dispute with Siegfried: see Struve (1969) pp. 34–7.

835 See above n. 449.

836 See above n. 121.

837 Eppo (Eberhard) of Zeitz (Naumburg): see above n. 46.

838 See above n. 500.

abbot of Fulda and the abbot of Hersfeld[839] because they both possessed very many churches with the right to collect tithes and countless estates in Thuringia and, if the Thuringians failed in the defence of their cause, the abbots themselves would fail with them. When in the public debate they were pressed to give up their tithes, at first they begged the archbishop in God's name to allow the lawful rights conferred on their monasteries in ancient times to be confirmed and to remain undisturbed, for the apostolic see had frequently confirmed them for the abbots in old and recent documents[840] and his predecessors, the archbishops of Mainz, men of the greatest distinction and holiness, up to the time of Archbishop Liutpold,[841] had never attempted to violate them. The archbishop countered this with the sharp reply that his predecessors had in their day governed the Church of God according to their own judgements and had given to their ignorant subjects, who were still more or less newly converted to the faith, *milk* to drink and *not strong meat*[842] and, showing wise management, they had made many concessions that they wished to be curtailed in the course of time by the diligence of their successors, when their subjects had become stronger in the faith. Now, however, when the Church had reached maturity, or rather old age, he would *regulate spiritual things with spiritual means*[843] and he would no longer provide small children with *milk* but adults with *solid food*[844] and demand from the sons of the Church the observance of the Church's laws. They must accordingly either withdraw from the unity of the Church or calmly accede to the laws of the Church.

Then the abbots again pleaded with him in God's name that, if there was no remnant of protection or hope for them in the authority of the

839 Widerad of Fulda (above n. 239) and Hartwig of Hersfeld (above n. 820). In the eighth century the archbishop of Mainz had been the sole tithe-holder in Thuringia but the abbeys of Hersfeld and Fulda had gradually acquired the right of tithes. A crucial complication was that in the time of Lul (754–86) the archbishop of Mainz held the abbatiate of Hersfeld in a personal union. See Meyer von Knonau (1894) pp. 188–9; Struve (1969) pp. 46–8; Struve (1970a) pp. 76–8; Vogtherr (1991) pp. 444–5.

840 Of these papal privileges for Hersfeld only John XII, *JL* 3723 (in which there is no mention of tithes) is authentic. Tithes are the subject of the spurious privileges of Stephen III, *JE* 2383–4 and Gregory IV, *JE* 2571.

841 Archbishop Liutpold of Mainz (above n. 92). Cf. Henry IV's grant to Mainz of *D.H.IV* 48 (14 February 1059): see Meyer von Knonau (1890) pp. 151, 658.

842 Hebrews 5:12.

843 I Corinthians 2:13. On the idea of the 'old age' of the Church see below p. 239 and n. 1267.

844 I Corinthians 3:1–2.

Roman pontiff, in the privileges of Charles[845] and other emperors, in the favour of his predecessors, the archbishops of Mainz, let him at least allow a division of those tithes, such as the decrees of the canons had judged to be fair and such as the other churches throughout the world regarded as customary: namely, that he should be content with a quarter in respect of the payments due to him and to his representatives and should allow the remaining three-quarters to the churches that had been entitled to them since ancient times.[846] The archbishop retorted that he had not exhausted himself with such hard labour and *rolled* this heavy *stone*[847] now for almost ten years with the intention of voluntarily giving up his rights when he had at last *obtained his wish*[848] and willingly agreeing to share with them the tithes that he had extorted with so great an effort.

A first and a second day had now passed by as this dispute continued and *the hazards of fortune made it uncertain*[849] which party would yield to the other. At this moment it seemed that *the situation would be transformed*[850] by the Thuringians rejecting the synod and appealing to the apostolic see. But the king, calling on God as his witness, declared that he would punish with death anyone who ventured to do this and that he would utterly destroy everything that he possessed and that the calamity of that day would not be effaced for many centuries thereafter. The abbot of Hersfeld was *terrified by the danger*[851] threatening his brethren and, therefore, since in this narrowly confined situation no other way of escape lay open to him, he left the matter to the decision of the king so that he might settle the case between him and the archbishop according to his judgement of what was good and equitable. A long consultation was held, therefore, after which, with the king acting as mediator, the abbot and the archbishop finally consented to this accord. The abbot was to receive two-thirds of the tithes in ten of his churches

---

845 On the privilege of Charlemagne granting tithes to Fulda and his privileges for Hersfeld granting the tithes of some estates in Thuringia see Holder-Egger, *Lamperti Annales* p. 143 n. 1.

846 A conflict between Mainz and Hersfeld in the 840s had been settled in 845, when the archbishop conceded a fourth part of the tithes in Thuringia: cf. the memorandum *On tithes in Thuringia*, found in the twelfth-century Hersfeld cartulary, printed by Holder-Egger in *Lamperti Opera* p. 356. See Struve (1969) p. 47.

847 Terence, *Eunuchus* V.8.55.

848 Livy VII.40.6. Cf. Horace, *Ars poetica* 76; Ovid, *Ars amatoria* I.486.

849 Cicero, *Oratio pro Marcello* 5.

850 Livy I.30.8.

851 *Ibid.*, II.12.12.

with the right to collect tithes, while the archbishop received one-third, but in his other churches half should be due to the abbot, half to the archbishop. Where a church with the right to tithes was the property of the archbishop, all the tithes there were granted to him. Moreover all the archbishop's manors, in whatever diocese they lay, were to remain entirely exempt from all demands for tithes. Once the abbot of Hersfeld had been *compelled to pass under the yoke*,[852] the Thuringians at once *lost all hope*[853] – for they had placed the greatest reliance on his sagacity and eloquence – and they resisted no longer and they declared that in future they would pay tithes without hesitation.

The abbot of Fulda remained steadfast and firm in his purpose for some days afterwards. But since he could neither recover the king's favour nor obtain permission to return to his own estates unless he yielded to the general opinion, he was at length overwhelmed by the difficulty of his situation and, *not* so much *through consultation as through* royal command and *fear*[854] of the king, he was compelled to accept these terms. In all his churches with the right to collect tithes he himself was to receive half of the tithes and the archbishop was to receive half but, as in the case of the archbishop, all his manors were to be free from all payment of tithes. Then the king – knowing that these proceedings would not be acceptable to the Roman pontiff – commanded both abbots, under the threat of the withdrawal of his favour, neither in person nor through an envoy or in any way whatsoever to appeal to the apostolic see against the decisions of the synod.[855]

When all the business that he had planned was thus completed according to his wishes, he hastened with all speed to Regensburg to celebrate the holy festival of Easter there.[856] And while he was spending Palm Sunday in the city of Augsburg,[857] he received into his favour Duke Rudolf of the Swabians and certain other men, who had been accused

---

852 *Ibid.* I.26.13; II.34.9 (a frequent usage). Cf. Caesar, *Bellum Gallicum* I.7, I.12.

853 Livy IX.2.12.

854 *Ibid.*, II.11.4.

855 See Struve (1969) p. 48. After Abbot Hartwig was forced to give way, a lively polemical activity began in Hersfeld. 'The essential element of this "Hersfeld programme" … was Lampert's *Vita Lulli* (above n. 834), which implicitly contrasted the conduct of Lul and Charlemagne, the benefactors of Hersfeld, with that of Siegfried of Mainz and Henry IV. See also above p. 29.

856 31 March. See Kilian (1886) p. 57; Meyer von Knonau (1894) pp. 194–5.

857 24 March. According to *Annals of Niederaltaich* 1073, p. 85, 'the king celebrated Palm Sunday in Eichstädt', which was preferred by Kilian (1886) pp. 57–8 and Meyer von Knonau (1894) p. 195 and n. 15.

a long time before of having evil designs against the State.[858] Then, as he had intended, he celebrated the holy festival of Easter in Regensburg and Whitsun in Augsburg.[859]

Pope Alexander, who was also called Anselm, died.[860] The Romans immediately, without consulting the king,[861] elected as his successor Hildebrand,[862] a man who was most learned in sacred literature and most renowned throughout the whole Church in the time of the previous popes for every kind of virtue. Since he burned most intensely with the zeal of God, the bishops of Gaul[863] immediately began to be troubled by great uneasiness, fearing that *a man of his ardent temper*[864] and passionate fidelity towards God would at some time judge them with great severity for their negligent conduct. They all decided unanimously, therefore, to approach the king and entreat him to declare that the election – which had been carried out without his commanding it – was invalid. They maintained that if he did not act quickly to anticipate the impetuous behaviour of the man, the evil consequences would affect no one more seriously than the king himself. The king immediately sent as his envoy Count Eberhard,[865] who was to meet the leading

---

858 Cf. *Annals of Niederaltaich* 1073, p. 85: 'he restored his favour to the dukes Rudolf and Berthold'. See above p. 163 and n. 824. See also Meyer von Knonau (1894) p. 195 and n. 15.

859 19 May. Cf. *Annals of Niederaltaich* 1073, p. 85: 'he held a conference of princes in Augsburg at the feast of Whitsun'; *DD.H.IV* 258–60 (20, 23–4 May, Augsburg). See Kilian (1886) p. 58; Meyer von Knonau (1894) p. 223.

860 Alexander II (above n. 358) †21 April. See Meyer von Knonau (1894) pp. 201–2.

861 For Lampert's use of this formula in accounts of papal elections see above 1054, 1057, 1058, 1063, pp. 62, 68, 72, 84. See Meyer von Knonau (1894) p. 209 n. 37; Krause (1960) pp. 164–6; Schneider (1972) p. 53 and n. 154; Robinson (1999) p. 129.

862 Gregory VII (above n. 194), elected 22 April. See Meyer von Knonau (1894) pp. 204–10; Krause (1960) pp. 159–69; Schneider (1972) pp. 23–35; Cowdrey (1998) pp. 72–4. For analysis of Lampert's version of the election see Meyer von Knonau (1894) pp. 841–2; Schneider (1972) pp. 52–4.

863 I.e. the German bishops. On this meaning of 'Gaul' see Lugge (1960) pp. 132–40, especially p. 132 n. 238. Evidence of opposition to Gregory's election within the empire is recorded by Abbot Walo of St Arnulf, Metz, *Letter* 1, p. 53: 'that devil of Vercelli [Bishop Gregory], together with his accomplices, labours to prevent your being confirmed in the see'. Schneider (1972) pp. 52–5 linked Lampert's report with the 'conference of princes in Augsburg' (see above n. 859) and with the excommunication of five advisers of Henry IV by Alexander II

864 Livy II.23.15; VI.11.6.

865 Probably Count Eberhard 'the Bearded' (†1078): see above n. 641. See Meyer von Knonau (1894) pp. 43 n. 6, 841 n. 160; Schneider (1972) p. 52. This Count Eberhard was one of the five royal advisers excommunicated by Alexander II in the Lenten synod of 1073: see Robinson (1999) pp. 125, 360–1. Lampert alone identified

Romans and ask them the reason why, contrary to the custom of their ancestors, they had appointed a pontiff of the Roman church without consulting the king and who was to command Hildebrand himself to resign from the office that he had unlawfully taken, if he did not give a suitable account of himself. Count Eberhard came to Rome and was received by Hildebrand in a friendly manner. After he had explained the king's commands to him, Hildebrand replied that, as God was his witness, he had never aimed at this high office out of ambition but that he had been elected by the Romans and had been compelled by violence to undertake the government of the Church.[866] Nevertheless he could by no means be forced to allow himself to be consecrated until he knew for certain from reliable envoys that both the king and the princes of the German kingdom had consented to his election. For this reason he had hitherto delayed his consecration and would doubtless continue to delay it until a trustworthy messenger coming from the court made known to him the king's will. When *this was reported to the king*,[867] he gladly accepted the explanation and announced his most joyful assent to his consecration, which was performed in the following year on the feast of the Purification of St Mary.[868]

Meanwhile those who were stationed in the castles mentioned above were an extremely serious threat to the people of Saxony and Thuringia.[869] Every day they *made incursions*[870] and seized everything that was in the villages and fields; they demanded insupportable tributes and taxes from the woods and the produce of the fields and they very frequently drove off whole herds of animals at a time under the pretence of a claim for tithes. They forced the inhabitants of the province – very many of whom were of distinguished birth and very prosperous property-

---

Eberhard as a royal envoy in 1073. In the similarly polemical version of Gregory VII's election by Bonizo of Sutri, *To a Friend* VII, p. 221, the royal envoy is identified as Bishop Gregory of Vercelli (Henry IV's Italian chancellor).

866 For this theme in Gregory VII's pronouncements on his election see *Register* I.3, 8, 70; III.10a; IV.28; VII.14a, 23, pp. 5, 13, 101, 270, 343, 483, 500. Cf. Lampert's criticisms of ambition above, 1064, p. 96 ('schism of Cadalus'); 1071, p. 145 (Abbot Rupert of Reichenau); below, 1075, p. 289 (abbacy of Fulda).

867 Livy XLV.5.10.

868 2 February 1074. But Gregory VII was actually consecrated on 30 June 1073: see Meyer von Knonau (1894) p. 221; Cowdrey (1998) p. 74. Ranke (1888) pp. 136–7 was the first to note that Lampert's account was chronologically impossible. See also Holder-Egger (1894) pp. 519–20; Meyer von Knonau (1894) pp. 841–2; Borino (1956) pp. 313–43; Krause (1960) pp. 164–9; Schneider (1972) pp. 52–4.

869 See above p. 164 and n. 829.

870 Livy XXII.6.8. See Billanovich (1945) p. 74.

owners – to serve them in the manner of common slaves. They violated their daughters and wives with the knowledge of the husbands and virtually before their very eyes. They carried off some of these women by force into the castles and treated them in the most lewd fashion whenever their lust prompted them and finally sent them back to their husbands with shameful reproaches. Any man among them who had dared to utter a sigh in the midst of such great evils and to alleviate and dissipate the grief within his mind even by the slightest complaint, was immediately thrown into chains as if he had perpetrated a serious injury against the king and he could not regain his freedom unless he had first redeemed his life and safety by parting with all his possessions.[871] And when they appealed every day from all sides in great numbers to the royal majesty – which before that time had usually been the sole refuge for all the afflicted – they were driven away with harsh invective and the king declared that they suffered in this way because they had unjustly withheld tithes and that he would inevitably coerce with armed might, like an avenger of God's cause, those who would not willingly accede to the laws of the Church.[872]

When, therefore, the king saw that all the inhabitants of that locality were *struck by terror*[873] and were entirely ready to accept whatever conditions he might impose, he began to plan a great stratagem that had not been attempted by any of his ancestors in former times: namely, to reduce all the Saxons and Thuringians to slavery and to add their estates to the public fisc.[874] Nevertheless he took care that this plan should not be divulged prematurely and fail in its purpose and offer the princes of the kingdom an occasion for just complaint. He therefore held a conference

---

871 Cf. Archbishop Werner of Magdeburg, letter to Archbishop Siegfried of Mainz of 1074/5 (cited in Bruno of Merseburg, *The Saxon War* c. 42, pp. 41–2): 'the great dangers, the great insults, the great losses that we have suffered in our own bodies, in our wives, in our possessions'; Bruno, *The Saxon War* c. 25, p. 29: 'From you who live in the vicinity they took your property into their castles against your will; they subdued your daughters and wives to their lust. They demanded your servants and your draught animals for their service and even placed their burdens, however dishonourable, on your shoulders.'

872 Cf. *Annals of Niederaltaich* 1073, p. 85: 'If anyone approached the court to bemoan these grievances, he seems to have been assailed with insults and driven away.' On Lampert's version of the significance of tithes see above n. 832.

873 Livy X.41.4.

874 Cf. *Casus monasterii Petrishusensis* II.31, p. 645: the king 'dwelled in Saxony so often that the province was known as the emperor's kitchen'. See also Rieckenberg (1942) pp. 95–6; Jordan (1970) p. 543; Leyser (1981) pp. 743–4; Leyser (1983) p. 434.

in secret with the king of the Danes[875] and made an agreement with him that, in return for a certain large area of Saxony that belonged to Margrave Udo,[876] he would provide him with help in accomplishing the plan that he was revolving in his mind. The king of the Danes would make war on the Saxons from one direction, while he himself assailed them from the other direction. He enjoined the same strategy on the other kings and peoples who were the neighbours of Saxony.[877]

When it seemed that he had enough support, he announced to all the princes of the kingdom an expedition against the Poles, alleging as his pretext that they had made war on the Bohemians, contrary to his prohibition, and had attacked their territory with fire and sword. As I said, this was a pretext that he had ready to hand.[878] For the rest, as *a widespread rumour*[879] subsequently declared, he wished, using the excuse of the Poles, to lead an army into Saxony, to *destroy* the Saxons *utterly*[880]

---

875 Swein Estrithson, king of Denmark (1047–74). This meeting was dated in 1071 by Adam of Bremen, *Gesta* III.60, p. 206: 'that famous conference of the emperor with the king of the Danes was held as an affront to the duke [of Saxony] in Lüneburg, where in the form of a treaty they vowed to take arms against the Saxons'. Lampert's own subsequent reference to this agreement in this same annal (below p. 194) in fact suggests a date earlier than 1073: 'the agreement that [Swein] had long ago concluded with the king'. Cf. Bruno of Merseburg, *The Saxon War* c. 20, pp. 25–6: at a secret meeting in Bardowick 'the king of the Danes swore to King Henry that he would bring what help he could by land and sea against [Henry's] enemies, and particularly against the Saxons, and King Henry promised to give him possession of all the regions bordering on his kingdom'. The purpose of this meeting is not known: it was perhaps linked with Swein's plans for the restructuring of the Danish church or with missionary or military initiatives concerning the Liutizi: see Meyer von Knonau (1894) pp. 73–4; Seegrün (1982) pp. 1–14.

876 Margrave Udo II (of Stade) of the Saxon Nordmark (above n. 168). Hucke (1956) p. 85 cited Lampert's anecdote as the explanation of Udo II's participation in the Saxon rebellion of 1073.

877 Cf. below p. 193, referring to the Liutizi, and Bruno of Merseburg, *The Saxon War* c. 36, pp. 37–8, mentioning the duke of Bohemia, the Liutizi, the kings Philip I of France and William I of England and the duke of Aquitaine.

878 Henry IV's intention was to punish Duke Boleslav II of Poland for his breach of the truce with Bohemia that the king had negotiated in October 1071: see above p. 151 and n. 747. It is clear from the Saxon legation to the king in early August, below p. 177, that the Saxons themselves were summoned to the expedition and believed that it was bound for Poland. See Meyer von Knonau (1894) pp. 222–3, 859; Robinson (1999) p. 72. Lampert's 'rumour' probably derived from the incident in August in Kappel near Hersfeld (recorded below p. 186): 'there were those [princes] who were of the opinion that, since they had come armed and prepared for the expedition against the Poles, the army should immediately be marched into Saxony'. See Meyer von Knonau (1894) pp. 256–7.

879 Livy I.7.2; XXV.17.4.

880 *Ibid.*, IX.45.17.

and to establish the people of the Swabians in their place.[881] For this people was most dear to him and he had raised very many of them – who were *descended from low-born ancestors*[882] and had virtually no ancestors at all – to the highest offices and made them into men of the first importance in the palace and all the business of the kingdom was settled according to their will. This conduct had made him an object of extreme hostility and detestation to the princes and very many of them would not tolerate his unseemly behaviour and absented themselves entirely from the palace, unless they received a summons to which a response was unavoidable.

The king, therefore, decided that his army should assemble for the expedition one week after the feast of the Assumption of Mary, the holy Mother of God.[883] And while everyone was anxiously and eagerly awaiting the outcome, he himself was now acting in a more headstrong and more outrageous manner even than usual. Neglecting the princes, he continually had only Swabians about him and it was from their ranks that he appointed his secret counsellors and it was they whom he made the administrators of both private and public affairs.[884] Then he repeatedly said in conversation that all Saxons had the status of slaves and he also sent envoys to chide some of them, asking why they did not, as befitted the rank of their ancestors, perform the service of slaves (to use his own expression) and pay from their income the sums owed by serfs to the royal treasury.[885] If they objected, he threatened to pursue

---

881 Lampert alone placed this emphasis on the Swabians in his polemic against the king's conduct in Saxony. Bruno of Merseburg, *The Saxon War* c. 21, p. 27, wrote that in 1073 the garrison of Lüneburg consisted of Swabians, '70 of his most trusted men'. But cf. c. 17, p. 24: 'When the nation of the Swabians heard of the calamity of the Saxons, they secretly sent envoys to them and concluded a treaty with them so that neither people would help the king in oppressing the other. For the king also wished to oppress the Swabians with violence and compel them to render tribute to him from their own estates.' *Annals of Niederaltaich* 1072, p. 84, reporting that the king 'raised up inferior men by means of riches and property', made no reference to Swabians.

882 Cicero, *De officiis* I.32.116. This description prompted the theory of Bosl (1950) pp. 82–8, that these Swabians were 'unfree knights', *ministeriales* from the royal household, whom the king encouraged to marry Saxon noblewomen, in order to settle his own adherents in the province. Against Bosl's theory see Fenske (1977) pp. 280–1; Wilke (1970) pp. 33–6; Robinson (1999) pp. 81–2, 356–9.

883 22 August. See Meyer von Knonau (1894) p. 222 and n. 60.

884 Lampert, 1071, p. 148, identified the Swabian adviser Liupold of Meersburg (above n. 728), whose brothers, the 'knights' Arnold and Berthold, appear in *D.H.IV* 243. See Robinson (1999) pp. 67, 359.

885 Cf. Archbishop Werner of Magdeburg, letter to Archbishop Siegfried of Mainz of 1074/5 (cited in Bruno of Merseburg, *The Saxon War* c. 42, pp. 41–2): the garrisons

them with all the strength of the kingdom and to drive them out of the kingdom, as though they had outraged the royal majesty.

From these and other indications of this kind the princes of Saxony recognised the evil that threatened their necks and immediately, being deeply disturbed by *the danger that came from two sides*,[886] they held frequent secret meetings and exhorted each other to offer their advice about what ought to be done.[887] A single wish united them all; all were of the same opinion, which they confirmed by an oath that they gave and received in turn: that they preferred to die and to undergo all extremes sooner than suffer the disgrace of losing the liberty that they had received from their ancestors. Among the leaders and standard-bearers of this sworn association were Bishop Bucco of Halberstadt,[888] Otto, formerly duke of Bavaria,[889] and Herman, brother of the Saxon duke Otto, who had died in the previous year.[890] As for Bucco, although he had been exasperated by the frequent injuries inflicted by the king, he was a man of such extraordinary sanctity and of such an excellent reputation in the Church of God that it is impossible to believe that he would have rushed into this daring enterprise for any other reason than zeal for God and a simple concern for the welfare of all.[891] In the case of the other two men, in addition to their adherence to the common cause of their people, they had ceased to support the king long before because of Magnus, the son of the Saxon duke Otto, whom the king, after receiving his surrender, had now held in prison for two years.[892]

They could not obtain pardon for him except on the condition that he renounced forever the duchy and the other properties that belonged to him by hereditary right from his deceased parents. Magnus declared

---

of the royal castles 'forced us to serve [the king] in the manner of slaves'; *Annals of Disibodenberg* 1075, p. 6: 'King Henry was planning to subject all the Saxons to slavery.'

886 Sallust, *Jugurtha* 38.5.

887 Cf. *Annals of Niederaltaich* 1073, p. 85: 'very many of the Saxon princes ... immediately held frequent secret meetings and anxiously discussed what they should do about these evils'.

888 Bucco (Burchard II) of Halberstadt (above n. 235).

889 Otto II of Northeim (above n. 261). See Lange (1961) p. 46.

890 Herman Billung, count (✝1086), brother of Duke Ordulf (Otto) Billung of Saxony (above n. 621) ✝28 March 1072.

891 On Lampert's presentation of Bucco-Burchard as an *exemplum* of piety see Struve (1970a) p. 105 n. 32. On the bishop's leading role in the conspiracy see Fenske (1977) p. 105.

892 Magnus Billung (above n. 621). See above 1071, p. 144 and n. 704.

that in no circumstances would he do so, even if he had to spend whatever remained of his life in prison and in chains; even if he must lay down his life amidst tortures and torments of every kind. And when the two princes achieved nothing by their humble supplication, nothing by offering money and countless estates, nothing *by calling to mind* their frequent *meritorious services* to the king himself and *to the State*,[893] finally Otto, the former duke of Bavaria, offered himself to the king – to be kept in chains as long as he wished and all his property to be divided up according to his pleasure, as if the earlier settlement had never been made – if only he might by his surrender secure the release of his kinsman, who had fallen into this calamity solely through his devotion to Otto's cause.[894] To this the king is said to have given *the* very *savage reply*[895] that Otto himself and everything that he possessed had long since fallen into the royal power as the lawful consequence of his surrender and that he had not yet been cleared of the offence of which he had previously been accused so that, according to the law of nations, the king had a right to the free surrender of Otto's person and his property.[896] These words, pronounced with bitterness, were received with even greater bitterness and were productive of deep hatred and anger.

The sedition instigated by these *leaders*[897] in a short time infected all the people of Saxony like a kind of madness so that every rank, every condition of men, every age group, provided only that they were fit to perform military service, with one mind and with one will, *issued a call to arms*[898] and promised on oath either to die without flinching or to set their people free. These princes were in that sworn association: Archbishop Wezilo of Magdeburg,[899] Bishop Bucco of Halberstadt, Bishop Hezelo

893 Livy III.56.9.

894 On the unconventional nature of this royal treatment of Magnus see Althoff (1991) pp. 323–4; Althoff (1997) pp. 50–1. On the polemical character of Lampert's report see Meyer von Knonau (1894) p. 236 and n. 84. The statement that Magnus was Otto's 'kinsman' is corroborated nowhere in the primary sources but was accepted without comment by Lange (1960) pp. 41, 46. According to Meyer von Knonau (1894) p. 236 n. 84, 'to inquire into this rhetorical flourish ... is not worth the trouble'.

895 Livy II.39.11.

896 On Lampert's concept of 'the law of nations' see Struve (1970a) p. 50; Dickerhof (1991) pp. 451–2, 454.

897 Livy II.16.3. See Billanovich (1945) p. 77.

898 Livy III.50.11; VII.12.3; X.32.9; XLI.26.2. See Billanovich (1945) p. 67.

899 Wezilo (Werner), archbishop of Magdeburg (1063–78). Bruno of Merseburg, *The Saxon War* c. 26, 39, pp. 30, 40, also identified Wezilo and his nephew, Bucco (Burchard II) of Halberstadt, as leaders of the Saxon opposition to the king. See Fenske (1977) pp. 105, 196–7; Robinson (1999) pp. 88–9.

of Hildesheim,[900] Bishop Werner of Merseburg,[901] Bishop Egilbert of Minden,[902] Bishop Imad of Paderborn,[903] Bishop Frederick of Münster,[904] Bishop Benno of Meissen,[905] Otto, the former duke of Bavaria, Margrave Udo,[906] Margrave Dedi and – more spirited and more implacable than any margrave – his wife, Adela;[907] Margrave Ekbert of the Thuringians, a boy still under the age of knighthood;[908] Count palatine Frederick,[909] Count Theoderic,[910] Count Adalbert,[911] Count Otto, Count Conrad and Count Henry.[912] Then there were more than sixty thousand of the common people, who with the utmost readiness promised their hands and their help in asserting the freedom of the fatherland and in defending the laws. And they said that this was truly an opportunity offered to them by heaven to discard the yoke of a most unjust lordship from their necks.[913]

900 Hezelo of Hildesheim (above n. 121). On his opposition to Henry IV and friendship with Bucco-Burchard see Erdmann (1938) pp. 125, 130, 138–9, 146; Fenske (1977) p. 105.

901 Werner, bishop of Merseburg (1059–93). Cf. Bruno, *The Saxon War* c. 39, p. 40. See Meyer von Knonau (1894) p. 251 n. 103; Fenske (1977) p. 106.

902 Egilbert, bishop of Minden (1055–80). See Meyer von Knonau (1894) p. 251 n. 103.

903 Imad of Paderborn (above n. 102). Cf. Bruno, *The Saxon War* c. 39, p. 40. See Meyer von Knonau (1894) p. 251 n. 103; Fenske (1977) p. 106.

904 Frederick, bishop of Münster (1064–84), brother of Margrave Dedi, was identified by Bruno, *The Saxon War* c. 27, p. 31, not as a rebel but as a royal envoy to the Saxons in summer 1073. See Fenske (1977) pp. 70–1; Robinson (1999) p. 73.

905 Benno of Meissen (above n. 494). See Meyer von Knonau (1894) p. 251 n. 103.

906 Margrave Udo II (of Stade) of the Saxon Nordmark (above n. 168). Cf. Bruno, *The Saxon War* c. 46, p. 45; *Annals of Disibodenberg* 1075, p. 7. See Fenske (1977) pp. 67–8; Robinson (1999) p. 74.

907 Margrave Dedi of Lower Lusatia (above n. 522) and Adela of Louvain (above n. 506). Cf. Bruno, *The Saxon War* c. 26, p. 30. See Fenske (1977) pp. 70, 73–4; Robinson (1999) p. 74.

908 Margrave Ekbert II of Meissen (above n. 504). See Fenske (1977) pp. 74–5; Robinson (1999) p. 74.

909 The Saxon count palatine Frederick II (of Goseck) (above n. 227). Cf. Bruno, *The Saxon War* c. 26, p. 30. See Fenske (1977) pp. 79–80; Robinson (1999) p. 74.

910 Theoderic II, count of Katlenburg (+1085), brother-in-law of Margrave Ekbert II. Cf. Bruno, *The Saxon War* c. 84, p. 80. See Fenske (1977) p. 79; Robinson (1999) p. 75.

911 Adalbert, count of Ballenstedt (+ *ca.* 1080), step-son-in-law of Margrave Dedi. See Fenske (1977) pp. 34–5, 80, 87, 89.

912 These three princes have not been identified: see Meyer von Knonau (1894) p. 251 n. 103. Lampert's list does not include Count Gebhard of Supplinburg and Meinfried, burgrave of Magdeburg, identified by Bruno of Merseburg, *The Saxon War* c. 46, 52, pp. 45, 50.

913 Cf. below 1075, p. 259: the king's scouts reported that the rebel Saxon army 'consisted of an absurd rabble, accustomed to farming rather than to military service'; Bruno, *The Saxon War* c. 31, p. 34: Henry IV described the rebels as 'rustic

No duke had yet been appointed in Saxony because (as was mentioned above) Duke Otto had departed this mortal life a little before and his son Magnus, to whom the duchy was due by lawful succession, was still kept prisoner in the castle of Harzburg. And because the king had fixed his gaze on Magnus's property, it was believed that he was waiting until Magnus was wearied by the weight of his misfortunes and the tedium of a long imprisonment and voluntarily gave up his rights and permitted the duchy to be given to whom the king wished.[914] Because Archbishop Liemar of Bremen,[915] Bishop Eppo of Zeitz[916] and Bishop Benno of Osnabrück[917] would not comply with the general will of their people, they were driven out of the territory of Saxony. They turned to the king and remained close to him during the whole period of this war, as his inseparable companions.[918]

Around 1 August,[919] therefore, when the conspiracy had already matured and had been sufficiently strengthened, they sent envoys[920] to the king, who was at that time stationed in Goslar, demanding that they should be released from the expedition that he had planned against the Poles. For they were *standing in readiness* day and night in full battle array *against*[921] their fiercest enemies, the Liutizi, and, if they relaxed their guard for a little while, they would see the enemy at once attacking their territory

men unskilled in war'. On the identity of these peasants see Baaken (1961) pp. 80–95 and the criticisms of his views by Fenske (1977) pp. 293–325.

914 See above p. 174. Cf. Bruno, *The Saxon War* c.19, p. 25: 'the king held Duke Magnus in prison for two whole years, so that throughout this time no one knew whether he was dead or alive'.

915 Liemar of Hamburg-Bremen (above n. 798).

916 Eppo (Eberhard) of Zeitz-Naumburg (above n. 46).

917 Benno II of Osnabrück (above n. 500).

918 Their presence at the royal court is evident in the diplomas: *DD.H.IV* 264–5, 267–9, 275, 283, 299 (Liemar of Hamburg-Bremen); *DD.H.IV* 264–5, 267–9, 283–4, 293, 295–7, 299 (Eppo-Eberhard of Zeitz-Naumburg); *DD.H.IV* 264–5, 293, 295–7, 299 (Benno II of Osnabrück). See Gawlik (1970) pp. 51–61, 138, 142–4. See also Fenske (1977) pp. 28–9, 60 n. 172; Robinson (1999) pp. 89, 363–4.

919 *Annals of Niederaltaich* 1073, p. 85 reported a delegation on 29 June: 'When … the king was celebrating the festival of the prince of the apostles in Goslar, very many Saxon princes arrived there to seek whether they could find an end to these evils.' Cf. Bruno of Merseburg, *The Saxon War* c. 23, p. 27: 'when the festival of the princes of the apostles Peter and Paul drew near, the king commanded all the princes of Saxony to meet in Goslar'. Lampert's later date suggested to Meyer von Knonau (1894) pp. 222–5, 238–9 and Lange (1961) p. 48 that Lampert was reporting a second legation to Goslar.

920 Three envoys, including Meinfried, burgrave of Magdeburg, according to the anonymous Henrician *Song of the Saxon War* I.37, p. 2.

921 Livy VI.39.5.

and destroying everything with fire and slaughter.[922] They had hardly
enough troops *to hold off their forces*:[923] it would be foolish, therefore, for
those who were incessantly troubled by local, indeed almost internal,
wars to open hostilities against a foreign people, living far away. They
demanded moreover that the king should order the demolition of the
castles that he had built on each of the mountains and little hills in
order to destroy Saxony; that he should make amends, according to
the adjudication of his princes, to the princes of Saxony whom he had
deprived of their property without a legal hearing;[924] that he should
occasionally leave Saxony, where he had now resided since boyhood
and more or less languished in inactivity and idleness, and visit also the
other regions of his kingdom;[925] that he should drive out of the palace
the utterly worthless men through whose advice he had *brought himself
and the State into extreme danger*[926] and allow the business of the kingdom
to be attended to and administered by the princes of the kingdom, to
whom it belonged;[927] that he should rid himself of the swarm of concubines whom he frequented with unblushing impudence, contrary to
canon law, and love and treat as his wife the queen whom he had chosen
according to the traditions of the Church to be his bedfellow and the
consort of the kingdom;[928] that he should now at least, having reached

922 On the Liutizi (above n. 147) cf. Bruno of Merseburg, *The Saxon War* c. 32, pp. 34–5.
But according to Brüske (1955) pp. 83–6, the confederation of the Liutizi was in
1073 beginning to disintegrate as a result of faction and the 1068–9 defeats inflicted
by German armies.

923 Livy II.53.1; cf. I.1.5; III.8.7; XXV.30.9.

924 Cf. Bruno of Merseburg, *The Saxon War* c. 26, p. 30.

925 A recurrent theme of Lampert's polemic against the king: see above, 1066, p. 109
and n. 458; 1070, p. 133; 1071, p. 135 and below, 1073, p. 182; 1074, p. 212; 1075,
p. 270. The analysis of Henry IV's itinerary in Kilian (1881) pp. 4–73, 137–44,
shows that, while Lampert exaggerated, it was true that in 1056–76 the king was
more often in Saxony than in any other region of the kingdom. In particular, he
visited his birthplace Goslar on thirty-two occasions. See also Rothe (1940) pp.
21–31; Wilke (1970) pp. 18–24, 30–3; Robinson (1999) pp. 78–80.

926 Livy XXVII.27.11.

927 Cf. Archbishop Werner of Magdeburg, letter to Archbishop Siegfried of Mainz of
1074/5 (cited in Bruno of Merseburg, *The Saxon War* c. 42, p. 41): 'Our lord the
king after coming of age rejected the advice of his princes, began to act on his own
authority and subjected himself to the mastery of those who took no account of
justice or goodness' See also above p. 173 and nn. 881–2. For Lampert's emphasis
on the rights of the princes in government see Struve (1970a) pp. 44, 46.

928 Queen Bertha (above n. 491). These allegations – probably arising from the divorce
proceedings of 1069 (see above p. 117) – are also found in Bruno, *The Saxon War* c.
6–10, pp. 16–19; Manegold of Lautenbach, *Ad Gebehardum* c. 29, pp. 362–3; Wido of
Ferrara, *De scismate Hildebrandi* c. 3, p. 536. See Robinson (1999) pp. 112–13.

the years of maturity and reason, give up the other wicked offences by which he had in his youth defamed the royal dignity. Finally they asked him in God's name freely to grant their just demands and not to compel them to resort to momentous and unprecedented action. If he did so, they would serve him with the utmost readiness, as hitherto, although only in the manner that was appropriate for free men born in a free empire to serve their king. But if not, they were Christians and they refused to be defiled by communicating with a man who had betrayed the Christian faith by committing offences worthy of death. If he had resolved to compel them by means of armed force, they themselves were lacking neither in weapons nor in experience of military affairs. They had sworn fidelity to him on oath but only if he wished to be a king *for the sake of building up the Church*[929] of God, not destroying it; if he governed justly, lawfully and in the manner of his ancestors; if he allowed each man's rank, his office and his rights to remain secure and inviolable. But if he was the first to violate these rights, they would no longer be bound by the sanctity of this oath but would thenceforward wage a just war, as if against a barbarian enemy and an oppressor of the name of Christ, and, as long as the last spark of life survived, they would fight for the Church of God, for the Christian faith and also for their own freedom.[930]

This message had a powerful effect on the king. But when his advisers said that such passionate anger would abate at the first *alarm of war*,[931] *he recovered his spirit*[932] somewhat, replied in a trifling and contemptuous manner to the envoys and sent them away with nothing certain to report.[933] When the envoys announced this to their fellows, a fierce anger blazed up in all their minds and they exhorted each other in their

---

929 I Corinthians 14:12.

930 Cf. Bruno, *The Saxon War* c. 25, p. 29 (a speech attributed to Otto of Northeim): 'Perhaps, as Christians, you are afraid to violate the oath that you swore to the king.... As long as, in my view, he was a king and behaved like a king, I kept the fidelity that I swore to him pure and inviolate, but after he ceased to be a king, he was no longer the man to whom I owed fidelity. It is not, therefore, against the king but against the unjust thief of my liberty, not against the fatherland but on behalf of the fatherland and of freedom, ... that I take up weapons.' On Lampert's justification of the rebellion see Struve (1970a) pp. 48 and n. 7, 99. See also Kern (1939) pp. 93–6.

931 Livy I.2.4. See Billanovich (1945) p. 124.

932 Judith 13:30.

933 Cf. *Annals of Niederaltaich* 1073, p. 85: 'after some days they were with difficulty admitted to the king's presence and, when their case was stated, they returned to their homes without honour and without a clear answer'. A similar but more elaborate report is found in Bruno, *The Saxon War* c. 23, pp. 27–8, who concluded: 'This was the day and this the cause that first began the war: this was the beginning of all the evils that followed.' See Meyer von Knonau (1894) pp. 238–9.

talks to avenge his contempt with their own hands. 'A character hardened in evil-doing cannot be softened,' they said, 'unless a stronger *force is applied*[934] and it does not feel the sensation of pain unless it is cut to the quick and the sword's point is driven closer to the innermost parts.'[935]

They therefore made for Goslar, *fully armed and in battle array*,[936] and there they pitched their camp at no great distance from the royal residence.[937] In their savage state of mind they would immediately have attacked the king and demanded their rights, this time not with rhetorical proofs but *with the terrors of war*,[938] had not Bishop Bucco of Halberstadt and a few more who knew well enough what was reasonable,[939] restrained the impetuosity of the turbulent crowd *with healthy moderation*.[940] When the king received the news of the nearby and indeed imminent danger, he was overwhelmed with dismay and he made for the Harzburg in all haste and brought there with him the insignia of the kingdom and as much of his treasure as he could in that hurry and confusion.[941] Bishop Eppo of Zeitz and Bishop Benno of Osnabrück were with him at that time and everything that he did was according to their advice now that the State was thrown into disorder, precisely as in earlier tranquil times.[942]

By chance Berthold, formerly duke of the Carinthians, had recently arrived to transact private business of some kind in the palace. To

---

934 Livy V.43.1; VIII.20.6.

935 According to Bruno, *The Saxon War* c. 24–6, pp. 28–31, these discussions took place in an assembly of the Saxons in the village of Hoetensleben, near Helmstedt (the place-name was a conjecture by H.-E. Lohmann, Bruno's editor), in which Otto of Northeim played a leading role. See Meyer von Knonau (1894) pp. 242–6; Lange (1961) p. 47.

936 Livy XXIX.2.4. See Billanovich (1945) p. 124.

937 According to Bruno, *The Saxon War* c. 27, p. 31, 'not long after' the assembly at Hoetensleben the rebels 'proceeded directly to the Harzburg, where the king was'. Cf. *Annals of Niederaltaich* 1073, p. 85: 'While the king was staying in the Harzburg, a place dear to him, and was providing royal entertainment for his close friends, it was suddenly reported by his followers that a great army of Saxons had encamped nearby.' This contradiction was discussed by Kilian (1886) pp. 58–60, who accepted Bruno's version (but see especially p. 60 n. 4: 'Goslar and the Harzburg are so close to each other that a repeated change of residence is not out of the question'). Meyer von Knonau (1894) pp. 239 n. 87, 246–7 and n. 93, accepted Lampert's version.

938 Livy VI.6.6. See Billanovich (1945) p. 124.

939 Cf. Bruno of Merseburg, *The Saxon War* c. 23, p. 28: 'had not Margrave Dedi by means of his prudence restrained their fury'.

940 Livy XLV.18.6.

941 According to *D.H.IV* 261, Henry IV was in the Harzburg on 26 July. See Meyer von Knonau (1894) p. 248.

942 See above p. 177 and n. 918.

this man the king exculpated himself with the most holy adjurations, denying that he had granted his duchy to another and claiming instead that it was on his own initiative that Markward had seized the territory of another man and that Berthold's rights were in no way diminished because a very foolish man had interfered with public offices without a royal command and without consulting the princes.[943] Although Berthold knew that this was false and that the king's ill will towards him had not been improved voluntarily but was corrected by the violent change in his fortunes, he nevertheless accepted the explanation and promised that he would never fail to serve the interests of the State. Because he was a man of excellent judgement, whose eloquence was agreeable to the people, the king sent him as his envoy to the Saxons, together with the aforementioned bishops.[944]

When they had reached them, the envoys requested the Saxons in God's name at once to abandon their weapons, for although they had taken them up for an honourable reason, they had *set a very bad example.*[945] Nor should they attempt an enterprise that was disproportionate and beyond their powers and that must be regarded with extreme disapproval by the other princes of the kingdom, since it was an enterprise that no people had ever attempted either in their memory or that of their ancestors. Their cause was just and it was the merciless severity of the king that through countless injuries had compelled them to resort to these extremes but they should nevertheless be mindful of their honour rather than their anger and they should defer to the royal majesty, which had always been safeguarded and inviolable even among barbarian nations. They must, therefore, abandon the clash of weapons and in tranquillity, their hostilities laid to rest, they should fix a time and place to which the king might summon the princes of the kingdom

---

943 On Duke Berthold I of Carinthia and Count Markward IV of Eppenstein see above p. 163 and nn. 824–5. The presence of Berthold in the Harzburg was recorded by Bruno, *The Saxon War* c. 27, p. 31. See Meyer von Knonau (1894) p. 818. For Lampert's emphasis on the princes' right to be consulted see Struve (1970a) pp. 44, 46.

944 I.e. the bishops of Zeitz-Naumburg and Osnabrück. But according to Bruno, *The Saxon War* c. 27, p. 31, 'The envoys were Bishop Frederick [of Münster (above n. 904)], Duke Berthold and Siegfried, the king's chaplain [the future Bishop Siegfried II of Augsburg]'. See Meyer von Knonau (1894) p. 250 and n. 101. Holder-Egger, *Lamperti Annales* p. 154 n. 1, suggested that Lampert assumed that Bishops Eppo-Eberhard and Benno II were the royal envoys because he himself saw them in August in the neighbourhood of Hersfeld, after they had fled with the king from the Harzburg (see below pp. 184–5).

945 Livy III.35.8. See Billanovich (1945) p. 124.

in order to clear himself of the charges against him according to their common judgement and to correct whatever seemed to be in need of correction.

In reply to this the Saxons said:[946] 'The other princes of the kingdom are not burdened with the same need to rebel that weighs on us. For while the other peoples were freed from their duties and almost all were on holiday, the king had selected us in particular – according to the saying of the prophet – to *thresh us with wagons of iron.*[947] Once his reign had begun, he never moved beyond our region; after taking away our inheritances, he also stole our freedom and, dishonouring all our birthrights, he threw upon us the yoke of harshest servitude. In order to oppress us, he imposed a garrison on every mountain and every little hill so that we were forced to pay to drink our own water and to purchase our own wood with money. He publicly prostituted our wives and daughters to his knights, as the victims of their lust and – what we regard as the most grievous of all the ills that we have suffered – he defiled our land with unheard-of inventions and with crimes not to be mentioned by a Christian mouth.[948] If this injury was one that we had in common with the other princes of the kingdom, our case should rightly be referred to their attention and judgement. Now, however, when we must either sink under the weight of our own misfortunes or *resist these injustices*[949] with our own courage, we have no interest in awaiting the judgement of other men on our miseries. If, therefore, the king ever finally feels shame and repents of his evil deeds, as proof that his penitence is not feigned, let him without any procrastination demolish the castles that he built to bring ruin to us;[950] let him restore the inheritances that were taken from us either by violence or by the perversion of justice; finally, let him swear to us an oath that he will never hereafter attempt to break the laws established for our people from the earliest times. Although we have often been deceived, often mocked *by peaceable words uttered in cunning,*[951]

946 According to Bruno, *The Saxon War* c. 27, p. 31, 'Duke Otto [of Northeim] gave the reply of all the Saxons'.

947 Amos 1:3.

948 Cf. the accounts of the Saxons' grievances above pp. 170–1, 177–9.

949 Livy III.37.8; Sallust, *Jugurtha* 14.25.

950 Cf. Bruno, *The Saxon War* c. 27, p. 31: 'They requested him to destroy the castles that he had built not for the defence but for the destruction of the kingdom: if he refused to do so, then they would understand why they had been built. They wished to defend their freedom and their property against the violence of all men with the help of divine mercy.' See Meyer von Knonau (1894) pp. 251 and n. 104, 858–9.

951 I Maccabees 7:10.

nevertheless if he does this, we shall somehow for the first time believe him when he promises what is good. But if he does not do this, we shall admit of no delay nor wait for the decisions of other peoples or other princes but shall endeavour to shake off the yoke that hangs over our necks and *we shall secure freedom*[952] for our children either by our death or by our victory.' With these words they dismissed *the envoys*. The latter were *sent* again *and sent back*[953] again and found the Saxons inflexible in that same purpose.

The Saxons therefore decided to set guards to keep watch on all the paths by which it was possible to come down from the castle, intending by a supreme effort to deny the king the opportunity of making his escape and *bringing the war to other*[954] parts of the kingdom. And certainly if they had attended to this properly, a task would have been fully accomplished at little cost and in a few days that was subsequently to be drawn out for so long a time and to drag all the provinces of the kingdom *to the verge of extreme danger.*[955] And this was not hidden from the king himself. He therefore eagerly sought by all the means at his disposal how *he might deceive the enemy's guards*[956] and transfer the war from the confinement of Saxony to the wide open spaces of the kingdom and especially to the lands of the bishops of the Rhineland, for he hoped that they would be faithful and supportive because of the frequent favours that he had conferred on them. The castle[957] had been sited on a very high hill and it could be approached only by a single path and that a very difficult one. A forest of enormous size shaded the other sides of the mountain and it extended from there, many miles wide, immense and uninterrupted, as far as the borders of Thuringia and therefore no amount of caution on the part of the besiegers could deprive those inside the castle of the means of going out or coming in.

952 Livy VIII.5.4.

953 *Ibid.*, XXIV.6.2.

954 *Ibid.*, XXI.21.3.

955 *Ibid.*, XXII.9.6.

956 *Ibid.*, XXII.22.17; XXIII.9.10.

957 I.e. the Harzburg, on the northern edge of the Harz mountains with the forest lying to the south. Cf. Bruno, *The Saxon War* c. 16, p. 22: Henry IV sought out 'high mountains with natural defences in deserted localities and began to build on them castles … To the first and greatest of these he gave the name Harzburg.' *Ibid.*, c. 27, p. 31: 'With the knowledge only of the few men to whom he had entrusted that castle, he abandoned Saxony by night, fleeing through the dense woodland that he had often passed through when he was seeking locations for his castles, and came to eastern Franconia with a few companions.' On the Harzburg see Spier (1967–8) pp. 185–201; Stolberg (1968) p. 137; Fenske (1977) pp. 29–33.

Taking the advice of his followers, the king frequently sent envoys to the Saxons, requesting peace and promising to amend all those matters that had caused them offence. All the Saxons eagerly fixed their attention on these proceedings and, as a consequence of the success of their enterprise, relaxed their guard with a premature sense of security. Then one night,[958] when they had not the slightest suspicion, the king himself took with him Duke Berthold and the two bishops mentioned above[959] and many other members of his household and, sending on ahead of him in the baggage both the insignia of the kingdom and as much of his treasure *as the time and the circumstances allowed*,[960] he secretly left the castle. He gave those who remained inside this task: that on the following day they should pretend, with all the skill in their power, that he was still present and remove from the minds of the enemy any suspicion that he had fled.

For three days they walked without food (so it is said) through the vast wilderness of the forest along a very narrow path, previously known to few, which a certain hunter, their guide on the journey, had discovered while very skilfully exploring the secret areas of the forest in his zeal for hunting. On all sides they looked anxiously around them for a glimpse of a sword and, hearing the sound of any gust of wind, they feared that the enemy was attacking and that death was already at their throats.[961] On the fourth day they reached Eschwege, *reduced* to extreme weakness by hunger, *sleeplessness and the exertions*[962] of the long journey. There they were somewhat refreshed by food and sleep and on the next day, that is, 13 August, they made for Hersfeld, since troops had already begun to flock to the king in great numbers. He remained in that place

---

958 9 or 10 August. Cf. *Annals of Iburg* 1073, p. 436: 'The flight of the king from the Harzburg on the nativity of St Laurence [10 August]' (= *Annales Patherbrunnenses* p. 95); *Annalista Saxo* 1073, p. 700: 'fifth Ides of August' [9 August]. These dates seem to have beeen deduced directly from Lampert's account: see Meyer von Knonau (1894) pp. 253–4 and n. 109.

959 Eppo (Eberhard) of Zeitz-Naumburg and Benno II of Osnabrück: see above pp. 177 and nn. 916–17; 181 and n. 944.

960 Livy XXXIII.48.6. Cf. Berthold of Reichenau, *Chronicle* 1073, p. 129: 'hastily gathering up his treasure, as far as the limited time permitted, he escaped from them with difficulty'.

961 Cf. *Annals of Niederaltaich* 1073, p. 85: 'After [the king] departed, Otto [of Northeim] strove to ambush him en route. Although he had a much greater force of knights, he nevertheless did not presume to encounter [the king] as he travelled and became aware of him.'

962 Livy XXXI.46.14. The royal estate of Eschwege on the River Werra in Hesse. See Kilian (1886) p. 60; Meyer von Knonau (1894) pp. 254–5.

for the following four days, preoccupied with the army, which he had summoned from every part of his kingdom for the expedition against the Poles.[963]

For now the day was at hand that he had fixed for the assembling of the troops.[964] Bishop Adalbero of Würzburg[965] and Bishop Herman of Bamberg[966] and very many other princes who were bound for the expedition had already arrived in the neighbourhood and, hearing what had happened, they came in great haste to the king, who was still stationed in Hersfeld. Duke Rudolf of the Swabians, together with the bishops of the Rhineland, Swabia and Bavaria, had pitched camp in the area of Mainz and awaited a messenger of the king, from whom he might obtain more reliable information about the place in which he ought to meet him. For he had heard that the king's mind had turned away from this expedition to other affairs of the kingdom but he had not learned for certain what had happened to force him suddenly to change his purpose. Nevertheless very many men said that Rudolf was aware of this conspiracy and was a participant in it and that he was advancing at a slow pace to the army, therefore, either so as not to be shamed into offering help to the king in so great a crisis contrary to his own intentions or so as not to be forced to betray prematurely his plans and the fact of his rebellion by refusing his help.[967]

The king therefore sent envoys with orders that both Rudolf himself and the other princes who were with him should hasten their journey as much as they could and meet him in the village that was called

---

963 Lampert alone recorded these details. Cf. *Annals of Niederaltaich* 1073, p. 85: 'the king passed into *Francia* and then as far as Bavaria'; Bruno, *The Saxon War* c. 27, p. 31: 'fleeing to eastern *Francia*'. See Kilian (1886) p. 60; Meyer von Knonau (1894) p. 255.

964 22 August. See above p. 173 and n. 883.

965 Bishop Adalbero of Würzburg (above n. 44). Lampert's report contradicts the claim of Frutolf of Michelsberg, *Chronica* 1072, p. 82, that Adalbero was a 'supporter' of the Saxon rebels.

966 Bishop Herman of Bamberg (above n. 449).

967 Cf. Bruno, *The Saxon War* c. 17, p. 24: 'When the nation of the Swabians heard of the calamity of the Saxons, they secretly sent envoys to them and concluded a treaty with them so that neither people would help the king in oppressing the other.' Lampert alone recorded these events. According to Meyer von Knonau (1894) p. 255 and n. 112, 'because all these events occurred in Hersfeld and its environs, [his account is] probably essentially a reliable source, at least as far as external events are concerned'. Meyer von Knonau, however, doubted the involvement of Rudolf of Swabia (above n. 203) in the Saxon rebellion, not least because of his close alliance with Duke Berthold I of Carinthia, who was the king's companion in the flight from the Harzburg.

Kappel, not far from Hersfeld.[968] When they had arrived there, the king *prostrated himself at their feet*[969] and entreated them by their reverence for God, Whom they had called to witness when they swore fidelity to him, to feel both compassion and indignation at his unhappy misfortunes. He had been deprived of the service that they all intended to perform by the malice of a few men who – forgetting the oath that they had sworn, *forgetting the favours*[970] by which again and again he had bound them to himself both privately and publicly – would have snatched away from him not only his kingdom but even his life, had he not evaded the danger and taken refuge in flight. The crime of injuring the royal majesty was not solely the concern of the king himself: it was an affront to the State[971] and to all those who had created him king and by whose help he ought to have been protected from wicked men. Accordingly they should all strive *to the utmost of their ability*[972] so that the royal dignity, which they had received from their ancestors as the most honourable and the most distinguished of ranks, should not fall into obscurity as a result of their inactivity. Nor should they leave such a very wicked deed unpunished and transmit it to their descendants as a precedent from their own times. In speaking of these matters, he drew tears from all those who were present both because of the shameful nature of his experiences and because of his presentation of his lamentable complaint.

There were those who were of the opinion that, since they had come *armed and prepared*[973] for the expedition against the Poles, the army should immediately be marched into Saxony and the wound recently and shamefully inflicted should be healed by the antidote of vengeance. Others considered that nothing should be undertaken in haste. The Saxons were a very hardy people and, by virtue of their inborn *ferocity*,

968 On the identification of Kappel see Kilian (1886) pp. 60–1; Meyer von Knonau (1894) pp. 256–7 and n. 114, on the polemical nature of Lampert's (uncorroborated) account.

969 Livy VI.3.4; XXXVI.35.3. Cf. the emphasis of Bruno, *The Saxon War* c. 30, p. 32, on Henry IV's 'humble entreaties'.

970 Livy VII.20.8.

971 Cf. Bruno, *The Saxon War* c. 30, p. 32: Henry claimed to have been 'unjustly driven out of the kingship of Saxony, which he had received both through inheritance from his father and through election by them all and therefore this act dishonoured not so much himself as all those [princes] who suffered contempt in his person'. The Saxon rebels were accused of a crime 'against the State' by Petrus Crassus, *Defensio Heinrici IV regis* c. 8, pp. 452–3 (mid–1080s). See Robinson (1978a) pp. 82–3.

972 Tacitus, *Agricola* 45; *Historia* 3.20.

973 Livy XXIX.2.4. See Billanovich (1945) p. 124.

very well versed in the skills of warfare. They had *moreover* been *driven wild*[974] by the frequent injuries that they had suffered and had now burst all the bonds of laws and justice and were firmly resolved either to die or to conquer. A delay must therefore be granted to the princes, during which they might return home, equip their troops and increase their supplies so that they would have the additional resources to last out the war, however much it was protracted. Since this opinion was approved by them all, the king decreed that the troops should assemble for the campaign on the seventh day after the feast of St Michael in a village belonging to the monastery of Hersfeld called Breitungen.[975] Taking with him the princes who had arrived, the king went to visit Tribur and other places in the vicinity of the Rhine.[976] He urgently sent envoys in all directions and implored not only the princes but also the common people not to desert him.[977] He gave away many gifts and promised many more and to some people he even restored the property that in previous years – *the period of good fortune,*[978] when he indulged himself entirely without restraint – he had seized from them by means of a false legal claim.

When the Saxons learned that the king had eluded their guards and had escaped into other regions of the kingdom, they were greatly saddened, believing, as the circumstances demanded, that henceforward they would have no leisure or freedom from care. This plague was not to be confined, as hitherto, *within the walls of their house.*[979] instead they must without any disguise wage a war on behalf of the State against the enemy of the State. It was therefore expedient for them to incite as many peoples and kingdoms as they could to attack the king. They immediately sent envoys to the Thuringians to seek their help and beg them also not to delay in taking up weapons themselves for the sake

---

974 Livy XXIII.5.12.

975 5 October in Frauenbreitungen on the River Werra. Lampert also referred subsequently (below, 1075, p. 252) to 'the property of the monastery of Hersfeld in the place called Breitungen'. On its location see Kilian (1886) p. 61; Meyer von Knonau (1894) p. 257 n. 115.

976 Cf. Berthold of Reichenau, *Chronicle* 1073, p. 129: the king 'came with a few followers to Worms'. This report, however, seems to confuse the events of August with those of the following December: see below p. 200. See Kilian (1886) p. 60; Meyer von Knonau (1894) p. 255.

977 Cf. Bruno, *The Saxon War* c. 30, p. 32: 'the king approached the individual princes of the German kingdom with humble entreaties'. See Meyer von Knonau (1894) p. 268.

978 Livy XXII.3.4. See Billanovich (1945) p. 127.

979 Cicero, *Oratio pro Rege Deiotaro* II.5.

of their own freedom and in response to the frequent insults that had exasperated them. The Thuringians held a very well attended assembly in the place called Tretenburg, where they listened to the legation of the Saxons and most eagerly gave their assent. No legation was ever received with more joyful shouts of approbation. Without delay they swore an oath that they would never desert the enterprise. They shared with the Saxons the same necessity for rebellion and they would therefore share the same danger: they would also, if God granted it, share the victory and they would fight to the last breath for their common good.[980]

They gave notice moreover to the abbot of Fulda and the abbot of Hersfeld and to the other princes who possessed any property in Thuringia that they should come on the appointed day to swear an oath with them to bring help to their people. If they did not do so, the rebels would immediately seize all their possessions.[981] Envoys of the king also came to the Thuringians, *promising* them *extraordinary*[982] marks of favour if they would repudiate their alliance with the Saxons and their participation in the war. But they were driven away with such violent reproaches that the fury of the people would have been unleashed against them, had not a few wise men intervened to urge restraint on account of *the law of nations*, which requires that honour should be shown to *envoys*.[983] At this time the archbishop of Mainz was staying in Erfurt. The Thuringians approached him and pressed him to consent to their common purpose and they would not permit him to depart from that region until he had given them hostages and confirmed his promise that he would take no measures against them either with weapons or with counsel. Some people believed, however, that both he and the archbishop of Cologne and also very many princes of the Rhineland were privy to this conspiracy and were participants in it from the beginning. They

---

980 Lampert alone referred specifically to the Tretenburg assembly (near Erfurt). Cf. Bruno, *The Saxon War* c. 28, p. 32: 'Certain of [the Saxons] crossed over to the Thuringians and, informing them of the whole sequence of events, admitted them into their alliance, after giving and taking oaths.' See Meyer von Knonau (1894) pp. 264–5; Robinson (1999) p. 76.

981 Widerad of Fulda (above n. 239) and Hartwig of Hersfeld (above n. 820). There is an allusion to this threat in Lampert, *Libellus de institutione Herveldensis ecclesiae*, prologus, p. 344, recording the sufferings of Hersfeld 'because of the violence of robbers, who left her nothing except the walls and stones' and 'their wicked suggestion' and 'conspiracy opposed to the State and the peace of the Church'. See Holder-Egger, *Lamperti Opera* p. XXXIV; Holder-Egger (1894) p. 183; Struve (1970a) p. 78.

982 Livy I.47.7.

983 *Ibid.*, XXI.25.7; XXX.25.10; XXXIX.25.10. For Lampert's idea of 'the law of nations' see Struve (1970a) p. 50; Dickerhof (1991) pp. 451–2, 454.

nevertheless did everything in their power to conceal this as long as the outcome of their undertaking was still in the balance.[984]

Since their plan was not to chase the king into the lands of the foreign peoples, therefore, they turned all their efforts to seize his castles. These, however, are the castles that he himself built after his father had died and that are still in the memory at the present time: Harzburg,[985] *Wigantestein*,[986] Moseburg,[987] Sachsenstein,[988] Spatenburg,[989] Heimburg,[990] Hasenburg.[991] *Vokenroht*[992] belonged to the Count palatine Frederick and the king had seized it from him by an act of legalised violence and placed his own garrison there. He had also taken possession of the Lüneburg, a very great fortress of the Saxon duke Otto,[993] situated on the frontier of the Saxons and the Liutizi, and he had placed there a body of picked

984 Lampert subsequently presented this rumour about Siegfried of Mainz (above n. 210) and Anno of Cologne (above n. 139) as fact: below, 1074, p. 212. See also below n. 1004. Cf. Siegfried of Mainz, letter to Pope Gregory VII, *Codex Udalrici* 40, p. 87, referring to 'such an abominable and unusual crime' and the 'inveterate stubbornness of the Thuringians'. See Meyer von Knonau (1894) pp. 265–6.

985 See above p. 183 and n. 957.

986 This castle has not been identified: see Fenske (1977) pp. 31–2.

987 According to Berges (1963) p. 133 and Stolberg (1968) p. 255, this was Meseburg, north of Goslar near Weddingen, where remains of a building have been found. Other possible sites are Moseberg, on the southern edge of the Harz mountains near Bad Sachsa, and Moseburg, on the eastern edge of the Harz, northwest of Stangerode, but no traces of building have been found here. See Fenske (1977) p. 31 n. 80.

988 On the southern edge of the Harz, 2.3 km west of Walkenried: see Stolberg (1968) pp. 331–2; Fenske (1977) p. 31 and n. 77; Robinson (1999) p. 83.

989 On the northern edge of the Hainleite hills,1 km south of Sondershausen: see Stolberg (1968) pp. 347–8; Fenske (1977) p. 31 n. 78.

990 On the northern edge of the Harz between Wernigerode and Blankenburg: see Stolberg (1968) p. 160; Fenske (1977) p. 31 n. 76.

991 On the southern edge of the Harz, 2 km east of the village of Haynrode: see Stolberg (1968) pp. 148–9; Fenske (1977) p. 31 n. 79.

992 Perhaps the 'destroyed royal castle' mentioned by a twelfth-century source in Volkenrode, part of Körner, northeast of Mühlhausen; alternatively sited on the southern edge of the Harz between Nordhausen and Stolberg: see Fenske (1977) p. 31 and n. 80. Meyer von Knonau (1894) p. 232 linked Lampert's reference to Count Frederick II of Goseck (above n. 227) with the report of Bruno, *The Saxon War* c. 26, p. 30: 'The count palatine Frederick complained that the great benefice that he held from the abbey of Hersfeld had been taken from him by an unjust command of the king'. There is, however, no evidence to link *Vokenroht* with Hersfeld.

993 Duke Ordulf (Otto) Billung of Saxony (above n. 621). Cf. Bruno, *The Saxon War* c. 21, p. 26: 'That castle, however, had always belonged to the kindred of Duke Magnus [Billung]'; c. 26, p. 30: 'Count Herman [Billung] told of the recent event, that the king cunningly seized his castle of Lüneburg, which had been left to him as his inheritance'; Adam of Bremen, *Gesta* III.60, p. 206. See Fenske (1977) p. 64.

knights, together with Eberhard, the son of Count Eberhard of Nellenburg.[994] He had done this for no other reason than that he claimed that
all that had belonged to the aforementioned duke had come under royal
control by right of surrender through the action of his son, Magnus.[995]
The king had begun to build very many other castles besides these but
the storm of war[996] had suddenly blown up and called him away from his
undertaking.

Herman, the brother of the Saxon duke, had already laid siege to the
Lüneburg, long before the king was forced to flee from Saxony,[997] and
in a few days he had forced the king's knights to surrender, since they
had begun their occupation of the castle without any plan and they had
no provisions. He nevertheless wished neither to release nor to punish
those whom he had defeated but kept them in the fortress, carefully
guarded so that they should not escape and sustained (as the prophet
says) by *scanty bread and little water*.[998] Herman sent word to the king that
if he wished to recover his besieged followers alive and well, he should
release Magnus, his brother's son, from captivity and send him back to
him. If he did not do so, Herman would treat them like enemies who
had unlawfully invaded foreign territory and *inflict capital punishment*,[999]
according to the laws of his people. For a long time the king remained
undecided about what to do. He knew of course that it would be inhuman
if he did not take care of his followers when they were in a situation
of great danger. But on the other hand he reflected how much his own
interests would suffer if he released and allowed to be his own master
that man from whose ruin he had promised himself the lordship of the
whole of Saxony, especially since it was to be feared that the recent

---

994 Eberhard, son of Eberhard III, count of Nellenburg (✝1078), brother of Archbishop
　　Udo of Trier. See Meyer von Knonau (1894) p. 259.

995 Magnus Billung: see above p. 133 and n. 621.

996 Livy III.7.3.

997 Count Herman Billung (above n. 890). Cf. Bruno, *The Saxon War* c. 21, p. 26:
　　'Herman waited until the king had left his territory and immediately surrounded
　　that same castle with a large force'. Bruno erroneously linked the beginning of the
　　siege with events of 1071: see Meyer von Knonau (1894) p. 260 n. 120. Meyer von
　　Knonau (1894) p. 260 suggested that Herman began the siege immediately after the
　　assembly of Hoetensleben (above n. 935). See also Fenske (1977) pp. 64–5; Althoff
　　(1991) p. 324; Robinson (1999) p. 90.

998 Isaiah 30:20. Cf. Bruno, *The Saxon War* c. 21, p. 26: 'except for a few loaves that the
　　monks [of the monastery of St Michael, Lüneburg] had left behind them on their
　　departure, it contained nothing to eat and hunger commanded them to leave the
　　castle'.

999 Livy III.18.10; XXXIII.28.15. See Billanovich (1945) p. 78.

injuries that he had inflicted, in keeping Magnus in prison now for three years, would cause him to trouble the State more grievously than all the rest of the rebels. *For* many *days* these *reflections kept him*[1000] in a state of anxiety and suspense. And assuredly avarice would have got the better of him and he would have neglected the safety of his knights in the interest of his personal profit, had not the princes of the kingdom – who were wearied by the repeated messages from the men who were besieged – unanimously approached the king and deflected him from his decision, not so much by begging him as by threatening and terrifying him. On the feast of the Assumption of St Mary,[1001] therefore, while he was still in Hersfeld, he sent envoys to release Magnus from his imprisonment and to restore him to his own people and to liberate from their state of siege and danger those men who were now being held in the aforementioned castle in order to be punished.

Assembling a great host from the neighbouring areas, the Thuringians laid siege to the castle of Heimburg and within a few days they had stormed it by force of arms, captured it and set it on fire.[1002] When the castle had been destroyed, they sent away those who were inside without punishing them in order to demonstrate that they had not taken up arms against the king out of hatred and enmity but only to rid themselves of the injustices that had overwhelmed their region as a result of false accusations. They immediately marched the army to another castle, which was called the Hasenburg and, as there was no hope of their being able to storm it because of the difficulties presented by the location, they pitched their camp all around it and preoccupied themselves with preventing anyone from going in or coming out, so that those who could not be assailed by human force might be reduced by the lack of provisions. They knew for certain that, however abundant

---

1000 Livy VII.39.11; XXXV.42.3.

1001 15 August. On the king's indecision cf. Bruno, *The Saxon War* c. 21, pp. 26–7: 'He did not wish to release the duke because he was safe from war in Saxony as long as he held him in chains.... If, however, he allowed so many of his most faithful followers – among whom were those who had noble and powerful kinsmen – to perish, he would never thereafter find anyone who was faithful to him and would never have a safe moment from their kinsmen.' See Meyer von Knonau (1894) pp. 259–61.

1002 Cf. *Annals of Niederaltaich* 1073, p. 85: 'after the king's departure the Saxons besieged his castle, named the Heimburg, received its surrender and destroyed it'; *Song of the Saxon War* I.87–138, pp. 3–5: 'the proud people of the Saxons ... first attacked the Heimburg', reinforced by 'the count palatine' (Frederick II of Goseck). Meyer von Knonau (1894) pp. 266–7 suggested that this was a joint Saxon–Thuringian operation.

were the food supplies that they had accumulated, they could not long sustain the great host that was inside the castle.[1003]

Meanwhile the king saw that the conspiracy was growing stronger from day to day and that the forces of the enemy were increasing and he was also greatly alarmed by the loss of his castles, hearing that some of them had already been captured and others were being attacked with the greatest exertion. He therefore asked the archbishops of Mainz and Cologne to hold a meeting with the Saxons and to attempt to find a settlement of these disorders. In obedience to this request, they summoned the princes of Saxony to meet them in the monastery of Corvey on 24 August to discuss the requirements of both sides.[1004] The archbishop of Cologne did not come on the appointed day: I do not know whether he was delayed by chance or whether it was intentional. He nevertheless sent envoys, who were to speak as his representatives, and he promised that he would most readily assent to all their reasonable decisions that were beneficial to themselves and to the State and that to the best of his ability he would devote his efforts to the common good.

The archbishop of Mainz remained with the Saxons who had come to meet him and endeavoured assiduously to pacify them and reconcile them with the king. But they, on the contrary, besides alleging their well known injuries, by means of which the king had inflicted serious harm on them, they drew attention to serious considerations that demonstrated that he could not continue to reign without causing great damage to the Christian religion. For he had perpetrated such crimes against his most intimate friends, against his wife,[1005] against his own sister, the abbess of Quedlinburg,[1006] against other persons

1003 See Meyer von Knonau (1894) pp. 267–8, 286; Robinson (1999) pp. 90–1.

1004 On the implausibility of this report see Meyer von Knonau (1894) pp. 270–1, 811–13; Jenal (1975) pp. 374–80; Robinson (1999) p. 91. Lampert's version of these events is contradicted by his own account of the situation of the king and Archbishop Siegfried (above p. 189 and n. 984) during August. It seems more likely that the archbishops negotiated with the rebels on their own behalf, unknown to the king: Siegfried of Mainz to obtain the Thuringian tithes and Anno of Cologne in support of his kinsmen, Archbishop Werner of Magdeburg and Bishop Burchard II of Halberstadt. This interpretation is perhaps supported by Bruno's undated account of Siegfried's negotiations with Werner, Burchard and Anno of Cologne (*The Saxon War* c. 18, p. 24) and by the incorrectly dated annal of Frutolf of Michelsberg, *Chronica* 1072, p. 82: the Saxons, 'so they say, made Siegfried, the metropolitan of the see of Mainz, ... their supporter. Some also declare that Archbishop Anno of Cologne ... was aware of this conspiracy.'

1005 Bertha of Turin (above n. 491). See above p. 178 and n. 928.

1006 Adelaide II, abbess of Quedlinburg and Gandersheim (†1096?), daughter of Emperor Henry III. Cf. Bruno, *The Saxon War* c. 9, p. 18: 'the dishonour that

very closely allied to him by the bonds of kinship, that, if they were judged according to the laws of the Church, he would be sentenced to the annulment of his marriage, the loss of the status of a knight and of all secular functions and above all the loss of the kingship.

After long discussion, therefore, they finally reached this conclusion. They decided that twelve hostages were to be provided from their own people and twelve from the king's side and they would serve as a pledge that the Saxons would come in safety to a conference with the other princes of the kingdom. The suit that they were bringing against the king was to be investigated and settled according to the judgement of the princes in the presence of the king himself, if this seemed to be expedient, and he was to refute the accusations brought against him, if he could do so. The day fixed for the giving and receiving of the hostages was 13 September in Thuringia in the place called Homburg.[1007] The day fixed for holding the conference with the princes was 20 October on the frontier of Thuringia and Hesse in the village called Gerstungen. The meeting broke up after reaching this agreement.

The Saxons, however, did not on that account slacken in their preparations for war and in besieging the king's castles. And when the news of what had been accomplished had been communicated to the king, it seemed to those who supported his party that it was deeply offensive to the royal majesty for him to give hostages on his behalf to the Saxons and the royal title was gravely insulted by being burdened with this most unseemly condition. The archbishops of Mainz and Cologne, therefore, travelled to Homburg on the appointed day and achieved an agreement that both sides should dispense with hostages and that they were merely to pledge their word that they would secure peace and by means of this guarantee they freed the princes who were about to come to the conference from all fear of danger.

Meanwhile the king sent envoys to the Liutizi, a people most hostile to the Saxons,[1008] and promised them an immense sum of money to wage

---

[Henry] inflicted on his sister ... the daughter of an emperor ... betrothed to Christ by means of the holy veil'; Manegold of Lautenbach, *Ad Gebehardum* c. 29, p. 363.

1007 On the River Unstrut, near Langensalza. Lampert alone recorded these events. See Meyer von Knonau (1894) pp. 271–2, 812–13.

1008 See above p. 178 and n. 922. On the polemical nature of Lampert's report see Meyer von Knonau (1894) pp. 286 ('greatly exaggerated by rumour'), 819. Cf. Bruno, *The Saxon War* c. 36, p. 38: in 1074 the king 'loosed in the pagan Liutizi the reins of the cruelty that they had always practised against the Saxons and allowed them to add to their territories as much of Saxony as they could'.

war against the Saxons, declaring that the latter were now preoccupied with internal conflicts and could easily be brought to utter destruction by *the shock of external warfare*.[1009] When the Saxons learned of this, they themselves also sent envoys to the Liutizi and promised them a much greater sum of money to abstain from their attack at such an unfavourable time. If they did not comply, they should not be deceived by false assumptions; for, if the Saxons were faced with that necessity, their power was sufficient both in the numbers and in the valour of their knights to deal with both enemies. Some of the barbarians cried out that they ought to accept the alliance and the money of the king; others, the alliance and the money of the Saxons. Because of the indiscipline of this *ignorant crowd*,[1010] the disagreement gave rise to conflict and they tore each other to pieces with such carnage that many thousands of men are said to have been killed in that fight. And for many days thereafter they raged with hostile swords against each other and against their own flesh and blood so that they were necessarily compelled to refrain from foreign wars.[1011]

It happened also that the king of the Danes, mindful of the agreement that he had long ago concluded with the king, landed in Saxony with an army conveyed by ships.[1012] The ships were dragged for a long distance overland to a river[1013] that seemed convenient for the completion of this enterprise and the king prepared to assail the region with fire and sword. But his army *declined to fight this campaign*,[1014] stating as their

1009 Livy II.42.3.

1010 *Ibid.*, I.19.4; II.45.5; XLV.23.8.

1011 Holder-Egger (1894) p. 530 noted here the stylistic influence of Justinus, *Epitome historiarum Philippicarum Pompei Trogi* III.2.1, XIII.6.17. According to Bruno, *The Saxon War* c. 32, pp. 34–5, the frozen rivers and marshes of Saxony in the winter of 1073–4 gave an enemy ready access to the province, so that 'the pagans could ... reduce all Saxony to ashes, had not God ... ordered them to remain quiet within their own frontiers'. See Brüske (1955) pp. 83–6 on the disintegration of the confederation of the Liutizi in the later eleventh century.

1012 King Swein Estrithson: see above n. 875. No other source mentions this campaign (although Bruno, *The Saxon War* c. 36, p. 38, recorded that in 1074 the king 'reminded the king of the Danes of the promise that he had confirmed on oath'). Meyer von Knonau (1894) pp. 286–7 suggested that it was an exaggerated version of rumours reaching Hersfeld. Holder-Egger, *Lamperti Annales* p. 164 n. 2 noted that Swein's principal preoccupation at this time was England. His son Cnut sailed there with a fleet of two hundred ships in 1075: see Stenton (1947) pp. 594–7, 603.

1013 Holder-Egger, *Lamperti Annales* p. 164 n. 2 and Meyer von Knonau (1894) p. 820 n. 102 suggested that Lampert derived this detail of his fictitious account from Regino of Prüm, *Chronicon* 888, 890, pp. 130, 135.

1014 Livy V.19.5; VII.11.5. See Billanovich (1945) p. 145.

objection that, whenever they themselves suffered attacks by foreign enemies, the Saxons were like a defensive wall and never inflicted any injuries upon them, when they had enough power to do so. Finally, if the Saxons somehow warded off the disaster that was bearing down on them at that moment, they would exact severe penalties for this unjust attack by the peoples of the Danes. Since they were uttering these opinions in private and in public, the king feared that he would *be deserted* by the troops *in* that *dangerous situation*[1015] and that he would become a laughing-stock among the enemy. He therefore ordered the ships to be dragged back and withdrew from Saxony without inflicting any damage in the region. Thus that raging heat of warlike preparations burned out without doing any harm.

On 20 October, according to the agreement, the princes of Saxony came to Gerstungen[1016] with fourteen thousand armed men, leaving behind the rest of the great army to guard the region and to lay siege to the castles. Present also, as representatives of the king, were the archbishop of Mainz, the archbishop of Cologne, the bishop of Metz,[1017] the bishop of Bamberg,[1018] Duke Gozelo of the Lotharingians,[1019] Duke Rudolf of the Swabians and Duke Berthold of the Carinthians, sent by the king to refute the allegations that the Saxons were bringing against him. He himself refused to come there and awaited the outcome of the proceedings in the city of Würzburg,[1020] in order to guard against aggravating the fury of the restless people by his presence and perhaps bringing evil consequences on himself. The princes of Saxony therefore *fell at the feet*[1021] of the princes who had come from the king and begged them in God's name to be attentive in their scrutiny and just in their judgement when sifting their case and to consider not how great and how unprecedented were the measures that they undertook against the State but

1015 Livy XXV.20.5.

1016 Lampert alone identified the place as Gerstungen. Cf. Berthold of Reichenau, *Chronicle* 1073, p. 129: 'A conference ... was held in Würzburg' by 'the Saxons', 'certain bishops and the dukes [of Swabia and Carinthia]'; *Song of the Saxon War* II.32–3, p. 8: 'The bishops, the foremost men, the counts and dukes joined with the Saxons *on the level plain* [Vergil, *Aeneid* VII.781].' See Meyer von Knonau (1894) pp. 287–8, 820–1; Robinson (1999) pp. 91–2.

1017 Herman of Metz (above n. 822).

1018 Herman of Bamberg (above n. 449).

1019 Duke Godfrey IV ('the Hunchback') of Lower Lotharingia (above n. 570).

1020 Cf. *D.H.IV* 264–5, issued on 27 October in Würzburg. See Kilian (1886) p. 62; Meyer von Knonau (1894) pp. 289–90.

1021 Livy VI.3.4; XXXVI.35.3.

what adversity had compelled them to resort to these extremes. Then, when they were granted the opportunity to speak, they one by one related the injuries that the king had inflicted on them as individuals and also the heinous offences that he had committed against their people, through which moreover he had dishonoured the very majesty of the title of king with unheard-of crimes. The princes who had come from the king were astounded and (in the words of the prophet) all men's *ears tingled*[1022] because of the enormity of the evildoing and they judged the Saxons to be blameworthy not because they had taken up arms for their freedom, for their wives and for their children, but because they had for so long borne with intolerable insults with the patience of women.

When they had consulted together for three whole days[1023] and had anxiously asked each other what ought to be done, they finally all agreed on this decision: that they should reject the king and elect another, who was suitable to govern the kingdom. Nevertheless they resolved not to be rash in making this public and not to do so until they could communicate this decision to the other princes of the kingdom, when the king had been drawn away to the more distant parts of the kingdom for the purpose of concluding a peace. They therefore ordered that a report should be spread abroad among the people that the princes of both parties had agreed on this judgement: that the Saxons were to propose to make appropriate amends to the king for the rash deeds that they had perpetrated against him and against the State but that the king was to promise the Saxons on oath both that they would not be punished for what they had done and that in the future they would be safe from that unjust treatment by which the king was alleged to have driven them to rebellion.[1024] The date fixed for completing these proceedings was the

1022 Jeremiah 19:3.

1023 On Lampert's tendency to report councils and conferences as lasting three days see Holder-Egger, *Lamperti Annales* p. 131 n. 2.

1024 Lampert's uncorroborated account of the proposed deposition of the king, a polemical claim influenced by his knowledge of the events of 1076–7 (cf. above, 1066, p. 111 and n. 469), contains obvious contradictions. See above p. 33 and Holder-Egger, *Lamperti Annales* p. 165 n. 4 ('What Lampert relates is ridiculous: that all the aforementioned princes, even the bishop of Bamberg and Duke Gozelo [Godfrey IV], were associated with a plan of this kind'); Meyer von Knonau (1894) pp. 820–1. Cf. Berthold of Reichenau, *Chronicle* 1073, p. 129: 'after many complaints about the intolerable injustices that they had suffered, nothing was done except that they disdainfully promised the king ... satisfaction'. According to the pro-Henrician *Song of the Saxon War* II.32–50, pp. 8–9, the Saxons 'seduced' the other German princes 'from the right way', so that the latter approved their conduct and undertook to exhort the king to 'restore the rights of their fathers' and pardon their rebellion.

festival of Christmas,[1025] which the king was to celebrate in Cologne. And they would certainly have appointed Duke Rudolf as king without any delay in that very place, had the latter not stubbornly resisted and sworn that he would never consent to this, unless an assembly was held, in which it was decided by all the princes that this could be done without incurring the disgrace of perjury and with his good name unimpaired.[1026]

The Saxons returned to their homeland in peace. The other princes set out for Würzburg to inform the king what had been achieved.[1027] Without any hesitation he immediately (as the common saying goes) *trod in the footsteps*[1028] of their decision and promised that, when peace was agreed, he would most readily take upon himself whatever conditions they had imposed. After celebrating the feast of All Saints[1029] in that same place, he decided to go to Regensburg, since he perceived that the princes of the Rhineland were already infected with a slight trace of the Saxon frenzy and from day to day were less and less well disposed and willing to show him obedience. And while in the course of the journey he was spending some days in Nuremberg, a certain man named Regenger,[1030] who had long remained at his side on the most intimate terms, suddenly burst on the scene and – it is uncertain whether he acted at the instigation of others or out of personal hatred for the king – reported to the dukes Rudolf and Berthold a serious accusation against the king. He said: 'I and very many others, whom the king expected to be useful agents of his most evil plan, were recently inveigled by him with many prayers and great promises in order that, when you and the other princes of the kingdom were meeting in Würzburg and you had withdrawn a short distance from the crowd to engage in a more secret conversation, we might attack you with our weapons and, by slaughtering *the instigators of*

1025 Cf. Berthold of Reichenau, *Chronicle* 1073, p. 129: the Saxons promised 'that at Christmas they would give [the king] satisfaction'.

1026 Cf. Gregory VII, *Register* VII.14a, c. 7, pp. 484–5 (Rudolf was 'compelled to assume the government of the kingdom'); Berthold of Reichenau, *Chronicle* 1077, p. 167. For the *topos* that reluctance was a necessary qualification for high office see Gregory I, *Regula pastoralis* I.6, 10, *MPL* 77, col. 19D–20A, 23AC. See Weiler (2000) pp. 1–42. See also above p. 33.

1027 The seven princes identified by Lampert in Gerstungen on 20 October appear in the intervention clause of *D.H.IV* 264, issued on 27 October in Würzburg.

1028 Livy IX.8.13; XXI.56.1; XXVII.34.7.

1029 1 November. See Kilian (1886) p. 62; Meyer von Knonau (1894) p. 291.

1030 Lampert alone identified Regenger by name. Cf. Berthold of Reichenau, *Chronicle* 1073, p. 129: 'one of the king's advisers'. Nothing further is known of him: see Robinson (1999) pp. 359–60.

the rebellion,[1031] we might free the king himself from danger and the State from turmoil. And the others indeed accepted the task most readily. I alone rejected the impious deed, both out of respect for justice and out of fear of the Judgement to come, and I tried to dissuade the king from his plan, as far as I dared to resist his inflexible purpose. For this reason he flared up against me with such intense indignation that he instantly removed me from attendance on his person, which (as you know very well) I have hitherto performed in a relationship of greater intimacy than the others, and he would have handed me over to his servants to be murdered, had I not avoided the impending peril by quickly leaving his living quarters.'[1032] After saying this, as proof of his trustworthiness he described the place, named the accomplices and said that, if the king denied the accusation, he was prepared to entrust the matter to divine judgement in single combat either with the king himself, if the laws permitted that, or with any other man.

The aforementioned dukes were powerfully affected by these words, since the man who made the accusation was far from being a person of low standing in the palace and he had an unimpeachable reputation among his fellows. Moreover one consideration above all inspired trust in his words: namely, that the king had long ago been charged with *having planned the murder of* certain other *princes*[1033] in a similar manner and also with having killed very many of his intimate friends. They therefore sent envoys to him and informed him that they were no longer bound by the obligation of the oath with which they had promised him fidelity and subjection, since he himself had been the first to betray the principle of fidelity and, while they were conducting negotiations in the interests of his safety, he had been devising plots against them. Unless he refuted the accusations, therefore, he should expect from them neither fidelity in time of peace nor help in time of trouble.

The king *reacted with* extreme *displeasure*[1034] to this and immediately made a public declaration about the insolence of Duke Rudolf. For in order to find an opportunity to take possession of the kingship – since

---

1031 Livy III.17.10. See Billanovich (1945) p. 77.

1032 The plot was also reported by Berthold of Reichenau, *Chronicle* 1073, p. 129: the unnamed royal adviser 'publicly accused [the king] in the presence of the afore-mentioned dukes [Rudolf and Berthold] of having made a plan with him and with his other close advisers to kill them all somehow or other'. See Meyer von Knonau (1894) pp. 291–2, 846–9; Robinson (1999) p. 93.

1033 Livy I.51.4. Cf. Bruno of Merseburg, *The Saxon War* c. 10–11, pp. 18–19.

1034 Livy I.9.6. See Billanovich (1945) p. 131.

he could not fasten upon the king any truthful accusation – he assailed him with false suspicions and skilfully fabricated rumours and tried to cast a shadow on his innocence. 'But let there be an end of the battles with words,' said the king; 'let there be no more of the cleverly contrived phantasms presented as evidence! I shall rebut the lie not with words but with my own hand and, setting aside the majesty of the royal title for a while in order to fight with Duke Rudolf himself, I shall expose the secret devices behind this fictitious accusation, by means of which he seeks to cloak his malice.[1035] Thus, if I lose the kingdom, it will be understood that I have lost it not through my own fault but through his deceit and through the breaking of his oath.' Then Udalric of Godesheim[1036] (who was one of those men accused of being appointed as accomplices in the plan and agents of the crime) strove to calm the king's indignation with gentle words and he begged him not to be so moved by the intensity of his anger as to offer to perform an action that was beneath the eminence of a king. It would be better and much more appropriate for Udalric to fight with Regenger or with any other man and declare his own and the king's innocence. And Udalric went at once to Duke Rudolf and said that he was prepared to disprove Regenger's lie in whatever way Rudolf himself might judge to be just. Rudolf did not accept this as amends nor did he openly reject it but he said that he would await the judgement of the other princes on this matter. The king made for Regensburg, as he had intended. He was *hated by all men and suspected by all men*[1037] and he himself had little faith in any man, since even those whom he had bound to himself in the most intimate friendship had deserted him at the first little cloud of the storm that was brewing.

Meanwhile the Saxons sent frequent envoys to urge the princes of the Rhine that either they should empower the Saxons to appoint a king or they themselves – since they were superior in rank and more numerous – should elect and enthrone anyone whom they wished, once the Saxons had approved the candidate, and they should not allow the State to fall

---

1035 Meyer von Knonau (1894) p. 847 contrasted 'this dramatically effective narrative of the imaginative and poetically gifted storyteller' with the laconic version of Berthold of Reichenau, *Chronicle* 1073, p. 130: the king 'waited for the day on which he could clear himself by judicial combat of the accusation'. For Lampert's interest in trial by combat and 'the judgement of God' see Struve (1970a) pp. 50–1, 117–18.

1036 Udalric of Godesheim (possibly Gosheim near Donauwörth) was one of the five royal advisers excommunicated by Pope Alexander II in 1073: see below, 1076, p. 308 and n. 1638. See Meyer von Knonau (1894) pp. 847 and n. 180; Robinson (1999) pp. 125, 359–60. Berthold of Reichenau's account does not mention Udalric.

1037 Livy XLII.42.5.

into utter devastation through the worthlessness of one man. Roused by
these messages, the archbishop of Mainz – to whom, before all others,
by virtue of the primacy of the see of Mainz, the authority to elect and
to consecrate a king was granted[1038] – summoned the princes from the
whole kingdom to Mainz, so that according to their common counsel
he might set up Duke Rudolf as king.[1039] When the king learned of this,
he took with him everyone whom he could attract to his party by gifts
or promises[1040] and returned from Bavaria in great haste, thinking that
above all his concern must be to hinder a development of such consequence. And when he had arrived near Worms in a place called Ladenburg, he was struck down by a very severe illness and was confined to
his bed for many days.[1041] This gave very great hope to his enemies that
such great disturbances and such great anger could be ended without
bloodshed. But the king hastened to Worms, even though he was
scarcely fully recovered from his sickness.

There he was received with great pomp into the city by the citizens. In
order to make their devotion to his cause more evident, the citizens had
shortly before driven the bishop's knights from the city when they had
attempted to prevent the king from entering. They would have seized
the bishop himself[1042] and put him in chains, had he not fled in time and
escaped from the city. When the king drew near, therefore, they went
out to meet him, *armed and well prepared,*[1043] not in order to resort to
violence but so that, seeing their great numbers, their weapons and
equipment, their throng of *young men at the ready,*[1044] he would be aware

1038 Cf. above, 1054, p. 63 and n. 127. See Thomas (1970) pp. 394–5; Boshof (1978b) pp.
      36–43.

1039 This claim has been discounted by historians – see Meyer von Knonau (1894) pp.
      292–3, 820–1 and n. 104; Thomas (1970) pp. 394–5 and n. 110; Robinson (1999)
      pp. 91–2 – except for Jakobs (1968) p. 266.

1040 Cf. *Song of the Saxon War* II.71–2, p. 9 describes the king's followers as 'a few
      Franci, the largest part Bavarians, some Swabians, small in numbers but not in
      strength'.

1041 Ladenburg was an estate of the church of Worms on the River Neckar. Kilian
      (1886) p. 63 conjectured that Henry IV arrived there 'about the beginning of
      December'. The report of Berthold of Reichenau, *Chronicle* 1073, p. 129, that the
      king 'came with a few followers to Worms, where he remained for some time in
      ill health', is erroneously placed between the escape from the Harzburg and the
      sojourn in Würzburg. See Meyer von Knonau (1894) p. 294; Robinson (1999) p. 93.

1042 Adalbert of Worms (above n. 626). Cf. Berthold of Reichenau, *Chronicle* 1073, p.
      130: the king 'entered Worms with the help of the citizens'. See Meyer von Knonau
      (1894) pp. 294–5; Kottje (1978) pp. 136–7; Robinson (1999) p. 93.

1043 Livy XXIX.2.4. See Billanovich (1945) p. 124.

1044 Livy XXXVII.16.8.

in the midst of his troubles how much hope he ought to place on them. They readily promised their help; they swore an oath; they offered to pay for the expenses of conducting the war from their personal resources, each *to the utmost of his ability*[1045] and they assured him that they would faithfully fight for his honour as long as they lived.[1046] Thus the king acquired a very well fortified city and thereafter this was his *headquarters in war*,[1047] this was *the bulwark of his kingdom*;[1048] this, whatever might befall, was the safest of refuges. For it was full of citizens and impregnable because of the strength of its walls; it was extremely rich by virtue of the fertility of the surrounding regions and very well provided with all the resources that are customarily used in war.

When those who had been summoned by the archbishop of Mainz to the assembly in Mainz heard that the king was rapidly drawing near, very many of them were struck with fear and failed to come there. Since the few who came did not dare to reach a decision on matters of such great importance without consulting the other princes, they departed disappointed and without achieving anything.[1049] The king sent envoys to them and, using many entreaties, with the greatest difficulty wrung from them the concession that they would meet him in Oppenheim for a private conversation.[1050] When they arrived there – after hostages had been given on both sides because they feared danger – the king *threw himself at their feet*[1051] and humbly begged them to remember that God was a just judge, to remember the oath by which they had bound themselves with God as their witness and in this time

---

1045 Tacitus, *Agricola* 45; Tacitus, *Historia* 3.20.

1046 Cf. *D.H.IV* 267 (issued on 18 January 1074 in Worms): the fidelity of the people of Worms was 'outstanding because when all the princes of the kingdom raged against us, they alone … adhered to us against the will of all'.

1047 Livy IV.31.8; XXII.1.2. See Billanovich (1945) p. 132.

1048 Livy XXXVII.18.3; XLIV.31.2. Between 1073 and 1075 Henry IV resided in Worms on at least twelve occasions: see Kilian (1886) pp. 143–4; Meyer von Knonau (1894) pp. 294–6, 307–9, 310–14; Kottje (1978) pp. 134–8, 157.

1049 Lampert alone recorded this assembly in Mainz. See Meyer von Knonau (1894) pp. 293, 296; Thomas (1970) pp. 394–5; Robinson (1999) p. 92.

1050 No other source mentions this meeting in Oppenheim (mid-way between Worms and Mainz). See Kilian (1886) p. 63; Meyer von Knonau (1894) p. 296: Lampert's report is 'in no way straightforwardly credible but tinged with many different prejudices'. Meyer von Knonau (1894) p. 848 also noted that this account closely resembles that of the meeting of the king and the princes at Kappel (see above p. 186 and n. 968) in structure and wording (including the same quotation from Livy).

1051 Livy VI.3.4; XXXVI.35.3.

of adversity to maintain their fidelity towards him. Whatever excesses he had committed in former times, they should pardon as the effect of youthful high spirits and of a time of life prone to vice.[1052] Henceforward, reformed by his experience of misfortune and strengthened by greater maturity both in years and in understanding, he would *put away childish things*[1053] and he would reflect upon and cherish whatever is virtuous, whatever is honourable, whatever belongs to the dignity of a king and finally whatever befits a man. To this they replied that it was useless for him to seek from them the fidelity that he himself had never shown either to God or to man. In his case they were never certain whether he was more dangerous and more untrustworthy in peace or war, towards friends or towards enemies; for only a few days before, while they were in Würzburg, negotiating in the interests of his safety, he was secretly recruiting executioners to kill them. If he wished to make any representations to the contrary or if he believed that he had been assailed with false accusations by a certain faction, let him permit Udalric of Godesheim *to fight hand to hand*[1054] with Regenger, as he had volunteered to do. If Udalric was victorious, the king would find thereafter that the princes were faithful and obedient towards him in perpetuity without any opposition. The king willingly accepted this proposition and decided that they should meet on a particular day after the octave of the feast of the Epiphany near Mainz on the island of the Rhine that is called Marsaue[1055] and allow the allegations of the two parties to be tried by the just judgement of God.

At that time those men who were in the Harzburg performed many outstanding deeds of military daring.[1056] For again and again they sallied forth into the neighbouring regions and plundered them and perpetrated great slaughter among the inhabitants and, before the Saxons could assemble in large numbers *to halt the attack*,[1057] they retreated into the castle. They proved particularly deadly, however, to the inhabitants of Goslar because of its proximity. For they killed very many of them and in their frequent incursions they laid waste to their estates,

---

1052 Cf. Henry IV, *Letter* 5, p. 9 (to Pope Gregory VII, 1073): 'partly through the impulses of deluding youth ... we have sinned'; Bruno of Merseburg, *The Saxon War* c. 31, p. 34: 'through the faults of his youth and his evil counsellors'.

1053 I Corinthians 13:11.

1054 Vergil, *Aeneid* XII.345.

1055 I.e. after 13 January 1074. See Meyer von Knonau (1894) p. 297.

1056 Cf. *Song of the Saxon War* I.139–237, pp. 5–7; Bruno of Merseburg, *The Saxon War* c. 29, p. 32. See Meyer von Knonau (1894) pp. 298–9.

1057 Livy II.53.1. See Billanovich (1945) pp. 85–6.

which were found outside the village, and prevented foreign merchants from bringing their customary merchandise there for fear of losing their lives. And when peace had been agreed between them for a short time, certain persons from the castle came to Goslar to transact some personal business there. When they were full of food and drink and had grown hot as a result of their excessive drinking – as drunkenness is accustomed to be the mother of quarrels – they began *to utter* impertinent and *uncouth speeches*[1058] directed against those with whom they were drinking and to reproach the Saxons with cowardice, saying that they had taken up arms against the king not with the courage of warriors but with the mentality of sheep. The Saxons who were present, becoming angry, began a fight, cut them to pieces and threw them out of doors.[1059] When the inhabitants of the Harzburg learned of this, they armed themselves *with eager diligence*[1060] to avenge their comrades and, because they considered that it would be dangerous to attack a village defended by brave men and protected on all sides by valleys and barriers, they prepared to defeat them by means of cunning.

There was in Goslar a certain burgrave named Bodo,[1061] who had been a great favourite of the king in peacetime and who now, when the State was in confusion, preserved his fidelity towards him undiminished, *but secretly, for fear of*[1062] the Saxons, lest he should be found out and should lose all his possessions through the machinations of the common people. On the instructions of those who were in the castle, he bribed the herdsmen who kept watch over the cattle of the men of Goslar to drive the herd to pasture a little further from the village. Riders sent from the castle drove them even further away. Some of their comrades, fully armed, hid themselves in the mountains and the forests. When the report reached Goslar that the cattle had been driven off, *there was a* unanimous *call to arms*[1063] and they all made a supreme effort to hurl

---

1058 Livy IV.53.11; V.49.7.

1059 Cf. *Song of the Saxon War* I.184–6, p. 6: 'when two young men from the Harzburg went down and wished to provide themselves with new weapons in Goslar, they were captured, stripped and raised upon a cross'.

1060 Plautus, *Trinummus* 1.2.29.

1061 Bodo, steward of Goslar. Cf. Bishop Hezelo of Hildesheim, letter to Henry IV (1075) in *Briefsammlungen* p. 30, a complaint about 'Boto, *advocatus* of Goslar'. See Meyer von Knonau (1894) p. 299; Wilke (1970) pp. 33–4; Fenske (1977) p. 83. Holder-Egger, *Lamperti Annales* p. 232 n. 3 identified with him the 'Count Bodo' mentioned below, 1075, p. 278 and n. 1462. On the title ascribed to him by Lampert, *prefectus*, see Niermeyer – van de Kieft (2002) pp. 1083–4.

1062 John 19:38.

1063 Livy III.50.11; VII.12.3. See Billanovich (1945) p. 67.

themselves into the battle. They did not trouble to wait for one another but each man *rode at full gallop*[1064] and strove as hard as he could to be the first to pursue the enemy and to snatch back the plunder. The enemy, pretending to flee, kept a short distance between themselves and those who were following them until they had drawn their incautious pursuers *into the area where the ambush had been prepared.*[1065] Then a shout went up on all sides and both those who had remained in the castle and those who had concealed themselves in the neighbouring mountains launched an attack on the pursuing forces and continued to cut down both stragglers and fugitives until they made an end of the slaughter not because reason prevailed but because they were overcome by horror and *sickened by the bloodshed.*[1066] This and other similar incidents prompted the Saxons to take possession of the hill next to the castle and to post knights there,[1067] who were *to keep watch* for enemy attacks *with the utmost vigilance*[1068] and without intermission. Nevertheless they failed to restrain their presumption by this means, for whenever the opportunity offered itself, the enemy perpetrated many hostile attacks both against those who were guarding them and against the other inhabitants of the province.

Meanwhile, as Christmas drew near, the knights of the king who were being besieged in the Hasenburg continually sent envoys to the king, asking him in God's name to devise a plan to set them free.[1069] For their provisions were running out and they were now wasting away from extreme hunger, so that unless he took urgent measures to assist them in their dangerous situation, either they must die or else they must submit to the power of their enemies. The king summoned the archbishops of Mainz and Cologne to an audience and begged them most insistently to meet the Saxons and negotiate with them to achieve at least a short cessation of hostilities and their withdrawal from besieging the castles. Although they knew beyond doubt that their efforts would be in vain, nevertheless, because he continued to importune them, they promised

1064 Caesar, *Bellum Civile* III.96; Livy I.27.7; III.46.6.

1065 Livy I.14.7; XXXV.29.3.

1066 *Ibid.*, XXVII.49.8.

1067 Cf. *Song of the Saxon War* II.91–2, p. 10: 'on the huge mountain that stood next to the [Harzburg] they constructed a castle'; Bruno of Merseburg, *The Saxon War* c. 29, p. 32: the Saxons 'built another castle of equal strength and placed a garrison there, who prevented reinforcements and provisions reaching the enemy'. See Meyer von Knonau (1894) pp. 299–300 and n. 197.

1068 Livy XXI.53.9.

1069 See above p. 189 and n. 991. See also Meyer von Knonau (1894) pp. 297–8.

to do what was asked of them and they immediately sent envoys to call on the princes of Saxony to meet them for a conference in Corvey in the week after Epiphany.[1070]

In this year after the outbreak of the Saxon war there was no further collection of tithes in Thuringia.[1071] The Thuringians rejoiced that they had found an opportunity to defend with military might the rights handed down to them by their ancestors, while the king lamented that, through his unbridled eagerness to obtain the tithes, he had almost lost both his kingdom and his life.

In this year also that most notorious man Egino, who had accused Duke Otto of Bavaria of that capital offence,[1072] was arrested in the course of a robbery and blinded by the local people. And he was reduced to such great poverty that afterwards he went about from door to door, begging for alms from the public. Moreover Count Giso[1073] and Adalbert[1074] with his four sons – who had incited that same reprobate to fabricate this tragic story – were killed by their enemies in a private quarrel in Hollende, Giso's own castle, and so God demonstrated the innocence of Duke Otto.

1074

The king celebrated Christmas in Worms but he lived there in a manner that did not at all match the magnificence of a king.[1075] For no food supplies[1076] were delivered to him from the royal estates nor did bishops

---

1070 I.e. the week after 6 January 1074. Lampert alone reported this royal summons to Siegfried of Mainz and Anno of Cologne: see Meyer von Knonau (1894) p. 298 and n. 196.

1071 Cf. Siegfried of Mainz, letter to Pope Gregory VII, *Codex Udalrici* 40, p. 87, referring to 'the inveterate stubbornness of the Thuringians ... refusing to pay tithes on their revenues'. See Meyer von Knonau (1894) p. 266; Struve (1970a) p. 77 n. 32.

1072 See above pp. 127 and n. 582, 157 and n. 789. See Fenske (1977) p. 92. On Lampert's idea of God's vindication of Otto of Northeim and the motif of divine judgement see Struve (1970a) p. 118 n. 18.

1073 Perhaps the Count Giso (†1073), father of Count Giso IV of Gudensberg (†1122) and possessor of the castle of Hollende near Wetter (Hesse). See Metz (1991) pp. 350, 352, 354–5, 366; Robinson (1999) pp. 67–8.

1074 Perhaps Adalbert, count of Schaumburg, in Hesse (†1073). See Metz (1991) pp. 337, 362.

1075 25 December 1073. Cf. Berthold of Reichenau, *Chronicle* 1074, p. 130: 'King Henry celebrated Christmas in Worms, although he was beset by the greatest dangers and difficulties.' See Kilian (1886) p. 63; Meyer von Knonau (1894) p. 297.

1076 On Lampert's term, *servicium*, see Niermeyer – van de Kieft (2002) p. 1259. See also Brühl (1968) pp. 132–9, 157–8; Metz (1971) pp. 257–91.

or abbots or the other holders of public office show him the customary service: instead whatever was needed for his daily subsistence was purchased at a low price.[1077] Nevertheless some of the princes were with him but they did not have that splendid retinue of servants nor that throng of knights and attendants to which they were accustomed. On the contrary, they had come to pay their respects to him with a few followers and dressed almost like persons of no consequence. They came so as not to be branded with open rebellion if they refused to come to court when summoned. The king, however, would by no means permit them to leave him, since he reckoned that, even if they were of little help to him, it would nevertheless fill the enemy with dread when they heard that persons of such distinction in the kingdom had been gathered together to oppose them.[1078]

The archbishops of Mainz and Cologne came on the appointed day to Corvey, as had been agreed,[1079] and, according to the commission that they had from the king, they requested the Saxons who had come to meet them there to withdraw their army from the siege of the castles. But they replied that they would by no means do so. Moreover they chided the archbishops angrily for *wasting time in consultations*[1080] and in demanding sometimes a conference, sometimes a truce. They had thereby increased the king's presumption and had destroyed the Saxons' greatest opportunity to claim their freedom. They should therefore depart and no longer mock them *with peaceable but treacherous words:*[1081] they had reached that point at which their business must now be settled not by means of womanish talk but by the weapons of war. It was only with difficulty that *the majority was calmed*[1082] by the wiser men among them and they agreed unanimously on the decision to meet in the week after the Purification of St Mary[1083] in Fritzlar and there to take counsel

---

1077 Cf. above, 1066, p. 109.

1078 Cf. *D.H.IV* 267 (issued on 18 January 1074 in Worms). The witnesses were Archbishop Liemar of Bremen and Bishop Eppo-Eberhard of Zeitz-Naumburg (on their presence at court see above, 1073, p. 177 and n. 918) and the bishops of Verdun, Bamberg and Basel, all of whom were the king's faithful advisers. See Meyer von Knonau (1894) p. 307 and n. 1; Robinson (1999) pp. 94–5.

1079 I.e. in the week 12–18 January 1074. Lampert alone reported this mission of Siegfried of Mainz and Anno of Cologne: see Meyer von Knonau (1894) pp. 309, 823.

1080 Livy VIII.11.3.

1081 I Maccabees 7:10.

1082 Livy III.49.7.

1083 I.e. the week after 2 February. Lampert again interpolated his polemical theme of the election of a new king: see Meyer von Knonau (1894) p. 823 and also above p. 33.

with the rest of the princes of the kingdom and to set up a ruler for the endangered State who would be acceptable to all men. They also sent word to the king to be present on the appointed day, if he judged it to be useful for him, and to demand his own rights not by means of letters and mediators but in person and with his own voice.

Three days after they reached this decision and departed, the Thuringians received the surrender of the men who were in the Hasenburg and who were overcome by hunger. They released them without punishment, set fire to the castle and immediately marched the army to another castle, which was called the Spatenburg.[1084] The siege of the castle of *Vokenroht*[1085] had begun a few days before. And because the queen was being kept safe there throughout the war,[1086] the abbot of Hersfeld[1087] went there on the king's orders and took her from there with the consent of the Thuringians and brought her to Hersfeld. She was pregnant and already from day to day she anxiously saw the birth drawing near. And after she had resided there for many days – for because of the disorder in the State the king did not know where he could send her to be kept in safety – she gave birth to a son on Wednesday 12 February.[1088] Since he was believed to be sick and to be on the point of dying, he was baptised at three days old by Bishop Ezzo of Oldenburg,[1089] who chanced at that time to be the guest of the abbot, and he was given the name of his great-grandfather Conrad. And since there were no other persons present who were worthy to perform that office, the abbot and some others of the brethren of the monastery of Hersfeld took him up from the holy baptismal font.

Regenger, who had proposed to fight against Udalric of Godesheim in

1084 See above p. 189 and n. 989.

1085 See above p. 189 and n. 992.

1086 Bertha of Turin (above n. 491). The queen had been in Würzburg on 27 October 1073 (cf. *D.H.IV* 264). *D.H.IV* 269, a donation to Bertha of 28 January (issued in Breitenbach), refers to 'Queen Bertha and the offspring conceived from us'. On the inaccuracies in Lampert's account see Holder-Egger (1894) pp. 190–2; Meyer von Knonau (1894) p. 310 and n. 4.

1087 Hartwig (above n. 820). See Feierabend (1913) pp. 111–12; Vogtherr (1991) p. 452.

1088 Conrad, duke of Lower Lotharingia (1076–87), king (1087–98) †1101. Cf. Lampert, *Libellus de institutione Herveldensis ecclesiae* II, p. 354: 'The empress gave birth to a little king in Hersfeld'; Berthold of Reichenau, *Chronicle* 1074, p. 131. (*Annals of Iburg* 1074, p. 436, give the date of birth and baptism as 14 February.) See Meyer von Knonau (1894) p. 327 and n. 27 ('as a monk of Hersfeld, Lampert … is here the classic witness').

1089 Ezzo, bishop of Oldenburg (?1055/60–1082). The child was named after Emperor Conrad II (above n. 1).

order to incriminate the king, was seized by a most fearful demon a few days before the duel was to take place and he died a horrible death.[1090]

Meanwhile the king saw that little by little the princes were deserting him and that the ferocity of his enemies grew stronger as a result of his forbearance towards them. Compelled both by his sense of shame and by the difficulty of his situation, he made up his mind to try the extreme hazard of his fortunes and to engage in battle with the Saxons as soon as he had the means to do so, choosing rather to lose his life with honour than to lose his kingdom with infamy. For he had greatly alienated his knights because he brought no help to his followers, who every day were attacked, overcome, driven out. While others fatigued themselves in their solicitude for his welfare, he himself idled within the walls of Worms in sluggish inactivity: now he desired to bargain with his life in order to cleanse himself of this offence. He therefore sent messages to all the princes of the kingdom and entreated them in God's name to come to his aid, *reminding* them *of the* many *marks of favour that he had bestowed*[1091] on them in the past and promising still more in the future.

And indeed many of the bishops immediately came to him[1092] but they were more ready to offer him advice than to provide him with soldiers.[1093] For they had left their knights at home and presented themselves with few followers and virtually as persons without a public office, with the intention namely of clearing themselves in his presence of the accusation of disobedience, while not greatly aiding his cause, of which they all most strongly disapproved. But the archbishop of Mainz, the archbishop of Cologne, the bishop of Strasbourg,[1094] the bishop of Worms

---

1090 On Regenger and Udalric see above pp. 197 and n. 1030, 199 and n. 1036. Cf. Berthold of Reichenau, *Chronicle* 1073, p. 130: 'that man who had betrayed him and who had come forward as his enemy, died a sudden death'. See Meyer von Knonau (1894) pp. 308–9, 847–8.

1091 Livy XXVII.17.12.

1092 Cf. *DD.H.IV* 268–9 (27–8 January). The intervention clause identifies the archbishops of Bremen and Trier and the bishops of Zeitz-Naumburg, Verdun, Eichstätt, Metz, Freising and Augsburg. See Meyer von Knonau (1894) p. 311.

1093 Cf. Berthold of Reichenau, *Chronicle* 1074, p. 130: the king 'assembled help from wherever and from whomsoever he could'; *Song of the Saxon War* II.119, p. 11: the royal army was 'small but distinguished by the great fame of its courage'; II.71–2, p. 9 (above n. 1040); Bruno of Merseburg, *The Saxon War* c. 31, p. 33: 'he gathered an army that was indeed large but not prepared to fight unless extreme necessity compelled it to do so'.

1094 Werner II (above n. 378) was to prove a consistently loyal supporter of Henry IV: see Robinson (1999) pp. 118, 155, 174, 175.

(whom he had previously driven out of his city)[1095] and in addition
all the dukes – of Bavaria,[1096] Swabia,[1097] Lotharingia,[1098] the Moselle
province,[1099] the Carinthians[1100] – and also the knights of the abbots of
Fulda[1101] and Hersfeld steadfastly opposed him. They refused to take up
arms to oppress innocent people, who, if they had indeed been guilty
of anything that ought to be punished by the sword of vengeance, had
been driven to it by an unavoidable and easily excusable necessity.

The king left Worms and came to Hersfeld with his army on 27
January.[1102] On that day a wonderful sign was seen in heaven. When the
sun rose, two columns, golden in colour and shining with a most magnificent splendour, also rose to the right and to the left and remained with
a reddish glow, retaining the same brightness, until the sun climbed
some degrees higher. During the previous night very many people also
saw a rainbow around the time of cock-crow in a totally clear heaven.
It was extraordinarily cold and everything was gripped by so great a
frost that the rivers not only were compacted with ice on the surface but
seemed most unusually to be totally transformed into ice.[1103] The army
therefore suffered severely from the lack of bread because, as a result of
the frozen condition of the rivers, the working of the mills everywhere
came to a halt and they could not grind the grain that they chanced to
have found.

On the day before he came to Hersfeld, the king sent the abbot of
Hersfeld to the Saxons, who were said to be assembled to the number
of forty thousand men and stationed on the further bank of the River

---

1095 Adalbert (above n. 626). This polemical version of the bishop's expulsion from
Worms (cf. above p. 200 and n. 1042) is found also in the *Annals of Weissenburg*
1074, p. 57: 'after removing the bishop, he made a residence for himself in Worms'.

1096 Welf IV (above n. 630).

1097 Rudolf (above n. 203).

1098 Gozelo-Godfrey IV of Lower Lotharingia (above n. 570). Cf. the opinion of Bruno
of Merseburg, *The Saxon War* c. 78, p. 77: 'Duke Godfrey ... was the greatest
enemy of Saxony'.

1099 Theoderic II (of Châtenois), duke of Upper Lotharingia (1070–1115).

1100 Berthold I (above n. 824).

1101 Widerad (above n. 239). Holder-Egger (1894) p. 191 argued that, if the Fulda and
Hersfeld knights declined to perform military service, it was because of the winter
weather and the king's tardiness in summoning the expedition.

1102 See Kilian (1886) p. 63; Meyer von Knonau (1894) p. 315.

1103 On the severity of the weather cf. *Song of the Saxon War* II.147–62, p. 12; Bruno of
Merseburg, *The Saxon War* c. 32, p. 34; *Annals of Iburg* 1074, p. 436.

Werra.[1104] He was to find out from them whether the king's messengers could go to them and return in safety. The king himself passed by Hersfeld and awaited the abbot's return in the nearby villages,[1105] almost two miles from the aforementioned river. He did not wish to move the camp any further until greater numbers of troops arrived and until he himself made more careful enquiries whether any hope remained of restoring peace. He had indeed heard that the Saxons had decided to deny him access to Thuringia and immediately to intercept him with an army drawn up for battle when he came to that same bank of the aforesaid river, which divided Hesse and Thuringia. The ice had made the river passable for travellers on foot. This circumstance inspired the king with an even greater fear: that the enemy, no longer hindered by any difficulty in their passage, might make a sudden attack on him, while he was still unprepared and no match for so great a host. For that reason he is said to have raged violently against his advisers for having allowed him to leave Worms and needlessly to rush headlong into so great a peril. For the Saxons were said to have such *a superabundance of troops*[1106] that they sent back to their homes, as superfluous to their needs, eleven thousand men, who had received a sudden summons to the expedition but who had brought no provisions with them.

Amidst these delays the king's army, more eager *for booty than for battle*,[1107] scoured the villages in the neighbourhood of Hersfeld far and wide and plundered them as if they were in enemy territory and, under the pretext of provisions needed to sustain the troops, they left the innocent inhabitants nothing except their pitiful existence. The king did not prevent this injustice since this was the price that he paid to make the troops more loyal to him. The estates of the monasteries of Fulda and Hersfeld were so weakened and exhausted by this devastation that it was with great difficulty that the brethren were restrained from leaving the monasteries as the food shortage grew worse.[1108] On his

---

1104 Cf. Bruno, *The Saxon War* c. 31, p. 33: the Saxons marched 'to the town called Vacha' (west of Hersfeld); *Song of the Saxon War* II.190, p. 13, numbered their army at sixty thousand. The mission of Abbot Hartwig on 26 January was reported only by Lampert. See Holder-Egger (1894) p. 192; Meyer von Knonau (1894) p. 317; Struve (1970a) p. 78.

1105 Cf. *DD.H.IV* 268–9, issued on 27–8 January in Breitenbach.

1106 Livy II.47.4; XXI.8.3; XXIV.48.7. See Billanovich (1945) p. 88. According to Bruno, *The Saxon War* c. 31, p. 33, 'the army of the Saxons was so great that it was believed to be double the size of the king's army'.

1107 Livy II.47.5; VII.16.4.

1108 Lampert, *Libellus de institutione Herveldensis ecclesiae*, prologus, p. 344, reflects

return from the Saxons the abbot of Hersfeld reported that, contrary to the general belief, their response had been mild and peaceable. For they were not so devoid of reason and not so forgetful of *the law of nations*, which was widely known even among the barbarian peoples, that they did not know that *envoys* must not be injured even in the cruellest hostilities.[1109] The Saxons had been compelled by extreme necessity to resort to warfare and they had not taken up arms to attack anyone but to defend themselves and to ward off injuries. If that necessity was removed, they would even now prefer peace to war and they would gladly put back their drawn swords into their sheaths. This reply was exceedingly welcome to those who were with the king.

Then four of the bishops[1110] were sent to negotiate peace with the Saxons and to promise in the king's name that he would most readily agree to all those reasonable demands that mediators chosen by both parties judged to be just, as long as they also, for their part, were satisfied with just conditions and preferred to encounter his clemency rather than his armed might. To this the Saxons replied that they demanded nothing except what they had already frequently demanded in their many embassies.[1111] This was, namely, that he should order without delay the demolition of the castles that he had constructed throughout . Saxony and Thuringia in order to oppress them; that he should restore to individual persons their inherited estates that had been seized from them by force or by legal subterfuge; that he should give back the duchy of Bavaria to Duke Otto, whom he had sought to destroy by shamelessly making use of the false accusation and the most wicked invention

---

the damage inflicted on Hersfeld through 'the violence of robbers, who left her nothing except the walls and stones'. Cf. *Song of the Saxon War* II.168–9, p. 12: 'eager flames devoured numerous villages roundabout'. See Holder-Egger (1894) pp. 192–3; Struve (1970a) p. 78.

1109 Livy XXI.25.7; XXX.25.10; XXXIX.25.10. Cf. above p. 188 and n. 983. For Lampert on 'the law of nations' see Struve (1970a) p. 50; Dickerhof (1991) pp. 451–2, 454.

1110 *Annals of Augsburg* 1074, p. 128 recorded that peace was made with the Saxons 'through Bishop Embriko of Augsburg'. It is not clear whether he participated in this mission or in that of the 'fifteen bishops' and other princes reported by Lampert below p. 214.

1111 Cf. Bruno's version of the Saxon demands (*The Saxon War* c. 31, p. 34): 'that [the king] should destroy his castles and never restore them again; that he should make no more depredations in their land; that he should settle all affairs in Saxony according to the Saxons' advice and should admit no foreigner as an adviser in their concerns; and that he should never take revenge on any of them for his expulsion.' See Meyer von Knonau (1894) pp. 321–2.

of a criminal;[1112] that he should guarantee freedom from punishment to the archbishop of Mainz, the archbishop of Cologne, Duke Rudolf and in short to all men who had deserted him during this time of discord[1113] or who had inflicted an injury on him through their attachment to the other party and that he should impose no penalties for this offence in perpetuity; that he should allow their people their freedom and their lawful rights from the earliest times to remain valid and inviolable; that he should not spend all his life only in Saxony in sluggish idleness but should now and then leave Goslar and travel around his kingdom, which through the industry of his ancestors extended very far and wide in all directions;[1114] that he should do justice to the churches and monasteries, the widows and orphans and the others who suffered through the perversion of law and that he should adorn the office of king, of which he was the titular representative, with the splendour of royal morals and royal deeds.[1115] If he promised most faithfully to perform these obligations and if he gave them as his guarantors, who would affirm that he was undoubtedly trustworthy, those same princes of the kingdom whom he now had as mediators to restore peace, they would be prepared to lay down their weapons, to uphold the peace and thereafter to live in obedience to his commands. If he did not promise, however, they were bound by their oath to fight tirelessly for their freedom, their rights, their fatherland as long as the last spark of *vital heat*[1116] survived.

This demand seemed to the king too harsh and he began *to shift* this way and that in his distress and *to appeal* to his princes by *the fidelity*[1117] that they owed him not to allow him – to the dishonour of all of them – to be *sent under the yoke*[1118] of such infamous conditions. Before all else he judged it intolerable that he should be forced to destroy his castles and to give

---

1112 On Otto of Northeim (above n. 261) and his accuser Egino see above p. 127 and n. 582. Bruno (*The Saxon War* c. 30, p. 33) claimed that the king 'promised Duke Otto ... the office that had been unjustly taken from him, together with an increase of power'. Bruno did not include Otto's claims among the Saxon demands (above n. 1111).

1113 On Siegfried of Mainz, Anno of Cologne and Rudolf of Swabia see above p. 189 and n. 984.

1114 A consistent theme of Lampert's polemic against the king: see above, 1066, p. 109 and n. 458; 1070, p. 133; 1071, p. 135; 1073, p. 178 and n. 925, p. 182; below 1075, p. 270. Bruno (above n. 1111) did not include this among the Saxon demands.

1115 For Lampert's idea of the duties of the just king see Struve (1970a) pp. 82, 96.

1116 Lucretius, *De rerum natura* III.129.

1117 Livy IV.14.4.

1118 *Ibid.*, I.26.13; II.34.9; Caesar, *Bellum Gallicum* I.7; I.12.

his enemies rewards instead of punishment. He therefore rejected the peace that was offered and on the following day he chose to muster the army and to draw up the troops in battle array. He sent messengers in all directions to where the princes were stationed, ordering that each of them should lead out his men in full battle formation. They all promised most readily that they would obey his command but after the messengers had returned, not one of the princes left his camp. They all refused to undertake such a nefarious action as to make war on those whose cause they believed to be entirely just.

On the other side the camp of the Saxons was shaken by a great conflict. All the common people raised a tumult against the princes because they had driven them into such great storms of war and all to no purpose. For now, when all the circumstances gave assurance of victory and the opportunity that they had longed for with the utmost eagerness since the beginning of the war was now smiling upon them precisely as they wished, they suddenly found themselves, like penitents, stretching out their hands in supplication and begging for peace. With womanish folly and childish levity they were delivering themselves up to be cheated again by the man who had so often cheated them before. The common people also earnestly pressed Duke Otto to assume office as their king, to serve as their leader in the forthcoming struggle and, since God was promising that their cause would prosper, not to deny them his powerful support.[1119]

The king was surrounded by those men on whose advice he had been accustomed to rely most closely.[1120] When they saw that he was moving heaven and earth in his efforts to escape from the Saxon conditions, they said: 'We have, O king, no other way. Either you must accept with equanimity the conditions that they have imposed or you must lose the kingdom and in addition put your life in great peril. You wish to do battle and ward off danger by force of arms? But how courageously, do you think, will this army strike against the enemy, when they did not

---

1119 This incident was reported only by Lampert, who characteristically exaggerated the role of Otto of Northeim and the fragility of Henry's regime: see Meyer von Knonau (1894) p. 324 and n. 1; Lange (1961) pp. 50–2. On Otto's standing cf. Bruno, *The Saxon War* c. 31, p. 34: the king 'knew that the plans of all [the Saxons] depended on' Otto; Bernold of St Blasien, *Chronicle* 1083, p. 268: 'Duke Otto, the most prudent knight whom [the anti-king] had left in Saxony as the chief of all his vassals'.

1120 *DD.H.IV* 267–9 (18, 27–8 January) identify the archbishops of Trier and Bremen and the bishops of Zeitz-Naumburg, Verdun, Bamberg, Basel, Eichstätt, Metz, Freising and Augsburg. See Robinson (1999) pp. 94–5.

even wish to leave their camp after the order was given to muster the army? A short distance away there is an innumerable army of enemies but more than all those enemies you ought to fear the men who stand at your side like close friends and who for the moment pretend to be loyal and address flattering words to you but only as long as they are not forced to do battle against those to whom they have bound themselves by an oath. If the war-trumpets sound and they are compelled to make a stand and, hard pressed and hemmed in on all sides, to kill or be killed, then certainly either they will flee in all directions in less time than it takes to say the word or they will desert you and cross over to the side of the enemy. It would have been better, therefore, not to leave Worms than, having advanced into *a situation of extreme danger*,[1121] to seek to test the loyalty of the princes at such an unfavourable time. Nevertheless, although your *hopes have been cancelled out*[1122] and you are surrounded on all sides by obstacles, one way of escape lies open if you promise without delay to do what is demanded of you. In this way you can fend off the savage valour and youthful exuberance of the enemy and escape the peril that threatens to seize you by the throat. Thereafter, when all these animosities have been laid to rest forever, you can strengthen your hold on the kingdom.'

After he had tried every possible evasion and all in vain, the king was now convinced not so much by reason as by necessity. At last he summoned the princes to a council and permitted them to regulate these great disturbances according to their own judgement, promising that they might undoubtedly rely on him to approve whatever they judged to be appropriate for the settlement of such great affairs. But they replied that there was absolutely no other way open to him of avoiding the battle, which now threatened him close at hand with drawn sword, than to do what the Saxons had demanded. When the king had promised to do this, calling the name of Christ to witness, fifteen bishops[1123] and such princes as were in the camp set out to the Saxons to inform them of the king's will. *Many opinions were expressed*[1124] there, many arguments were sought to counter them, since no proposals seemed to the Saxons to be sufficiently secure, given their mistrust of the king's savage disposition and their frequent opportunities of testing his reliability. After a long drawn out debate they finally agreed to the restoration of

1121 Livy XXII.9.6.
1122 *Ibid.*, III.58.6; XXXV.31.7.
1123 See above n. 1110.
1124 Livy II.55.11.

peace on this condition. If the king, remembering the injuries inflicted on him, ever tried to revoke his decision or to invalidate any of the measures that they had been compelled by supreme necessity to take, they would all resort again to their weapons, bound by the same oath that bound them now; *they would oppose such a wrong*[1125] and with the consent of all the princes of the kingdom they would depose him from the kingship, as one who was manifestly guilty of breaking his oath.[1126] With these words, still in their serried ranks, they marched off to meet the king face to face on the very day of the feast of the Purification of St Mary.[1127] They were preceded by those bishops and other princes who had been the mediators in this restoration of the peace. When they arrived, the king received them in honourable fashion, bestowed the kiss of peace and confirmed with the authority of his own voice the peace conditions, which he had made public through his intermediaries.

When everything had thus been settled according to their wishes, he rewarded with the magnificence befitting a king those men who had shown great enthusiasm for his cause. After he had permitted every man to depart to his own home, he joined the Saxons and set out for Goslar.[1128] He sent messengers in all directions, sending word that the army should withdraw from the siege of the castles. He ordered that those who were in the castles should henceforward *undertake no hostile activities*[1129] against the inhabitants of the province but that as soon as they had consumed the provisions that had been accumulated in sufficient quantities to sustain them during a long war, they should surrender the castles themselves to the local inhabitants to be destroyed from the very foundations. Although the Saxons were very suspicious

1125 *Ibid.*, III.37.8; Sallust, *Jugurtha* 14.25.

1126 Holder-Egger, *Lamperti Annales* p. 180 n. 1, noted that the reference to Henry's deposition must have been a polemical invention of Lampert.

1127 2 February. Lampert subsequently identified the meeting-place as Gerstungen: below, pp. 218, 240 and 1075, p. 269. The date is corroborated in *Annals of Augsburg* 1074, p. 128 and Berthold of Reichenau, *Chronicle* 1074, p. 130, who added: 'Fearing the shock of war, [the Saxons] came to surrender with this stipulation, that the fortifications about which the quarrel had arisen should be destroyed.' *Song of the Saxon War* II.180–4, p. 13 claimed that the Saxons 'surrendered themselves and all their possessions' to the king: it was 'a triumph the like of which has not happened since the time of Charles [the Great]'. According to Bruno of Merseburg, *The Saxon War* c. 31, p. 34, 'the king promised most faithfully to perform all' the Saxon demands (above n. 1111). See Kilian (1886) p. 64; Meyer von Knonau (1894) p. 326; Giese (1979) pp. 158–9; Vogtherr (1991) p. 452; Robinson (1999) pp. 95–7.

1128 Cf. Berthold, *Chronicle* 1074, p. 131; *Song of the Saxon War* II.210, p. 13; Bruno, *The Saxon War* c. 31, p. 34. See Kilian (1886) p. 64; Meyer von Knonau (1894) p. 327.

1129 Livy XLII.14.3.

of this delay, they were not greatly concerned about it, since they knew that the king had been placed in their power and could not put up any opposition to their common decision.

When the king arrived in Goslar, the young men who were in the Harzburg and whom he regarded with great admiration because of their successes,[1130] loudly condemned the peace agreement and because, according to the prophet, *deceit prospered under* their *hands*,[1131] they promised him that they had the strength to achieve many deeds of immeasurable magnificence, if he continued the war. As proof of their courage, they boastfully pointed to the tombstones of the men of Goslar who had been slaughtered, standing along the whole distance between Goslar and the Harzburg for almost two miles. Hearing this, the king, accustomed as he was to adversity and being of an age that is greedy for military glory, gradually returned to his old inclinations and to his former inflexible attitude and now he deeply regretted the agreement that he had made.[1132] When he was asked by the Saxons to keep his promises, he began once more to shift his ground, making crafty replies, and to demand that *the fulfilling of the terms of the agreement should be postponed*[1133] until there was a general hearing in an assembly of the princes of the kingdom to decide in detail what would best serve the honour and the needs of the State. When they gave their assent to this, the king commanded that the princes from the whole of the kingdom should meet in Goslar on 10 March.

On the appointed day not one of the other princes appeared there.[1134]

1130 *Song of the Saxon War* II.217–18, p. 14: 'Firstly he endowed the foremost men of the Harzburg with the gifts that they deserved.'

1131 Daniel 8:25.

1132 Cf. Archbishop Werner of Magdeburg, letter to Archbishop Siegfried of Mainz (1074/5), cited in Bruno, *The Saxon War* c. 42, p. 42: 'We have knocked down all the castles and other fortifications that [the king] ordered to be destroyed in our territory, except for those that he allowed to stand, against our will.' Bruno himself wrote, c. 33, p. 35: 'he began, remembering his true self, to seek opportunities so as not to have to destroy his castles immediately, as he had promised'. According to *Song of the Saxon War* II.215–16, p. 14, the king 'summoned to himself all the guards of the castles and commanded that the castles should throw open their gates'. The poet said nothing of the promise to destroy the castles. Berthold of Reichenau, *Chronicle* 1074, p. 130, wrote that the Saxons had stipulated (at Gerstungen) 'that the fortifications ... should be destroyed and this was subsequently carried out'. Cf. *Annals of Weissenburg* 1074, p. 57: 'In this same year the castles that the king built, causing offence to Saxony, were demolished.' See Meyer von Knonau (1894) pp. 329–30.

1133 Livy III.9.12; III.44.12. See Billanovich (1945) pp. 139–40.

1134 Lampert alone reported these events. Meyer von Knonau (1894) pp. 329–30, 823–5 analysed the contradictions in his account.

The Saxons and Thuringians were present with an innumerable host, summoned according to their oath from the whole of Saxony and Thuringia. They pitched their camp not far from Goslar and sent envoys to the king to negotiate with him the conditions relating to the peace that had been agreed between them. For three whole days[1135] they eagerly pressed him, sometimes imploring him, sometimes threatening *the terrors of war*.[1136] The king tried to evade their unrelenting pressure by giving them slippery answers. Sometimes he made a pretext of the absence of the princes, to whose discretion the judgement of this matter principally belonged. Sometimes he begged with might and main that, while all the other conditions remained in place according to their agreement, they might allow him at least the castles, which he had built at enormous cost to defend the kingdom. If these were exempted, he would easily accept the loss of the other terms of the agreement because he hoped always to have a place of refuge in these castles, whatever might befall and to use them to impose a permanent punishment on the Saxons for the insult that they had now inflicted on him. He had already rejected the pleas of the envoys and ignored the advice of his confidants and remained stubborn and inflexible in his purpose, when suddenly news came that the Saxons, dispensing with the mediators through whom the negotiations had previously been conducted, were marching on the palace, *armed and fully equipped*,[1137] and that they no longer demanded the fulfilment of what had been promised but wished to bid him farewell and set up a king whom they would thereafter have as their leader in war.[1138]

The king received the unanimous backing of the archbishop of Bremen, the bishop of Zeitz, the bishop of Osnabrück and the others who had been driven from Saxony because of their zealous partisanship for the king, were deprived of their property and suffered great dishonour and

---

1135 On Lampert's custom of describing councils and conferences as lasting three days (cf. above 1071, p. 150 and n. 737; 1073, p. 196 and n. 1023) see Holder-Egger, *Lamperti Annales* p. 131 n. 2.

1136 Livy VI.6.6. See Billanovich (1945) p. 124.

1137 Livy XXIX.2.4. See Billanovich (1945) p. 124.

1138 Cf. Bruno, *The Saxon War* c. 33, p. 35: when Henry tried to go back on his promise to destroy the castles, the princes, 'wishing to please him', sought to exempt the Harzburg but 'the people insisted urgently that it should be destroyed and if that did not happen, they declared that the rebellion would begin anew'. Holder-Egger, *Lamperti Annales* p. 182 n. 2, notes that (as above p. 215 and n. 1126) the reference to Henry's deposition was a polemical invention of Lampert.

ignominy.[1139] They implored him in God's name to pity if not his own, then at least their misfortunes, for they had been driven from their sees because of the hatred with which he himself was regarded and they now for almost a whole year led lives beset by every kind of misery. They had unfailingly preserved their loyalty towards him in adversity and they had withstood everything that happened contrary to their wishes and had shared his troubles. Now that God *in a benevolent change of fortune had restored*[1140] such violent storms *to their former state, let him rejoice in his lot*[1141] and now that he found himself in a safe anchorage, let him hereafter take care that no such shipwreck happened again. But if he wished once more to disturb and confound the tranquillity and the settlement that through heaven's grace had now been reached in keeping with his honour and according to his wishes, let him see for himself what the outcome would be. Already reduced to utter exhaustion by their previous misfortunes, they for their part must thereafter acquiesce in whatever the time and place demanded of them and submit to the demands of their people so as not to be driven out of their country once again.

During this conversation the king saw that the Saxons had now filled the entrance hall of the palace *with an armed host* and in their wild agitation made a loud noise, *ready to do violence.*[1142] He was at last persuaded by the *double danger*[1143] to agree that within a year he would do justice to Duke Otto, who was claiming the duchy of Bavaria, according to the judgement of the princes;[1144] that he would certainly destroy all his castles without delay but on condition that the Saxons and Thuringians should likewise demolish those of their own castles that had been built during his reign;[1145] and that all the rest of the promises that he had made in Gerstungen would be kept with complete fidelity. The

---

1139 On Liemar of Hamburg-Bremen (above n. 798), Eppo (Eberhard) of Zeitz-Naumburg (above n. 46), Benno II of Osnabrück (above n. 500) see above p. 177 and n. 918.

1140 Horace, *Epodi* XIII.7.8.

1141 *Ibid.*, XIV.15.

1142 Livy I.52.5; VI.18.7.

1143 Sallust, *Jugurtha* 38.5; Tacitus, *Annales* 4.59.

1144 See above pp. 130 and n. 592, 211 and n. 1112. For Lampert's emphasis on 'the judgement of the princes' see Struve (1970a) p. 46.

1145 According to Spier (1962) p. 31, Henry's castles served as a 'counter-system against the threat of the aristocratic castles' of the region. See also Spier (1967–8) pp. 185–201; Fenske (1977) pp. 29–30; Robinson (1999) pp. 82–3.

violent restlessness[1146] of the Saxons would not grant him any delay in performing what he had promised. He therefore sent messengers in all directions and caused *Vokenroht* and Spatenburg[1147] and the other castles that had been the subject of the public debate to be set on fire and entirely destroyed. In the case of the Harzburg only the walls were demolished and as much was done as would weaken the fortifications and remove the difficulty of access to the castle.[1148] The condition of the rest of the buildings remained unimpaired because a church had been built there and the site had been designated for the foundation of a congregation of canons.[1149] After peace with the Saxons was thus restored, the king withdrew from Goslar and went to Worms and spent the whole of Lent there[1150] and abstained thereafter from all military preparations.

The common people of Saxony, however, and especially those who lived in the little village in the neighbourhood of the Harzburg, were certainly displeased that any part of the Harzburg still remained standing. They considered that nothing had been achieved by their great exertions as long as that castle was still standing intact, which had been the source and origin of all the disasters that they had endured and which had reduced the neighbouring villages, once very prosperous, to a dreadful empty wilderness.[1151] The king had not dedicated it to divine worship but under the pretext of religion he had acquired a stronghold for his cruelty. He intended in a short while to begin the war anew and, when the anger of the Saxons had cooled down, to have a place from which he might once again send out his knights to cause destruction in Saxony

1146 On the translation of Lampert's term *improbitas* see Holder-Egger, *Lamperti Annales* p. 183 n. 3.

1147 See above p. 189 and nn. 992, 989.

1148 Cf. Bruno of Merseburg, *The Saxon War* c. 33, p. 35: the king 'secretly ordered certain of his men who had long been his friends to pull down only the outer part of the ramparts ... and after this slight damage had been repaired, [the castle] would remain sound'.

1149 On this foundation see Spier (1962) pp. 31–7; Weinfurter (1991) pp. 86–7.

1150 I.e. 5 March – 19 April. *D.H.IV* 271 was, however, issued on 22 March in Fritzlar. Cf. Bruno, *The Saxon War* c. 34, p. 36: the king 'left Saxony before the end of March and travelled, by no means joyfully, to the inhabitants of the Rhineland and the other regions of *Francia*'. See Kilian (1886) pp. 64–5; Meyer von Knonau (1894) p. 331.

1151 Cf. Archbishop Werner of Magdeburg, letter to Archbishop Siegfried of Mainz (1074/5), cited in Bruno, *The Saxon War* c. 42, p. 42: 'the peasants, like ignorant peasants and men who had endured many evils from that same castle'; Bruno, *The Saxon War* c. 33, p. 35: 'when the peasants had gained power over that place from which they had formerly suffered many evils'.

and to bring them back safely and the more embittered he was by the
successes of the Saxons now as he departed, the more violent would
be his conduct towards them then, when they were defeated. They
spread these rumours among their ranks with wild cries and roused
themselves into a state of great savagery.

On the third day after the king's departure, therefore, without the knowledge of the princes and without their being consulted, the common
people banded together and made an attack on the Harzburg.[1152] They
threw down what remained of the walls even to the foundations and
they scattered the stones far and wide. They did the same to the rest of
the buildings, which had been preserved intact by the permission of the
princes. They set fire to the church, which in the interests of expediting
the work had meanwhile been most finely constructed with wood; they
looted the treasures; they broke the altars in pieces. Finally, so that
the king should be left with no motive for rebuilding the castle, they
exhumed the bodies of his son and his brother,[1153] whom he had interred
there in order to make the place more acceptable to the people, and they
did everything that they could so that the mountain was levelled and
could no longer be of service in the conduct of a war. The abbot from
the neighbouring monastery[1154] *arrived opportunely*[1155] to snatch away
from the raging mob the relics of the saints,[1156] which had been torn
out when the altars were broken up, and the exhumed bodies of the
deceased and he transported them with honour to his own monastery.

1152 Cf. below, 1075, p. 253, on the Saxon princes' determination 'to refute the accusation and declare their innocence' of involvement in the attack on the Harzburg.
Cf. Werner of Magdeburg, letter to Siegfried of Mainz, cited in Bruno, *The Saxon
War* c. 42, p. 42: 'you will recognise that we are innocent'; Bruno, *The Saxon War*
c. 34, p. 36: 'the princes of Saxony ... sought to pacify [the king] ... by clearing
themselves of having planned or willed the offence'. See Meyer von Knonau (1894)
pp. 331–3; Giese (1991) p. 294; Rösener (1991) p. 61; Robinson (1999) pp. 97–8.

1153 Henry IV's son (name unknown: see above, 1071, p. 151 and nn. 741–2) and Henry
III's son, Duke Conrad II of Bavaria (see above, 1055, p. 68 and n. 158). Cf. Werner
of Magdeburg, letter to Siegfried of Mainz, cited in Bruno, *The Saxon War* c. 42, p.
42; Bruno, *The Saxon War* c. 33, pp. 35–6; *Song of the Saxon War* III.1–23, pp. 14–15;
Frutolf of Michelsberg, *Chronica* 1073 (*sic*), p. 82. On the significance of these royal
graves see Leyser (1979) p. 93; Weinfurter (1991) p. 86; Robinson (1999) p. 98.
Reuter (1991b) p. 297 and n. 3 argued that the burial of Conrad (✝1055) implies a
date of foundation of the Harzburg congregation at the end of the reign of Henry
III.

1154 For the conjecture that this was Herrand, abbot of Ilsenburg, later bishop of
Halberstadt (1090–1102), nephew of Bishop Burchard II of Halberstadt, see
Meyer von Knonau (1894) p. 333 n. 36.

1155 Livy XLII.59.7.

1156 On this relic collection see above, 1072, pp. 157–8 and nn. 792–4.

When the rumour of this outrage reached the princes of Saxony, it struck them with great terror. For they feared that the king, provoked by so great an injury, might pretend that they themselves had broken the treaty and, deriving from this a just reason for renewing the war, he might incite the whole military strength of the kingdom against them. Desiring to anticipate this outcome in a carefully considered manner, the princes punished severely those who had committed such a crime.[1157] Then they sent envoys to the king, imploring him in God's name to regard them as blameless: they had been neither accomplices in nor instigators of so great an offence and they took this event no less seriously and were no less angered by it than he himself. If, however, he had no faith in their denials, they were ready to prove the truth of their statements by whatever means would satisfy him and to free themselves of the suspicion of breaking the peace. The king was violently enraged that they had by these recent outrages aggravated the old wound, which had not yet been covered with a scar. He said: 'Since the secular laws make no headway against the violence of the Saxons and since I have been abandoned by my troops and have no power to avenge my wrongs with military force, I am now compelled by necessity to have recourse to the laws of the Church and, where human aid fails, I shall invoke the help of heaven.' He immediately sent envoys to Rome to appeal to the apostolic see[1158] against those men who had burned down a church, broken up altars, desecrated graves and, out of hatred for one of the living, had *raged* with barbarous cruelty against *the ashes of the buried.*[1159]

The king celebrated Easter in Bamberg.[1160] With him were the archbishop of Mainz, Duke Berthold of the Carinthians and very many of those who had deserted him during the Saxon war.[1161] For since he had pardoned the

---

1157 Cf. Bruno, *The Saxon War* c. 34, p. 36: the Saxon princes sought to pacify the king 'by punishing those who were involved in the offence in any way that he wished'.

1158 There is no trace of such a mission in the letters of Pope Gregory VII. Perhaps Lampert was thinking of the mission recorded by Bruno, *The Saxon War* c. 64, p. 56, sent to Rome after 25 October 1075: see Meyer von Knonau (1894) p. 564 and n. 153.

1159 Horace, *Epodi* XVI.11–14.

1160 20 April. Cf. Berthold of Reichenau, *Chronicle* 1074, p. 131; Marianus Scottus, *Chronicon* 1096 [=1074], p. 561. (Bernard of Hildesheim, *De damnatione schismaticorum* II.36, p. 43, dated the occasion in 1075.) See Kilian (1886) p. 65; Meyer von Knonau (1894) p. 373.

1161 Siegfried of Mainz (above n. 210) was in the royal entourage in Nuremberg a few days after Easter: see Meyer von Knonau (1894) p. 377. On Berthold I of Carinthia (above n. 824) see above p. 209 and n. 1100. Cf. Berthold, *Chronicle* 1074, p. 131: 'Duke Rudolf and the other rebels were reconciled to the king.'

Saxons for the offence of rebellion, he had no legitimate cause of anger in the case of the other princes of the kingdom who had been associated with their conspiracy.

At that same time events occurred in Cologne worthy of the sympathy and the tears of all good men. It is uncertain whether the cause was the unreliability of the common people or whether it was the doing of those who desired to take revenge on the archbishop[1162] on behalf of the king. The latter alternative particularly suggested itself for the following reason. When the men of Worms won universal renown because they had kept faith with the king in adversity and had expelled from the city their bishop, who attempted to rebel against the king,[1163] the men of Cologne, emulating their *very evil example*[1164] and their dedication to the royal cause, wished likewise to gratify the king by some outstanding act of villainy. Chance brought them a suitable opportunity to execute their wicked plan. The archbishop celebrated Easter in Cologne and with him was the bishop of Münster,[1165] whom he had invited because of their intimate friendship to share in the joys of so great a festival. When the holy days of Easter were almost over and the bishop was preparing to depart, the men who managed the archbishop's domestic affairs were ordered to provide a suitable ship for the bishop's journey. After seeking out and inspecting all the ships, they took possession of one that belonged to a certain very rich merchant, because it seemed suitable for that purpose; they threw out the merchandise that it contained and ordered it to be speedily made ready for the archbishop's service. When the servants who had the responsibility of guarding the ship opposed them, they were threatened with violence if they did not quickly carry out their commands.[1166]

1162 Lampert provided the only detailed report of the rising against Archbishop Anno II of Cologne (above n. 139). The only contemporary allusion to the event is in the letter of Anno to Archbishop Udo of Trier, in *Briefsammlungen* pp. 90–1. The account in *Vita Annonis archiepiscopi Coloniensis* II.21, pp. 492–4 (see below n. 1541), is closely based on that of Lampert. See Meyer von Knonau (1894) pp. 391–9, 804–7; Strait (1974) pp. 25–30; Diederich (1975) pp. 167–82; Schieffer (1991) pp. 14–15; Stehkämper (1991) pp. 93–8, 111–13.

1163 On Bishop Adalbert of Worms (above n. 626) see above 1073, p. 200 and n. 1042.

1164 Livy III.35.8. See Billanovich (1945) p. 124.

1165 20 April. Bishop Frederick of Münster (above n. 904). See Meyer von Knonau (1894) p. 393. On the evidence that Anno and Frederick were fellow pupils in the cathedral school of Paderborn in the 1030s (*Vita Meinwerci episcopi Patherbrunnensis* c. 160, p. 140) see Meyer von Knonau (1890) p. 185 n. 31; Meier (1987) p. 9 and n. 24.

1166 In commandeering the ship of a Cologne merchant, Anno violated an ancient

The servants ran as fast as they could to report the matter to the ship owner and to ask what they ought to do.

The ship owner had a grown-up son, who was outstanding as much for his daring as for his strength and who was especially esteemed and beloved by the foremost men of the city[1167] both because of his family connections and because of his meritorious conduct. Taking with him his servants and young men from the city, as many as he could gather to help him in the haste of the moment, he rushed with all speed to the ship and, after the archbishop's servants continued to demand stridently that the ship should be unloaded, he violently drove them away. When subsequently the provost of the city[1168] arrived to intervene in this business and started a new disturbance, he drove him back, vanquished him and put him to flight with the same steadfastness of purpose. And now his friends and those of the other faction were hastening fully armed to his assistance and the situation *seemed to be developing into a* great *crisis*[1169] and a dangerous battle. When the news reached the archbishop that the city had been thrown into confusion by a most violent uproar, he hurriedly sent forces *to calm the agitation*[1170] of the people and, full of anger, he threatened that at the next session of his court he would inflict on those factious young men the punishment that they deserved. The archbishop was indeed a man renowned for every kind of virtue, whose uprightness had very often been demonstrated in the affairs both of the State and of God's truth. But among such great virtues there appeared one fault, like a small *mole on a* very beautiful *body*:[1171] namely, when his anger was kindled,[1172] he could not sufficiently govern his tongue but hurled challenges and the most offensive insults

---

mercantile privilege, confirmed by Emperor Louis the Pious (814–40): see Ennen (1977) p. 125 n. 63; Stehkämper (1991) p. 93.

1167 On Lampert's term, 'foremost men' (*primores*) of the city see Strait (1974) pp. 28–9; Stehkämper (1991) pp. 94, 111.

1168 Holder-Egger, *Lamperti Annales* p. 186 n. 4 and Meyer von Knonau (1894) p. 806 n. 56 identified Franco as the *advocatus* of the city in charters of Anno for 1061 and 1074. On the office of 'advocate of the city' see Strait (1974) pp. 11–12, 23, 25–6; Stehkämper (1991) pp. 92–3.

1169 Livy II.18.2; XXIV.6.1; XXV.3.19.

1170 *Ibid.*, III.50.12.

1171 Horace, *Satirae* I.6.66.

1172 The significance of this defect is emphasised in the account of Anno's deathbed vision, below, 1075, p. 000. See Struve (1970a) pp. 110–11 and n. 68 ('Perhaps Lampert himself had previously experienced this anger in Bamberg').

against everyone *without respect of persons.*[1173] When he had somewhat abated his anger, he severely censured himself for this conduct.

It was only with difficulty that the strife was interrupted for a short time. But *the young man* was of a *warlike* disposition and *elated by* his initial *success*[1174] and he did not cease to bring about general confusion. He traversed the city and disseminated among the people various statements about the arrogance and severity of the archbishop, who so often issued unjust commands, so often deprived innocent persons of their possessions and so often attacked the most respectable citizens with the most shameless words. It was not difficult to transform men of that kind, like *the leaf which is borne away by the wind,*[1175] into everything that you might wish. For, being brought up from their earliest years among the delights of the city, they had no experience of warfare and, being accustomed after they had sold their merchandise to discuss military affairs over their wine and sumptuous food, believed that everything that came into their minds was as easy to perform as it was to speak of and they did not know how to judge the outcome of such events. Moreover there came into their minds the remarkable and outstanding deed of the men of Worms, who had driven their bishop out of the city when he began to act in a rather haughty manner.[1176] Since they were superior in numbers to those men and better provided with wealth and weapons, they considered it dishonourable that they should be thought inferior to them in courage and that they should with unmanly subservience allow the archbishop to rule over them for so long with his tyrannical arrogance. The prominent men made senseless plans; the common people raged,[1177] rendered ungovernable by their *zeal for novelties,*[1178] and, seized by the spirit of the devil, they *issued a call to arms*[1179] throughout the whole city. And now their plan was not to expel the archbishop from the city, as the men of Worms had done, but, if they were able to do so, to inflict every kind of torture and butcher him. It was the nativity of the blessed martyr George, which in that year fell on the Wednesday in

---

1173 I Peter I.17.

1174 Livy III.11.6; XXVIII.6.8; XLII.66.3. See Billanovich (1945) p. 80.

1175 Job 13:25.

1176 See above 1073, p. 200 and n. 1042; 1074, p. 222 and n. 1163.

1177 On Lampert's term, 'the common people' (*vulgus* or *populus*), see Stehkämper (1991) pp. 112–13. For Lampert's aristocratic contempt for them (cf. below, 1075, p. 274: 'the disposition of the common people is always fickle and untrustworthy') see Struve (1970a) pp. 40–2.

1178 Sallust, *Catilina* 37.1.

1179 Livy III.50.11. See Billanovich (1945) p. 67.

Easter week,[1180] and the archbishop celebrated mass at the church of the blessed George.[1181] When he preached his sermon to the people, with a presentiment of the future, although he himself was unaware of the evil that threatened him, he bore witness to his hearers that the city had been delivered into the power of the devil and would very soon perish unless they hastened to deflect the wrath of God, which already hung over them, by means of acts of penitence.

After midday, therefore, *as the day already inclined*[1182] towards evening, when drunkenness had been added to anger, like oil to fire, they rushed from every part of the city to the archbishop's palace. They attacked him while he was dining with the bishop of Münster in a much frequented place; they brandished weapons and threw stones; they killed some of the bystanders, subdued the rest with blows and wounds and put them to flight. Meanwhile very many people caught sight of the instigator of such violent passions, the devil himself, running ahead of the raving people, clad in helmet and mail, hurling lightning in a fearful manner with his fiery sword, and there was no one like him. While he sounded a war trumpet to urge those who were hesitating to follow him into the battle, in the midst of the attack, as he rushed forward, shouting loudly, to break open the bars on the gates, he suddenly vanished from the sight of those who were following him. The archbishop was extricated by his followers with the greatest difficulty from the ranks of his enemies and *the dense cloud of missiles*[1183] and removed to the church of St Peter[1184] and his followers not only fastened the doors with bolts and bars but also moved great blocks in front of them.

Outside *the vessels* of the devil raged and *roared* like *water overflowing*, full of *the wine* of God's *fury*[1185] and, running to and fro through the inner rooms of the archbishop's palace, they broke open the doors, plundered his treasures, chopped up the wine casks and, when with excessive haste they poured away the wine, which had been accumulated with the greatest effort so that it would remain in use for a long time, they found themselves in a cellar that was suddenly filling up and – it is laughable

1180 23 April.

1181 Founded by Anno II in 1059 as a spiritual centre for a growing settlement outside the southern Roman wall of the city: see Stehkämper (1991) pp. 82, 86–7, 144–6; Schieffer (1991) pp. 9, 18.

1182 Genesis 24:63.

1183 Livy XXI.55.6.

1184 I.e. the cathedral church of Cologne. See Coué (1991) pp. 375–6; Stehkämper (1991) pp. 87–9.

1185 The quotation is a composite of Job 3:24, Jeremiah 25:15 and Isaiah 13:5.

to relate – were at risk from the unexpected flood and almost drowned. Others burst into the archbishop's chapel and despoiled the altar; they *touched the holy vessels with* their *polluted hands;*[1186] they stole the archiepiscopal vestments. While they were turning all the liturgical vessels upside-down with curious – or rather, furious – diligence, they found there a certain man, who out of fear had hidden himself in a corner. Supposing him to be the archbishop, they killed him and sarcastically congratulated themselves on having at long last imposed some moderation on a most impudent tongue. When they learned that they had been deceived by the resemblance between the two men and that the archbishop was in the church of St Peter, where he was safeguarded both by the holiness of the place and by the strength of the walls, they crowded together from all sides and laid siege to that church. They tried with all their might to break down the walls and finally they threatened to set fire to the building if the archbishop was not quickly handed over to them.

Then those who were inside the church saw that the minds of the people were firmly resolved on his murder and that the men were driven not solely by drunkenness, which tends to disappear with time, but also by long-standing hatred and a kind of insane rage. They advised the archbishop to change his clothes and to try to flee from the church and escape the notice of the besiegers. If he did this, he would release the sacred building from the danger of a conflagration and free himself from the peril of death. The moment was opportune and promised safety in flight. The uproar had now lasted until midnight; everything was shrouded in darkness and gloom so that it was far from easy for anyone to identify the faces of those whom he encountered. A narrow passage opened out of the church into a dormitory and led in turn from the dormitory into the churchyard and to a certain canon's house, which was built next to the city wall. A few days before the outbreak of violence that canon had obtained permission from the archbishop to break through the city wall and make a little backdoor for himself. Thus God in His mercy provided for the archbishop's deliverance. The archbishop was led out this way; four horses were quickly brought to carry him and his attendants and he set off, making use most conveniently of the darkness of *the obscure night*[1187] so as not to be recognised by those whom he might meet. After a short time he found the bishop of Münster and, now surrounded by a large number of companions

---

1186 A composite of II Maccabees 5:16, 4:48 and Isaiah 59:3.
1187 Vergil, *Aeneid* IV.123.

appropriate to that situation, he reached the place called Neuss.[1188]

Meanwhile those men who surrounded the church caused the walls to shake with repeated blows from battering-rams. There was a confused cry from the rioters, who called upon Almighty God to witness that the archbishop would not escape their hands, that he would not evade the vigilance of the besiegers, even if he transformed himself into the smallest creeping thing of the earth. For their part, the men who were besieged cunningly mocked the efforts of their oppressors, now pleading with them, now promising that they would search for the archbishop with the greatest care and, if they found him, they would surrender him to the besiegers, until they supposed that the archbishop had ridden far enough away and had already reached a place of safety. Then at last they threw open the doors and permitted them to enter and to search as much as they pleased and they added that it was useless to seek within the walls of the church a man whom they knew for certain to have left the city *at the first onset of the agitated crowd,*[1189] while it was still broad daylight, so that he could by now have reached a distant region. The conjecture must be that he had spent the night in assembling troops from all directions and that he would arrive early in the morning to take possession of the city with military might. When they had entered, therefore, and very assiduously turned the whole of the interior of the church upside-down in the course of their search, they finally and with difficulty accepted as true the fact that they had been deceived. They then turned their attention from their eager searching to the defence of the city and assigned a great number of armed men to the ramparts on all sides.

Meanwhile they seized one man from the crowd and hanged him over the gate of the city in order to dishonour the archbishop. They did this in order to satisfy the fury that carried them away headlong and not because they could accuse the wretched man of any offence worthy of hanging. They also threw a certain woman down from the highest part of the walls and killed her by breaking her neck. The charge that they brought against her was that she had the reputation of very often driving men out of their minds by means of magical arts. They ought, however, to have punished this crime at a more appropriate time and in a calmer frame of mind. They had also resolved – *if* God, being mindful

---

1188 An archiepiscopal property that was the nearest inhabited place on the same side of the Rhine: see Schieffer (1991) pp. 15, 21.

1189 Livy II.17.3; II.56.14.

of His servants, *had not shortened the days*[1190] of their madness – to
slaughter all the monks of St Pantaleon because, after their predecessors had been expelled by the archbishop, these monks had introduced
there a new and unaccustomed form of the religious life.[1191] Moreover
they ordered *some energetic young men*[1192] to go to the king as quickly as
they could to inform him what had happened and to suggest that he
should come as soon as possible to take possession of the city, which was
without a ruler now that the archbishop had been expelled. *The welfare
of the city* and its most important interests *depended on his*[1193] trying
to arrive there before the archbishop, who was setting great plans in
motion to avenge his injuries. For three days[1194] they were *driven hither
and thither by* such *violent passions.*[1195]

After the news was heard throughout the province and spread abroad
by frequently repeated rumours that the men of Cologne had assailed
their archbishop with reproaches and dishonourable treatment and had
driven him from the city, all the people were struck with horror at the
unprecedented character of the event, at the cruelty of the crime and at
the drama of human affairs:[1196] that a man of such great virtues in Christ
could suffer such unworthy treatment in the sight of God. His great
generosity towards the poor, his manifold piety in heavenly matters,
his great restraint in human affairs, his passionate zeal in correcting the
laws, his unrestrained severity in pursuing evildoers were proclaimed
by the voices of all men and the remembrance of these qualities won
him the favour of the common people to an extraordinary degree. They
all exclaimed that this violation of the majesty of the episcopal title
dishonoured themselves more than it did the archbishop and that it
was better for them to die than to allow the most shameful acts of their
times to go unpunished. They therefore *issued a call to arms*[1197] for four
or five miles on all sides.[1198] Many thousands of men gathered together

---

1190 Mark 13:20.

1191 See above p. 152 and n. 749.

1192 Livy III.46.5. See Billanovich (1945) p. 144 n. 1.

1193 Livy III.46.5; IV.31.4.

1194 23–5 April.

1195 Livy I.48.7.

1196 Sallust, *Jugurtha* 14. On Lampert's predilection for the image of 'the world as a
theatre' see Struve (1970a) pp. 122–3 and n. 49 and above p. 47.

1197 Livy III.50.11. See Billanovich (1945) p. 67.

1198 Cf. Anno, letter to Archbishop Udo of Trier, in *Briefsammlungen* p. 90: 'rumour has
divulged to you the great offences that my citizens have perpetrated against me

more quickly than can be related[1199] and no one *who was old enough to be able to bear arms refused to perform military service*[1200] in such a pious cause. *Forming a dense crowd,*[1201] they asked the archbishop – using compulsion when he showed hesitation – to hasten as soon as possible to recover the city. They would fight on his behalf and, if the need arose, they would freely embrace death, like sheep for their shepherd, like sons for their father. If the men of Cologne did not hurry to receive him on his arrival and make amends for their offence according to his own judgement, either they would throw in burning brands and consume the people together with the city or they would demolish the wall and conduct him back to his episcopal throne over a heap of the slain.

Thus on the fourth day after his departure[1202] the archbishop approached the city, surrounded by a large number of troops. When this became known to the men of Cologne and they realised that they *could not withstand an attack by so great* and so fierce *a host*[1203] either on the wall or in a battle, then for the first time their fury began to abate and their drunkenness to disappear. Thoroughly terrified, *they sent peace envoys*[1204] to meet the host, confessing themselves to be guilty and declaring that they were prepared to pay every penalty that might be decreed, if only their lives were spared. The archbishop replied that he would not refuse pardon to those who were properly repentant. Then after the celebration of mass in the church of St George he summoned by virtue of his episcopal authority those men who had driven a bishop from his own see, who had defiled the church with murder, who had made an attack on the church of St Peter and violated the other laws of religion with their barbarous endeavours, to make amends. They all immediately came in procession, barefoot and wearing woollen garments next to their skin,[1205] after obtaining a safe-conduct with the greatest difficulty from the host that surrounded the archbishop, so that they might be allowed to do this without danger. For this host angrily reproved him

---

and you have learned how I was restored to my throne by those who were outside'.

1199 Vergil, *Aeneid* I.142; Horace, *Satirae* II.2.80.

1200 Livy III.42.6; V.19.5; VII.11.5.

1201 *Ibid.*, VIII.11.5. See Billanovich (1945) p. 146.

1202 26 April.

1203 Livy I.41.4; XL.58.2. See Billanovich (1945) pp. 86–7.

1204 Livy II.18.9; IX.45.1. See Billanovich (1945) p. 146.

1205 On correct penitential conduct: Gregory VII, *Register* IV.12, p. 313: 'barefoot and clad in woollen garments'.

for showing excessive mercy because he wished to have the people's favour, while by not punishing this offence he was encouraging impious men to dare to do even more wicked deeds.

The archbishop ordered the men of Cologne to be present at St Peter's the following day to perform penance according to canon law for so abominable an offence. He himself went to St Gereon[1206] and decided to spend the night there outside the city. He feared that, now the city had been surrendered, the power of his *impetuous host* of followers *could not be held*[1207] in check and that they would vent their rage on the people all too harshly, inflamed partly by the injustice that had been committed, partly by the desire for plunder. He therefore urgently requested those men who were with him who came from the surrounding countryside to go in peace, each one to his own home. For he had made sufficient use of their services and had obtained clear evidence of what the sheep felt for their shepherd and the sons for their father. The most arduous part of the task had been accomplished by means of their great courage: whatever remained to be done could now be easily completed by the warriors of his own household. *Because it was good, fortunate and suitable to do so,*[1208] they should return to their homes, taking with them this hope: that gratitude for this service would remain in his heart forever, whether he lived or died. After he had with great difficulty achieved their departure, he ordered his knights – as many as he thought sufficient *to suppress any commotions in the city,*[1209] should they chance to recur through the fickleness of the common people[1210] – to precede him into the city. He himself would follow next day, when, thanks to the care of those men who had gone in advance, he might guard against any ambushes that might perhaps be lurking in the city.

During the night six hundred or more of the wealthiest merchants fled from the city[1211] and went to the king to entreat him to intervene to

---

1206 An early ninth-century foundation of canons, north of the city. See Semmler (1959) pp. 173–4; Stehkämper (1991) pp. 86–7, 97.

1207 Livy XXIII.14.8.

1208 *Ibid.,* III.34.2; III.54.8; VIII.25.10.

1209 *Ibid.,* III.41.8. See Billanovich (1945) pp. 147–8.

1210 See above n. 1177.

1211 Cf. Anno, letter to Archbishop Udo of Trier, in *Briefsammlungen* p. 90: 'I ought to have punished the abominable temerity [of the citizens] on that same day [27 April] with the sword of anathema, according to canon law.... But because ... a party of insolent men secretly withdrew during the night, threatening to perpetrate more grievous acts than they had already done, I excommunicated them on the advice of the bishops whom the pope sent to us' (see below nn. 1218–22).

assist them against the archbishop's severity. After entering the city, the archbishop waited for three whole days[1212] for the rest of the citizens to attend according to the agreement but they failed to present themselves to propose some form of reparation. The archbishop's knights would not tolerate this insulting behaviour and – as very many men declare, without the knowledge and advice of the archbishop – snatched up their weapons, attacked the houses and plundered the possessions of those who opposed them; some they laid low, others they took prisoner and threw into chains. In a word – since we are compelled to tell the truth – they accomplished the work of just revenge with greater ferocity than befitted the good name of so great an archbishop. But the more serious diseases require a more violent remedy.

The son of the merchant mentioned above, who first roused the people to insurrection, and a few other men were blinded; some were beaten with rods and their hair was cut off. All the citizens were punished with a very heavy fine on their personal property and were forced to take an oath that henceforward, as much as they could with advice and with weapons, they would defend the city for the archbishop against acts of violence by all men and that they would always regard those citizens who had fled from the city *as their most dangerous enemies*[1213] until they had made appropriate amends to the archbishop. Thus the city, which shortly before had possessed the largest population of citizens and which, after Mainz, was the chief and principal city of Gaul,[1214] was suddenly reduced virtually to a wilderness. The streets of Cologne previously could scarcely accommodate the dense crowds of passers-by but now a human being rarely appeared there and dreadful silence took possession of all the places formerly given over to desire and pleasure. Clear portents had foretold that this was about to happen. A certain stranger had arrived in the city in this same year to celebrate the festival of Palm Sunday.[1215] He saw in a dream a raven of fearfully monstrous size flying over every part of Cologne, its loud and dreadful croaking driving the people hither and thither, stupefied by such a sight. The dreamer then saw a man outstanding both in his beauty and

---

Lampert exaggerated the number: Meyer von Knonau (1894) pp. 391 and n. 110, 397; Stehkämper (1991) p. 97.

1212 27–9 April.

1213 Livy VIII.31.1.

1214 On the status of Cologne see Coué (1991) pp. 373–4. See also Thomas (1970) pp. 371–2, 384; Boshof (1978b) pp. 36–43. For 'Gaul' as Germany see Lugge (1960) pp. 132–40, especially p. 132 n. 238.

1215 13 April.

his raiment, who drove the raven, still uttering its terrible sounds, out of the city and who freed the people – whose minds were full of dismay and who now dreaded every kind of misfortune – from their ground-less fears. When the horror-struck dreamer asked those around him the meaning of his dream, he was told that because of the sins of the people the city had been delivered into the power of the devil but had been freed through the intervention of the martyr George and had escaped the fate of imminent destruction, predestined by God.

After the king had celebrated the festival of Easter in Bamberg,[1216] he proceeded to Nuremberg,[1217] where he met the legates of the apostolic see. These were his mother, the empress,[1218] the bishop of Ostia,[1219] the bishop of Palestrina,[1220] the bishop of Chur[1221] and the bishop of Como.[1222] They were sent by the Roman pontiff[1223] to bring some order, if they could, to the situation in Gaul, which had now been in confusion for a long time. Nevertheless they would not agree to speak directly to the king, even though they were very often requested to do so, until he had performed penance according to the laws of the Church and had been absolved from excommunication by their judgement; for he had been denounced to the apostolic see as guilty of the heresy of simony for having sold ecclesiastical offices.[1224] The legates therefore demanded in the name of the Roman pontiff to be permitted to hold a synod in Gaul, subject to the permission of the bishops. This was emphatically rejected by all the bishops as contrary to custom and utterly unfavourable to their own interests.[1225] They declared that the privilege of exercising this authority

---

1216 20 April. Cf. Berthold of Reichenau, *Chronicle* 1074, p. 131. See Kilian (1886) p. 65; Meyer von Knonau (1894) p. 373.

1217 Cf. Berthold, *Chronicle* 1074, p. 131; Bonizo of Sutri, *To a Friend* VII, pp. 221–2. See Kilian (1886) p. 65; Meyer von Knonau (1894) pp. 377–81, 843; Erdmann (1938) p. 236 and n. 2; Robinson (1999) pp. 132–3; Gresser (2006) pp. 123–6.

1218 Empress Agnes (above n. 30). Cf. Gregory VII, *Register* I.85, p. 121 (to Agnes). See Black-Veldtrup (1995) p. 97.

1219 Gerald, cardinal bishop of Ostia (1072/3–1077).

1220 Hubert, cardinal bishop of Palestrina (?1073–?1082).

1221 Henry I, bishop of Chur (1070–8).

1222 Rainald, bishop of Como (1061–84).

1223 Pope Gregory VII (above n. 194). His allusions to the events in Nuremberg: *Register* II.30, p. 163 (to Henry IV); *Epistolae Vagantes* 14, p. 36 (to the German princes). See Cowdrey (1998) pp. 98–9.

1224 Lampert was inaccurate in reporting that Henry IV had been excommunicated and that the legates refused to negotiate with him. On the polemical character of this report see Ranke (1888) pp. 138–9; Meyer von Knonau (1894) p. 843.

1225 The plan for a legatine council of the whole German Church was foiled by the

had never been granted to anyone other than the Roman pontiff himself. For the Roman pontiff had indeed intended to investigate the cases of all the bishops and abbots who had purchased their holy offices with money and to depose them. For this reason he had already suspended the bishop of Bamberg[1226] and some others from all the functions of the divine office until they came into his presence and, by means of a satisfactory explanation, proved that they had been wrongfully accused of the offence of heresy.[1227] Because of the king's hatred for the bishop of Worms[1228] and certain other men who had displeased him during the Saxon war, he eagerly desired that they also would find themselves involved in these accusations and in the certainty of his hopes he took for granted that they would suffer the loss of their offices. But because there was no hope that so important a case could be settled by legates, a decision was taken to refer it to the judgement of the Roman pontiff himself.

After sending the legates away, the king prepared to lead to Hungary an expedition, which was not announced in the customary manner but which consisted of an *army* gathered together *in a hasty and disorganised fashion.*[1229] For he had learned that Salomon, king of the Hungarians,[1230] had been attacked by Geisa, the son of Bela,[1231] had already been defeated in three battles, had *lost his army* and had *with difficulty escaped*[1232] from the kingdom. The king intended to aid him in his misfortune and to discharge the duties of kinship, which he had contracted when he gave Salomon his sister[1233] in marriage. It was also in the king's own interests to do so because Salomon had promised him a large part of his kingdom if his enemies were defeated and he himself was restored

---

bishops, led by Archbishop Liemar of Bremen and Archbishop Siegfried of Mainz. See Meyer von Knonau (1894) pp. 379–81; Erdmann (1938) pp. 238–9; Schneider (1972) pp. 83–5; Cowdrey (1998) pp. 112, 114, 599; Robinson (1999) p. 133.

1226 Cf. below, 1075, p. 246. It was not until 1075 that Bishop Herman I of Bamberg (above n. 449) was suspended by a papal synod. See Schieffer (1972) pp. 22–46; Schieffer (1975) pp. 55–76; Cowdrey (1998) pp. 110, 113–14, 118, 120, 124–7.

1227 In the Lent synod of 1075 Bishops Werner of Strasbourg and Henry of Speyer, together with Herman of Bamberg, were suspended: Gregory VII, *Register* II.52a, p. 196.

1228 Adalbert of Worms (above n. 626). See above p. 200 and n. 1042.

1229 Livy XLI.10.3.

1230 King Salomon (above n. 250). See Meyer von Knonau (1894) pp. 384–8; Boshof (1986) p. 186.

1231 King Geisa (Magnus) of Hungary (above n. 258), son of King Bela I (above n. 248).

1232 Livy XXIII.11.9.

1233 Judith-Sophia (above n. 251).

to the kingship with the king's assistance. When the king arrived in Regensburg,[1234] however, he was closely followed by envoys sent by his advisers to inform him that William, named 'the Bastard', king of the English[1235] – inveigled by an empty promise from the archbishop of Cologne[1236] – was rapidly advancing with a great army, prepared to seize the royal residence of Aachen. The king was struck with terror by such dreadful news and, reckoning that attention to his personal concerns ought to take precedence of foreign affairs, he abandoned the expedition to Hungary and returned with all speed to the Rhine. He celebrated Whitsun in Mainz,[1237] where he was received and entertained by the archbishop of Mainz amidst splendour and affability.

From there the king had decided to go to Cologne, boiling with rage and uttering menaces against the archbishop of Cologne. The latter, however, sent messengers to meet him and tell him that the accusation was an utterly false tale, like the fictions of the theatre, which his enemies had invented against him: those very same men who shortly before had driven him from the city and who now spread lies to crush him since they could not do so by means of weapons. He was not so devoid of reason or so careless of the common good that he would betray his fatherland to barbarians in order to avenge a personal injury. Nor had he lived his life since boyhood in such a frivolous manner that anyone of sound judgement could suspect him of such folly. He obtained through the envoys the opportunity to come into the royal presence and he met the king in Andernach.[1238] The king insisted with the greatest severity on a public investigation of the information that he had been given and the archbishop cleared himself by means of an oath of the offence of

1234 Cf. *D.H.IV* 273, issued on 25 May in Regensburg. See Kilian (1886) p. 65; Meyer von Knonau (1894) p. 388.

1235 William I ('the Conqueror'), king of England (1066–87).

1236 The reworking of Lampert's account in *Vita Annonis archiepiscopi Coloniensis* II.22, p. 495, states that the envoys' news was 'false'. But cf. *Vita Annonis* I.30, pp. 478–9: Anno was 'united in friendship with the kings of the English and the Danes and frequently honoured with their gifts and legations'. A different version of the rumour appears in Bruno of Merseburg, *The Saxon War* c. 36, pp. 37–8: Henry IV summoned the aid of William I. Holder-Egger, *Lamperti Annales* p. 195 n. 4, noted that the English and Norman sources show William I to have been in Normandy at this time. See Meyer von Knonau (1894) p. 390 and n. 108.

1237 8 June. Cf. *D.H.IV* 274 (issued 12 June in Mainz). See Kilian (1886) p. 66; Meyer von Knonau (1894) p. 399.

1238 Meyer von Knonau (1894) p. 401 and n. 131 considered that Lampert's details of the royal itinerary are 'hardly to be doubted' but that the accompanying information is 'very uncertain'. See also Kilian (1886) p. 66 (Henry IV 'came probably at the beginning of July to Andernach on the Rhine'); Stehkämper (1991) p. 100.

which he had been accused, namely betraying the State. As for the rest of the charges that were brought against him, the king declared that he pardoned the offences for the sake of their long-standing friendship and of the episcopal office and that he had no wish to make demands according to his rights. The king's fury was thus held in check for the time being but not extinguished and he proceeded to Cologne.[1239] There on the next day he held a court of justice in public, hoping that an accusation from those whom the archbishop had punished for the injuries that he had suffered would give him the opportunity to provoke an insurrection and drive him from the city again or at least to find him guilty of treason for oppressing the innocent by means of false charges. But the archbishop *dashed away* all the crafty accusations against him *like spiders' webs*[1240] by the truth of his replies and the impressive character of his statements.

When the king *saw that* the archbishop was *protected in all respects*[1241] by his innocence, the blamelessness of his life and also his wisdom and that there was no way of reaching him with an accusation, he turned to other ways of inflicting injuries upon him. He demanded of the archbishop, not with entreaties, as was appropriate, but by the imperious exercise of his authority that he should pardon the men of Cologne who had committed those rash actions and reconcile the excommunicates to the Church. He was moreover to give the king six hostages from among his knights as a guarantee that he would keep faith with him perpetually.[1242] The archbishop refused both these demands with great firmness of purpose. The hostages he refused because none of the previous kings had made such a demand of any of his predecessors; the reconciliation of the excommunicates he refused, however, because the laws of the Church forbid excommunicates to be received into the Church unless they make appropriate amends through penitence. The king uttered violent menaces, threatening that he would inflict every kind of misfortune on him and destroy all his possessions with fire and sword. The archbishop remained firmly resolved in his purpose, saying indeed that he was prepared to die, if the king had conspired with the men of Cologne to kill him but he would never turn from right to wrong through the

1239 See Kilian (1886) p. 66. On Lampert's polemical version of the events in Cologne see Meyer von Knonau (1894) pp. 401–2, 807–8; Stehkämper (1991) pp. 98–101.

1240 Isaiah 59:5; Job 8:14.

1241 Livy II.6.1; III.44.4.

1242 Cf. the revised version of Lampert's account in *Vita Annonis archiepiscopi Coloniensis* II.21, p. 494. See Meyer von Knonau (1894) pp. 807–8 and n. 64 ('the number six in connection with the hostages … is again one of Lampert's favourite numbers'); Stehkämper (1991) pp. 100–1.

desire to preserve his life. *For a long time the outcome of the conflict was uncertain*[1243] and the adherents of the two men were full of disquiet about the consequences of such a sorry spectacle. At last the king was prevailed on by those men whose advice he most valued to change his attitude. He declared that he preferred to compete with the archbishop *in performing good deeds rather than evil ones*[1244] and, if he found him faithful to himself and devoted to the interests of the State, he would henceforward regard him as the foremost of his friends. After reconciling himself with the archbishop in this manner, he came to Aachen and protected that part of the kingdom, as far as he could, against the danger of the invasion of the barbarians that had been widely rumoured.[1245]

Ruthard, abbot of the monastery of Hersfeld, died on 9 June.[1246] He was extremely learned in the holy Scriptures and so skilful in speaking that no man of that time discoursed of the word of God with more eloquence or with more penetration or with more refinement. On the other hand, he was rather more negligent in his observance of the holy *Rule* than *morals and the times*[1247] required. According to the incomprehensible judgement of God, Who chides *those whom He loves and chastises every son whom He receives*,[1248] that man lost his reason before the time of his death[1249] and for two whole years and six months he was very cruelly tormented both by madness and by epilepsy. He died, however, a full year and six months after he had resigned the office of abbot.[1250] Nevertheless, whenever he recovered a little from his insensibility and dullness of mind, he repented and deplored this action so that it was doubtful whether he was weakened more seriously and more painfully by his disease or by his sorrow.

In the middle of July, when the king had returned from Lotharingia to Worms,[1251] envoys from the king of the Hungarians[1252] once more approached him, most strenuously begging him – mindful of their

1243 Livy XXVII.14.6; XXVIII.14.12; XXXIII.18.16.

1244 *Ibid.*, VII.20.8.

1245 See Kilian (1886) p. 66; Meyer von Knonau (1894) p. 402.

1246 Ruthard: above n. 234. See also Meyer von Knonau (1894) p. 173 and n. 107.

1247 Cicero, *Actio in Verrem* II.25; *Oratio I in Catilinam* 2.

1248 Hebrews 12:6.

1249 Cf. Lampert, *Libellus de institutione Herveldensis ecclesiae* II, p. 354: 'Ruthard subsequently became insane.'

1250 See above, 1072, p. 162 and n. 819.

1251 See Kilian (1886) p. 66; Meyer von Knonau (1894) p. 402.

1252 Salomon (above n. 250): see above p. 233 and n. 1230.

kinship, *mindful of the boyhood that they spent*[1253] together – to come as rapidly as possible to the aid of the king who had been expelled. Since their pleas were very slow to move him and his mind was fixed on his personal concerns, they gave him twelve hostages as confirmation of their promise that, if their king was restored to the kingship with his help, he would thereafter pay tribute to Henry and obey his commands and he would surrender to him six of the most strongly fortified cities in Hungary as a pledge that his fidelity would never be broken.[1254] Once he was hired at this price, the king immediately sent messengers in all directions with the customary summons to the princes to join the expedition. But some of them pleaded that they had been given insufficient time; others pleaded scarcity of resources; very many alleged that their wealth had been too much exhausted by the Saxon war and yet others offered another kind of excuse: all simultaneously *refused to take part in the expedition.*[1255]

Lest so great and so favourable an opportunity that had chanced to be offered to the State should come to nothing because of his own inactivity, the king – contenting himself merely with common soldiers and the knights of his own household – marched into Hungary with a hostile army and passed through some of its provinces, bringing devastation with him.[1256] When Geisa, who had seized control of Hungary, learned of his arrival, he strove with the greatest energy to make preparations so that, in the places where an enemy invasion was feared, men would find no food and animals no fodder. He himself withdrew with all his followers to a certain island, which because of the difficulty of the terrain was totally inaccessible to the enemy. The king's army had made no provisions for the conduct of war on so large a scale and immediately suffered so very severe a famine that in a short time plague and hunger consumed very many of the men and almost all the animals. The king was forced by this disaster to leave Hungary without accomplishing anything noteworthy and he returned to Worms after the feast of St

---

1253 Horace, *Carmina* I.36.7.8. Salomon was Henry IV's brother-in-law. On his boyhood exile at the imperial court see above 1061, p. 78.

1254 Cf. Gregory VII, *Register* II.13, p. 145 (to King Salomon, 28 October 1074): 'you have received [St Peter's] kingdom [of Hungary] from the king of the Germans as a benefice'. See Cowdrey (1998) pp. 443–4.

1255 Livy V.19.5; VII.11.5. See Billanovich (1945) p. 145.

1256 Cf. Berthold of Reichenau, *Chronicle* 1074, p. 131. On the Hungarian expedition in August see Meyer von Knonau (1894) p. 404; Boshof (1986) p. 186; Robinson (1999) p. 99.

Michael.[1257] There he set the business of the kingdom in order, as far as the time and his resources allowed, before returning to Regensburg.[1258] His intention was to spend the time that remained until Christmas in travelling through the cities of Bavaria and Swabia.[1259]

Pope Hildebrand, in the frequent synods that he had held with the bishops of Italy, had already decreed that, according to the ordinances of the ancient canons, priests should not have wives; that those who were married should either dismiss their wives or be deposed and that no one at all was to be admitted to the priesthood unless he made a vow of perpetual chastity and of celibate life.[1260] After he had published this decree throughout Italy, he sent numerous letters to the bishops of Gaul, commanding them to do the same in their own churches and to exclude all women without exception from living with priests under pain of perpetual anathema.[1261] At once the whole company of the clergy violently denounced this decree. They cried out that this man was assuredly a heretic and that his teaching was insane and that he had forgotten the word of the Lord, which says: '*Not all men can receive this saying: he who is able to receive this, let him receive it*'[1262] and the apostle: 'He who *cannot contain* himself, *let* him *marry; for it is better to marry than to burn.*'[1263] With this unreasonable demand he was forcing men to live in the manner of the angels and, in refusing to allow nature to follow its

---

1257 29 September. See Kilian (1886) p. 67; Meyer von Knonau (1894) p. 404.

1258 Cf. *D.H.IV* 276 (issued 26 November in Regensburg). See Kilian (1886) p. 67; Meyer von Knonau (1894) pp. 405–6.

1259 Cf. Berthold, *Chronicle* 1074, p. 131: 'During the autumn he went again to Bavaria…. From there by way of Augsburg and Reichenau he reached the city of Strasbourg.' See Kilian (1886) p. 67; Meyer von Knonau (1894) p. 407.

1260 Gregory VII (above n. 194) had held a single reforming synod in, Rome, 9–15 March 1074. Cf. Marianus Scottus, *Chronicon* 1096 [=1074], p. 560: 'The pope … forbade priests, deacons and all clerks to have wives and to live at all with women'; Sigebert of Gembloux, *Chronica* 1074, p. 362: 'Pope Gregory celebrated a synod … and removed married priests from the divine office.' See Meyer von Knonau (1894) pp. 347–50; Barstow (1982) pp. 67–8; Cowdrey (1998) pp. 242–8, 550–3; Gresser (2006) pp. 117–23.

1261 Cf. Gregory VII, *Register* II.25, p. 157 (to Archbishop Anno of Cologne, 18 November 1074): 'by your admonitions you are to cause priests, deacons and subdeacons to live chastely'. Gregory VII's letters *Epistolae Vagantes* 6–11, pp. 14–26, may also have been sent in 1074: see Cowdrey, *Epistolae Vagantes* pp. 160–1. Lampert may also have been thinking of the numerous papal letters of 1075 to German bishops: see Barstow (1982) pp. 218–19 n. 43.

1262 Matthew 19:11, 12.

1263 I Corinthians 7:9.

usual course, he unloosed the reins of fornication and impurity.[1264] If he continued to maintain his view, they preferred to give up the priesthood rather than their marriages and then he – who *held* men *to be of no account*[1265] – would see where he might obtain the services of angels to rule over the people throughout the Church of God. The pope nevertheless insisted on his decree and constantly sent out legates to accuse all the bishops of negligence and idleness and to threaten that he would proceed against them with apostolic punishment, unless they quickly performed the task that had been imposed on them.

The archbishop of Mainz[1266] knew that the effort would cost them dear, to tear up by the roots a custom that had been implanted for so long a time and to restore a world that was now in its old age[1267] to the principles of the Church in the days of its infancy. He therefore dealt in a rather moderate manner with the bishops and at first he granted them a delay of half a year and an opportunity for reflection and exhorted them to do of their own free will what it was necessary to do and thus deprive both himself and the Roman pontiff of the need to take severer measures against them. Finally in the month of October he assembled a synod in Erfurt,[1268] where he now applied more pressure. Setting aside all subterfuge, they were to renounce their marriages on the spot or to resign the ministry of the holy altar. The bishops countered with many arguments by means of which they sought to evade his urgency and persistence and to overturn his decision. Their arguments, their pleadings and their prayers, however, achieved nothing whatsoever against the authority of the apostolic see, which – so the archbishop claimed –

1264 Cf. the arguments of Sigebert of Gembloux, *Apology against those who slander the masses of married priests* pp. 437–48, perhaps composed in 1074 in response to Gregory VII's decree: see Barstow (1982) pp. 141–50. Cf. also Sigebert, *Chronica* 1074, pp. 362–3 and Ps.-Udalric, *Letter on the chastity of the clergy* pp. 255–60, perhaps composed in 1074/5 in the diocese of Constance: Robinson (1989) pp. 179–80.

1265 Job 18:3. Cf. Livy IV.25.11.

1266 Siegfried of Mainz (above n. 210) received the letter of Gregory VII, *Epistolae Vagantes* 6, pp. 14–15, reporting the decrees of the papal synod of either 1074 or 1075, including the prohibition that 'those who commit the crime of fornication must not celebrate mass nor serve at the altar in the lesser orders'. The archbishop was urged 'to tear up these offences by the roots from [his] churches'.

1267 For the eleventh-century idea that the world was now in its old age and near its end see Miccoli (1966) pp. 301–3. See also Struve (1970a) pp. 69–70.

1268 Lampert alone recorded this synod. Holder-Egger, *Lamperti Annales* p. 200 n. 1 suggested that the events described here actually occurred in Siegfried's synod of October 1075, reported below, p. 272. See also Meyer von Knonau (1894) pp. 410–13; Gresser (2006) p. 125 n. 70.

compelled him to make this demand, which was against his own will. The bishops went out, as if to consult together, and they decided that they should not return to the synod but instead that they should all depart for their homes without seeking permission to do so. Some of them even cried out in wild confusion that it seemed to them a better plan to go back to the synod and cast the archbishop down from the episcopal throne before he pronounced his accursed judgement against them. They should punish him with death, as he deserved, and thus transmit an extraordinary reminder to posterity so that thereafter none of his successors would attempt to practise such chicanery against the office of the priesthood. When their plots were reported to the archbishop, he was admonished by his followers to forestall the incipient commotion by the timely management of affairs. He sent messengers outside to request them to calm themselves and return to the synod. He declared that he would at the first favourable opportunity send envoys to Rome and, using whatever arguments he could, cause the lord pope to draw back from this harsh purpose.

On the following day, when laymen and clergy had been admitted together into the session of the synod, the archbishop reopened the old quarrel about the payment of tithes.[1269] As if nothing had been decided by the Saxon war, nothing by the terms on which peace had been agreed shortly before in Gerstungen,[1270] he began once more to accuse all the Thuringians of unjustly withholding tithes and did not take into consideration that this issue was the source and starting-point of all the disasters by which the State had now been very unhappily tormented for very many years.[1271] The Thuringians were extremely indignant at this, since after their recent success in war they were in the highest spirits and they had persuaded themselves, totally groundlessly, that once *the king* had been defeated and *had received a taste of* their *daring*,[1272] henceforward no bishop would ever again dare to trouble them about this matter. At first, however, they replied in moderate language, reminding him that they had agreed to the restoration of peace in Gerstungen solely on condition that their rights, as decreed and established from early times, should remain theirs, perpetually

1269 See above 1073, p. 168 and n. 855.

1270 See above p. 215 and n. 1127. The issue of the Thuringian tithes was not included in the agreement in Gerstungen of 2 February.

1271 On what Holder-Egger (1894) p. 186 called Lampert's 'fantasy' about the importance of the Thuringian tithes controversy see above p. 164 and n. 832.

1272 II Maccabees 13:18.

inviolate. When, in repeating these claims, they seemed to be *telling a tale to deaf*[1273] ears, they suddenly *rushed out of the session in a* wild *rage,*[1274] *issued the call to arms,*[1275] rapidly gathered together a huge crowd and burst into the synod. They would have seized the archbishop even as he was seated on his episcopal throne, had not the archbishop's knights made a timely intervention and by means of soothing and reasonable speeches rather than by armed resistance – since *they were inferior in strength*[1276] – restrained the raging mob from attacking.[1277] The synod was thus broken up and the archbishop and all the clergy who were attending, overwhelmed by utter terror, sought here and there for hiding-places in every corner of the church. The archbishop immediately departed from Erfurt and spent the remainder of the year until Epiphany[1278] in Heiligenstadt. On all the feast days during the sacred celebration of mass he called on all those men who had disrupted the holy synod to do penance on pain of episcopal excommunication.

1075

The king celebrated Christmas in Strasbourg.[1279] Very many of the princes were present, whom he had summoned to the festival from everywhere in the kingdom with a particular purpose. *He set forth to them his secret plan*[1280] and inveigled them in every possible way to resume the Saxon war. He distributed many gifts on the spot and promised more in the future. He left out no one, not even a man of the lowest status, if only

---

1273 Terence, *Heautonitimorumenos* II.1.10.

1274 Livy XXIV.26.12.

1275 *Ibid.,* III.50.11. See Billanovich (1945) p. 67.

1276 Livy XXVI.25.10; XXV.27.8; XLII.65.6.

1277 Cf. Siegfried of Mainz, letter to Gregory VII in *Codex Udalrici* 40, p. 87: 'when I admonished them to obey Almighty God, they on the contrary besieged me and my followers with an armed band drawn indiscriminately from among the common people.' Cf. also Gregory VII, *Register* III.4, pp. 248–50 (3 September 1075), rejecting Siegfried's excuses. See Meyer von Knonau (1894) pp. 412–13.

1278 6 January 1075. Siegfried thus withdrew beyond the River Werra into northwestern Thuringia: see Meyer von Knonau (1894) p. 413 and n. 150.

1279 25 December 1074. Cf. Berthold of Reichenau, *Chronicle* 1075, p. 132: 'The king celebrated Christmas ceremoniously in Strasbourg, glorying in the great numbers of his magnates who were present.' See Kilian (1886) p. 67; Meyer von Knonau (1894) pp. 410, 415.

1280 Judith 2:2. Cf. Berthold, *Chronicle* 1075, p. 132: the king devised 'an artful plan, that while publicly announcing another Hungarian expedition ..., he would use the army for a surprise attack on Saxony'. See Meyer von Knonau (1894) pp. 415–16 and n. 152.

he was thought to be useful in such a great undertaking and the king had not rendered him faithful and submissive to himself by the giving and receiving of oaths. What principally moved them all to give their consent was the promise, which he confirmed to them individually by means of an oath, that, if he regained Saxony and Thuringia with their help, he would surrender both provinces to them to be divided among themselves and to be held by them as their right in perpetuity. His anger was so violent that he desired nothing more than the blood of those men who had offended him. He had, however, now kept this entirely secret for a whole year so that, whenever the princes of Saxony had come to him, he received them in a magnificent fashion and, when they were absent, he frequently sent them peaceful and respectful messages.

A few days later he came to Mainz[1281] and there he was met by the king of the Russians, whose name was Demetrius.[1282] He brought the king inestimable riches in *vessels of gold and silver and* extremely precious *garments*[1283] and requested that he would aid him against his brother,[1284] who had driven him by force from the kingdom and who had seized the kingship with tyrannical ferocity. Burchard, the provost of the church of Trier,[1285] was immediately sent by the king to confer with the usurper about the wrongs that he had inflicted on his brother and to admonish him to resign of his own accord from the kingship that he had unjustly usurped: otherwise he would very soon experience the might and the weapons of the German kingdom. Burchard seemed suitable for this embassy because the prince to whom he was sent was married to his sister[1286] and it was for this reason that he had pleaded most urgently with the king and obtained the concession that in the meantime no severer measures would be ordered against the usurper. Until the envoys returned, the king of the Russians was entrusted by the king to

1281 See Kilian (1886) p. 67; Meyer von Knonau (1894) p. 481.

1282 Isjaslav-Demetrius, grand prince of Kiev (1054–78), son of Jaroslav I.

1283 I Kings 10:25.

1284 Svjatoslav, grand prince of Kiev (†1076). Cf. Sigebert of Gembloux, *Chronica* 1073, p. 362: 'Two brothers who were kings of the Russians were contending for the kingdom and one of them, being expelled from participation in the kingship, appealed to Emperor Henry, submitting himself and the kingdom of the Russians to him, if he was restored to the kingship with [Henry's] help.' See Meyer von Knonau (1894) pp. 481–2; Vlasto (1972) pp. 287–91.

1285 Burchard, provost of the cathedral of Trier, son of the Saxon noblewoman Ida of Elsdorf. See Meyer von Knonau (1894) p. 482; Jakobs (1968) pp. 202–3.

1286 Oda, daughter of Ida of Elsdorf. Cf. the genealogy in *Annales Stadenses* 1112, pp. 319, 320. See Meyer von Knonau (1894) p. 482 and n. 51; Jakobs (1968) pp. 185, 202–3 and n. 22.

ʼthe protection of the Saxon margrave Dedi,[1287] who had escorted him to Mainz.

It happened at this time that the church of Bamberg was shaken by a serious scandal. Bishop Herman had built at his own expense a church in honour of the blessed James in Bamberg outside the wall[1288] and there he had brought together a congregation of twenty-five clergy, distinguished for their learning, their morals and the discipline of the canonical way of life and he had made sufficient provision for them in respect of their food and clothing. When the clerk whom he had appointed to rule the congregation succumbed to illness and breathed his last, Herman seized the opportunity to expel the clerks and hand over the place itself, together with all its appurtenances, to Abbot Ekbert of St Michael[1289] to establish a monastery there. He did this, not because he had taken exception to any misconduct on the part of the clerks – since, as I said, they led a most honourable life according to the laws of the Church – but because, delighting in the purity of the monastic way of life, he desired, if it was possible, that this should be the only form of the religious life throughout his diocese. Having indeed *a zeal for God but not according to knowledge*,[1290] he *strove after the beauty of Rachel to such an extent that* he believed that *the fruitfulness of Leah*[1291] ought not to be admitted to the bedchamber of the heavenly Bridegroom.

The clerks who had been expelled were greatly angered at being deprived without cause of the ecclesiastical endowment that maintained them. The clergy of the cathedral church of Bamberg were also aggrieved both on the clerks' and on their own account because the fact that the bishop esteemed the monastic order so highly was greatly injurious to their own order. They therefore addressed to him their combined entreaties, beseeching him in God's name not to snatch away without a legal investigation and hearing, from men who were not accused of any crime, the benefices that they had received according to canon law for their maintenance in the Church. Nor should he allow

---

1287 Margrave Dedi of Lower Lusatia (above n. 522).

1288 Bishop Herman I of Bamberg (above n. 449) had founded St James in Bamberg as a congregation of regular canons in 1071/2. See Hallinger (1950) pp. 354–5; Struve (1969) pp. 29–30; Schieffer (1972) pp. 22–30; Cowdrey (1998) p. 113.

1289 Abbot Ekbert of Münsterschwarzach, of Michelsberg and of St James, Bamberg (above n. 718). See Hallinger (1950) pp. 353–6.

1290 Romans 10:2.

1291 Gregory I, *Registrum* I.5, *MGH Epistolae* 1, 7, referring to Genesis 29:16–17, 30–1, and adding the interpretation: 'I loved the beauty of the contemplative life like unfruitful Rachel ... but Leah ... [is] the active life, fecund but blear-eyed.'

those men, who had been deprived of the wages of spiritual service and who besides had no personal property, to be exposed to the scorn of laymen. The bishopric of Bamberg possessed few congregations of clerks and consequently was in need not so much of monks as of clergy, whose support would be useful to the people in processions on festal days and in the accommodation of guests. Moreover the church that the bishop had recently built was situated in a much frequented place in the midst of streams of people flocking this way and that and separated from the cathedral church of Bamberg by thirty paces at most and therefore much more suitable for clerks than for monks. Monks indeed are set apart from the multitude, since they are commanded *to sacrifice the abominations of the Egyptians to the Lord* their God and, as it is written, to go *three days' journey into the wilderness,*[1292] so that, if they sacrifice what laymen revere and regard as of the utmost importance, they do not do so before the eyes of laymen, who would be tempted to evil and would pelt them with the stones of their derision and defame the holy and apostolic life. Although monks, as the more honourable and the more exalted part of the body of Christ, cling more closely to God, clerks ought not on that account to be cut off entirely from the Church like rotten limbs. For although *stars differ from other stars in glory,*[1293] nevertheless by their diversity they adorn the single face of heaven in a most becoming manner and, although *the members* are dissimilar and perform distinct functions, nevertheless by means of their harmonious, albeit different, service they fulfil the needs *of one* and *the same body.*[1294]

The bishop was to be moved neither by reasoning nor by pleading and he declared that the honour that he paid to monks was in no way prejudicial to clerks. As for the property, however, which he had accumulated by his own efforts to be used for the poor: it was his personal possession and it was a matter for his own judgement whether he conferred it on clerks or on monks. The clerks, who were deeply distressed both by their personal poverty and by their insulting treatment, assailed the ears of the king and of all the princes of the kingdom with the daily recital of their wrongs. When they found no help anywhere and no hope of redress, they turned to the greatest source of strength, which in holy Church is always *the one and only means of assistance*[1295] *in the time*

1292 Exodus 8: 26–7. See Struve (1969) pp. 29–31.

1293 I Corinthians 15:41.

1294 Cf. I Corinthians 12:12–26.

1295 Livy III.4.9.

of greatest need.[1296] they made their way to Rome. They told the Roman pontiff the whole sequence of events in the history of their misfortunes and earnestly begged for the protection of the apostolic see against the violence of so great a perverter of the law.[1297]

At the same time envoys appeared on behalf of all the clergy of Bamberg. They reiterated the complaint and strongly criticised the indulgence of the Roman pontiff, asking why he allowed the Church of God for so long to be stained by communion with a heretic, who stole *into the sheepfold* not, like *the shepherd, by the door* but, like *a thief and a robber*[1298] by means of simoniacal heresy and the squandering of huge sums of money. When he was accused before his predecessor, Pope Nicholas,[1299] of so great an offence, as is commonly said, he put out *the fire with a sword.*[1300] that is, he cleared himself of heresy by means of perjury. Although utterly unlearned,[1301] he had shamelessly taken possession of the episcopal throne and the holy office of preaching, contrary to the holy canons. Before he became a bishop, he had achieved fame and came to public attention in the city of Mainz, where he was brought up,[1302] by committing all the capital crimes and every kind of infamy. After he was appointed to administer the heavenly talents, he practised the financial skills and the arts of usury, in which he had been trained since boyhood with ever greater care, so that, when he laid hands by shameful means on the abbeys and churches situated within his diocese, he then sold

1296 *Ibid.,* III.55.3.

1297 Lampert subsequently (below, 1076, p. 312 and n. 1665) emphasised the role of 'Poppo, the provost of Bamberg, whose partisanship and whose exertions had been principally responsible for the deposition of Bishop Herman of Bamberg'. Cf. Gregory VII, *Register* III.1, p. 242: 'Poppo, the provost of your church'. In the letters of Gregory VII and the other documents recording the proceedings against Herman there is no reference to the case of St James, Bamberg. See Meyer von Knonau (1894) pp. 462–72; Schieffer (1972) pp. 22–30; Schneider (1972) pp. 73–4, 124–5, 127; Meier (1987) pp. 39–43; Cowdrey (1998) pp. 113–14.

1298 John 10:1, 2.

1299 Not Nicholas II but Alexander II: cf. above, 1070, p. 126 and n. 566. See Meyer von Knonau (1894) p. 800 n.40; Schieffer (1971) pp. 158–60

1300 Horace, *Satirae* II.3.275.

1301 Cf. Gregory VII, *Register* II.76, p. 239: 'a certain illiterate man, ruined by the heretical wickedness of simoniacal infidelity, had intruded into that church'; Bruno of Merseburg, *The Saxon War* c. 15, p. 22: the king 'gave, or rather sold for an enormous sum of money, the bishopric of Bamberg ... to a certain mercenary man, who knew better how to count the various sorts of money than to read the text of any book correctly'.

1302 Cf. above 1065, pp. 107–8: '*vicedominus* of Mainz'. See Meyer von Knonau (1890) p. 456 and n. 113.

them in the most shameful manner and he reduced to utter poverty the community of the church of Bamberg, which shortly before had been exceedingly wealthy and abounding in every kind of property. Now in addition to all his other evil deeds, in order the more readily to practise his wolfish savagery *in sheep's clothing*[1303] and the more easily to abuse the innocence of simple people, the angel of *Satan* was *transformed into an angel of light.*[1304] He expelled the clergy from their churches without any investigation and he established the monastic life in all the places that he could, not so much as a lover of the religious life but as a cunning hypocrite. Finally the envoys from Bamberg implored the pope that Simon Peter should at last awaken and lift up the staff of pastoral zeal against *the wolf* that wickedly *snatched and scattered the sheep*[1305] of God and that once again he should send Simon the magician – who was setting out *the tables of the moneychangers*[1306] and the coins *in* the Church *of God – to perdition*, together *with* his *money.*[1307]

The Roman pontiff had already long before suspended him from the ministry of the holy altar.[1308] He was, however, exasperated by the account now given to him and without delay he excommunicated him on the following grounds: that he had long stood accused of the most serious offences and, although he had often been summoned to Rome during the past two years to defend himself, he had disdained to come.[1309] The pope also ordered that their church should be restored to those clerks who were complaining that they had been expelled by means of a legal subterfuge. Furthermore he sent a letter to the clergy of Bamberg,[1310] commanding them to withdraw from communion with Herman, and he declared in the most solemn terms that, although Herman might at some time regain the right of communion, he would thenceforward never in his lifetime recover the office of bishop, which he had usurped against the laws of the Church.

1303 Matthew 7:15.

1304 II Corinthians 11:14.

1305 John 10:12.

1306 Matthew 21:12.

1307 Acts 8:20.

1308 Cf. above 1074, p. 233 and n. 1226.

1309 He had been summoned only to the Lent synod of February 1075 (Gregory VII, *Register* II.29, p. 162) and he had responded by sending a messenger and a letter of excuse (*Codex Udalrici* 43, pp. 91–2).

1310 Gregory VII, *Register* III.1, pp. 242–4 (20 July), informing the clergy and people of Bamberg that he had deposed Herman from the episcopal and priestly offices and excommunicated him 'until he presents himself for an apostolic hearing'.

When this was reported to the Bamberg clergy by their envoys and their reliance on so important a promise provoked their old anger, they concealed for the time being the coming of the legation from the apostolic see and sent to the bishop, who remained at that time in Bamberg, giving him notice to leave the city as soon as possible.[1311] He could no longer be their bishop both because he had purchased the bishopric by means of simoniacal heresy, contrary to the decrees of the Church and because, as a man totally without learning, he could not administer it. To this dreadful message they added a serious insult. A certain *young man* from the body of the clergy with *the boldness of* his nature and *his age*[1312] cited a short verse from the Psalter, saying: 'If you explain to me correctly not the mystical sense, not the allegorical signif- icance but the meaning word for word, like a trustworthy interpreter,[1313] I shall proclaim you as certainly most worthy of the office of bishop, free from any investigation and acquitted of all the offences of which we accuse you.' The bishop was astounded at this extraordinary conduct and asked in an agitated manner what was the matter and what was the cause of this unaccustomed violence of tone on the part of clergy who had previously been so mild-mannered. After he had countered their harsh speeches with even harsher replies, suddenly the legates of the apostolic see made their appearance. In addition to the letter that they carried in their hands, they made an oral pronouncement in the name of the Roman pontiff that henceforward he no longer possessed the rights and the power of the office of bishop. He was informed that he had been cut off by the sword of papal excommunication from the body of the universal Church because, although he had so often been summoned to Rome by papal letters, he had omitted to clear himself of the offence

---

1311 Herman learned the papal decision when he was two days' journey from Rome (in April). Cf. Gregory VII, *Register* III.3, p. 247 (to Henry IV); Meinhard, master of the cathedral school of Bamberg, letter to certain Bamberg canons, *Brief- sammlungen* pp. 243–6; letter of the Bamberg clergy to Bishop E. (Embrico of Augsburg?), *Codex Udalrici* 44, pp. 93–7. On the discrepancy between Lampert's account and these documents see Meyer von Knonau (1894) p. 802: the account 'is a synopsis of the rumours about the case that reached Lampert from the Bamberg clergy and was revised by him in his usual manner'. See also Meyer von Knonau (1894) pp. 464–5; Struve (1969) pp. 29–30; Schieffer (1972) pp. 22–60; Cowdrey (1998) p. 125.

1312 Livy VI.23.3; VIII.30.4. See Billanovich (1945) p. 67.

1313 Cf. the anecdote of Bruno of Merseburg, *The Saxon War* c. 15, p. 22, about Herman's mangling of the text of Genesis 1:2, intended to illustrate the bishop's inability 'to read the text of any book correctly, let alone understand or expound it'. For the mystical, allegorical and literal senses of the Bible see Smalley (1952) pp. 1–26.

of simoniacal heresy of which he had been accused.[1314] The legates also commanded the Bamberg clergy no longer to show him the honour and reverence due to a bishop but to withdraw entirely from communion with him lest they be judged to be transgressors of the decrees of the Church and share with him the same punishment of excommunication.

This was when the bishop first became aware that he had been trapped by the deceptions of his clergy. They urgently pressed him to resign and to withdraw from the episcopal office as soon as possible, since he could not offer a satisfactory justification of his conduct and they called on God to witness that they would not perform the divine services in the church if he remained in it. Full of doubt and confused, the bishop sent a message to the archbishop of Mainz. The latter was his most trusted friend,[1315] whom he had often placed under an obligation to him by many favours, both in private and public affairs, and who had been his confidant and associate in all the measures that he had taken in obtaining and in administering the bishopric. Herman asked him to come as quickly as possible and, by whatever means he could, to check the boisterous conduct of the clergy and their internal strife. The archbishop did not delay in coming and endeavoured to persuade the clergy, as he had been requested to do. He declared that they should not forget the demands of decency and propriety and vent their anger without any cause against their bishop, whom they ought for God's sake to revere in the place of a father, since he had not knowingly provoked them by any word or any deed that they could justly call into question. If by chance he had unknowingly done something or other that caused them distress, he was prepared – after he himself had acted as investigator and judge – to make amends in any way he could to those who were offended. They should bear in mind not so much his innocence as their own honour and reputation, lest the rest of the clergy throughout the world should be encouraged by this example to despise their bishops and this noxious disease of rebellion and obstinacy, beginning among the clergy of Bamberg, should infect the whole body of the Lord's flock. The clergy, however, would hear nothing of conciliation, *nothing of extenuation*.[1316] They silenced him with loud

1314 Cf. Gregory VII, *Register* II.76, pp. 239–40 (20 April); III.1, pp. 242–4 (20 July), both addressed to the clergy and people of Bamberg.

1315 According to the letter of the Bamberg clergy, *Codex Udalrici* 44, p. 94, the visit of Siegfried of Mainz (above n. 210) was unexpected: 'Lo! God so ordained that the lord metropolitan arrived.' On Herman's acquaintance with Siegfried see above n. 1302.

1316 Livy II.3.4; XXXV.21.10.

reproaches, saying most justly that the sentence of papal excommunication ought to be put into effect also against the archbishop himself, since he had by means of simoniacal heresy consecrated as bishop a man branded with every kind of infamy, who possessed nothing of the character, nothing of the learning appropriate to the priesthood. The archbishop could not use ignorance *to plead as an excuse for* his *sins*[1317] since, as one who had long observed him in his own house and had been on the closest terms with him, he knew very well his conduct and his whole way of life. He himself had also been present, as mediator and confidant, in all the dealings that occurred when Herman was purchasing the bishopric.

The archbishop saw that the clergy were firmly intent on conflict and could by no means be appeased. In order to leave no effort on behalf of his friend untried and unattempted, he decided to go to Rome, taking Herman with him.[1318] He hoped that the Roman pontiff could be won over either by money or by supplication and that he would absolve Herman from the offence and from the anathema. Once the journey had begun, however, he reflected that it was hardly safe enough to bring Herman to Rome before he had discovered the attitude of the Roman pontiff. He therefore persuaded Herman to remain in one of the more distant properties of the church of Bamberg to await his return, while he himself with a few companions hastened to Rome, as he had intended.[1319] When he arrived there, it was with the greatest difficulty that he succeeded in being received by the Roman pontiff. Now he who had prepared himself to defend another man against accusations found himself facing charges on his own account: namely, that he had consecrated the bishop of Bamberg in the full knowledge of his simoniacal heresy and thus was almost in danger of losing his office. Finally at his departure he was commanded to withdraw entirely from communion with Herman and to inform all the princes of the German kingdom of the sentence of papal excommunication that had been promulgated against him. At the first favourable opportunity he was to consecrate

---

1317 Psalm 140:4.

1318 'That Siegfried and Herman went to Rome together ... is quite erroneous': Meyer von Knonau (1894) p. 464 n. 26. Herman was accompanied by the provost Poppo and other Bamberg clergy: cf. Gregory VII, *Register* III.1, p. 242; letter of the Bamberg clergy, *Codex Udalrici* 44, p. 95.

1319 According to the letter of the Bamberg clergy pp. 94–5, Siegfried 'had arrived [in Rome] unexpectedly' and attended the papal assembly of 12 April in which he 'proclaimed [Herman] without question to be a simoniac'. See Meyer von Knonau (1894) pp. 464–5; Cowdrey (1998) p. 125.

another bishop for the people of Bamberg in place of Herman.[1320]

When the bishop of Bamberg learned this, he judged that henceforward he had no hope left unless it was to be found in the mercy of the
Roman pontiff. He hired the services of men who were to defend his
case before the apostolic see with their oratorical skills and set off for
Rome. But the firmness of the Roman pontiff and his invincible opposition to avarice refused to hear the arguments of human deceit. With
many tears, many pleas, many disquisitions composed according to the
art of rhetoric he was able with difficulty to achieve only this: that he
would be absolved from excommunication on condition that, as soon as
he had returned to his own land, he entered a monastery.[1321] There he
should ever afterwards abstain from all worldly activities and lament
the scandal that his ambition had caused to the Church by appropriate
acts of penance. He thus returned to his homeland and reported the
commands of the Roman pontiff to his knights, among whom he had
made himself extremely popular by his prodigal generosity.[1322] They
strongly resisted these commands, saying that it was most shameful
and something that in the memory of *ancestors in times past*[1323] had never
happened in the churches of Gaul, that a bishop was deposed without a
public hearing and a trial according to canon law, which was inappropriate even for the lowest ranks of the clergy. They regarded this not
as an injustice against him personally but rather as a general affront
affecting all those who were obliged to give their aid in defending the
dignity of the church of Bamberg and had sworn fidelity on oath to
their bishop. They would therefore do their utmost before they would
allow the honour of that church, which had been preserved up to the
present day, to be defiled by so infamous a precedent. Encouraged by

1320 Gregory VII, *Register* III.2, p. 245 (20 July) orders Siegfried to arrange for the
appointment of a new bishop in Bamberg 'so that you may be proved to put right
your negligent conduct in the case of the aforesaid simoniac'.

1321 Herman was in the vicinity of Rome in April (see above n. 1311). Gregory VII,
Register III.3, p. 247: 'when he had approached very near to Rome, he halted his
journey, ... sending his envoys ahead well supplied with gifts.... When the event
proved contrary to his hopes, he hastily withdrew, all too certain of his condemnation, and, duping the clergy who were with him with smooth and deceptive
promises, said that if he could return to his homeland, he would retire from
episcopal office and take upon himself the profession of the monastic life.' See
Meyer von Knonau (1894) pp. 464–7; Cowdrey (1998) p. 125.

1322 Cf. Gregory VII, *Register* VI.19, pp. 430–1, ordering Herman, Udalric, Frederick,
Mazelin, Herold, Wirinto and Gotebold, 'knights of the church of Bamberg', to
surrender the properties of the church of Bamberg that they had received from
Bishop Herman.

1323 Esther 14:5.

these promises, the bishop disregarded the decree of the Roman pontiff and returned to Bamberg. During the four or five weeks that he stayed there, except for the service of the altar, in all other respects, as far as the external administration of the bishopric was concerned, he did not relinquish any of his rights. For he considered the excommunication to be invalid because – such was his captious reasoning – it had not been promulgated against him according to canon law. In these days divine service was not performed in public in the city of Bamberg since the clergy shunned and thoroughly detested communion with him. He spent the remaining part of the year on the more distant properties of the church of Bamberg under the protection of his knights. But neither the king nor any bishop – nor any other person of sound judgement – wished to have contact with him.[1324]

The king celebrated Easter in Worms.[1325] Certain of the princes of Saxony had decided to go there to pay their respects to him but during their journey envoys who had been sent to meet them, urged them to return to their homes with all speed: for it would hardly be prudent for them to come face to face with the king, whom they had not yet appeased by making appropriate amends after inflicting such severe injuries.[1326] It was then that they first became aware of the calamity that hung over them. The king had already accumulated provisions in great numbers and made all the preparations necessary for conducting a war. With the customary official proclamation he announced to all who were in the kingdom an expedition against Saxony and appointed the day and the place for the assembling of the army: namely, on 8 June[1327] in the

1324 According to Gregory VII, *Register* III.3, p. 247, if Henry IV's 'royal power had not checked him, [Herman] would have brought [his church] into utter confusion'. Cf. Bruno of Merseburg, *The Saxon War* c. 15, p. 22: 'although [Herman] did not spare either his own gold or that of the church that he had received to govern, in order to obtain the king's favour, he was deposed on the advice of that same king and the bishopric was given to another man'. See Meyer von Knonau (1894) pp. 469–70; Schneider (1972) p. 127.

1325 5 April. So also Berthold of Reichenau, *Chronicle* 1075, p. 134 but according to Bruno of Merseburg, *The Saxon War* c. 44, p. 43, 'in Mainz'. Meyer von Knonau (1894) p. 483 followed Lampert and Berthold.

1326 The arrival of Saxon envoys at the royal court in Eastertide was reported by Bruno, *The Saxon War* c. 41, 44, pp. 41, 43. See Meyer von Knonau (1894) p. 489.

1327 Cf. Henry IV, *Letter* 6, p. 10, to Abbot Theoderic and the monks of St. Maximin in Trier (1075): 'We have ordered our expedition against the Saxons and have decided, if God permits it, to begin it on 6 June.' Meyer von Knonau (1894) p. 495 n. 59 suggested that there was a scribal error in the extant copy of this letter and preferred Lampert's date, since he was likely to be well informed about any event involving Hersfeld property.

place called Breitungen, a property of the monastery of Hersfeld.[1328] He also sent envoys to the Saxons, who had gathered in great numbers in Goslar to make their plans, to tell them that he remembered well the grave insults that he had suffered, the outrage inflicted on the royal majesty and the shameful flight to which he had been forced to resort, to save himself when in extreme danger of his life. He said that he was not directing this accusation against all the Saxons in general. There were a few princes who had inflamed to this madness the inexperienced crowd, which with its innate fickleness was always *eager for novelties.*[1329] It was on these men that he would inflict the punishment with armed might – since he could not do so by legal measures – for inciting discord and throwing the State into confusion. He therefore requested the other Saxons and commanded them on pain of losing his favour not to support the enemies of the State with their weapons or their wealth. If they were obedient, he would pardon them for their former offence, in having previously been allies and partners in such an extraordinary crime. If they did not obey, however, they would thereafter have no excuse for the sinful conduct that they had committed knowingly and with forewarning.

To this the Saxons replied:[1330] 'The message of your envoys is most welcome. Unless our princes promise to make amends befitting the greatness of the royal majesty for all the offences with which they are charged, we shall without delay either take them prisoner and keep them in chains to await the king's judgement or reduce all their property to ashes and force them to flee far from Saxony. If, however, they are prepared, under conditions that are just and appropriate to the title of king, either to clear themselves of the accusations or to atone for their sinful conduct, we beg and implore the king in God's name to be mindful of his honour rather than his anger and not to undertake any measures against them that are unworthy of him before holding a public hearing and a judicial investigation by the other princes. Instead he should fix a day, designate a place and give them a safe-conduct to come there and to present their defence so that there would be a just trial according to the legal proceedings of the palace and he should either punish them if they were convicted of the offences or acquit them if they were innocent.

1328 Cf. above p. 187 and n. 975.

1329 Sallust, *Jugurtha* 19.46. Cf. Livy I.8.6.

1330 Bruno of Merseburg's version of 'the frequent embassies [that] they sent to the king and all the princes': *The Saxon War* c. 45, pp. 43–4. See Meyer von Knonau (1894) pp. 493–4.

But if his unbridled wrath permitted no amends to be made and could be extinguished by no other means than by the blood of our princes, what was the good of *darkening counsel*[1331] with ambiguous replies? We consider that it would be the height of disloyalty to abandon our princes and deliver them up to be slain for our sakes, when we know for certain that they took up arms against the king not out of personal hatred or for their own gratification but solely to preserve our safety and to maintain our freedom. We therefore humbly beg that the same pardon should be granted to us and to them for those acts of presumption or, if no sacrifice of humble submission can atone for what we have done, let the same punishment be imposed on us and on them.'

Then Bishop Bucco of Halberstadt, Archbishop Wezel of Magdeburg, Duke Magnus of Saxony, Otto the former duke of Bavaria and the other princes[1332] against whom the king's dark threats were particularly directed, stated that they were totally unaware of having violated by any deed or word the peace that had been agreed the previous year in Gerstungen.[1333] For if the king suspected that it was at their instigation or on their advice that the church on the Harzburg was burned down, the treasures were plundered and the bodies were torn out of the tombs or that anything else was done contrary to the terms of that treaty, they were prepared, under any conditions that the rest of the princes of the kingdom judged to be equitable, to refute the accusation and declare their innocence. Moreover they would at their own expense rebuild that church more splendidly than it was before and improve it with more handsome decorations. They would also replace many times over everything that the senseless common people, incited by the evil spirit, had laid waste, plundered and desecrated in their impious rashness.[1334]

1331 Job 38:2.

1332 Bucco (Burchard II) of Halberstadt (above n. 235), Wezilo (Werner) of Magdeburg (above n. 899), Magnus Billung (above n. 621), Otto of Northeim (n. 261). Cf. Bruno, *The Saxon War* c. 45, pp. 43–4: 'the king offered his pardon to the archbishop of Magdeburg and certain others', 'if they would abandon [the king's] enemies and surrender to him Bishop Burchard of Halberstadt, Duke Otto and the count palatine Frederick [II of Goseck], together with others whom he might subsequently ask for'. See Lange (1961) p. 55. On Lampert's claim that Henry IV regarded Wezilo as an enemy see Meyer von Knonau (1894) p. 827 and n. 121.

1333 See above 1074, p. 215 and n. 1127.

1334 No such offer is made in the letter of Archbishop Werner of Magdeburg to Archbishop Siegfried of Mainz (1074/5), cited in Bruno, *The Saxon War* c. 42, p. 42: 'As for the destruction of his monastery, the desecration of the tombs of his son and brother and the dispersal of their bones, when you hear how it was done, you will recognise that we are innocent.' See above 1074, p. 220 and nn. 1151–2.

In addition to all this they would readily give him as much gold and silver and as many of their estates as his sense of decency and the royal majesty would permit him to accept, if only he would once more show his favour and, being appeased, *put* back *into its sheath the sword*,[1335] which in his anger he had brandished over their necks, threatening the destruction of the whole of Saxony. If, however, he was inflexibly opposed to all their prayers and humble petitions, they would never thereafter take up arms against him nor face him in battle but, when he came, they would meet him with bare feet and stretch out their necks to receive his sentence, even though he pronounced it in anger.[1336] With these words they sent away the king's messengers and they themselves at once sent messengers of their own to the king, bearing the same reply.

When the king learned of their arrival, he ordered that they were on no account to be admitted to his presence. He let them know through secret intermediaries that they should depart as soon as possible and should not be so rash as to allow themselves to be seen by one on whom they had inflicted great injuries. Otherwise he would use against them the power of royal coercion, as enemies of the State and usurpers of the kingdom, who, under the pretext of acting as envoys, spread their lies among the people *in order to inveigle the princes*[1337] and hinder the king's expedition. The envoys thus returned without accomplishing anything. Again and again the Saxons sent other envoys but they all met with the same inflexibility and found both the doors and the ears of the king firmly closed against them.[1338] On one occasion, when one of the envoys seized the opportunity of the place and the time to rush unexpectedly into the king's presence and began to express what he had been commissioned to say, he had scarcely uttered the opening words of his speech before he was commanded to be silent and he was turned out amidst great indignation. He was led, or rather dragged away by

---

1335 John 18:11.

1336 According to Bruno, *The Saxon War* c. 45, p. 44, the Saxons replied that they would surrender those whom the king identified as his enemies 'on condition that they would be judged by the princes of both parties, so that their sentence would condemn them if they were convicted or, if they were found to be guiltless, restore them to the king's favour, together with all the Saxon people'.

1337 Livy XXI.22.1.

1338 Cf. Werner of Magdeburg, letter to Siegfried of Mainz, cited in Bruno, *The Saxon War* c. 42, p. 42: 'we very frequently sent an embassy to our lord the king, like humble slaves, with earnest supplication'; Bruno, *The Saxon War* c. 41, p. 41: 'our princes individually and collectively sent incessant embassies to the king, sometimes with a letter, sometimes without a letter ... but they had received no gentle reply from him'.

Udalric, a certain royal guard, to be kept in prison until the next day but the next morning he evaded his guards and with difficulty he escaped with his life.[1339]

Then the Saxons approached Duke Rudolf, Duke Berthold, Duke Gozelo and the rest of the princes who had been their fellow conspirators in the previous war.[1340] Sending frequent envoys, *they implored them to be loyal*[1341] to them, reminded them of the treaty that they had made and called on them in the name of God, in whose name they had sworn oaths in one and the same service, to stand by them in their time of danger. They urged them that, just as they had previously shown their good will when they were waging war, so now, since they repented having gone to war, they should not withdraw their aid and counsel in restoring peace. But the sagacity of the king – he was wise beyond his years to a remarkable degree – had hedged them in on all sides and had closed up all approaches and means of access. For he had taken an oath from all his princes that they would receive no envoys from the Saxons without consulting him, that they would not support them openly with their weapons or secretly with their advice and that they would never address him with prayers and humble petitions on their behalf until he himself, as judge and witness, acknowledged that the stain of dishonour that the Saxons had imposed on him had been washed away by a fitting punishment. Thus in whatever direction they turned, whatever route they considered, the Saxons found everything locked up, impenetrable, obstructed.

Accordingly they held frequent meetings throughout Saxony and Thuringia to consider what was to be done and they discussed and examined all the measures that seemed to promise some remedy to so great an evil. Since no hope of human help could be descried in any direction, they decided unanimously that henceforward they must seek relief from God, who alone could soften the inflexibly savage disposition of the king and unravel the tangled situation. They therefore ordered that throughout Saxony and Thuringia the inhabitants should set aside their more elegant clothing and dress in sackcloth and woollen garments. They should abstain from food and drink on prescribed days;

1339 Lampert alone recorded this incident and identified Udalric: see Meyer von Knonau (1894) p. 827.

1340 Rudolf of Swabia (above n. 203); Berthold I of Carinthia (above n. 824); Godfrey IV of Lower Lotharingia (above n. 570). On 'the treaty that they had made' see above 1073, p. 196 and n. 1024.

1341 Livy III.44.7; III.45.9; III.56.8. See Billanovich (1945) p. 143.

they should give alms to the poor, each according to his personal means, and walk through the churches barefoot, beseeching God amidst general lamentation to reach out His hand – which, when human help is everywhere at an end, can now alone bring relief to those who are besieged on all sides – to free them. Furthermore, if they were willing, on the day on which the king's army was required to assemble in Breitungen according to the official announcement, the Saxons and Thuringians should establish their camp in the place called Lupnitz,[1342] six miles distant from them, and again and again they should din the ears of the king and his princes with repeated prayers. If they were successful, they should give thanks to God; but, if not, they should await his arrival in that place, engage in battle and entrust their cause to God, the most just of judges.[1343]

Messengers also arrived, on the one hand from the Liutizi, on the other from the Poles, both promising their help, alliance and equal participation in all their military undertakings. They declared that they were prepared on any day that the Saxons chose to send very large numbers of armed troops into Saxony or, if they preferred this, they would act as an outpost, continually on the lookout for the Danes and other peoples who were rumoured to have been incited by the king to invade Saxony[1344] so that the Saxons might be relieved of this part of their responsibilities while they were preoccupied elsewhere. The spirits of the Saxons were somewhat revived by this news and they went their separate ways. They spent such time as remained until the day of the assembling of the army in fasting and nightly vigils; they tirelessly occupied the churches; they swathed themselves in ashes and hair shirts; they devoted the nights and the days equally to prayer. In short, they omitted no kind of religious observance that has been established by the tradition of the Church to appease God. But the wrath of God that had broken out against them was greater than could be extinguished by tears or soothed by sacrifices and services.

1342 East of Eisenach. See Meyer von Knonau (1894) pp. 496 and n. 63, 828, noting (p. 874 n. 2) that the army never reached Lupnitz.

1343 On the idea of battle as a form of trial by ordeal see Cram (1955) pp. 13–16; Struve (1970a) p. 121 and n. 41. On the polemical character of Lampert's account of the measures taken by the Saxons and Thuringians see Meyer von Knonau (1894) p. 828.

1344 Bruno of Merseburg, *The Saxon War* c. 36, p. 48, identified the Liutizi as the allies of Henry IV. For the Hersfeld rumours about the Liutizi and the Danes see above pp. 193–4 and nn. 1008, 1012. See also Meyer von Knonau (1894) p. 828.

The king celebrated Whitsun in Worms[1345] with only a few princes, since each was personally preoccupied with the preparations for the expedition. On the appointed day[1346] the king came to Breitungen with an innumerable host of men. It was indeed the unanimous opinion of all men that *never* in the most distant memory of their ancestors *had an army as great*, as powerful, as well equipped for war, *been*[1347] assembled in the German kingdom by any king.[1348] All the bishops in the kingdom, all the dukes, all the counts, all the holders of ecclesiastical and secular offices had assembled, bringing all their strength and all their power to this war. No one at all was absent, unless he could perhaps plead the excuse of some extremely serious and inescapable emergency. The archbishop of Cologne[1349] had obtained exemption on the grounds that it would be an act of impiety for him to be an onlooker at the disaster that was to overwhelm his brother, the archbishop of Magdeburg and his nephew, the bishop of Halberstadt. The king was not reluctant to grant this because, after the archbishop's original desertion, he had *always* regarded him *with hatred and suspicion*.[1350] The bishop of Liège,[1351] who in addition to his advanced age was worn out by a long illness, had in the meantime received the queen[1352] under his protection and for this reason he also was released from military service. Nevertheless both men sent their knights in very large numbers.

The duke of the Bohemians[1353] was also present, attended by so great a troop of men that, deluded by vain hopes, he believed that his forces alone were sufficient to fight the Saxon war. Abbot Widerad of Fulda, *apart from the fact that* from his earliest years *he had been* severely *lame*

1345 24 May. Cf. *D.H.IV* 278, issued in Worms on 28 May. See Kilian (1886) p. 67; Meyer von Knonau (1894) pp. 495–6.

1346 8 June. See above p. 251 and n. 1327.

1347 Livy XLII.51.11.

1348 Cf. the description of the army in *Song of the Saxon War* III.57–93, pp. 16–17. See Meyer von Knonau (1894) pp. 496–7.

1349 On the kinship of Anno of Cologne (above n. 139) with Wezilo (Werner) of Magdeburg (above n. 899) and Bucco (Burchard II) of Halberstadt (above n. 235), of the family of Steusslingen, see Fenske (1977) pp. 100–4, 195–6; Robinson (1999) pp. 47, 88–9, 100, 358.

1350 Livy V.20.7; XLI.24.18; XLIV.24.7.

1351 Dietwin of Liège (above n. 687) died the following 23 June: see below p. 270. Cf. Gregory VII, *Register* II.61, p. 216, referring to his 'old age' and 'bodily weakness'. See Meyer von Knonau (1894) p. 497.

1352 Bertha of Turin (above n. 491). See Meyer von Knonau (1894) p. 513.

1353 Vratislav II of Bohemia (above n. 746). See Meyer von Knonau (1894) p. 497; Wegener (1959) p. 117; Robinson (1999) p. 100.

in one foot,[1354] for the past two years had been so weakened by palsy that he could go nowhere except when supported by a stick or by the shoulders of his servants. Even this poor state of health, however, could not exempt him from military service since the king was concerned above all to make this the most impressive of expeditions by including the banners and insignia of all his princes. When the abbot travelled to the place of assembly of the army, seated in a wagon in the extreme heat of the summer, he was stifled by the *confused* din *of the surrounding crowd*[1355] and by the quantity of swirling dust and he almost breathed his last. After he had been brought back to the monastery, he indeed recovered from his stupor after a little while but he could no longer utter a word and for the next six weeks he was consumed by the most severe bodily suffering. On 16 July he was released from human cares. He clearly was a man with an ardent faith in God but he was utterly hated by all his monks because in his time the reputation of Fulda had been seriously eroded by many disasters and almost completely blotted out.[1356] But let us return to the narrative from which we have digressed.

Scouts sent by the king to observe the army of the Saxons reported back that they were in numbers and in weapons the equals of the royal army and in their other military preparations they were even superior.[1357] They had brought together a large quantity of materials and also enough provisions to last a long time. Undaunted by the approach of so great a host of enemies, they had placed their camp nearby. After the exertions of the march they had pitched their tents and were now unconcernedly giving themselves up to recreation. They had decided to send envoys to beg for peace and, if they were unsuccessful, they would accept battle with the oncoming enemy on equal terms.[1358] This report was received by those who were with the king *in an offhand and scornful manner*.[1359] They

---

1354 Einhard, *Life of Charles the Great* c. 22, p. 27. On Widerad of Fulda (above n. 239) cf. Marianus Scottus, *Chronicon* 1097 [=1075], p. 561. See Meyer von Knonau (1894) p. 546 and n. 131 (on the date of Widerad's death); Robinson (1999) p. 100.

1355 Livy II.22.6; II.28.6. See Billanovich (1945) p. 154.

1356 Cf. above, 1063, p. 91.

1357 Cf. *Annals of Disibodenberg* 1075, p. 7: 'after carefully observing the [Saxon] army, the king's spies came to their lord and falsely declared that the Saxons were preparing for battle.' See Meyer von Knonau (1894) pp. 498 n. 66, 880.

1358 Cf. Berthold of Reichenau, *Chronicle* 1075, pp. 134–5: '[The Saxons' and Thuringians'] agreed intention nevertheless was that they would humble themselves and surrender to the king.... If not, however, they would rather perish as innocent victims fighting for their lives.'

1359 Livy II.56.12.

boasted indiscriminately that, given their numbers and their courage, they would not find even armies of iron and steel invincible. For they had with them knights of the greatest distinction, who had spent their whole lives in military service: the individual princes had recruited them with the greatest care from every part of the world. Their opponents consisted of an absurd rabble, accustomed to farming rather than to military service.[1360] They had advanced into battle, contrary to their habits and training, driven not by martial instincts but by their fear of the princes. They would therefore not wait for battle to be joined so that they might fight hand to hand with drawn swords and either kill or be killed but, even before the battle began, they would be terrified simply by the sound of the rapidly advancing army and the shouts of the enemy, they would be put to flight and routed. The king was afraid not so much of being defeated in the battle as of being overwhelmed by prayer and supplication. He feared that his princes would consider it irreligious to make war on men who showed themselves most ready to make peace on any conditions and that the opportunity of avenging the dishonour inflicted on him – which he desired more ardently than anything else – would be torn from his hands. To prevent this from happening, he exerted himself to the utmost so that the armies would engage in battle before the envoys of the Saxons could come to sue for peace. Duke Rudolf of the Swabians strove his hardest to achieve this same object because in the previous year he had been suspected of seeking to obtain the kingship and he wished most eagerly to remove this suspicion by these new efforts to serve the king.[1361]

The king set out from Breitungen and on the first day he arrived in Oberellen.[1362] The following day with excessive haste he completed a march of almost two days and set up camp in Behringen,[1363] at no great

1360 Cf. *Song of the Saxon War* III.100–26, pp. 17–18: 'All the farmers broke their farm implements and made weapons from them.... The fields lay neglected, deprived of their cultivators.' See Fenske (1977) pp. 55–6; Rösener (1991) p. 61; Robinson (1999) pp. 101–2.

1361 Cf. Bruno of Merseburg, *The Saxon War* c. 44, p. 43: 'Duke Rudolf of the Swabians, who had not forgotten the treaty that the Saxons had suddenly made with the king, incited the king not to overlook the injury that had been so insolently inflicted on him and all his princes without imposing punishment and he promised to assist him with the strength in his power.' For Lampert's version of the suspicions against Rudolf see above 1073, p. 197 and n. 1026.

1362 On 8 June the royal army moved east and crossed the River Werra to Oberellen, west of Eisenach: see Kilian (1886) p. 68; Meyer von Knonau (1894) pp. 499, 874–5.

1363 On the morning of 9 June the royal army reached Behringen, a village between Eisenach and Langensalza. Cf. Bruno, *The Saxon War* c. 46, p. 44. On Lampert's

distance from the Saxons. After they had pitched their tents, the men scattered in various directions to provide themselves with the means to restore their weary and exhausted bodies. The king had also lain down on a bed in order to recover from fatigue. Suddenly Duke Rudolf appeared and announced that the Saxons were only a short distance away[1364] and – it was uncertain whether they were careless or ignorant of their enemies' arrival – were indulging in feasting and drinking and foolish games. It was as if they considered that at this moment they might with impunity thus shamelessly bring before the eyes of the king those weapons that they had taken up against the State and against the ancestral laws. This dishonour to the German kingdom could not be effaced in all the centuries to come. The duke was therefore of the opinion that, since the greater part of the day still remained, they should draw up their forces and join battle or, if the enemy refused to do battle and remained in the safety of their camp, they should move the army and storm the camp. The king thanked him, sinking to the ground, and promised, calling on God to be his witness, that, as long as he lived, he would never forget this service. Thus they both hurried from the tent. When the signal for battle was given, all their men quickly appeared and took possession of the length and breadth of the open field, each of the dukes separately drawing up his forces in battle array.[1365] Because neither *the lie of the land* nor the size of the army *would permit*[1366] all the troops to attack simultaneously as a single force, Duke Rudolf was given the task of fighting with his followers in the front line. For it was a special

---

confused account of 'a march of almost two days' accomplished 'with excessive haste' on 9 June, see Holder-Egger, *Lamperti Annales* p. 217 n. 2: 'In order to depict the king as thirsting for the Saxons' blood, Lampert fell into an error through his inordinate zeal, since the journey from Oberellen to the village of Behringen would certainly not have required two days.'

1364 Cf. Bruno, *The Saxon War* c. 46, p. 44: 'The Saxons placed their camp in the neighbourhood of Nägelstedt [near Langensalza] and waited for the king to summon them to a council.'

1365 The battle of Homburg on the River Unstrut, 9 June 1075. See Meyer von Knonau (1894) pp. 496–506, 874–84; Cram (1955) pp. 139–40; Giese (1979) pp. 159–61; Robinson (1999) pp. 100–2. Holder-Egger (1894) pp. 533–4 strongly criticised Lampert's description of the battle. According to Struve (1970a) p. 87, however, the concrete facts in Lampert's account 'largely agree with Bruno's description and are also confirmed by the evidence of other sources'. Lampert was best informed about the royal army and this may well have been his source of information, especially the Hersfeld and Fulda contingents of knights. 'In the case of the Saxon army he lacked such reports and thus was obliged to fill the blanks in his information by borrowing from classical authors.' See also below n. 1375 and also above p. 8.

1366 Livy V.49.4; IX.41.6. See Billanovich (1945) p. 126.

privilege of the Swabians, conferred on them by law from ancient times, that in every expedition of the German king they must form the advance guard of the army and engage in battle first.[1367] The rest of the forces were ordered to station themselves close to the fighting men and to rush to their aid, as the situation demanded. The king was in the fifth division, which he had assembled from the most carefully selected young men who had fully proved their fidelity towards him and whom he had equipped with the greatest splendour.[1368] Thus they advanced slowly in serried ranks towards the camp of the Saxons.

The Saxons had very foolishly persuaded themselves that the distance between them and the king could hardly be traversed in a single day by a lightly burdened rider, let alone by an army weighed down by supplies and other baggage. They had absolutely no suspicion that the king would reach them on that day.[1369] They were therefore resting with a delusive sense of security and they *had turned* all their attention from weapons *to the care of their bodies.*[1370] *Suddenly they saw* that the heavens were darkened *by a cloud of dust,*[1371] that an army innumerable *beyond the sands of the sea*[1372] had taken possession of the whole breadth of the nearby plain *like locusts in their numbers,*[1373] that it had already traversed nearly half of the intervening distance and that it was moving with a somewhat accelerated pace to overwhelm the camp itself, if they did not hasten their departure. *Alarmed by this unexpected attack* and accusing each other of

1367 Cf. Berthold of Reichenau, *Chronicle* 1075, p. 135: Henry IV sent 'the dukes of the Swabians and the Bavarians ... to make the first charge, as the Swabian law requires'; *Song of the Saxon War* III.57–8, 140–1, pp. 16, 18: 'the Swabians, the Bavarians, who were foremost in the king's army'. See Waitz (1878) pp. 181–2; Meyer von Knonau (1894) p. 875 n. 6; Maurer (1978) pp. 151–2.

1368 Cf. Berthold, *Chronicle* 1075, p. 135: the king remained 'at the rear with his elite warriors '. In his account of the battle of the Lech (955), Widukind of Corvey, *Res Gestae Saxonicae* III.44, pp. 124–5, recorded that Otto I was stationed in the fifth division, 'which is called the royal legion', with his elite troops.

1369 Cf. Bruno, *The Saxon War* c. 46, p. 44: a messenger 'declared that the king was advancing with his whole army. At first [the Saxons] did not believe it and when they realised that it was all too true, there was no time for consultation or for setting the army in order for battle'; Berthold, *Chronicle* 1075, p. 135: 'the first surprise attack'. The claim that the Saxons were unprepared is found in the other anti-Henrician accounts – Bonizo of Sutri, *To a Friend* VII, p. 233 ('the unprepared Saxons'); *Annals of Disibodenberg* 1075, p. 7 ('unaware and unprepared') – but not in the royalist *Song of the Saxon War.*

1370 Livy IV.52.3.

1371 *Ibid.,* XXI.33.21; cf. IX.43.12. Cf. *Song of the Saxon War* III.130–1, p. 18.

1372 Jeremiah 15:8.

1373 Judges 6:5.

idleness because they had not detected the enemy earlier, they immediately raised their voices to heaven in a call to arms; *they caught up their weapons*[1374] and burst out of the gates.[1375] A few men protected their bodies with coats of mail; the rest rushed out, impatient of delay and did not remember to put on again the garments that they had taken off a short while before, when they gave themselves up to an all too ample leisure. No man took heed of a more dilatory comrade but all came running indiscriminately, according to how rapidly or how slowly they had laid hands on their weapons. Very many of the Saxons were encamped at a considerable distance beyond the River Unstrut and they received the news of the unfortunate outcome of the engagement before they received the call to join battle.[1376] Because of the lack of time they were not permitted to draw up their forces in order of battle nor to encourage the troops nor to secure the camp with the usual sentinels nor to make any of the other preparations that normal military usage demands. The unexpected arrival of the king had prevented all such measures.

They finally and with difficulty recovered their breath after that initial confusion and pressed together in a very dense throng, positioning themselves with no regard for order. *Without waiting for the signal*,[1377] as is the custom with those about to engage in battle, they *spurred on their horses*[1378] and with a supreme effort they rushed headfirst against their enemies, not far from Homburg.[1379] The Swabians would *not have been able to withstand the attack*[1380] *even for a moment*,[1381] had not Duke Welf[1382] with the Bavarian army hastened to join them, as they were moved from their position and were already being forced back. The first onset of the battle used up the javelins and the throwing-spears. They continued

---

1374 Livy V.49.5; XXXVIII.30.8. See Billanovich (1945) p. 156.

1375 See Struve (1970a) p. 86: 'Lampert, who did not experience the engagement as an eyewitness, clothed the reports that reached him in the sumptuous garment of an ancient battle description.' The Saxon army is, therefore, placed in a fortified Roman camp, which Lampert derived from his knowledge of Livy: see above p. 9.

1376 Cf. *Annals of Disibodenberg* 1075, p. 7: 'The Saxons were scattered over the breadth of the land.'

1377 Livy XXXI.36.3.

1378 *Ibid.*, II.20.2; IV.33.7.

1379 See above 1073, p. 193 n. 1007.

1380 Livy VI.33.10; VII.12.4; XL.58.2. See Billanovich (1945) pp. 86–7.

1381 Galatians 2:5.

1382 Welf IV (above n. 630). On his role in the battle: Berthold of Reichenau, *Chronicle* 1075, p. 135; *Annales Einsidlenses* 1075, p. 146; *Historia Welfonum Weingartensis* c. 13, p. 461.

the struggle with swords, *a type of fighting in which* the Saxon knights greatly *excelled.*[1383] They were girded with two or three swords and they attacked with such force and so great a ferocity and struck home with such skill as to fill even their enemies with wonder no less than with terror. There Margrave Ernest of the Bavarians[1384] – a man of very great renown in the kingdom and famous for his many victories against the Hungarians – was seriously wounded. After he had been brought back to the camp only half alive, he died the next day. There fell Count Engelbert[1385] and two sons of Count Eberhard of Nellenburg;[1386] there fell very many Swabian noblemen, very many Bavarian noblemen. Very few men left the battle without wounds. Duke Rudolf was frequently assailed by many swords and, although all *the blows were turned aside by the* extremely sturdy *coat of mail*[1387] that he wore as a protection, he nevertheless suffered many bruises from the constant battering of his limbs.[1388]

In the Saxon *army the courage* of Otto, the former duke of Bavaria, *shone out*[1389] with particular spendour.[1390] Supported by very valiant young men, at one moment he was in the front line, urging them to fight. He was to be found fighting hand to hand wherever the enemy pressed forward more fiercely. He struck with his sword at the faces of those who hemmed him in; *he used the sword* to clear *a path* for himself through the ranks of *the enemy on all sides.*[1391] At the next moment he was at the rear of the army, shouting encouragement to those men who hung back; he reminded them of the cause for which they had taken up arms and entreated them all in God's name together to lay claim to their freedom through their own efforts, as they had so often solemnly sworn to do.

1383 Livy III.2.12; cf. XXVIII.37.6.

1384 Ernest, margrave of the Bavarian Ostmark (✝1075). Cf. *Annals of Disibodenberg* 1075, p. 7; *Annales Einsidlenses* 1075, p. 146.

1385 Engelbert, count in Bavaria (✝1075). See Meyer von Knonau (1894) p. 880 n. 23.

1386 Henry and Eberhard, sons of Count Eberhard of Nellenburg (above n. 994). Cf. *Annales Einsidlenses* 1075, p. 146.

1387 Livy XXXV.35.19.

1388 Cf. Bruno of Merseburg, *The Saxon War* c. 46, p. 45: 'We have learned that our Margrave Udo [II (of Stade) of the Saxon Nordmark] struck his cousin Duke Rudolf vigorously in the face and if the nose-guard of his helmet had not sturdily defended him, he would have cut off entirely the upper part of his head.'

1389 Livy I.42.3. See Billanovich (1945) p. 159.

1390 Otto of Northeim (above n. 261). Cf. Arnulf of Milan, *Liber gestorum recentium* V.3, p. 222. See Lange (1961) p. 55.

1391 Livy III.48.6; VII.33.10. See Billanovich (1945) p. 159.

Strenuously indeed *he performed the duty* both *of an* excellent *soldier and of the best of commanders.*[1392]

The battle had now dragged on from midday until the ninth hour and the situation now was that *the two armies of two*[1393] kingdoms, Swabia and Bavaria, were in retreat. A series of messengers reported to the king that their men were in the greatest danger, when suddenly from one side Count Herman of Gleiberg[1394] and from the other the knights of Bamberg advanced to the attack. Now the duke of the Bohemians, now Duke Gozelo of the Lotharingians[1395] – who had previously been plagued by many envoys and humble pleas from those in peril in the battle – each sent in his troops with their horses at the gallop. The Saxons *could no longer withstand the strength of this host*[1396] and they gradually fell back. Although for a long time Duke Otto had made a great effort to revive an army that was now ready to flee, *entreating, rebuking,*[1397] reproaching their lack of skill and their idleness, at last they turned tail and fled in all directions. Then indeed – as is always the case when enemies flee, *the most cowardly* and the most courageous are usually equal in daring, *equal in glory*[1398] – all the divisions in the king's army, reduced to a state of disorder, even all the common people and peasants, who performed the servile labour needed in the camp, quickly broke away to pursue the fugitives. They almost killed their horses in spurring them on; they flew over the widest fields more swiftly than can be told and they trod underfoot whatever stood in their way. They captured and plundered the Saxon camp and drove out the fugitives who had returned to the camp, seeking a hiding-place there. All the places through which fugitives had passed, for two or three miles roundabout[1399] were stained with the blood of the slain and piled high with heaps of corpses. Furthermore, because the dust stirred up by the horses' hooves robbed men's eyes

1392 Sallust, *Catilina* 60.

1393 Livy II.6.5.

1394 Herman II, count of Gleiberg (a neighbour of Hersfeld in Hesse). See Meyer von Knonau (1894) pp. 502, 876; Metz (1991) pp. 360–1.

1395 Duke Vratislav II (above n. 746) and Duke Godfrey IV of Lower Lotharingia (above n. 570). Cf. Berthold of Reichenau, *Chronicle* 1075, p. 136: 'receiving help on both flanks from Duke Godfrey and the duke of the Bohemians'. On the role of 'the distinguished Duke Godfrey' cf. *Song of the Saxon War* III.79–80, 201, pp. 17, 20.

1396 Livy XL.58.2. See Billanovich (1945) pp. 86–7.

1397 II Timothy 4:2.

1398 Sallust, *Jugurtha* 53.

1399 Cf. Berthold, *Chronicle* 1075, p. 136: 'They cruelly pursued the fugitives for nearly two miles.'

of their vision and their power of discrimination, with their clouded eyesight they could not easily distinguish allies from enemies[1400] and they killed very many of their own comrades, supposing them to be enemies.

The princes and noblemen of Saxony, with the exception of two men of middling rank,[1401] all escaped alive and unharmed because they made very skilful use of their knowledge of the locality, of the heavy darkness and of the swiftness of their horses. On the other hand, the savagery of the enemy raged uncontrollably against the common foot soldiers, who had still remained in the camp while the cavalry were fighting. The enemy's conduct so far exceeded the bounds of moderation that, forgetful of the Christian dread of wrongdoing, their victims seemed to them to be not men but cattle to be slaughtered. The River Unstrut also swallowed up a very large number of them, who threw themselves headlong into it for fear of the swords that threatened them.[1402] *The night made an end of the slaughter.*[1403] Because it was thought to be unsafe to pursue the fugitives beyond the river,[1404] the knights turned back in search of plunder. They found in the enemy camp so great an abundance of food, so great a mass of gold and silver and precious garments that they seemed to have encountered the king's army not to wage war but to give a banquet and to display the splendour of their treasures.

A little after sunset the king returned to the camp amidst shouts of congratulation from the knights, as is the usual practice. He was cheerful and glowing with joy because he had subdued his most dangerous enemies in a notable victory. Everywhere his knights were boasting loudly that they had killed some or other of the foremost princes of Saxony with their own hands. When, however, on their return to the battlefield, one of them found that his lord or his father or his brother[1405] or his kinsman or someone bound to him by any tie of relationship had

---

1400 Cf. Bruno of Merseburg, *The Saxon War* c. 46, p. 45: 'so great a cloud of dust was thrown up that each man could hardly distinguish between friend and enemy'.

1401 Cf. Bruno, *The Saxon War* c. 46, p. 45: 'of the middling rank Folcmar and Suidger died'. Bruno also recorded the death of Count Gebhard of Supplinburg (father of Emperor Lothar III). Holder-Egger, *Lamperti Annales* p. 221 n. 2, noted that 'it is not easy to believe that Lampert was unaware of this'.

1402 Cf. *Song of the Saxon War* III.186–98, p. 20.

1403 Livy XXIV.32.9. See Billanovich (1945) p. 162.

1404 *Song of the Saxon War* III.199–202, p. 20, reported that Duke Godfrey IV continued the pursuit beyond the River Unstrut.

1405 Cf. Bruno, *The Saxon War* c. 46, p. 45: 'In that battle brothers were on different sides, fathers were divided against sons.'

fallen in battle, all joy turned to grief and song *turned to the voice of those who weep.*[1406] The whole camp echoed with wailing and shrieking. They spent the following day[1407] in the same camp and covered the slain with earth. They sent back those among the dead who were more illustrious and more wealthy to be buried, each in the land of his origin.[1408] They cared for the wounded and they sent those whose wounds had rendered them unfit for military service in future to be cared for by their kindred in their homelands. It was not easy to calculate *how many thousands had been killed* on this side and on the other *in that battle.*[1409] Nevertheless it is undisputed that more noblemen fell on this side and more of the common people died on the other side and that, because of the loss of men of the greatest distinction, the victors suffered more damage than the defeated.[1410]

To the grief and distress that afflicted them all was added the severer pain and the penance of learning that the princes of Saxony – who on the previous day had been reported in *a widespread but groundless rumour*[1411] to have been slaughtered to the last man – were, every one of them, alive and, full of courage, were once again assembling fresh troops to renew the struggle. It was extremely hard for them to bear and they complained quite openly among themselves that at the greatest sacrifice to themselves and without the slightest advantage to the State they had defiled their hands with the blood of the harmless common people. The king himself very much feared that his army, repenting that they had shed so much blood to no purpose, would henceforward *refuse to perform military service*[1412] on religious grounds, since they could not serve without committing a sin and gravely offending God. To this most evil state of affairs the archbishop of Mainz applied a most evil remedy. After a consultation with a few of the king's close associates

1406 Job 30:31.

1407 10 June. On the significance of the victors remaining on the battlefield see Cram (1955) pp. 139–40.

1408 Cf. Bruno, *The Saxon War* c. 47, p. 45: 'the king ... caused his dead to be buried or to be brought back for burial in their homeland'.

1409 Livy XXVII.1.13. According to Berthold of Reichenau, *Chronicle* 1075, p. 136: 'almost eight thousand of [the Saxons] perished'; 'more than 1,500 of [the royal army] were killed'.

1410 Cf. Bruno, *The Saxon War* c. 46, p. 45: 'our men ... left the king with the glory of victory but with great losses among his men. For ... of that party there died eight princes no less noble than the king himself.'

1411 Livy XXVIII.24.2; XXXIII.44.7.

1412 *Ibid.*, V.19.5; VII.11.5. See Billanovich (1945) p. 145.

he suddenly appeared in public and imposed an over-hasty sentence of excommunication on the princes of Thuringia, without a canonical summons to a synod and without a synodal hearing and an investigation according to canon law.[1413] The reason for the sentence was that in the previous year in Erfurt, when the archbishop had held a synod in order to lay claim to tithes, the Thuringians had attacked him with drawn swords.[1414] Lest anyone should accuse him of having, contrary to canon law, assailed wretched men, who were currently involved in such inextricable difficulties, at such an unfavourable time – when they were tossed about on all sides by the tumult of war and did not have the leisure to present a defence but were obliged to preserve their lives by means of flight or by using weapons – the archbishop said that he had received permission from the Roman pontiff to cut them off from the Church by a lawful anathema without the delay required by law, without a judicial examination, on any day that he chose. No sensible man, however, could be unaware of the principal purpose of this measure: namely, that the king's army would henceforward wage war on the Thuringians more readily and more confidently in the belief that in killing them – if they were slain after their excommunication – they would not be guilty of the sins nor liable to the penalties that the laws of the Church prescribe for murderers.

The army therefore moved away from the battlefield and, passing through Thuringia, entered Saxony, laying waste all the surrounding territory with fire and sword. The troops found such great wealth in every single village – it was indeed a most fertile region and hitherto untouched by any wars – that the plentiful supply satisfied the fastidious palates even of the very greedy common people of the camp, who follow the army only in the hope of plunder.[1415] The king, however, constantly sent envoys to the princes of Saxony both in his own name and in the names of his princes, exhorting them to surrender and in future to *place*

1413 Meyer von Knonau (1894) pp. 506 n. 72, 813–14, considered this report improbable and typical of Lampert's hostility towards Siegfried of Mainz (above n. 210). He argued that, if Siegfried had acted in this way, he would hardly have been approached by the king's enemies to act as a mediator after Homburg – cf. the letter of Archbishop Werner of Magdeburg in Bruno, *The Saxon War* c. 48, pp. 46–7 – or used by Henry IV himself as a mediator (see below p. 268 and n. 1420).

1414 See above pp. 239–40 and n. 1268.

1415 Cf. Archbishop Werner of Magdeburg, letters, cited in Bruno, *The Saxon War* c. 49, 51, pp. 47–8, 48–50; Berthold, *Chronicle* 1075, p. 136: *Song of the Saxon War* III.229–53, pp. 21–2; Bruno, *The Saxon War* c. 47, pp. 45–6. See Meyer von Knonau (1894) pp. 506–7.

their hopes on his clemency *rather than their weapons,*[1416] of which they *had made a trial* on that one occasion *without success.*[1417] But the Saxons had clear evidence of the passionate hatred that he felt for them and they judged it to be utter madness to hasten to offer power and authority over their lives to one whose anger they had proved themselves unable to appease with so many urgent prayers before the expedition. Nevertheless they sent him a message in the humblest terms that they had always preferred peace to war and his clemency to his displeasure. If they could have purchased peace at any price other than their own blood, they would never have gone so far as to dare to attempt to take those extreme measures. If, however, now at least, after the defeat that they had suffered, God had *touched* his *heart*[1418] so that he sympathised with the misfortunes of those whom he had overthrown almost to the point of destruction, they would joyfully welcome this. They would erase from their hearts all the injuries by means of which he had sated his anger and his hatred against them and henceforward they would be faithful and devoted to him. But, if this could not be achieved other than by their surrender, then it would be more advisable for them to save their good name and to preserve their freedom unimpaired by dying in battle in the sight of all rather than to surrender and then to be slaughtered like cattle or to suffer a long imprisonment and furthermore to be tormented by hunger and thirst and other tortures and lead a life *more melancholy than any death.*[1419]

Finally at the king's command the archbishop of Mainz and certain other princes set out and negotiated face to face with the Saxons about these same matters.[1420] They implored them in God's name that, after they had committed their cause so inauspiciously to the arbitration of battle and had suffered a defeat that would not be effaced for many centuries to come, they should now at least, compelled by their misfortune, give up their folly and avoid *bringing* themselves and *their people to* utter *destruction*[1421] through their inflexibility and foolhardiness. They pledged their

1416 Livy II.39.8; III.53.3.

1417 *Ibid.*, I.45.3; II.35.8.

1418 Jeremiah 4:18.

1419 Livy IX.6.3.

1420 Siegfried of Mainz, letter to Pope Gregory VII (July/August) in *Codex Udalrici* 45, pp. 97–100, refers to the 'obstinacy' of the Saxons and Thuringians but says nothing of the archbishop negotiating with them. Meyer von Knonau (1894) pp. 561–2, 829–30, suggested that Lampert's implication of Siegfried in these unsuccessful negotiations was part of his polemic against the archbishop.

1421 Livy XXXII.22.6.

word before the face of the all-seeing God that, if the Saxons voluntarily surrendered, on the same day or a very short time afterwards they would be released from their capitulation and their offices, benefices, estates and other possessions would be theirs without reservation. For their part, the Saxons replied that they had in fact knowledge and experience both of the princes' trustworthiness and of the king's harsh and implacable disposition, when – after the peace agreement that in the previous year in Gerstungen the king had solemnly confirmed with the approbation of the princes[1422] – he had so cruelly punished them for the fault that he had previously pardoned and the trustworthy princes had offered them no help or protection whatsoever in their perilous situation. It was in vain therefore that the princes asked them to put their trustworthiness to the test, as if it was an unknown quantity, when to their own detriment they had experienced it with total clarity in the fields of Thuringia. Thus the Saxons remained steadfast and immovable in their determination. They established themselves in very well fortified places not far from Magdeburg[1423] because, although they had an abundance of troops, they had nevertheless decided henceforward to abstain from battles, unless they were unavoidably compelled to fight. Margrave Udo and the bishop of Merseburg,[1424] however, together with a few other members of the nobility of Saxony, agreed to surrender. Of these, Margrave Udo gave his son[1425] as a hostage on his behalf and was immediately released from his capitulation. The bishop was sent to the monastery of Lorsch; the others were entrusted to various princes to be kept under guard for the time being.

The king came with his army as far as Halberstadt and continued, as he had begun, to lay waste the surrounding territory with fire and sword.[1426] He also went on to Goslar with only a few followers in order

---

1422 See above 1074, p. 215 and n. 1127.

1423 Cf. Bruno, *The Saxon War* c. 47, p. 46: 'Our princes entered various fortresses'; c. 52, p. 50: 'Almighty God ... miraculously defended the city and the whole diocese [of Magdeburg] from the cruel attack of the king', who 'never entered that diocese'.

1424 Margrave Udo II of the Saxon Nordmark (above n. 168) and Bishop Werner of Merseburg (above n. 901). Cf. *Song of the Saxon War* III.252, p. 22: 'very many [Saxons] sought out the king's camp and surrendered themselves and their possessions'.

1425 Meyer von Knonau (1894) pp. 512–13 and n. 81 and Fenske (1977) p. 68 suggested that this was his eldest son, Henry, the future Henry III, count of Stade and margrave of the Saxon Nordmark (†1087). See also below, 1076, p. 331 and n. 1745.

1426 See Kilian (1886) p. 69; Meyer von Knonau (1894) p. 507 and n. 75; Giese (1979) p. 160.

to spare that very wealthy place, which was always most dear to him;[1427] for he feared that, if he brought a great host with him, the place would suffer plunder and damage. Since his army was afflicted more and more each day by hunger and thirst – for the old corn had been consumed partly by fire and partly by the needs of so great a host and the new corn was not yet ripe[1428] – and since there was no hope that this war could be prosecuted without a lengthy period of truce and greater expenditure, the king was prevailed on by the princes to leave Saxony. He marched through the territory of Thuringia and arrived in Eschwege. There he dismissed his army, after receiving from the princes a binding promise to bring a greater number of troops, more lavishly equipped, to Gerstungen on 22 October.[1429]

At this time the king received the news that Bishop Dietwin of Liège – a man adorned with many virtues, who had now been discharging the duties of a bishop for very many years – had departed this life.[1430] Through the intervention of Duke Gozelo and because of the latter's outstanding service in the war, the king immediately appointed Henry, a certain canon of Verdun, who was a close relative of the duke, as Dietwin's successor.[1431] The duke was placed under a great obligation to the king by this favour and he promised his fullest support in the forthcoming expedition.

After dismissing the army, the king came in great haste to Worms. Not long afterwards Burchard, provost of the church of Trier, who had gone to the king of the Russians as a royal envoy, returned.[1432] He

1427 Cf. Bruno, *The Saxon War* c. 53, p. 50: 'the king had come to Goslar, accompanied by the army'. For Lampert on Goslar see also above 1066, p. 109 and n. 458; 1070, p. 133 and n. 624; 1071, p. 135. See Rothe (1940) pp. 21–31; Wilke (1970) pp. 18–24, 30–3; Robinson (1999) p. 80.

1428 Cf. Bruno, *The Saxon War* c. 53, p. 51: 'he could not remain long with an army in this land because hunger in that year had on that occasion proved useful to us and the month of July showed that the fruit was not yet ripe'.

1429 Cf. the version of Berthold of Reichenau, *Chronicle* 1075, p. 136: 'After they had ranged through [Saxony] and laid waste a large part of it with fire and plunder, they returned home with their purpose not accomplished and the king somewhat displeased.' See Kilian (1886) p. 69; Meyer von Knonau (1894) pp. 511–12.

1430 Dietwin of Liège (above n. 687) died on 23 June. See Meyer von Knonau (1894) p. 513.

1431 Henry, bishop of Liège (1075–91). Cf. *Chronicon sancti Huberti Andaginensis* c. 28, p. 587: Duke Godfrey IV of Lower Lotharingia (above n. 570), 'who then chanced to be staying with King Henry', 'immediately sent to Henry, the archdeacon of Verdun, and ordered him without any delay to come to him'. See Meyer von Knonau (1894) pp. 515–17; Zielinski (1984) p. 41.

1432 On the mission of Burchard of Trier (above n. 1285) to Grand prince Svjatoslav of Kiev (above n. 1284) see above p. 242.

brought the king so great a quantity of gold and silver and precious garments that no one could remember such treasure being brought into the German kingdom on a single occasion in the past. In return for this payment the king of the Russians desired only that the king should offer no help against him to his brother, whom he had expelled from the kingdom.[1433] The king of the Russians could certainly have achieved this free of charge because the king was preoccupied with the internal warfare of his own kingdom and by no means had the leisure to wage foreign wars against such distant peoples. The circumstances of the moment made this great gift even more valuable. For the king's *treasury* had *been emptied by* the enormous expense of the recent *war*[1434] and the troops were urgently and forcibly demanding payment for the military service that they had lately performed. If the king had failed to satisfy these demands with a royal distribution of wealth, there was no doubt that he would have found that the troops were not to be depended on for that part of his plans that remained to be accomplished and that, it was feared, would certainly be the more difficult part.

The archbishop of Mainz was enraged with the bishop of Halberstadt because it seemed that he was principally responsible for the refusal of the Saxons to agree to a surrender. He therefore prepared to defeat him with spiritual weapons since he could not do so by military means. He sent him an envoy and summoned him to a synod. He charged him with the offence of oath-breaking for this reason: he himself, as military commander, had led a well equipped army against the State and against the king, to whom he had promised fidelity by means of an oath. He plotted to depose him from his bishopric on this pretext, if he could put his wishes into effect. He did not reflect upon the fact that he himself was equally guilty of the same offence because both he and all the princes of the kingdom who were now in the king's party had initially conspired in this same war against the king.[1435] But the messenger was detained by his fear of the enemies through whose lands he was required to travel so that he did not inform the bishop of the date within the legal time limit, as custom requires. Thus the senseless plan was abandoned as capriciously as it had been initiated.

1433 Grand prince Isjaslav-Demetrius of Kiev (above n. 1282).

1434 Livy V.20.5; XXII.32.5.

1435 On the leading role of Burchard II (Bucco) of Halberstadt (above n. 235) in the Saxon rebellion see above, 1073, p. 174 and n. 891. For Lampert's portrayal of Siegfried of Mainz as a conspirator against Henry IV see above, 1073 pp. 189 and n. 984, 195 and n. 1016.

Nevertheless the archbishop assembled a synod in Mainz in October of the same year.[1436] Among the other bishops who came together there was the bishop of Chur.[1437] He brought a letter and instructions from the apostolic see, according to which the pope commanded him, under the threat of losing his office and his holy orders – as he had also previously commanded in many legations – to force all the priests who were within his diocese either immediately to abandon their wives or forever to renounce the ministry of the holy altar.[1438] When the bishop expressed the wish to do this, the clergy who were seated all around him sprang up and both silenced him with their outcry and raged against him with their fists and with such contortions of their whole bodies that he despaired of being able to leave the synod with his life. Thus he was at length defeated by the sheer difficulty of his task and he decided in future to have nothing whatever to do with such a question and to leave it to the Roman pontiff to bring to a successful conclusion by his own efforts, when and how he wished, a cause that he had so often propounded without any effect.

Bishop Henry of Speyer was carried off by sudden death,[1439] after he had already with childish carelessness squandered almost all the treasures of the church of Speyer and given away its estates to his knights as benefices, to such an extent that scarcely half a year's expenses could be paid from the remaining income of the church. A certain clerk named Huzman, who immediately succeeded the deceased in the bishopric,[1440] saw a vision of his death that is worthy of remembrance. He thought that he was standing in the choir in Speyer with the bishop and the other clergy and, lo and behold! three men entered the choir, one a

---

1436 According to Berthold of Reichenau, *Chronicle* 1075, p. 134, 'the lord pope commanded that a general council should be held in Mainz', which Siegfried arranged for 17 August but his suffragans failed to comply. *Codex Udalrici* 45, pp. 97–100, is Siegfried's letter of apology to the pope. See Meyer von Knonau (1894) pp. 560–2, 570; Gresser (2006) pp. 139–40.

1437 It is not clear whether Bishop Henry of Chur (above n. 1221) participated in the council as papal legate or simply as a suffragan of Mainz: see Schumann (1912) p. 28; Gresser (2006) p. 140. Meyer von Knonau (1894) p. 570 n. 158 suggested that Henry might have been acting as the messenger of the king.

1438 Cf. Gregory VII, *Register* III.4, p. 250: 'as you have received instructions from the apostolic see, you are to make careful inquiries about simoniacal heresy and the fornication of the clergy and are to punish according to the law whatever offences you find to have been committed in the past'. There is no evidence in the letter of the threat to Archbishop Siegfried mentioned by Lampert.

1439 Henry of Speyer (above n. 498) †26 February. See Meyer von Knonau (1894) pp. 483–4 and n. 54.

1440 Huzman, bishop of Speyer (1075–90).

man of advanced age with venerable white hair and two youths, whose function seemed to be to serve the older man. After they had stood for some time in silence in the midst of the choir, the older man said to the youths who stood next to him: 'Why do you delay in performing what you were commanded to do?' But they replied: 'It is for you, father, first to pass sentence on him and then we shall carry out your judgement without delay.' And he said: 'Because of the many evil deeds that he has perpetrated against this place and against the holy Mother of God, the sentence has gone forth from God that he is to be killed.' At these words they seized the bishop, beheaded him and suspended his body on the wood of the cross that was raised up high in that church. When next morning the horrorstruck clerk related his dream to the bishop, he seemed to the bishop to be talking nonsense. Because of his physical health and the continued vigour of all his limbs the bishop had no premonition of such an imminent death. And lo and behold! on the seventh day after this, when he was standing in the choir with the brethren for the vesper service, he suddenly felt a sting, as a very small pustule developed in his neck. This gradually swelled to an enormous size and he died before midnight.[1441]

After the withdrawal of the king's army from Saxony the Saxons and Thuringians once more held frequent assemblies in which the common people raged against the princes and the princes against the common people with the most grievous animosity. The common people were inflamed with anger because the princes had most insistently urged and incited them to take up arms against the king and then, when it came to the battle, they fled and made their escape, leaving the common people to the enemy, to be overthrown, trampled underfoot and *slaughtered like helpless cattle*.[1442] The princes were angry with the commoners because, while they had advanced into battle and – considering their numbers – had fought most effectively, the commoners had remained in camp,

1441 The contemporary Swabian chroniclers linked Henry's death with his condemnation as a simoniac in Gregory VII's Lenten synod of 1075. According to Bernold of St Blasien, *Chronicle* 1075, p. 254, 'On the very same day that his case was being examined in Rome, that is, on 24 February, he became ill in Speyer. Then on 26 February, when he was the subject of a definitive sentence of condemnation by Pope Gregory in the Roman synod, he died a pitiful death.' Cf. Bernold's polemic, *De incontinentia sacerdotum* V, p. 26. According to Berthold of Reichenau, *Chronicle* 1075, p. 133, 'rising from the table after a delicious meal (as was his custom), his throat was suffocated by a stab of pain so very sharp and lethal that afterwards he could very rarely utter a word and it was with difficulty that he survived until the morning of the next day'.

1442 Livy III.47.7.

inactive and at their ease and had brought to the endangered princes only vain hopes of assistance and none of the help and support that they had long expected.[1443]

Then, however, all the Saxons united in turning with the greatest hostility upon all the Thuringians. They declared that there would be more justice in making war on them than on the king because, when the Saxon army was put to flight, the Thuringians had stationed themselves on all the roads and crossroads and attacked the fugitives, plundered them, *inflicted injuries* on them and drove them, *dishonoured*[1444] and stripped of all they possessed, from their territory. The altercations seemed now *to be leading to* great *violence*[1445] and to evil consequences. But the bishop of Halberstadt and Otto, the former duke of Bavaria, by whose advice the Saxon war was principally conducted,[1446] soothed the tempers of the savage host. They entreated them in God's name not to turn their weapons – those weapons that they had taken up as friends to defend their liberty – now, as though carried away in a diabolical fury, against their own hearts. Nor should they by this *internal turmoil*[1447] revive the courage and the boldness of their enemies, who had won a lamentable victory over them. They perceived, moreover, that the commoners had been broken by the first failure; they already regretted the war and were likewise weary of it. They also feared – since the disposition of the common people is always fickle and untrustworthy[1448] – that the commoners would seize the princes and surrender them to the king and purchase their own safety with the blood of the princes. They therefore proposed to reestablish peace and recommended that, since the first defeat that they had suffered had inspired in them a

---

1443 The version of Bruno of Merseburg, *The Saxon War* c. 54, p. 51, however, represents the rebels as united in their determination 'not, as before, to flee but bravely to fight for their freedom'. Lampert's account of dissension among the rebels was accepted by Meyer von Knonau (1894) pp. 518–20 and n. 89; Fenske (1977) pp. 56–7; Giese (1979) p. 160; Robinson (1999) pp. 101–2.

1444 Livy XLI.18.3.

1445 *Ibid.*, I.9.6. See Billanovich (1945) pp. 140–1.

1446 For Lampert's account of the leadership of Burchard II (Bucco) of Halberstadt (above n. 235) and Otto of Northeim (above n. 261) of the Saxon rebellion see above, 1073, p. 174 and n. 891. On the attitude of Otto of Northeim cf. Berthold, *Chronicle* 1075, p. 136: 'Otto the former duke and Duke Magnus and the other Saxon magnates remained obstinately rebellious and combative and still in the same treacherous state of mind as before.'

1447 Livy II.31.10; II.32.10; V.12.7; XXXIV.25.6.

1448 See above p. 224 and n. 1177.

loathing and a horror of war, they should now turn all their efforts towards calming the king's anger against them.

This proposal was heard and received with great rejoicing by all the people. After consulting together, they immediately sent the archbishop of Bremen and Margrave Udo[1449] to the king to plead with him in God's name that, at least now that he was satiated with their blood, he might set a limit to his anger and refrain from the total extermination of that small remnant of the Saxon people that had survived that most horrible slaughter. Let him instead fix a day and a place where they might be allowed to come in safety and to defend their cause. They were prepared to make the desired reparation, according to the judgement of all the princes of the kingdom, for every wrong by which he claimed to have been injured: they would, in short, propose any amends, they would freely suffer everything, saving solely their lives and liberty, if only he would delay the expedition against them, which, so they had heard, he had announced to all the princes of the kingdom.[1450] To this the king replied that he would not refuse pardon either to them or to anyone else making lawful amends for his wrongdoing. In so serious and so dreadful a case, however, he would not and must not pass sentence too hastily. He should wait until the princes of the kingdom met together, for an insult to the royal majesty brought dishonour to them all and it was by their courage that war was to be waged, just as it was by their advice that peace was to be restored. The princes' advice was especially necessary because the Saxons had already on many occasions deceived him by promising good will and peace. He had fixed 22 October as the date for the princes to assemble the army in Gerstungen for the expedition.[1451] If the Saxons truly repented of the crime that they had committed, let them come there in order to receive in that place whatever judgement the princes of the kingdom considered appropriate to their rash conduct.

When the Saxons were informed of this, they were seized by great apprehension. They all eagerly directed their thoughts and their

---

1449 Archbishop Liemar of Hamburg-Bremen (above n. 798) and Margrave Udo II of the Saxon Nordmark (above n. 168). See Meyer von Knonau (1894) p. 519.

1450 Cf. Archbishop Werner of Magdeburg, letter to Archbishop Siegfried of Mainz and Bishop Adalbero of Würzburg, cited in Bruno, *The Saxon War* c. 48, p. 47: 'Now that so much blood has been shed, let [the king] do what he could have done before the bloodshed. Let him give us the opportunity to meet you and Dukes Rudolf, Berthold and Godfrey and let us set aside our own will and suffer the judgement imposed by your wisdom in any matter in which we seem to you to be guilty.'

1451 See above p. 270 and n. 1429.

endeavours towards appeasing the king's anger by whatever means
they could. Above all their concern was to avert the expedition that
had been planned with such a cruel intention. They recalled how great
a disaster they had experienced from the previous expedition and they
knew beyond a doubt that the renewal of the war after their defeat
would now bring them an even more dangerous enemy. They therefore sent the messengers mentioned above, together with the bishop of
Hildesheim,[1452] and ordered them with all their might to beseech not
only the king but also all the princes to restore peace. They promised
to make complete reparation for their misdeeds, even over and above
what was required by law or was appropriate to their lineage. Furthermore, lest their words should not be trusted, they handed over to the
envoys themselves as many hostages as they wished to take, on whose
account they bound themselves never to break their promises as a
result of carelessness, of danger or of a sudden change in their circumstances. The king, however, learned from secret informers what they
were attempting to do and he tried by all means to deny to the envoys
of the Saxons any opportunity of speaking to him before the preparations for the expedition were complete. He thus averted the possibility
that the princes of the kingdom would be moved by their supplications and their humble promise of reparation and would respond
more mercifully to them. He, on the contrary, considered that it would
better serve both his honour and his wrath, if it could be done, to
revive the old enmities with new pretexts for conflict and to aggravate with fresh strokes the old wound that he feared had been covered
too quickly with a scar. To achieve this, he used a new and carefully
chosen artifice. He pretended that he had been summoned to Hungary
by Salomon, king of the Hungarians, the husband of his sister,[1453] in
order to settle by means of confidential talks the dispute between him
and Geisa, who had driven him out of the kingdom.[1454]

Using the pretext of this journey, the king deceived all the princes of
the kingdom and set out for Bohemia.[1455] He had none of the princes

---

1452 Holder-Egger, *Lamperti Annales* p. 224 n. 3, conjectured that Bishop Hezelo of
Hildesheim (above n. 121), whom Lampert identified as one of the leaders of the
rebellion in 1073 (above p. 176 and n. 900), had been restored to royal favour,
perhaps in Goslar in July (when, according to Bruno, *The Saxon War* c. 53, p. 50,
the king 'had been received by certain of our bishops in triumphal glory').

1453 King Salomon of Hungary (above n. 250), husband of Judith-Sophia (above n. 251).

1454 King Geisa of Hungary (above n. 258).

1455 Lampert alone reported this expedition to Bohemia: see Kilian (1886) pp. 69–70;
Meyer von Knonau (1894) p. 521 and n. 9, dating the expedition in September.

with him except Count Herman of Gleiberg[1456] but he was accompanied
by almost five hundred swiftly moving horsemen, specially chosen for
so important a task, who had left behind the baggage and the other
burdensome apparatus of war and had equipped themselves only for the
journey and for battle. In Bohemia he joined forces with the Bohemian
duke[1457] and army and directed his course to Saxony, following secret
and very difficult roads. He hoped that, when he made his unexpected
attack, he would find them yawning, as the saying goes, and easily
overpower them or, if they offered resistance, he would then have a just
cause for making war on them and for refusing to accept the offered
reparation. He therefore advanced as far as the city of Meissen, situated
on the frontier of Bohemia and Saxony. After he had been peacefully
received into the city by the citizens, he arrested the bishop of that
city[1458] and plundered all his possessions. He declared the bishop guilty
of treason for the sole reason that for the whole period of the Saxon war
he had sent to him no messengers or letters, as evidence that he had
preserved his fidelity to the State.[1459] The bishop was notwithstanding
a man who lived in the poverty befitting a churchman and there was
little or nothing of military ostentation about him. While he might
perhaps wish to oppose the State, he could not bear arms against it and
it was not of great importance whether he was the friend or enemy of
one party or the other.

The king proceeded a little further, burned a number of villages and
received the surrender of very many free born men.[1460] Suddenly the
scouts who had been sent in advance reported that the rumour of his
planned attack had long since reached the Saxons, that they had assembled more than fifteen thousand armed men and had pitched their camp
not far away. They were prepared to engage with them and join battle

---

Lampert's formulation, 'using the pretext of this journey', resembles his account
of the king's reasons for the expedition against Poland in 1073: 'this was a pretext
that he had ready to hand' (above p. 172 and n. 878).

1456 Count Herman II of Gleiberg (above n. 1394). On these specialised military
preparations see Meyer von Knonau (1894) p. 522 and n. 91. Meyer von Knonau
suggested that Herman's being a neighbour of Hersfeld would account for
Lampert's being well informed about this expedition.

1457 Duke Vratislav II of Bohemia (above n. 746).

1458 Benno of Meissen (above n. 494).

1459 Lampert himself had already identified Benno as one of the leaders of the Saxon
rebellion: above, 1073, p. 176 and n. 905.

1460 *Song of the Saxon War* III.256–66, p. 22, gives an imprecise account of an autumn
incursion into Saxony, without referring to Bohemia. See Meyer von Knonau
(1894) p. 524 n. 93.

the next day unless the king voluntarily accepted their offer of amends and their peace conditions. Finally the scouts reported that it would imperil his own safety and that of all his followers if he wished to advance further or even to wait in their camp until the next day, especially since they were hemmed in on all sides and no way of escape was open to them and they could not ward off the danger with armed might because they were unequal in numbers to that great host. All those who were with the king *were struck with consternation and the greatest apprehension.*[1461] They strongly berated the folly of one who – in pursuing his preoccupation with his own success in such an extreme manner and, impatient of delays, in hastening with unbridled presumption to bring to an end a war of many years with one decisive blow – had with childish light-mindedness betrayed himself and his followers to the enemy. Obeying their admonitions, the king returned as quickly as he could to Bohemia, from where he had sallied forth.

As he departed, he was pursued by certain swiftly moving horsemen from the Saxon army, without the knowledge of their princes, and they would have overwhelmed him before he left Saxony, had not Count Bodo[1462] tricked them by means of this stratagem. He had gone to the Saxons as a spokesman from the king to summon them to surrender or, more properly speaking, to entrap them with an empty promise of pardon so that they would not pursue him after his withdrawal. When Bodo departed from the Saxons' camp, he realised that they were carefully following his tracks. He could have returned to the king in a single day's journey but by taking long, circuitous routes and long *roundabout ways,*[1463] he scarcely completed the journey in three days and, as a result of this delay, the king evaded the enemy and was able to escape to safety.[1464] The king was thus freed from danger and after a few days he brought his troops back to Regensburg.[1465] They were *weakened*

1461 Livy II.37.9; III.30.5. See Billanovich (1945) p. 168.

1462 Holder-Egger, *Lamperti Annales* p. 232 n. 3, identified this Count Bodo with the Bodo, steward of Goslar, mentioned above, p. 203 and n. 1061. Meyer von Knonau (1894) p. 525 and Meyer von Knonau (1904) p. 408 identified him as the Bavarian Count Boto of Botenstein.

1463 Martial, *Epigrammaton* IX.100.

1464 Holder-Egger, *Lamperti Annales* pp. 232 n. 4, 273 n. 2, noted the improbably close resemblance between this account and Lampert's later, also uncorroborated, description of the royal incursion into the march of Meissen in 1076 (below p. 329 and n. 1738). In both cases the king is represented as being saved by chance from defeat by the Saxons.

1465 See Kilian (1886) p. 69; Meyer von Knonau (1894) p. 525.

by their exertions and lack of sleep[1466] but especially by hunger and thirst, almost to the point of total exhaustion. By this time the day was close at hand on which the army was to assemble for the expedition. There the king found the envoys of the Saxons, who had now been waiting a long time for his return. By delaying his answer, he kept them long in suspense so that they could not return to their compatriots until the very moment when the expedition was imminent and the enemy's sword was hovering over their necks. It was about this time that Margrave Dedi died,[1467] after being consumed by a long illness. The king gave his march to the Bohemian duke as a reward for the military service that he had performed,[1468] even though Adela, the wife of the margrave,[1469] had shortly before sent him her son[1470] – to whom the march ought to be given according to hereditary succession – as a hostage on her behalf. Moreover the margrave himself after peace had been restored in Gerstungen[1471] had always preserved inviolate his fidelity towards the king and the State.

Meanwhile the Saxons and Thuringians in the ebb and flow of their troubles *fluctuated between hope and fear,*[1472] between peace and war, between threatening and pleading and, although they held frequent consultations, they could not reach a resolution about what they should do, where they should turn and how they should unravel the intricacies of their situation. Some were of the opinion that, since the king had set his mind inexorably on the extermination of the whole Saxon people, they should destroy by fire whatever was left of Saxony and Thuringia after the enemy army had departed and they should withdraw beyond the River Elbe with all their followers. Others thought that they should summon from their land the Liutizi, that people most hostile

---

1466 Livy XXXI.46.14. Meyer von Knonau (1894) p. 525 n. 94 noted the resemblance between this passage and the account of the sufferings of the royal entourage escaping from the Harzburg (above, 1073, p. 184 and n. 962), including Lampert's characteristic reference to 'three days'.

1467 Margrave Dedi of Lower Lusatia (above n. 522). See Meyer von Knonau (1894) p. 526 and n. 96.

1468 Cf. Cosmas of Prague, *Chronica Boemorum* II.39, p. 141. Cf. Meyer von Knonau (1894) p. 526; Schramm (1968) p. 350; Fenske (1977) p. 74. See also below, 1076, pp. 329–30 and n. 1739.

1469 Adela of Louvain (above n. 506).

1470 Henry I of Eilenburg, margrave of Meissen and of Lower Lusatia (✝1103). Cf. *Annalista Saxo* 1070, p. 697. See below, 1076, p. 331 and n. 1746.

1471 See above 1074, p. 215 and n. 1127.

1472 Livy XLII.59.8.

to Christendom,[1473] and use a barbarian army against a barbarous
and implacable enemy. Others suggested that they should rebuild the
castles throughout Thuringia and Saxony that the king had ordered
to be demolished and, *since they could not* defend themselves *by their
weapons,*[1474] they should seek their safety in those inaccessible places
until the wrath of the Lord had burned itself out. But the common
people *transferred* all their hopes *from* weapons *to prayers.*[1475] They had
unhesitatingly and firmly resolved that, if prayers were ineffective, they
would bear any treatment, however shameful and cruel, rather than
engage in conflict and once more hazard a throw of *the uncertain dice of
fortune,*[1476] which they had experienced once before in that unfortunate
battle. The princes, on the contrary, who had originally fanned the flames
of the commoners' fury, eagerly urged and implored them to remember
their former courage and to *bring no reproach on* their *honour.*[1477] they
should not now most shamefully abandon an undertaking that they
had begun with outstanding success. That their enterprise had fared
badly in the first clash of arms was to be explained as follows. They had
neither king nor prince, *under whose leadership and authority* they were
compelled – being bound by an oath of military service – *to wage war*[1478]
and at whose command they pitched camp, advanced into battle, *came to
blows with the enemy*[1479] and performed the rest of the duties required by
military discipline. If this difficulty was removed, henceforward there
would be no king and no army that could not be conquered by the
valour of the Saxons. There was therefore a single remedy for their bad
situation and their much worse future prospects, which would also be a
powerful weapon against the arrogance of their enemies. They should
choose a king for themselves and swear an oath to him that they would
fight to the death for the fatherland, for wives, for children, for the laws
and for their freedom. When they had wasted sometimes seven days,
sometimes fourteen days in continuous discussions concerning these
and other resolutions of the same kind, they returned home, in all cases
more uncertain in their minds than when they had come. Thus after they
had considered everything and investigated everything in the course of

1473 On the Slav confederation of the Liutizi see above p. 66 n. 147.

1474 Livy II.40.2. See Billanovich (1945) p. 168.

1475 Livy III.28.9; IV.10.4. See Billanovich (1945) p. 90.

1476 Cf. Lucan, *Pharsalia* VI.7; Sallust, *Jugurtha* 7, 62. On fortune as a motif in Lampert's
work see Struve (1970a) p. 115 and n. 6.

1477 I Maccabees 9:10.

1478 Livy VIII.12.6; X.18.1. See Billanovich (1945) p. 168.

1479 Livy IX.5.10.

their discussions, they believed – in the light of the recent *memory of the defeat that they had suffered*[1480] – that nothing in their conclusions was safe enough, nothing was reliable enough.

The king came to Gerstungen, according to the agreement, on 22 October. All the bishops and counts of the German kingdom also came there. Duke Theoderic of the Moselle region was present; Duke Gozelo of Lotharingia was present,[1481] accompanied by such a large number of troops, so well provided with military equipment and drawn from the whole region that he governed by such a very strict process of recruitment that they alone seemed entirely to surpass the rest of the king's army in their numbers and the splendour of their military preparations. Other dukes – namely Duke Rudolf of the Swabians, Duke Welf of the Bavarians and Duke Berthold of the Carinthians[1482] – refused their help when the king requested it. For, as they said, they regretted that so much blood had been shed in vain during the previous expedition.[1483] They were also shocked by the king's harsh and implacable spirit, since his blazing anger could not be *extinguished* either by the tears of the Saxons or *by the streams of blood*[1484] overflowing the fields of Thuringia. Nevertheless the rest of the princes, who had assembled in great numbers, had brought together an army that was large and strong enough, although it was very far from equalling the army that the earlier expedition had gathered together.[1485]

The Saxons and Thuringians, now aroused by the extreme danger of their situation, assembled in very large numbers and pitched their camp not far from the royal estate of Nordhausen.[1486] They sent the archbishop

1480 *Ibid.*, XXII.61.13. See Billanovich (1945) p. 170.

1481 Duke Theoderic II of Upper Lotharingia (above n. 1099) and Duke Godfrey IV of Lower Lotharingia (above n. 570). On the proceedings in Gerstungen see Kilian (1886) p. 70; Meyer von Knonau (1894) pp. 527–33; Robinson (1999) p. 102.

1482 Rudolf of Swabia (above n. 203), Welf IV of Bavaria (above n. 630) and Berthold I of Carinthia (above n. 824).

1483 Cf. Bruno of Merseburg, *The Saxon War* c. 54, p. 51: 'For after they returned from the previous battle, Dukes Berthold and Rudolf were moved by divine mercy to show remorse and in fear of God they publicly fasted for forty days and made a firm vow to God that they would no longer fight for the king against the innocent Saxons.'

1484 Livy XXVIII.23.3.

1485 Cf. Bruno, *The Saxon War* c. 54, p. 51: 'Nevertheless the king's army was not as ready for battle as before … and a great part of the earlier host was missing.'

1486 Cf. Bruno, *The Saxon War* c. 54, p. 51: 'Both armies met in the place called Ebra' (southwest of Sondershausen). Both authors refer to the northern part of Thuringia, close to the Harz region.

of Bremen,[1487] the bishop of Hildesheim and Margrave Udo[1488] to meet the king in Gerstungen, urgently requesting that he should dispatch to them princes from his entourage, whom he himself should choose. They were prepared, after consultation with these princes, to give their assent most readily to everything that accorded with justice. The king rejected this request and declared that his princes had not gathered together from such distant regions of the kingdom to pronounce sentence but to call their enemies to account by means of their military might for the injuries that they had all inflicted on the State. The humble supplication of the Saxon envoys with the greatest difficulty extorted from the king his consent to their request but none of the princes would agree to perform the office of royal envoy.[1489] For each of them feared either that they would be branded by the king with treachery if they treated the Saxons too mercifully or that they would be denounced by the Saxons for the offence of lying if they promised them pardon for their wrong-doing, which the Saxons knew without a doubt that they would never obtain from the king. Three days were taken up with these delays.[1490] The envoys continually came and went and dinned the ears of the king and all the princes with the same speeches. The king did not on that account postpone the expedition but drew up the army in battle array, caused the military banners to be carried in front of the army and every day they advanced at a slow pace, laying waste the land.

At length it pleased the king to send to the Saxons the archbishop of Mainz, the archbishop of Salzburg,[1491] the bishop of Augsburg and the bishop of Würzburg.[1492] With them was Duke Gozelo, who exercised the

1487 Liemar of Bremen (above n. 798). Cf. Adam of Bremen, *Gesta*, verse epilogue, p. 282, alluded to Liemar's mediation: 'You bring back peace to the churches, after it was put to flight by ancient disputes; now conflict arises anew and you unite discordant minds with the kiss of peace.'

1488 Hezelo of Hildesheim (above n. 121) and Udo II of the Saxon Nordmark (above n. 168). See above pp. 275–6 and nn. 1449, 1452.

1489 This is contradicted by a letter of Bishop Embriko of Augsburg to Bishop Burchard II of Halberstadt (October 1075), in *Briefsammlungen der Zeit Heinrichs IV.*, pp. 100–1, in which Embriko offered himself 'in friendship' as a mediator, together with the archbishops of Mainz and Salzburg, Bishop Altman of Passau and Duke Berthold of Carinthia.

1490 See Meyer von Knonau (1894) pp. 531 n. 103, 831 and n. 129 on Lampert's 'customary time scheme' of three days of negotiations.

1491 Gebhard, archbishop of Salzburg (1060–88).

1492 Embriko of Augsburg (above n. 366) and Adalbero of Würzburg (above n. 44). Cf. Embriko's letter to Burchard of Halberstadt (above n. 1489), inviting him 'to commit [his] cause to the archbishops of Mainz and Salzburg and to the bishop of Passau and Duke Berthold and in addition to me, the least of these'. According to

greatest authority in that expedition: he was the supreme power and the central point around which all activity turned. For although he was very small in stature, misshapen, with a hunchback, he nevertheless towered above the rest of the princes because of the splendour of his wealth and the number and excellence of his knights but also because of his mature wisdom and perfect eloquence.[1493] The Saxons had wished for precisely these five men to attend their conference since they had learned that they were men of the most steadfast fidelity and truth and the Saxons believed that whatever they promised would undoubtedly be ratified.

When the five men came to the camp of the Saxons, the princes of Saxony *fell at their feet*[1494] and implored them in God's name to have pity on their misfortunes. It was the severity of the king that had first compelled them to dare to perpetrate this monstrous crime and, now that they were defeated and destroyed almost to the point of extermination, with insatiable hatred he condemned them to deadly torments. If, however, they were permitted to defend their innocence as prescribed by the laws, according to judicial procedures and the customs of their ancestors, they would easily refute the accusation and prove that they had not violated the conditions of peace that they had accepted in Gerstungen[1495] by any rash undertaking. If they could not prove it, however, they would not refuse to pay the penalties that the laws and decrees of their ancestors had established for those who were guilty of similar offences. But a new form of cruelty had now been devised, which denied the innocent the possibility of disproving accusations, which would not accept reconciliation, which would not allow reparation to be made. Instead the poison of the king's displeasure, once absorbed, penetrated so deeply into his heart that it could be checked by no other antidote than the extermination of the whole Saxon people. The envoys should therefore remember the changeable character of human affairs and should look to themselves lest the contagion of *this noxious precedent,*[1496] which originated with the Saxons, should perhaps at some time or other infect the rest of the princes of the kingdom. The envoys should so now intervene

---

Berthold of Reichenau, *Chronicle* 1075, p. 137, 'following the reckless persuasions of the bishops, especially those of Mainz and Augsburg, and also of Duke Godfrey and others', the Saxons surrendered to the king.

1493 Cf. the description of Duke Godfrey IV of Lower Lotharingia above 1070, p. 126 and n. 570; below 1076, p. 308 and n. 1643.

1494 Livy VI.3.4; XXXVI.35.3. On Lampert's use of this quotation see above 1073, p. 195 and n. 1021. See also Meyer von Knonau (1894) p. 831.

1495 See above 1074, p. 215 and n. 1127.

1496 Livy II.43.10.

in the unhappy fortunes of the Saxons, they should so mix this cup of *poison and wormwood*[1497] and give it to the Saxons to drink, as men who knew full well that in a short time they also must drink from this same cup. The Saxons, for their part, now that *their hopes had been taken away from them*,[1498] would henceforward pay no heed to their own welfare. They had firmly resolved that they would perform without hesitation whatever they were advised, recommended or ordered to do and they would never again allow the existence of the whole State to be endangered by the zeal shown by others for their party.

To this the five envoys replied that they did not absolutely disapprove of the cause for which the Saxons had first taken up arms against the king and that they were displeased by the king's unyielding hatred and his fixed determination to destroy the Saxons. Nevertheless all the princes of the kingdom had agreed that in the light of the outrage that they had perpetrated against the State – a deed unheard of in recent times or for many centuries in the past – the Saxons could make amends to the king and the State by no other means than by surrendering unconditionally. It would be the envoys' duty, if the Saxons acted on this advice of theirs, to see to it that they experienced no threat to their safety, their honour and their personal possessions as a result of this surrender. The common people of Saxony protested loudly against this speech. It seemed indeed to all of them to be harsh and intolerable to give power and the right of jurisdiction over their lives to a man of whose cruelty they had received such clear proofs. This was he who after the devastation of Thuringia and Saxony, after the killing of many thousands of men, *still breathed threats and slaughter*[1499] and incited all the kingdoms of the world against them. Even in favourable circumstances nothing could ever impose a limit on his anger: not piety, not compassion, not respect for God or men. It would be better for them to engage in open conflict and die in battle like men of courage rather than offer themselves as a ridiculous spectacle to their enemies as exiles, as prisoners, *as victims* slaughtered *like cattle*.[1500] The envoys, on the contrary, continued to press them,[1501] begging them to accept their salutary advice lest that small

1497 Jeremiah 9:15.

1498 Livy III.58.6; XXXV.31.7.

1499 Acts 9:1.

1500 Livy III.47.7.

1501 Lampert subsequently (below, 1076, p. 315 and n. 1683) recorded that Otto of Northeim was also involved in the process of persuasion: 'he had taken such trouble to persuade the rest of the princes to surrender'.

remnant of the Saxon people that had survived the slaughter and the devastation should needlessly despair and go to their ruin. The envoys declared that they felt the very greatest solicitude, if not for the welfare of the Saxons, then for their own reputations. For they would certainly incur a stain on their characters and become subjects of reproach, which would not thereafter be effaced either by the passage of time or by subsequent virtuous conduct, if the least breath of misfortune touched, however slightly, persons who had trusted in their good faith. They would therefore go to the king and learn for certain whether they could pledge their faith and promise a pardon without fear of repudiation and they would report back to them what they had learned the next day.

The king most thankfully welcomed the peace agreement. He promised and – according to a widespread rumour, repeated by very many people – even swore an oath that, if they surrendered, he would take no measures against them except according to the will and the judgement of those through whose efforts and through whose service he had been given this *bloodless victory*.[1502] There were now frequent comings and goings. The Saxons, opposing the advice to surrender, repeatedly called for weapons to be placed in readiness and for the banners to be brought forward for battle because they thought that anything was safer than relying on the faith of the king. But Duke Gozelo and those who were with him showed the greatest energy in these negotiations and they suppressed the uproar, now with threats, now with blandishments. They promised and – because their hearers placed little faith in words – they also confirmed on oath that the Saxons would not experience any loss of life, of liberty, of estates, of benefices or of any other possessions but, after they had shown honour to the king's countenance and the majesty of the kingdom by performing a brief act of reparation, they would immediately be released from their surrender and they would be restored to their homeland and to freedom with no reduction in their rank or circumstances.[1503]

No words, no oaths, no promises could remove the fears of the princes of Saxony. But because *with their inferior numbers and strength*[1504] they had no reasonable hope of meeting the enemy in battle and because the

1502 Livy IV.17.8; VII.8.7. See Billanovich (1945) p. 171.

1503 Cf. Bruno of Merseburg, *The Saxon War* c. 54, p. 51: the envoys promised the Saxons 'that they would remain neither in a harsh nor in a long captivity' and the king swore to his princes 'that at the beginning of next November he would release them all to their homes in peace and with his grace'.

1504 Livy XXXVIII.13.2.

war could not be drawn out any longer – for the people had long ago become weary of war and extremely eager to restore peace[1505] – at last, after long consultations, after many subterfuges, weeping and fetching heavy sighs from the depths of their being, they agreed to surrender and decided *to make trial of* the princes' *good faith* and the king's *mercy*[1506] at the peril of their own lives. When this immediately began to be rumoured throughout the king's army, there was great joy and there were fervent expressions of thanksgiving. They considered the victory to be more distinguished than every other triumph and more splendid than any plunder because they were freed of the necessity of fighting once again with those men who in the first attack had extinguished almost all the lights of Swabia and Bavaria and who in their defeat inflicted lamentable losses on the victors.

The next day the king took his seat to receive the Saxons in the middle of an open and level field in the place called Spier.[1507] The whole army was formally invited to view this spectacle and in the midst of the densely packed crowd was an open space, where the Saxons would be visible to the whole army when they passed through it. Firstly, the princes of Saxony and Thuringia were conducted into the field in order: Archbishop Wezilo of Magdeburg, Bishop Bucco of Halberstadt, Otto, formerly duke of Bavaria, Duke Magnus of Saxony and his uncle, Count Herman, the count palatine Frederick, Count Theoderic of Katlenburg, Count Adalbert of Thuringia[1508] and the counts Ruotger,[1509] Sizzo,[1510] Berengar[1511] and Bern.[1512] Then followed all the free-born men, who *because of the renown of their family* or *the splendour of their wealth stood out*[1513] somewhat

---

1505 Cf. above pp. 274 and n. 1448, 280. See also Fenske (1977) p. 56.

1506 Livy XLIV.9.1.

1507 'On 27 October': Kilian (1886) p. 70; '25 October': Holder-Egger, *Lamperti Annales* p. 238; 'at the end of October': Meyer von Knonau (1894) p. 533. Lampert alone provided the place-name Spier (south of Sondershausen). See Meyer von Knonau (1894) pp. 533–4; Fenske (1977) p. 56; Giese (1979) pp. 161–2; Robinson (1999) p. 102.

1508 Archbishop Wezilo (Werner) of Magdeburg (above n. 899), Bishop Bucco (Burchard II) of Halberstadt (above n. 235), Otto of Northeim (above n. 261), Magnus Billung (above n. 621), Herman Billung (above n. 890), Frederick II of Goseck, Saxon count palatine (above n. 227), Theoderic II of Katlenburg (above n. 910), Adalbert of Ballenstedt (above n. 911).

1509 Ruotger, count in the Werratal in western Thuringia (above n. 614).

1510 Sizzo, a Thuringian count, probably of Schwarzburg-Käfernburg. See Fenske (1977) p. 81 and n. 309.

1511 Perhaps Berengar, count of Sangerhausen. See Fenske (1977) p. 81.

1512 Count Bern has not been identified.

1513 Einhard, *Life of Charles the Great* c. 2, p. 4.

among the people. As had been agreed, they surrendered unconditionally to the king.[1514] The king entrusted them to his princes to be kept under guard, individual Saxons to individual princes, until a general consultation could be held and a decision was reached about them. Shortly afterwards he broke the treaty and, making light of the binding oath by which he had committed himself, he caused them to be conveyed away to Gaul, Swabia and Bavaria, to Italy and Burgundy.[1515] He also divided their benefices among those of his knights whose services he had particularly relied on in the Saxon war.[1516] Remaining for a few days in Thuringia, he repaired the castle of Hasenburg and placed a garrison there, as a precaution against an uprising after his departure on the part of the fickle and volatile common people.[1517] In addition he set a time-limit for all free-born men *who had* either *been absent by chance* or withdrawn themselves *through fear*.[1518] If they had not come to surrender before that date, they were to be pursued with fire and sword, as public enemies, by all men who cared for the welfare of the State. After disbanding his army, the king thus returned as a conqueror and celebrated the nativity of St Martin in Worms.[1519]

Meanwhile the king was urgently pressed by the Roman pontiff through frequent legations and by the clergy of Bamberg through their continual supplications to provide a ruler for the church of Bamberg, which had now been vacant for a long time.[1520] For although the former bishop, as was mentioned above,[1521] lived on the more distant properties of the

---

1514 Cf. *Song of the Saxon War* III.286, p. 23: 'they surrendered to the king without any conditions'.

1515 Cf. Berthold of Reichenau, *Chronicle* 1075, p. 137: the king 'commanded that they should be brought to various fortresses and prisons and should be held captive there'; Bruno of Merseburg, *The Saxon War* c. 55, p. 51: 'The king placed our princes in various prisons.' The *Chronicon Gozecense* I.13, pp. 145–6 (composed *ca.* 1150), referring to 'the broken treaty', claims that the Saxon count palatine Frederick was sent to Pavia.

1516 Cf. Berthold, *Chronicle* 1075, p. 137: the king 'then seized the possessions of certain of them, claiming to do so by royal authority'; Bruno, *The Saxon War* c. 56, p. 52: 'he lavished on his parasites the property of our men who were captives, which ought to have remained inviolate if their fidelity to him had been inviolate'.

1517 Cf. above p. 274 and n. 1448. For Hasenburg see above n. 991. Cf. Bruno, *The Saxon War* c. 56, p. 52: the king 'then entrusted the castles and whatever fortifications Saxony still possessed to his followers'. See Meyer von Knonau (1894) pp. 539–40 and n. 120.

1518 Livy II.23.12.

1519 11 November. See Kilian (1886) p. 70; Meyer von Knonau (1894) p. 540.

1520 Gregory VII, *Register* III.3 (20 July), III.7 (early September), pp. 246–7, 258–9.

1521 Herman I of Bamberg (above n. 449). See above p. 251 and n. 1324.

church under the protection of his knights, contrary to the prohibition, he nevertheless made no attempt to exercise the powers of the episcopal office, being deterred by his scruples arising from the papal anathema. He had always stood at the king's side in the most helpful manner in peace and in war, when the State was tranquil and when it was in confusion. When the rest of the princes of the kingdom were *offended because of* the king, he alone was *never offended* but, in all the disasters that had befallen the king, he had *borne the burden and heat of the day*[1522] with him with unshaken loyalty. The king, however, never said the slightest word to contradict the bishop's detractors. On the contrary indeed he did not seem to be at all reluctant to hear the accusations against the bishop because – so very many men explained his attitude – his purpose was that this deposition should open up the way for proceedings against the bishop of Worms and some other bishops.[1523] For it was supposed that he had long been devoting his utmost efforts to contriving a false accusation against them in revenge for their previous rebellion.

The king therefore went to Bamberg and caused Rupert, provost of Goslar,[1524] to be consecrated in Herman's place on the nativity of St Andrew the apostle.[1525] Rupert was a man whose reputation among the people was very bad because he was on the most intimate terms with the king and was always privy to all his secrets and he was believed to be the foremost instigator of the measures that the king had undertaken in the State that were wrong and at variance with the royal dignity.[1526] The knights of the church of Bamberg indeed most violently condemned the fact that in the lifetime of the previous bishop, who had neither

1522 Matthew 26:33; 20:12. On Herman's loyalty to the king cf. *D.H.IV* 270 (March 1074): 'Bishop Herman ..., who in all our trials faithfully adhered to us'.

1523 Adalbert of Worms (above n. 626). On 'the king's hatred for the bishop of Worms and certain other men who had displeased him during the Saxon war' see above 1074, p. 233.

1524 Rupert, bishop of Bamberg (1075–1102).

1525 30 November. Cf. Gebhard of Salzburg, *Epistola* (1081) p. 279: 'when the king had celebrated the birthday of the apostle Andrew in Bamberg' (cited in Hugh of Flavigny, *Chronicon* II, p. 431). See Kilian (1886) pp. 70–1; Meyer von Knonau (1894) pp. 541–2.

1526 Cf. below 1076, p. 320: Rupert 'was rougher and of a more savage temper than the rest of his intimates and had often proved his loyalty towards him in adversity'; Berthold of Reichenau, *Chronicle* 1075, p. 138: 'a certain Rupert, ... who was his chosen confidential adviser, but who was unacceptable to almost all the clergy and people'; Bruno of Merseburg, *The Saxon War* c. 15, p. 22: after Herman's deposition 'the bishopric was given to another man, not one who was more worthy of the bishopric because of his life and his wisdom but one who was in every respect a stronger supporter of the king's misdeeds'.

been summoned to a synod in accordance with canon law nor judged according to the canons, another bishop had been appointed to succeed him, thus defiling the chastity of the church of Bamberg. As for the clergy, although they were extremely displeased by the character of the man who had been consecrated – for indeed he did not *have a good report from those that are outside*[1527] – they nevertheless preferred to have anyone whatsoever rather than receive again the man against whom they had appealed to the apostolic see and about whose way of life and whose appointment they had published a mournful tragedy, to be recited in a theatre whose audience was this whole world.[1528]

The next day, when the king held a meeting with the princes to elect the abbot of Fulda,[1529] there was a violent dispute between the abbots and the monks, who had flocked together in great numbers from various places. As in a contest in officially convened public games, each man ran the race to the utmost of his ability. One man *promised mountains of gold,*[1530] another promised vast benefices from the lands of Fulda, a third promised more than the customary services to the State: none of them paid any heed to moderation or discretion in his promises. *What morals, what times!*[1531] O *abomination of desolation standing* in the place *where it ought not to stand*[1532] and Mammon, in our times publicly *sitting in the Temple of God and exalting himself above every so-called god or object of worship.* [1533] Abbots and monks were dragged headlong by the spirit of ambition to such an extent that they were *not deterred* from their covetousness by reverence for Christianity or by the habit of a strict religious community and ultimately not even *by the recent example*[1534] of the bishop of Bamberg, whom they had seen the day before deprived both of episcopal office and of communion for no other reason than that he had made his way into holy orders by the unlawful distribution of wealth.

1527 I Timothy 3:7.

1528 Cf. Meinhard of Bamberg, *Letter* 32, in: *Briefsammlungen der Zeit Heinrichs IV.*, p. 229. On Lampert's use of the image of the theatre see Struve (1970a) pp. 122–4 and above p. 47.

1529 1 December. The vacancy was caused by the death of Abbot Widerad on 16 July: cf. above p. 258. See Meyer von Knonau (1894) pp. 546–7; Feierabend (1913) pp. 133–4; Vogtherr (1991) p. 455.

1530 Terence, *Phormio* I.2.18. The same quotation is used in Lampert's polemic against monks obsessed with 'money and profit' above, 1071, p. 153 and n. 759.

1531 Cicero, *Oratio I in Catilinam* I.2. See above p. 6 and n. 25.

1532 Mark 13:14.

1533 II Thessalonians 2:4.

1534 Livy XXXI.12.2.

The king thoroughly detested their shameless conduct, as was fitting. As he was being urged from all sides in unmannerly fashion by men who dinned his ears with their prayers, suddenly – moved, it is believed, by the divine spirit – he summoned into his presence a certain monk of Hersfeld, named Ruozelin.[1535] This monk had come to the court at the command of his abbot on the business of his monastery. He suspected nothing at all and he almost died of shock at the unexpected and miraculous event, when the king offered him the pastoral staff. The king was the first to elect him abbot and he then strenuously urged the others, both monks and knights, to consent to his election. When all who were present had given their assent with joyful shouts of approval, he was commanded to accept the office of abbot. After he had put up a long resistance, now pleading his inexperience, now his bad health, now the absence of his own abbot, at last, giving way to the prayers and earnest entreaties of the bishops who were present, he reluctantly agreed to accept the office.

There was a similar case after the recent death of Abbot Udalric of Lorsch.[1536] The monks and the knights had come to the court unanimously agreed on the election of the provost[1537] and they believed that the king would not think differently from them because of the many services by means of which, while he was provost of the monastery, he had with the greatest courtesy and eagerness earned the esteem and love of the king. The king, however, suddenly took the hand of another monk of the same monastery, whose name was Adalbert,[1538] who had arrived with the other brethren and who had never imagined such a development. The king drew him forward and gave the pastoral staff to him, *astounded as he was by the strangeness of the event,* while all the rest were *struck with amazement.*[1539]

When Bishop Herman of Bamberg learned that another man had been put in his place as bishop, since all hope of recovering his office in future had now been taken from him and there was no longer any way open

1535 Ruozelin (Ruthard), abbot of Fulda (1075–96). A hostile reference to Ruozelin's election is found in Herrand of Halberstadt, *Epistola de causa Heinrici regis* p. 289 (1094/5).

1536 Udalric of Lorsch (above n. 352) +24 November: see Meyer von Knonau (1894) pp. 547–8; Feierabend (1913) pp. 101–2.

1537 Holder-Egger, *Lamperti Annales* p. 241 n. 3, identified this provost as Sigelaus. Cf. *Chronicon Laureshamense* p. 409.

1538 Adalbert, abbot of Lorsch (1075–7).

1539 Livy I.47.9; I.59.2.

to him of fending off the judgement of the Roman pontiff, he withdrew into the monastery named Schwarzach. There he received the habit of the holy way of life under Abbot Ekbert.[1540] He immediately set out for Rome, taking his abbot with him. After he had humbly performed penance for his disobedience at the apostolic see, he was both freed from excommunication and obtained permission to exercise the priestly ministry but not the office of bishop.

The death of Archbishop Anno of Cologne[1541] made this year, which was already *marked by many disasters*,[1542] to be predominantly a year of mourning. After a long illness, by means of which the Lord had refined his *chosen vessel* in *the furnace*[1543] of the tribulations of this transitory state to be purer than *gold*, cleaner than *fine gold*,[1544] he endured a blessed death on 4 December and was removed from men to the angels, from mortality to immortality. This was demonstrated by the signs and wonders that the Lord deigned to make manifest every day at his tomb in order to refute those shameless men who, shortly before, were enviously slandering his life, which was most holy and entirely untouched by any blemish of this world, as far as is possible for a human being, and who tried to blacken with false rumours the *pearl of great price*,[1545] which had long been intended for the diadem of the King of Heaven.

He was educated both in divine and in secular literature in the school of the church of Bamberg.[1546] When he came to maturity, he became known to Emperor Henry, not through the recommendation of his

---

1540 Abbot Ekbert of Münsterschwarzach (above n. 718) died 1 December 1075, according to evidence cited by Meyer von Knonau (1894) p. 96 n. 105. Cf. Berthold of Reichenau, *Chronicle* 1075, pp. 137–8: 'After a pretended conversion he was soon reconciled by the pope and entered the monastery of Schwarzach, where he made his profession as a monk.' See also Meyer von Knonau (1894) p. 544; Cowdrey (1998) pp. 126–7.

1541 For Lampert's attitude towards Anno of Cologne (above n. 139) see Meyer von Knonau (1894) pp. 599–601, 808; Struve (1970a) pp. 107–12. The ensuing account of Anno's personality and career was used extensively in the biography of Anno composed by a monk of Siegburg: see Wattenbach – Holtzmann (1967–71) pp. 649–50; Jakobs (1968) p. 255 n. 7; Struve (1969) pp. 71–84. Cf. *Vita Annonis archiepiscopi Coloniensis* I.2–5, 16–17, 19–21, 22–4, 28, 33; II.10, 20–1, 23, 25, pp. 467, 474–7, 480, 487, 492, 495, 497.

1542 Livy IV.12.6. Cf. III.32.4.

1543 Proverbs 17:3; Acts 9:15.

1544 Isaiah 13:12.

1545 Matthew 13:46.

1546 Anno was educated in Bamberg, either in the cathedral school or in the church of St Stephan (a canonical foundation). See Struve (1969) pp. 22, 28; Lück (1970) pp. 60–2; Märtl (1991) p. 331.

ancestry – for he was born of a family of middling rank[1547] – but solely because of the pre-eminence of his wisdom and virtue. He was received into the palace by the emperor and in a short time he had attained the foremost position in the emperor's favour and regard before all the clergy who laboured in the palace.[1548] He was loved by all good men for this reason in particular: that he held fast absolutely to what was just and virtuous and in all legal cases he defended the principle of justice, as far as was possible in his position, not speaking only for the sake of flattery like the rest but contradicting others with great freedom. Besides his intellectual gifts and the distinction of his character, he was splendidly furnished with physical advantages. He was tall in stature, with a handsome face and *adroit in speech* and he showed the greatest endurance in vigils and in fasting. In short, he was abundantly *provided* with the gifts of *nature* to perform every kind of *good*[1549] work. After spending only a few years in the palace, he obtained the archbishopric of Cologne,[1550] accompanied by the high hopes of the emperor and of all those who knew him. Thereafter he conducted himself in all the affairs both of the Church and of the State as one who was equal to the office that he had received and he appeared conspicuous among the rest of the princes of the kingdom by virtue both of the pre-eminence of his more elevated office and of every kind of virtue. He punctiliously *rendered unto Caesar the things that are Caesar's and unto God the things that are God's.*[1551] For he displayed the majesty and the secular pomp of the name of Cologne before the eyes of the people almost more ostentatiously than any of his predecessors and yet amidst all the great commotion of business his indomitable spirit never slackened in its devotion to heavenly concerns. He tortured his body with frequent fasting and forced it into submission. He very frequently spent the night in prayer and walked barefoot through the churches, *content*[1552] *to have only a single*

1547 For Anno's membership of the Swabian family of Streusslingen see Lück (1970) pp. 9–31. Zielinski (1984) pp. 22–3 dismissed the suggestion that Lampert's term 'of middling rank' indicated the status of 'unfree knights' or *ministeriales*. On this suggestion see Lück (1970) p. 26 n. 118. On Lampert's 'aristocratic outlook' and his hostility towards the low-born advisers of Henry IV see Struve (1970a) pp. 39–45.

1548 On Anno's service in the imperial chapel of Henry III see Fleckenstein (1966) pp. 245–6, 261–4, 268–70, 277–8, 294–5, identifying him as a chaplain, a canon of Bamberg and Hildesheim and provost of Goslar.

1549 Livy II.45.15; III.12.5. Struve (1970a) p. 106 and n. 38 compared this passage with the description of Gunther of Bamberg, above, 1065, p. 107 and n. 442.

1550 Cf. above, 1056, p. 65.

1551 Luke 20:25.

1552 Sulpicius Severus, *Vita Martini* c. 2.

boy in attendance. He spent the day indeed in settling private or public business but he spent the whole night in the service of God. *Great was* his *benevolence* towards the poor, towards pilgrims, towards clergy and monks and his generosity was *extraordinary.*[1552] He did not overlook a single congregation in his diocese but, when he departed this life, he left each one enriched with estates, buildings, revenues by a special act of donation. It was assuredly believed beyond all doubt by everyone that, since Cologne was founded, *the wealth and renown* of the church of Cologne *had* never *grown*[1553] so greatly through the exertions of a single bishop. In judging the cases of his subjects, he was not diverted from the truth either by hatred or by favour but in all instances he always followed without any deviation the straight line of justice that was set down for him. He was *not partial in respecting the person of the poor* or in *honouring the person of the mighty*[1554] so as to subvert justice. Then indeed he preached the word of God so clearly, so excellently, that his discourse seemed to be able to draw tears even from hearts of stone and, when he delivered his exhortations, the whole church always echoed with the wailing and lamentation of the remorseful crowd.

He founded two congregations of clergy in Cologne entirely at his own expense: one in honour of St Mary in the place called *ad Gradus*, the other in honour of St George the martyr outside the city wall.[1555] He also established three congregations of monks at his own cost in different places: one on the mountain that is named Siegberg after the river that flows by it; another in the land of the Slavs in the place called Saalfeld;[1556] the third in the region of Westphalia, in the place called Grafschaft.[1557] He provided them all with the most majestic buildings and adorned them with the most exquisite church ornaments and enriched them with the most extensive estates, sufficient for the needs of the many brethren. When he perceived that in all the monasteries of the German kingdom that ancient fervour for the discipline of the *Rule* had grown absolutely cold and that the monks had transferred all their thoughts and exertions from the common life to their own personal concerns,

---

1553 Livy I.3.4; XXI.7.3; XLIV.25.2.

1554 Deuteronomy 1:17; Leviticus 19:15. Cf. above, 1072, p. 157 and n. 788.

1555 On the canonical foundations at Mariengraden and St George see Oediger (1954–61) pp. 249, 280–1 (nos. 862, 970); Semmler (1959) p. 178; Schieffer (1991) pp. 8–10.

1556 Siegburg, on the River Sieg (1068?), and Saalfeld (1063–4): cf. above, 1071, p. 152 and n. 749.

1557 The abbey of Grafschaft in the Sauerland (1072): see Oediger (1954–61) pp. 298–9 (no. 1014); Semmler (1959) p. 64.

his *mind was* gravely *troubled* by the anxious thought that despite this enormous *expenditure*[1558] he would achieve nothing worthy of God.

Meanwhile it happened that he went to Rome on the business of the State. While he was travelling through certain regions of Italy to support the princes of that kingdom so that they did not desert the king,[1559] he turned aside to pray in a certain monastery, the name of which was Fruttuaria.[1560] There he admired the way of life of the monks, which was very strict and accorded with the traditions of the *Rule*, and on his return he brought away with him some of those who were most practised in the service of God and installed them in Siegburg in order to transmit the model of that same discipline to Gaul.[1561] Since the earlier monks of Siegburg, whom he had received from St Maximin, did not wish to comply with their ordinances, he sent them back in an honourable manner to their former place.[1562] The rest of the bishops of Gaul imitated his action. They summoned monks – some from Gorze, some from Cluny, some from Siegburg, some from other monasteries – and each bishop established a new school of divine service in his monasteries.[1563] In short, the desire to imitate this fortunate development so grew in strength that we now see few monasteries in Gaul that have not already submitted to the yoke of this new institution.

When he saw that his monks were living a life of the strictest discipline, such as he had encountered in Fruttuaria, and that the rumour of their way of life, spreading far and wide, had fired many men with contempt for the world and inspired them to submit to their direction to be trained in the way of God, the archbishop gave heartfelt thanks to God

---

1558 Livy I.55.7.

1559 Referring to Anno's third journey to Italy above, 1070, p. 125 and n. 565, Lampert reported that Anno had been 'summoned by the lord pope' (Alexander II).

1560 The abbey of Fruttuaria (diocese of Ivrea, Piedmont). Cf. *D.H.IV* 233, issued for Fruttuaria 'through the intervention' of Empress Agnes and Archbishop Anno of Cologne (15 June 1070); privilege of Pope Alexander II, *JL* 4675 for Fruttuaria, 'at the request of the beloved and venerable Archbishop Anno of Cologne' (1070), *Italia Pontificia* 6/2, 151 (no. 10). For the influence of Fruttuaria on monastic reform in Germany see Semmler (1959) pp. 35–7, 241–2, 255–7; Jakobs (1968) pp. 242–59 and above p. 18.

1561 According to *Vita Annonis* I.23, p. 476, Anno brought twelve monks from Fruttuaria. See Semmler (1959) p. 35.

1562 On the significance of the abbey of St Maximin in Trier as a reforming monastery see Hallinger (1950) pp. 1041–2; Semmler (1959) p. 35.

1563 Cf. above, 1071, p. 154 and n. 765. See Jakobs (1961) pp. 152–89; Jakobs (1968) pp. 1, 258 and n. 21, 271–90 ; Jakobs (1973) pp. 102–8; Schmid (1973) pp. 295–319. On 'Gaul' (Germany) see above n. 241.

that he had *not been confounded in* his *hope*.[1564] He also devoted the most
careful attention to their needs so that they lacked nothing that would
assist bodily weakness. He honoured and revered them as his lords and
was so submissive and obedient not only to the abbot[1565] but also to the
deacons of the monastery[1566] that, however deeply involved he was in
important business of his own or of the State, he at once freed himself
from his task and arose at their first command and performed all that
they commanded as if he were a common serf. Whenever he could be
present, he himself every day carried the food, which had been prepared
with the greatest care; he himself set the food before them and mixed
their drink and he himself waited on them as they ate, more ready and
quicker than any servant to serve in every way. He also observed the
silence and the other customs of the monastery, whenever he lodged
with them as their guest, and did so with care and anxiety, as if he had
to answer for his errors every day in their chapter and have judgement
passed on him. This was his endeavour and this his conduct in Siegburg
as in Saalfeld and in Grafschaft.

He was frequently on the most hostile terms with the king and he
rebuked him loudly and with the utmost ferocity for the many measures
contrary to justice and the public good that were undertaken in the
State every day at his command or with his permission. Hence the king
in his rage very often threatened to destroy all his possessions with
fire and sword[1567] but he also very often approached him with humility
and softened his anger with the most handsome promises. He offered
to make over to him legal rights and power over both himself and the
whole kingdom if only he found him faithful towards him and not so
hostile towards all his wishes. To this the archbishop replied that his
service would always be forthcoming in all the measures attempted by
the king that were correct and accorded with royal magnanimity. If,
however, the king was corrupted by the suggestions of wicked men
and wished to act wrongly and contrary to the laws and ordinances
of his ancestors, the archbishop could not be bought at any price or
be compelled by any terror to give his consent and lend his authority
to these measures. At one time indeed he was received by the king on
terms of the greatest intimacy and virtually as a partner in the kingship

1564 Psalm 118:116.

1565 Erpho, abbot of Siegburg († 1076).

1566 According to *Rule of Benedict* c. 21, a *decanus* was a monk placed at the head of a
group of ten monks. See Niermeyer – van de Kieft (2002) p. 400.

1567 Cf. above, 1074, pp. 234–5 and nn. 1236, 1239.

but at another time, since he hated intensely and attacked with great ferocity the wrongdoing in the kingdom, he was turned out of the palace with reproaches and insults and the whole strength of the kingdom was brought into action *to annihilate his name*[1568] completely. His dispute with the king was protracted for very many years through these violent changes. Reason could not check the licentious conduct of the king nor his advancing age nor the chiding of his friends. Instead from day to day he became worse and, breaking through all the restraints of human – not to say Christian – decency, he rushed headlong into every shameful act that came into his mind.[1569] Since the princes were now overwhelmed with fear, there was no one who dared to rebuke, even with the slightest word, the sinner who was indiscriminately bringing all divine and human laws into confusion.

At length the archbishop concluded that the king's wickedness had come to a head and that his disposition towards evil deeds was so ingrained that it could not be corrected by time or reason and almost a year before the outbreak of the Saxon war he begged to be freed henceforward from the external business of the State.[1570] When he had obtained permission to depart, he withdrew into the monastery of Siegburg and there he spent what remained of his life in vigils and fasting, in prayers and almsgiving and he never went anywhere else unless he was drawn away by an extreme and unavoidable emergency.[1571] If the reader wishes to know more about what he achieved or what he suffered in the course of administering the State, he should return to the earlier pages of this little book and he will find the individual events set out in detail in the order and according to the time at which they happened.

1568 Livy VI.2.2. Holder-Egger, *Lamperti Annales* p. 246 n. 2 described this passage as 'a mendacious exaggeration'.

1569 Cf. above, 1073, p. 164.

1570 Cf. above, 1073, p. 163 and n. 828, referring to 25 December 1072.

1571 Lampert identified Anno as a mediator in Saxony above, 1073, p. 192 and n. 1004, p. 204 and n. 1070. Meyer von Knonau (1894) p. 591 n. 182 noted that none of the charters issued by Anno in the last two years of his life was dated in Siegburg. According to *Vita Annonis* II.24, p. 496, Anno went to Saalfeld during the winter of 1074–5, returning to Siegburg by way of the abbey of Hersfeld, where he celebrated the Feast of the Purification (2 February 1075), an incident surprisingly not mentioned by Lampert. According to Struve (1970a) p. 109, this account of Anno's life in Siegburg 'corresponded to Lampert's ideal of sanctity' and was intended as a deliberate contrast with Henry IV, 'the embodiment of evil'. Struve (pp. 111–12 and n. 79) noted that Lampert's description of Anno's asceticism closely resembled his account of the piety of Archbishop Lul of Mainz, founder of Hersfeld: *Vita Lulli* c. 7, pp. 317–18.

But the pious Lord, who *rebukes and chastens those whom* He *loves*,[1572] also permitted this soul so dear to Him, to be tried by many misfortunes before the day of his summons so that the furnace of the troubles of this transitory world *purged* him *of* all *the dross*[1573] of worldliness. Firstly, when the Saxon war began, a storm of the severest persecution overwhelmed his brother, Archbishop Wezilo of Magdeburg, and his nephew, Bishop Bucco of Halberstadt.[1574] Since Archbishop Anno did not *assist* the king against them *with sufficient energy*[1575] – to be sure, he was inhibited by the laws of nature and family affection – *he became an object of hatred and suspicion*[1576] and he was accused of oath-breaking and treachery by the king,[1577] who was intent upon the destruction of the whole Saxon people. The citizens of Cologne, to whom shortly before he had been especially beloved and welcome, were induced by gifts and promises to kill him.[1578] After this evil had somehow or other been overcome, two of his servants, who lived in his house as trusted members of the household, plotted against him and they would have butchered him, he meanwhile suspecting nothing of the kind, had not the mercy of God prevented this evil deed. He gave to another servant – whom he had bound to himself on terms of special trust by the gifts that he had conferred on him – a personal letter, which, to ensure greater secrecy, he had written with his own hand on a writing tablet, to be delivered to the bishop of Halberstadt. In this letter he comforted and instructed his nephew, who was being buffeted and almost shipwrecked by the great storms of misfortune that assailed him from all sides. But the servant conjectured from such a painstaking and secret process of preparation that the letter's contents were hostile to the king and the State and he brought it to the king. Thereafter the king reproached the archbishop with the letter as evidence of a breach of fidelity[1579] and

1572 Revelation 3:19.

1573 Isaiah 1:25.

1574 Wezilo (Werner) of Magdeburg (above n. 899), Bucco (Burchard II) of Halberstadt (above n. 235).

1575 Livy XXII.6.2. See Billanovich (1945) p. 100.

1576 Livy XLI.24.18; XLIV.24.7.

1577 Cf. above 1073, p. 188 and n. 984; 1074, pp. 212 and n. 1113, 222; 1075, p. 257 and n. 1349. See Meyer von Knonau (1894) pp. 593–4, 805; Jenal (1975) pp. 398–402.

1578 Holder-Egger, *Lamperti Annales* p. 247 n. 3, drew attention to Lampert's account of the rising, above, 1074, p. 222 and n. 1162, which states that 'it is uncertain ... whether it was the doing of those who desired to take revenge on the archbishop on behalf of the king'. See Meyer von Knonau (1894) pp. 805, 807; Stehkämper (1991) p. 99.

1579 Holder-Egger, *Lamperti Annales* p. 248 n. 1 linked this passage with Lampert's

he planned, if there was an opportunity, to kill him and bring about the complete destruction of all that he possessed. There was another man among his servants, whom he had secured for the service of the church of Cologne through his own efforts and whom he had always cherished with the most tender affection and had enriched with all kinds of property, to a degree even above the rank in which he was born. That man was suddenly puffed up with the insolence of a serf and began to reject the yoke of servitude to the church. He *declared* himself *to be a free man*[1580] by means of the unreasonable proceedings of a secular court, which was a great affront to the archbishop.

Then indeed he *was made bitter*[1581] and he *suffered wound upon wound*[1582] through the deaths of many who were dear to him[1583] so that such a violent whirlwind of tribulation could shake even a heart of stone and a building *founded on a rock.*[1584] Finally *Satan* was also given power over his flesh and he was *afflicted with loathsome sores*[1585] on both feet so that the putrid flesh gradually turned into liquid. Then the skin came away and, when the flesh had wasted away, the bones were laid bare in a manner horrible to behold. This disease first devoured the feet, then the legs and the thighs in a pitiable way and so after long torments it penetrated to the vital organs.[1586] Then it sent the soul, purer than *silver, tried, refined* and *purified seven times*[1587] from this *house of clay*[1588] into *a house not made with hands, eternal in the heavens.*[1589]

---

reference above, 1074, p. 235 and n. 1239, to 'the offence of which [Anno] had been accused, namely betraying the State'. On this letter to Bucco (Burchard) of Halberstadt see also Meyer von Knonau (1894) pp. 805–6; Jenal (1975) pp. 400–1.

1580 Livy VIII.5.4. There seems to be a reference to this incident in *Vita Annonis* II.10, p. 487.

1581 Revelation 10:10.

1582 Job 16:15.

1583 *Vita Annonis* III.1–3, pp. 498–9, identified 'the boy Anno', the son of the archbishop's sister (✝23 May), and Herman, the prior of Siegburg (✝1 June). See Meyer von Knonau (1894) p. 595.

1584 Luke 6:48.

1585 Job 2:7.

1586 *Vita Annonis* III.5, p. 500 refers to 'a pain in the right foot' and states that Anno's sufferings lasted 'about nine weeks'. See Meyer von Knonau (1894) p. 595.

1587 Psalm 11:17.

1588 Job 4:19.

1589 Mark 14:58; II Corinthians 5:1.

Almost half a year before he departed this life[1590] a clear revelation
had made him certain of this outcome. For it seemed to him that he
was entering a certain house that was resplendent with great beauty
inside and out. And lo! there were seated in judges' chairs, as though
formally summoned to a council, Archbishop Heribert of Cologne,[1591]
Archbishop Bardo of Mainz,[1592] the archbishops Poppo and Eberhard
of Trier,[1593] Bishop Arnold of Worms[1594] and very many other bishops
of Gaul, some of whom he had known during their lifetimes, others he
knew of only by reputation or from his reading. They were all *clothed
in* episcopal *robes*[1595] and wore garments as white *as snow.*[1596] It seemed
to him that he himself was clad in totally white and precious garments
but part of his shining clothing, that namely by which the breast was
covered, was covered by a dark patch, filthy and unbecoming, and this
greatly detracted by its unpleasantness from the splendour of the rest of
his attire. He was suffused with blushes on this account and he tried to
cover and conceal it with his hand so as not to offend the sight of those
who looked at him. He saw moreover that a seat of remarkable beauty
had also been prepared for him among them. When, glowing with joy
and exultation, he hastened to occupy it, Bishop Arnold of Worms rose
and in a gentle voice forbade him to sit down. He said that the venerable
fathers who sat there would not admit him into their company precisely
because this filthy stain sullied his garment. When he was commanded
to leave the place, he went out in tears, his spirit utterly broken. That
same bishop followed him and said, '*Be of good cheer,*[1597] father. Simply
give orders that this stain darkening your garment should be washed
away as quickly as possible because in a few days time *you will obtain
your wish*[1598] and receive permission to sit down in the fellowship of
this blessed house and of the holy fathers whom you have beheld.' The
next morning, when he had described the vision to a certain member
of his household, the latter wisely interpreted the vision and said, 'This

---

1590 I.e. June 1075. But below, p. 300 and n. 1600, Lampert stated that 'he had seen the
    vision during Lent' (18 February – 4 April).
1591 Heribert, archbishop of Cologne (999–1021).
1592 Bardo of Mainz (above n. 91).
1593 Poppo, archbishop of Trier (1015–47); Eberhard of Trier (above n. 474).
1594 Arnold (Arnulf) I of Worms (above n. 38).
1595 Revelation 7:9.
1596 Exodus 4:6.
1597 I Kings 21:7.
1598 Livy VII.40.6.

stain besmearing your garment is, I believe, father, nothing other than the memory of the wrongdoing of your citizens, who drove you out of Cologne last year[1599] and whose action you ought long ago, with a view to God's compassion, to have pardoned. This memory – if I may say so by your good leave – has taken hold of your heart more strongly than is reasonable and consumes your mind with the bitterest affliction, contrary to divine law. It darkens and obscures the brightness of the rest of your holy way of life with its offensive gloom.' The archbishop was convinced by the evidence of his own conscience and did not contradict what he heard. He humbly confessed his guilt and immediately sent messengers in all directions to summon to him all the citizens of Cologne whom he had excommunicated and driven out of the city as a punishment for the wrong that had been done to him. On the following Easter festival[1600] – for he had seen the vision during Lent – he most generously restored to them not only ecclesiastical communion but also all the possessions that had been taken from them. Thus that fierce storm, raised by the devil, that had shaken the whole of Cologne, was at rest. The father acknowledged his sons, the sons their father; the archbishop was freed from bitterness, the people from fear and disquiet, the city from desolation.

The archbishop had from the beginning provided for his burial in Cologne in the church of blessed Mary called *ad Gradus*. Afterwards he was offended by the foolhardiness of the people of Cologne in raging against him with unheard-of fury and he considered that not only his spirit but also his body should be transferred from Cologne to Siegburg and he decided by all means to be buried there. When the day of his summons was approaching and he was lying sick in Cologne and was at the end of his strength, he learned that the people of Cologne were very much aggrieved that they were to be cheated of a treasure that was so much desired. Recovering his spirits a little, he sat up in his bed and allowed the archbishop's pallium to be placed on him so that his words would have more authority. He then charged the members of his household under oath, calling on God to witness that they should not allow him to be placed anywhere other than Siegburg. What he commanded was therefore performed.[1601] For he

1599 Cf. above, 1074, pp. 222–8.

1600 5 April. Lampert alone recorded this reconciliation of Anno and the citizens. See Meyer von Knonau (1894) p. 593 and n. 186; Oediger (1954–61) pp. 314–15 (no. 1046); Schieffer (1991) p. 15.

1601 *Vita Annonis* III.8, p. 501, places Anno's action at a much earlier stage of his illness. The burial took place in Siegburg on 11 December. See Meyer von Knonau (1894) pp. 596–8.

died soon afterwards[1602] and with *the greatest splendour*, through the great endeavours of the clergy and people and amidst the loud *lamentations of the matrons*[1603] of Cologne, he was brought to Siegburg and buried in the middle of the church. There every day many favours of heavenly assistance are shown through his intervention to believers who request them.

1076

The king celebrated Christmas in Goslar.[1604] He had summoned all the princes of the kingdom there to hold a general consultation and reach a decision about the princes of Saxony, who had come to surrender. Apart from the duke of the Bohemians,[1605] however, very few princes arrived. Nevertheless from those who had come the king demanded and obtained an oath that after his death they would elect as their king no one except his son, who was still a child of tender age.[1606] There Otto, the former duke of Bavaria, was released from the terms of his surrender after giving his two sons[1607] as hostages on his behalf. He was received by the king not only into favour but also into a relationship of so great an intimacy that henceforward the king communicated to him all his plans both concerning personal matters and concerning the State on more familiar terms than the rest of his close advisers.[1608]

1602 4 December. See Meyer von Knonau (1894) p. 597 and n. 195.

1603 Livy II.16.7.

1604 25 December 1075. Cf. Berthold of Reichenau, *Chronicle* 1076, p. 142; Bernold of St Blasien, *Chronicle* 1076, p. 255; Bruno of Merseburg, *The Saxon War* c. 57, p. 52. See Kilian (1886) p. 71; Meyer von Knonau (1894) p. 583.

1605 Duke Vratislav II of Bohemia (above n. 746). Cf. Berthold, *Chronicle* 1076, p. 142: 'the Saxons were greatly enraged against him and not entirely faithful to him'; Bruno, *The Saxon War* c. 57, p. 52: 'he summoned the bishops of his party and celebrated Christmas ... in no festive spirit'. See Meyer von Knonau (1894) p. 583; Robinson (1999) p. 104.

1606 Conrad (above n. 1088). Cf. Bernold of St Blasien, *Chronicle* 1076, p. 255: 'The king ... compelled certain men to swear that they would elect his son to the kingship after him.' See Meyer von Knonau (1894) p. 584; Goez (1996) p. 4; Robinson (1999) pp. 103–4.

1607 Probably the younger sons of Otto of Northeim (above n. 261), Siegfried and Cuno, because their elder brother, Henry 'the Fat', seems (on the evidence of *D.H.IV* 277) to have been performing the office of count in the Germarmark at this time: see Lange (1961) pp. 58–60 and n. 268.

1608 Cf. Bruno, *The Saxon War* c. 57, p. 53: 'he was frequently admitted to the king's counsels and thanks to his wisdom in a short time he brought it about that the king himself decided whatever pertained to the royal honour especially on [Otto's] advice. Finally he now began to regard as his most faithful adviser him whom he had considered his fiercest enemy.' See Meyer von Knonau (1894) p. 585 n. 177;

There was no mention of the rest of the Saxons who had surrendered.

The clergy and people of Cologne had also flocked there in great numbers to elect an archbishop for themselves. The king offered them a certain Hildolf, a canon of Goslar,[1609] and he eagerly pressed them to elect him. They resisted with all their might, objecting that he was a man of very small stature with a contemptible countenance, that he was low-born and that he could lay claim to none of the intellectual or physical qualities befitting so great an ecclesiastical office.[1610] This shameful affair inspired such intense hatred against Hildolf on the part of all those who were in the royal court that, whenever he appeared in public, they all assailed him with uncouth shouts and songs, as if he were some monster of ancient times, and threw stones and dirt at him or whatever else chanced to be found by the furious people. But the king recalled the firmness of character of Archbishop Anno and his invincible opposition to his criminal endeavours and he deliberately devoted his efforts to appointing a successor to Anno whose readiness to serve him he could exploit at will to achieve everything that he wished. When after long and strenuous efforts he could by no means obtain his election, the king sent the men of Cologne back to their homes without achieving their purpose. He commanded them to return to his presence in the middle of Lent, in a state of mind less ill-advised, if that was possible.[1611] He solemnly declared that, as long as he lived, they would have either Hildolf or no one as their archbishop.

Also present in Goslar were the legates of Pope Hildebrand,[1612] who gave notice to the king that he was to appear before a synod in Rome on the Monday of the second week in Lent[1613] to defend himself against the

---

Lange (1961) pp. 58–9; Fenske (1977) pp. 62–3.

1609 Hildolf, archbishop of Cologne (1076–8).

1610 Cf. Berthold of Reichenau, *Chronicle* 1076, p. 138: 'a canon of Goslar and a royal servant, who was with difficulty appointed by royal authority, against the protests of the clergy and people'; Bernold of St Blasien, *Chronicle* 1076, pp. 254–5: '[Anno's] equal neither in birth nor in character'. See Meyer von Knonau (1894) pp. 646–7; Zielinski (1984) p. 26; Schieffer (1991) pp. 15–16.

1611 6 March: see below p. 309.

1612 Not the legates of Pope Gregory VII (above n. 194) but the king's own envoys returning from Rome, Radbod, Adelpreth and Gotteschalk, who brought the pope's ultimatum letter of 8 December 1075, *Register* III.10, p. 267. They arrived on 1 January 1076, according to Bernold, *Chronicle* 1076, p. 255. See Meyer von Knonau (1894) pp. 612–13; Cowdrey (1998) pp. 133–5; Robinson (1999) pp. 140–3.

1613 21 March 1076. The Lenten synod probably took place from 14 to 20 February. For the actual message of the pope to Henry IV, cf. Gregory VII, *Epistolae Vagantes* 14, p. 38: through the envoys, 'his own vassals', 'we secretly admonished him

charges that were made against him. If he did not do so, he should know that he would without any delay be cut off from the body of holy Church by papal excommunication on that very same day. This legation moved the king to extreme anger. After the legates had been driven away with violent invective,[1614] he at once commanded the bishops and abbots who were in his kingdom to assemble in Worms on Septuagesima Sunday. He wished to discuss with them if any course of action lay open to him to depose the Roman pontiff;[1615] for he believed that his own safety and the stability of the kingdom hinged entirely on Hildebrand's ceasing to be pope.

At that same time it happened that at the instigation of Satan the pope was struck by a very heavy misfortune. A certain prefect of the city of Rome named Quintius,[1616] who was extremely *eminent* throughout Italy *by virtue of the distinction of his birth* and the splendour of his *riches*,[1617] made many unlawful inroads on the possessions of the Roman Church. When complaints against him were brought to the pope, the latter very frequently rebuked him in mild terms but, when these private reproofs

---

to perform penance for his offences' and dismiss his excommunicated advisers. According to 'divine and human laws', the king's offences deserved excommunication and deposition but 'if he wished to receive our admonitions and correct his life', Gregory would 'rejoice in his salvation and honour'. Cf. the version of the message given by Bernold of St Blasien, *Chronicle* 1076, p. 255: Gregory informed Henry 'that he would be excommunicated in the next Roman synod if he did not come to his senses'; and Bernold, *De damnatione scismaticorum* III, p. 49: 'King Henry ... knew in advance that he would be excommunicated in the next Roman synod'. (similarly Berthold of Reichenau, *Chronicle* 1075, p. 140). Anti-Henrician polemicists like Lampert argued that the king, having been summoned to the synod and having failed to attend, deserved excommunication and deposition according to canon law. The pro-Henrician polemicist Wido of Ferrara, *On the schism of Hildebrand* I.3, p. 537, summarised the Gregorian argument: 'after [the king] had been summoned once and again and, to speak the truth, very frequently commanded to come to Rome and after he had for a long time strongly resisted and had refused to come to his senses, [the pope] ... excommunicated him and removed him from the office of kingship.' Cf. *Vita Altmanni episcopi Pataviensis* c. 13, p. 233.

1614 Cf. Berthold of Reichenau, *Chronicle* 1076, p. 143: Henry was 'greatly angered after the departure of [Radbod, Adelpreth and Gotteschalk]'.

1615 24 January 1076. Lampert subsequently reported that Gregory VII 'was ordered to resign the papal office', which is corroborated by Henry IV, *Letters* 10–12, pp. 13, 15, 17 (below p. 306 and n. 1630). Zimmermann (1970) pp. 121–31 argued that Henry IV planned the pope's deposition, as Lampert claims here, but could not obtain a sentence of deposition from the council of Worms and therefore called on him to abdicate.

1616 Cencius Stephani (†1077), son of the Roman prefect Stephen. The Roman prefect at this time was another Cencius (†1077), son of the prefect John Tiniosus. See Borino (1952) pp. 373–440; Cowdrey (1998) pp. 326–8.

1617 Einhard, *Life of Charles the Great* c. 2, p. 4.

achieved nothing, he finally excommunicated him,[1618] thinking that he might at least by this means restrain his wickedness. This measure, however, drove Quintius into even greater insanity. On the very night of Christmas, in the company of armed men, he unexpectedly burst into the church in which the pope, clad in his pontifical vestments, stood at the holy altar, celebrating the liturgy of the mass.[1619] He seized the pope by the hair – it is monstrous even to say it – and violently dragged his victim with many insults out of the church. Before the rumour of the event could spread through the city and the people could rush out in great numbers to bring help, he carried the pope off to a strongly fortified house. The news of such a dreadful deed immediately *filled the whole city.*[1620] On all sides *there was a call to arms.*[1621] Rich and poor, noble and low-born, all unanimously came running and in the darkness of daybreak they at once set to work with all their might to storm the house of Quintius. If the latter had not – foreseeing the disaster that threatened him – hastened to release the pope, they would have pulled down the house to its foundations and killed everyone in it. The fury of the violently excited crowd was with great difficulty held in check through the intervention of the pope.[1622] The Romans reacted to what had been done with extreme anger and destroyed all the possessions of Quintius with fire and sword both inside and outside the walls. Quintius himself, on the other hand, was no less active in perpetrating acts of military daring, burning and destroying all the possessions of the Roman church that he could reach. Thus this conflict lasted for many days with heavy losses on both sides.[1623]

1618 According to Paul of Bernried, *Life of Pope Gregory VII* c. 46, p. 293, Cencius was excommunicated by Alexander II. Cf. the versions of Cencius's relations with Gregory VII in Bonizo of Sutri, *To a Friend* VII, pp. 227–8, 231; Beno of SS Martino e Silvestro, *Gesta Romanae ecclesiae* I.8, p. 372. See Meyer von Knonau (1894) pp. 421–2; Cowdrey (1998) p. 326.

1619 Cencius abducted the pope during the midnight mass of Christmas Eve 1075 in the basilica of S. Maria Maggiore. Cf. Berthold of Reichenau, *Chronicle* 1076, pp. 142–3; Bernold of St Blasien, *Chronicle* 1076, p. 255; Bonizo of Sutri, *To a Friend* VII, pp. 232–3; Paul of Bernried, *Life of Pope Gregory VII* cc. 49–56, pp. 295–301. See Meyer von Knonau (1894) pp. 586–7; Borino (1952) pp. 431–6; Cowdrey (1998) p. 327.

1620 Livy III.69.2; V.39.4; XXII.56.4. Cf. Berthold, *Chronicle* 1076, p. 143; Paul of Bernried, *Life of Pope Gregory VII* c. 51, p. 297.

1621 Livy III.50.11. See Billanovich (1945) p. 67.

1622 Cf. Bernold, *Chronicle* 1076, p. 255; Bonizo, *To a Friend* VII, p. 233; Paul of Bernried, *Life of Pope Gregory VII* c. 56, p. 301.

1623 According to Berthold, *Chronicle* 1076, p. 143, Cencius 'fled from the city by night', 'seized a very strong fortress in the neighbourhood and there he lived by robbery,

On the appointed day the king came to Worms. The bishops and abbots also came in very large numbers.[1624] It was also convenient for the transaction of such important business that one of the Roman cardinals appeared. This was Hugh, nicknamed 'the White', whom a few days earlier the pope had removed from his office because of his foolishness and his disorderly conduct.[1625] He brought with him something like a tragedy on the subject of the life and appointment of the pope with theatrical inventions. These concerned his origins, his way of life from his earliest youth, the corrupt manner in which he gained possession of the apostolic see and the shameful acts, incredible to relate, which he committed both before and after he received the papacy. They most gratefully accepted the testimony of the cardinal, as though it was sent to them from heaven, and they were very ready to follow his counsel.[1626] They pronounced judgement that a man who had polluted his life with such disgraceful acts and such great offences could not be pope and did not now possess and had at no time ever possessed the power of binding and loosing according to the privilege of the Roman see.

While all the rest of the bishops unhesitatingly subscribed the document of his condemnation, Bishop Adalbero of Würzburg and Bishop Herman of Metz[1627] resisted for some time, saying that it was

---

plunder and bloodshed ... for two years'. See Borino (1952) pp. 436–7; Cowdrey (1998) p. 327.

1624 24 January 1076: see Kilian (1886) p. 71; Meyer von Knonau (1894) p. 613. For the attendance of the bishops in Worms cf. Henry IV, *Letters* appendix A, p. 65. On the council of Worms see Meyer von Knonau (1894) pp. 613–28; Schneider (1972) pp. 146–53; Cowdrey (1998) pp. 135–8; Robinson (1999) pp. 143–6; Gresser (2006) pp. 142–7.

1625 Hugh Candidus, cardinal priest of S. Clemente (?1049–85), cardinal bishop of Palestrina (?1085–99). Bonizo of Sutri, *To a Friend* VII, p. 234 and Donizo of Canossa, *Vita Mathildis* I, p. 377, also placed Hugh Candidus at the council of Worms. Bonizo claimed (p. 230) that Hugh had been deposed at the papal synod of Lent 1075 but there is no reference to him in the synodal proceedings (Gregory VII, *Register* II.52a, pp. 196–7). See Lerner (1931) pp. 50–1; Hüls (1977) p. 159.

1626 Cf. Bonizo, *To a Friend* VII, p. 234: 'taking the advice of Hugh Candidus, [Henry] sent a letter, which he forced his bishops to subscribe, renouncing the lord pope'. Hugh's allegations appear in the letter of the German prelates at the council of Worms in Henry IV, *Letters* appendix A, pp. 65–8. On Lampert's use of theatrical imagery see Struve (1970a) p. 123 and n. 53 and above p. 47.

1627 For the presence in Worms of Adalbero of Würzburg (above n. 44) and Herman of Metz (above n. 822) cf. Henry IV, *Letters* appendix A, p. 65. *Chronicon episcoporum Hildesheimensium* c. 17, p. 854 recorded the secret resistance of Hezelo of Hildesheim. Cf. Bruno of Merseburg, *The Saxon War* c. 65, p. 57: the king 'compelled them to renounce their subjection and obedience to Hildebrand.... The few who were the originators of this plan did so willingly but very many wrote the letter of renunciation in fear of death.'

extremely unsuitable and contrary to the principles of canon law that any bishop should be condemned in his absence, without a general council being held, without the legally required and suitable accusers and witnesses, when the offences with which he was charged were not yet proven and this applied even more emphatically to the case of the Roman pontiff, against whom no accusation by any bishop or archbishop was to be accepted.[1628] But Bishop William of Utrecht, who was a very staunch supporter of the cause of the king, issued violent threats, saying that they should either subscribe the condemnation of the pope together with the rest of the bishops or immediately renounce the king, to whom they had promised fidelity on oath. This bishop was at that time much loved and highly esteemed by the king and the king had made him responsible, after himself, for the administration of all private and public affairs. He was a man of very great learning in secular literature but so swollen with pride that even he could scarcely tolerate himself.[1629] In the name of all the bishops and abbots who had assembled there a letter full of insults was therefore sent to Rome, in which the Roman pontiff was ordered to resign the papal office, which he had usurped in defiance of the laws of the Church, and was informed that whatever he enacted, commanded or decided after that day would be regarded as invalid.[1630]

The envoys, making a supreme effort to hasten their journey, as they were commanded to do, entered Rome on the day before the holding of the synod that had been announced and they delivered the letter.[1631] They

---

1628 A summary of the regulations in the Pseudo-Isidorean Decretals intended to inhibit judicial proceedings against bishops and of the decree of Pseudo-Symmachus (501) that the pope could not be judged: see Robinson (1988) p. 269; Zimmermann (1968) pp. 2–3. On Lampert's use of the term 'general council' see Gresser (2006) p. 577.

1629 On the character of William of Utrecht (above n. 369) cf. Bruno, *The Saxon War* c. 74, pp. 76, 77: 'an eloquent man'; 'that wise man, honourable in all things, had he not been infected by the poison of avarice'; Jocundus, *Translatio sancti Servatii* c. 74, p. 121: 'most learned in divine and human literature, most admired among the friends of the king'.

1630 Cf. Henry IV, *Letter* 11 (to Gregory VII), p. 15: 'I command you to step down'. Cf. also Letter 10 (to the Romans), p. 13: 'you are to compel him to step down, if he refuses to do so'; Letter of the German prelates at Worms in Henry IV, *Letters* appendix A, p. 68: 'henceforward you will not be regarded as pope by any of us.'

1631 The bishops of Speyer and Basel and Count Eberhard 'the Bearded' brought the letters of the king and the prelates to Piacenza, where a council of Italian bishops called on the pope to abdicate. Roland, a canon of Parma, then brought to Rome the letters informing the pope of the conciliar decisions. See Meyer von Knonau (1894) pp. 629–30; Cowdrey (1998) pp. 138–9; Robinson (1999) p. 147; Gresser (2006) pp. 147, 149.

then performed the rest of their office, according to their instructions, with a speech that was no less abusive than what was written in the letter.[1632] The pope was unmoved by the harshness of the message. The following day,[1633] when the clergy and people had assembled at the synod in great numbers, the pope caused the letter to be read out for them all to hear. Then, according to the decision of all the bishops who had assembled there, he excommunicated the king[1634] and with him Archbishop Siegfried of Mainz, Bishop William of Utrecht and Bishop Rupert of Bamberg.[1635] As for the rest of those who had participated in this conspiracy, the pope set a date[1636] by which they were to present themselves in Rome to offer a defence of this new and extraordinary rebellion against the apostolic see. If they did not do so, they would receive the same sentence of excommunication as the others. The pope had moreover long before excommunicated Bishop Otto of Regensburg, Bishop Otto of Constance, Bishop Burchard of Lausanne,[1637] Count

1632 Cf. Empress Agnes, letter to Bishop Altman of Passau in Hugh of Flavigny, *Chronicon* II, p. 435: 'The envoys of my son the king came into the synod and in the presence of all they told the pope on my son's behalf that he should rise and renounce the apostolic see, which he had acquired not canonically but by robbery.' Cf. also Bonizo of Sutri, *To a Friend* VII, p. 234; Donizo of Canossa, *Vita Mathildis* I, pp. 377–8.

1633 The Lenten synod probably took place from 14 to 20 February (see above n. 1613). The synodal protocol gives no precise dates: Gregory VII, *Register* III.10a, pp. 268–71. Like Lampert, Bruno of Merseburg, *The Saxon War* c. 68, p. 60, and Bonizo, *To a Friend* VII, p. 235, placed the sentence of excommunication 'on the following day'. See Meyer von Knonau (1894) pp. 632–45; Cowdrey (1998) pp. 140–2; Robinson (1999) pp. 148–9; Gresser (2006) pp. 149–56.

1634 Cf. the synodal protocol: *Register* III.10a, pp. 270–1: 'excommunication of Henry, king of the Germans'. Holder-Egger, *Lamperti Annales* p. 255 n. 1, noted that 'Lampert did not say – what I do not believe that he was unaware of or omitted by accident – that the king was deprived of the kingship and that his subjects were absolved from the oath taken to him'.

1635 The synodal protocol records the excommunication of Siegfried of Mainz (above n. 210) and his suspension from his office: *Register* III.10a, p. 268. The protocol does not specifically mention William of Utrecht or Rupert of Bamberg (above n. 1524) but suspends from their offices those bishops 'who willingly consented to [Siegfried's] schism' (p. 268). See Gresser (2006) pp. 153–4 and n. 264.

1636 The synodal protocol defers the suspension of those bishops 'who did not willingly consent' to the proceedings at Worms until 1 August, on condition that before this date they or their envoys 'offered satisfaction' in the pope's presence (pp. 268–9).

1637 There is no other report of a papal excommunication of Burchard, bishop of Lausanne (1056–88) or of Otto of Regensburg (above n. 245). In the case of Otto of Constance (above n. 743) cf. Bernold of St Blasien, *Pro Gebhardo episcopo Constantiensi epistola apologetica* c. 4, p. 109: 'Pope Gregory VII … deprived Bishop Otto of Constance by synodal judgement of office and communion', referring to the Lenten synod of 1076; Berthold of Reichenau, *Chronicle* 1076, p. 153. See Meyer von Knonau (1894) p. 642 and n. 34; Gresser (2006) p. 154 and n. 267.

Eberhard, Udalric and some others whom the king used as advisers in preference to all others.[1638]

When Duke Gozelo of the Lotharingians was on the frontier of Lotharingia and Flanders in the city called Antwerp, he was murdered[1639] – so it was believed – through the cunning of Count Robert of Flanders.[1640] For one night, when all were at rest and he had withdrawn to satisfy a need of nature, an assassin stationed outside the house stabbed him through the buttocks and fled in all haste, *leaving the weapon in the wound.*[1641] The duke survived for barely seven days after receiving the injury; he departed this life on 27 February and was buried next to his father[1642] in Verdun. He was a great source of strength and of great influence in the German kingdom since (as has often been said already),[1643] although he appeared contemptible because of the smallness of his stature and his hunchback, he nevertheless far surpassed the rest of the princes in the splendour of his wealth and the numbers of his knights, men of the greatest courage, and also in the maturity of his judgement and finally in the moderation that characterised his whole life.

When the conference in Worms was at an end, the king hurried back to Goslar.[1644] There he satisfied the anger that for a long time had been

1638 Probably Count Eberhard 'the Bearded' (above n. 641) and Udalric of Godesheim (above n. 1036), two of the 'five members of the household of the king of the Germans, on whose advice churches are sold', excommunicated by Gregory VII at the Roman synod of Lent 1075 (*Register* II.52a, p. 196). They had already been excommunicated by Alexander II in 1073: see Robinson (1999) pp. 125, 360–1.

1639 The murder of Gozelo-Godfrey IV of Lower Lotharingia (above n. 570) was placed in Vlaardingen by *Chronicon sancti Huberti Andaginensis* c. 31, p. 588. Cf. Sigebert of Gembloux, *Chronica* 1076, p. 363, Jocundus, *Translatio sancti Servatii* c. 56, p. 115, and Laurence of Liège, *Gesta episcoporum Virdunensium* c. 7, p. 494: 'in Frisia'. See Meyer von Knonau (1894) pp. 651–2 and n. 54; Mohr (1976) pp. 62–6; Werner (1991) pp. 401–2; Robinson (1999) pp. 147–8.

1640 Robert I of Flanders (above n. 654). Cf. *Chronicon sancti Huberti Andaginensis* c. 31, p. 588: 'by certain close friends of Count Robert of Flanders'. According to *Annales Egmundenses* 1075, pp. 447–8: 'by a certain Giselbert, the personal servant of Theoderic, son of Count Florentius' (i.e. by a servant of Count Theoderic V of Holland, Robert I's stepson). Bernold of St Blasien, *Chronicle* 1076, p. 256, identified the assailant as 'a certain cook'. See Meyer von Knonau (1894) pp. 650–2 and n. 54; Werner (1991) p. 387.

1641 Livy I.40.7.

1642 Duke Godfrey III, 'the Bearded' (above n. 33). Cf. Laurence of Liège, *Gesta episcoporum Virdunensium* c. 7, p. 494. The date is given as 26 February by *Annales Egmundenses* 1075, p. 448, and the local evidence cited by Meyer von Knonau (1894) p. 652 n. 55.

1643 See above 1070, p. 126 and n. 570; 1075, pp. 282–3 and n. 1493.

1644 See Kilian (1886) p. 71; Meyer von Knonau (1894) p. 645.

raging incessantly against the Saxons and he inflicted on them every kind of cruelty. He removed to the farthest regions of the kingdom those Saxon princes who had come to surrender[1645] and permitted his supporters to plunder their property according to their pleasure.[1646] Every day he issued the most ferocious commands, urging the submission of those who had not yet surrendered and he threatened that, if they did not give themselves up as soon as possible, they would be attacked with fire and sword and driven far away from the land of their birth. Then he restored all the castles that he had ordered to be destroyed in the previous year,[1647] which involved a supreme effort and much toil and hardship on the part of the local inhabitants. He also constructed new castles on all the mountains and hills throughout Saxony that seemed to offer only the slightest possibility of warding off attack[1648] and he placed garrisons in those castles that the Saxons had surrendered into his power. And *evils,* misfortune *and desolation increased*[1649] throughout all Saxony and Thuringia beyond anything in the memory of *our ancestors long ago.*[1650]

When he was on the point of departing from Goslar, on 6 March he gave the archbishopric of Cologne to Hildolf, as he had stubbornly intended to do from the first. Only three of the clergy of Cologne were present and also very few of the knights. Indignation held back the rest of the clergy and people from coming to give their assent.[1651] The king consulted those who were present about his election almost contemptuously and, as the usual saying is, *in an off-hand manner*[1652] and he would

---

1645 See above 1075, p. 287 and n. 1515.

1646 Cf. Bruno of Merseburg, *The Saxon War* c. 56, p. 52: 'Then he lavished on his parasites the property of his captives, which should have remained theirs unimpaired, if his faith had been untainted.'

1647 See above 1074, p. 218 and n. 1145.

1648 Lampert subsequently identified 'another castle on the mountain called the Steinberg', below p. 315 and n. 1681. No other source refers to the building of new castles. Bruno, *The Saxon War* c. 56, p. 52, reported that the king 'commended the cities and castles and whatever fortifications he held in Saxony to his followers and commanded them to exercise a tyranny throughout the whole of the region'. See Meyer von Knonau (1894) p. 645 and n. 40; Fenske (1977) p. 29.

1649 I Maccabees 1:10; Hosea 12:1.

1650 Esther 14:5.

1651 On the appointment of Hildolf (above n. 1609) see above p. 302 and n. 1611. Cf. Berthold of Reichenau, *Chronicle* 1076, p. 138: 'against the protests of the clergy and people'. See Kilian (1886) p. 71; Meyer von Knonau (1894) p. 647; Schieffer (1991) p. 16.

1652 Seneca, *Epistolae* 10.

certainly have treated them with ridicule and derision if they had not immediately approved him. And lest perhaps a commotion might be generated against him by dissension among the people because of a deferral of his consecration, he at once set out for Cologne. There he caused him to be consecrated by Bishop William of Utrecht and, so that the latter would not cause any delay in the consecration, he promised the bishopric of Paderborn to his nephew.[1653]

The king celebrated Easter in Utrecht[1654] and there he conferred the duchy of Lotharingia on his son Conrad[1655] but granted the march that is called Antwerp to Godfrey, the nephew of Duke Gozelo and son of Count Eustace,[1656] an energetic young man, very eager for military action.

At that same time Duke Rudolf of the Swabians, Duke Welf of the Bavarians, Duke Berthold of the Carinthians, Bishop Adalbero of Würzburg, Bishop Herman of Metz and many other princes[1657] met to consult together and discuss what should be done about the great misfortunes that assailed the State. For the king still remained after the Saxon war the same man that he had been before: nothing had changed his inconstancy, his cruelty, his intimacy with and reliance on the most wicked men. His outstanding victory over the Saxons had achieved only this: that he obtained power and jurisdiction over all their lives and he

1653 For Henry IV in Cologne see Kilian (1886) p. 71; Meyer von Knonau (1894) p. 648. The kinsman of William of Utrecht (above n. 369) has not been identified. Cf. Berthold, *Chronicle* 1076, p. 147: 'The bishop of Utrecht, however, had previously received this [bishopric] from the king to be given as a gift to a certain kinsman of his, on condition that he would not oppose the consecration of the bishop of Cologne ... but that he himself would consecrate him.' Berthold added that William was subsequently 'deceived' by the king, who broke his promise. (Bishop Imad of Paderborn had died on 3 February.) See Meier (1987) p. 38.

1654 27 March. Cf. Berthold, *Chronicle* 1076, p. 147; Bruno of Merseburg, *The Saxon War* c. 74, p. 76. See Kilian (1886) p. 71; Meyer von Knonau (1894) pp. 650, 658–9.

1655 Conrad (above n. 1088). Cf. Berthold, *Chronicle* 1076, p. 146: 'The king caused his own son, who was barely two years old, to rule over [the duchy].'

1656 Godfrey V (of Bouillon), duke of Lower Lotharingia (1087–96), advocate of the Holy Sepulchre (ruler of Jerusalem, 1099–1100), son of Ida, sister of Gozelo-Godfrey IV of Lower Lotharingia (above n. 570) and of Eustace II, count of Boulogne (†1086/8). See Meyer von Knonau (1894) pp. 658–9; Mohr (1976) pp. 62–6; Robinson (1999) p. 148.

1657 Rudolf of Swabia (above n. 203), Welf IV of Bavaria (above n. 630), Berthold I of Carinthia (above n. 824), Adalbero of Würzburg (above n. 44), Herman of Metz (above n. 822). Berthold, *Chronicle* 1076, p. 146 identified the conspirators as 'the patriarch of Aquileia, the bishops of Salzburg, Passau, Worms ... and Würzburg and almost all the Saxons and the dukes Rudolf, Berthold and Welf and a considerable number of the other princes of the kingdom'. See Meyer von Knonau (1894) pp. 673–4 and n. 88; Robinson (1999) p. 152.

rampaged with complete impunity, destroying all their possessions and committing every shameful act that came into his head. The princes felt that no hope and no defence was left for them in the future if they chanced – as was only human – to offend him, since he had perpetrated such abominable cruelties against those who had surrendered, against the oath that he had sworn[1658] and the promise made by the princes. This consideration had greatly perturbed not only the princes at this meeting but all the princes of the kingdom and especially those on whose advice the princes of Saxony had put themselves in danger. A great conspiracy therefore came into being and grew in strength from day to day, since they all drew courage and confidence above all from the fact that a daily stream of messengers from Italy reported that the king had been excommunicated by the Roman pontiff.[1659] Encouraged by this news, the bishop of Metz and many others, unknown to the king, permitted some of the princes of Saxony, whom they had received from the king to be kept under guard, to return to their homes as free men.[1660]

Bishop William of Utrecht (as was mentioned above)[1661] stubbornly defended the cause of the king, contrary to what was good and right. In his zeal for the king's party he furiously delivered many defamatory speeches against the Roman pontiff on almost every feast day during the celebration of mass, calling him an oath-breaker, an adulterer and a false pope and declaring that he had frequently been excommunicated both by him and by the rest of the bishops.[1662] Shortly after the king had

---

1658 See above 1075, p. 287 and n. 1515.

1659 According to Bruno of Merseburg, *The Saxon War* c. 74, p. 76, it was in Utrecht that the envoy of Henry IV first brought news of the excommunication. See Meyer von Knonau (1894) p. 660. The earliest dated letter of Gregory VII informing the Germans of the excommunication is that of 25 July 1076 (*Register* IV.1, pp. 289–92) but the undated letter, *Epistolae Vagantes* 14, pp. 32–40, was probably earlier. Gregory's detailed defence of the excommunication, *Register* IV.2, pp. 293–7, is dated 25 August and addressed to Herman of Metz.

1660 Cf. Bruno, *The Saxon War* c. 82, p. 78: 'When King Henry's excommunication and deposition became known, all those who held our men captive ... sent them back to their homeland without a ransom and without Henry's knowledge.' Lampert subsequently identified Herman Billung as one of the princes released 'by the good natured persons who were keeping them prisoner': below, p. 314. See Meyer von Knonau (1894) pp. 675–6.

1661 On the partisanship of William of Utrecht (above n. 369) see above p. 306 and n. 1629.

1662 According to Hugh of Flavigny, *Chronicon* II, p. 458 and Bruno, *The Saxon War* c. 74, p. 76, William of Utrecht excommunicated Gregory VII on Easter day 1076. See Meyer von Knonau (1894) pp. 660–2; Schneider (1972) p. 166; Robinson (1999) p. 149.

departed from Utrecht, where he had spent the feast days of Eastertide, the bishop was suddenly seized by a very serious illness. Oppressed by the most severe torments of body and soul, he cried aloud with pitiful lamentations to all those who were present that through the just judgement of God he had lost both this present life and eternal life. This was because he had exerted himself to assist the king in all the wrongdoing that he had planned and, in the hope of obtaining his favour, he had heaped harsh reproaches on the Roman pontiff, a most holy man of apostolic virtues, although he knew full well that he was innocent. With these words (so they maintain) he died without receiving communion and without making any act of penitence.[1663] Conrad, the chamberlain of the archbishop of Mainz, succeeded him in the bishopric.[1664] The bishopric of Paderborn, however, was obtained by Poppo, the provost of Bamberg, whose partisanship and whose exertions had been principally responsible for the deposition of Bishop Herman of Bamberg from his bishopric.[1665]

Rupert, the former abbot of Reichenau, had received from the bishop of Bamberg the government of a certain monastery in the territory of Alsace, named Gengenbach.[1666] While he was striving there with excessive eagerness for temporal riches according to his custom, being preoccupied in overcoming the poverty of the place through his own efforts, he was killed, together with another, a young monk[1667] whose character was full of promise and who had followed him from the monastery in Bamberg. The perpetrators were the serfs of the monastery of Gengenbach, whom the abbot, wishing to defend the possessions of

---

1663 27 April. Cf. Bernold of St Blasien, *Chronicle* 1076, p. 256: William, 'who had greatly reviled the pope, was punished after Easter by sudden death'; Bruno, *The Saxon War* c. 74, p. 76: 'in the same place in which [William] disparaged the Roman pontiff, ... he himself was seized by an evil disease'; Berthold of Reichenau, *Chronicle* 1076, p. 147; Hugh of Flavigny, *Chronicon* II, pp. 458–9; Paul of Bernried, *Life of Pope Gregory VII* c. 80, pp. 323–4. On the statement that William died excommunicate and impenitent cf. Gregory VII, *Register* IV.6, pp. 303–4. See Meyer von Knonau (1894) pp. 669–70 and n. 83; Cowdrey (1998) pp. 142, 144; Robinson (1999) p. 151.

1664 Conrad, bishop of Utrecht (1076–99).

1665 Poppo, bishop of Paderborn (1076–83). On his role in the deposition of Herman of Bamberg cf. Gregory VII, *Register* III.1, p. 242. See above 1075, p. 245 and n. 1297. See also Meier (1987) pp. 38–43.

1666 Rupert of Reichenau (above n. 706) had received the abbacy of Gengenbach from Herman of Bamberg after the death of Abbot Acelin in 1074: see Meyer von Knonau (1894) p. 409. But cf. Lampert's statement above, 1072, p. 161 and n. 812: 'that all access ... to any ecclesiastical office was closed to him forever'.

1667 'His chaplain, named Otto', according to the *Annales Gengenbacenses* 1075, p. 390.

the monastery and his own rights, had proceeded to control by violent means.[1668]

After their princes had been sent into exile, the Saxons were consumed by weariness and grief and there seemed to be no means of escape from their misfortunes. The king's friends, scattered over the mountains and hills, threatened their lives and did not allow them to hold assemblies, as they had done before, to take counsel together or to seek any means of regaining their safety. In addition they plundered the fields and the villages every day; they levied the most troublesome tributes on the region;[1669] they fortified their castles, making the maximum use of the labour of the local people and at their expense and they enforced impossibly severe penalties for their previous rebellion. There were two sons of a certain Count Gero,[1670] who were indeed sufficiently well born but because of their lack of personal possessions they were of no repute and of no importance among the princes of Saxony. At the time of the surrender they had fled beyond the River Elbe and there awaited the outcome of these events, for it was easy for them to be overlooked by the king or held in contempt by him because their names were so little known. When they saw the evils that had befallen – namely, that the consequence of the surrender of the princes was that *the liberty* of the fatherland *had been* utterly *betrayed*[1671] and, as the king had always intended, the whole Saxon people had been driven under the yoke of servitude – they nevertheless rejoiced exceedingly that, although they were exiled from their homeland, although they had lost their fortresses and their hereditary lands and had been left *destitute of everything*,[1672] they had not met with that turbulent shipwreck of surrender with the rest of the princes of Saxony. Since they were driven by need, they assembled a

---

1668 Rupert's death is dated 12 November 1075 by Meyer von Knonau (1894) p. 409 and n. 147. According to the *Annales Gengenbacenses* 1075, p. 390, Rupert was killed when he intervened to prevent trespass on the abbey's lands by 'certain of his knights, H. and his son, C.'. Cf. Berthold of Reichenau, *Chronicle* 1073, p. 130: Rupert 'was killed by a certain servant of the church because of a benefice that [the abbot] wished to take away from the man'.

1669 Cf. Bruno of Merseburg, *The Saxon War* c. 60, p. 54: the king departed, 'leaving among us men who were to demand tribute from our regions'; c. 84, p. 80: (the princes' exhortation to the Saxons) 'Refrain from paying tributes, lay hold of the possessions that are freely yours'. See Meyer von Knonau (1894) p. 648.

1670 Theoderic, count of Brehna and William, count of Camburg, sons of Gero, count of Brehna (Wettin prince, brother of Margrave Dedi I of Lower Lusatia). See Meyer von Knonau (1894) pp. 713–14; Fenske (1977) pp. 53–4, 73; Robinson (1999) p. 152.

1671 Livy III.28.13; IV.13.9.

1672 *Ibid.*, IV.10.7.

considerable force of men who were in the same situation as themselves
and they began to earn their living by robbery. Very often, when the
opportunity occurred, they tried to resist the king's tax collectors and to
repel their unjust demands by force. After they had met with success on
one or two occasions, they were joined in large numbers by the knights
of the princes who had been banished and also by all the free-born men
who had not yet surrendered and who *preferred* to face any dangers
rather than *make a* further *trial of* the king's *reliability.*[1673] Within a few
days it became a very great host, so that they believed themselves to be
equal not only to ambushes and small clandestine attacks in the manner
of highway robbers but also to open force and direct encounters with
their enemies. Moreover the local people – to whom it seemed that in the
midst of the final darkness of despair a light of salvation and consolation
had shone from heaven – all promised with the utmost readiness to be
their allies and to give their assistance in public affairs. For they judged
it to be better to suffer an honourable death for the fatherland, for their
wives and children, than to lead amidst such great troubles a life that
was *more unhappy than any death.*[1674]

Meanwhile Herman, the uncle of Duke Magnus,[1675] and very many
others of the princes who had surrendered – who (as mentioned
above)[1676] had been freed, without consulting the king, by the good-
natured persons who were keeping them prisoner – returned, bringing
unexpected joy to all men and removed every trace of hesitation that
still remained in their minds. For a stroke of good fortune so great
and so unlooked for appeared to them all as clear evidence of *God's
mercy being mindful of them.*[1677] They therefore *armed their young men*[1678]
and, moving through Saxony, they quickly regained possession of
all the castles in which the king had placed garrisons, some of them
surrendering, others being taken by storm.[1679] When they had taken
the plunder, they released unharmed those who were inside the castles,

---

1673 *Ibid.,* XLIV.9.1.

1674 *Ibid.,* IX.6.3.

1675 Count Herman Billung (above n. 890), uncle of Duke Magnus Billung of Saxony
(above n. 621). Cf. Bruno, *The Saxon War* c. 84, p. 80: 'Herman, uncle of Duke
Magnus, … arrived somewhat earlier than the rest'. See Meyer von Knonau (1894)
pp. 675–6.

1676 See above p. 311 and n. 1660.

1677 Psalm 24:16; Psalm 68: 17.

1678 Livy I.14.4; III.8.7. See Billanovich (1945) p. 180.

1679 Cf. Bruno, *The Saxon War* c. 84, p. 80: 'they drove Henry's garrisons out of all the
castles and restored them freely to those to whom they belonged'.

after obtaining from them an oath that they would not thereafter enter Saxony with hostile intent. As for the friends of the king and all those, whoever they might be, who had refused to promise their help to the common enterprise, they destroyed all that they possessed and drove them far away from Saxony. *And deliverance prospered by their hands*[1680] to recover their former freedom.

Otto, the former duke of Bavaria, still resided alone in the castle of Harzburg. The king had delegated to him his authority and the administration of public affairs throughout the whole of Saxony and in addition he had given him the task of building up the castle of Harzburg with all his might, together with another castle on the mountain called the Steinberg, which is near Goslar.[1681] The Saxons sent envoys to him, calling on him to discontinue the building work, which, unmindful of the fatherland, *unmindful of freedom*,[1682] he had undertaken with the purpose of destroying his people. Instead he should diligently search for a plan to rescue the princes since he himself had very earnestly persuaded them to surrender. Indeed many people had long been of the firm opinion that he had taken such trouble to persuade the rest of the princes to surrender in order that their blood might appease the king's anger against himself and in order to purchase his own safety by the destruction of his people.[1683] This was now clearly evident since, while the other princes had been banished to the most distant regions of the earth, he himself had received dominion over the whole of Saxony from the king as the price of his betrayal and he was now the king's executioner carrying out his cruel measures and the savage perpetrator of all the king's savage plans. It would therefore be beneficial for his reputation and his honour if he tried to expiate the disgrace of such great infamy by some distinguished service for his fatherland and to bring help to his people, who wished to recover their land and their freedom by means of their weapons. Finally, the Saxons declared that, if Otto did not voluntarily acquiesce in their advice, they would without doubt resort to force and destroy all his possessions and drive him far away from Saxony, as was fitting for a traitor to the fatherland and a deserter from their party.

1680 I Maccabees 3:6.

1681 On the role of Otto of Northeim (above n. 261) see above p. 301 and n. 1608. On the Steinberg (west of Goslar) see Meyer von Knonau (1894) p. 645; Lange (1961) p. 61; Fenske (1977) p. 29.

1682 Livy II.10.8.

1683 See above 1075, p. 284 and n. 1501.

In reply Otto implored them most earnestly in God's name to proceed more mildly and more peaceably. What they were striving to do for the common good would be more readily achieved by reason than by rashness. He would immediately send a message, urging the king with all his might to release the princes from the terms of their surrender, to demolish the castles that he had built because of the fear inspired in him by the former rebellion and to restore to the people of the Saxons the freedom, the laws and the rights of their ancestors, which had been snatched away by force and which they had so often tried to regain with their weapons. If the king accepted his advice, Saxony would be freed without bloodshed from the need to wage a grievous war, the outcome of which was uncertain. If the king did not agree, however, Otto declared that he could not be prevented by love of the office that had been conferred on him nor by the fear of death nor by the sanctity of the oath from defending, aiding and upholding the common cause of his fatherland and his ancestors with all the courage that he could muster to the last gasp. With these words he dismissed the envoys of the Saxons and immediately sent his own envoys to the king, as he had promised. He also withdrew the garrisons from both of the mountains of which he had taken possession and henceforward he enjoyed affable and companionable relations with the Saxons.[1684]

When the king received the bad news of the events in Saxony and learned also that the rest of the princes had held frequent assemblies and taken counsel together and that they were planning rebellion, he was driven in different directions, now by anger, now by anxiety, and distressed by indecision about which disease to cure first. But being more inclined to go where anger drove him, he considered leading the army to attack the city of Metz and seek revenge on the bishop of that place because, without consulting him, he had released the princes entrusted to his keeping.[1685] But thinking over the disturbed condition

---

1684 Lampert alone reported Otto's change of alliance. Significantly, *The Saxon War* of Bruno of Merseburg, likewise an admirer of Otto of Northeim, says nothing of Otto's activities between December 1075 and October 1076. Meyer von Knonau (1894) pp. 679 and n. 97, 714–15, 834–5, argued that Lampert, 'outstandingly favourable to Otto' (p. 715), contrived to disguise the fact that this latest change of sides was entirely Otto's own free decision. But Lange (1961) p. 63 and Fenske (1977) p. 63 took Lampert's account at face value. See also Robinson (1999) pp. 152–3.

1685 On Herman of Metz (above n. 822) and the prisoners see above p. 311 and n. 1660. No other source mentions the plan to attack Metz. Henry IV was certainly in Lotharingia during March and April: cf. above p. 310 and n. 1653 and *D.H.IV* 283, issued on 21 April in Aachen. See Kilian (1886) p. 72; Meyer von Knonau (1894) pp. 667, 675–6. Holder-Egger, *Lamperti Annales* p. 262 n. 2, and Meyer von Knonau

of the State, the doubtful loyalty of the princes and *the exhaustion* of the troops *after the* recent *wars*,[1686] he concluded that it would be the height of insanity to attempt any difficult undertaking in haste and his mind shifted away from rash and impetuous measures to more peaceful plans.

He therefore sent messengers in all directions and commanded all the princes of the kingdom to meet him at Whitsun in Worms[1687] in order – so he claimed – to consult together about what ought to be done. On the appointed day, although the rest of the princes assembled in fairly large numbers, there was no sign of any of the aforementioned dukes,[1688] who were feared to be a danger to the State and according to whose decision the most important public affairs ought primarily to be settled in peaceful times. Thus that assembly of princes accomplished nothing and the king's wishes were brought to naught. He issued a further command that they should present themselves on the Nativity of St Peter the apostle in Mainz[1689] and to his order he now added an urgent plea. But on that occasion not one of them paid heed either to his plea or to his command, for they all adhered firmly and unshakeably to their decision to rebel. Those who had assembled there disagreed among themselves with shameful animosity. For now *Satan* was *loosed from his prison*[1690] and fought not only with corporeal but also with spiritual weaponry against the peace of the Church and he actively sought

---

(1894) p. 676 n. 89 noted Lampert's inaccurate chronology of events in spring 1076.

1686 Livy XXX.44.4.

1687 15 May. Cf. Henry IV, *Letter* 13, p. 20: a summons to an unnamed bishop 'to come to Worms at Whitsun' to decide on proceedings against Gregory VII.

1688 Rudolf of Swabia (above n. 203), Welf IV of Bavaria (above n. 630), Berthold I of Carinthia (above n. 824): see above p. 310 and n. 1657. Among those present were the archbishops of Mainz and Cologne and the bishops of Bamberg, Naumburg and Utrecht: cf. *D.H.IV* 284 (issued on 23 May in Worms). On the failure of this assembly cf. Berthold of Reichenau, *Chronicle* 1076, pp. 147–8. See Kilian (1886) p. 72; Meyer von Knonau (1894) pp. 676–7; Schneider (1972) pp. 166–7, 170; Robinson (1999) p. 151; Gresser (2006) pp. 158–9.

1689 29 June. Cf. Berthold, *Chronicle* 1076, p. 148: 'they met once again in Mainz on the feast-day of the apostles Peter and Paul and ... very rashly excommunicated [Gregory VII]'. See Kilian (1886) p. 72; Meyer von Knonau (1894) pp. 681–3 and n. 99; Schneider (1972) pp. 171–2; Robinson (1999) pp. 151–2; Gresser (2006) pp. 159–60. On the lack of detailed information in Lampert's account of the assemblies of Worms and Mainz see Holder-Egger, *Lamperti Annales* p. 263 n. 2. On Lampert's failure to mention the excommunication of the pope see Ranke (1888) pp. 142–3, arguing that Lampert's attention was mainly fixed on the resumption of the Saxon rebellion and that he had little understanding of the issues in the dispute between the king and the pope. See also Meyer von Knonau (1894) p. 683 n. 99.

1690 Revelation 20:7.

to destroy the souls of those whose bodies he slaughtered so that they would not have eternal life.

Archbishop Udo of Trier,[1691] who had recently returned from Rome, refused to communicate with the archbishop of Mainz, the archbishop of Cologne[1692] and very many others who were more assiduous in their attendance on the king than the rest and whose advice the king followed in all matters. Udo gave as his reason the fact that both they and the king himself had been excommunicated by the Roman pontiff. Nevertheless Udo had been granted the right – which he had extorted from the pope with great difficulty by the most urgent pleading – to speak to the king, but only to speak to him: he was not permitted to eat or drink or pray or have any other kind of communication with him. Udo's weighty influence inspired very many others, whose faith in God was purer and who were more concerned about the dignity of the State, gradually to distance themselves from the palace precisely in order not to be defiled by contact with the men mentioned above. They also refused to return to the king, although they were frequently ordered to appear, judging it better to offend the king rather than God and to meet with injuries to the body rather than to the soul. Their opponents, on the contrary, raged, howled, raved and hurled threats and insults in all directions. They declared the sentence of the Roman pontiff to be unjust and therefore to be regarded as invalid. For he had excommunicated them in a fit of reckless fury rather than in a judicious manner, without summoning them to a synod according to canon law or investigating their case according to the canons or convicting them of the offence with which they were charged or obtaining a confession, as canon law requires.[1693] They declared that the archbishop of Trier

---

1691 Udo of Trier (above n. 483). Cf. the papal letter to Udo in April, Gregory VII, *Register* III.12, p. 273: 'we ask and admonish you to correct by appropriate amendment the offence that you have committed through the persuasion of the schismatics' and the reference to him on 25 August in *Register* IV.2, p. 297, as 'our brother, the venerable archbishop of Trier'. See Meyer von Knonau (1894) pp. 681, 683 n. 99; Schneider (1972) p. 171; Erkens (1987) pp. 24–7; Robinson (1999) pp. 151–2.

1692 For the presence of Siegfried of Mainz (above n. 210) and Hildolf of Cologne (above n. 1609) in the king's council in Worms on 15 May see above n. 1688. Hildolf was not excommunicated in the synodal protocols of February 1076 (see above p. 307 and n. 1635) but was guilty of communicating with the excommunicate king.

1693 Cf. Berthold of Reichenau, *Chronicle* 1076, p. 148: those present at Mainz on 29 June 'declared ... that the anathema pronounced by the pope ... against the king and against the other members of his alliance was unconsidered, unjust and of no weight'.

and the others who had for so long been conspiring with him *to overturn the State*[1694] had a purpose quite different from what they claimed. Their intention was not so much to confer authority on the holy see as to seek an opportunity to undermine the office of king and to cloak their deeply rooted hatred of the king with the new term 'religious duty'. They believed that the king would be rightly protecting his honour if he speedily drew the sword – which, according to the word of the apostle, he had received for *the punishment of evil*[1695] men – against his enemies and if, showing contempt for their empty excuses and deceptions, he inflicted on the clearly guilty intriguers against the kingdom the penalty that they deserved. It was not difficult for them to incite the mind of the king to anger, since it was by its very nature savage and implacable.

The king saw that the princes, under the pretext of religious obligation, were one by one deserting him and that, now that the empire was deprived of their help, it was futile to issue threats that he had not the power to carry out. He resolved, as the present circumstances indeed demanded, to be guided by expediency rather than anger and therefore *tried* again and again *to soften the* hostile *attitude*[1696] of the princes with soothing messages. Nevertheless – it is astonishing to relate – despite the severe difficulties of his situation and the great mass of dangers that was assailing him, he could not be prevailed on to release the princes of Saxony from the terms of their surrender and this was the cause of that *blaze of ill will*[1697] and hatred that flared up against him. On the contrary, *greatly alarmed by the recent cases*[1698] of those princes who had released very many of their prisoners without consulting him,[1699] the king gave orders that those who still remained in prison should be guarded with the utmost care, so that they did not escape. He therefore repeatedly sent word to those princes to whom he had entrusted prisoners to *remember the favours* that he had *conferred on them*,[1700] to remember the oath by which they had confirmed their fidelity to him to keep the prisoners who had been consigned to their custody with undiminished loyalty until he demanded them back from them. They were not to be

1694 Livy III.17.2.

1695 I Peter 2:14; cf. Romans 13:4.

1696 Livy XXXVIII.48.11.

1697 *Ibid.*, III.11.10; XL.5.1; XLIII.16.2.

1698 *Ibid.*, XXXI.12.2.

1699 See above p. 311 and n. 1660.

1700 Livy XXIV.13.2.

misled by the infamous example of other princes, who, without being commanded to do so, released those who had surrendered, because they wished to avenge themselves on the king for their personal injuries, and who thereby inflicted on the State a very great disaster and a shameful stain that would not be washed away for many centuries.

The king indeed was enraged with everyone and – so it seemed – thirsted for everyone's blood. Nevertheless his anger was especially directed against the bishop of Halberstadt, whom he pursued with implacable hatred, both as the leader of the whole Saxon rebellion and as the instigator and supporter of all the evils that had occurred.[1701] Had he not been prevented by reverence for the office of bishop and the promise made at the time of the surrender, the king would have taken his life after inflicting every kind of torture. The king had entrusted him to the keeping of Bishop Rupert of Bamberg, since the latter was rougher and *of a more savage temper*[1702] than the rest of his intimates and had often proved his loyalty towards him in adversity. Subsequently, however, when the princes were thinking of rebellion and the king saw that the State was once again agitated by new storms, although he did not distrust Rupert's diligence as a guard, he was nevertheless afraid that during this long imprisonment some chance act of negligence might suddenly allow enemies to use violence or deception against him. The king therefore summoned the prisoner to the palace and caused him to be kept there under the most careful guard sometimes among his chamberlains and sometimes among the cooks and amidst the filth of the kitchens in the most shameful conditions until he had devised a place of exile that corresponded to his deadly hatred of the bishop.[1703]

At that same time the king had with him his sister, the wife of King Salomon of the Hungarians.[1704] After her husband had been driven out

1701 For this view of the role of Burchard II (Bucco) of Halberstadt (above n. 235) see above 1073, p. 174 and n. 891; 1075, p. 274 and n. 1446.

1702 Livy XXI.5.12. See Billanovich (1945) p. 80. On the character of Rupert of Bamberg (above n. 1524) see above 1075, p. 288 and n. 1526.

1703 The presence of Burchard at the royal court may have been linked with his attendance at the council of Worms, 24 January 1076: cf. Henry IV, *Letters* appendix A, p. 65. Erdmann (1938) pp. 145–8 suggested a different version of Burchard's treatment, on the basis of a letter, perhaps from Bishop Hezelo of Hildesheim to Henry IV, December 1075 (*Briefsammlungen der Zeit Heinrichs IV.*, p. 69), in which the author thanked the king for behaving 'more humanely to my friend, the lord B. [Burchard?]'. See also Fenske (1977) p. 107 and n. 40.

1704 Judith-Sophia (above n. 251), wife of Salomon (above n. 250): see above 1074, p. 233 and n. 1230.

of his kingdom, he had judged that, while he was in arms and ready for battle, nowhere was safer for her to remain than with her brother, until he had recovered his kingdom, if it could be done, and he might be allowed to give himself up to the enjoyment of married life. When after a long time she was now preparing to return to her husband, who was living in Hungarian territory, the king, thinking her a suitable person to perform this cruel duty, asked her to take the bishop of Halberstadt with her and arrange for him to be banished to a place from which there would thereafter be no opportunity of returning to the German kingdom. She agreed to his request and, placing him on board a ship, she sent him on in advance with her own men, with the intention of following him a few days later, after she had made the necessary preparations for her departure.[1705]

That same bishop had a knight named Udalric,[1706] a very rich man with many estates in Bavaria and also especially dear to and esteemed by the king. When he learned of the evils that were in store for the bishop, he was moved by compassion and by his reflections on the uncertain nature of human affairs that so great and distinguished a man – who would have been a strong pillar and support of the State, if the king's foolhardiness had not brought all divine and human laws into confusion – should now perish as a consequence of so dreadful a punishment. Udalric therefore approached the bishop shortly before his ship set sail and gave him a full exposition of what the king had decided to do about his case. His safety was at stake, unless the gracious heavens, which alone had the power to do so, helped him in his dangerous situation. Udalric further informed him that his estates and a strongly fortified castle were not far from the banks of the River Danube and advised him that, once arrived by ship at that precise place, he should frequently

---

1705 The report of Burchard's escape in Bruno of Merseburg, *The Saxon War* c. 83, pp. 78–9, claims that 'when Henry was by the Danube, ... he entrusted Bishop Burchard to his brother-in-law [Salomon], who was now about to return to his fatherland'. This reference to Henry IV does not accord with what is known of his itinerary: see Kilian (1886) p. 72; Meyer von Knonau (1894) p. 680. Holder-Egger (1894) pp. 522–5 argued that Bruno's account was in general more accurate since his information, unlike Lampert's, was derived directly from Burchard's own circle. On Burchard's escape see Meyer von Knonau (1894) pp. 681–1, 835–9; Fenske (1977) p. 107; Robinson (1999) p. 152.

1706 Bruno, *The Saxon War* c. 83, p. 79, refers only to 'a certain Udalric'. Holder-Egger, *Lamperti Annales* p. 266 n. 2 questioned whether this might be the 'Udalric, whom they called "the very rich"', mentioned by Frutolf of Michelsberg, *Chronica* 1099, p. 118, i.e. Count Udalric of Passau (†1099). Holder-Egger noted that Lampert's claim that 'this Bavarian was a vassal of the bishop of Halberstadt' was 'certainly false'. See also Meyer von Knonau (1894) pp. 836 n. 145, 839.

ask the men with whom he was sailing to bring the ship to land and make it possible for him to step on land for a little, under the pretext of resting or some other necessary purpose that would assist the success of his device. Udalric declared that he was mindful of the fidelity that he owed him; he would do all that he could to the utmost of his ability and if God showed him a way of rescuing the bishop, he would make the attempt. The bishop did as he had been instructed and, as soon as he came near the aforementioned place, he feigned an illness, the effect of continual sailing on a body unaccustomed to it, and declared that unless rapid action was taken, the sick man would finally succumb to death. He easily persuaded the sailors – whose respect for the office of bishop caused them to behave with great humanity towards him – to bring the ship to land as often as he wished and to give him the opportunity of leaving the ship and recovering his strength on land as often as he pleased. The remoteness of the region, the large number of guards and the weak condition of the sick man dispelled any fear, any suspicion of flight or ambush. He frequently left the ship and returned to it, looking about him in all directions and surveying everything with a vigilant eye. Nowhere, however, was there a sign of the promised deliverance, nowhere a ray of hope.

It happened to be the feast of the Nativity of the blessed John the Baptist.[1707] In the morning, as they were sailing by, he caught sight of a church close to the river bank and asked the sailors to land the ship so that he might go into the church and celebrate mass on that most holy day. They agreed and he entered the church and, clad in the priestly vestments according to solemn custom, he began to offer the life-giving eucharistic sacrifice. While they were all giving their full attention to the mass, the aforementioned Udalric – taking advantage of the situation, of which he had been accurately informed through the careful efforts of his scouts – suddenly surrounded the church with a large band of armed men. He entered discreetly, concealing for the time being the purpose for which he had come, and silently and peacefully awaited the completion of the holy office. When the mass was over, he ordered his followers to run to the ship with all speed and to bring from it all the bishop's possessions. He himself, surrounded by a troop of the most courageous young men, greeted the bishop as he was coming out of the church. He offered him the kiss of peace and bade

1707 24 June. In Bruno's version (c. 83, p. 79) the bishop, accompanied by a single chaplain, deceived the sailors into setting him on land and he went in search of 'a solitary house not far from the riverside' about which Udalric had informed him.

him as quickly as possible to mount the horse that he had provided as the most suitable for his flight. When the men who had brought the bishop there, wondering what was happening, after futile debates had recourse to their weapons, Udalric ordered them to remain still, if they had any concern for their lives and safety. They should lay down their arms, return peacefully to their ships and be thankful that no *penalties were exacted*[1708] for the offence that they had committed against so great a bishop. If they continued to provoke him with empty words and irrational actions, their impudence would easily be checked by swords. It was more appropriate for the bishop to perform his episcopal duties for the church of Halberstadt, to which he was appointed bishop, than for them. Since the sailors were *inferior in numbers* and *in courage*,[1709] they thought that it would be rash to decide the issue by fighting and they returned to their ships with saddened and subdued spirits. The bishop withdrew to a castle that was not far away and remained there for a few days until the notoriety of the event had died down and until all those who might perhaps be eager to ambush him on his return journey had abandoned their exertions. At last he put on layman's clothing by means of which he might deceive those whom he encountered and he hastened into Saxony.[1710] The Saxons had already given up any hope of his return and he was suddenly restored to them like one who had escaped alive from hell.

When the king received the news of these events,[1711] he was extremely vexed and discontented that such great efforts had ended in nothing, that he had been deprived of his revenge for such atrocious insults and that his enemies had had restored to them, unpunished, the man who was the supreme hinge upon which the whole of the Saxon war turned.[1712] He could moreover be in no doubt that the fires of Saxon fury, which had for a little while been dormant, would immediately be rekindled through the instigation of this bishop and would very soon flare up into a vast conflagration. Nor could he doubt that the bishop would be all the more dangerous when he remembered that after his

---

1708 Ovid, *Fasti* IV.230; *Metamorphoses* VIII.531.

1709 Livy XXXVIII.13.2.

1710 According to Bruno (c. 83, p. 79), 'Udalric received the bishop and, resting by day but hastening by night, ... he brought him to Halberstadt'.

1711 In the version of Bruno (c. 85, p. 80), 'when Henry heard all this news, his mind was extremely disturbed and he came to Mainz', i.e. to the assembly of 29 June: see above n. 1689. See Meyer von Knonau (1894) pp. 682, 837.

1712 Cf. above, 1073, p. 174 and n. 891; 1075, p. 274 and n. 1446 (identifying Burchard and Otto of Northeim as the ringleaders); 1076, p. 320 and n. 1701.

surrender he had experienced no mercy and no humanity at the hands of the king. Furthermore the king feared that the rest of the princes who had surrendered might also escape in the same way and that, if they gained their freedom against his will, he would lose the advantage of that remarkable victory and that toilsome surrender. After mature reflection on all these matters, he finally decided henceforward to proceed in another way and prepared to overcome the Saxons now with their own weapons and their own strength, since external force had so often attempted but failed to achieve their conquest. This was indeed a wise resolution since it is well known that *every kingdom* is more quickly weakened and destroyed by domestic and internal dissension than *by any other power*[1713] or any other disaster.

The king therefore commanded the archbishop of Magdeburg, the bishop of Merseburg,[1714] the bishop of Meissen, Duke Magnus, the count palatine Frederick[1715] and in addition all the princes of Saxony and Thuringia who were still held prisoner to be recalled from their exile. He summoned them to his presence in a kindly manner and he declared that, although he could, according to the laws of the royal palace, *impose on them the ultimate penalty*[1716] and he would be right to do so after being provoked by them so often with grievous insults, nevertheless, remembering their birth and remembering their courage, which could contribute both to the honour and to the defence of the State, he pardoned their dreadful actions. What was more, as the price of their release he asked only that henceforward they remained faithful and trustworthy in precarious times and provided help in restoring order to the kingdom and in checking those who caused dissension, especially those who every day disturbed the Saxons – a straightforward people who knew nothing of wicked and cunning devices – with their internal disagreements. If they did so, rather than abandoning their loyalty with their former fickleness, he would regard them as the foremost among his friends and, when the opportunity arose, he would confer favours upon them, in keeping with the generosity of a king.

1713 Matthew 12:25; Luke 11:17.

1714 Wezilo (Werner) of Magdeburg (above n. 899) and Werner of Merseburg (above n. 901). According to Bruno, *The Saxon War* c. 86, p. 81, these two churchmen were sent to the Saxons as the king's envoys. See Meyer von Knonau (1894) p. 683; Robinson (1999) p. 152.

1715 Benno of Meissen (above n. 494); Magnus Billung, duke of Saxony (above n. 621); Frederick II (of Goseck), Saxon count palatine (above n. 227). See Meyer von Knonau (1894) p. 837 and n. 149.

1716 Livy XXIV.14.7.

For their part, although they knew that what he said was false and that he had relaxed the natural inflexibility of his temper out of necessity rather than compassion, nevertheless, because of their longing to escape punishment, they gladly embraced what was on offer. They promised whatever he commanded, they repeatedly confirmed their promises by swearing oaths and, when they received leave to depart, they each joyfully returned to their homeland.

The king (as we mentioned above)[1717] had been strongly advised by Otto, the former duke of Bavaria, to look to the troubled condition of Saxony as soon as possible. The king had sent word to Otto to meet him on a specific day in Saalfeld so that they might have a discussion together and determine what needed to be done. Afterwards, however, he changed this plan, placing his reliance instead on those whom he had released from the terms of their surrender, with whose help he would be able to satisfy his anger in a suitable manner against the Saxons who had injured him. On the appointed day he sent messengers[1718] in his place to Duke Otto in Saalfeld and they told him to gather together as many troops as he could and to hasten to meet the king in the march of Meissen. After leading his army through Bohemia, the king would arrive there and, if God answered his prayers, he would reward according to their deserts the sons of Count Gero,[1719] who had so inauspiciously issued a call to arms to *the ignorant masses.*[1720] He sent the same message also to the princes of Saxony and Thuringia, whom he had recently sent back to their fatherland, beseeching them to be thankful for the indulgence that had been shown to them and to dissuade all whom they could from allying themselves with those desperate men. He required them to be present, armed and well prepared to give their aid in affairs of State on the appointed day and in the designated place.

The king himself, as he had decided, hastened into Bohemia, taking with him a very small number of knights from the German army, while all the rest remained totally unaware of what he was endeavouring to do. There he joined forces with the Bohemian duke[1721] and his forces and

1717 See above p. 316 and n. 1684. Lampert alone reported the king's relations with Otto of Northeim (above n. 261) in summer 1076: see Meyer von Knonau (1894) pp. 715–16 and n. 167; Lange (1961) pp. 63–4.

1718 Lampert subsequently identified Bishop Eppo (Eberhard) of Zeitz (Naumburg) as the envoy to Otto: see below p. 327 and n. 1726.

1719 Count Theoderic of Brehna and Count William of Camburg, sons of Count Gero of Brehna: see above p. 313 and n. 1670.

1720 Livy I.19.4; II.45.5; XLV.23.8.

1721 Duke Vratislav II of Bohemia (above n. 746). Lampert alone reported a royal

unexpectedly invaded the march of Meissen but he did so either more confidently or else more carelessly – I do not know which – than was appropriate for so great an enterprise. For he was deceived by the vain hope that every hindrance and every difficulty in accomplishing the enterprise would be dispelled by the diligent efforts of Duke Otto and the other princes whom, so he fondly imagined, he had placed under an obligation by the favour that he had bestowed on them.

But Duke Otto knew that the Saxon people had just causes for rebellion and he had already for a long time been working on the king by the frequent sending of envoys, so that he would remove the reasons for war and the causes of resentment, confirm to the Saxons that their laws and rights would remain in force and curb rioters by means of justice rather than weapons. The king would then save himself such great hardships and spare the great quantity of blood that must be shed if there was a battle and he would without difficulty enjoy forever the service of a most splendid people. For this was the difference between a king and a tyrant: the latter extorted obedience from unwilling subjects by means of force and cruelty, while the former governed his subjects and issued his commands according to the laws and customs of his forefathers.[1722] But that king had been born and brought up to exercise power and, as befitted such high birth and the high offices and titles of his lineage, he always showed a royal spirit in all his troubles and he would rather die than suffer defeat. He thought it a blot of irremediable disgrace if he received an injury and did not avenge it: nay, he considered it the supreme honour, comparable in value to life itself to allow nothing that happened amiss to go unavenged. For this purpose he had drawn to himself men who were skilled in such endeavours, born indeed of middling rank[1723] but very *ready to give advice and to act,*[1724] and who, as

---

expedition to Bohemia: see Kilian (1886) p. 73; Meyer von Knonau (1894) pp. 715–16. The incompletely dated *D.H.IV* 285 places Henry IV in Regensburg on either 27 July or 27 August. Holder-Egger, *Lamperti Annales* p. 270 n. 1, noted that a visit to Regensburg on either on these dates would not preclude an expedition such as Lampert reported here. See Kilian (1886) p. 73; Meyer von Knonau (1894) pp. 715–16.

1722 Bruno of Merseburg, *The Saxon War* c. 25, p. 29, also applied to Henry IV this distinction between king and tyrant. Carlyle (1915) p. 132 detected here and in Lampert's statement the influence of the political ideas of Isidore of Seville, *Etymologiae* IX.3.4–22. Isidore was directly cited in a long digression by Berthold of Reichenau, *Chronicle* 1077, p. 178: 'if they oppress the people with a most cruel power and domination ..., why are they not to be properly called the most powerful kind of tyrants rather than use the name of kings ...?'

1723 Cf. above 1073, p. 173 and n. 882, p. 178. See Struve (1970a) p. 43.

1724 Livy II.33.5.

the prophet says, *spoke to* him *smooth things and divined*[1725] errors for him. Through their flatteries they inflamed his diseased mind, which was in any case inclined to wrath and rashness, as if they invited him to every-thing that gave him pleasure. With the purpose of making their work more necessary for him, they put the greatest efforts into ensuring that the State was troubled by continual misfortunes. The king used these most wicked men as his advisers; he strongly resisted the princes of the kingdom when they urged him to do what was right and did not permit them to advise him unless he chanced to find himself in some inextri-cable emergency. On the contrary he desired, if the opportunity arose, to suppress their authority and to obliterate it entirely, so that no one would oppose and no one would condemn him when he threw himself with unbridled freedom into every activity that suggested itself to him.

Duke Otto was therefore greatly enraged that the king, against his advice, was once again making war on Saxony. He declared to Bishop Eppo of Zeitz, who (as was mentioned above)[1726] had met him in Saalfeld, acting as the king's envoy, that he had given the king his advice about what was best both for his honour and for the good of the State. But since the king trusted senseless flatterers more than he did Otto and placed more hope and reliance on the Bohemian forces than on the strength of the German army, the outcome of his undertakings would be his own concern. Otto himself would have neither the glory if the enterprise prospered nor the dishonour if it failed. He would not now, moreover, be bound by any religious consideration by the oath of fidelity that he had sworn to the king, since the latter did not listen to him when he gave him correct and useful advice. He was furthermore commanded by the king to take up his arms *to shed innocent blood*[1727] in the manner of the heathen, in violation of the laws of God, the honour of the empire and the salvation of his soul. Accordingly he regarded himself as released from any reproach of oath-breaking and he would henceforward freely defend the cause of his people, which was a just cause, with his weapons and his wealth, as far as he was able.

The other princes both of Saxony and Thuringia also made the same declaration. Even if they had most ardently wished to do so, they could

---

1725 Isaiah 30:10; Ezekiel 13:6.

1726 Lampert failed to mention Eppo (Eberhard) of Zeitz-Naumburg (above n. 46) when he reported that the king 'sent messengers' to Saalfeld: see above p. 325 and n. 1718. On these negotiations see Meyer von Knonau (1894) pp. 716–17; Lange (1961) pp. 63–4.

1727 Jeremiah 22:17.

not provide the king with the help that he requested, since their knights unanimously *declined to perform* that unpropitious *military service*[1728] against their fatherland and their kinsmen. For now they did not act as previously, irresolute in their loyalty with vacillating minds that *wavered between hope and fear*,[1729] but instead in a spirit of unanimity, inflexible in their opposition, they had entered into a conspiracy to rebel. They had not rushed to arms, as the common people had done on the previous occasion, violently roused by the crafty urging of the princes,[1730] but all the inhabitants of the province had resolved together *to wage war*, not *under the leadership and at the command*[1731] of the princes but according to their own endeavours and at their own personal expense. They were prepared to fight for themselves and, if God permitted it, to conquer for themselves. They were not expecting a reward from anyone for their military service except *to secure the safety of their wives and children*[1732] and to shake off the yoke of the most burdensome slavery from their necks. In fact they even threatened the princes that, if they attempted to resist or restrain them, they would scatter or burn all their possessions and drive them far away from their homeland.[1733] They had, in short, undertaken to pursue their enterprise with the intention that either they would be completely victorious or they would perish. Their zeal had been kindled by utter desperation because in recent years they had received clear evidence that the defeated would have no hope of pardon from the king, since neither the voluntary surrender of the princes nor the immense bloodshed in Thuringia had quenched the savagery of his feelings and his immovable hatred for the very name of Saxony.[1734]

When the rumour spread throughout Saxony, therefore, that the king was ravaging the march of Meissen (which bordered on the Saxon kingdom) with fire and sword, they issued a call to arms. Many thousands of men soon flocked together, burning with the irresistible desire to

1728 Livy V.19.5; VII.11.5. See Billanovich (1945) p. 145.

1729 Livy XLII.59.8.

1730 Cf. above, 1073, p. 176 and n. 913.

1731 Livy VIII.12.6; X.18.1. See Billanovich (1945) p. 168.

1732 Regino of Prüm, *Chronicon* 906, p. 151.

1733 Cf. Lampert's version of the threats of the Saxon rank and file to their princes, above, 1075, p. 252: to 'reduce all their property to ashes and force them to flee far from Saxony'.

1734 Cf. above, 1075, pp. 268 ('the Saxons had clear evidence of the passionate hatred that [the king] felt for them'); 279 ('the king had set his mind inexorably on the extermination of the whole Saxon people'); 283 ('with insatiable hatred [the king] condemned them to deadly torments').

do battle, and they set off, unanimous in their eagerness to encounter the enemy. But since this crowd, all too numerous and hindered by its weaponry and other baggage, was unable to maintain the desired rate of progress, the sons of Count Gero,[1735] taking with them seven thousand lightly armed riders, with the greatest exertions hastened to the encounter with a most ardent longing to accomplish their task as quickly as possible. If they had happened to overtake the king and to engage with him in battle when their troops were so exasperated and so inflamed with the desire to fight, then – so many people suppose – the Saxon war, which had endured for so many years, would have been ended easily and rapidly and the king and all his entourage would have met either with certain death or with dishonour that would be hard to efface. For, apart from the Bohemian army, which had shown itself *unequal in* its weapons, *its numbers and its courage*[1736] to so great a task, the king had very few men with him, since he had thought it superfluous to impose on German knights the hardship of so distant a campaign. He hoped (as was mentioned above)[1737] that as a result of the exertions of Duke Otto and the others whom he had released from the terms of their surrender, free of ransom, all the forces of the Saxons would easily be rendered ineffective and troops sufficient even for more extensive wars would be at his disposal on the stated day and in the appointed place.

It happened at that time that, through God's merciful care for the safety of the king, the River Mulde, which separated the two armies, was extremely swollen by the recent torrential rain and denied them any possibility of making the crossing. The king made very good use of this flood for his own purposes. Without waiting for the waters to recede, he turned back to Bohemia and, returning hurriedly through Bavaria, he retreated to Worms, full of distress and regret that such great efforts had come to nothing.[1738] On parting from the Bohemian duke, he had given him the march of Meissen, as a reward for the loyalty that he

---

1735 Count Theoderic of Brehna and Count William of Camburg, sons of Count Gero of Brehna (above n. 1670). See Meyer von Knonau (1894) p. 717.

1736 Livy XXXVIII.13.2.

1737 See above p. 325.

1738 Kilian (1886) p. 73 and Meyer von Knonau (1894) p. 719 and n. 172 dated the king's return to Worms in August. Holder-Egger, *Lamperti Annales* p. 273 n. 2, noted the close resemblance between the account of this expedition to the march of Meissen and that of 1075, which again only Lampert reported (above p. 278 and n. 1464). Both involved the duke of Bohemia; both brought the king into danger, from which he was saved by chance. Holder-Egger concluded that 'very little of [these two accounts] seems to be true'.

had shown in a difficult situation.[1739] This march, however, belonged to Margrave Ekbert, who was the son of a cousin of the king and a boy still considerably under the age for bearing arms.[1740] As soon as the floods subsided and the river became passable, Ekbert joined forces with the Saxons, pressed on to Meissen and attacked and regained possession of all the castles in which the Bohemian duke had placed garrisons. He placed his own knights there, who in the future were to maintain a tireless watch against enemy incursions. Everyone was amazed that the king had not been restrained from perpetrating this injury by consideration for Ekbert's age and their kinship.

Meanwhile Duke Rudolf of the Swabians, Duke Welf of the Bavarians, Duke Berthold of the Carinthians, Bishop Adalbero of Würzburg, Bishop Adalbert of Worms and others[1741] who were disturbed by the danger to the State held a meeting in the place called Ulm[1742] and decided that everyone who desired the good of the State should assemble in Tribur on 16 October. Then, disgusted by these evils, they would make an end of the various mischiefs that had now disturbed the peace of the Church for many years. They announced this to the princes of Swabia, Bavaria, Saxony, Lotharingia and Franconia and implored them all as a body to discard all excuses and set aside every personal consideration so that each and every one of them might devote his utmost efforts to

1739 On the investiture of Vratislav II (above n. 746) with the march see above, 1075, p. 279 and n. 1468. Cf. Bruno of Merseburg, *The Saxon War* c. 36, p. 38, claiming that Henry promised 'the city of Meissen with all its appurtenances' in 1074; Cosmas of Prague, *Chronica Boemorum* II.39, p. 141, stating that in 1087 'Vratislav ... entered Meissen, which Emperor Henry had formerly given up to him to be held in perpetuity'. See Meyer von Knonau (1894) pp. 718–19; Schramm (1968) p. 350; Fenske (1977) pp. 74–5.

1740 Cf. Bruno, *The Saxon War* c. 56, p. 52: 'Margrave Ekbert ... wholeheartedly adhered to the king, as his very close kinsman'. Count Ekbert II of Brunswick, margrave of Meissen (above n. 504) was the son of Margrave Ekbert I of Meissen (above n. 177), who was the grandson of Empress Gisela from her first marriage, while Henry IV was her grandson from her third marriage. See Fenske (1977) pp. 23 n. 41, 75 n. 270; Robinson (1999) p. 80.

1741 Rudolf of Swabia (above n. 203), Welf IV of Bavaria (above n. 630), Berthold I of Carinthia (above n. 824), Adalbero of Würzburg (above n. 44), Adalbert of Worms (above n. 626). (The first four names occur in the list of conspirators above p. 310 and n. 1657.) According to Bernold of St Blasien, *Pro Gebhardo episcopo Constantiensi epistola apologetica* c. 5, p. 110, Bishop Altman of Passau was present in Ulm as a papal legate and there restored Bishop Otto of Constance to communion. This incident is also mentioned in Berthold of Reichenau, *Chronicle* 1077, p. 170.

1742 According to Bernold, *Pro Gebhardo* c. 5, p. 110, the meeting was held 'in the autumn'. Meyer von Knonau (1894) p. 725 suggested September. See also Schneider (1972) p. 172 and n. 552; Cowdrey (1998) pp. 144–5; Robinson (1999) pp. 153–4; Gresser (2006) pp. 162–3.

the common good. While everyone awaited this event with anxiety and amazement, the archbishop of Mainz,[1743] and very many others who had hitherto vigorously supported the party of the king, abandoned him and joined the princes mentioned above, blazing with the most fiery zeal for the betterment of the condition of the kingdom. A wonderful and unexpected development, which removed the obstacles that might have delayed their plans, was the fact that the hostages – by means of whom some of the princes had guaranteed their fidelity to the king during the previous year – were suddenly restored to those who had given them. The king himself sent back one of the two sons of Duke Otto;[1744] the prince who had received the other son from the king to keep under guard, sent him back to his unsuspecting father without the king's knowledge.

The son of Margrave Udo[1745] and the son of Adela, the widow of Margrave Dedi,[1746] were both little boys of tender years, well below the age of maturity and, while they were imprisoned in the fortress of a certain Eberhard, a servant of the king,[1747] they offered a striking proof of the extreme nobility of their character, which it would be worth-while for posterity to remember.[1748] The king had commanded that same Eberhard, either because of the distinction and greatness of their families or out of sympathy for the weakness of the very young, to tend

1743 On the conduct of Siegfried of Mainz (above n. 210) see Meyer von Knonau (1894) p. 728; Thomas (1970) p. 397; Cowdrey (1998) p. 150. He first appeared openly as the king's enemy at the assembly of Forchheim in March 1077: see Robinson (1999) p. 167.

1744 Probably either Siegfried or Cuno, the younger sons of Otto of Northeim (above n. 261): see above p. 301 and n. 1607. That some hostages were not released at this time is evident from the demands of the king's opponents at the assembly of Tribur, as reported by Berthold of Reichenau, *Chronicle* 1076, pp. 153–4: 'that the hostages of the Saxons should be returned to them'.

1745 Probably Henry (the future Count Henry III of Stade, margrave of the Saxon Nordmark), son of Margrave Udo II of the Saxon Nordmark (above n. 168). See above, 1075, p. 269 and n. 1425.

1746 Henry I of Eilenburg (later margrave of Meissen and of Lower Lusatia), son of Adela of Louvain (above n. 506) and her late husband, Margrave Dedi of Lower Lusatia (above n. 522). See above, 1075, p. 279 and n. 1470.

1747 Eberhard, who is mentioned in no other source, is described by Meyer von Knonau (1894) p. 836 as 'a royal *ministerialis*'. See also Zotz (1991) p. 44. On the possible location of his fortress see Meyer von Knonau (1894) p. 837 n. 148.

1748 For this account see Meyer von Knonau (1894) pp. 728–9, 836–7 and n. 148. In this footnote Meyer von Knonau argued that the story of this adventurous escape is implausible, since Henry of Eilenburg, whose parents married in 1069, can have been no more than seven in 1076 and Lampert represents both boys as approxi-mately the same age.

them with the utmost kindness and to allow them occasionally to play
games with boys of their own age so that they would not pine away as
a result of inactivity or the weariness of continual captivity. The boys'
parents made the same request and they frequently sent small presents
to the guards. Eberhard did as he was bidden and permitted them to play
sometimes inside the fortress and sometimes outside in the presence
of guards, suspecting no harm from those at an age that was artless
and unaware of deception. Now and then he also went hunting in the
woods that bordered on the fortress and allowed them to go with him,
mounting them on horses, which at their age they were scarcely capable
of riding, so that they might refresh their spirits, weighed down by
sorrow and weariness, by means of this consoling activity. Since he did
this on numerous occasions, custom bred trust on the part of the guards
and trust bred negligence, so that from day to day they treated the boys
more indulgently and relaxed the strictness of their careful vigilance.
They finally ceased to be at all suspicious and let them do whatever they
wished without anyone to watch over them. Wherever they found an
opportunity and a sufficiently secluded place, therefore, the boys began
to talk together, to recall their homeland and their parents, to bewail
the vexations of life in a foreign land and they encouraged each other
to attempt some plan that would, with God's help, achieve their escape.

One day when according to his custom the aforementioned Eberhard
had gone hunting, taking the boys with him, they chanced to encounter
a wild beast and they all, as usually happens, ran hither and thither with
confused shouts in their impetuous efforts to pursue it. The little boys
realised that they were alone, that there was not a single guard, that
all those who had gone out together to hunt were intent only on the
progress of the hunt and oblivious of everything else. The boys *set spurs
to their horses*[1749] with all the power of which they were capable and flew
more quickly than words can describe through the dense woodland,
the steep paths in the mountains, the hollows of the valleys,[1750] heedless of
or indifferent to their danger. They did not give a particular direction to their journey, unacquainted as they were with that land, but,
blindly loosing the reins, they rushed headlong wherever the impulse
of the horses carried them. After they had passed through the woods
at a rapid pace, they reached the River Main. There they came upon
a fisherman in a fishing skiff, preoccupied with catching fish. They
begged him to convey them to Mainz and offered him the cloaks that

1749 Livy II.20.2.
1750 Regino of Prüm, *Chronicon* 866, p. 91.

they were wearing as the price of their passage since nothing else was available. The fisherman was either attracted by the price or moved by compassion for them in their dangerous situation – for he could easily divine this from their agitation and the rest of their physical demeanour – and he kindly received them in his boat, covered them with the equipment that was in the boat so that they would not be recognised by their pursuers and carried them to Mainz, as they had requested. Their horses swam across the river and ran along the opposite bank at a moderate pace level with the boat in a remarkable manner so that when the boat moved, they moved at the same time and when it came to a halt, they likewise halted. You might suppose that the irrational beasts possessed human souls. When the boys came to Mainz, they recovered their horses[1751] and secretly slipped into a house close to the riverside, where they entreated the lord of the household in God's name not to betray them to anyone. They said that they were very closely related to the archbishop of Mainz and if he brought them to him safe and sound, showing himself to be completely trustworthy, he would receive a reward appropriate to his deserts both from the archbishop himself and from the rest of their kinsmen, who were prominent among the princes of the kingdom by virtue of their wealth and the particular eminence of their rank.

Not long afterwards Eberhard appeared, raging and gnashing his teeth in his uncontrollable wrath. He had learned from reliable informants where the boys had found lodgings and was preparing *to storm* the house and to break down the doors, *using the utmost force*[1752] and the greatest exertions. He threatened *to set the roof on fire*[1753] if the king's hostages were not surrendered quickly. The whole city *rushed to view the spectacle*[1754] and there was a disorderly and discordant outcry as the crowd shouted according to their party allegiance, some on one side and some on the other. When the news of the disturbance in the city reached the archbishop of Mainz, he immediately sent Count Conrad, from the castle that is called Lützelburg,[1755] who then happened to be

---

1751 Meyer von Knonau (1894) p. 837 n. 147 noted that this detail places Mainz on the wrong side of the Rhine.

1752 Livy X.I.7. See Billanovich (1945) pp. 185–6.

1753 Livy XXVIII.20.7. See Billanovich (1945) p. 186.

1754 Livy XXIX.26.7.

1755 Conrad I, count of Luxemburg (✝1086). Bernold of St Blasien, *Chronicle* 1086, p. 287, however, characterised Conrad as 'a tireless supporter of Henry [IV]'. See Twellenkamp (1991) pp. 476, 490.

with the archbishop, with a force of armed men. Arriving on the scene, Conrad found Eberhard raving beyond all the bounds of moderation and assailing all those who opposed him, now with force, now with threats. Conrad repelled his attack on the house, loading him with insults. He took the boys and handed them over to the archbishop. The latter rejoiced exceedingly that he had removed this particular impediment that had hindered the cause of the princes who were planning to take up arms for the common good. He sent the boys back to their parents, taking every precaution against their being waylaid on the return journey.

On the appointed day the princes of Swabia and Saxony met in very great numbers in Tribur, according to their agreement.[1756] They were firmly resolved to displace King Henry from the government of the kingdom and to elect another king, whom they would choose by general agreement.[1757] Among those present were legates of the apostolic see, Patriarch Sigehard of Aquileia[1758] and Bishop Altman of Passau, a man who followed an apostolic way of life and possessed great virtues in Christ and to whom the pope had assigned his own authority in settling ecclesiastical cases.[1759] There were also some

1756 16 October: see above p. 330. Frutolf of Michelsberg, *Chronica* 1076, p. 84, gave the date 14 September. The place-name Tribur is given only by Lampert and the fragmentary *Annals of Iburg* p. 436. Berthold of Reichenau, *Chronicle* 1076, p. 152, placed the meeting of the princes in Magdeburg, which Meyer von Knonau (1894) p. 727 n. 178 explained as a scribal error for Madenburg (near Speyer), where there was perhaps a preliminary meeting before the main assembly in Tribur. The location is described in Bruno of Merseburg, *The Saxon War* c. 88, p. 82 as 'on the Rhine, opposite the town called Oppenheim'. On the assembly in Tribur see Meyer von Knonau (1894) pp. 729–35, 885–93; Erdmann (1937) pp. 361–88; Erdmann (1940) pp. 486–95; Schneider (1972) pp. 171–87; Beumann (1973) pp. 33–44; Hlawitschka (1974) pp. 25–45; Cowdrey (1998) pp. 150–3; Robinson (1999) pp. 155–8.

1757 Bruno of Merseburg, *The Saxon War* c. 88, p. 82 also referred to 'the election of a new king, on account of which they had assembled'. According to Berthold of Reichenau, *Chronicle* 1076, p. 152, however, 'the magnates of the kingdom decided that they should hold a conference with [the king] ... in which it would become lawful for them to serve their king and lord after he had been admonished and converted to penitence and reconciled'. This is the attitude of the only eyewitness account of Tribur, a letter by an unknown bishop, edited by Holder-Egger (1906) pp. 183–93. Erdmann (1937) p. 376 noted that 'from the outset only one party of princes sought a new election; the others certainly wished to humble Henry, but also to keep him as king'. Thus Lampert and Bruno represented the views of the former party, 'the deposition faction', while Berthold presented the attitude of the moderate majority of the princes at Tribur. See also Robinson (1999) pp. 155–6.

1758 Sigehard of Aquileia (above n. 509) is identified only by Lampert. Bruno, *The Saxon War* c. 88, p. 82 referred only to 'the patriarch'.

1759 On Altman of Passau (above n. 452) cf. Berthold, *Chronicle* 1076, p. 153: 'the bishop of Passau, to whom [Gregory VII] had long before granted the office of papal

laymen who, forsaking great riches, had spontaneously devoted themselves to a life of deprivation and poverty for God's sake. They had been sent by the Roman pontiff to bear witness publicly to all men throughout Gaul that King Henry had been excommunicated on just grounds and to promise the support of papal approval and authority in the election of another king.[1760] They refused to associate with any prince or any private individual who had had any connection with King Henry by word or deed after his excommunication until he had performed penance publicly and been absolved from the anathema by Altman, the vicar of the Roman pontiff.[1761] They were equally careful to avoid associating with those who participated in the prayers of married priests or those who had acquired their ecclesiastical ordinations by paying for them.

They consulted together continuously for seven days[1762] and diligently debated what ought to be done and how to assist a State that was already in danger and threatened by shipwreck. They looked back upon the whole course of the king's life *from his tenderest years* (as men say)[1763] and the shameful and dishonourable actions by which he had defiled both his own good name and the dignity of the empire when he had scarcely reached adulthood. They considered the injuries that he had inflicted on individuals and those that he had perpetrated against all men in general when he first reached the years of manhood. They reflected that he had excluded the princes from his friendship and had raised *men of the lowest*

---

representative'; Bruno, *The Saxon War* c. 88, p. 82: 'the bishop of Passau, the legate of the Roman pontiff'.

1760 Cf. Bernold of St Blasien, *Chronicle* 1076, p. 257: 'Brother Kadaloh, who had left the secular career of a knight and converted to religion, brought the pope's legation to the assembly of Oppenheim, the pope having laid this duty on him.' On the attitude of the pope cf. Gregory VII, *Register* IV.3, pp. 298–300, of 3 September, addressed to the faithful in Germany, which referred to the election of a new king as a last resort, to be used only 'if [the king] was not wholeheartedly converted to God'.

1761 Cf. Berthold of Reichenau, *Chronicle* 1076, p. 153: Altman had 'the responsibility of reconciling according to canon law all – except only the king – who came in a fitting manner to perform reparation and worthy penitence.... Among these were the archbishop of Mainz with his vassals, the bishops of Trier, Strasbourg, Verdun, Liège, Münster, the bishop elect of Utrecht, the bishops of Speyer and Basel ... and very many abbots and also a large crowd of greater and lesser men.' Cf. also Bernold of St Blasien, *Pro Gebhardo episcopo Constantiensi* c. 5, p. 110: see above n. 1741.

1762 16–22 October. Berthold of Reichenau, *Chronicle* 1076, p. 153, referred to 'ten days'.

1763 Horace, *Carmina* III.6.24.

rank[1764] and of no ancestry to the highest honours. He spent nights no less than days in consultations with them and finally he plotted the destruction of the nobility, if it could be done. They recalled that he had left the barbarian peoples undisturbed[1765] but with all his might had drawn his sword against the peoples subject to him and proceeded to slaughter them with the cruelty of an enemy. They considered how loathsome, how contemptible, how endangered by internal strife and how bloody he had made the kingdom that he received from his ancestors in a most peaceful condition, abounding in everything that was good. They observed that churches and monasteries had been destroyed, that income intended to provide food for the servants of God had been diverted to pay for the service of knights, that zeal for religion and for the concerns of the Church had been transformed into a preoccupation with the weapons of war and the construction of fortresses. These were intended not to ward off the violent attacks of the barbarians but to rob the fatherland of peace and to place the yoke of hardest slavery on the necks of free men.[1766] They saw that there was no comfort anywhere for widows and orphans, no refuge for the oppressed and for the falsely accused. There was no respect for the laws, no discipline in men's conduct; neither the authority of the Church nor the dignity of the State remained in being. Thus the sacred and the profane, the divine and the human, right and wrong had been thrown into confusion and become indistinguishable through the rashness of one man. Accordingly, there was but a single remedy for such great misfortunes: that man should be removed and as soon as possible another king should be elected, who would *rein in the licentiousness that had* for so long *gone beyond*[1767] all bounds and support the ruins of the tottering world upon his shoulders.

King Henry had gathered the adherents of his party together and stayed in the village called Oppenheim, so that the River Rhine divided the two camps.[1768] Every day he sent numerous envoys to the princes,

---

1764 Livy I.47.11; XXIV.23.10. On this complaint cf. above, 1073, pp. 173 and n. 882, 178; 1076, p. 326 and n. 1723.

1765 Cf. above, 1073, pp. 177–8 and n. 922.

1766 Cf. above, 1073, pp. 164, 170–1, 178.

1767 Horace, *Carmina* IV.15.9.

1768 Tribur and Oppenheim (south of Mainz) were identified only by Lampert and the fragmentary *Annals of Iburg* p. 436. Cf. Berthold of Reichenau, *Chronicle* 1076, p. 153: 'After [the princes] had assembled there [in Magdeburg, perhaps meaning Madenburg: see n. 1756] ..., the king ... set up camp beside the Rhine in the village of Oppenheim'; Bruno of Merseburg, *The Saxon War* c. 88, pp. 82–3: 'the Saxons ... arrived on the Rhine, opposite the town called Oppenheim ... but Henry

promising that everything that displeased them would be corrected in future. He promised that, if he lived, he would cancel out the memory of old injuries by means of the favours that he would confer in future times. Henceforward he would take no initiative in the government of the State without a general consultation. Finally he declared that he would willingly surrender his rights and make over to them the right and the power to govern and to order the whole kingdom according to their own wishes,[1769] as long as they *allowed in a spirit of patience*[1770] only the outward signs – the royal title and the reverence due to a king – to remain lawfully his. For once he had received these in a lawful manner, he could not lose them without involving them all in the utmost disgrace. The princes should not allow the splendour of the German kingdom, which had remained pure and undefiled throughout all the past centuries, to become contaminated in their time by the stain of such an unseemly example. If, however, they found it too difficult to credit his words, because they had been deceived so often by his lofty promises, he was prepared to pledge his faith by means of whatever oaths and whatever hostages they wished that no lapse of time and no change of circumstances or reversal of fortunes would ever destroy this good will that he felt towards them.

To this the princes replied that there was no longer any reliable evidence by means of which the king's faith, so often tried and tested, could be proved or guaranteed. For on so many occasions he had promised by all that was holy before the eyes of the all-seeing God that he would amend his conduct but, as soon as the crisis that currently beset him had passed by, he *broke* all the chains by which he had bound himself, *as if they were spiders' webs.*[1771] He always began afresh with unbridled liberty on his *career of evildoing,* like *a horse plunging*

---

was in the city of Mainz on the other bank of the Rhine'. Oppenheim is identified in other narrative sources as the meeting-place of both the princes and the royal party: see Meyer von Knonau (1894) p. 889. Lampert's version of the two meeting-places has been accepted in the modern secondary literature (above n. 1756).

1769 Holder-Egger, *Lamperti Annales* p. 278 n. 4 and 279 n. 1, observed that 'in his anger and hatred Lampert was led into extreme folly, so as to represent the king as speaking in this way'. See also Meyer von Knonau (1894) p. 886. In the version of Berthold of Reichenau, *Chronicle* 1076, p. 152, Henry IV was 'threatening and proud in his exhortations and persuasions'. According to Bruno of Merseburg, *The Saxon War* c. 88, p. 82, the king 'sent envoys, who tried to move [the princes] to compassion, so that they would deign to accept that, having been sufficiently reproved, he was now corrected'.

1770 Livy X.41.13. See Billanovich (1945) p. 101.

1771 Isaiah 59:5; Job 8:14. Cf. above, 1074, p. 235 and n. 1240.

headlong into battle[1772] and was worse than before. 'We have not rushed forward in a rash and over-hasty manner to resort to these extreme measures. We have previously tried every way, every expedient by which the character of this hopeless man, inflexible and inured to evil, might somehow be softened. But the chronic disease is already deeply rooted in his innermost being and admits of no hope, no remedy and defeats all the skill and all the persistence of the healers. In truth, while we are earnestly striving to humour his light-mindedness and, under the pretext of the oath of fidelity, we respond with womanly patience to all the wrong that he tries to do, the condition of the State is undermined, the serenity of the Church is disturbed, the majesty of the empire is destroyed, the authority of the princes is cancelled, morality is perverted, the laws fall into decay and, according to the saying of the prophet, *swearing and lying and killing and stealing and committing adultery have broken all bounds and blood follows blood.*[1773] In short, the whole practice of justice and piety, religion and honour has become neglected and is no longer cultivated. Nevertheless we have borne with this, as long as it threatened only to damage this temporal existence and only to sully men's reputation and good name – although men ought not to have to bear such things – lest we should seem to act in a hasty and shameless manner against the oath by which we were bound and, in our efforts to preserve our own fame, we should suffer the shipwreck of our souls.[1774] But now because of his disgraceful actions[1775] the king has been cut off by the sword of papal anathema from the body of the Church and we cannot have contact with him without losing the communion of the Church and departing from the faith, and the Roman pontiff has by his apostolic authority released us from the fidelity by which we were bound to the king through many oaths. It would certainly be the height of madness, therefore, not to seize the opportunity of salvation offered by heaven *with open hands* (as the saying is)[1776] and not to enact at such an appropriate time the plan

---

1772 Jeremiah 22:17; 8:6.

1773 Hosea 4:2.

1774 Cf. Bruno of Merseburg, *The Saxon War* c. 25, p. 29: 'Perhaps, as Christians, you are afraid to violate the oath that you swore to the king.'

1775 Lampert here implied that it was because of the princes' grievances that Henry IV had been excommunicated. Gregory VII, *Epistolae Vagantes* 14, pp. 38–9, had informed the German faithful during the summer of the three reasons for the excommunication: association with excommunicates, failure to perform 'penance for the guilty actions of his life' and daring 'to breach the unity of holy Church'.

1776 Jerome, *Letter* 53 (to Paulinus) c. 10, *MPL* 22, col. 549. Cf. above, 1059, p. 75 and n. 222.

of action that had been under deliberation for so long. For both secular and ecclesiastical laws permit it; the time and the place smile upon it; finally, everything that is advantageous to peace or war favours the execution of so great an enterprise.[1777] We therefore despise the secret devices and the empty assertions by means of which the king once more tries to find a way to reach our necks and our throats with his sword. We remain unalterably determined to provide ourselves without delay with a man who will lead us and fight the war of the Lord to attack and destroy *every lofty ambition* on the part of any man raising and *exalting himself against* the righteousness and truth *of God*[1778] and the authority of the holy Roman church.' With these words they dismissed the king's envoys.

Again and again the king sent other envoys and omitted no form of entreaty that he considered likely to hinder that great undertaking of the princes. But the latter remained firm and immovable in their resolve. *It* now *seemed* from the point of view of both parties *that events were moving towards*[1779] a great crisis. Finally the princes prepared to appoint another king immediately, to cross the River Rhine – for the archbishop of Mainz[1780] had assembled all the boats on that side of the river – and to make an attack on King Henry the following day.[1781] Since his hope of obtaining a delay was gone, the king ordered his followers, who were scattered through the neighbouring villages, to assemble in one place and to arm themselves so that, when the enemy advanced to the opposite bank of the river, they should at once meet them in battle. *While they were* all *eagerly and anxiously awaiting this decisive event,*[1782] behold! at first light on the following day[1783] – which, it was feared, would bring the utmost

---

1777 Holder-Egger, *Lamperti Annales* p. 280 n. 3, interpreted this passage as 'Lampert's address to the brethren of Hersfeld, wishing to persuade them to abandon the party of King Henry'.

1778 II Corinthians 10:5.

1779 Livy II.18.2; XXIV.6.1; XXV.3.19.

1780 On Siegfried of Mainz (above n. 210) and the 'deposition faction' see above p. 331 and n. 1743.

1781 This planned attack on the king is mentioned only in Lampert's account. The other detailed reports – the eyewitness account by an unknown bishop in Holder-Egger (1906) pp. 183–93; Berthold of Reichenau, *Chronicle* 1076, pp. 152–4; Bruno of Merseburg, *The Saxon War* c. 88, pp. 82–3 – refer only to a sequence of negotiations. Holder-Egger, *Lamperti Annales* p. 281 n. 1, noted that 'the extreme absurdity of this narrative is revealed when the princes, preparing to make war on the king, are said suddenly to have changed their minds'.

1782 Livy II.18.4; XXI.53.9.

1783 Holder-Egger, *Lamperti Annales* p. 281, suggested the date '*ca.* 25 October'.

harm to the State – the Swabians and Saxons[1784] sent envoys to the king who made the following statement. Although he had never shown any concern for justice or the laws either in war or in peace, they nevertheless wished to deal with him according to the laws and, although the offences of which he was accused were glaringly obvious to everyone, they would nevertheless refer the case without prejudice to the judgement of the Roman pontiff. They would propose to the pope that he would come to Augsburg at the Purification of St Mary[1785] and there hold a very well attended council of the princes of the whole kingdom. After examining the statements of both parties, he himself would either pass sentence on the accused or absolve him, according to his own judgement.[1786] But if the king was not absolved from excommunication through his own fault before the anniversary of the day on which he was excommunicated, his case would be lost irrevocably.[1787] Thereafter he could not lawfully regain the kingship because, according to the laws, one who had experienced a year as an excommunicate could no longer

1784 Lampert's account does not refer to the role of the papal legates in the negotiations, which were regarded as crucial by Meyer von Knonau (1894) pp. 730–1; Erdmann (1937) pp. 379–80; Cowdrey (1998) p. 151; Robinson (1999) pp. 155–8.

1785 2 February: so also Berthold of Reichenau, *Chronicle* 1076, p. 156; Bernold of St Blasien, *Chronicle* 1076, p. 257. Cf. Bruno of Merseburg, *The Saxon War* c. 88, p. 83: 'they sent an envoy to request the pope to come to Augsburg at the beginning of February'. According to the letter of the anonymous eyewitness in Holder-Egger (1906) p. 189, 'the time for the accomplishing of this [the reconciliation of the king with the pope] was designated as Epiphany [6 January], the place as Augsburg'. Hlawitschka (1974) p. 44 convincingly suggested that the copyist here erroneously substituted the term *epiphania* for *hypante* in the original letter, i.e. the Greek term for the feast of the Purification.

1786 Cf. Bruno of Merseburg, *The Saxon War* c. 88, p. 83: the pope would 'either absolve [the king] or bind him still more strongly'. A different emphasis appears in the letter of the anonymous eyewitness in Holder-Egger (1906) pp. 188–9: 'the excommunicate should be reconciled to the Church in the presence of the excommunicator either by proving his innocence or by making appropriate satisfaction for his fault'. I.e. even if the pope judged the king to be guilty, Henry would still be absolved from excommunication after performing penance. Cf. Berthold of Reichenau, *Chronicle* 1076, p. 156: the king 'should meet [the pope] in the presence of the magnates of the kingdom in Augsburg to be heard by him and to be reconciled'.

1787 Cf. Berthold, *Chronicle* 1076, p. 154: 'if through his own fault he remained excommunicate for over a year, they would no longer have him as king'; Bruno, *The Saxon War* c. 88, p. 83: 'if Henry IV ... had not been absolved from excommunication by the pope at the beginning of the month of February, he was by no means ever again to be called their king'. While Lampert presented this condition as part of the original agreement reached in Tribur, Berthold reported it as a last-minute condition imposed after Henry had agreed to the other terms. Bruno reported both this condition and the invitation to the pope as late conditions imposed after a general settlement had been reached.

govern.[1788] If he willingly accepted the conditions offered to him and promised to be subject to the Roman pontiff in all things and obedient to his commands,[1789] the princes would regard the following as a test of his good faith. He must immediately banish from his company and his entourage all those whom the pope excommunicated.[1790] He himself must dismiss his army and withdraw to the city of Speyer, contenting himself there solely with the company of the bishop of Verdun[1791] and a few servants, whom the princes judged to be untouched and uncontaminated by this excommunication. He must meanwhile live as a private individual; he must not enter a church; he must take no measures in public affairs on his own authority; he must make no use of royal pomp and magnificence nor of the insignia of the royal office according to custom until his cause had been decided by the synod.[1792] Moreover in the case of the city of Worms – which, after the bishop[1793] had been expelled and the sanctuary of divine service had been destroyed, he had *made* into a citadel of war and *a den of thieves*[1794] – he must remove his garrison, restore the city to the bishop of Worms and in addition ensure by means of oaths and hostages that the bishop need not in future fear a rebellion or a plot on the part of the citizens.[1795] Furthermore, if he deviated from any one of these conditions, they would regard themselves as released from all blame, from all the obligations of their

---

1788 Bonizo of Sutri, *To a Friend* VIII, p. 239: the German princes 'did not wish to break their law, which prescribed that an excommunicate who was not absolved from his excommunication before a year and a day, should lose his office and all his authority'. Holder-Egger, *Lamperti Annales* p. 281 n. 5, commenting on Lampert's reference to 'the laws', referred to the canon law tradition recorded in Gratian, *Decretum* C.XI q.3 c. 36–7.

1789 This was the most important condition imposed on the king, prompting Henry's 'Promise of Oppenheim': Henry IV, *Letters*, appendix B, p. 69. Cf. Henry IV, *Letter* 14, pp. 20–1. See Meyer von Knonau (1894) pp. 732–4; Erdmann (1937) pp. 90–103; Schneider (1972) pp. 173–86; Cowdrey (1998) pp. 151–2; Robinson (1999) pp. 156–8.

1790 Cf. Berthold of Reichenau, *Chronicle* 1076, p. 154: 'the king should separate himself entirely from his excommunicated followers'.

1791 Theoderic, bishop of Verdun (1046–89).

1792 Cf. Berthold, *Chronicle* 1076, p. 155: 'in Speyer, living in the customary manner of the penitent, together with the guardians and stewards who had been allotted to him by the magnates of the kingdom'.

1793 Adalbert (above n. 626). See above 1073, p. 200 and n. 1042.

1794 Matthew 21:13.

1795 Cf. Berthold of Reichenau, *Chronicle* 1077, p. 168: 'The citizens of Worms also conspired in a rebellion against the king [the anti-king Rudolf] and their bishop'. See Büttner (1973) pp. 355–6.

oath of fidelity, from all accusations of treachery in no longer waiting
for the judgement of the Roman pontiff and taking counsel together to
consider what was in the best interests of the State.

Since all the king's hopes and his whole freedom of action had been
reduced almost to nothing, he was exceedingly glad that he had escaped
for the present from the disaster that threatened him, albeit on such
degrading conditions. He therefore very readily promised obedience
in all respects. He at once commanded the archbishop of Cologne, the
bishop of Bamberg, the bishop of Strasbourg, the bishop of Basel, the
bishop of Speyer, the bishop of Lausanne, the bishop of Zeitz and the
bishop of Osnabrück[1796] to leave his camp, together with Udalric of
Godesheim, Eberhard,[1797] Hartman[1798] and all the other excommunicates,
of whose aid and advice he had hitherto been very glad to make use.[1799]
He also sent envoys to Worms and ordered that the knights whom
he had stationed there as a garrison should depart and that the city
should stand open to the bishop. After he had sent back to their various
homes the other men who had assembled in large numbers to offer him
their help, the king then went to Speyer with a few followers, according
to the agreement. There he spent some time living a retired life, his
conduct restricted by the conditions and regulations that the princes
had prescribed.[1800]

After the men of Worms had surrendered and restored the city to
the bishop in an entirely peaceful condition, the Swabians and Saxons
returned to their homelands joyful and triumphant. They immediately

---

1796 Hildolf of Cologne (above n. 1609), Rupert of Bamberg (above n. 1524), Werner II of
Strasbourg (above n. 378), Burchard of Basel (above n. 773), Huzman of Speyer (above
n. 1440), Burchard of Lausanne (above n. 1637), Eppo (Eberhard) of Zeitz-Naumburg
(above n. 46), Benno II of Osnabrück (above n. 500). According to Berthold, *Chronicle*
1077, p. 153, the bishops of Strasbourg, Speyer and Basel were among those restored
to communion by Altman of Passau during the assembly of Tribur.

1797 Udalric of Godesheim (above n. 1036) and probably Count Eberhard 'the Bearded'
(above n. 641), two of the five royal advisers excommunicated by Gregory VII in
1075: see above p. 308 and n. 1638.

1798 Hartman, probably one of the five excommunicated royal advisers, is mentioned in
no other source. See Meyer von Knonau (1894) p. 730 and n. 187; Robinson (1999)
p. 360.

1799 Holder-Egger (1894) p. 198 conjectured that Abbot Hartwig of Hersfeld was one
of these 'other excommunicates' and that Lampert here deliberately concealed this
fact.

1800 Cf. Berthold, *Chronicle* 1076, p. 155: see above n. 1792. See Kilian (1886) p. 74;
Meyer von Knonau (1894) pp. 739–40, 890 and n. 16; Cowdrey (1998) p. 153.

sent envoys to Rome,[1801] who informed the pope of the course of events and earnestly entreated him not to decline the invitation to appear in person on the appointed day to put an end to these great calamities, the civil wars throughout Gaul. The king knew for certain that his *preservation depended entirely on*[1802] whether he was absolved from excommunication before the anniversary of his sentence. He did not consider it safe in regard to his own interests to wait for the arrival of the Roman pontiff in Gaul and thus to deliver up his cause to be decided by so hostile a judge and by such inflexible accusers. He therefore concluded that it would be best for him in the present state of his affairs to meet the Roman pontiff inside Italy, while he was travelling to Gaul and to try by every means in his power to obtain absolution from the anathema. When he had achieved this, the rest of his difficulties would easily be removed since considerations of religion would no longer prevent him from holding talks with the princes and taking counsel with them and from calling on his friends to fulfil their duty of fidelity in time of trouble.[1803] A few days before Christmas, therefore, he left the city of Speyer and began his journey, together with his wife and his little son.[1804] On his departure from the kingdom there was in his entourage no free-born man from among all the Germans except one and he was remarkable neither for his birth nor for his riches.[1805] Since he was concerned about the expense of

1801 Cf. Berthold, *Chronicle* 1076, p. 154: 'The magnates of the kingdom ... sent in great haste to Rome envoys whose testimony could be relied on and who had been present at all the negotiations' in Tribur; Bruno of Merseburg, *The Saxon War* c. 88, p. 83.

1802 Livy III.46.5.

1803 Cf. Berthold, *Chronicle* 1076, pp. 156–7: the king 'strove to meet [the pope] before he entered our region. For he decided to force him to his own way of thinking either by terrifying him ... or with the help of the Romans and his other advisers, who might be corrupted by large bribes and thus made [the king's] inseparable supporters'. Bernold of St Blasien, *Chronicle* 1077, p. 257: 'Henry the so-called king despaired of his own cause and therefore avoided a public hearing.' See Meyer von Knonau (1894) pp. 739–40 and n. 199; Cowdrey (1998) pp. 154–5; Robinson (1999) pp. 158–9.

1804 Bertha of Turin (above n. 491) and three-year-old Conrad (above n. 1088). Cf. Berthold, *Chronicle* 1077, p. 157: 'he took his wife and son'. Their departure was 'around 20 December', according to Kilian (1886) p. 74. See also Meyer von Knonau (1894) pp. 741–2; Cowdrey (1998) p. 155.

1805 Berthold, *Chronicle* 1077, p. 157, refers to 'his magnificent retinue of followers', Bruno, *The Saxon War* c. 88, p. 83, to 'a great army'. Lampert subsequently contradicted himself below, 1077, p. 346 and n. 1819, referring to 'all the king's advisers' in his entourage in Gex. The reference to the absence of 'free-born men' in the royal entourage continues the polemic noted above, 1073, p. 173 and n. 882, 178; 1076, pp. 326 and n. 1723, 336 and n. 1764.

so long a journey, he appealed to many men to whom he had often shown favour in the days when the State was in a sound condition. There were, however, exceedingly few who were moved either by the remembrance of former acts of kindness or by *the drama of human affairs*[1806] unfolding before them and who relieved his needs to some degree. From the height of fame and power he had suddenly reached that state of distress and adversity. The other excommunicates likewise hastened their journey into Italy with the utmost impatience,[1807] such was their eagerness to obtain absolution as quickly as possible. Nevertheless because of their fear of the princes or rather of the Roman pontiff, they would not allow the king to travel in their company.

The merciless rigour of the winter in this year lasted so long and was so much harsher than usual that the River Rhine was held in the grip of ice from the feast of St Martin[1808] until almost 1 April and was able to bear travellers on foot. In very many places the vines withered completely because their roots were dried up by the cold.

1077

The duke of the Poles, who had for many years been obliged to pay tribute to the German kings and whose kingdom had long ago been conquered by the valour of the Germans and reduced to a province, became suddenly puffed up with pride.[1809] For he perceived that the German princes were preoccupied with *the dissension in their homeland*[1810] and were by no means in a position to make war on foreign peoples. He therefore usurped for himself the office of king and the royal title,

1806 Sallust, *Jugurtha* 14. Lampert's predilection for the image of 'the world as a theatre' was discussed by Struve (1970a) pp. 122–3 and n. 49. See also above p. 47.

1807 Berthold, *Chronicle* 1077, p. 155, identified 'the bishop of Toul, together with the bishop of Speyer and many others, on whom the bishop of Passau imposed this duty'.

1808 11 November. Cf. Berthold, *Chronicle* 1076, pp. 154–5: 'the harsh and snowy winter and uninterrupted cold weather' lasted from 'around 1 November ... until 15 March' ('the Rhine and likewise the Po, to say nothing of other rivers, were frozen so hard that for a long time they presented all travellers with an icy road that was like solid land'); Bernold of St Blasien, *Chronicle* 1077, p. 257: from 31 October until 26 March; Sigebert of Gembloux, *Chronica* 1076, p. 363: from mid-November until the spring equinox. See Meyer von Knonau (1894) p. 750 and n. 7.

1809 Duke Boleslav II of Poland (above n. 745). Cf. Bernold of St Blasien, *Chronicle* 1077, p. 257: 'The duke of the Poles crowned himself king.' Significantly, *Chronicae Polonorum* I.22–30, pp. 439– 42 consistently referred to Boleslav II as 'king' from his accession in 1058. See Meyer von Knonau (1894) pp. 745–6.

1810 Livy II.42.3.

put on the diadem and was consecrated king by fifteen bishops on the very day of Christmas.[1811] When this news soon afterwards reached the German princes, for whom the dignity of the State was a matter of great concern, it had a serious effect on them. They were enraged with one another because, while they vented their fury against themselves and their very existence in internal disputes, they had allowed the power and the influence of the barbarians to grow to such an extent that the duke of Bohemia had now for the third time passed through the German kingdom, devastating it with fire and sword,[1812] and now the duke of the Poles had in a shameless manner aimed at the royal title and the royal diadem to the dishonour of the German kingdom, contrary to the laws and rights of their ancestors.

King Henry set out for Italy and celebrated Christmas in Burgundy, in a place called Besançon,[1813] with some appearance of splendour, considering his dangerous situation. He was received and entertained by Count William, the kinsman of his mother,[1814] whose most ample and flourishing properties were in that region. This was the reason for his abandoning the direct route and turning aside into Burgundy: that he had learned for certain that the dukes Rudolf, Welf and Berthold had acted in advance to place guards on all the roads and all the approaches leading to Italy, which are commonly called mountain passes, so that he might have no opportunity there of crossing into Italy.[1815] After observing the festival of Christmas, he set out from that place and, when he had arrived in the place called Gex,[1816] he met his mother-

1811 Meyer von Knonau (1894) p. 746 n. 213 suggested that 'fifteen' might be an error for 'five', the current number of dioceses in Poland.

1812 On this recent expedition of Duke Vratislav II of Bohemia (above n. 746) see above p. 326 and n. 1721.

1813 25 December 1076. Cf. Berthold of Reichenau, *Chronicle* 1077, p. 157: 'The king celebrated Christmas *as best he could* in Besançon.' See Kilian (1886) p. 74; Meyer von Knonau (1894) p. 742.

1814 William, count of Burgundy (✝1087), cousin of Empress Agnes (above n. 30).

1815 Rudolf of Swabia (above n. 203), Welf IV of Bavaria (above n. 630), Berthold I of Carinthia (above n. 824). Gregory VII, *Register* IV.12, p. 312, referring to his plans to travel to Germany, noted that 'one of the dukes was to meet us at the mountain passes'. The papal letter used the same term, *clusae*, that Lampert found it necessary to explain here: see Niermeyer – van de Kieft (2002) p. 252. On Henry IV's route see Meyer von Knonau (1894) p. 742 and n. 201.

1816 Cf. Berthold, *Chronicle* 1077, p. 157: 'he crossed the Rhone at Geneva'. Kilian (1886) p. 74 (and the older historical literature) identified the place name as *Cinis*, perhaps Chêne (near Geneva). Holder-Egger's edition, *Lamperti Annales* p. 285 n. 2, adopted the reading *Civis* and suggested that this was a scribal error for 'Jais', the modern Gex. See also Meyer von Knonau (1894) pp. 748–9 and n. 6.

in-law[1817] and her son, named Amadeus,[1818] who enjoyed outstanding authority, the most ample possessions and the greatest renown in those regions. They gave the king an honourable reception on his arrival. Nevertheless they refused to allow him to cross their frontiers unless he granted them five of the bishoprics of Italy neighbouring their own possessions as the price to be paid for his journey. This seemed to all the king's advisers[1819] too harsh and intolerable. But he was burdened by the inescapable need to purchase the right to continue his journey by whatever means he could and they were not at all influenced either by considerations of kinship or by compassion at so wretched a situation. Finally, after much time and effort had been spent in these discussions, it was concluded with great difficulty that they would agree to accept a certain province in Burgundy, very well supplied with possessions of all kinds, as a reward for granting the king the right to cross their territory.[1820] Thus God's displeasure estranged from the king not only those men who were bound to him by oaths and by frequent acts of favour but also his friends and family connections.

Another difficulty immediately succeeded that of securing permission to make the crossing. The winter was very harsh and the mountains through which the journey was to be made reached up to an immense height and thrust their peaks almost into the clouds. *They were so thickly covered with* a huge mass of snow and *ice*[1821] that they did not allow a traveller on horseback or on foot to step on *the steep and slippery slopes*[1822] without being in danger. But the anniversary of the day on which the king had incurred excommunication was close at hand and admitted of no delays in pressing on with the journey. For he knew that it had been decided by the universal judgement of the princes that, unless he obtained absolution from the anathema before that day, his case would be lost forever and he would lose the kingdom without any possibility of recovering it in the future.[1823] He therefore hired certain natives of

1817 Adelaide of Susa, margravine of Turin (?1015–91), mother of Queen Bertha.

1818 Amadeus II, count of Savoy (✝1080), son of Adelaide and her third husband, Count Otto of Savoy.

1819 See above, 1076, p. 343 and n. 1805.

1820 Lampert alone reported this transaction: see Meyer von Knonau (1894) pp. 748–9. According to Previté-Orton (1912) pp. 237–8, the province was North Bugey or Tarentaise or a 'grant of immunity for the Savoyard possessions scattered outside their own *comitatus*'.

1821 Livy XXI.32.7.

1822 *Ibid.* XXI.35.12; XXI.36.7.

1823 Between 14 and 20 February: see above, 1076, p. 307 and n. 1633. See also above,

the region, who were skilled and well accustomed to *the rugged summits of the Alps*.[1824] They were to lead his entourage over the steep mountain and the huge mass of snow and to smooth the unevenness of the path by whatever means they could for those who were following. When, with these men as their guides, they had with great difficulty reached the summit of the mountain,[1825] there was no possibility of advancing further. For the mountain side was precipitous and, so they said, slippery because of the icy cold and seemed to rule out entirely any hope of a descent. In that situation the men tried to overcome every danger using their own strength, *now crawling on their hands and feet,*[1826] now clinging to the shoulders of their guides and also occasionally, when a foot slipped on an icy surface, falling and rolling down for a considerable distance. At last with difficulty and for a time at serious risk of their lives they reached the plains. The queen[1827] and the other women who were in her service were placed on the hides of oxen and *the guides who had been hired to lead the expedition*[1828] dragged them down behind them. Some of *the horses* they lowered down the mountainside by means of certain contrivances; others they spancelled and *dragged down* but many of these died while they were being dragged and very many were crippled: very *few* were able *to escape the peril*[1829] safe and sound.

After the rumour spread through Italy that the king had come, that he had surmounted the fearsome obstacle of the peaks and was now

---

1076, p. 340 and n. 1787.

1824 Livy XXI.35.4. See Billanovich (1945) p. 191.

1825 Mont Cenis: see Kilian (1886) p. 74; Meyer von Knonau (1894) pp. 750–1. Eleventh-century German kings usually travelled to their Italian kingdom by way of the Brenner but in December 1076 the Alpine passes in southern Germany were in the hands of the 'deposition faction': see above p. 345 and n. 1815. See Schrod (1931) pp. 16–17; Zimmermann (1975) p. 154; Robinson (1999) pp. 159–60. On Lampert's account of Henry IV's crossing of the Alps see Meyer von Knonau (1894) p. 751 n. 8: 'This very lively description, which has achieved a certain fame, is further evidence of Lampert's narrative art'. Struve (1970a) p. 91 suggested that because of Lampert's pilgrimage to Jerusalem (see above, 1058, p. 73), during which he spent the winter in the mountainous territory on the Bulgarian–Hungarian frontier, 'he could well have been in a position to describe Henry IV's arduous crossing of the Alps from his own viewpoint'. For the influence of the account of Hannibal's crossing the Alps in Livy XXI see Billanovich (1945) pp. 190–3 and above p. 8.

1826 Livy XXI.36.7. Cf. Berthold of Reichenau, *Chronicle* 1077, p. 157: 'undertaking a most desperate journey, with difficulty he climbed and crawled up the Alps'.

1827 Bertha of Turin (above n. 491): see above p. 343 and n. 1804.

1828 Livy XXI.34.3. See Billanovich (1945) p. 192.

1829 Livy XXI.33.5.

within the frontiers of Italy,[1830] all the bishops and counts of Italy eagerly crowded around him. They received him with the greatest honour, as befitted the greatness of the royal office, and within a few days an enormous army, too great to be counted, had flocked to him. For from the very beginning of his reign there were always those who longed for his arrival in Italy because that kingdom was continually troubled by wars and rebellions, together with freebooting and various acts of violence by private individuals. It was hoped that all the offences that wicked men dared to commit against the laws and ancestral rights would be amended by exercising royal authority. Since moreover there was a widespread rumour that the king was hastening with implacable determination to depose the pope, they rejoiced greatly that they were being offered an opportunity to revenge themselves in a suitable manner on him for the injury that he had previously inflicted on them when he suspended them from the communion of the Church.[1831]

Meanwhile the pope had been requested in a letter from the German princes who had assembled in Oppenheim to meet them on the feast of the Purification of St Mary[1832] in Augsburg to investigate the case of the king. Against the will of the Roman princes, who advised him against undertaking that journey because of the uncertain outcome of the business,[1833] the pope left Rome. He exerted himself to be present on the appointed day, hastening his journey as much as he could.[1834] Matilda, the widow of Duke Gozelo of the Lotharingians and the daughter of Margrave Boniface and Countess Beatrice,[1835] provided him with an

---

1830 Cf. Berthold of Reichenau, *Chronicle* 1077, p. 157: Henry 'hastily entered Lombardy by way of the bishopric of Turin. Gathering men wherever he could, he came from there to Pavia, where he also drew to himself from all sides a crowd of excommunicated bishops.' See Kilian (1886) p. 75; Meyer von Knonau (1894) pp. 752–4.

1831 Cf. Berthold, *Chronicle* 1077, pp. 157–8: Henry 'announced to [the bishops] ... that he would exhort the pope to examine not only his own case but also the sentence of excommunication wrongfully imposed on them. They, however, strongly urged him on the contrary not even to recognise him as pope'; Bonizo of Sutri, *To a Friend* VIII, p. 240: 'There are those who say that he wished to capture the pope unawares, which seems likely enough'; Bruno of Merseburg, *The Saxon War* c. 89, p. 83: 'it was announced to the pope that Henry ... wished to appoint another pope in his place'.

1832 2 February: see above, 1076, p. 340 and n. 1785.

1833 Cf. Gregory VII, *Epistolae Vagantes* 17, p. 48 ('setting aside the advice of almost all our faithful men'); no. 18, p. 50 ('against the will and the advice of the Romans'); *Epistolae Vagantes* 19, p. 50 ('against the will of almost all our faithful').

1834 Cf. Gregory VII, *Epistolae Vagantes* 17, pp. 46–8: 'we ... have decided ... to hasten our journey so that we wish to be in Mantua on 8 January'.

1835 Matilda, margravine of Tuscany (1046–1115), widow of Gozelo-Godfrey IV of

escort. Already in the lifetime of her husband she had lived at a very great distance from him and claimed for herself a kind of widowhood since she did not wish to follow her husband to Lotharingia and live outside her native land.[1836] Her husband was immersed in the affairs of the duchy that he administered in Lotharingia and he scarcely visited the Italian march once in three or four years. After his death[1837] Matilda stayed at the side of the Roman pontiff as his virtually inseparable companion and devoted herself to him with extraordinary compassion.[1838] A great part of Italy obeyed her authority and she possessed an abundance of all the property that mortals most prize, greater than the rest of the princes of that land.[1839] Wherever the pope had need of her help, therefore, she was there with all speed and zealously served him, as a father or a lord. For this reason she could not escape the suspicion that she was guilty of an incestuous passion.[1840] The king's supporters and especially the clergy – whom the pope had forbidden to contract unlawful marriages against the ordinances of the canons – spread far and wide the story that day and night the pope shamelessly luxuriated in her embraces and that she refused to marry a second time after she lost her husband because she was preoccupied with her clandestine passion for the pope.[1841] But it was clearer than day to all men of sound judgement that what they said was false. For it was the case both that

---

Lower Lotharingia (above n. 570), daughter of Margrave Boniface of Canossa (above n. 110) and Margravine Beatrice of Tuscany (above n. 111).

1836 *Chronicon sancti Huberti Andaginensis* p. 583: '[Gozelo-Godfrey's] wife Matilda left him and returned to Lombardy and when her husband rather frequently commanded her to return, she did not obey.' He visited her in Italy 'but he did not obtain marital favour from her and, rejected by her and driven out of Italy, he returned to Lotharingia'. Two letters of Gregory VII urge Matilda not to abandon her marriage and take the veil: *Register* I.47, p. 71 ('I have restrained you from deserting others in order to provide salvation of your soul alone'); I.50, p. 77 (Matilda should not 'leave the world with all its cares'). See Cowdrey (1998) pp. 97, 299; Hay (2008) pp. 43–4.

1837 26 February 1076: see above, 1076, p. 308 and nn. 1639, 1642.

1838 See Simeoni (1947) pp. 353–72; Cowdrey (1998) pp. 299–300, 302–3; Hay (2008) pp. 59–100.

1839 The march of Tuscany *ca.* 1077 consisted of the region of central Italy north of the papal patrimony, extending from the area of Mantua, north of the River Po, to the River Arno and to the west of the Apennines: see Overmann (1895) pp. 1–40.

1840 Cf. Lampert's formulation above, 1062, p. 81 and n. 268, concerning the relations of Empress Agnes and Bishop Henry II of Augsburg.

1841 Cf. Letter of the German prelates at Worms to Gregory VII (January 1076) in Henry IV, *Letters*, appendix A, p. 68: 'you have filled the whole Church with, as it were, a stench of the most grievous scandal because you live together with another man's wife in a closer intimacy than is necessary'.

the pope led a life of such distinction and such apostolic virtue that his exalted personal conduct would not suffer the slightest blemish from an injurious rumour and that, if Matilda committed any offence, she could never have concealed it in a very populous city and amidst so great a concourse of servants. Moreover the signs and wonders that were quite often wrought through the prayers of the pope[1842] and his most fervent zeal for God and for the Church's laws sufficiently protected him against the venomous tongues of detractors. While the pope was hastening to Gaul, therefore, he unexpectedly heard that the king was now in Italy. On the advice of Matilda,[1843] he changed course and made for a certain very well fortified castle, which was called Canossa.[1844] He wished to wait until he had carefully investigated the king's reason for coming and whether he came to seek pardon for what he had done or whether he came, *full of animosity*,[1845] to avenge the injury of his excommunication with military might.

When Bishop Theoderic of Verdun,[1846] a man who had shown the most steadfast fidelity to the king, wished to follow the king shortly after he set out for Italy, he was captured by Count Adalbert of the castle called Calw.[1847] He was plundered of all the supplies that he had gathered together with the greatest care for so long a journey. He was held in prison by Adalbert for a long time and was finally released and allowed to go free only after giving him whatever was demanded as the price of his ransom and in addition after taking an oath that he would never impose either a spiritual or a corporal punishment on Adalbert. When Bishop Rupert of Bamberg was travelling through Bavaria on his way to Italy, he also was captured by Welf, the duke of the Bavarians. The latter took away all the bishop's personal property but he restored to the church of Bamberg in their entirety the episcopal vestments and the rest of the ecclesiastical apparatus that he found among his treasures. The bishop himself he kept in close confinement in a strongly fortified castle from Christmas to the feast of the holy apostle Bartholomew[1848]

1842 Cf. the miracle recorded by Paul of Bernried, *Life of Pope Gregory VII* c. 22, p. 272.

1843 Cf. Gregory VII, *Epistolae Vagantes* 19, p. 50: 'against the will of almost all our faithful except Matilda'; Arnulf of Milan, *Liber gestorum recentium* V.8, p. 228: 'relying on the help of Matilda, he came into Italy'. See Hay (2008) p. 70.

1844 The fortress of Matilda of Tuscany, southwest of Reggio. Cf. Bonizo of Sutri, *To a Friend* VIII, p. 240: 'the very secure fortress of the most excellent Matilda'.

1845 Livy IV.32.10.

1846 Theoderic of Verdun: see above p. 341 and n. 1791.

1847 Adalbert II, count of Calw (†1099). See Meyer von Knonau (1894) p. 755.

1848 25 December 1076 – 24 August 1077. On Rupert of Bamberg (above n. 1524) and

and he could not be induced by the prayers or bribed by the gifts of his friends to let him go free.

The rest of the bishops and the laymen whom the pope had excommunicated and whom for this reason the king had been compelled by extreme necessity to banish from his side evaded the guards who were blockading the mountain passes[1849] and reached Italy unharmed. When they found the pope in Canossa, they humbly begged him, with bare feet and wearing woollen garments next to their skin, for pardon for presuming to rebel and for absolution from excommunication.[1850] The pope said that mercy must not be denied to those who truly acknowledged their sin and deplored it but that their long period of disobedience and the shame of a sin that had long been widely known ought to be destroyed and purified by the fire of a penance that should last even longer. If thereafter they truly repented their action, *they would patiently submit*[1851] to whatever cauterisation, in the form of ecclesiastical rebuke, the pope applied to heal their wounds. For if their pardon came too easily, the dreadful and violent offence that they had ventured to commit against the apostolic see would seem to be little or nothing. When they professed that they were ready to endure everything that he inflicted on them, the pope commanded that all the bishops should be kept separate from one another and imprisoned alone in individual cells. They were not to have any conversation with anyone but in the evening they were refreshed with a moderate quantity of food and drink. The pope also imposed on the laymen a penance suitable to each individual, according to their age and strength. After he had thus tested them for some days, he finally summoned them to him and gently rebuked them for the offences that they had committed, admonished them not to offend in the same way in future and absolved them from excommunication. When they departed, he commanded above all, repeating it again and again, that they should not have any kind of contact with King Henry until he had made amends to the apostolic see for the injury

---

Welf IV of Bavaria (above n. 630) see Meyer von Knonau (1894) p. 755.

1849 See above p. 345 and n. 1815.

1850 These 'bishops and laymen' are identified below, p. 357 and n. 1879: 'the bishop of Zeitz and the bishop of Vercelli and and Margrave Azzo'; p. 363 and n. 1900: 'Archbishop Liemar of Bremen, Bishop Eppo of Zeitz, Bishop Benno of Osnabrück, Bishop Burchard of Lausanne, Bishop Burchard of Basel and the laymen Udalric, Eberhard, Berthold'. Berthold of Reichenau, *Chronicle* 1077, pp. 161, 162, identified the bishops of Naumburg (Zeitz) and Vercelli and the archbishop of Bremen and the bishops of Strasbourg, Lausanne and Basel.

1851 Livy X.41.13. See Billanovich (1945) p. 101.

that he had done or bring him their help in any way to overturn the State and disturb the peace of the Church. Nevertheless the pope also permitted them all without exception to speak to the king so that he might be incited to do penance and be called back from *the evil course*[1852] on which he seemed to be borne headlong.

Meanwhile King Henry summoned Countess Matilda to a conference[1853] and sent her to the pope, laden with prayers and promises. He sent with her his mother-in-law and her son[1854] and also Margrave Azzo[1855] and the abbot of Cluny[1856] and some others of the foremost princes of Italy, whose opinion he did not doubt would carry great weight with the pope. The king begged that he might be absolved from excommunication and that the pope should not be over-hasty in placing his reliance on the German princes, who had been inflamed to accuse the king by the sting of envy rather than by zeal for justice. When the pope had heard the message of these envoys, he said that it was entirely inappropriate and utterly at odds with the laws of the Church that the case of the accused should be discussed in the absence of the accusers.[1857] On the contrary, if the king believed in his own innocence, he should with confidence and free of any particle of fear make his appearance in Augsburg on the day on which the rest of the princes

---

1852 Jeremiah 22:17.

1853 On the role of Matilda (above n. 1835) cf. Gregory VII, *Register* IV.12, p. 313 ('our daughter Matilda'); Berthold of Reichenau, *Chronicle* 1077, p. 159 ('primarily through the mediation and help of Margravine Matilda'); Arnulf of Milan, *Liber gestorum recentium* V.8, p. 229 ('through the great prudence of Matilda their treaties of peace were confirmed'). Donizo of Canossa, *Vita Mathildis comitissae metrica* II, p. 381, represented Henry IV saying to Matilda, 'Powerful cousin, go and cause me to be blessed!' Cf. the well known miniature depicting this scene in the codex of the *Vita*, Vaticanus latinus 4922, with the caption, 'The king ... kneels to Matilda' (facsimile at *MGH SS* 12, 366, *tabula* III, image 7).

1854 Margravine Adelaide of Turin (above n. 1817) and Count Amadeus II of Savoy (above n. 1818). Cf. Gregory VII, *Register* IV.12, p. 313 ('our daughter Countess Adelaide'); Berthold, *Chronicle* 1077, p. 159 (Henry's 'mother-in-law Adelaide', likewise a margravine').

1855 Lampert alone mentioned the involvement of Margrave Albert Azzo II of Este (above n. 630).

1856 Abbot Hugh I ('the Great') of Cluny (above n. 810), godfather of Henry IV. Cf. Gregory VII, *Register* IV.12, p. 313; Berthold, *Chronicle* 1077, p. 159; Arnulf of Milan, *Liber gestorum recentium* V.8, p. 229; Donizo of Canossa, *Vita Mathildis comitissae metrica* II, p. 381, and in the miniature in Vaticanus latinus 4922 (above n. 1854). See Diener (1959) p. 366; Kohnle (1993) pp. 111–14.

1857 Here, as above, 1076, p. 338 and n. 1775, Lampert implied that Henry IV had been excommunicated because of the princes' grievances against him. See also above, 1076, p. 302 and n. 1613.

had decided to meet.[1858] There, after the arguments of both parties had been examined, the pope would not be diverted by hatred or by favour from right to wrong but would deliver the most just judgement that he could on the individual issues according to the laws of the Church. To this the envoys replied that there was nowhere in the world that the king would evade the judgement of the pope, whom he knew to be a totally uncorrupted vindicator and guardian of justice and innocence. But the anniversary of the day on which he had been excommunicated was now close at hand and the princes of the kingdom eagerly, apprehensively and in great suspense awaited the outcome of this troubling affair. For if he was not absolved from excommunication before this day, according to the laws of the palace he would henceforward be regarded as unworthy of the office of king and would no longer be entitled to a hearing to maintain his innocence.[1859] He therefore begged very strenuously – and he was prepared to *deserve* this by every kind of *amends* that the pope commanded – that he might in the meantime be absolved only from the anathema and might receive *the grace of the communion of the Church*.[1860] He would answer in full all the charges that his accusers had brought against him on whatever day and in whatever place the pope ordered, as if nothing had been decided by these present proceedings. Then according to the pope's judgement he would either keep his kingdom if he cleared himself of the charges or would bear the loss of it with equanimity if his cause failed.[1861]

The pope resisted for a long time, for what he feared in the king was the

---

1858 2 February 1077: see above, 1076, p. 340 and n. 1785.

1859 See above, 1076, pp. 340–1 and nn. 1787–8. On 'the laws of the palace' see Struve (1970a) pp. 49–50 and n. 17.

1860 Holder-Egger, *Lamperti Annales* p. 291 n. 2 detected here a direct borrowing from Gregory VII, *Register* IV.12, p. 312. See also Meyer von Knonau (1894) p. 896 and nn. 5–6; Struve (1970a) pp. 88–9: 'Lampert drew his knowledge of the facts from Gregory VII's letter.' On Lampert's formulation 'absolved only from the anathema' cf. Berthold of Reichenau, *Chronicle* 1077, p. 160: the pope 'would not refuse to receive [Henry] into the Christian communion (but only into communion)'; Bernold of St Blasien, *Chronicle* 1077, p. 257: 'the concession not of the kingship but only of communion'. Cf. the emphasis in Gregory VII's pronouncement of 7 March 1080, *Register* VII.14a, p. 484: 'I restored to him communion alone but I did not install him in the kingship'. See Morrison (1962) pp. 121–48; Miccoli (1966) pp. 203–23; Schneider (1972) pp. 206–7; Beumann (1973) pp. 49–55; Cowdrey (1998) pp. 162–4; Robinson (1999) pp. 162–3.

1861 Cf. Gregory VII, *Register* IV.12, pp. 313–14: 'the whole conduct of this business has so far been suspended'; Oath of Henry IV, *Register* IV.12a, pp. 314–15: the king promised to 'do justice according to [the pope's] judgement or make an agreement according to his counsel'.

changeable nature of the young mind and the disposition to go wherever flatterers urged him to go. But at length he was overcome by the insistence of those who urged him and by the weight of their opinions.[1862] 'If he truly repents his conduct,' said the pope, 'as evidence of true and heartfelt repentance, let him resign the crown and the rest of the royal insignia into our power and let him declare that after behaving in so insolent a manner, he was henceforward unworthy of the title and the office of a king.' This seemed to the envoys to be too harsh.[1863] They earnestly pressed the pope to moderate his decision and *not* entirely *to break a bruised reed*[1864] by the rigour of his judgement. At last he was with great difficulty prevailed on to allow the king to come into his presence and, if he performed a true penance for his actions, he might now atone by obeying the decrees of the apostolic see for the guilt that he had incurred by inflicting injury on the apostolic see.

The king came, as he had been commanded,[1865] and since that castle was surrounded by a triple wall,[1866] he was received within the second circle of the walls. His whole entourage was left outside[1867] and he himself, *laying aside his royal garb*, with nothing of the king in his

---

1862 Cf. Gregory VII, *Register* IV.12, p. 313: 'At last, overcome by ... such great supplication on the part of all who were present there, we at last ... received him into the grace of communion'.

1863 Only Lampert reported this demand. Cf. Berthold of Reichenau, *Chronicle* 1077, pp. 160–1: the pope would absolve Henry 'if he would come without delay to confirm on oath ... those conditions of obedience and reparation that [the pope] would now impose on him.... [Henry] and all his followers judged this proposal to be very harsh.'

1864 Isaiah 42:3.

1865 There is no hint of a command in Gregory VII, *Register* IV.12, pp. 312–13: the king 'arrived with a few followers' and 'remained for three days before the castle-gate' until the pope was reluctantly persuaded by the mediators to receive him. Cf. Berthold, *Chronicle* 1077, p. 160: Henry 'unexpectedly rushed up to the gate of the castle' and 'although he received no answer and no word of invitation from the pope, ... he begged with all his might for permission to enter'; Donizo of Canossa, *Vita Mathildis comitissae metrica* II, p. 381: 'The pope granted permission to the king to come into his presence.'

1866 Cf. Vergil, *Aeneid* VI.549 ('surrounded by a triple wall'); Ovid, *Fasti* III.801 ('enclosed by a triple wall'). Tondelli (1952) pp. 365–71 reported that the archaeological evidence from the castle of Canossa confirmed Lampert's description of the 'triple wall'. But see Struve (1970a) p. 89 n. 7.

1867 Below p. 357 and n. 1879 Lampert identified 'the bishop of Zeitz and the bishop of Vercelli' in the presence of pope and king. Cf. Berthold, *Chronicle* 1077, p. 162 identified 'the five bishops of Strasbourg, Bremen, Lausanne, Basel and Naumburg [Zeitz] and the other magnates'.

appearance, with no display of splendour, *with bare feet*[1868] he remained fasting from morning to evening,[1869] waiting for the judgement of the Roman pontiff. He did this on the second day and on the third day. At last on the fourth day he was allowed to come into the pope's presence and after many arguments and counter-arguments he was finally absolved from excommunication on these conditions.[1870] On whatever day and in whatever place the pope chose, he was to attend a general council to which the German princes had been summoned and he was to answer the accusations that were made against him. The pope himself would act as judge of the case, if it seemed expedient to do so, and according to his judgement the king would either keep the kingdom if he cleared himself of the charges or bear the loss of it with equanimity if his offences were proved and he was declared henceforward to be unworthy of the office of king according to the laws of the Church. Whether he retained or lost the kingdom, he should never at any time avenge himself on any man for this injury. But until that day on which his case was investigated according to the law and decided, he should use none of the adornments of royal apparel and none of the insignia of the office of king; he should take none of the measures in the government of the State that customarily belonged to his jurisdiction and should reach no legally binding decision.[1871] Finally he should

---

1868 Holder-Egger, *Lamperti Annales* p. 292 n. 3, again detected a direct borrowing from Gregory VII, *Register* IV.12, p. 313: 'laying aside all his royal garb, in a wretched condition, with bare feet and clad in wool'. Cf. Berthold, *Chronicle* 1077, p. 160; Bruno of Merseburg, *The Saxon War* c. 90, p. 84; Bonizo of Sutri, *To a Friend* VIII, p. 241; Donizo of Canossa, *Vita Mathildis* II, p. 381.

1869 Lampert alone mentioned fasting: see Struve (1970a) p. 89 n. 8.

1870 Henry IV 'remained for three days before the castle-gate', according to Gregory VII, *Register* IV.12, p. 313. Cf. Berthold, *Chronicle* 1077, p. 160 ('for three days'); Donizo of Canossa, *Vita Mathildis* II, p. 381 ('for three days'). The chronology of *Vita Anselmi episcopi Lucensis* c. 16, p. 18, contradicts that of Lampert: 'finally on the third day' the king received absolution. According to Donizo, Henry IV began his penance on 25 January, that is, the feast of the Conversion of St Paul. Hence Cowdrey (1998) p. 156 n. 354 suggested that the king's conduct was intended to evoke Paul's three-day fast at Damascus (Acts 9:8–9). The oath of Henry IV at Canossa, recorded in Gregory VII, *Register* IV.12a, pp. 314–15, is dated 28 January. See Kilian (1886) pp. 75–6; Meyer von Knonau (1894) pp. 759–64, 894–903; Morrison (1962) pp. 121–48; Miccoli (1966) pp. 203–23; Schneider (1972) pp. 201–213; Beumann (1973) pp. 49–55; Struve (1995) pp. 44–5; Cowdrey (1998) pp. 162–4; Robinson (1999) pp. 162–3; Reuter (2006) pp. 147–66; Hay (2008) p. 70.

1871 In the oath of Henry IV, Gregory VII, *Register* IV.12a, pp. 314–15, the king promised, firstly, to 'do justice according to [the pope's] judgement or make an agreement according to his counsel' and, secondly, guaranteed the safety of the pope and his entourage and legates if they crossed the Alps or travelled in the imperial territories. The other 'conditions' detailed here are Lampert's polemical

appropriate nothing that belonged to the kingdom, nothing that was a possession of the State except for the requisition of the royal services[1872] that he himself and his men needed for their sustenance. Moreover all those who had sworn fidelity to him on oath should meanwhile remain free and unencumbered before God and before men of the obligation of this oath and of the duty of preserving fidelity towards him. He was to banish forever from his intimate acquaintance Bishop Rupert of Bamberg and Udalric of Godesheim[1873] and the rest of those men to whose advice he had surrendered both himself and the State. If he cleared himself of the accusations against him and continued to be powerful and *strengthened in the kingdom*,[1874] he should always be subject to the Roman pontiff and obedient to his orders[1875] and should reach agreement with him and be his fellow worker to the utmost of his ability in correcting whatever evil customs had grown up contrary to the laws of the Church. Finally, if he failed to perform any one of these conditions, this absolution from the anathema, which he had now been seeking with so great a longing, would become invalid. Indeed he would be regarded as having already been convicted and as having confessed his guilt and he would never again obtain a hearing for professions of his innocence. The princes of the kingdom would be freed from the need for any further judicial proceedings and from all the obligations of their oath of fidelity and would set up another king on whose election they were all agreed.[1876]

---

elaborations. A similar version appears in Bruno of Merseburg, *The Saxon War* c. 90, p. 84: the pope 'ordered him not to put on any royal adornment until he himself permitted it'.

1872 On Lampert's term, *servitia*, see Niermeyer – van de Kieft (2002) p. 1259. See also above, 1074, p. 205 and n. 1076.

1873 Rupert of Bamberg (above n. 1524), who was currently in captivity (above p. 350 and n. 1848) and Udalric of Godesheim (above n. 1036). According to Berthold of Reichenau, *Chronicle* 1077, p. 162, the pope reminded Henry of 'the need to beware of the anathema imposed on the Lombards'. Cf. Bruno, *The Saxon War* c. 90, p. 84: the pope commanded Henry 'to avoid those who had been excommunicated and neither eat nor speak with them'; Bonizo of Sutri, *To a Friend* VIII, p. 241: 'the king and all those who had been absolved from excommunication were commanded to beware of association with excommunicates'.

1874 II Chronicles 1:1.

1875 Lampert used this same formulation in his reference to Henry IV's 'Promise of Oppenheim': cf. above, 1076, p. 341 and n. 1789.

1876 Lampert here returned to the theme of the deposition of Henry IV that recurs throughout his work: see above, 1066, p. 111 and n. 469; 1073, p. 197 and n. 1026, p. 200 and n. 1039; 1074, pp. 206, 217 and n. 1138; 1076, p. 334 and n. 1757, 336.

The king joyfully accepted the conditions[1877] and promised that he would keep them all, using the most sacred declarations in his power. Nevertheless there was no strong inclination to trust the man who made the promise. But the abbot of Cluny pledged his word before the eyes of the all-seeing God, since he declined to swear an oath because of his monastic vow.[1878] After relics of the saints had been brought, the bishop of Zeitz and the bishop of Vercelli and Margrave Azzo[1879] and the other princes who had made this agreement also confirmed on oath that the king would do what he promised and that he would not be drawn away from his decision by any difficulty that might arise or by any change in the varying circumstances of existence.

After he had been absolved from excommunication in this way, the pope celebrated *the solemn rites of the mass*. When he had prepared the sacred offering, *he called the king*, together with the rest of the company, who were present in great numbers, *to the altar* and, holding *the Lord's body in his hand*,[1880] he said, 'I long ago received from you and your supporters letters in which you accused me of having seized the apostolic see by means of simoniacal heresy and of having polluted my life with certain other offences both before and after I received the office of bishop, which according to the regulations of the canons should have barred me from all access to holy orders.[1881] And although I am able to refute the accusations by means of the testimony of many witnesses who are certainly satisfactory – of those namely who know in its entirety the whole course of my life from my earliest years and those who were responsible for my elevation to the office of bishop – nevertheless, lest it should seem that I rely on human rather than divine testimony, I

1877 Lampert's 'conditions' purport to refer to the agreement recorded in the oath of Henry IV, Gregory VII, *Register* IV.12a, pp. 314–15 (see above n. 1871).

1878 Hugh I of Cluny (above n. 810). Cf. Gregory VII, *Register* IV.12, p. 313: 'We have also received confirmation of [the guarantees contained in the oath of Henry IV] through the hands of the abbot of Cluny'. See Kohnle (1993) p. 113.

1879 Eppo (Eberhard) of Zeitz-Naumburg (above n. 46); Gregory, bishop of Vercelli (1044–77), chancellor for the Italian kingdom; Albert Azzo II of Este (above n. 630). Cf. Berthold of Reichenau, *Chronicle* 1077, p. 161: 'Two bishops, Naumburg and Vercelli, were chosen to take the oath on [Henry's] behalf, besides the other members of his entourage'. According to the archival version of the oath of Henry IV noted in the apparatus criticus of *Register* IV.12a, p. 315, 'Of the king's party there were present the archbishop of Bremen, the bishops of Vercelli and Osnabrück and the abbot of Cluny and many noblemen.'

1880 Regino of Prüm, *Chronicon* 869, p. 97. Lampert borrowed phrases from Regino's report of the encounter of Pope Hadrian II and King Lothar II: see below n. 1882.

1881 Cf. Letter of the German prelates at Worms to Gregory VII (January 1076) in Henry IV, *Letters*, appendix A, pp. 66–8.

shall remove every trace of an obstacle for everyone on the shortest route to providing the proof. Behold the body of the Lord, which I shall consume: let it be for me today a test of my innocence, so that Almighty God will today by[1882] *His judgement* either absolve me from the suspicion of the offence of which I am accused, *if I am innocent*, or remove me by sudden death, *if I am guilty*.' After he had begun, *as is customary*, by pronouncing these and other dreadful words, in which he prayed that God, the most just judge of his cause and the defender of his innocence, would be present, he took part of the Lord's body and ate it. After he had consumed it with complete confidence, the people rejoiced at this proof of his innocence and applauded, praising God, for some considerable time. When he had at last obtained silence, the pope turned to the king and said, 'Do, therefore, my son, if it pleases you, what you have seen me do. Day after day the princes of the German kingdom din our ears with their accusations; they have piled upon you a great mass of capital offences, for which they considered that you ought to be suspended not only from any part in the government of the State but also from the communion of the Church and from every kind of secular activity until your last breath. Most particularly they request that a day and a place be appointed and a hearing arranged in which the accusations that they bring against you are to be investigated according to canon law. You know very well that human judgements are very often untrustworthy and in political debates false statements are sometimes more persuasive than true ones. For men listen with pleasure to falsehood that is decorated with ornamental words because of the genius of eloquent men and the richness and pleasantness of their speech, while they despise truth that does not rely on the support of eloquence. Since, therefore, I desire to give you good advice, because

1882 Lampert used here the formulas of a trial by ordeal (*MGH Leges, sectio V, Formulae, Ordines iudiciorum Dei* pp. 610, 611, 617, 703, 704). According to his account, the pope himself first took the sacrament to prove his innocence of the offences alleged against him at the council of Worms, then called on Henry to submit to the same ordeal to prove that the princes' accusations against him were false. This the king feared to do. Lampert was imitating the narrative of Regino of Prüm, *Chronicon* 869, p. 97 (see above n. 1880), who reported that Pope Hadrian II imposed such an ordeal on King Lothar II during the celebration of mass. For the historiographical discussion of this aspect of Lampert's account of Canossa see Ranke (1888) p. 147; Holder-Egger (1894) pp. 557–9; Meyer von Knonau (1894) pp. 900–1; Struve (1970a) pp. 118–21. The interpretation of the communion in Canossa as a trial by ordeal is found also in Bonizo of Sutri, *To a Friend* VIII, p. 241: 'if [Henry] had indeed humbled himself in mind and body ..., then the sacrament would prove to him the means of salvation.... If, however, he thought otherwise, ... after the morsel, Satan would enter into him.'

you have humbly sought the protection of the apostolic see in your time of adversity, do as I counsel. *If you know that you are innocent*[1883] and that your reputation has been assailed by your rivals with false accusations in a malicious prosecution, take the shortest way of freeing the Church of God from scandal and yourself from the uncertain outcome of this long conflict. Eat this remaining part of the Lord's body so that you may prove your innocence with God as your witness and *every mouth* of those who gabble *iniquity* against you *may be stopped.*[1883] I myself shall thenceforward be the advocate of your cause and the most vigorous defender of your innocence. The princes will be reconciled with you; the kingdom will be restored to you; all the storms of civil war, by which the State has been troubled for so long, will be laid to rest forever.'

The king was *thunderstruck by this unexpected development.*[1884] His response was to become violently agitated, to be evasive, to take counsel with his intimate friends apart from the rest of the company and in his agitation to consider what must be done and how he might escape the need to undergo so fearful a trial. When he finally *recovered his spirit,*[1885] he replied to the pope and began to make a pretext of the absence of the princes who had hitherto preserved their fidelity towards him undiminished in misfortune. If he could not consult them and in particular if his accusers were absent, whatever justification he offered to prove his innocence to the few people who were present would be regarded as invalid and entirely without force among the unbelievers. He therefore urgently requested the pope to defer the entire case to a general assembly and to a universal hearing so that, when the accusers had gathered there and both the accusations and the persons of the accusers had been investigated according to the laws of the Church, he might refute the charges under whatever conditions the princes of the kingdom judged to be fair.[1886] The pope assented to his request without

1883 Romans 3:19; Psalm 62:12.

1884 Livy XL.15.14.

1885 Judith 13:30.

1886 Henry IV ultimately declined to receive communion, according to Lampert, because he was afraid to submit to the ordeal. Lampert was clearly aware of Regino of Prüm, *Chronicon* 869, pp. 97–8 (see above nn. 1880, 1882), who recorded that the guilty King Lothar II underwent the ordeal, receiving communion from the pope, and died within the year. Berthold of Reichenau, *Chronicle* 1077, p. 162, also claimed that the king avoided receiving the sacrament but did not ascribe to the communion the character of an ordeal: 'The king declared that he was unworthy to share [the eucharist] and he went away without receiving communion.' That Henry actually received communion was confirmed by Gregory VII, *Register* IV.12, p. 313: 'we at last released him from the bond of anathema and received him

difficulty. When divine service was over, he invited the king to a meal.[1887] After he had entertained him and carefully instructed him about all the matters to which he must pay attention, he parted from him most kindly and sent him back in peace to his followers, who had remained at some distance from the castle.[1888] The pope also sent Bishop Eppo of Zeitz in advance of the king so that he might, on the pope's behalf, absolve from excommunication those who had unthinkingly communicated with the excommunicate king before he was absolved from the anathema. The pope thus kindly guarded against the king's defiling with a stain his newly received communion with the Church.[1889]

When Bishop Eppo arrived and explained to the Italians the purpose of his mission, a fierce storm of *anger and displeasure*[1890] arose against him. They all began to rage with fierce words and gestures, to cry out against the papal mission with shouts of mockery and to overwhelm the envoy with the most unseemly insults and curses that their anger suggested to them. They declared that they considered as worthless an excommunication pronounced by that man, whom all the bishops of Italy had long ago excommunicated on just grounds, who had seized the apostolic see by means of simoniacal heresy and who had defiled it with murders and polluted it with adulteries and other capital offences.[1891] They considered that the king had not acted as befitted his dignity and had *inflicted a stain on* his *honour*[1892] never to be effaced because he subordinated the royal majesty to a man who was a heretic and disgraced by every kind

into the grace of communion'. Cf. Bonizo of Sutri, *To a Friend* VIII, p. 241; Donizo of Canossa, *Vita Mathildis comitissae metrica* II, p. 382.

1887 Cf. Berthold, *Chronicle* 1077, p. 162; Bonizo, *To a Friend* VIII, p. 241; Donizo, *Vita Mathildis* II, p. 382.

1888 See above p. 354 and n. 1867. According to Donizo, *Vita Mathildis* II, p. 382, the king returned to Reggio: see Kilian (1886) p. 76; Meyer von Knonau (1894) p. 764.

1889 This account seems to be contradicted by Berthold, *Chronicle* 1077, p. 163: 'the pope reluctantly gave [Henry] permission during his expedition through Lombardy to receive service from [the Lombards] but only what was necessary and on condition that he avoided any communion with them, as required by canon law'. Hence Holder-Egger, *Lamperti Annales* p. 298 n. 3, argued that Eppo (Eberhard) of Zeitz-Naumburg (above n. 46) was more likely to have been sent not as a papal legate but as Henry's envoy to the Lombards. See also Meyer von Knonau (1894) p. 764 and n. 29; Vogel (1983) pp. 20–1.

1890 Livy II.58.6. See Billanovich (1945) p. 194.

1891 Cf. Gregory VII, *Epistolae Vagantes* 19, p. 52: 'it is sad to tell and abominable to hear how great was the pride and how great the malicious purposes [the Lombard bishops] directed against us'. On the hostility of the Lombard bishops towards the pope see Arnulf of Milan, *Liber gestorum recentium* V.8, p. 229.

1892 I Maccabees 9:10.

of shameful act. He, whom they had provided for themselves as the
protector of justice and the defender of the laws of the Church, by his
most dishonourable submission clearly betrayed the Catholic faith, the
authority of the Church and the dignity of the State. They themselves
had inflicted on the pope all the injuries that they could in order to
avenge the king and now – it is shameful even to say it – the king had
abandoned them in the midst of storms and disorders, he had consulted
only his own interests and restored good relations with the enemy of
the State for the sake of his personal needs. These were the principal
complaints that the princes of Italy *raised and disseminated everywhere*[1893]
among the people and in a short time they had kindled enormous hatred
against the king. Finally, there was a fully fledged uprising in which
there was among them all a single will and a single opinion: that after
the father – who by his own actions had rendered himself unworthy of
exercising power – had resigned his office, they should make his son[1894]
their king, even though he was not yet of age and too young to deal
with the affairs of the kingdom. They would then set out with the boy
for Rome and elect another pope, through whose means the boy would
at once be consecrated emperor and all the measures of this apostate
pope would be annulled.

When news of so dangerous a conspiracy was brought to the king, he
hastily sent those of the princes who were with him to pacify the anger
of the exasperated people by whatever means they could and with all
the diligence of which they were capable. The Italians should not take
amiss what he had been compelled to do by extreme necessity in the
interests of the common good and they should not interpret it as an
insult directed against themselves. It was impossible to satisfy either
the German princes, who were plotting with all their might to snatch
the kingdom from him by means of legal subterfuge, or the Roman
pontiff, who was sending bolts of lightning in all directions with the
spiritual sword in order to undermine the condition of holy Church,
except by being absolved from excommunication before the appointed
day. Now he was freed from all the difficulties by which his enemies had
obstructed his path and he would henceforward transfer all his attention

---

1893 Livy VI.3.9: VIII.292.

1894 Lampert alone reported this scheme to enthrone the three-year-old Conrad (above
n. 1088). Berthold of Reichenau, *Chronicle* 1077, pp. 171–2, reported that, on his
return to Germany, Henry left his son behind as his father's representative in
Italy, in the care of the archbishop of Milan and the bishop of Piacenza, the pope's
principal opponents in Lombardy. See Meyer von Knonau (1900) p. 20; Goez
(1996) pp. 7–8. This was perhaps the basis of Lampert's garbled account.

and all his efforts to avenging both his own and their injuries. When at
length the conflagration of this violent disturbance had with difficulty
been not so much extinguished as restrained, very many of the princes
angrily withdrew *from the camp and returned* to their homes *without
being ordered to do so.*[1895] The rest of the princes concealed their anger for
the time being and received the king peaceably when he returned. But
they neither showed him the customary deference nor rendered him
their service on the same lavish scale as they had previously done and
as befitted the magnificence of a king. Instead with averted eyes and
hostile thoughts far and wide in every corner they grumbled about his
shallowness and his folly and accused him of negligence because, after
Italy, threatened with disasters, had awaited him for so long and so
anxiously wished for his coming, he had in the end brought her no hope
and no protection. When he travelled through Italy so that he might,
according to royal custom, do justice to those who had suffered oppres-
sion or malicious prosecution, he was not received in the cities nor was
he met by processions with torches and shouts of approval, as had been
customary in the case of the previous kings.[1896] Instead he was bidden
to remain outside and to pitch his camp in the suburbs. There they
supplied him with provisions to feed the army but in limited quantities
and barely enough for their needs, rather than the usual splendour and
abundance of royal banquets. They did this so that they could not be
accused too soon of openly deserting the king and they posted guards
in every location so that those who were perhaps willing to plunder the
fields and villages might be held in check by armed force.

The king was alarmed by this unexpected state of affairs and repented
too late that he had so rashly placed his trust in the previously untried
fidelity of a people unknown to him and that in leaving German territory he had changed his enemy and not escaped from enmity. He was
oppressed by deep disquiet and fear and nowhere could he find a way
out of his difficulties except perhaps by seeking reconciliation, by
whatever means was possible, with the Italians whom he had offended.
He considered therefore that the sole remedy for this situation was to

1895 Livy II.44.11.

1896 Cf. Berthold, *Chronicle* 1077, p. 164 described Henry as 'scouring that region
during the whole of Lent [1 March – 15 April] and most eagerly gathering
together copious quantities of gold, silver and precious garments'. The king
visited Piacenza, Verona and Pavia, issuing a series of diplomas: *DD.H.IV* 286–91.
Six judicial hearings (*placita*) took place between 17 February and 1 April: *I Placiti
del 'Regnum Italiae* 3, nos 438–43. See Meyer von Knonau (1894) pp. 765–8 and
(1900) pp. 12–13; Vogel (1983) pp. 29–32.

break the treaty that he had concluded with the Roman pontiff so that the beginning of the restoration of harmony would be the point from which the discord had originated. He recalled to their former position in his favour and intimacy Udalric of Godesheim[1897] and the rest of those whom the pope had removed from his company by that most stern anathema and he once more sought their advice on personal affairs and matters of State on the same exclusive and privileged terms to which he had formerly been accustomed. Then he continually complained of and disparaged the Roman pontiff in an assembly of princes, alleging that it was his plotting that had incited all those whirlwinds and storms of most violent agitation that had shaken the State. He had been the originator and the inciter of all the evils that had happened in the Church of God in recent memory. The king therefore exhorted them all to act as one *under his command and guidance*[1898] in seeking revenge on the pope for such great injuries. He then scornfully *tore asunder* like *spiders' webs*[1899] all the conditions and all the bonds of ecclesiastical laws by means of which the pope had restricted him according to apostolic authority for the sake of his salvation. Casting aside all the restraints imposed by the fear of God, the king was borne along with unbridled liberty in every direction prompted by his will. Through these measures the anger of the Italians gradually began to be pacified, their fury to die down and their good will towards the king to grow warmer. Hence from day to day a larger and larger crowd flocked to him, they supplied increasingly abundant provisions to the army and they now most readily promised their labour and support in all endeavours that he commanded. The German princes who were with him at that time were Archbishop Liemar of Bremen, Bishop Eppo of Zeitz, Bishop Benno of Osnabrück, Bishop Burchard of Lausanne, Bishop Burchard of Basel and the laymen Udalric, Eberhard,[1900] Berthold[1901] and almost all the others whom the legates of the apostolic

1897 On Udalric of Godesheim (above n. 1036) see above p. 356 and n. 1873.

1898 Livy VIII.12.6; X.18.1. See Billanovich (1945) p. 168.

1899 Isaiah 59:5; Job 8:14. Cf. above, 1074, p. 235 and n. 1240, 1076, p. 337 and n. 1771.

1900 Liemar of Hamburg-Bremen (above n. 798), Eppo (Eberhard) of Zeitz-Naumburg (above n. 46), Benno II of Osnabrück (above n. 500), Burchard of Lausanne (above n. 1637), Burchard of Basel (above n. 773), Udalric of Godesheim (above n. 1036) and probably Count Eberhard 'the Bearded' (above n. 641).

1901 Probably Berthold, brother of Liupold of Meersburg (see above, 1071, p. 148 n. 728), identified in *D.H.IV* 243 of 30 July 1071 ('knight') and in Bruno of Merseburg, *The Saxon War* c. 81, p. 78 ('Berthold, the king's adviser'). See Robinson (1999) p. 359.

see in Oppenheim separated from his company because of his excommunication. When these men, who had now been received back into communion, learned that the king had also been reconciled with the Church,[1902] they unanimously flocked to him and thereafter they stood by him as his inseparable companions on his earthly pilgrimage.

Meanwhile the bishops of Mainz, Würzburg and Metz, the dukes Rudolf, Welf and Berthold and very many other German princes met to reflect on the needs of the State.[1903] They decided that the princes of Saxony and all those who were concerned about the wellbeing of the State should assemble in Forchheim on 13 March,[1904] should take counsel together and should determine what ought to be done, especially since conditions were peaceful as a result of the king's absence, and offered them a suitable opportunity for their deliberations and consultations. They also wrote to the Roman pontiff that, since he had been circumvented by the cunning of the king and was unable to appear in Augsburg on the feast of the Purification of St Mary[1905] according to his promise, he should at least be present in Forchheim on the appointed day and should wield the authority of the apostolic see to calm the storms of civil war, by which the State was so long endangered.[1906]

The pope still remained in Canossa and in other very strong fortresses in the neighbourhood,[1907] with the intention of not returning to Rome

---

1902 See above p. 351 and n. 1850.

1903 Siegfried of Mainz (above n. 210), Adalbero of Würzburg (above n. 44), Herman of Metz (above n. 822), Rudolf of Swabia (above n. 203), Welf IV of Bavaria (above n. 630), Berthold I of Carinthia (above n. 824). According to Berthold of Reichenau, *Chronicle* 1077, p. 164, 'they assembled in Ulm after Christmas' and he added, 'few met there, the others being hindered by the excessive snow and the bitter cold of the winter'. Cf. Paul of Bernried, *Life of Pope Gregory VII* c. 88, p. 330 ('in Ulm in Swabia'). See Meyer von Knonau (1894) pp. 775–6: Vogel (1983) pp. 40–6; Cowdrey (1998) p. 168; Robinson (1999) p. 166.

1904 Similarly Berthold, *Chronicle* 1077, p. 164: 'on 13 March in Forchheim, where, after holding a conference ..., they might settle decisively what seemed to them best to do in the case of the kingdom, the Church and the need to preserve their own lives'. Cf. Paul of Bernried, *Life of Pope Gregory VII* c. 88, pp. 330–1: 'in Forchheim on 12 March to elect a new king'.

1905 2 February: see above, 1076, p. 340 and n. 1785.

1906 Cf. Berthold, *Chronicle* 1077, p. 165: 'they sent a suppliant letter ... to the lord pope ... and asked that he should send a letter indicating his views, together with his envoys, as soon as possible'; Paul of Bernried, *Life of Pope Gregory VII* c. 88, p. 331: 'they also sent envoys requesting the advice and help of the lord pope'. The envoy of the 'deposition faction' was identified by Gregory VII, *Epistolae Vagantes* 19, p. 52 as 'our son, Rapoto'.

1907 Gregory VII stayed in a number of fortresses near Canossa: Carpi, Bianello, Ficarolo, Carpineto (1 March – 28 June). See Gregory VII, *Register* IV.13–28, pp.

before he completed the journey that he had planned and – if God was gracious to him and his efforts were attended with success – restored peace to the Church of God. Numerous rumours had already reached him long before that the king had changed his mind, that *his attitude* towards the pope *was hostile*,[1908] that he expressed contempt for the conditions according to which he had been absolved from excommunication and that he was fully determined to conquer the laws of the Church with military force. When he received the letter of the princes, therefore, he sent one of the cardinal bishops of the Roman church named Gregory[1909] and others whom he thought suitable for that task, who were to say to the king that it was time that he fulfilled his promises. The princes of the German kingdom would meet in Forchheim on 13 March to restore order, if God granted their prayers, to the condition of the State. Let the king therefore come, as he promised, and with the pope presiding as advocate and judge,[1910] let him answer the charges with which he was assailed by his slanderers, of which, as he himself declared, he was innocent. He would contribute much before God and before men both to his own concerns and to his salvation, if he freed the Church from scandals, the State from civil wars and himself from the stain of a most shameful reputation. For on that day the accusations that were brought against him would be investigated according to synodal procedure and either he would receive the kingdom or he would lose it irrevocably. To the legates who brought these injunctions the king – concealing somewhat unsuccessfully the thoughts that were troubling him – replied that he had entered Italy for the first time since he had obtained the kingdom and so he was now involved in many great affairs of State and he could not leave the province so soon without settling

---

316–47. He returned to Rome by 16 September: *Register* V.3, pp. 350–1. On the pope's continued hope to travel to Germany cf. Gregory VII, *Epistolae* Vagantes 19, p. 52; *Register* IV.23–4, pp. 334–8. See Meyer von Knonau (1900) pp. 78–81; Vogel (1983) pp. 23–5; Struve (1995) p. 45; Cowdrey (1998) pp. 167–8; Robinson (1999) p. 165; Hay (2008) pp. 71–3.

1908 Livy II.35.6.

1909 Probably Cardinal deacon Gregory (title church unknown, *ca.* 1073 – *ca.* 1098). See Hüls (1977) p. 249.

1910 It is clear from Gregory VII, *Epistolae Vagantes* 19, p. 52, that the pope did not expect Henry IV to appear at Forchheim: his concern was to secure 'the agreement of the king' for his own journey to Germany. Cf. Berthold of Reichenau, *Chronicle* 1077, pp. 165–6: the pope was ready to come to Germany 'but only if he received from the king himself a guarantee of peace and fidelity'; Paul of Bernried, *Life of Pope Gregory VII* c. 89, p. 331: Cardinal deacon Gregory 'was to investigate whether the king, who still remained in Lombardy, was willing to assure the safety of the assembly and to grant the lord pope safe-conduct to German territory'.

these matters. For if he did that, he would very seriously offend the Italians, whom he had kept in suspense for a long time as they anxiously awaited his arrival. Besides, the day that had been fixed for holding the assembly was very near at hand and he could not cover so great a distance in so short an interval of time, however fast his horses might be, even if he was not delayed by any external hindrances. With these words he dismissed the legates.

The pope was now made more certain of the king's change of heart and of the other matters with which rumour had already long before acquainted him. He immediately sent Abbot Bernard of Marseilles, a man whose way of life was outstanding and who possessed many virtues in Christ, and also another Bernard, a cardinal deacon of the holy Roman church,[1911] to meet the princes of the German kingdom who (as was mentioned above) were about to assemble in Forchheim on 13 March, and to inform them in a methodical manner about what had happened. He had made the greatest possible effort to fulfil his intention of being present on the day and in the place appointed, to discuss what would be generally advantageous to holy Church. He had, however, been so beset by the efforts of the lord Henry, who had *taken possession of* all *the mountain passes*[1912] through which he could have made the crossing, so that he could neither advance safely into Germany nor return safely to Rome.[1913] He therefore advised them in the meantime to order, by whatever means they could, both their own affairs and the kingdom of the Franks – which had for so long been plagued by the childish light-mindedness of a single individual[1914] – until, if God willed it, when the difficulty of travelling had been removed, he himself should

---

1911 Bernard, abbot of St Victor in Marseilles (1064–79). Cardinal deacon Bernard (title church unknown): see Hüls (1977) pp. 245–6. On their legation see Meyer von Knonau (1894) p. 778; Schumann (1912) pp. 36–44; Cowdrey (1998) pp. 169–75.

1912 Livy XXXIX.20.6.

1913 Gregory VII, *Register* IV.23, p. 335 (31 May 1077) says nothing of having been hindered by Henry IV but requests his legates in Germany to urge Henry and Rudolf (elected anti-king by the 'deposition faction' at Forchheim) 'to open up a way of crossing there in safety'.

1914 Cf. Gregory VII, *Epistolae Vagantes* 19, p. 52: 'As for the king, we cannot much rejoice that he should simply walk obediently in the ways that he has promised us, especially since, as a result of his presence, certain very wicked men are emboldened rather than fearful in their conduct towards us and the apostolic see in respect of the evil that they have done.' Berthold of Reichenau, *Chronicle* 1077, p. 166, gave a polemical paraphrase of this letter ('there was little reason for his subjects to rejoice, as far as hopes for his penitence and his progress were concerned') in justifying the election of a new king at Forchheim.

come and, after they had taken counsel together, should be able to decide according to the laws of the Church whatever would best serve the interests and the honour of all men and the peace of the Church.

Like a languid poet, now faint with exhaustion at the end of the work and *overwhelmed by the sheer quantity of the subject-matter*,[1915] here at last we bring to an end a volume that has been extended, so it seems, to a very great length. If therefore it happens that someone who comes after us should choose to put his hand to writing the remaining part of this narrative, he will find a suitable beginning for his work in the election of King Rudolf.[1916]

1915 Sulpicius Severus, *Vita Martini* c. 26.

1916 Robinson (1978b) pp. 538–50 argued that a continuation of Lampert's work was written (by an unknown author), of which traces survive, notably in the polemic composed by an anonymous monk of Hersfeld in the early 1090s, *The preservation of the unity of the Church*. See above p. 17.

BIBLIOGRAPHY

Primary sources

Adam of Bremen, *Gesta Hammaburgensis ecclesiae pontificum*, MGH SS rer. Germ. [2] (1917) trans. F. J. Tschan, *History of the archbishops of Hamburg-Bremen* (New York, 1959)

Annales Egmundani, MGH SS 16, 442–79

Annales Einsidlenses, MGH SS 3, 145–9

Annales Gengenbacenses, MGH SS 5, 389–90

Annales Hildesheimenses, Quedlinburgenses, Weissenburgenses et Lamberti pars prior, MGH SS 3, 18–116

Annales necrologici Fuldenses, MGH SS 13, 161–218

Annales Patherbrunnenses = P. Scheffer-Boichorst, *Eine verlorene Quellenschrift des XII. Jahrhunderts aus Bruchstücken wiederhergestellt* (Innsbruck, 1870) pp. 92–170

Annales Romani, MGH SS 5, 468–80

Annales Sangallenses maiores, MGH SS 1, 72–85

Annales Stadenses, MGH SS 16, 283–378

Annalista Saxo, MGH SS 6, 553–777

Annals of Augsburg = *Annales Augustani*, MGH SS 3, 123–36

Annals of Benevento = *Annales Beneventani*, MGH SS 3, 173–85

Annals of Corvey = *Annales Corbeienses*, MGH SS 3, 2–18

Annals of Disibodenberg = *Annales sancti Disibodi*, MGH SS 17, 6–30

Annals of Iburg = *Annales Yburgenses*, MGH SS 16, 434–8

Annals of Niederaltaich = *Annales Altahenses maiores*, MGH SS rer. Germ. [4] (1891)

Annals of Ottobeuren = *Annales Ottenburani*, MGH SS 5, 1–9

Annals of Weissenburg = *Annales Weissenburgenses* in *Lamperti Opera*, MGH SS rer. Germ. [38] (1894) pp. 9–57

Anonymous of Hasenried, *On the bishops of Eichstädt* = *De episcopis Eichstetensibus*, MGH SS 7, 253–66

Anonymous of Hersfeld, *The preservation of the unity of the Church*: see *Liber de unitate ecclesiae conservanda*

Anselm of Besate, *Rhetorimachia*, MGH Quellen zur Geistesgeschichte 2 (1958)

Anselm of Liège, *Gesta episcoporum Leodiensium*, MGH SS 7, 189–234

Arnulf of Milan, *Liber gestorum recentium*, MGH SS rer. Germ. [67] (1994)

Beno of SS. Martino e Silvestro, *Gesta Romanae ecclesiae contra Hildebrandum*, *MGH Libelli* 2, 369–80

Benzo of Alba, *Ad Heinricum IV. imperatorem libri VII. Sieben Bücher an Kaiser Heinrich IV.*, *MGH SS rer. Germ.* 65 (1996)

Bernard of Hildesheim, *De damnatione scismaticorum* = Bernold, *De damnatione scismaticorum* II

Bernold of St Blasien (of Constance), *Chronicle* trans. I. S. Robinson, *Eleventh-century Germany: the Swabian Chronicles* (Manchester–New York, 2008) pp. 245–337 = Bernold, *Chronicon* in *Die Chroniken Bertholds von Reichenau und Bernolds von Konstanz, MGH SS rer. Germ. nova series* 14 (2003) pp. 383–540

Bernold of St Blasien (of Constance), *De damnatione scismaticorum, MGH Libelli* 2, 26–58

Bernold, *De incontinentia sacerdotum, MGH Libelli* 2, 4–26

Bernold, *Pro Gebhardo episcopo Constantiensi epistola apologetica, MGH Libelli* 2, 108–11

Berthold of Reichenau, *Chronicle* trans. I. S. Robinson, *Eleventh-century Germany: the Swabian Chronicles* (Manchester–New York, 2008) pp. 99–244 = Berthold, *Chronicon* in *Die Chroniken Bertholds von Reichenau und Bernolds von Konstanz, MGH SS rer. Germ. nova series* 14 (2003) pp. 161–381

Bonizo of Sutri, *To a Friend* trans. I. S. Robinson, *The Papal Reform of the Eleventh Century* (Manchester–New York, 2004) = Bonizo, *Liber ad amicum, MGH Libelli* 1, 568–620

Briefsammlungen der Zeit Heinrichs IV., MGH Die Briefe der deutschen Kaiserzeit 5 (1950)

Bruno of Merseburg, *Saxon War* = *Saxonicum bellum: Brunos Buch vom Sachsenkrieg, MGH Deutsches Mittelalter* 2 (1937)

Burchard of Worms, *Decretum, MPL* 140, 337A–1058C

Casus monasterii Petrishusensis, MGH SS 20, 621–82

Chronicae Polonorum, MGH SS 9, 418—78

Chronicle of Monte Cassino = *Chronica monasterii Casinensis, MGH SS* 34 (1980)

Chronicon episcoporum Hildesheimensium, MGH SS 7, 845–73

Chronicon Gozecense, MGH SS 10, 140–57

Chronicon Laureshamense, MGH SS 21, 334–453

Chronicon sancti Huberti Andaginensis, MGH SS 8, 565–630

Codex Hirsaugiensis, MGH SS 14, 254–65

Codex Laureshamensis ed. K. Glöckner 1 (Darmstadt, 1929)

Codex Udalrici ed. P. Jaffé, *Bibliotheca rerum Germanicarum* 5 (Berlin, 1869), 17–469

Cosmas of Prague, *Chronica Boemorum, MGH SS rer. Germ.*, n.s. 2 (Berlin, 1955)

Deeds of the bishops of Cambrai = *Gesta pontificum Cameracensium, MGH SS* 7, 442–89

Die ältere Wormser Briefsammlung ed. W. Bulst, *MGH Briefe der deutschen Kaiserzeit* 3 (Hanover, 1949)

Dietwin, bishop of Liège, Letter to Bishop Imad of Paderborn, *MGH SS* 11, 434

Donizo of Canossa, *Vita Mathildis comitissae metrica*, *MGH SS* 12, 348–409

Einhard, *Life of Charles the Great* = *Vita Karoli Magni*, *MGH SS rer. Germ.* [25] (1911)

Ekkebert of Hersfeld, *Vita sancti Haimeradi*, *MGH SS* 10, 595–607

Frutolf of Michelsberg, *Chronica* (Ausgewählte Quellen zur deutschen Geschichte des Mittelalters 15: Darmstadt, 1972) pp. 48–121, trans. T. J. H. McCarthy, *Chronicles of the Investiture Contest. Frutolf of Michelsberg and his continuators* (Manchester–New York, 2014)

Gebhard of Salzburg, *Epistola*, *MGH Libelli* 1, 261–79

Genealogia Wettinensis, *MGH SS* 23, 226–30

Gesta archiepiscoporum Magdeburgensium, *MGH SS* 14, 376–416

Gesta episcoporum Halberstadensium, *MGH SS* 23, 73–123

Gesta Treverorum, *MGH SS* 8, 111–200

Gratian: *Decretum magistri Gratiani* ed. E. Friedberg (Corpus Iuris Canonici 1: Leipzig, 1879)

Gregory VII, *Registrum*, *MGH Epistolae selectae* 2 (1920, 1923); trans. H. E. J. Cowdrey, *The Register of Pope Gregory VII 1073–1085* (Oxford, 2002)

Gregory VII, *The Epistolae Vagantes of Pope Gregory VII* ed. H.E.J. Cowdrey (Oxford, 1972)

Gundechar, *Liber pontificalis Eichstetensis*, *MGH SS* 7, 239–53

Haimo, *Vita Willihelmi abbatis Hirsaugiensis*, *MGH SS* 12, 209–25

Heinrici III Diplomata: Die Urkunden Heinrichs III., *MGH Diplomata* 5 (1931)

Heinrici IV Diplomata: Die Urkunden Heinrichs IV., *MGH Diplomata* 6/1–3 (1941, 1959, 1978)

Henry IV, *Letters* = *Die Briefe Heinrichs IV.*, *MGH Deutsches Mittelalter* 1 (1937), trans. T. E. Mommsen, K. F. Morrison, *Imperial Lives and Letters of the eleventh century* (New York, 1962)

Herman of Reichenau, *Chronicle* trans. I. S. Robinson, *Eleventh-century Germany: the Swabian Chronicles* (Manchester–New York, 2008) pp. 58–98 = Herman, *Chronicon*, *MGH SS* 5, 67–133

Herrand of Halberstadt, *Epistola de causa Heinrici regis*, *MGH Libelli* 2, 287–91

Historia martyrum Trevirensium, *MGH SS* 8, 220–3

Historia Welforum Weingartensis, *MGH SS* 21, 454–71

Hugh of Flavigny, *Chronicon*, *MGH SS* 8, 280–502

Isidore of Seville, *Etymologiae seu origines*, ed. W. M. Lindsay (2 volumes: Oxford, 1911)

Italia Pontificia ed. P. F. Kehr, 1–8 (Berlin, 1906–35)

Jocundus, *Translatio sancti Servatii*, *MGH SS* 8, 85–126

Jordanes, *Getica* [*De origine actibusque Getarum*], *MGH Auctores antiquissimi* 5, 53–138

Lampert of Hersfeld, *Annales* = *Lamberti Hersfeldensis Annales* ed. F. L. Hesse and G. Waitz, *MGH Scriptores* 5, 134–263

Lampert of Hersfeld, *Annales* in *Lamperti monachi Hersfeldensis Opera*, ed. O. Holder-Egger, *MGH SS rer. Germ.* [38] (1894) pp. 3–304

Lampert of Hersfeld, *Annales*, ed. O. Holder-Egger, revised A. Schmidt, W. D. Fritz (Ausgewählte Quellen zur deutschen Geschichte des Mittelalters. Freiherr-vom-Stein-Gedächtnisausgabe 13: Darmstadt, 1962)

Lampert of Hersfeld, *Annalium pars prior* see *Annales Hildesheimenses*

Lampert of Hersfeld, *Libelli de institutione Herveldensis ecclesiae quae supersunt* in *Lamperti monachi Hersfeldensis Opera*, ed. O. Holder-Egger, *MGH SS rer. Germ.* [38] (1894) pp. 343–54

Lampert of Hersfeld, *Vita Lulli archiepiscopi Mogontiacensis* in *Lamperti monachi Hersfeldensis Opera*, ed. O. Holder-Egger, *MGH SS rer. Germ.* [38] (1894) pp. 305–40

Laurence of Liège, *Gesta episcoporum Virdunensium et abbatum sancti Vitoni*, *MGH SS* 10, 486–516

Liber de unitate ecclesiae conservanda, *MGH Libelli* 2, 173–284

Life of Pope Leo IX trans. I. S. Robinson, *The Papal Reform of the Eleventh Century* (Manchester–New York, 2004) = *Die Touler Vita Leos IX.*, *MGH SS rer. Germ.* [70] (2007)

Mainzer Urkundenbuch 1, ed. M. Stimming (Darmstadt, 1932)

Manegold of Lautenbach, *Liber ad Gebehardum*, *MGH Libelli* 1, 308–430

Manegold of Lautenbach, *Liber contra Wolfelmum*, *MGH Quellen zur Geistesgeschichte* 8 (1972)

Marianus Scottus, *Chronicon*, *MGH SS* 5, 481–562

Meinhard of Bamberg, *Letters* = *Briefsammlungen der Zeit Heinrichs IV.* pp. 107–31

Oediger, F. W. (1954–61), *Die Regesten der Erzbischöfe von Köln im Mittelalter* 1 (Publikationen der Gesellschaft für Rheinische Geschichtskunde 21: Bonn)

Otloh of St Emmeram, *Liber Visionum*, *MGH Quellen zur Geistesgeschichte* 13 (1989)

Paul of Bernried, *Life of Pope Gregory VII* trans. I. S. Robinson, *The Papal Reform of the Eleventh Century* (Manchester–New York, 2004) pp. 262–364 = Paul of Bernried, *Vita Gregorii VII papae* ed. J. M. Watterich, *Pontificum Romanorum Vitae* 1 (Leipzig, 1862), 474–545

Peter Damian, *Letters* = *Die Briefe des Petrus Damiani*, *MGH Die Briefe der deutschen Kaiserzeit* 1–4 (Munich, 1983–93)

Petrus Crassus, *Defensio Heinrici IV regis*, *MGH Libelli* 1, 432–53

I Placiti del 'Regnum Italiae' ed. C. Manaresi 3 (Fonti per la Storia d'Italia 97: Rome, 1960)

Pseudo-Udalric, *Letter on the chastity of the clergy* = *Epistola de continentia clericorum, MGH Libelli* 1, 255–60

Ralph Glaber, *Vita domni Willelmi abbatis* in Rodolfus Glaber, *Opera* ed. J. France, N. Bulst, P. Reynolds (Oxford, 1989) pp. 254–98

Regino of Prüm, *Chronicon, MGH SS rer. Germ.* [50] (1890)

Rudolf of St Trond, *Gesta abbatum Trudonensium libri I–VII, MGH SS* 10, 213–72

Rule of Benedict = *Regula Benedicti, Corpus Scriptorum Ecclesiasticorum Latinorum* 75 (Vienna, 1960)

Sigebert of Gembloux, *Apology against those who slander the masses of married priests* = *Apologia contra eos qui calumniantur missas coniugatorum sacerdotum, MGH Libelli* 2, 437–48

Sigebert of Gembloux, *Chronica, MGH SS* 6, 268–374

Song of the Saxon War = *Carmen de bello Saxonico, MGH SS rer. Germ.* [17] (1889) pp. 1–23

Sulpicius Severus, *Vita Martini episcopi Turonensis* in *Sulpicii Severi Opera, Corpus Scriptorum Ecclesiasticorum Latinorum* 1 (Vienna, 1866) pp. 107–37

Theoderic of Tholey, *Vita et passio Conradi archiepiscopi Treverensis, MGH SS* 8, 212–19

Thietmar of Merseburg, *Chronicon, MGH SS rer. Germ.*, nova series 9 (Berlin, 1935), trans. D. A. Warner, *Ottonian Germany* (Manchester–New York, 2001)

Triumphus sancti Remacli Stabulensis de coenobio Malmundariensi, MGH SS 11, 433–61

Vita Altmanni episcopi Pataviensis, MGH SS 12, 226–43

Vita Annonis archiepiscopi Coloniensis, MGH SS 11, 462–514

Vita Anselmi episcopi Lucensis, MGH SS 12, 1–35

Vita maior Bardonis archiepiscopi Moguntini, MGH SS 11, 322–42

Vita Meinwerci episcopi Patherbrunnensis, MGH SS rer. Germ. [59] (1921)

Walo, abbot of St Arnulf, Metz, *Letters* = *Die Briefe des Abtes Walo von St. Arnulf von Metz* ed. B. Schütte, *MGH Studien und Texte* 10 (Hanover, 1995)

Wido of Ferrara, *On the schism of Hildebrand* = *De scismate Hildebrandi, MGH Libelli* 1, 529–67

Widukind of Corvey, *Res Gestae Saxonicae, MGH SS rer. Germ.* [60] (1935)

Secondary works

Althoff, G. (1991), 'Die Billunger in der Salierzeit' in *Die Salier und das Reich* 1, 309–29

Althoff, G. (1997), *Spielregeln der Politik im Mittelalter. Kommunikation in Frieden und Fehde* (Darmstadt)

Arbusow, L. (1963), *Colores rhetorici. Eine Auswahl rhetorischer Figuren und Gemeinplätze als Hilfsmittel für akademische Übungen an mittelalterlichen Texten* (second edition: Göttingen)

Baaken, G. (1961), 'Königtum, Burgen und Königsfreie. Studien zu ihrer Geschichte in Ostsachsen' in *Vorträge und Forschungen* 6 (Constance–Stuttgart) pp. 9–95

Barstow, A. L. (1982), *Married priests and the reforming papacy. The eleventh-century debates* (Texts and Studies in Religion 12, New York–Toronto)

Berges, W. (1963), 'Zur Geschichte des Werla-Goslarer Reichsbezirks vom 9. bis zum 11. Jahrhundert' in *Deutsche Königspfalzen. Beiträge zu ihrer historischen und archäologischen Erforschung* 1 (Göttingen), 113–57

Beumann, H. (1950), *Widukind von Korvei. Untersuchungen zur Geschichtsschreibung und Ideengeschichte des 10. Jahrhunderts* (Weimar)

Beumann, H. (1965), 'Widukind von Korvei als Geschichtsschreiber und seine politische Gedankenwelt', *Westfalen* 27 (1948), 161–76; reprinted in *Geschichtsdenken und Geschichtsbild im Mittelalter* ed. W. Lammers (Wege der Forschung 21: Darmstadt) pp. 135–64

Beumann, H. (1973), 'Tribur, Rom und Canossa' in *Investiturstreit und Reichsverfassung* pp. 33–60

Billanovich, G. (1945), *Lamperto di Hersfeld e Tito Livio* (Opuscoli Accademici. Serie Liviana 8, Padua)

Black-Veldtrup, M. (1995), *Kaiserin Agnes (1043–1077). Quellenkritische Studien* (Münstersche Historische Forschungen 7, Cologne–Weimar–Vienna)

Borino, G. B. (1952), 'Cencio del prefetto Stefano l'attentatore di Gregorio VII', *Studi Gregoriani* 4, 373–440

Borino, G. B. (1956), 'Perché Gregorio VII non annunciò la sua elezione ad Enrico IV e non ne richiese il consenso', *Studi Gregoriani* 5, 313–43

Boshof, E. (1978a), 'Lothringen, Frankreich und das Reich in der Regierungszeit Heinrichs III.', *Rheinische Vierteljahrsblätter* 42, 63–100

Boshof, E. (1978b), 'Köln, Mainz, Trier. Die Auseinandersetzung um die Spitzenstellung im deutschen Episkopat in ottonisch-salischen Reichskirche', *Jahrbuch des kölnischen Geschichtsvereins* 49, 19–48

Boshof, E. (1986), 'Das Reich und Ungarn in der Zeit der Salier', *Ostbairische Grenzmarken* 28, 178–94

Boshof, E. (1991), 'Bischöfe und Bischofskirchen von Passau und Regensburg' in *Die Salier und das Reich* 2, 113–54

Bosl, K. (1950), *Die Reichsministerialität der Salier und Staufer* (Schriften der MGH 10/1, Stuttgart)

Bresslau, H. (1878), 'Heinrich II. und die Salier, 1002–1125', *Jahresberichte der Geschichtswissenschaft* 1, 139–47

Bresslau, H. (1879, 1884), *Jahrbücher des Deutschen Reichs unter Konrad II.* 1, 2 (Leipzig)

Brühl, C. (1968), *Fodrum, Gistum, Servitium regis* 1 (Cologne–Graz)

Brüske, W. (1955), *Untersuchungen zur Geschichte des Lutizenbundes* (Münster)

Bühler, A. (2001), 'Kaiser Heinrich IV. und Bertha von Turin. Eine schwierige Ehe im Spiegel der Urkunden', *Archiv für Kulturgeschichte* 83, 37–61

Büttner, H. (1949), 'Das Erzstift Mainz und die Klosterreform im 11. Jahrhundert', *Archiv für mittelrheinische Kirchengeschichte* 1, 30–64

Büttner, H. (1966), 'Abt Wilhelm von Hirsau und die Entwicklung der Rechtsstellung der Reformklöster im 11. Jahrhundert', *Zeitschrift für Württembergische Landesgeschichte* 25, 321–38

Büttner, H. (1973), 'Die Bischofsstädte von Basel bis Mainz in der Zeit des Investiturstreites' in *Investiturstreit und Reichsverfassung* pp. 351–61

Bulst-Thiele, M. L. (1933), *Kaiserin Agnes* (dissertation, Göttingen)

Carlyle, A. J. (1915), *A History of Medieval Political Theory in the West* 3 (Edinburgh–London)

Coué, S. (1991), 'Acht Bischofsviten aus der Salierzeit – neu interpretiert' in *Die Salier und das Reich* 3, 347–413

Cowdrey, H. E. J. (1970), *The Cluniacs and the Gregorian reform* (Oxford)

Cowdrey, H. E. J. (1998), *Pope Gregory VII (1073–1085)* (Oxford)

Cram, K.-G. (1955), *Iudicium belli. Zum Rechtscharakter des Krieges im deutschen Mittelalter* (Beihefte zum Archiv für Kulturgeschichte 5, Münster–Cologne)

Dickerhof, H. (1991), 'Wandlungen im Rechtsdenken der Salierzeit am Beispiel der *lex naturalis* and des *ius gentium*' in *Die Salier und das Reich* 3, 447–76

Diederich, T. (1975), 'Anno und seine Kölner' in *Sankt Anno und seine viel liebe statt. Beiträge zum 900jährigen Jubiläum* ed. G. Busch (Siegburg) pp. 167–82

Diener, H. (1959), 'Das Itinerar des Abtes Hugo von Cluny' in *Neue Forschungen über Cluny und die Cluniacenser* ed. G. Tellenbach (Freiburg)

Eckhardt, K. A. (1964), *Eschwege als Brennpunkt thüringisch-hessischer Geschichte* (Marburg)

Ennen, E. (1977), *Gesammelte Abhandlungen zum europäischen Städtewesen und zur rheinischen Geschichte* (Bonn)

Erdmann, C. (1935), *Die Entstehung des Kreuzzugsgedankens* (Stuttgart)

Erdmann, C. (1937), 'Tribur und Rom. Zur Vorgeschichte der Canossafahrt', *Deutsches Archiv* 1, 361–88

Erdmann, C. (1938), *Studien zur Briefliteratur Deutschlands im elften Jahrhundert* (Schriften der MGH 1, Leipzig)

Erdmann, C. (1940), 'Zum Fürstentag von Tribur', *Deutsches Archiv* 4, 486–95

Erkens, F.-R. (1987), *Die Trierer Kirchenprovinz im Investiturstreit* (Passauer Historische Forschungen 4, Cologne–Vienna)

Fauser, A. and Gerstner, H. (1953), *Aere perennius. Jubiläumsausstellung der Staatlichen Bibliothek Bamberg zur Feier ihres 150-jährigen Bestehens* (Bamberg)

Feierabend, H. (1913), *Die politische Stellung der deutschen Reichsabteien während des Investiturstreites* (Historische Untersuchungen 3, Breslau)

Fenske, L. (1977), *Adelsopposition und kirchliche Reformbewegung im östlichen Sachsen* (Veröffentlichungen des Max-Planck-Instituts für Geschichte 47: Göttingen)

Fleckenstein, J. (1966), *Die Hofkapelle der deutschen Könige 2* (Schriften der MGH 16/2: Stuttgart)

Fleckenstein, J. (1973), 'Hofkapelle und Reichsepiskopat unter Heinrich IV.' in *Investiturstreit und Reichsverfassung* pp. 117–40

Franke, T. (1987), 'Studien zur Geschichte der Fuldaer Äbte im 11. und frühen 12. Jahrhundert', *Archiv für Diplomatik 33*, 55–238

Frech, G. (1991), 'Die deutschen Päpste – Kontinuität und Wandel' in *Die Salier und das Reich 2*, 203–32

Freise, E. (1981), 'Roger von Helmarshausen in seiner monastischen Umwelt', *Frühmittelalterliche Studien 15*, 180–293

Gawlik, A. (1970), *Intervenienten und Zeugen in den Diplomen Kaiser Heinrichs IV. (1056–1105)* (Kallmünz)

Gawlik, A. (1978), Introduction to *Die Urkunden Heinrichs IV.*, MGH Diplomata 6/3 (Hanover)

Gfrörer, A.F. (1861), *Papst Gregorius VII. und sein Zeitalter 7* (Schaffhausen)

Giese, W. (1979), *Der Stamm der Sachsen und das Reich in ottonischer und salischer Zeit* (Wiesbaden)

Giese, W. (1991), 'Reichsstrukturprobleme unter den Saliern – der Adel in Ostsachsen' in *Die Salier und das Reich 1*, 273–308

Giesebrecht, W. von (1885, 1890), *Geschichte der deutschen Kaiserzeit 2, 3* (fifth edition, Leipzig)

Glaeske, G. (1962), *Die Erzbischöfe von Hamburg-Bremen als Reichsfürsten (937–1258)* (Hildesheim)

Goez, E. (1995), *Beatrix von Canossa und Tuszien. Eine Untersuchung zur Geschichte des 11. Jahrhunderts* (Vorträge und Forschungen, Sonderband 41: Sigmaringen)

Goez, E. (1996), 'Der Thronerbe als Rivale: König Konrad, Kaiser Heinrichs IV. älterer Sohn', *Historisches Jahrbuch 116*, 1–49

Gresser, G. (2006), *Die Synoden und Konzilien in der Zeit des Reformpapsttums in Deutschland und Italien von Leo IX. bis Calixt II. 1049–1123* (Konziliengeschichte Reihe A: Paderborn–Munich–Vienna–Zürich)

Hainer, C. (1914), *Das epische Element bei den Geschichtsschreibern des Mittelalters* (dissertation: Gießen)

Haller, J. (1938), 'Die Überlieferung der Annalen Lamperts von Hersfeld' in *Wirtschaft und Kultur. Festschrift für A. Dopsch* (Baden b. Wien–Leipzig) pp. 410–23

Hallinger, K. (1950–1951), *Gorze-Kluny. Studien zu den monastischen Lebensformen und Gegensätzen im Hochmittelalter* (Studia Anselmiana 22–5: Rome)

Hallinger, K. (1958–60), '*Cluniacensis sanctae religionis ordinem elegimus: Zur* Rechtslage der Anfänge des Klosters Hasungen', *Jahrbuch für das Bistum Mainz* 8, 224–72

Hauck, A. (1954), *Kirchengeschichte Deutschlands* 3 (eighth edition: Berlin–Leipzig)

Hauck, K. (1959), 'Zum Tode Papst Clemens II.', *Jahrbuch für fränkische Landesforschung* 19, 265–74

Hay, D. J. (2008), *The military leadership of Matilda of Canossa, 1046–1115* (Manchester–New York)

Heyck, E. (1891), *Geschichte der Herzöge von Zähringen* (Freiburg i.B.)

Heyen, F. J. (1964), 'Die Öffnung des Paulinus-Gruft in Trier im Jahre 1072 und die Trierer Märtyrerlegende', *Archiv für mittelrheinische Kirchengeschichte* 16, 23–66

Hlawitschka, E. (1974), 'Zwischen Tribur und Canossa', *Historisches Jahrbuch* 94, 25–45

Hlawitschka, E. (1991), 'Zur Herkunft und zu den Seitenverwandten des Gegenkönigs Rudolf von Rheinfelden. Genealogische und politisch-historische Untersuchungen' in *Die Salier und das Reich* 1, 175–220

Höss, I. (1945), *Die deutsche Stämme im Investiturstreit* (dissertation, Jena)

Holder-Egger, O. (1884), 'Über die Vita Lulli und ihren Verfasser', *Neues Archiv* 9, 283–320

Holder-Egger, O. (1892), 'Ein Brief Erzbischof Udos von Trier', *Neues Archiv* 17, 487–9

Holder-Egger, O. (1894), 'Studien zu Lambert von Hersfeld', *Neues Archiv* 19, 141–213, 369–430, 507–74

Holder-Egger, O. (1906), 'Fragment eines Manifestes aus der Zeit Heinrichs IV.', *Neues Archiv* 31, 183–93

Holtzmann, R. (1941), *Geschichte der sächsischen Kaiserzeit (900–1024)* (Munich)

Hucke, R. G. (1956), *Die Grafen von Stade 900–1144. Genealogie, politische Stellung, Comitat und Allodialbesitz der sächsischen Udonen* (Stade)

Hüls, R. (1977), *Kardinäle, Klerus und Kirchen Roms 1049–1130* (Tübingen)

Jakobs, H. (1961), *Die Hirsauer* (Cologne–Graz)

Jakobs, H. (1968), *Der Adel in der Klosterreform von St. Blasien* (Kölner Historische Abhandlungen 16, Cologne–Graz)

Jakobs, H. (1973), 'Rudolf von Rheinfelden und die Kirchenreform' in *Investiturstreit und Reichsverfassung* pp. 87–115

Jenal, G (1974, 1975), *Erzbischof Anno II. von Köln (1056–75) und sein politisches Wirken* 1, 2 (Stuttgart)

Johanek, P. (1991), 'Die Erzbischöfe von Hamburg-Bremen und ihre Kirche im Reich der Salierzeit' in *Die Salier und das Reich* 2, 79–112

Joranson, E. (1928), 'The great German pilgrimage of 1064–65' in *The Crusades and other historical essays* ed. L. J. Paetow (New York) pp. 3–43

Jordan, K. (1970), 'Sachsen und das deutsche Königtum im hohen Mittelalter', *Historische Zeitschrift* 210, 529–59

Kehr, P. F. (1930), 'Vier Kapitel aus der Geschichte Kaiser Heinrichs III.', *Abhandlungen der Preußischen Akademie der Wissenschaften, phil.-hist. Klasse* 3, 1–61

Keller, H. (1986), *Zwischen regionaler Begrenzung und universalem Horizont. Deutschland im Imperium der Salier und Staufer 1024–1250* (*Propyläen Geschichte Deutschlands* 2: Berlin)

Kern, F. (1939), *Kingship and Law in the Middle Ages*, trans. S. B. Chrimes (Oxford)

Kilian, E. (1886), *Itinerar Kaiser Heinrichs IV.* (Karlsruhe)

Kohnle, A. (1993), *Abt Hugo von Cluny (1049–1109)* (Beihefte der Francia 32: Sigmaringen)

Kottje, R. (1978), 'Zur Bedeutung der Bischofsstädte für Heinrich IV.', *Historisches Jahrbuch* 97–98, 131–57

Krause, H.-J. (1960), *Das Papstwahldekret von 1059 und seine Rolle im Investiturstreit* (Studi Gregoriani 7: Rome)

Krüger, K. H. (1976), *Die Universalchroniken* (Typologie des sources du moyen âge occidental 16, Turnhout)

Lange, K.-H. (1961), 'Die Stellung der Grafen von Northeim in der Reichsgeschichte des 11. und 12. Jahrhunderts', *Niedersächsisches Jahrbuch für Landesgeschichte* 33, 1–107

Lerner, F. (1931), *Kardinal Hugo Candidus* (Beiheft 22 der Historischen Zeitschrift: Munich–Berlin)

Leyser, K. (1979), *Rule and conflict in an early medieval society. Ottonian Saxony* (London)

Leyser, K. (1981), 'Ottonian government', *English Historical Review* 96, 721–53

Leyser, K. (1983), 'The crisis of medieval Germany', *Proceedings of the British Academy* 69, 409–43

Lintzel, M. (1956), 'Die Mathildenviten und das Wahrheitsproblem in der Überlieferung der Ottonenzeit', *Archiv für Kulturgeschichte* 38, 152–66

Lübeck, K. (1942), 'Der kirchliche Rangstreit zu Goslar', *Niedersächsisches Jahrbuch für Landesgeschichte* 19, 96–133

Lübeck, K. (1947), 'Die Zehntstreitigkeiten zwischen Hersfeld und Halberstadt', *Archiv für katholische Kirchenrecht* 122, 296–323

Lück, D. (1970), 'Erzbischof Anno II. von Köln: Standesverhältnisse, verwandtschaftliche Beziehungen und Werdegang bis zur Bischofsweihe', *Annalen des Historischen Vereins für den Niederrhein* 172, 7–112

Lugge, M. (1960), *'Gallia' und 'Francia' im Mittelalter. Untersuchungen über den Zusammenhang zwischen geographisch-historischer Terminologie und politischem Denken vom 6.–15. Jahrhundert* (Bonner Historische Forschungen 15: Bonn)

Märtl, C. (1991), 'Die Bamberger Schulen – ein Bildungszentrum des Salierreichs' in *Die Salier und das Reich* 3, 327–45

Maurer, H. (1978), *Der Herzog von Schwaben* (Sigmaringen)

Maurer, H. (1991), 'Die Konstanzer Bischofskirche in salischer Zeit' in *Die Salier und das Reich* 2, 155–86

Meier, G. (1987), *Die Bischöfe von Paderborn und ihr Bistum im Hochmittelalter* (Paderborn–Munich–Vienna–Zürich)

Metz, W. (1971), 'Tafelgut, Königsstrasse und Servitium regis in Deutschland vornehmlich im 10. und 11. Jahrhundert', *Historisches Jahrbuch* 91, 257–91

Metz, W. (1991), 'Wesen und Struktur des Adels Althessens in der Salierzeit' in *Die Salier und das Reich* 1, 331–66

Meyer, O. (1973), *Oberfranken im Hochmittelalter* (Bayreuth)

Meyer von Knonau, G. (1890, 1894, 1900, 1903, 1904), *Jahrbücher des Deutschen Reiches unter Heinrich IV. und Heinrich V.* 1–5 (Leipzig)

Miccoli, G. (1966), *Chiesa gregoriana* (Florence)

Mitteis, H. (1927), *Politische Prozesse des früheren Mittelalters in Deutschland und Frankreich* (Sitzungsberichte der Heidelberger Akademie der Wissenschaften, philosophische-historische Klasse 1926/7, 3. Abhandlung, Heidelberg)

Mohr, W. (1976), *Geschichte des Herzogtums Lothringen* 2 (Saarbrücken)

Moore, R. I. (1977), *The origins of European dissent* (London)

Morrison, K. (1962), 'Canossa. A revision', *Traditio* 18, 121–48

Müller, E. (1901), *Das Itinerar Kaiser Heinrichs III. (1039–1056) mit besonderer Berücksichtigung seiner Urkunden* (Historische Studien 26, Berlin)

Munier, C. (2002), *Le Pape Léon IX et la Réforme de l'Eglise, 1002–1054* (Strasbourg)

Munk Olsen, B. (1985), *L'étude des auteurs classiques latins aux XIe et XIIe siècles* 2 (Paris)

Niermeyer, J. F. – van de Kieft, C. (2002), *Mediae Latinitatis Lexicon Minus* 1–2 (second edition, Leiden)

Oexle, O. G. (1978), 'Memorialüberlieferung und Gebetsgedächtnis in Fulda von 8. bis zum 11. Jahrhundert' in *Die Klostergemeinschaft von Fulda im früheren Mittelalter* ed. K. Schmid 1 (Münstersche Mittelalter-Schriften 8, Munich), 136–77

Overmann, A. (1895), *Gräfin Mathilde von Tuscien. Ihre Besitzungen. Geschichte ihres Gutes von 1125–1230 und ihre Regesten* (Innsbruck)

Petrucci, E. (1977), *Ecclesiologia e politica di Leone IX* (Rome)

Poole, R. L. (1934), *Studies in chronology and history* (Oxford)

Previté-Orton, C. W. (1912), *The early history of the house of Savoy (1000–1233)* (Cambridge)

Ranke, L. von (1886), *Weltgeschichte* 7 (Munich—Leipzig)

Ranke, L. von (1888), 'Zur Kritik fränkisch-deutscher Reichsannalisten', *Abhandlungen der Preußischen Akademie, philosophische-historische Klasse* (1854) pp. 436–58; reprinted in *Sämtliche Werke* 51–52 (Leipzig) pp. 125–49

Reinhardt, U. (1975), *Untersuchungen zur Stellung der Geistlichkeit bei den Königswahlen im Fränkischen und Deutschen Reich (751–1250)* (dissertation, Marburg)

Reuter, T. (1991a), *Germany in the early Middle Ages, 800–1056* (London–New York)

Reuter, T. (1991b), 'Unruhestiftung, Fehde, Rebellion, Widerstand: Gewalt und Frieden in der Politik der Salierzeit' in *Die Salier und das Reich* 3, 297–325

Reuter, T. (2006), 'Contextualising Canossa: excommunication, penance, surrender, reconciliation' in T. Reuter, *Medieval Polities and Modern Mentalities* ed. J. L. Nelson (Cambridge) pp. 147–66

Rieckenberg, H. J. (1942), 'Königsstrasse und Königsgut in liudolfingischer und frühsalischer Zeit (919–1056)', *Archiv für Urkundenforschung* 17, 32–154

Robinson, I. S. (1978a), *Authority and resistance in the Investiture Contest. The polemical literature of the eleventh century* (Manchester–New York)

Robinson, I. S. (1978b), 'Zu den Hasunger Annalen', *Deutsches Archiv* 34, 538–50

Robinson, I. S. (1988), 'Church and papacy', *The Cambridge History of Medieval Political Thought c.350 – c.1450* ed. J. H. Burns (Cambridge) pp. 252–305

Robinson, I. S. (1989), 'Bernold von Konstanz und der gregorianische Reformkreis um Bischof Gebhard III.' in *Die Konstanzer Münsterweihe von 1089 in ihrem historischen Umfeld* ed. H. Maurer (Freiburg) pp. 155–88

Robinson, I. S. (1999), *Henry IV of Germany, 1056–1106* (Cambridge)

Robinson, I. S. (2004a), *The papal reform of the eleventh century: Lives of Pope Leo IX and Pope Gregory VII* (Manchester–New York)

Robinson, I. S. (2004b), 'Reform and the church, 1073–1122', *The New Cambridge Medieval History* 4/1 (Cambridge), 268–334

Robinson, I. S. (2008), *Eleventh-century Germany: the Swabian chronicles* (Manchester–New York)

Rösener, W. (1991), 'Bauern in der Salierzeit' in *Die Salier und das Reich* 3, 51–73

Rothe, E. (1940), *Goslar als Residenz der Salier* (Dresden)

Schieffer, R. (1971), 'Die Romreise deutscher Bischöfe im Frühjahr 1070. Anno von Köln, Siegfried von Mainz und Hermann von Bamberg bei Alexander II.', *Rheinische Vierteljahrsblätter* 35, 152–74

Schieffer, R. (1972), 'Spirituales latrones. Zu den Hintergründen der Simonie-prozesse in Deutschland zwischen 1069 und 1075', *Historisches Jahrbuch* 92, 19–60

Schieffer, R. (1975), 'Hermann I., Bischof von Bamberg', *Fränkische Lebensbilder* 6, 55–76

Schieffer, R. (1985), 'Lampert von Hersfeld' in *Die deutsche Literatur des Mittel-alters. Verfasserlexikon* 5 (Berlin–New York) cols 513–20

Schieffer, R. (1991), 'Erzbischöfe und Bischofskirche von Köln' in *Die Salier und das Reich* 2, 1–29

Schmale, F.-J. (1979), 'Die "Absetzung" Gregors VI. in Sutri und die synodale Tradition', *Annuarium Historiae Conciliorum* 11, 55–103

Schmeidler, B. (1920), 'Lampert von Hersfeld und die Ehescheidungsangele-genheit Heinrichs IV. im Jahre 1069', *Historische Vierteljahrschrift* 20, 141–9

Schmid, K. (1973), 'Adel und Reform in Schwaben' in *Investiturstreit und Reichs-verfassung* pp. 295–319

Schmid, K. (1984a), 'Salische Gedenkstiftungen für *fideles, servientes* und *milites* in *Institutionen, Kultur und Gesellschaft im Mittelalter* ed. L. Fenske, W. Rösener, T. Zotz (Sigmaringen) pp. 245–64

Schmid, K. (1984b), 'Die Sorge der Salier um ihre Memoria' in *Memoria. Der geschichtliche Zeugniswert des liturgischen Gedenkens im Mittelalter* ed. K. Schmid and J. Wollasch (Munich) pp. 666–726

Schmid, P. (1926), *Der Begriff der kanonischen Wahl in den Anfängen des Investi-turstreits* (Stuttgart)

Schmidt, T. (1977), *Alexander II. und die römische Reformgruppe seiner Zeit* (Päpste und Papsttum 11: Stuttgart)

Schneider, C. (1972), *Prophetisches Sacerdotium und heilsgeschichtliches Regnum im Dialog 1073–1077* (Munich)

Schneider, R. (1991), 'Landeserschließung und Raumerfassung durch salische Herrscher' in *Die Salier und das Reich* 1, 117–38

Schramm, P. E. (1955), *Herrschaftszeichen und Staatssymbolik* (Schriften der MGH 13/2, Stuttgart)

Schramm, P. E. (1968), 'Böhmen und das Regnum. Die Verleihungen der Königswürde an die Herzöge von Böhmen' in *Adel und Kirche. Festschrift für Gerd Tellenbach* ed. J. Fleckenstein and K. Schmid (Freiburg–Basel–Vienna) pp. 221–36

Schrod, K. (1931), *Reichsstraßen und Reichsverwaltung im Königreich Italien* (Stuttgart)

Schumann, O. (1912), *Die päpstlichen Legaten in Deutschland zur Zeit Heinrichs IV. und Heinrichs V. (1056–1125)* (dissertation, Marburg)

Schwartz, G. (1913), *Die Besetzung der Bistümer Reichsitaliens unter den sächsischen und salischen Kaisern mit den Listen der Bischöfe, 951–1122* (Leipzig–Berlin)

Seegrün, W. (1982), 'Erzbischof Adalbert von Hamburg-Bremen und Gottschalk, Großfürst der Abodriten (1043–1066/72)' in *Beiträge zur mecklenburgischen Kirchengeschichte* ed. B. Jähnig (Cologne–Vienna) pp. 1–14

Seibert, H. (1991), 'Libertas und Reichsabtei: Zur Klosterpolitik der salischen Herrscher' in *Die Salier und das Reich* 2, 503–69

Semmler, J. (1956), 'Lampert von Hersfeld und Giselbert von Hasungen. Studien zu den monastischen Anfängen des Klosters Hasungen', *Studien und Mitteilungen zur Geschichte der Benediktinerordens und seiner Zweige* 67, 261–76

Semmler, J. (1959), *Die Klosterreform von Siegburg. Ihre Ausbreitung und ihr Reformprogramm im 11. und 12. Jahrhundert* (Rheinisches Archiv 53: Bonn)

Simeoni, L. (1947), 'Il contributo della contessa Matilde al papato nella lotta per le investiture', *Studi Gregoriani* 1, 353–72

Simon, G. (1958, 1959), 'Untersuchungen zur Topik der Widmungsbriefe mittelalterlicher Geschichtsschreiber bis zum Ende des 12. Jahrhunderts', *Archiv für Diplomatik* 4, 52–118; 5, 73–154

Smalley, B. (1952), *The study of the Bible in the Middle Ages* (Oxford)

Spier, H. (1962), 'Die Harzburg als salische Residenz. Versuch einer typologischen Bestimmung', *Harz-Zeitschrift* 14, 31–7

Spier, H. (1967–8), 'Die Harzburg Heinrichs IV. Ihre geschichtliche Bedeutung und ihre besondere Stellung im Goslarer Reichsbezirk', *Harz-Zeitschrift* 19–20, 185–204

Staab, F. (1991), 'Die Mainzer Kirche: Konzeption und Verwirklichung in der Bonifatius- und Theonesttradition' in *Die Salier und das Reich* 1, 31–77

Stehkämper, H. (1991), 'Die Stadt Köln in der Salierzeit' in *Die Salier und das Reich* 3, 75–152

Steindorff, E. (1874, 1881), *Jahrbücher des Deutschen Reiches unter Heinrich III.* 1, 2 (Leipzig)

Stengel, E. E. (1955), 'Lampert von Hersfeld der erste Abt von Hasungen' in *Aus Verfassungs- und Landesgeschichte. Festschrift für Theodor Mayer* 2 (Lindau–Constance) pp. 245–58

Stenton, F. M. (1947), *Anglo-Saxon England* (second edition, Oxford)

Stenzel, G. A. H. (1828), *Geschichte Deutschlands unter den Fränkischen Kaisern* 2 (Leipzig)

Störmer, W. (1991), 'Bayern und der bayerische Herzog im 11. Jahrhundert' in *Die Salier und das Reich* 1, 503–47

Stolberg, F. (1968), *Befestigungsanlagen im und am Harz von der Frühgeschichte bis zur Neuzeit* (Hildesheim)

Strait, P. (1974), *Cologne in the twelfth century* (Gainesville, Florida)

Struve, T. (1969,1970a), 'Lampert von Hersfeld. Persönlichkeit und Weltbild eines Geschichtsschreibers am Beginn des Investiturstreits', *Hessisches Jahrbuch für Landesgeschichte* 19, 1–123; 20, 32–142

Struve, T. (1970b), 'Die Ausfahrt Roberts von Flandern', *Zeitschrift für Deutsche Philologie* 89, 395–404

Struve, T. (1984a), *Regesten des Kaiserreiches unter Heinrich IV.*, 1056 (1050)–1106 1 (J. F. Böhmer, *Regesta Imperii* III.2,3: Cologne–Vienna)

Struve, T. (1984b), 'Zwei Briefe der Kaiserin Agnes', *Historisches Jahrbuch* 104, 411–24

Struve, T. (1985), 'Die Romreise der Kaiserin Agnes', *Historisches Jahrbuch* 105, 1–29

Struve, T. (1995), 'Mathilde von Tuszien-Canossa und Heinrich IV.', *Historisches Jahrbuch* 115, 41–84

Taviani-Carozzi, H. (1996), 'Une bataille franco-allemande en Italie: Civitate (1053)' in *Peuples du Moyen âge: problèmes d'identification* ed. C. Carozzi, H. Taviani-Carozzi (Aix-en-Provence) pp. 181–211

Tellenbach, G. (1988), 'Der Charakter Kaiser Heinrichs IV.' in *Person und Gemeinschaft im Mittelalter* ed. G. Althoff, D. Greuenich, O. G. Oexle, J. Wollasch (Sigmaringen) pp. 345–67

Thomas, H. (1968), *Studien zur Trierer Geschichtsschreibung des 11. Jahrhunderts, insbesondere zu den Gesta Treverorum* (Rheinisches Archiv 68: Bonn)

Thomas, H. (1970), 'Erzbischof Siegfried I. von Mainz und die Tradition seiner Kirche', *Deutsches Archiv* 26, 368–99

Tondelli, L. (1952), 'Scavi archeologici a Canossa. Le tre mura di cinta', *Studi Gregoriani* 4, 365–71

Twellenkamp, M. (1991), 'Das Haus der Luxemburger' in *Die Salier und das Reich* 1, 475–502

Verlinden, C. (1935), *Robert Ier le Frison, comte de Flandre: étude d'histoire politique* (Paris)

Vlasto, A. P. (1972), *The entry of Slavs into Christendom: an introduction to the Medieval History of the Slavs* (Cambridge)

Vogel, J. (1983), *Gregor VII. und Heinrich IV. nach Canossa* (Arbeiten zur Frühmittelalterforschung 9: Berlin–New York)

Vogel, J. (1984), 'Rudolf von Rheinfelden, die Fürstenopposition gegen Heinrich IV. im Jahre 1072 und die Reform des Klosters St. Blasien', *Zeitschrift für die Geschichte des Oberrheins* 132, 1–30

Vogtherr, T. (1991), 'Die Reichsklöster Corvey, Fulda und Hersfeld' in: *Die Salier und das Reich* 2, 429–64

Wadle, E. (1973), 'Heinrich IV. und die deutsche Friedensbewegung' in *Investiturstreit und Reichsverfassung* pp. 141–73

Waitz, G. (1878), *Deutsche Verfassungsgeschichte* 8 (Kiel)

Wattenbach, W. – Holtzmann, R. (1967–1971), *Deutschlands Geschichtsquellen im Mittelalter. Deutsche Kaiserzeit. Die Zeit der Sachsen und Salier* ed. F.-J. Schmale 2 (Darmstadt)

Wegener, W. (1959), *Böhmen / Mähren und das Reich im Hochmittelalter* (Cologne–Graz)

Weiler, B. (2000), 'The *rex renitens* and the medieval ideal of kingship, ca. 900 – ca. 1250', *Viator* 31, 1–42

Weinfurter, S. (1991), 'Herrschaftslegitimation und Königsautorität im Wandel: die Salier und ihr Dom zu Speyer' in *Die Salier und das Reich* 1, 55–96

Weinfurter, S. (1992), *Herrschaft und Reich der Salier. Grundlinien einer Umbruchzeit* (Sigmaringen)

Wendehorst, A. (1991), 'Bischöfe und Bischofskirchen von Würzburg, Eichstätt und Bamberg' in *Die Salier und das Reich* 2, 225–49

Werner, M. (1991), 'Der Herzog von Lothringen in salischer Zeit' in *Die Salier und das Reich* 1, 367–473

Wilke, S. (1970), *Das Goslarer Reichsgebiet und seine Beziehungen zu den territorialen Nachbargewalten* (Göttingen)

Zielinski, H. (1984), *Der Reichsepiskopat in spätottonischer und salischer Zeit (1002–1125)* 1 (Stuttgart)

Zimmermann, H. (1968), *Papstabsetzungen des Mittelalters* (Graz–Vienna–Cologne)

Zimmermann, H. (1970), 'Wurde Gregor VII. 1076 in Worms abgesetzt?', *Mitteilungen des Instituts für Österreichische Geschichtsforschung* 78, 121–31

Zimmermann, H. (1975), *Der Canossagang von 1077* (Akademie der Wissenschaften und der Literatur: Mainz 1975, no. 5)

Zotz, T. (1982), 'Pallium et alia quaedam archiepiscopatus insignia' in *Festschrift für Berent Schwineköper* ed. H. Maurer and H. Patze (Sigmaringen) pp. 155–75

Zotz, T. (1991), 'Die Formierung der Ministerialität' in *Die Salier und das Reich* 3, 3–50

INDEX